The Failed Century of the Child

Governing America's Young in the Twentieth Century

Between 1900 and 2000, an unprecedented American effort to use state regulation to guarantee health, opportunity, and security to the country's children failed to reach its goals. The achievements envisioned were enormously ambitious and reflected entrenched but self-contradictory values and Americans' inconsistent expectations of government. As such, a "failed" century deserves a mixture of rebuke and cautious admiration.

Starting with the young, American public policy transformed individuals into strings of measurable characteristics. People became statistics, and if society could just get the measurements right, social policy said, progress would be possible. But children proved hard to quantify. Policies based in optimistic faith in the powers of applied scientific truth revealed perils implicit in acceptance of poorly understood social science paradigms. Definitions changed, as psychology or sociological or statistical theory changed, and good intentions foundered, as experts fiercely challenged each other's conclusions and public policies sought to respond.

Judith Sealander is Professor of History at Bowling Green State University. Her previous books include *As Minority Becomes Majority: Federal Reaction to the Phenomenon of Women in the Work Force* (1983); *"Grand Plans": Business Progressivism and Social Change* (1989); *Women of Valor: The Struggle Against the Great Depression* (1990), coauthored with Bernard Sternsher; and *Private Wealth and Public Life: Foundation Philanthropy and the Re-shaping of American Social Policy* (1997), which won the 1998 Ohio Academy of History Book Prize. She is the recipient of numerous teaching awards and research fellowships from the National Endowment for the Humanities, the American Association of Colleges, the Rockefeller Archive Center, and the Indiana University Center for the Study of Philanthropy.

The Failed Century of the Child

Governing America's Young in the Twentieth Century

JUDITH SEALANDER

Bowling Green State University

PUBLISHED BY THE PRESS SYNDICATE OF THE UNIVERSITY OF CAMBRIDGE
The Pitt Building, Trumpington Street, Cambridge, United Kingdom

CAMBRIDGE UNIVERSITY PRESS
The Edinburgh Building, Cambridge CB2 2RU, UK
40 West 20th Street, New York, NY 10011-4211, USA
477 Williamstown Road, Port Melbourne, VIC 3207, Australia
Ruiz de Alarcón 13, 28014 Madrid, Spain
Dock House, The Waterfront, Cape Town 8001, South Africa

http://www.cambridge.org

© Judith Sealander 2003

First published 2003

Printed in the United States of America

Typeface Sabon 10/12 pt.   *System* LATEX 2$_\varepsilon$ [TB]

A catalog record for this book is available from the British Library.

Library of Congress Cataloging in Publication Data
Sealander, Judith.
The failed century of the child : governing America's young in the twentieth century /
Judith Sealander.
p.   cm.
Includes bibliographical references and index.
ISBN 0-521-82878-3 – ISBN 0-521-53568-9 (pkb.)
1. Children–Government policy–United States–History–20th century.   2. Child
welfare–United States–History–20th century.   3. Children–Services for–United
States–History–20th century.   I. Title.
HV741.S383   2003
362.7'0973'0904–dc21   2003048460

ISBN 0 521 82878 3 hardback
ISBN 0 521 53568 9 paperback

For Fuji Kawashima

Contents

Acknowledgments   *page* ix

   Introduction   1

PART ONE: CHILDREN'S WELFARE

1   Juvenile Justice: From "Child Saving" to "Public Accountability"   19
2   "The Pontius Pilate Routine": Government Responses
   to Child Abuse   53
3   "Illusory Promises": State Aid to Poor Children   92

PART TWO: CHILDREN'S WORK

4   "Inducting into Adulthood": State Reactions to the Labor
   of Children and Adolescents   137

PART THREE: CHILDREN'S EDUCATION

5   "Laying Down Principles in the Dark": The Consequences of
   Compulsory Secondary Education   187
6   The Return of the Infant School: Twentieth-Century
   Preschool Education   222
7   Public Education of Disabled Children: "Rewriting One
   of the Saddest Chapters"   259

PART FOUR: CHILDREN'S HEALTH

8   "Shaped Up" by the State: Government Attempts to Improve
   Children's Diets, Exercise Regimes, and Physical Fitness   293

9 Mandatory Medicine: Twentieth-Century Childhood
Immunization   323

Conclusion: Two Cheers for a "Failed" Century   355

Index   365

Acknowledgments

Oscar Wilde once remarked, "When people talk to us of others they are usually dull. When they talk to us of themselves, they are nearly always interesting... if one could shut them up." I hope I avoid the former sin here, since the people of whom I wish to talk have made the journey toward completion of this book so satisfying.

Willard Gatewood and Ellis Hawley read and improved several drafts of this manuscript. Decades of friendship with these exemplars have spoiled me. I never doubted that either would refuse my request for help. I knew even before receiving thick packages of carefully marked pages back in the mail that I would, once again, benefit from their keen editorial skills and their enormous store of knowledge about American politics and society. Only those fortunate enough to have been a student of Willard or Ellis can realize the degree to which any acknowledgment's tribute is pitifully insufficient thanks. Well, I never actually *was* Ellis's student.

Colleagues, fellow scholars, and friends scrutinized chapters or entire drafts of this book, and I thank them. Gary Hess read every chapter in at least one version. His comments helped me reshape my arguments about the American juvenile court, while his thoughts about the CCC changed what I eventually decided to say about it. Don Rowney's ideas about framing the introduction were enormously helpful, as were Marty Sklar's. Ed Berkowitz's criticism was brilliant. Jim Smith's questions were crucial as I struggled to state this study's central arguments. Dan Nelson helped me through thickets of confusion about child labor statistics. Roger Daniel's tough dismissal of early chapter drafts made me rethink the book's organization. Walt LaFeber set me straight on American basketball. An exchange with Stan Katz about the role of courts in the twentieth century was illuminating. Maris Vinovskis took time to discuss themes and suggest additional reading. He even emptied out a few shelves in his office and mailed me a box of books and offprints.

Jack Benge brought a lawyer's keen mind to the topic. Matt Musteric, Jim Buss, and Pete Genovese were geniuses at helping me track down errant statistics and incomplete citations. They also helped construct this volume's graphs and charts. Heartfelt thanks to all.

Mary Beth Zachary and Coleen Parmer of Bowling Green's Jerome Library were efficient, enthusiastic, and good humored, even as I pushed my interlibrary loan borrowing privileges to the brink. Both are paragons among librarians. Marnie Imhoff's enthusiasm for this project at an early stage buoyed me, as have conversations with Tom Rosenbaum, Kathy McCarthy, Ham Cravens, Ruth Crocker, and Peggy Giordano.

Cambridge sent my submitted manuscript to three readers. As is customary, I did not know who had been asked. Each returned an intelligent, extremely useful assessment. I am indebted to all three and delighted to be able to thank two by name, since, many months later, Ellen Fitzpatrick and Don Critchlow chose to shed their anonymity. Because I rank both among our profession's most astute analysts of twentieth-century American social policy, I congratulate my good fortune and Alia Winters of the Press for choosing so wisely. In this, and in many other ways, Alia was an ideal editor. In like fashion, Laura Lawrie was a skilled copy editor.

Fuji Kawashima is that rarity – a genuinely self-sacrificing academic leader. I laud his honor, celebrate the pleasure our friendship brings me, and dedicate this book to him.

My final debt is my greatest – that owed my amazing husband, Jerry Friedman. He read, reread, and reread yet again, every draft of every chapter. No one has given me better advice. That, however, is the least of it. On our first date, Jerry announced we'd stay home. He'd stocked up on Ken Russell videos and prepared a stack of tuna fish sandwiches. I told him I'd never met anyone with such terrible taste. We stayed up all night talking. A few weeks later we married. Decades have passed. Jerry still skewers my arguments and causes my heart to race. I am blessed.

Introduction

Why the Failed "Century of the Child"?

Between 1900 and 2000, an unprecedented American effort to use state regulation to guarantee health, opportunity, and security to the country's children did not meet its own goals. The achievements envisioned were enormously ambitious. They also reflected entrenched but self-contradictory values and Americans' inconsistent expectations of government. As such, a "failed" century deserves a mixture of rebuke and cautious admiration.

In the same breath, Americans celebrated individuals, family, and community but rarely acknowledged the inherent conflicts that accompanied such catholicity. Governments rarely established clear hierarchical priorities when the interests of the young, their elders, and the general public did indeed clash. Failure to do so produced unexpected, even nonsensical, consequences that these pages dissect. At best, it nourished ambivalence about responsibilities for children, reflected in public policy's frequent inability effectively to draw the lines – between proper parental discipline and child abuse – between medical privacy and mandatory immunization of all children – between a disabled child's right to education and a school system's need to balance a budget. That contributed to the country's failure to achieve the goals symbolized by the phrase, "century of the child." In 1900, well-read Americans discussed a just-published book, *The Century of the Child*. Its Swedish author, Ellen Key, predicted that children's welfare would be central to any definition of twentieth-century progress.[1] Nowhere did this really happen, certainly not in the United States.

Reiterated in these pages is another reason for, again, a mirror of powerful contradictions in American cultural and political beliefs. Americans lauded democracy and tried hard to implement it. They also embraced

---

[1] One wonders if very many of the American Progressives who copied the title actually read the book itself, as the socialist Key opposed most forms of public schooling and included diatribes against capitalism as harmful to children. Ellen Key, *The Century of the Child* (London, 1900).

prejudices that divided society by race, ethnic origins, class, and gender. A genuine egalitarianism justified many of the new duties twentieth-century American governments assumed as overseers of the young: no child should be hungry – no child should suffer injury at the hands of relatives – all should be educated. The idea that its children would grow up to be citizens with equal opportunity, even if they had been born poor or to foreign parents, was an audacious vision – not shared to such an extent by any other developed nation in the twentieth century. In unintended ways, this emphasis on commonality encouraged failure.

This book examines numerous ways activist state policies that emphasized universality, objectivity, and democracy deepened racial and class separations. A juvenile justice philosophy that said all wayward children should be "rehabilitated," not punished, wavered as young African Americans in great numbers finally exited the Jim Crow South and entered urban courtrooms. "IQ" exams "sorted" students and magnified existing prejudices. After all – didn't they prove that the poor, the nonnative, or the black child was quantifiably inferior?[2]

Starting with the young, American public policy transformed individuals into strings of measurable characteristics. People became statistics – points on a normal distribution, deviations from a population mean.[3] That also complicated efforts to improve childhood through state action. If society could just get the measurements right, social policy said, progress would be possible. But children proved hard to quantify. Policies based in optimistic faith in the powers of applied scientific truth revealed instead the perils implicit in acceptance of incompletely developed and poorly understood social science paradigms. Definitions changed, as psychology or sociological or statistical theory changed, and good intentions foundered, as experts fiercely challenged each other's conclusions and public policies sought to respond. Who among the young was "crippled" – then "handicapped" then "disabled"? Who should decide? How should society react?

This twentieth-century enthusiasm for numeric judgment produced another phenomenon important to this study of childhood policy: age-grading. From the seventeenth to the nineteenth century, ability often mattered more than age. Men in colonial Massachusetts who wished to be spared militia training had to demonstrate physical weakness – not proof that

---

[2] By the 1920s, some southern states made it illegal for a public school classroom to include even *teachers* and pupils who were members of different races, and many policy debates in the early twentieth century were distinguished by efforts to decide who, among non-African Americans, was "good enough" to be classified as white. For a fascinating account of these social policies, see Morton Keller, *Regulating a New Society: Public Policy and Social Change in America, 1900–1933* (Cambridge, MA, 1994), 248–75.

[3] For further elaboration of this argument, see Olivier Zunz's fine book, *Why The American Century?* (Chicago, 1998), 48–68. The above sentence paraphrases one original to Zunz: 49.

they had passed a certain chronological benchmark.[4] Adolescent boys in nineteenth-century American common schools struggled to learn their letters alongside four- or five-year-old children.[5]

State efforts to regulate children's lives made one kind of statistical measurement pervasive in America: division by years. Children studied in carefully separated cohorts, and school systems accepted "social" promotion so that same-age groupings would not be split. When faced with illiterate high school seniors, policy makers then demanded that graduation be based on measurable academic standards, though what those standards should be stimulated unending dispute.

So, too, did decisions about what age was appropriate for full or part time paid work, marriage, alcohol consumption, the right to drive, or, even, the imposition of the death penalty. Their daily lives transformed by government institutions organized by age, kids turned to those born at the same time, and youth "peer cultures" frightened the adults whose policies greatly encouraged their growth.

Twentieth-century Americans fancied themselves the planet's most ardent individualists but marched through life in age-graded ranks. They said they opposed intrusive government but accepted "help" for children that increased intrusive government. This exercise in collective self-deception, finally, weakened the chances that the century of the child would achieve its dreams, because it meant that the programs this book analyzes often functioned as a shield for a more controversial aim – the establishment of federally imposed uniformity of law.

Many reforms these chapters examine, such as an effort during the 1920s and 1930s to ratify a constitutional amendment giving the U.S. Congress the right to control the paid labor of all individuals under the age of eighteen, went far beyond powers most Americans were willing to grant local and state authorities, much less federal officials. Its supporters eventually abandoned the proposed Child Labor Amendment. Nonetheless, the odor of deception clung to child advocacy. Rightly so. Throughout the century reformers whose vision centered on a socially activist federal government urged change for the children. Marian Wright Edelman, founder of the Children's Defense Fund, actually admitted it in print in 1987. "Because we recognized that support for whatever was labeled black and poor was shrinking ... new ways had to be found to articulate and respond to the continuing problems of poverty and

---

[4] John Demos, *Past, Present, and Personal: The Family and Life Course in American History* (New York, 1986), 142.

[5] Maris Vinovskis remarks that twentieth-century age-grading transformed American public schools, but notes that "how, when, and why this remarkable" change occurred has been "seldom remarked upon." Maris Vinovskis, with David Angus and Jeffrey Mirel, "Historical Development of Age Stratification in Schooling," in Maris Vinovskis, *Education, Society, and Economic Opportunity: An Historical Perspective on Persistent Issues* (New Haven, 1995), 171–92. Quotation: 176.

race."[6] One does not have to oppose Edelman's goal to recognize the costs exacted by her strategy, one shared by generations of other "progressives." The idea that childhood policy cloaked other aims took hold, and for good reason. It frequently did.

Support of programs for the young, most important, local and state funds for schooling, peaked in the 1970s. For the rest of the century, voters around the country defeated school bonds. In Washington, politicians restricted many other "childhood" programs – from aid to poor youngsters to job training initiatives. Ironically, the early twentieth-century reformers who practiced the nonpartisan politics of child saving – in part, in hopes of shifting more political power to the national government – helped set in motion hugely important changes. By the 1990s, the nation's regions *were* less distinctive. Many aspects of American culture *had* nationalized. The issue-based politics childhood policy symbolized *was* far more important, as party loyalty waned, but the country's elderly, not its children, most benefited, as the recipients of federally sponsored programs of retirement stipends and medical care.[7] Of course, old people voted; children did not.

A Broad Brush and a Big Canvas

Twentieth-century "child saving's" ambitious agenda transformed social attitudes toward childhood, parental duty, and family functions, while changing more than a hundred million youngsters' actual experiences of life. Moreover, many new supervisory duties given governments demanded intellectual reconceptions of the state. The subject is an enormous one, organized here topically into four sections that analyze public policies affecting children's welfare, work, education, and health. Several themes link these otherwise disparate subjects. The enduring legacies of early-twentieth-century Progressive reform underpinned a large number of government initiatives. Dramatic changes in the composition of twentieth-century American households and workplaces exercised a powerful demographic imperative to which public policy reacted, often inadequately or with confusion. The enormous growth in the twentieth century of the law and social sciences as professions profoundly altered public governance of the young. Finally, the persistence of federalism meant that divided bureaucracies disputed changed rules for childhood.

This book begins with some of the oldest duties accepted by states – to punish wrongdoers and succor the poor – then considers increasing novel

---

[6] Marian Wright Edelman, quoted in Theda Skocpol, "From Beginning to End: Has Twentieth Century U.S. Social Policy Come Full Circle?" in Morton Keller and R. Shep Melnick, *Taking Stock: American Government in the Twentieth Century* (New York, 1999), 266.

[7] For an informative discussion of the rise of "interest group" politics in twentieth-century America, see Jack Walker, *Mobilizing Interest Groups in America: Patrons, Professions, and Social Movements* (Ann Arbor, 1991).

innovations.[8] It analyzes juvenile justice, twentieth-century responses to child abuse, state aid to poor children, regulation of child labor, and government work programs for adolescents. It examines the creation of comprehensive systems of compulsory public high schools, the expansion of formal education for very young and disabled children, and efforts to improve and regulate children's diets, play, and exercise, and, finally, it investigates the impact of required immunization against infectious childhood diseases.

Such an overview necessarily employs a broad brush and a big canvas. The huge body of scholarship about American children in the twentieth century is immensely valuable. This book would not exist without it. However, this enormous literature is largely unintegrated. Histories of juvenile justice pay little attention to developments in child psychology, despite the fact that the juvenile court owed its birth to the growth of psychology as a distinct profession. Medical studies track the history of polio from its first appearance in the United States in epidemic form in 1916 to its defeat in the early 1960s. They do not speculate about the ways that a new, virulent childhood disease helped alter public education policy. Students of one subject rarely speculate about these kinds of connections. Did the "crusade" to end child labor really substitute the opportunities of free education for the dangers of factories? An answer to just that one question demands an understanding of the interactions between labor and education policy.

Moreover, most histories of twentieth-century laws and regulations are "snapshots" – pictures of a specific policy initiative over a relatively restricted period. This study focuses longitudinally and broadly – seeking to capture a complex landscape of change. It synthesizes work from many different disciplines as it investigates the transformation of American childhood into a public concern and a different experience. It utilizes the insights of many of the sociologists, psychologists, legal scholars, political scientists, economists, and historians who write about American education, medicine, law, social work, labor, and the history of the family. It surveys recent scholarship and reviews the literatures produced by earlier generations of experts on children. It is also based on a wide variety of primary and archival materials.

The stories these sources reveal are of public responses to the concept of *childhood*. This is not an attempt to survey the actual lives of twentieth-century children in the United States, although real children appear now and then as actors. The semantics are important. In some way, all societies throughout recorded time seem to have differentiated a state of human biological immaturity. The word "childhood" encompasses perceptions about the nature and importance of those differences. Cultural, political, and economic forces have always shaped such attitudes, but, nowhere, apparently,

---

[8] The oldest of all state functions has been armed conflict, but American armies of the twentieth century, while young, were not composed of children, at least as childhood was socially constructed. Therefore, state war making will not play a major part in this story.

have children ever grown up outside of the constraints of childhood – some system of adult understandings of who their young were and what they should do.[9]

It is conceptions of childhood that twentieth-century American governments helped to reshape, with varying impact on the experience of youth. Unquestionably, new regulations required that millions of twentieth-century youngsters behave differently than had their predecessors in earlier centuries. What the young actually thought about these demands remains largely unstudied. Often governments judged children's needs on scales tipped by perceptions of parental worthiness. Even when that did not happen, policies depended on adult ideas about who children were.

The anthropologists and sociologists who sought to understand "children's culture" warned that it was far more complex than most analysts imagined. Although their physical appearance made it impossible for these social scientists to pass for real children, some adopted a role they called "least adult." As did Margaret Mead in Samoa, they tried to blend in as participant observers, and reported back that children's worlds were exotic terrains, dominated by rituals, secrecy, and heavy reliance on nonverbal signals.[10]

However, the Samoans famously tricked Margaret Mead. Had the "least adults" been given the right passwords? If children created their own culture, to what extent could adults ever understand it? Could written records help? Adults, after all, wrote the vast majority of autobiographies, and viewed their own beginning years through older eyes.[11] Until the twentieth century,

---

[9] Documenting such differences poses huge problems. Material culture can be tricky. For instance, through the early nineteenth century, wealthy American adult women, not little girls, were the proud owners of most dolls. Many items now perceived as "toys" did not play such a role in earlier ages. Through the seventeenth century, documents variously referring to adult slaves, servants, or even prisoners, often used the term "child." For discussions of efforts to use evidence from material culture to assess historical childhood, see Antonia Fraser, *A History of Toys* (London, 1966); Karin Calvert, *Children in the House: The Material Culture of Early Childhood* (Boston, 1992). For discussion of written documents, see Roger Chartier, Ed., *A History of Private Life: The Passions of the Renaissance* (Cambridge, MA, 1989). Nonetheless, most historians of childhood now argue that no society thought its young were "miniature adults" – to use French historian Phillipe Aries's famous phrase. Aries's *Centuries of Childhood*, which appeared in a French edition in 1939 but not in English until 1962, stirred enormous debate among social historians for the last thirty years of the twentieth century. Many of Aries's critics, however, neglected to note that his comment about "miniature adults" was secondary to his central concern – idealizations of family life. For a summary of the debate about Aries, see Hugh Cunningham, *Children and Childhood in Western Society Since 1500* (New York, 1995), 9–12, 57.

[10] For an introduction to the anthropological literature that analyzes children's cultures, see Patricia Adler and Peter Adler, Eds., *Sociological Studies of Child Development* (Boston, 1986); John Clauson, Ed., *Socialization and Society* (Boston, 1986).

[11] For a discussion of the nature of autobiographies of childhood, see Richard Coe, *When the Grass Was Taller: Autobiography and the Experience of Childhood* (New Haven, 1984).

few bothered to ask such questions. Understanding twentieth-century state regulation of children's lives requires a larger framework that explains why an intense focus on children has been a relatively recent development and, even in the nineteenth and twentieth centuries, a trend largely confined to developed countries.

A Brief History of Children and Childhood

Before the early nineteenth century, the average child was the dead child. For most of human history, probably seven out of ten children did not live past the age of three.[12] Yet, despite high infant mortality, children were a greater presence in every society than they would be in the nineteenth and twentieth centuries. They were much more visible and, certainly, audible. When most people died before the age of forty, the greatest percentage of any population was under the age of ten, although, since at least the fourteenth century throughout the West pervasive late weaning helped prevent conception, and childbearing was widely spaced. Couples wed in their mid-twenties, and marriages generally ended with one spouse's death within two decades. Throughout that time, a wife usually gave birth every two or three years, but only a tiny fraction of parents raised all their young past infancy. The birth of children and the burial of children episodically marked family life, and an eldest surviving child likely had left home before the youngest was born.[13]

In such a world "civilization . . . stunted growth, spread disease, and shortened life spans."[14] Cycles of growth and collapse characterized all societies, even wealthy ones whose cities inevitably outstripped the capabilities of the outlying countryside. Urban areas were so unhealthy that none expanded through natural increase. Elites hoarded resources; war and epidemic regularly raged; the most technologically advanced cultures fell into ruin. Calamity dogged prosperity for centuries, and societies full of children offered their vulnerable young little but suffering.[15]

---

[12] Phillipe Aries, *Centuries of Childhood* (New York, 1962), 2.

[13] For overviews of family life in Western society since 1500, see Hugh Cunningham, *Children and Childhood in Western Society*, 79–111. See also Richard Smith and Keith Wrightson, Eds., *The World We Have Gained: Histories of Population and Social Structure* (Oxford, UK, 1986).

[14] This is the theme of John Coatsworth's 1996 presidential address to the American Historical Association, in which Coatsworth argued that, prior to the twentieth century, no peoples anywhere expected to enjoy prolonged eras of physical well-being. John Coatsworth, "Welfare," *American Historical Review* 101 (1996): 2.

[15] For example, Europe recovered from the devastation of the fourteenth-century plague, only to see population growth slow dramatically again in the seventeenth century – because of war and widespread malnutrition. For discussion of these historical patterns, see William Baumol, Richard Nelson, and Edward Wolff, Eds., *Convergence of Productivity: Cross National Studies of Historical Evidence* (New York, 1994).

Sometime around the middle of the seventeenth century, things changed. Adults started to live longer, and families produced fewer children. Although these trends were by no means uniform, they were the first signs of a monumental transformation: the growth in the Western world of "modern" information-rich societies in which ordinary people changed jobs, residences, even their legal and cultural status.[16]

Well before most of their people left the farm, areas in North America and northern Europe began to experience sharp declines in births. The Industrial Revolution accelerated this demographic one. New crops, higher productivity, efficient transportation, and better sanitation gradually improved the lives of millions of people, chief among them children, more of whom survived infancy.[17]

Modernization improved human prospects throughout the West, but not in simple linear fashion. Significant percentages of nineteenth-century Americans consumed a diet inferior to the one enjoyed by their colonial grandfathers.[18] Conditions in hugely overcrowded cities worsened in both the United States and Europe before they began to improve.[19] Hundreds of thousands of children grew up only to endure lives of brutally hard labor in mines and mills.

Nonetheless, as actual children's survival chances improved, adults attached greater importance to the abstract phenomenon of childhood, nowhere more so than in parts of colonial America. At a time when perhaps as many as one third of all children in eighteenth-century France were abandoned, Puritan leaders of the Massachusetts Bay Colony punished the practice and demanded that parents feed, shelter, and train their children.[20] The young in the American colonial South fared far less well. Rectification of highly imbalanced sex ratios in both black and white populations came

---

[16] For good introductions to modernization theory, see Nick Eberstadt, Ed., *Fertility Decline in the Less Developed Countries* (Englewood Cliffs, NJ, 1981); Michael Teitelbaum, *The British Fertility Decline: The Demographic Transition in the Crucible of the Industrial Revolution* (Princeton, 1984); Richard Brown, *Modernization: The Transformation of American Life, 1600–1865* (New York, 1976).

[17] Baumol, Nelson, and Wolff, *Convergence of Productivity.*

[18] Economic historians use patterns in rise and fall of median heights as a marker of nutritional levels within a society. By this measure, mid-nineteenth-century Americans were unhealthier than their late-eighteenth-century ancestors. See John Komlos and Joo Han Kim, "On Estimating Trends in Historical Heights," *Historical Methods*, 23 (1990): 116–20.

[19] For a good overview of the nineteenth-century health crusades that improved life, especially in urban areas, see Allan Brandt and Paul Rozin, Eds., *Morality and Health* (New York, 1997).

[20] Most abandoned children died – within a few months at foundling hospitals, much more quickly if simply left out of doors. Victoria Getis and Maris Vinovskis, "History of Child Care in the United States Before 1950," in Michael Lamb and Kathleen Sternberg, Eds., *Child Care in Context: Cross Cultural Perspectives* (Hillside, NJ, 1992), 188–9.

slowly, and, through the mid-eighteenth century, fewer stable households existed, even among free whites.[21]

Still, throughout America, children emerged as individuals, especially by the early nineteenth century, an era that lauded the "self-made" man. As late as the mid-seventeenth century, states punished whole families for the crimes of particular members.[22] By the nineteenth century, that was anathema – in law at least – in the United States and most of Europe.[23]

And a dramatically new idea emerged in societies that praised "go-ahead spirit": the future was going to be better than the past.[24] Rapid technological innovation encouraged such belief – as well as a larger sense of life as a succession of stages, all perhaps quite different. Toll roads, canals, steamships, and railways made the world both larger and smaller. Millions no longer lived and died in the same spot, surrounded by kin.[25] For the first time, great numbers of people experienced mass dislocation as a potential source of opportunity, not woe. Change was the future. Who better symbolized it than the young? Why not begin to view childhood as another, quite separate "place"?

The Nineteenth Century and Child Saving

Individualism, faith in progress, and unprecedented mobility paralleled another phenomenon: the growing importance of family privacy and an enlarged nurturant role for mothers. An ideology that praised mothers as particularly fond of children was peculiarly modern – and simultaneously sentimentalized family life, motherhood, and children themselves.

This nineteenth-century emphasis on the young as uniquely attractive was not entirely new. As early as the mid-eighteenth century, the French

[21] For more information on southern colonial family history, see Allan Kulikoff, *Tobacco and Slaves: The Development of Southern Cultures in the Chesapeake, 1680–1800* (Chapel Hill, 1986). For discussion of slave family life, see Philip Morgan, *Slave Counterpoint: Black Culture in the Eighteenth Century Chesapeake and Lowcountry* (Chapel Hill, 1998), 498–519.

[22] The notion of individualized punishment spread from the West to the rest of the world from the eighteenth through the twentieth century, but in an incomplete fashion. Witness the fact that in the year 2000 the ruling Islamic Taliban in Afghanistan reimposed sentences on whole families for the moral infractions of members. See M. J. Gohari, *Taliban: Ascent to Power* (New York, 2001).

[23] Richard Coe argues that a separate literature meant to educate or amuse children would have been hard for adults to imagine creating prior to the early seventeenth century. Coe, *When the Grass Was Taller*, 26–29.

[24] John Demos discusses the history of American nineteenth-century admiration for "go ahead spirit," in "History and the Formation of Social Policy towards Children: A Case Study," David Rothman and Stanton Wheeler, Eds., *Social History and Social Policy* (New York, 1981), 317–19.

[25] Richard Coe asks: Had millions not made such kinds of travel the turning points in their own lives, would the idea of an autonomous "place" for childhood have resonated so deeply? Coe, *When the Grass Was Taller*, 26–29.

philosopher Jean-Jacques Rousseau celebrated children as imaginative, un-selfconscious creatures, with lessons to teach their elders.[26] After 1830, Victorians on both sides of the Atlantic elevated these ideas into a virtual cult of childhood. An age roiled by change glorified stable marriage. For the first time in history, the Industrial Revolution allowed tens of millions of ordinary people, mostly Europeans, to travel the globe seeking employment or adventure. Americans made folk heroes of the man on the move – the wanderer – the Huck Finn quick to abandon civilization and light out for the territories. They also praised the home fires many eschewed, either voluntarily or through force of circumstance. A distinction between the glorification of children as symbols of fantasy, innocence, and freedom and the lives of actual children should be drawn. Only prosperous families could afford to shield their young. Still, ideology mattered, even when reality came up short. Victorian adults could locate in sentimentalizations of childhood longings their own lives did not easily accommodate.[27] And the sentimentalized nineteenth-century child became a twentieth-century publicly regulated one.

The Demographics of Modernization and the "Century of the Child"

This book examines child saving's enduring legacies. It also argues that demography played a crucial role in shaping the century of the child. As nineteenth-century American society enshrined the family as a safe center for civilizing forces in times of rapid change, the idea of the child as the "heart of the home" gained emotional force. However, the "home" itself was already in decline. Modernization ensured that. Institutions as varied as common schools, charity hospitals, and orphanages took over some of the social roles once centered in families, and parents exercised reduced economic control over older youths.[28] By 1900, the United States was thoroughly modern – a country in which the economic, social, and emotional roles of private households diminished even further.

A new kind of family began to emerge, with fewer children, but also fewer dead children. Only in the middle of the twentieth century did a funeral for

---

[26] Jean-Jacques Rousseau, *Emile*, which first appeared in 1762 and has been in print almost continuously since (edition used: B. Gagnebin, Paris, 1969), 245–300. The historian John Boswell notes, however, that Rousseau did not practice what he preached – at least with his *own* children. All five were abandoned to foundling hospitals, acts Rousseau never publicly regretted. John Boswell, *The Kindness of Strangers: The Abandonment of Children in Western Europe from Late Antiquity to the Renaissance* (New York, 1988), 424.

[27] "Child saving" was not just an American phenomenon but also spread throughout much of the developed world. To explore its ramifications over a century's time in the United States, however, is a sufficiently large task, although references to European counterparts appear in these chapters, with notations to differences.

[28] For discussion of the changing economic and social roles of families in the nineteenth century, see Kurt Kreppner and Richard Lerner, Eds., *Family Systems and Life-Span Development* (Hillsdale, NJ, 1989).

a baby become an event few American parents experienced. As children themselves became a smaller percentage of the national population, policy expanded the chronological sphere of childhood.

This book contrasts that socially constructed change with one modernization also encouraged: longer lifetimes. In the twentieth century, mortality and morbidity rates declined for everybody, not just children. Add rapidly declining fertility, and a country that saw itself as young was in fact quickly graying.

Despite twentieth-century social policy's emphasis on the importance of giving the young expanded opportunities to enjoy good health, education, and a decent standard of living, the needs of elders trumped those of children, especially after 1935. In a society where income equalled worth even remote connections to the workplace through marriage earned "entitlements" for millions of old people. Children, however, were segregated within the world of paid employment – restricted by labor law, the demands of compulsory education, and major changes in the American economy.

In fact, children increasingly led separate lives from adults, a trend furthered by age-graded public policy. Visitors to the nineteenth-century United States were surprised by the speed with which children struck out on their own and by the degree to which most of the old seemed to live alone. By the end of the twentieth century, the fastest growing type of American household was one composed of only one person, and youngsters became invisible to greater proportions of people.[29] Children, for most of human history the demographic majority, became an isolated minority, banned from many workplaces and residential communities.[30]

Much American support for children and those who spent the most time with them took the form of earnest words of praise, not adequately funded budgets. Despite periodic alarm about a "crisis" in public education, the juvenile courts, foster home care, or child protective service systems, workers in these child-centered jobs enjoyed neither good pay nor high status.

And U.S. families, rather than booming, experienced a late-twentieth-century "bust." Those who lamented the decline of families often underestimated the degree to which significant numbers of children in the early twentieth century lived with only one parent. But the demograpy of families, and inevitably, the patterns of childhood, *had* changed by the end of the twentieth century. Since the peak of the "Baby Boom" in the early

---

[29] For further exploration of these nineteenth-century demographic precedents, see Andrew Achenbaum, *Old Age in the New Land* (Baltimore, 1978); for the demographics of age in the twentieth century, see Peter Peterson, *Gray Dawn: How the Coming Age Wave Will Transform America – And the World* (New York, 1999), 70–152.

[30] Peterson, *Gray Dawn*, 150–62. Residential communities' bans on those under age eighteen were one of the few forms of category-specific age discrimination allowed by late-twentieth-century American courts.

1960s, American birthrates declined dramatically, and ever-larger numbers of couples remained childless, most of them voluntarily. Their mothers were among the most fertile in the country's history, but almost one quarter of American women born between 1950 and 1965, the daughters of the "Baby Boom," never had any children at all. By the 1970s, organizations promoting a "child-free" way of life, such as the Childfree Network and the National Organization of Non-Parents, emerged.[31] For many, childlessness was a cause, not an affliction.[32] By the 1990s, far more American homes contained pets than children, and bizarre battles occurred in city parks around the country, as owners defied city ordinances and demanded that their dogs run free, while parents claimed that fear of animal attacks kept their children from enjoying green spaces.[33]

Moreover, the rates of childbearing among couples who later divorced, or who never married, soared after 1970. The impact of that changing demography was enormously important to the success – and the failure – of children's policies – from efforts to end child abuse to plans to reduce impoverishment among the young. By the end of the century, one in three American children lived in a home headed by only one adult, usually their mother, though one of the first surprises of the 2000 Census was the doubling of single-parent households headed by fathers between 1990 and 2000.[34] Once again, contradictions surfaced. As public regulations chronologically lengthened "childhood" – real American children increasingly grew up fast in homes where the one adult present struggled with the shock waves of

---

[31] Scattered individual rebellions long predated the 1970s organized opposition to a cult of motherhood in the United States. For instance, in 1957 journalist Roslyn Smith penned a sarcastic piece published in the widely circulated *American Mercury.* "The poor childless couple," she wrote, "You just have to look at them to see the terrifying emptiness – He looks boyish, unlined and restful. She's slim, well-groomed, and youthful. It isn't natural." Roslyn Smith, "Pity the Childless Couple," *American Mercury* 84 (1957): 76–78.

[32] For further analysis of this phenomenon, see Elaine Tyler May, *Barren in the Promised Land: Childless Americans and the Pursuit of Happiness* (New York, 1995). By the end of the 1990s, in some circles, parents had become SITCOMS (single income, two children, oppressive mortgage) and those without children were THINKERS (two healthy incomes, no kids, early retirement). For explications of the pro- and antichild debate that raged at the end of the century, see Elinor Burkett, *The Baby Boon: How Family-Friendly America Cheats the Childless* (New York, 2000); Sylvia Ann Hewlett and Cornell West, *The War Against Parents* (New York, 1998).

[33] For a summary of such end-of-century struggles, see Emily Gest, "Running With the Dogs: Pols Polled on Leash Laws," *New York Daily News*, August 25, 2001.

[34] By the year 2000, almost one sixth of single-parent households were headed by males, up from under one tenth in 1970, although such families were not evenly distributed. Single fathers in 2000 were more likely to be white men in their forties or older, with college degrees and professional jobs, while single mothers were, far more typically, poorly educated, young, and poor. As an indication of the cultural shift, however, the publication of advocacy books arguing that fathers could be good single parents mushroomed at the end of the century. For an example, see Armin Brott, *The Single Father* (New York, 2000).

divorce or battled poverty. While regulatory lines hardened, the social divisions between youth and adulthood blurred. Everyone wore blue jeans; adolescents and their mothers similarly agonized over what to wear on an important date. An age-graded society had difficulty agreeing what was age-appropriate.

Finally, major demographic shifts in the composition of the twentieth-century American workforce affected public policy as well. Only a minority of American fathers had ever been sole supporters of wives and offspring. Farming required the labor of whole families, and, through the early twentieth century, the children of the working class provided at least one half of the income for families headed by unskilled laborers and almost 40 percent for those in which fathers practiced a craft. They were even more important income earners for the very large numbers of families disrupted by deaths, illness, or a father's desertion.[35] A historic substitution, however, transformed the demographics of the twentieth-century American economy, and affected all classes. Beginning in significant numbers in the 1930s, wives slipped quietly into the labor force, initially earning rebuke. By the end of the century, the employed wife was, by far, the most typical married woman in the United States. Children, in contrast, were part-time teenage workers, employed, as had been their counterparts of earlier generations, in low-wage jobs, but, in a striking difference, mostly keeping their earnings for themselves.

This book examines the formative importance of these demographic changes. It also notes the crucial ways that physical and social science theory anchored policy innovations.

Hard Science, Social Science, State Policy, and Childhood

Through regulating childhood, twentieth-century American governments championed new medical and social scientific advice. As scientific expertise flourished in the twentieth century, adults acquired more information about children than ever before, and growing numbers of specialists debated how to apply this knowledge. Ordinary parents, however, gradually accepted the idea that childrearing was a complicated process that required the guidance of professionals, many from disciplines that had not even existed before 1900.[36] The experts "led" parents, and "led" policy, but both were confused by a lack of consensus.

---

[35] Selma Cantor Berrol estimates that as late as 1908 children provided 45 percent of the family income for Massachusett's mill workers and that in many immigrant communities through the middle to late nineteenth century children provided 65 percent of total income. Selma Cantor Berrol, *Growing Up American: Immigrant Children in America, Then and Now* (New York, 1995), 662.

[36] Such acceptance was by no means universal, and this book explores ways that twentieth-century Americans also loathed "experts."

Despite ongoing disagreement, social science expertise, even more than the insights of "hard" science, played a crucial role in the creation of twentieth-century social policies affecting childhood. Psychological and sociological theories grounded a wide variety of government initiatives, sometimes long after their original proponents abandoned them. This book examines the uses and misuses of social science ideas – in the juvenile courts, which initially accepted theories that said young children could not lie – in the rise of public preschool – justified by studies of children's cognitive development – in government work programs for adolescents – backed by sociological "opportunity theory" – in intelligence testing – important to the evolution of compulsory education.

Politicians and social scientists often made enduring bad marriages of convenience. These chapters examine the well-worn routes trod by the latter as they journeyed between academic postings, government hearings, places on blue ribbon panels, and appointments as public policy advisers. They also investigate the usually unacknowledged cycles through which social science ideas moved, losing cachet, only to be revived in altered form and couched in different language by another generation ignorant of the work of predecessors. Increasingly, however, social scientists battled lawyers or backed up lawyers. The impact of a much larger American legal profession is another *leit motif* of twentieth-century American childhood policy.

A Litigious Century

In the years between 1890 and 1960, the United States grew from 68 million to over 183 million people. Its legal population, however, remained static – one in every one thousand people. Then, for four decades, membership metastasized – to one in every 364 Americans by 1984, to one in 267 by 1999. The nation burst at the seams with lawyers, who now looked more like the people they represented. A profession whose membership was 95 percent male in 1960 was one, only twenty years later, in which one in five attorneys was a woman. By the end of the century, one half of the entrants to American law schools were women, and about one tenth were black, roughly equivalent to their percentages within the general population.[37]

These changes in the size and nature of the legal profession in the twentieth century intersected in profound ways with government programs that made new demands of childhood, especially since litigation was a powerful weapon that Americans treated with insufficient caution. Once a dispute moved into

---

37 For a good summary of these changes, see Robert Nelson, David Trubeck, and Rayman Solomon, Eds., *Lawyers' Ideals/Lawyers' Practices: Transformations in the American Legal Profession* (Ithaca, NY, 1992).

a courtroom, both sides adopted more extreme positions.[38] Advocacy gr
challenging required vaccinations demanded that immunizations against
lio or diphtheria be guaranteed absolutely risk free – although most scient
thought that impossible. Parents of disabled kids argued that the Educati
of All Handicapped Children Act's mandate that every child be giv
"appropriate" public education meant that their offspring should be se
at state expense to private boarding schools.

If lawyers were important, so, too, were judges. Broadened laws o
standing permitted those not immediately affected to sue. Class action law
changed, so that suits could be so general that resulting decisions often
seemed more like statutes than traditional legal opinions. Equity law allowed
different kinds of uses of injunctions. Courts were still crucial policy makers
within the twentieth-century "administrative" state, and judges often acted
as *de facto* administrators.[39]

These developments necessitate the exploration of another theme: federalism. Despite the growing importance of Washington, an examination of
the ways twentieth-century society governed the young reveals that federalism, with its systems of shared, disputed, and negotiated power, remained
strong.

Childhood Policy and the Endurance of Federalism

As much as Washington mattered, so did Springfield, and so did more than
three thousand county seats. A synthetic look at a range of decisions affecting children's lives helps correct an overemphasis on the twentieth-century
federal government's supremacy, even as it acknowleges that many children's
advocates throughout the century were fervent supporters of nationally imposed regulations. Routes to reform sometimes wound through state capi-
tols or local courthouses on their way to the Potomac. Those who wanted
to change balances in power – either to favor greater state autonomy or to
tilt toward more centralized authority – frequently used the improvement
of children's lives as a battle cry. Sometimes they succeeded; sometimes they
failed, and ideas too far ahead of shared public opinion eventually faded.

Almost always, successful consensus-building occurred incrementally.
Powerful coalitions sometimes depended on temporary unions of opponents.
Some of these initiatives were federal. Often, they were not. Throughout the
twentieth century, local officials made many important decisions affecting

---

[38] For further discussion of these points, see Jeffrey Rosen, *The Unwanted Gaze: the Destruc-
tion of Privacy in America* (New York, 2000); Lawrence Friedman and George Fisher, Eds.,
The Crime Conundrum: Essays on Criminal Justice (New York, 1997).

[39] Nonetheless, scholarship about American government has, since the 1980s, focused heavily
on the growth of "administrative capacity." For examples of such scholarship, see Richard
Harris and Sidney Milkis, *The Politics of Regulatory Change: A Tale of Two Agencies* (New
York, 1996); Marc Eisner, *Regulatory Politics in Transition* (Baltimore, 1993).

children. Municipal and county officials ran school systems, oversaw children's protective services, and actually administered health-delivery and welfare programs. Most juvenile offenders encountered local and county officers of the court. Under the umbrella of federal labor law, state and municipal officials established, interpreted, and administered regulations affecting underage workers.

Throughout the century, "saving the children" was a common justification for increases in federal authority, but it also rallied support for expanded state authority at lower levels. Before Social Security's Aid to Dependent Children provisions spawned federal agencies, counties and cities employed the same agenda – cash assistance for impoverished mothers and their children – to justify their own administrative expansion. Bureaucracies facing crisis often articulated new "threats" to children.

A highly pluralistic American state proved adept at what a frustrated U.S. Senator George McGovern once condemned as "Alphonse-Gaston routines," as each level of government blamed another for mistakes.[40] Nonetheless, Americans resisted periodic campaigns to streamline public authority, preferring divided control. This greatly influenced the subject this book first examines, twentieth-century state responses to youthful crime.

The century began with hugely optimistic predictions that – at all jurisdictional levels – American justice would "treat," rather than censure, its young. It ended with calls for the abolition of the juvenile courts created to achieve such rehabilitation of criminal and wayward children.

---

[40] McGovern, then Chair of the Senate Committee on Nutrition and Human Needs, made the comment when complaining about ways that the U.S. Agriculture Department, State Departments of Education, and local school districts continually passed the buck among themselves, each blaming the other for failure to deliver enough lunches to poor children, but his comment could be applied generally. "Statement of Senator McGovern," Hearings before the Select Committee on Nutrition and Human Needs of the United States Senate, Ninetieth Congress, Second Session (Washington, DC, 1969): 3480.

PART ONE

CHILDREN'S WELFARE

I

Juvenile Justice

From "Child Saving" to "Public Accountability"

When twentieth-century American governments tried to control the misbehavior and crime of children, they did not assume new state duties. Organized societies had always created systems of rules and punishments. Juvenile
justice, therefore, provides an appropriate topic with which to begin analysis
of childhood policy. A desire to maintain order linked twentieth-century officials with their predecessors through the millennia. Between 1900 and 2000,
in addition, children's bad behavior followed predictable patterns. Male adolescents, proportionally, were greater lawbreakers than any other segment
of society, five times more likely than were girls to be arrested. Moreover,
young criminals were primarily thieves. In this, they repeated the actions of
their fellows in other eras and in other societies, as did the alarmed responses
of adults.[1]

That reaction was predictable. With reason, almost all societies have
treated young, unmarried males as threats to social stability.[2] They were –
and are. However, the ways that American governments responded in the
twentieth century to the need to make adolescents obey the rules moved into
uncharted territory. The juvenile court was an American creation, which
no other country embraced so enthusiastically. And while it was a new bureaucratic manifestation of an old state function, it mirrored larger developments: the rise of social science, the legal profession's unprecedented growth,
adult concerns about the threats posed by the very adolescent peer cultures
that public policy's separations of children into age-specific categories encouraged, and finally, public reaction to the fact that minorities – who by

---

[1] The numbers and percentages were not exactly the same, but extremely similar. For reviews
of statistics on twentieth-century juvenile crime, see United States Department of Health,
Education, and Welfare, Social Security Administration, Children's Bureau, Division of Reports, "The Children's Bureau and Juvenile Delinquency: A Chronology of What the Bureau
Is Doing and Has Done in the Field," (Washington, DC, 1960), 1–34.

[2] Eugene Bjorklun, "Teaching About Juvenile Justice," *Social Studies* 79 (1988): 97–102.

mid-century had far greater access to guns – committed a disproportionate number of crimes. An institution first shaped by the idea that a child could not really commit a crime and needed treatment, not punishment, was far different decades later.

In 1920, the country had three hundred full-time juvenile courts, by century's end ten times that number, and more than three thousand separate courts annually heard more than 750,000 cases.[3] But this much-enlarged system increasingly rejected separate punishment regimes for the young criminals Florida Representative Bill McCollum called "animals...feral, presocial beings."[4] States rushed to lower the age at which an individual could be imprisoned for life. Many stipulated age thirteen. A few set no age limit. *Amnesty International* reported that between 1979 and 1998 only eight juveniles under the age of eighteen were executed worldwide. Three of those eight were American citizens, theoretically linking American juvenile justice with the harsh eye-for-an-eye punishment practiced by Pakistan and Rwanda.[5] In the year 2000, several dozen boys between the ages of ten and thirteen sat in jails, arraigned as adult felons for murder, awaiting trials that could sentence them to death or life in prison. A Florida sixth grader carried a toy fire truck to his pretrial hearing.[6]

Why did the nation's justice system demand "ever-tougher" responses to serious juvenile crime? What had happened to a country that once embraced an image of unruly and criminal children as innocent and redeemable? The history of the American juvenile court provides a lesson in the unexpected consequences of the 1960s "due process" and civil rights revolutions, which granted children new legal rights and encouraged massive internal migrations of African Americans out of the South. By the end of the century, juvenile courts talked of protecting society, not curing the "disease" of youth crime.

The "State as Sorrowing Parent": The Philosophy of Juvenile Justice

One wonders how Edith Abbott and Sophonisba Breckinridge, both members in good standing of the nation's first generation of professional sociologists, would have assessed that fateful change. For them, the proper role for

---

[3] Hunter Hurst and Patricia McFall Tarbet, *Organization and Administration of Juvenile Services: Probation, Aftercare, and State Institutions for Delinquent Youth* (Pittsburgh, 1993), 4–11.

[4] Quoted in Barry Glassner, "School Violence, The Fears, The Facts," *New York Times*, August 13, 1999.

[5] The remaining five adolescents were executed in Pakistan, Rwanda, Bangladesh, and Barbados. John Watkins, *The Juvenile Justice Century: A Sociolegal Commentary on American Juvenile Courts* (Durham, NC, 1998), 221.

[6] Rick Bragg, "When a Child Is Accused of Killing and a Law Stays Firm," *New York Times*, June 22, 2000.

the state was to be a "sorrowing parent...no longer a power demanding vindication or reparation."[7]

In 1900, the nation's first juvenile court, based on these principles, opened its doors in Chicago, with University of Chicago professors Abbott and Breckinridge among its most ardent supporters. By 1927, when all but two states embraced the new institution, 368 existed.[8] Municipal or circuit systems housed most. Even in jurisdictions lacking separate juvenile branches, municipal judges no longer mixed cases involving children and adults on the same docket.[9]

Advocates of children's courts described the innovation as the birth of a different kind of American justice. It was, but one with a long incubation. Throughout the nineteenth century, support for different law enforcement standards for children and adults gradually gained increasing numbers of defenders. Between the 1840s and the 1870s, a majority of states enacted "infancy defense" laws, which defined those under age ten as incapable of the capacity to understand the consequences of their actions.[10] States also built special rural prisons for adolescents.

"Reformatories" operated on the theory that young offenders should be segregated from the corrupting influences of adult miscreants, protected from idleness, and forced to rethink the bad lessons taught them by their old neighborhoods, often the slums of the nation's burgeoning cities. Very few of the children sent off to be so "reformed" had trials or legal counsel.[11]

The juvenile court, therefore, built on nineteenth-century precedent, although few of its supporters emphasized that fact. Rather, with characteristic exuberance, Progressive reformers proclaimed the advent of a new age, one in which children would never be thrown into jail with hardened adult felons, one in which the wisdom of emerging social science disciplines would turn delinquent, dependent, and abused children into productive citizens, one in which a juvenile court would retain guardianship power indefinitely.

The breadth of its orbit distinguished the new juvenile court from its nineteenth-century antecedents. The early-twentieth-century social reformers who made the court a special cause emphasized that it should reach troubled children, not just children in trouble with the law. Many other states copied the categories created by the pioneering Illinois Juvenile Court Act of 1899 and established juvenile courts to act "for the state, as a parent" for

---

[7] Sophonisba Breckinridge and Edith Abbott, *The Delinquent Child and the Home* (New York, 1912), 205.

[8] By the end of the 1920s Maine and Wyoming were the only two states left that resisted the juvenile court trend and lacked any such institutions.

[9] United States Children's Bureau, "Children in the Courts: Tenth Report," Publication 250 (Washington, DC, 1940), 3–5.

[10] For an historical overview of the "infancy defense," see Andrew Walkover, "The 'Infancy Defense' in the New Juvenile Court," *UCLA Law Review* 31 (1984): 503–20.

[11] Anthony Platt, *The Child Savers: The Invention of Delinquency* (Chicago, 2d ed. 1977), 50–54.

children who were: "abused or abandoned," "beggars," living with "disreputable" adults, "in danger of corruption," found gambling, in saloons, or wandering the streets late at night. Almost as an afterthought, courts added that they would also "parent" youngsters "accused of criminal conduct."[12]

In practice, most juvenile courts delegated the care of abused children to private charity societies or child welfare agencies. Hence, the focus here will be on the group that most concerned juvenile justice: delinquent children. But that category alone was a large one and included more children defined as unruly than it did criminal. The juvenile court, in theory, did what any good parent should. It called children to task for misbehavior. In fact, signs of waywardness were more important than evidence of crime. Caught early, misbehavior could be changed.

The juvenile court, then, did not just amend traditional legal structures. It challenged them outright. The new institution's most colorful defender, Colorado's Judge Ben Lindsey, demanded that the word "courts" never be used. Call them instead "institutions for human relations."[13] Lindsey's theoretical justification, if not his name, stuck.

The ideal juvenile court was a social welfare agency – disassociated from traditional common law doctrines about crime and punishment. In 1922, C. C. Carstens, Director of the Child Welfare League of America, outlined the "four essential elements of any court worthy of the name."

First: The judge of the court had to be patient, with time for the "stupidest parent" and the "meanest youngster."

Second: Most children should be sent home immediately, where, with the help of a skilled probation officer, they and their families would learn better ways of adapting to society.

Third: "Privacy" was crucial. No publicity of any kind should surround court proceedings.

Fourth: Most important, the court should ally itself with "other children's and social agencies in the community."[14]

To reinforce that agenda, juvenile tribunals banished procedures and terminology shared with traditional courts. The changes demanded two

---

[12] Author's paraphrase of the categories of children listed in "An Act to Regulate the Treatment and Control of Dependent, Neglected, and Delinquent Children," *Code of the Laws of Illinois for 1899* (Springfield, IL, 1900), 131–33.

[13] Ben Lindsey and Rube Borough, *The Dangerous Life* (New York, 1931), 109. Lindsey, a relentless self-publicist, turned out to be too colorful for his own good. In the 1920s the "champion of children" achieved notoriety as the "corruptor of youth" as he toured the country advocating the right to divorce by mutual consent. Charles Larsen, "Ben Lindsey: Symbol of Radicalism in the 1920s," in Harold Hyman and Leonard Levy, Eds., *Freedom and Reform: Essays in Honor of Henry Steele Commager* (New York, 1967), 257–62.

[14] C. C. Carstens, "The Contribution of the Juvenile Court to the Child-Welfare Movement," in United States Children's Bureau, "The Practical Value of Scientific Study of Juvenile Delinquents," Publication 96 (Washington, DC, 1922), 9–10.

unsubstantiated leaps of faith: that the interests of the state, children, and parents were identical, and that judicial procedures involving children were civil, not criminal, in nature.

Therefore, a child had no need for legal counsel, jury intervention, the right to receive notice of charges, or the chance to confront and cross-examine witnesses at trial. No "trials" took place. Instead, a judge consulted with the child's probation officer, then faced the young offender. The "meeting," not "court," room was child-friendly and included chairs built for small bodies. Judges wore suits, not black robes. As Judge Julian Mack, one of the forces behind the Chicago Juvenile Court, explained, the state's sole interest was "protection" of errant children. Therefore, the court did not ask questions about proof of guilt or proper punishment. It wanted to see a plan to "reform" a youngster's habits.[15]

Juvenile judges conducted "adjudicatory meetings," at which they read "dispositions" rather than sentences into the record. Proceedings were non-adversarial, and sanctions were indeterminate. Who knew how long it might take to modify bad behavior? "Dispositions" were not punishments for specified crimes; they were corrective measures taken to alter personality and actions.[16] Indeed, " . . . the child who breaks a law is not a lawbreaker; crime is not a crime when committed by a juvenile, and so far as children are concerned, things are not at all what they seem."[17] The help of trained specialists in "child helping" was obviously necessary.

Scholars of the juvenile court have correctly seen it as victory for the emerging professions of social work and psychology, allied with Progressivism's women's clubs and other social reform institutions. The former disciplines were just two among many that created university departments, graduate degrees, national associations, and credentialing procedures during the Progressive era. Indeed, the professionalization of society was one of the early twentieth century's chief characteristics.[18]

During decades when most Americans thought age fourteen to be an appropriate chronological benchmark for legal full-time work, and judged

---

[15] Julian Mack, "The Juvenile Court," *Harvard Law Review* 23 (1909): 102–04.

[16] For further discussion and justifications of this terminology, see Thomas Eliot, *The Juvenile Court and the Community* (New York, 1914), 7–23.

[17] Charles Hoffman, Judge of the Hamilton County (Ohio) Juvenile Court, quoted in "The Practical Value of Scientific Study of Juvenile Delinquents": 19.

[18] For the importance of professionalization to Progressive "child saving," see Joseph Hawes, *The Children's Rights Movement: A History of Advocacy and Protection* (Boston, 1991), 28–43; Hamilton Cravens, *The Triumph of Evolution: American Scientists and the Heredity-Environment Controversy, 1900–1941* (Philadelphia, 1978). For contemporary accounts by some leading early twentieth century social workers and psychologists, see Miriam Van Waters, "The Juvenile Court from the Child's Viewpoint," in Jane Addams, Ed., *The Child, the Clinic, and the Court* (New York, 1925), 217–38; William Thomas and Dorothy Thomas, *The Child in America: Behavior Problems and Programs* (New York, 1928); Helen Jeter, *The Chicago Juvenile Court* (Chicago, 1922).

those over age sixteen to be adults, juvenile justice claimed control over a much larger group of adolescents. Most offenders who appeared in juvenile court were between the ages of twelve and eighteen, but the courts' champions routinely called them "boys and girls," "lads," "children," even "needy little ones."[19] Such language use was not necessarily consciously evasive, but, notably, court advocates rarely used the nineteenth-century term, "delinquents," or the word that best characterized the youngsters involved, although prominent juvenile court supporter psychologist G. Stanley Hall popularized it. They were "adolescents."[20]

The juvenile courts' creators extended the chronological definition of childhood far beyond an age that early-twentieth-century Americans still agreed merited nonpunitive supervision, especially if the individuals in question had broken windows, stolen property, or been found swigging gin in a saloon. Such teenagers, hailed before a "children's" judge, often towered over him and couldn't squeeze into the scaled-down furniture court enthusiasts so lovingly described.

The image of the juvenile judge as kindly "father," supporters soon learned, caused problems. As Miriam Van Waters, a psychologist who served as a consultant to one of the country's largest juvenile courts in Los Angeles, wrote in 1925, "If we say to Joe, age nine, 'We are going to treat you as your father,' what image arises in his mind?" The child was just as likely to envision the man who beat him or who said in court, "Take Joe; he is nothing but a burden and an expense" as he was to see a good man with only his interests in mind.[21]

Who else to choose? As admirers embellished the philosophy of juvenile justice, they borrowed a lexicon of medical terminology, during an era when the wide publicity accorded major breakthroughs, including identification of the microbes that caused cholera and typhoid fever, won physicians new popular admiration. The judge was a "doctor"; his courtroom was a "clinic"; young offenders were "patients" who could not be blamed for "getting sick."[22] Juvenile delinquency was a disease of childhood, just as was measles or whooping cough.[23] How did the philosophy of juvenile

---

[19] For further examples of such language, see "Proceedings of the State Conference of Charities, Remarks of Mary Edna McChristie," *The Indiana Bulletin* 135 (1923): 295–99.

[20] For Hall's own assessment of the impact of his studies of adolescence in the early twentieth century, see G. Stanley Hall, *Life and Confessions of a Psychologist* (New York, 1924), 354–420.

[21] Van Waters, "Juvenile Court from the Child's Viewpoint," 220.

[22] Mack, "The Juvenile Court," 104–106.

[23] By the early twentieth century an antitoxin to prevent diphtheria and a vaccine against rabies also became available. For discussions of the professions of medicine and bacteriology in the nineteenth and early twentieth centuries, see Howard Berliner, *A System of Scientific Medicine: Philanthropic Foundations in the Flexner Era* (New York, 1985); James Burrow, *Organized Medicine in the Progressive Era: The Move to Monopoly* (Baltimore, 1977); Nancy Tomes, *The Gospel of Germs: Men, Women, and the Microbe in American Life* (Cambridge, MA, 1998).

justice, based on a treatment model, and embellished with medical jargon, translate into actual practice?

"It Is Clear It Will Not Prevent Delinquency": The Juvenile Court Through Mid-Century

In 1923, Mary Edna McChristie, a probation officer who worked for the Court of Domestic Relations in Cincinnati, Ohio, estimated that fewer than 7 percent of the some three hundred specialized juvenile courts in the country carefully followed philosophies of rehabilitative probation.[24] McChristie's number was a plausible guess, based on conversations with dozens of court officials. Juvenile courts rarely possessed the resources to act as "clinics" curing the "diseases" of childhood crime and disobedience.

Although the phenomenon of separate judiciary systems for children and adults had become near-universal by the late 1920s, in no state was it uniform. In some areas, juvenile courts were independent. In others, they served as branches of existing criminal courts, especially county circuit courts. They sometimes were divisions of civil courts with probate or chancery jurisdiction. Some were truly "children's courts" that dealt solely with unruly and criminal children. Others had the authority to adjudicate offenses by adults against children, such as desertion or physical abuse. A few juvenile courts doubled as divorce courts.

Some jurisdictions considered anyone under the age of eighteen to be a child. Others listed boys under sixteen as children but labeled girls up to age twenty-two as "underage." A small number dealt only with boys. All reviewed the cases of children who had broken laws, as well as those who engaged in activities considered unsuitable for children. In fact the average child who came before a court during the first half of the twentieth century was a "pre" delinquent, not a lawbreaker.[25]

Probation and rehabilitation were the watchwords of juvenile justice philosophy, and most children brought before courts did receive probation. In Los Angeles, Denver, Milwaukee, Chicago, and Boston – the five big cities with the country's best-known courts, where new cases averaged between seven hundred and one thousand per year – over two thirds of all

---

[24] "Remarks of Mary Edna McChristie," 295.

[25] For a summary of the variety of forms "juvenile" courts assumed within the first two decades of their existence, see United States Children's Bureau, Katharine Lenroot and Emma Lundberg, "Juvenile Courts at Work: A Study of the Organization and Methods of Ten Courts," Bureau Publication 141 (Washington, DC, 1925), 6–28; United States Children's Bureau, Bernard Flexner and Rueben Oppenheimer, "The Legal Aspect of the Juvenile Court," Bureau Publication 99 (Washington, DC, 1922). For overviews of the court between 1900 and 1950, see United States Children's Bureau, "The Children's Bureau and Juvenile Delinquency: A Chronology of What the Bureau Is Doing and Has Done in This Field" (Washington, DC, 1960), 1–24.

children went home on probation.[26] That remained true, not just through mid-century, but until its end. Most crimes, especially against property, were never solved, and eight out of ten apprehended offenders immediately pled guilty, avoided trial, and left – sentenced with a fine or a warning.[27]

Most twentieth-century adults brought to court plea-bargained as well, but, in the case of children, carefully supervised probation attuned to social science methods was supposedly crucial to rehabilitation. A widely circulated Children's Bureau manual on selection and training procedures for the position advised that a probation officer should have college training, and, preferably, additional graduate work in psychology, sociology, social work, or "home economics." He or she should see each "young charge" with great frequency, visit homes, schools, or workplaces, and meet parents, siblings, teachers, employers. The Bureau included lists of other suggested activities: trips to physicians and clinics if a probation officer noticed signs of illness, jaunts to zoos and parks, drives in the country. It noted, approvingly, the case of one woman probation officer who supervised mothers' grocery shopping habits and persuaded all members of families under her watch to "take regular baths."[28] Remember, the Bureau preached, probation work is not just a job: "It is a spiritual thing."[29] The description better fit the few dozen indefatigable, highly educated, professional women employed as members of the Children's Bureau's small staff than it did the thousands of probation officers at work around the country.

Before 1920, most juvenile courts lacked the funds to pay probation officers. Louise deKoven Bowen, a wealthy Chicago socialite deeply involved with the Juvenile Court Committee formed at Jane Addams's famous settlement, Hull House, was a typical volunteer and a dedicated, if patronizing, supervisor of her young probationers. She averaged more than ten hours daily – doing everything from pulling down bed covers to check if sheets were clean, to assuring worried parents that the ingredient

---

[26] For reviews of these courts, see United States Children's Bureau, "Juvenile Courts at Work: A Study of the Organization and Method of Ten Courts" (Washington, DC, 1925). For scholarly analysis, see Peter Holloran, *Boston's Wayward Children: Social Services for Homeless Children, 1830–1930* (Toronto, 1987), 197–245; Steven Schlossman, *Love and the American Delinquent: The Theory and Practice of "Progressive" Juvenile Justice, 1825–1920* (Chicago, 1977); Mary Odem, *Delinquent Daughters: Protecting and Policing Adolescent Female Sexuality in the United States, 1885–1920* (Chapel Hill, 1995).

[27] For discussions of patterns in sentencing, see "Juvenile Justice Symposium: Panel Two: Dealing with the Problem of Discretion," *Pepperdine Law Review* 23 (1996): 881–95. Of course the twentieth century was in no way unique in being a period when most reported crimes were never solved – although record keeping documented that fact more clearly than had previous eras.

[28] United States Children's Bureau, "Probation in Children's Courts," Publication 80 (Washington, DC, 1921), 19.

[29] *Ibid.*, 17.

in bowls of soup served their children at school was not worms, but vermicelli.[30]

However, courts found that such enthusiasm for one-on-one work with primarily impoverished delinquents soon waned. The job of probation officer became a paid one, but not a well-paid one. Through the 1940s few made more than $1,000 per year, and until mid-century the minority who worked full-time made salaries that paralleled those of relatively inexperienced schoolteachers.[31] Jurisdictions did not establish the kind of rigorous employment standards the Children's Bureau considered vital. Indeed, most had no guidelines of any sort. The job was, usually, a part-time patronage position, controlled by the political party in power. Attempts in cities to screen applicants through examination met fierce resistance from ward bosses. In the rare instances when reformers were victorious, as in Chicago, and imposed merit testing, a less-than-ideal applicant pool surfaced. More than nine hundred men and women took Chicago's first examination in 1912. Created by the same Hull House reformers who had helped write the 1899 Illinois Juvenile Court Act, the test demanded that applicants produce written answers to such questions as "What is a juvenile delinquent?" and "Why do you want this job?" to be graded by majority vote of the Juvenile Court Committee. Eighty-one, out of nine hundred, applicants passed. One failure, who answered, "a delinquent is a no-account bum," got a job anyway.[32] Even probation officers with minds more open to all possibilities usually supervised eighty or more children.[33]

The most talented supervisor would have been hard pressed to "rehabilitate" anyone when he or she worked fifteen hours per week with such a staggering number of children. If the well-trained juvenile court probation officer who worked exhaustively with each problem child was largely mythical, so, too, was the wise physician-judge.

Unburdened by the presence of juries or defense and prosecuting attorneys, and able to impose indeterminate sentences, juvenile court judges

[30] For Bowen's own account of her work with the Chicago Juvenile Court, see Louise deKoven Bowen, *Growing Up with a City* (New York, 1926), 105–21. For analysis of the role of women reformers in the first decades of the juvenile court, see Elizabeth Clapp, "Welfare and the Role of Women: The Juvenile Court Movement," *Journal of American Studies* 28 (1994): 360–83.

[31] For discussions of the problems of finding highly qualified probationers officers and paying them good wages, see "Memo: Welfare and Youth Interests, Problems," The Rockefeller Family Archives, Record Group 2 (OMR) Folder 81, The Rockefeller Archive Center, Tarrytown, New York (hereafter RAC).

[32] Another whose test received a failing mark followed Mrs. Bowen around for several days threatening to kill her. *Ibid.*, 114–17.

[33] Katharine Lenroot, "Juvenile Detention Homes." Paper read before the International Association of Policewomen, Milwaukee, Wisc., June 21, 1921, Transcript in Records of the Bureau of Social Hygiene (hereafter BSH), Series 3, Box 14, Folder 241, RAC; Charles Chute to Harrison Dobbs, January 25, 1933, BSH, Series 3, Box 14, Folder 240, RAC.

exercised enormous, largely unmediated, power over those brought into their courts. Very few were Solomons. Most juvenile courts were linked to municipal or circuit systems, with traditions of election of judges.

The apolitical figure searching dispassionately for the causes of the "disease" of delinquency was in reality a politician. And party politics often got ugly. In Chicago, Judge Richard Tuthill's efforts to create a merit-based code of employment for anyone connected with his court unleashed a campaign of abuse, during which Democratic ward heelers organized door-to-door visits in ethnic neighborhoods, stirring up trouble. Yes, they lied to worried parents, often immigrants with little English and scant understanding of American law, the juvenile court authorized "snatching" raids and sold kidnapped youngsters to lonely, childless couples.[34] An angry crowd mobbed the Cook County Juvenile Court Building, briefly holding Judge Tuthill prisoner.

Most juvenile judges faced more mundane problems: budgetary shortfalls and bureaucratic struggles over turf. The "juvenile court" in a rural area of the country usually consisted of a judge's office, where, two or three afternoons a month, children received separate attention. In 1927, Sydnor Walker, a social worker employed by the Laura Spelman Memorial, a Rockefeller philanthropy committed to the promotion of child welfare issues, investigated juvenile justice in Virginia. Judges were members of circuit courts with heavy case loads. Left "very much to shift for themselves," they stole the unreimbursed time they gave to juvenile work from busy schedules. Many paid secretaries responsible for keeping records on youthful offenders out of their own pockets.[35]

If the juvenile court through mid-century lacked well-trained probation officers and politically disinterested judges, it also generally failed to achieve its goal to "keep children out of jail." Most children who appeared in a court received probation and returned home, but, in any large city, in any given year, hundreds of juveniles remained in "detention." The fact that the word "jail" was not used meant little to children in confinement, who, with no right to a trial at all, much less a speedy trial, could be held indefinitely. In fact, many spent weeks or months behind locked doors before a judge ever saw them, even if they were never charged with a specific offense. This was especially true of girls. Boys most commonly faced burglary charges and appeared before juvenile judges because police officers caught them. Girls, far more often, were status offenders, charged with "incorrigibility," and hauled before a court by an angry parent.

34 Jeter, *The Chicago Juvenile Court*, 6–8; for additional information on the early problems of the Chicago Juvenile Court, see "Annual Report of the Juvenile Protective Association of Chicago," Paper of Ernest Burgess, Box 12, Folder 2, Department of Special Collections, Regenstein Library, the University of Chicago, Chicago, IL (hereafter UC).

35 Sydnor Walker, "Trip to Virginia – Report on June 6–10, 1927," Records of the Laura Spelman Rockefeller Memorial (hereafter LSRM), Record Group 3.7, Box 87, Folder 910, RAC.

Ann, a sixteen-year-old brought before the Ohio Cuyahoga County Juvenile Court in 1924, fit that pattern. Her parents filed a charge of incorrigibility when the girl disobeyed their direct orders not to go out with the truck drivers who delivered materials to the cardboard box factory where she glued labels. When Ann ran away with one, her exasperated father notified the court. Brought back to Cleveland by the police, Ann impressed the judge as someone who "might give in to temptation again." After hearing from the girl's Polish immigrant father that neither he nor his wife could keep Ann home at night, the court detained the girl indefinitely, sending her to the Cleveland Detention Home. Ann claimed that she had learned her lesson, but the disbelieving judge suspected that she was "too fond of good times" and "too exhibitionistic" to shape up on her own.[36]

If girls stole out of windows to meet their boyfriends, boys stole. More often than girls, they ended up in actual jails, especially in rural states without separate juvenile facilities. A Children's Bureau investigation of detention practices in North Dakota and Georgia in 1929 discovered that more than 80 percent of boys in custody shared cells with adults. One Bureau field agent found boys kept in a drunk tank crawling with rats; another discovered a "juvenile detention" facility in Georgia where boys were indeed isolated, but kept in rows of iron cages five feet high and eight feet wide. Juvenile justice was supposed to rehabilitate, but in most circumstances, "that's the theory – not the reality."[37]

Dozens of critics agreed, most prominently the Harvard-based criminologists Sheldon and Eleanor Glueck, who, between 1930 and 1934 published several volumes of results from their investigations of the life histories of teenagers paroled from the Massachusetts Reformatory for Boys. Five years after release, over 85 percent of the youths in the Gluecks' samples had committed an offense, usually another theft.[38]

---

[36] Ann was one of three girls whose case studies Olive Hoover presented to earn her Master's degree in Social Work at Ohio State University in 1925. Olive Hoover, "Girls in Juvenile Court" (MA Thesis, Ohio State University, 1925), 76–91.

[37] Katharine Lenroot to Ruth Topping, May 28, 1929, BSH, Series 3, Subseries 3, Box 13, Folder 236, RAC. Since the Bureau of Social Hygiene, founded by John D. Rockefeller Jr. to investigate crime and vice, helped fund Children's Bureau investigations into conditions of juvenile detention in America, the Bureau routinely corresponded with the BSH and regularly sent along draft and final versions of reports.

[38] Sheldon and Eleanor Glueck, *Five Hundred Criminal Careers* (New York, 1930), 167–69. Other experts agreed with the Gluecks that the juvenile courts did not rehabilitate. Some even went further. Richard Cabot, a physician who taught social ethics at Harvard, wrote, "Those who sentimentally declared that the criminal was just like the rest of us knew little about the criminal....Most of us go wrong, but can learn to do better....The criminal is the person who cannot be taught better." For Cabot, criminals could be of any age, and the juvenile court was one of the most "dubious" developments of the twentieth century. Richard Cabot, "One Thousand Delinquent Boys: First Findings of the Harvard Law School's Survey of Crime," *Survey* 70 (1934): 40.

Why should we be surprised, countered the journalist Albert Deutsch in 1950. His popular book, *Our Rejected Children*, called the average state reformatory a "hell hole."[39] Who cared whether government officials had renamed most "training schools"? They didn't reform, and they didn't train, but were instead "slums" in rural settings.[40]

Nineteenth-century reformatories were in the countryside, separating the city kids who occupied them from old haunts. Boys not hired by area farmers as day laborers worked in an institution's own fields. Those who tried to escape or resisted orders faced beatings.[41] In Deutsch's account, little had changed. Most of the country's ninety-odd mid-twentieth-century training schools still housed boys, although a few accepted girls. A majority were still prison farms, which, contrary to juvenile justice's emphasis on individual attention, housed hundreds or, sometimes, even thousands of adolescents. Rigidly imposed order prevailed.

At the Illinois Sheridan Training School, boys marched to fields under the eye of armed guards on horseback. At the Lancaster School in Ohio, the more than 750 boys serving time chanted their serial numbers and surnames, whenever spoken to by an adult. When at meals or while at work in the school's orchards and dairy barns, all boys were silent. They knew a rubber-coated wooden stick would bloody the backs of those who chanced conversation.[42]

A series of conferences sponsored by the United States Department of Justice confirmed some of Deutsch's claims. Common disciplinary practices at training schools included whipping with wire coat hangers and wooden paddles, use of leg irons, and handcuffing inmates to beds at night.[43]

Superintendent Albert Jessup, head of the Indiana State School for Boys, endorsed such punishments and stressed his refusal to employ a staff psychologist. "Wouldn't stand to have one around,'" he said, "...They're always digging into sex, as if every problem leads to sex, or away from it." Here, he said, "We use *applied* psychology": a leather paddle "applied" to a bare back.[44]

---

[39] Albert Deutsch, *Our Rejected Children* (New York, 1950), 18.

[40] *Ibid.*, 22.

[41] John Watkins, *The Juvenile Justice Century*, 25–31.

[42] Albert Deutsch, *Our Rejected Children*, 22–38.

[43] The Children's Bureau produced a transcript of the 1946 conference, whose eight hundred participants included social workers, juvenile judges, prison officials, psychologists, and criminologists. "Children in the Community," Bureau Publication 317 (Washington, DC, 1946). Conferences held in 1950 and 1952 repeated similar charges.

[44] Quoted in Albert Duetsch, *Our Rejected Children*, 47–48 (emphasis in original). Hardened prison wardens were not the only ones skeptical of "psychological rehabilitation." For decades, the private correspondence of prominent social workers, such as Lawrence Dunham of the Rockefeller philanthropic network, resonated with doubts about rehabilitation. In 1931, Dunham described a luncheon hosted by the National Probation Society, at which the featured speaker was New York Governor Franklin Roosevelt. Dunham acidly noted, "The luncheon cost $2.00. The food was good. On the basis of $1.85 for the food

Jessup's sour joke reflected the reality of juvenile justice. It had never realized it rehabilitative ideal. In 1934, Children's Bureau chief Grace Abbott, like her sister Edith a prominent University of Chicago-trained sociologist, publicized a nagging conviction previously restricted to private conversations. Since its creation by Congress in 1912 as a federal agency within the United States Department of Labor with a mandate to investigate the circumstances and institutions under which American children lived, her Bureau had scrutinized juvenile justice. In her final *Annual Report*, an ailing Abbott wearily concluded that, "It is clear after thirty years of experience that we cannot expect the juvenile courts as now organized to prevent delinquency."[45] And, by the 1950s, the prevention of delinquency was a highly publicized concern as politicians confronted a "youth crime wave."[46]

The Teenager as Thug

Juvenile justice philosophy proclaimed that there were no bad children, only bad environments, and that children could not be criminals. Such ideas conflicted not just with the different reality of juvenile courts but, increasingly, with public perceptions of threats posed by adolescents.

By the mid-1950s, the teenager as thug was big news. Newspapers carried front-page stories about spoiled, violent American adolescents. Pundits blamed James Dean, blue jeans, comic books, even, implausibly enough, "Howdy Doody" – the number-one show for children on the brand new televisions that centered many American living rooms.[47]

Worries that American teenagers were self-indulgent materialists long predated the 1950s. By the 1990s, Miriam Van Waters was long forgotten, but

and $0.15 for the speeches, the expenditure was perhaps justified. The outstanding event was the Governor's statement that the percentage of probation cases in which rehabilitation was effected was 80%. He said there were no figures in the state of New York to support this contention, and everybody present knew there were no figures anywhere to support it." Lawrence Dunham to Ruth Topping, March 17, 1931, BSH, Series 3, Box 14, Folder 238, RAC.

[45] Grace Abbott, "Report of the Chief of the United States Children's Bureau," *Annual Report of the Secretary of Labor* (Washington, DC, 1934), 93. Abbott retired to return to teach at the University of Chicago, but she lived only another four years, dying in 1938.

[46] "Statement of Senator Robert Hendrickson of New Jersey," Hearings before the Subcommittee to Investigate Juvenile Delinquency of the Committee of the Judiciary, United States Senate, Eighty-Third Congress, Second Session, On S. Res. 89 (Washington, DC, 1955): 2 (hereafter Hearing, S. Res. 89).

[47] By late-twentieth-century standards, the three most popular children's shows in the 1950s: "Howdy Doody," featuring the eponymous puppet, the cowboy drama "Hopalong Cassidy," and "Super Circus," featuring, naturally, televised circus acts, were tame. But critics at the time charged that they were "saturated in violence, twice more violence than occurs in adult television." "Testimony of Reverend Emmett Parker, National Council of Churches," Hearing, S. Res. 89, 12–13.

in the 1920s the psychologist attached to the Los Angeles Juvenile Court was a bestselling author. "The fact is," she told her readers in 1925, "to possess a radio is the only thing that keeps a modern child in nights, and then he is vastly discontented if the performance is limited to his home city."[48]

Two decades later, the problem of "discontented" adolescents worried the nation. The "youth crime wave" of 1954–1964 tapped deep fears about a changing American culture in which teenagers were out of control. During the 1930s, the Depression shattered millions of American families, and, at a minimum, at least three hundred thousand boys hit the road as jobless wanderers. World War II returned prosperity, but it did not restore traditional roles for American teenagers. Far more than Rosie the Riveter, an adolescent without a nickname symbolized the industrial triumph of the Home Front. Hundreds of thousands of children flooded into war work, while state and federal factory inspectors looked the other way. Between 1940 and 1945, statistics recorded a 300-percent increase in legal child labor alone.[49]

By the 1950s, a "shook-up" generation shook up adults. The increases in crime committed by those under age eighteen were real, the result of higher percentages of adolescents within the national population. The "Baby Boom" had begun during, not after, the war. Couples unsure of their financial future, who had long delayed marriage, finally tied the knot and immediately began families. Others, embolded by the booming war economy, married at younger ages and also had children. More American women in their thirties and their teens were first-time brides than ever before. By 1955, America's birth rate rivaled that of India, and the first group of children born during the war had just entered adolescence. In 1961, there were almost 50 percent more boys and girls in the ten-to-eighteen-year-old age group among the country's inhabitants.[50]

---

[48] Van Waters, "Juvenile Court from the Child's Viewpoint," 221. This phrase appeared in the article Waters wrote for *The Child, The Clinic* but it was a popular tag line in her speeches as well. By the 1930s Waters had abandoned juvenile justice and taken a position as the Supervisor of the Reformatory for Women at Framingham, Massachusetts. As she wrote to Lawrence Dunham, "I have a bad opinion of the work of specialized courts for adolescents." Miriam Van Waters to Lawrence Dunham, BSH, Series 3, Box 11, Folder 214, RAC.

[49] In contrast to a large, scholarly literature on women workers during the war, the subject of child labor is still quite understudied. For a summary of the Home Front impact of child work during the war, see Gertrude Folks Zimand, *Child Labor after Ten Years of Federal Regulation* (New York, 1948), 3–9. See also Joseph Hawes, *Children Between the Wars: American Childhood, 1920–1940* (Boston, 1997); William Tuttle, *Daddy's Gone to War: The Second World War in the Lives of American Children* (New York, 1993).

[50] For discussions of the impact of the Baby Boom, see Judith Sealander, "The Baby Boom," in Joseph Hawes and Elizabeth Nybakken, Eds., *American Families* (Westport, CT, 1991); Landon Jones, *Great Expectations: America and the Baby Boom Generation* (New York, 1980); Jessica Weiss, *To Have and To Hold: Marriage, the Baby Boom, and Social Change* (Chicago, 2000).

Boys in that cohort have always been disproportionately responsible for crime. In urban areas youthful gangs flourished. In New York City, for instance, the Vampires, Dragons, and Egyptian Kings terrorized neighborhoods. School superintendents reported increases in rapes and stabbings.[51]

A clear national portrait of juvenile crime, especially one that accurately compared teenage Baby Boomers with earlier generations, was difficult to draw. The FBI released a *Uniform Crime Report* in 1957 that indicated a 55 percent increase in arrests of minors between 1949 and 1956. The much-larger percentages of American adolescents accounted for some of that jump. But many of the offenses most frequently connected with juvenile arrests were new ones. Cities such as Chicago, Cleveland, and Cincinnati imposed nightly curfews on all under age sixteen. Was being arrested while out after 10 P.M. really evidence of a huge increase in youthful crime? Moreover, a generation with greater access to automobiles also got pulled over far more frequently for traffic violations. These kinds of minor crimes also swelled statistics.[52]

Moreover, political agendas abetted fears spawned by actual increases in teenage offenses. Two ambitious men, J. Edgar Hoover of the Federal Bureau of Investigation and Senator Estes Kefauver of Tennessee, riveted the nation with terrifying stories. Hoover warned that a "flood tide" of youth violence engulfed the nation.[53] Kefauver had presidential ambitions, ultimately unfulfilled. Nonetheless, was it any accident that Kefauver opened his Senate Hearings on Juvenile Delinquency in 1955 to television cameras and proclaimed that no town in America was safe from out-of-control teenagers?[54]

While most violent crime involving youngsters occurred in big cities, Americans throughout the country agonized.[55] Did "Sultans of Smut" target "impressionable" adolescents?[56] Were "blue jeans and motorcycle jackets" for boys and "V-neck blouseless sweaters" on girls responsible

---

[51] For a good case study of the growth of gangs in the 1950s, see Eric Schneider, *Vampires, Dragons, and Egyptian Kings: Youth Gangs in Postwar New York* (Princeton, 1999).

[52] These are points made by James Gilbert, *A Cycle of Outrage: America's Reaction to the Juvenile Delinquent in the 1950s* (New York, 1996), 66–69.

[53] J. Edgar Hoover quoted in *Ibid.*, 72.

[54] *Ibid.*, 143–62. The Kefauver Hearings were among the first to be televised from gavel to gavel.

[55] *Ibid.*, 67–69.

[56] Once again, J. Edgar Hoover was the author of the chilling phrases. "Testimony of J. Edgar Hoover," *Obscene and Pornographic Literature and Juvenile Delinquency*, Interim Report of the Subcommittee to Investigate Juvenile Delinquency to the Committee on the Judiciary, Pursuant to S. Res. 62 (Washington, DC, 1956), 4–5. In 1993, a tell-all biography alleged that Hoover himself was a secret cross-dressing homosexual with a taste for lurid pornography, an ironic coda for the man who made himself famous in the 1950s as the nation's number one enemy of smut. Anthony Summers, *Official and Confidential: The Secret Life of J. Edgar Hoover* (New York, 1993).

for juvenile delinquency?[57] Even if they did not live in a gang-infested inner-city neighborhood, adults recognized that American culture *had* changed. Although its exact extent was hard to quantify, the juvenile "crime wave" spurred by the Baby Boom symbolized that fact. American teenagers had more disposable income than ever before, more mobility as automobile sales surged, and more independence. They spent increased time with each other and less time with those of other ages, including their parents.

Perceptions that its rehabilitative ideal had failed, coupled with public anxiety about perceived increases in adolescent crime, helped transform the juvenile court. So, too, did changed social science theories about child development.

No Longer Innocents: Changes in Concepts of Child Development

In the early twentieth century, American sociologists and psychologists developed theories about the unique malleability of the young that buttressed the juvenile court's new approach. By mid-century, however, their successors questioned some of these concepts. In revising theories of child development they also, at least implicitly, challenged the juvenile court. If postwar teenage crime waves helped doom Progressive era philosophies of juvenile justice, so, too, did changing social science theories about the competence of children.

Many of the country's first child psychologists thought that children could not be criminals because they were incapable of criminal motivation. Adult neglect was to blame for youthful error. In 1926, Commerce Secretary Herbert Hoover reflected this idea when he said that "after reckless waste" the country had finally begun to " ... swing from correction to conservation of the young lives that represent our highest natural resource." Experiments such as the juvenile court, directed to the "betterment of innocent childhood," indicated that "as a nation we are growing up."[58]

That kind of sentimental rhetoric had long colored political declarations. It remained a staple after 1950, but within social science circles the image of a blameless and rehabilitatable child lost luster. Developmental psychologists began to argue that even very young children could understand the basic rules of an orderly society. Some even thought that at age three or four many children could form criminal intent. If that were true for toddlers, all the more so for adolescents. Teenagers should be

---

[57] Dress codes in public schools were not new to the "standards" movement of the 1990s. Joseph Manch, Associate Superintendent of the Buffalo, New York, schools, asserted, "Sloppy dress leads to delinquency." "Teen Monkey Suits," *Newsweek* 69 (1957): 102.

[58] Herbert Hoover, "The Search for the Perfect Child," *Forum* 76 (1926): 537.

held to task for the harm they did.[59] Only infants should benefit from an "infancy defense."

The rhetoric of juvenile justice never reflected its reality. However, during the court's first decades, its language fit neatly with psychological theory – especially Behaviorism's mantra that children were emotionally plastic and much more easily influenced by training than were adults. After all, John Watson, one of the movement's most prominent popularizers, told parents in his bestselling *Psychological Care of Infant and Child* that "almost nothing is given in heredity."[60]

Juvenile court philosophy also reflected vague cultural attitudes popular since the mid-nineteenth century, which portrayed children as purer than their elders. However, by World War II, a fearful public heard politicians' and social scientists' warnings. The "innocent lad" became a sneering, deceitful, crime-prone gang member. When first published in the 1930s, the Gluecks' statistics-packed studies of juvenile delinquency attracted a largely academic audience. By the late 1940s, however, Sheldon Glueck was nationally known – his popular following swelled by frequent congressional appearances. Glueck, never a juvenile court advocate, warned his now much-larger audience that adolescents, far from being easily rehabilitatable, were the members of society most receptive to Fascist thinking.[61]

In the early twentieth century, Americans made best sellers of many of dime-novelist Horatio Alger's 150 titles. The teenagers in almost all were good boys – full of "pluck" who just needed a little "luck" to succeed. In 1944, another runaway literary success featuring an adolescent boy had a far more ominous theme. The protagonist in Robert Lindner's *Rebel Without a Cause* loathed his father, his town, and everything else. When the book became a movie in 1955, girls all over the country swooned over James Dean's sullen, sex-obsessed "rebel." Their parents looked past the tight white t-shirt and saw trouble.[62]

If the juvenile court ideal floundered amidst unrealized expectations and changing popular and professional ideas about childhood, it also faced juridical challenge.

---

[59] For a good summary of the impact of such theories on the "infancy defense" and on notions of criminal culpability among children, see Gary Melton, "Taking *Gault* Seriously: Toward a New Juvenile Court," *Nebraska Law Review*, 68 (1989): 153–60.

[60] John Watson, *Psychological Care of Infant and Child* (New York, 1928), 15. In the same volume, Watson also said that "The world would be considerably better off if we were to stop rearing children for twenty years (except those reared for experimental purposes) and were then to start again with enough facts to do the job with skill and accuracy," 12.

[61] This charge was widely publicized in the years just after the end of World War II. See James Gilbert, *A Cycle of Outrage*, 40–41.

[62] The movie greatly toned down the book, whose full title was *Rebel Without a Cause: The Hypnoanalysis of a Criminal Psychopath* (New York, 1944). For discussion of popular reaction to James Dean, see John Howlett, *James Dean: A Biography* (London, 1975), 80–95.

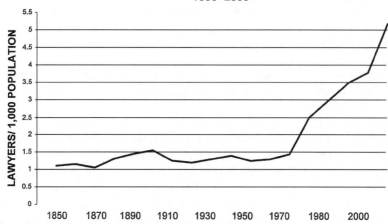

RATIO OF LAWYERS TO POPULATION, UNITED STATES, 1850–2000

FIGURE I.I   The rise of lawyers. Sources: Barbara Curron, et al., *The Lawyer Statistical Report: A Statistical Portrait of the U.S. Legal Profession* (Chicago, 1985); Clara Carson, *The Lawyer Statistical Report: The U.S. Legal Profession* (Chicago, 1994); The National Center for Youth Law (Oakland, CA, 2000).

The Rise of Lawyers and the Rise of "Children's Rights"

The postwar "teenage crime wave" was just one signal of a society on the brink of consequential change. In the two decades between 1945 and 1965, protest movements led by blacks and women reshaped American law as they argued that an equal guarantee of due process was a crucial civil right. By the mid-1960s, these large-scale changes in the practice of American law reached the juvenile courts.[63] However, they had been decades in the making and were connected to an immensely important transformation of the American legal profession.

Only in the last forty years of the twentieth century did the United States become a country with the developed world's highest percentage of lawyers. In common with many others, attorneys in early-twentieth-century America tried to increase their status and income through professionalization. They developed local, state, and national bar associations, established codes of ethics, and hammered out details of disciplinary procedures. Led by the

---

[63] Good introductions to the broader subject of civil rights and law in America since 1945 include: Jerold Auerbach, *Unequal Justice: Lawyers and Social Change in America* (New York, 1976); Jonathan Black, *Radical Lawyers: Their Role in the Movement and in the Courts* (New York, 1971); Jonathan Caspar, *Lawyers Before the Warren Court: Civil Liberties and Civil Rights, 1957–1966* (Urbana, 1972); Ann Fagan Ginger and Eugene Tobin, Eds., *The National Lawyers Guild: From Roosevelt Through Reagan* (Philadelphia, 1988); Kenneth Clark, "The Social Sciences and the Courts," *Social Policy*, 17 (1986): 33–38.

American Bar Association, its membership ranks top-heavy with better-paid, urban practitioners, attorneys established institutions that formalized study of the law. By 1920, these law schools commonly refused admittance to anyone without an undergraduate college degree. They also rarely admitted blacks, women, or recent immigrants. Written bar examinations became standard and required applicants to provide proof of residency, American citizenship, and good character.

The hurdles to a life at the bar rose. No longer could anyone able to find a mentor with whom to apprentice eventually put out a shingle. The legal profession became whiter, more male, and more restrictive. Lawyers' fees began their historic twentieth-century ascent, but growth in status took longer. An older nineteenth-century reputation lingered among a public that regarded attorneys-at-law as meddlers and tricksters.[64]

The champions of the juvenile court manipulated such stereotypes, even though some were also judges. That did not necessarily mean they were denigrating their own. Although many had legal training, often acquired through informal reading of the law, most judges in early-twentieth-century America were not practicing attorneys. Indeed, as late as 1960, only 6 percent of all members of local and county judiciaries – the domains of the juvenile courts – had passed a state bar examination.[65]

Indeed, supporters justified the juvenile court's banishment of counsel as highly beneficial. Ben Lindsey proclaimed that, in his chambers, "no lawyers" ever arose to "ostentatiously declaim – to the resentment of a youthful witness."[66] Judge Hugo Pam, of Illinois' Cook County Superior Court, assured reporters that efforts by the American Bar Association to open juvenile courtrooms to the public were the work of "ignorant...reactionaries" intent on ruining efforts to give "half a million children...real boy and girlhoods."[67] By the 1960s, a significantly enlarged American bar began to argue that what was really ruinous was the

---

[64] Of course, many argued that such a reputation never really disappeared in the twentieth century, either. For discussions of the American legal profession in the early twentieth century, see Terence Halliday, "Six Score Years and Ten: Demographic Transitions in the American Legal Profession, 1850-1980," *Law and Society Review* 20 (1986): 53–78; Barbara Curran, "American Lawyers in the 1980s: A Profession in Transition," *Law and Society Review* 20 (1986): 19–52; Richard Abel, "The Transformation of the American Legal Profession," *Law and Society Review* 20 (1986): 7–18; Kermit Hall, Ed., *The Legal Profession: Major Historical Interpretations* (New York, 1987); Robert Nelson, David Trubeck, and Rayman Solomon, Eds., *Lawyers' Ideals/Lawyers' Practices: Transformations in the American Legal Profession* (Ithaca, NY, 1992).

[65] Curran, "American Lawyers," 33.

[66] Lindsey and Borough, *The Dangerous Life*, 103. Worth noting: Lindsey also derided the social workers Colorado law required him to consult about juvenile cases as "scientific robots, jabbering away always of records, statistics, standards, and the need of more workers to roll up more records, statistics, and standards." *Ibid.*, 248.

[67] "Stenographic Report of Judge Pam's Comments," *The Indiana Bulletin* 133 (1923): 125.

juvenile court's denial of children's basic legal rights, including the right to counsel.

Changed governmental responses to young offenders were part of a larger extension of equal legal protections to blacks, criminal defendants, women, and alien residents.[68] The juvenile court was just one arena where some members of a different American legal profession reinterpreted legal precedent.

The percentages of people who practiced law in the United States spiralled during the last four decades of the twentieth century. For almost one hundred years, between 1850 and 1940, lawyers' proportions within the larger population remained relatively constant. Indeed, between 1910 and 1930, the figure even dipped slightly, although generally one attorney per every one thousand adults was the ratio repeated decade after decade. Then, beginning in 1940, and at a rate unprecedented in the history of the industrialized world, both numbers and percentages of lawyers in America soared, and great numbers of practitioners were younger, female, or members of minorities.[69] A profession with about three hundred thousand members as late as 1970 had more than a million thirty years later.[70]

The late twentieth century was a time when the country's economy generally boomed. However, that was true during the years just before World War I as well, when both reputations and percentages of lawyers stagnated. America's economy became national, then global, without prompting a great increase in legal practice. But, as governments at all levels grew in the late twentieth century, so, too, did lawyers' fortunes. Government growth paralleled the appearance of an engorged American bar.[71]

In 1970, there were three lawyers for every one thousand American adults – in 1999 almost six. A much bigger profession created "a new political class" that wielded enormous influence over public policy making. The gross revenues of the country's top one hundred firms doubled between 1988 and 1998 – from $10.6 billion to $23.1 billion. That kind of concentrated money spelled clout.[72]

---

[68] Gary Debele argues that the 1954 Supreme Court decision in *Brown v. Board of Education* was a seminal turning point in this "due process revolution." Gary Debele, "The Due Process Revolution and the Juvenile Court: The Matter of Race in the Historical Evolution of a Doctrine," *Law and Inequality* 5 (1987): 513–48.

[69] Most analysts attribute the early-twentieth-century declines in percentages of lawyers to stiffer standards for entrance into the profession.

[70] Curran, "American Lawyers," 20; "Lawyers Contend with State and Federal Efforts to Restrict Their Rising Power," *New York Times*, August 5, 1999; Barbara Curran and Clara Carson, *The Lawyer Statistical Report: The U.S. Legal Profession in the 1990s* (Chicago, 1994).

[71] Halliday, "Six Score Years and Ten," 67–70.

[72] "Lawyers Contend with State and Federal Efforts to Restrict Their Rising Power."

Childhood was only one of a multitude of phenomena that the state now supervised, as the growth of regulations paralleled the rise of lawyers' power. Many of the leaders of struggles demanding equality for blacks, women, and many other groups were lawyers themselves, who either challenged existing law or demanded increased state responsibility to ensure social justice. Undoubtedly, tens of thousands of these attorneys sincerely viewed the law as a powerful tool of social reform, but it also paid the rent. It requires no conspiracy theory to recognize that, while the entrance of attorneys *en masse* into previously hostile juvenile courts was a victory for children's individual due process rights, it was also a significant expansion of employment opportunities for those with JDs.

The growth of the legal profession was a spectacular example of an important development: the emergence of a service sector economy. In the 1960s, for the first time, white- and pink-collar workers outnumbered manual and industrial laborers. Marking another crucial demographic change, a majority of all adult women now worked outside their homes. In one of the most consequential internal migrations in U.S. history, African Americans left the South in the early 1940s, pulled by wartime work opportunity and pushed by changes in southern agriculture that concentrated land ownership and reduced demand for tenant labor. Within fifteen years, the country's most rural minority became thoroughly urbanized. Blacks' demands for justice stimulated others to rethink their own situations. And, all of these revolutions were *televised*.

In an incendiary climate that combined the rise of lawyers with the rise of rights, the Supreme Court turned its attention to the juvenile bench. Between 1900 and 1966 no cases involving juvenile justice reached the United States Supreme Court. Why? Lawyers file appeals. And lawyers and due process procedure were notably absent from the American juvenile court.[73] However, in three landmark rulings handed down between 1966 and 1970 the High Court examined a system it had long ignored. Ironically, Morris Kent, the sixteen-year-old confessed rapist whose case inaugurated a precedent-shattering series of Supreme Court decisions, was by no means the kind of boy who usually stood before juvenile courts during their first fifty years.

The Supreme Court and the Juvenile Court

Kent's case, however, raised just the sort of question that lawyers from the American Civil Liberties Union (ACLU) wanted to test – the right of juveniles to receive "fair hearing" before their transfer to an adult court. Between 1966

---

[73] An influential survey published in the *Harvard Law Review* in 1966 concluded that during the courts' first half century lawyers appeared on behalf of juvenile clients in fewer than 5 percent of all cases that went to hearing. "Juvenile Delinquents: The Police, State Courts, and Individualized Justice," *Harvard Law Review* 79 (1966): 775–810.

and 1970, three pivotal Supreme Court rulings, beginning with *Kent v. United States*, undermined legal justifications for separate juvenile justice.

In each of these cases, *Kent, in re Gault*, and *in re Winship*, ACLU intervention was crucial. The organization's agenda, however, was far more ambitious – the reform of criminal procedure at all levels. Founded in 1917 to protest the wartime Espionage and Sedition Acts' restrictions on free speech, the ACLU saw defense of the Bill of Rights as its central mission. In the 1960s, as legal challenges to Jim Crow spilled out into the streets, the ACLU took up the cause of criminal defendants.[74]

By the time Morris Kent's appeal reached it, the Warren Court had already extended rules about the exclusion of evidence, required states to provide counsel to indigent defendants, and demanded that access to counsel during police interrogations not be denied.[75] The *Kent* decision, then, fit within a bigger framework: the reassessment of constitutional standards for the administration of criminal justice in America.

Throughout their history, juvenile courts had only occasionally considered the violent crimes of repeat offenders, but all juvenile court statutes included provisions that allowed the waiver of felony offenses to adult jurisdictions.[76] Therefore, the decision by a juvenile court judge in Washington, DC, to transfer Morris Kent for trial as an adult invoked well-established precedent.

In 1961, an intruder smashed the glass door of an apartment in the District, then beat and raped its female occupant. Acting on several tips, DC police took Kent into custody. He was already well-known to local law enforcement, on probation for a series of earlier offenses, including four housebreakings.

Given Kent's record, the DC Juvenile Court remanded him for trial as an adult, where he was found guilty of the housebreaking and robbery charges, but, strangely, declared "not guilty by reason of insanity" for the rape – which

---

74 For discussions of the history of the American Civil Liberties Union, see Samuel Walker, *In Defense of American Liberties: A History of the ACLU* (New York, 1990); Diane Garey, *Defending Everybody: A History of the American Civil Liberties Union* (New York, 1998); Peggy Lamson, *Roger Baldwin: Founder of the American Civil Liberties Union: A Portrait* (Boston, 1976).

75 For a legal history that places other Warren Court criminal procedures decisions within the context of changes in juvenile justice, see Christopher Manfredi, *The Supreme Court and Juvenile Justice* (Lawrence, KS, 1998), 48–52; for overviews of the Warren Court, see Bernard Schwartz, *Super Chief: Earl Warren and His Supreme Court – a Judicial Biography* (New York, 1983); Mark Tushnet, Ed., *The Warren Court in Historical and Political Perspective* (Charlottesville, VA, 1993). The most important cases of the early 1960s revising the rights of the accused include *Mapp v. Ohio* (1961) exclusion of evidence, *Gideon v. Wainwright* (1963) the right of the indigent to legal counsel, and *Escobedo v. Illinois* (1964) conduct of police interrogations.

76 For a discussion of waiver in the juvenile courts, see United States Children's Bureau, "Juvenile Court Standards," Bureau Publication 121 (Washington, DC, 1934).

he admitted.[77] Since both activities occurred simultaneously, the jury's decision was nonsensical, especially since the ninety-year prison term given for the housebreaking offense was strikingly harsh. A bizarre sentence, however, was not the basis of Kent's appeal. As was customary, the sixteen-year-old had been handed over to an adult court without a prefatory hearing. A majority ruling written by Johnson appointee Abe Fortas, the Court's most junior member, declared that Morris Kent's due process rights had been violated. Rather than "informal, compassionate treatment" the juvenile court imposed "arbitrary" punishment.[78] *Kent v. United States* declared that a formal hearing, at which the accused juvenile had a right to have counsel present, must precede any waiver to an adult court. Morris Kent was free.[79] Soon, too, was Gerald Gault, whose case provided an even greater challenge to juvenile court procedures.

Gault was the kind of kid the juvenile courts traditionally handled. For such an important Supreme Court ruling, *in re Gault* revolved around a very insignificant alleged offense. On June 8, 1964, a Gila County, Arizona, sheriff arrested fifteen-year-old Gerald at the trailer court where he lived. A female neighbor filed a complaint charging that the boy had phoned her to ask, "How big are your bombers?" Accused of making an obscene telephone call, Gault appeared before a juvenile judge the next day, the first time that either he or his parents learned why he had been detained. Noting that the boy was on probation for throwing rocks, the court sent Gault for an indeterminate period to Fort Grant Industrial School. In Arizona, a juvenile judge could keep Gerald there for six years until the boy reached the age of twenty-one.

Gerald Gault admitted dialing the telephone but denied uttering the fatal words. Instead, he called his neighbor a mean old lady who disliked him. Arizona state law imposed a maximum fine of $50 for the offense of uttering an obscenity in the presence of a woman or child. But, even though Gerald Gault denied doing so, and his accuser never appeared as a witness, he was not "sentenced" for this "crime." His case was "disposed" for "treatment." Gault's parents decided to fight back. They demanded that their son be released from Fort Grant, which was in fact an actual fort, built in the late nineteenth century to protect settlers and abandoned by the Army in 1905. Ever since 1912, the crumbling structure had housed Arizona's largest boys' reformatory. Amelia Lewis, a New York lawyer and ACLU stalwart who

---

[77] In its majority opinion the Supreme Court found the decision baffling, as have almost all subsequent scholarly analyses of the case. "Apparently," the Court ruled " ... the jury found that the robberies that anteceded the rape ... were not the product of mental disease ... " while the rape that occurred simultaneously, was. Most High Court rulings make for relatively dry reading. The language of disbelief in this one leaps off the page. *Kent v. United States*, No. 104, 383 U.S. 541; 86 S. CT 1045, 1966, at 11.

[78] *Ibid.*, 22.

[79] But not for long. Kent was soon rearrested, charged, and convicted, this time legitimately in adult court, for burglary.

had recently retired to Arizona for the sun, instead volunteered to help the Gaults on a pro bono basis.

In 1967, Abe Fortas, again writing for the majority, famously declared that "being a boy does not justify a kangaroo court." *In re Gault* extended a child's rights to receive prompt notice of charges, to enjoy legal counsel, provided at state cost if necessary, to confront and cross-examine witnesses, and, finally, to refuse to answer questions that might cause self-incrimination.[80] Fortas's challenge to juvenile justice could not have been clearer: "The exalted idea of immunizing juveniles from 'punishment' for 'crimes'" has, he said, "failed of achievement since the beginning."[81] Juveniles who faced a loss of liberty could not be denied the protections of the Bill of Rights.

In 1970, *In re Winship* reinforced that decision. The case began in 1967, when a furniture store clerk in New York City found cash missing from her purse, which she had left in an open employee's locker located next to the store's men's restroom. A day later, when police arrested twelve-year-old Samuel Winship for allegedly defacing a brick wall, someone noticed his physical similarity to the description the clerk had given of the boy she saw running from the store. Winship said he had been home in bed, an alibi his uncle verified. But the juvenile judge who heard the case thought Samuel's uncle was lying. Even though an extensive search of the boy's home failed to turn up any suspicious stash of money, Winship was sent, like Gerald Gault, to a training school. *In re Winship* mandated that the "reasonable doubt" standard used in adult trials must also apply to juvenile cases. Had it been used, the judge who sentenced Samuel Winship could not have said that the boy had been proven guilty of theft, beyond any reasonable doubt.[82]

After 1970, the Supreme Court backed away from its frontal assault on the distinctive legal procedures of the juvenile court. Earl Warren retired, and the court's impassioned advocate of juvenile justice due process, Abe Fortas, resigned in disgrace, hounded from the High Bench by financial scandal.[83] In 1971, for instance, the Court refused to extend to juvenile defendants the

---

[80] *In re Gault* has been the topic of extensive commentary. For one of the clearest summaries of the impact of the case, see Christopher Manfredi, *The Supreme Court and Juvenile Justice*, 53–130.

[81] *In re Gault, Et Al.*, No. 116, 387 U.S. 1; 87 S. CT 1428, 1967, at 44.

[82] For an astute assessment of the *Winship* ruling, see Bernard Schwartz, *The Ascent of Pragmatism: The Burger Court in Action* (Reading, MA, 1990), 341–48.

[83] In 1968 Lyndon Johnson nominated Fortas for the vacant position of Chief Justice. During Senate confirmation hearings Dixiecrats within the Democratic Party, led by Sam Ervin, exposed several highly questionable retainer fees Fortas had accepted. For further details of the scandal and Fortas's connections with Lyndon Johnson, see Laura Kalman, *Abe Fortas: A Biography* (New Haven, 1990); Bruce Murphy, *Fortas: The Rise and Ruin of a Supreme Court Justice* (New York, 1988); Robert Shogan, *A Question of Judgment: The Fortas Case and the Struggle for the Supreme Court* (Indianapolis, 1972); John Massaro, "LBJ and the Fortas Nomination for Chief Justice," *Political Science Quarterly*, 97 (1982–83): 603–21.

right to a jury trial. At the end of the century most juvenile court systems still operated without juries.[84]

Post–"Rights Revolution" Juvenile Justice

Between 1966 and 1970, the U.S. Supreme Court opened Pandora's Box. It did not close. The *Kent, in re Gault,* and *in re Winship* rulings disputed the two underlying premises of juvenile justice: that children, legal institutions, and families all shared the same goals, and that juvenile courts were civil, not criminal. During the last three decades of the century, state legislatures responded to the Supreme Court's demand that juvenile court procedures be formalized by rewriting juvenile codes. Barry Felt, a University of Minnesota law professor, argued that the juvenile court, once an "informal welfare agency," was now a "scaled-down, second-class criminal court."[85] In fact, the changes were not that simple.

State legislatures around the country did respond with revised legal codes that substituted "punishment" for "treatment," but they also abolished many "status" offenses, based upon age and inapplicable to adults. Youngsters who drank beer, copped cigarettes, or got pregnant might or might not attract the attention of a government official – from a school vice principal enforcing a smoking ban, to a child welfare social worker concerned about the living circumstances of an unwed teen. But such children were no longer of much interest to juvenile courts.

For the rest of the century, two widely divergent approaches to juvenile justice battled for dominance. Some policy makers urged that Massachusetts be a model for the nation. In 1972, state legislators decriminalized status offenses and shuttered the state's five juvenile training schools. Advocates of the new "diversion" policy said that the only activity for which training schools trained was crime. Instead, Massachusetts kept a tiny group of youths deemed serious threats to public safety in high-security institutions and sent the rest to community programs that emphasized behavior modification. The only children in juvenile court, Massachusetts lawmakers declared, should be lawbreakers. The only ones incarcerated should be proven dangerous. The rest should be "diverted."[86]

---

[84] For discussion of the 1971 *McKeiver v. Pennsylvania* ruling on jury trials and on subsequent use of juries in juvenile court for the rest of the century, see Joseph Sanborn, "The Juvenile, The Court, or the Community: Whose Best Interests Are Currently Being Promoted in Juvenile Court?" *The Justice System Journal* 17 (1994): 249–65; Joseph Sanborn, "The Right to a Public Jury Trial: A Need for Today's Juvenile Court," *Judicature*, 76 (1993): 230–38.

[85] Barry Felt, "Juvenile (In)Justice and the Criminal Court Alternative," *Crime and Delinquency* 39 (1993): 403.

[86] For an overview of the policy changes in Massachusetts, see "Rise of Juvenile Courts," *The Congressional Quarterly Researcher*, 4 (1994): 178–83.

If Massachusetts' approach won advocates, so, too, did the "get-tough" legislation passed by Washington State in 1977, which required mandatory sentences for particular crimes, specifically emphasized the rights of victims and society, and lowered the age at which teenagers accused of felonies could be transferred to adult courts. Nowhere in the Washington State Juvenile Justice Act were the "best interests of the child" or the pursuit of "rehabilitation" even mentioned as policy goals. Not only did Washington legislators consider children fully capable of criminal intent and activities, they wanted to lock up more of them.[87]

Late-Twentieth-Century Trends in Juvenile Justice

Both the Massachusetts and Washington State models were influential, as fifty state legislatures struggled to revise juvenile codes. If children had a constitutional right to many of the same due process guarantees given adults, many state laws stipulated, they also should be held responsible for their acts. By the end of 1997, new laws were in place in all fifty states authorizing prosecution of children age fourteen or older for felonies and easing transfer procedures from juvenile to adult courts for a variety of offenses. Some states abolished any age minimum for particularly heinous crimes, such as premeditated murder. Others automatically transferred accused juvenile felons to adult jurisdictions. The nature of the offense, not the needs of the offender, determined government reaction.

But, arguing that no person should be deprived of liberty for behavior that was not defined as criminal, many states coupled tougher policies with a general decriminalization of status offenses. The broad juvenile court category of "incorrigibility" disappeared. Children who disobeyed their parents ceased to line juvenile court hallways.[88]

By the end of the century, several trends were clear. Confinement for status offenses declined dramatically, resulting in significant drops in incarceration of girls in state reformatories. Teenage boys, in contrast, were confined in higher numbers, but generally, for far shorter periods. Indeterminate sentencing gave way to jail terms of six to nine months for all but the most serious crimes. Finally, the percentages of youths charged with major felonies sent to adult courts, and then to adult prisons, soared.[89]

[87] Thomas Castellano, "The Justice Model in the Juvenile Justice System: Washington State's Experience," *Law and Policy* 8 (1986): 479–506.

[88] For good summaries of late-twentieth-century trends, see Ralph Rossum, "Holding Juveniles Accountable: Reforming America's Juvenile Justice System," *Pepperdine Law Review* 22 (1995): 907–31.

[89] "Blended" sentencing often applied, as states struggled to create new models for juvenile justice. Sometimes youths convicted of a major felony, like murder, served time in a juvenile correctional facility until they reached a certain age, after which they were transferred to an adult prison. Sometimes juveniles sentenced as adults served time in special age-segregated

The "new" transformed courts, which proclaimed "accountability," not "treatment," as their primary goal, tried to do just that. However, critics wondered whether the changes were not primarily cosmetic. Some charged that there were high levels of noncompliance with post-*Gault* procedural requirements. Others doubted if "tougher" juvenile law had any impact on crime rates, especially in a system far more likely to incarcerate black and other minority offenders. Calls for further reforms clashed with demands that the entire juvenile system be abolished. Was the claim that "nothing worked" true? Would an aging society solve the problem of juvenile crime no matter what – simply because crime rates hinged on the percentages of youngsters under age nineteen in the population?

"Nothing Works"? Juvenile Justice At the End of the Century

By the late twentieth century, the idea that criminal children could be reformed no longer enjoyed widespread support. Americans were not inclined to support policies that promised rehabilitation for any lawbreaker – of any age. However, no one philosophy replaced the idea that incarceration "reformed," and those who experienced the realities of juvenile justice described systems in chaos.

During the 1990s, police referred more than a million and a half delinquency cases to prosecutors annually. Just over half produced what adult criminal courts called indictments. Of these, most suspects pled guilty and plea bargained, as did their adult counterparts. About one in ten youths brought before a court landed in prison.[90]

Judges, probation officers, prosecutors, and public defenders all described "assembly-line" justice. In most big cities, judges heard sixty to seventy cases per day, averaging about ten minutes on each. *In re Gault* demanded that juveniles receive legal counsel, and, after 1970, most did. But few hired their own lawyers. Neither they nor their families had the money. Rather, harrassed public defenders represented the vast majority.

Thirty-one-year-old Lisa Macfarlane, an attorney for Seattle's King County Juvenile Court, faced the kind of crushing work load overwhelming most courts. On an ordinary day, she arrived downtown before 8 A.M., prepared to represent from seven to ten youngsters. That number often escalated – depending on how many teens police apprehended on outstanding

facilities that were part of adult correctional systems. Sometimes they were sentenced and incarcerated as adults, with no concessions at all made for age.

[90] This figure was lower than was true in adult cases, but not drastically lower. Regardless of age most defendants in courts pleaded guilty, and both prosecutors and defense lawyers agreed, even if not openly, they *were* guilty. About one in five adult offenders did jail time. The rest, like juvenile offenders, plea bargained for lighter sentences. Travis Hirschi and Michael Gottredson, "Rethinking the Juvenile Justice System," *Crime and Delinquency* 39 (1993): 267–71.

warrants. Usually, Macfarlane managed to meet with the client she represented before they stood before a judge, but not always. Even in the best of circumstances her consultations usually occurred hurriedly in a hallway. Young, female, and on-the-verge-of-burnout after two years on the job, Macfarlane was the kind of public defender most adolescents saw.[91]

Colleagues around the country echoed Macfarlane's frustration. Indeed, Washington State's King County Court was one of the better-rated systems in the nation. In New Orleans, juvenile court public defenders had no offices, no access to telephones, no budget for recordkeeping, much less any computer technology, and almost no chance to discuss cases – in the hallways, or anywhere else – before a hearing.[92]

Throughout the century, most children who appeared before a juvenile court received probation, but probation officers were always underpaid and overworked. By the 1980s, they were full-time employees, and much more likely to be college graduates, with degrees in social work or criminal justice. But, as did their part-time predecessors, they faced near-impossible expectations. Laura Donnelly, a probation officer for the Cook County Juvenile Court, averaged caseloads of from forty-five to sixty youngsters, each of whom she was supposed to visit at home and school several times weekly. Had she been able to compare her job with a counterpart who worked for the same court in 1930 she might have been surprised by similarly unreachable demands. Laura Donnelly regularly put in twelve-hour days. She managed to see most of her young clients a few times a month.[93] Like Lisa Macfarlane, she plotted escape to another career.

The "new" juvenile justice was supposed to be offense-oriented and sensitive to victims' rights, but victims often felt victimized all over again. Most juvenile courts did not have their own warrant officers but instead depended on local police to find children who failed to appear for hearings. Often, the accused just never showed up, and witnesses grew sick of wasting hours and days in court, only to hear – one more time – that the case in question had been rescheduled.[94]

---

[91] David Gering, "Defending Juveniles in Court," *ABA Journal* 6 (1988): 54–57.

[92] Fox Butterfield, "With Juvenile Courts in Chaos, Critics Propose Their Demise," *New York Times*, July 27, 1997.

[93] *Ibid.*

[94] The frustration was certainly not limited to juvenile courts, but critics suggested that the percentage of cases dropped simply because the accused repeatedly failed to appear was higher in juvenile court. Victims who had to take unpaid time off from work, arrange child care, or otherwise disrupt their lives, only to find that the case had been yet again rescheduled for another day, were understandably furious. For accounts of the actual workings of late-twentieth-century juvenile courts, see William Ayers, *A Kind and Just Parent: The Children of Juvenile Court* (Boston, 1997); Edward Humes, *No Matter How Loud I Shout: A Year in the Life of the Juvenile Court* (New York, 1996).

Finally, courts originally created to give "individualized" attention and treatment to troubled children depersonalized them. In Los Angeles, judges presiding over twenty-eight courtrooms conducted more than eleven hundred delinquency hearings per day. Among themselves lawyers and judges referred to this "tidal flow" of humanity by numbers or acronyms. A kid might be a "607 (b)" – the relevant paragraph in the statute connected to the alleged offense. More commonly he was an "NFC" – another teenager with "no fuckin' chance."[95]

"He" was the right pronoun. Although female crime rates rose, especially after 1960, the decriminalization of most status offenses more than compensated, and fewer girls appeared in juvenile courts. Most offenders were still boys. The disparity most pervasive in juvenile justice, however, was racial, not gender-related. Minority youths were treated more harshly than white teenagers charged with comparable offenses at every step through the juvenile justice system. Throughout the century, criminologists focused on one question: why were young Latinos and African Americans responsible for a disproportionate number of crimes? By the 1980s, statistics indicated that they committed more than one half of all homicides in the country. However, together, the two groups constituted less than one quarter of the nation's population. No explanation was definitive, although some analysts attributed the ratios to higher birthrates in minority communities, since male adolescents were always the most crime-prone in any society. Others thought that those who experienced economic and social discrimination often learned to react with high levels of physical aggression and criminality.[96] Only in the 1990s did another question finally win significant attention: why were minority youths far more likely to be apprehended than were whites?

Once arrested for the same alleged crime, blacks and Latinos were nine times more likely than were white counterparts to be sentenced to prison. There was no getting around the fact that judges, even black judges, saw a baggy-jeaned black teenage boy scowling before the bench as a career-criminal-in-the-making, while they saw a baggy-jeaned white teenage boy scowling before the bench as potentially worthy of probation.[97]

---

[95] Humes, *No Matter How Loud I Shout*, 77.

[96] For a summary of these arguments, see Margaret Zahn, "Homicide in the Twentieth Century United States," in James Inciardi and Charles Faupel, Eds., *History and Crime: Implications for Criminal Justice Policy* (London, 1980), 111–17; Elizabeth Pleck, *Domestic Tyranny: The Making of American Social Policy against Family Violence from Colonial Times to the Present* (New York, 1987), 221–22.

[97] Ellen Poe-Yamagata and Michael Jones, *And Justice for Some: Disparities in American Justice* (New York, 2000). The costs for the report, one of the most extensive reviews ever made of America's juvenile justice system, were underwritten by the U.S. Justice Department, as well as six leading American foundations: the Ford Foundation, the MacArthur Foundation, the Rockefeller Foundation, the Johnson Foundation, the Annie Casey Foundation, and the Soros' Open Society Institute.

Until the 1940s, African-American adolescents were not a regular presence in juvenile courts, which remained concentrated in the country's cities.
Indeed, as members of a minority trapped as indebted tenants in the Jim
Crow South, they were largely invisible to the greater society. The country
did not pay much attention to the criminal behavior of black teenagers until
they congregated in urban neighborhoods and formed their own distinctive
peer cultures. Behind the transformation of the American juvenile court was
an unspoken racial agenda – white fear of black gangs, now increasingly
armed with easily acquired lethal weapons – and white belief that gentle
"treatment" would never "rehabilitate" youthful black offenders.

With no clear system of collective beliefs to direct policy, juvenile justice at the end of the century experimented. Dozens of states and localities
tried the approach Massachusetts initiated and "diverted" accused offenders
into alternative programs – from drug rehabilitation centers to after-school
mandatory community service.

In Ohio, for example, the Department of Youth Services kept one quarter
of its budget, dividing the other 75 percent into eighty separate accounts,
one for each county in the state. Each county had to pay $75 per day to
cover the costs of each youngster sent into the correctional system. Each
month, any unused funds went to the county to be used for child welfare
programs. During 1996, the first year the experiment was fully implemented,
the state recorded a 50 percent drop in the number of juveniles incarcerated
in state jails.[98] Ohio officials claimed a victory, and diversion programs,
which usually included counseling and other treatment options, won vocal
supporters around the country.

Others, however, challenged diversion's success.[99] Judge Margaret
Driscoll's bewildered summary of a diversion program meant to reduce in-
clinations to violence among juvenile offenders illustrated another enduring problem: misunderstood social science theory. Driscoll, a superior court
judge in Bridgeport, Connecticut, was not Superintendent Jessup, "applying"
psychology with a leather strap, but she was certainly another monument to
social science theory's power to confuse. Stumbling through testimony before Pennsylvania Senator Arlan Specter's Subcommittee on Juvenile Justice,
she said:

In Maine (it) is very eclectic kind of treatment. It is a changing of the whole thought
process. In fact, they have a whole diagram that the youngsters seem to understand,
I do not seem to understand, in which they could tell you, there are quotations from

---

[98] Ayers, *A Kind and Just Parent*, 200.

[99] The debate about diversion continued throughout the eighties and nineties. For typical arguments on each side, see David Shichor, "Historical and Current Trends in American Juvenile
Justice," *Juvenile and Family Court Journal* 34 (1983): 61–74; Patrick Tamilia, "In Search of
Juvenile Justice: From Star Chamber to Criminal Court," *Akron Law Review* 29 (1996):
509–29.

the study I have read, how their thoughts are changed over a period of time, how the way they decide if they do, to do this, then one kind of thought comes, if they do something else, another thought.[100]

By the end of the century, a mounting chorus of critics had another thought: abolish the juvenile court. They argued that since the watershed Supreme Court decisions of the 1960s, children's courts closely paralleled the adult system. Why not save money and merge the two?[101]

Others warned it was better to "leave bad enough alone." If juvenile courts were terrible, adult courts were worse. In the 1990s, judges declared individual prisons or entire systems in twenty-four states to be in violation of the Eighth Amendment's prohibitions against cruel and unusual punishment. Almost every other jurisdiction in the country faced similar charges.[102]

One fact was indisputable. By the late twentieth century, significantly more Americans under age eighteen had their cases heard in adult court and served time alongside adults in adult prisons, a clear challenge to juvenile justice's mandate that children be isolated. And youths did not just serve adult time; they were executed.

In 1989, the United States Supreme Court held that the imposition of capital punishment on individuals over age fifteen did not violate the Eighth Amendment and upheld a death sentence for a Kentucky sixteen-year-old convicted of the rape and murder of a gas station attendant during a botched robbery.[103] By 2000, the United States led every other country in the world in the number of children under age eighteen executed by the state. It also

---

[100] "Testimony of the Honorable Margaret Driscoll," Hearing, Preventive Detention, 40. When asked, Judge Driscoll could not remember the name of the study she read.

[101] For arguments for and against the abolition of the juvenile court, see Michael Burke, "This Old Court: Abolitionists Once Again Line up the Wrecking Ball on the Juvenile Court When All It Needs Is a Few Minor Alterations," *Toledo Law Review* 26 (1995): 1027–55; Janet Ainsworth, "Re-Imagining Childhood and Reconstructing the Legal Order: The Case for Abolishing the Juvenile Court," *North Carolina Law Review* 69 (1991): 1083–88; Katherine Hunt Federle, "The Abolition of the Juvenile Court: A Proposal for the Preservation of Children's Legal Rights," *Journal of Contemporary Law* 16 (1990): 23–51; Irene Merker Rosenberg, "Leaving Bad Enough Alone: A Response to the Juvenile Court Abolitionists," *Wisconsin Law Review* 73 (1993): 163–85.

[102] Rosenberg, "Leaving Bad Enough Alone," 181–82; Hunter Hurst, "Crime Scene: Treating Juveniles as Adults," *Trial* 33 (1997): 34–37.

[103] *Stanford v. Kentucky*, No. 87-5765, 492 U.S. 361; 109 S. CT, 2969, 1989. Of the four justices who dissented, only one, John Paul Stevens, was still alive in 2000. Of the three others, Justice Harry Blackmun died March 4, 1999, Justice Thurgood Marshall died on January 24, 1993, and Justice William Brennan died July 24, 1997 (http// supct.law.cornell.edu/supct/cases/judges/htm). Analysts argued that presidential appointments made during the first years of the twenty-first century would help decide whether American justice became more or less willing to impose the death penalty on juveniles. As the century ended, decisions at state levels hinted at greater harshness, not more leniency.

outranked every other developed country in the numbers of children indicted for murder who potentially could receive the death penalty. As states abandoned status crime, they amended laws excluding children from the punishments of life imprisonment or execution. Five states removed all age limits to execution. Others declared that anyone over age twelve could face the death penalty. The American Civil Liberties Union charged that children in adult prisons faced repeated rapes and beatings, and that, in 1994 alone, adult prisoners murdered forty-five children.[104]

California's Gang Violence and Juvenile Crime Prevention Act of 1998 typified a late-century punitive approach. Prosecutors no longer needed to receive permission from a juvenile judge before charging a youth age fourteen or older as an adult. Any child between ages fourteen and nineteen convicted of a felony automatically entered an adult prison. Vandalism resulting in more than $400 damage was a felony offense. The names of juvenile suspects were no longer confidential. Known gang members convicted of minor offenses, such as underage drinking, got mandatory six-month terms in adult corrections. A majority of gang members targeted for special attention by police were either African Americans or Latinos. The bill faced court challenges, but voters loved it.[105]

It certainly symbolized a real shift in mood since the creation of the juvenile courts. If early-twentieth-century Americans sentimentalized children's innocence, late-twentieth-century citizens exaggerated their brutality. Between 1980 and 1992 the country experienced another juvenile "crime wave" – a "boomlet" as the children of Baby Boomers themselves reached adolescence, and, once again, the number of young males in society rose. Experts disputed the exact span of years involved and the extent of the problem, but interestingly, almost all agreed that, after 1992, juvenile crime declined, just as most members of the Baby Boomlet reached their twenties.[106]

The average "delinquent" in 1900 was a boy caught stealing. So, too, in 2000, although thirty years of failed wars on drugs had filled the nation's jails to overflowing with Americans who used or sold narcotics, and many offenders were under age eighteen. The apprehensive adults who responded favorably to initiatives that imposed adult sanctions on children

---

[104] See, for example, "An Answer to Overcrowded Prisons: Smaller Prisoners," advertisement paid for by the American Civil Liberties Union, *New York Times*, August 6, 2000. No reliable national statistics on the exact scale of the problem of rape and assault within end-of-the-century American prisons existed. However, academic studies of sample groups of inmates reported that at least one in five reported forced sexual contact after incarceration. The ACLU charged that those already-high rates were worse for adolescents. "Rape in Prison," *New York Times*, April 22, 2001.

[105] Evelyn Nieves, "California Toughens Penalties for Young Criminals," *New York Times*, March 6, 2000.

[106] "Hopeful Signs on Juvenile Crime," *New York Times*, August 17, 1996.

thought that violent crime among youth, especially minority youth, was dramatically increasing. It wasn't. The same year that California Governor Pete Wilson introduced the Gang Violence and Juvenile Crime Prevention Act, state law enforcement arrested seventy-six thousand youngsters. Only two thousand fell within any category involving violence. Most were alleged thieves.[107]

But beliefs often confound reality, shaping and reshaping policy. Most late-twentieth-century young criminals did not commit rape, murder, or assault. However, the tiny percentage who did possessed a gun.[108] In a nation awash in powerful weapons, underage Americans had no trouble getting one. The "feral animal" with a Saturday night special tucked in the waistband of his jeans, or worse yet, an entire arsenal in his backpack, replaced early-twentieth-century reformers' appealing, teachable child. Both existed, of course, but, most importantly, as symbols.

However, as symbols, they also represented a disturbing reality. By the 1990s, Americans killed each other at much higher rates than did the citizens of any other developed country. U.S. homicide rates averaged about ten per one hundred thousand residents, greatly higher than in any other advanced nation. Another statistic set the United States apart. Everywhere men committed most homicides, but in no other country was murder an activity so concentrated among young males between the ages of fifteen and twenty-five. Both the perpetrators and victims of American killings were much more likely to be – at least chronologically – still boys. In the nine years that separated 1984 and 1993, the homicide rate for fourteen- to seventeen-year-olds tripled. Criminologists countered that only about 1 percent of all youth crime involved life-threatening violence.[109] However, Americans who thought that the country's male adolescents had unique access to weapons that could instantly turn a robbery-gone-bad into a murder were also right.

An adolescent thief wore the face of juvenile crime at century's beginning and end. However, the boys in Ben Lindsey's courtroom *were* different. New immigrants and the poor were overrepresented there as well, but in 1900 child criminals almost never possessed a powerful firearm. The handful who did were rarely ever African American. By the 1990s, that was no longer

107 "California Toughens Penalties for Young Criminals," *New York Times*, March 6, 2000. Males between the ages of twenty and thirty still committed most of the rapes, murders, assaults, and armed robberies in the country. "Number in Prison Grows Despite Crime Reduction," *New York Times*, August 10, 2000.

108 "Guns: Weapon of Choice," *Congressional Quarterly Researcher* 4 (1994): 183.

109 For further discussion of the differences in age-specific crime in the United States and other countries, see Rosemary Gartner, "Age and Homicide in Different National Contexts," in Lawrence Friedman and George Fisher, Eds., *The Crime Conundrum*, 61–74. See also: Richard Gill, *Posterity Lost: Progress, Ideology, and the Decline of the American Family* (Lanham, MD, 1997), 35–38.

true. Even if nonviolent property crime was the constant in twentieth-century juvenile courts, the image of adolescent boys brandishing lethal handguns exercised a powerful influence on juvenile justice policy, and on American responses to teenage males. Adult optimism created the juvenile court. Adult fear changed it.

Critics argued, correctly, that children had much more to fear from adults.

2

"The Pontius Pilate Routine"

Government Responses to Child Abuse

The champions of the juvenile court thought it would help mistreated children, not just reform those who bad behavior demanded gently corrective treatment. However, a new system of children's justice was not the only reform Progressives proposed to combat child abuse. As the century began, tens of thousands of "anticruelists" searched city neighborhoods for evidence of child abuse.[1]

The results of their investigations riveted a public that opened newly fat daily newspapers to read the terrible details of a particularly heinous assault: a toddler impaled to a table with a heavy serving fork; a baby mutilated by over five hundred human bite marks; an infant plunged into a tub of boiling water.[2] Then for about forty years, between 1925 and 1962, child abuse disappeared as a burning public policy topic, only to reemerge as an enduring late-twentieth-century political controversy.

Perpetual disagreement confused efforts to assess the extent and impact of child abuse. Some experts claimed that more than three million children a year suffered abuse, while others countered that the real number was closer

---

[1] By 1910 all states and most large cities had enacted a wide variety of law forbidding cruelty to children and animals. Indeed, when the American Humane Association, the country's largest anticruelty organization, published an annotated list of protective laws at state and local levels, the tables filled 110 pages of text. Roswell McCrea, Tables I and II: "Summary of Laws for Animal and Child Protection," in *The Humane Movement: A Descriptive Survey* (New York, 1910), 322–432. At the end of the twentieth century, the American Humane Association remained an influential advocate for increasing legal penalties for child abuse.

[2] For examples from widely reported newspaper summaries, see Worcester Branch of the Massachusetts Society for the Prevention of Cruelty to Children, *Second Annual Report* (Boston, 1912), 3–6 (hereafter, Worcester). For additional reviews of early- (and late-) twentieth-century cases, see Child Abuse Prevention Act, 1973, Hearings before the Subcommittee on Children and Youth of the Committee on Labor and Public Welfare, United States Senate, Ninety-Third Congress, First Session (Washington, DC, 1973): 144–52 (hereafter Hearing, Abuse, 1973).

to six thousand.³ Some thought that U.S. prisons teemed with criminals who had been intentionally injured when young.⁴ Others weren't so sure. Warnings echoed that battering killed more of the country's children than did infectious disease and that the United States led all other developed nations in the number of infants who died at the hands of their parents.⁵ However, no one came close to providing statistics that definitively proved these claims.⁶

By century's end, the "child abuse industry" was a multibillion-dollar employment bonanza for armies of lawyers, social workers, and therapists.⁷ But Americans generally thought child abuse policy to be a dismal failure.⁸ It was – correctly condemned by child psychiatrist Reginald Lourie as a "Pontius Pilate routine" where all involved adults sought to blame someone else.⁹ As had juvenile justice, child abuse policy derailed. This chapter investigates why that happened through an examination of the rise of child protection as a public concern. It assesses reasons why child abuse disappeared and

---

³ Statement of Congresswoman Patricia Schroeder, "Child Abuse Prevention and Treatment in the 1990s: Keeping Old Promises, Meeting New Demands," Hearing before the Select Committee on Children, Youth, and Families, House of Representatives, One Hundred Second Congress, Second Session, Hearing Held in Denver, Colorado, September 15, 1991 (Washington, DC, 1992): 75. This statement reviewed a variety of statistical summaries about child abuse (hereafter Hearing, New Demands).

⁴ Statement of Perry Duryea, Speaker, New York State Assembly, "Report of the Select Committee on Child Abuse," Mimeographed Pamphlet (New York, 1972), 7.

⁵ See Opening Statement of Congressman Fortney Stark, "Child Abuse Prevention," Hearing before the Subcommittee on Labor, Social Services, and the International Community of the Committee on the District of Columbia, House of Representatives, Ninety-Third Congress, Second Session (Washington, DC, 1974): 21 (Hereafter Hearing, Prevention).

⁶ As Dr. Dan Sosin, Director for Science, National Center for Injury Prevention and Control at the Centers for Disease Control, noted: "Problems with child abuse and neglect statistics are not easily overcome. Mortality statistics are generally the most reliable injury data we can get, but they are limited by the accuracy of the information recorded on them. As you can imagine, making the determination of intent (abuse, neglect, accident) is difficult and laden with legal ramifications. For example, suffocation may overlap with Sudden Infant Death Syndrome which is a non-intentional (and otherwise unexplained) cause of death. Many categories of cause are not terribly helpful and cannot accurately distinguish between child abuse and non abuse." Communication with author, November 6, 2000.

⁷ For a trenchant take on the emergence of the "child abuse industry," see Lela Costin, Howard Jacob Karger, and David Stoesz, *The Politics of Child Abuse in America* (New York, 1996), 107–34.

⁸ Steady declines in public faith in policy solutions to child welfare problems, be it crime, or abuse, or poverty, had occurred ever since the mid-1970s. Summaries of the polls commissioned by the National Committee for the Prevention of Child Abuse (NCPCA) can be found in "Reauthorization of the Child Abuse Prevention and Treatment Act (CAPTA)," Hearing before the Subcommittee on Children, Family, Drugs, and Alcoholism of the Committee on Labor and Human Resources, United States Senate, One Hundred Second Congress, First Session, April 16, 1991 (Washington, DC, 1992): 81–86 (hereafter Hearing, Reauthorization, 1991).

⁹ "Remarks of Reginald Lourie," April 24, 1973, Hearing, Abuse, 1973, 566.

then reemerged as a hot-button policy issue. Finally, it analyzes the consequences of state and federal passage of child abuse reporting and prevention laws.

The Rise of Public Child Protection

Before the late nineteenth century, public officials rarely interfered with a family's right to discipline resident children. A handful of criminal cases involved children permanently injured by repeated brutal beatings, but even then, most accused parents were not convicted.[10] Nonetheless, Victorian adults gradually embraced the idea that the defenseless should be protected, although animals first caught their attention.

Leagues that emphasized the need for kinder treatment of dogs and cats flourished during the Gilded Age, as did organizations that raised money to buy blankets and public drinking fountains for horses. New laws forbade the torture of animals. Hundreds of cities around the country made the then-common boys' game of burning kittens alive illegal, punishable by fine.[11]

The movement's acceptance, especially by an urban elite, reflected the influence of two larger intellectual phenomena: nineteenth-century Darwinianism and Romanticism. The publication of Charles Darwin's *Origin of Species* in 1859 had a huge, but divisive, impact. "Social" Darwinists, led by the British philosopher Herbert Spencer, concluded that human society, too, operated by rules under which only the fittest survived and argued that it was inevitable that the weak perish. Critics challenged that view and argued that *Origin of Species* proved something very different – the strong ties between humans and other animals.[12]

If Darwin's ideas had a formative influence on the nineteenth century, so, too, did Romanticism – which said that nature was beautiful; animals noble, children innocent. Embarking on crusades that earlier generations would have found puzzling, nineteenth-century reformers founded "Bide-A-Wee Homes" for stray cats, demanded that softer paving stones be used on city streets to prevent unnecessary laming of horses, and distributed pamphlets urging people never to rob birds' nests or chase butterflies. Coincident

---

[10] Mason Thomas, "Child Abuse and Neglect: Historical Overview, Legal Matrix, and Social Perspectives," *North Carolina Law Review* 50 (1972): 302–3.

[11] For a discussion of this history and a directory of all local humane societies in existence in America by the year 1900, see Appendix II: "Directory" in Rosewell McCrea, *The Humane Movement*, 157–215.

[12] A number of analysts have noted the importance of Darwin's ideas to the creation of a Victorian child saving ethos. See Linda Gordon, *Heroes of Their Own Lives: The Politics and History of Family Violence* (New York, 1988), 36–48; Thomas Jordan, "Victorian Child Savers and Their Culture: A Thematic Evaluation," *Mellen Studies in Sociology* 19 (1998): 13–36.

with the decline of the nation's rural population, a love for the unspoiled countryside blossomed.[13]

Moreover, a late-nineteenth-century generation with a keener sense of the importance of the natural environment reared sons who incorporated conservation into public policy.[14] By the early twentieth century, the federal Interior Department supervised a system of national parks and forests. States and localities followed the example.

Ordinary citizens, who for much of the nineteenth century slaughtered tens of millions of native animals, often just for sport, mourned the extinction of species. The world's last passenger pigeon had a name and a special cage at the Cincinnati Zoo. On September 1, 1914, Martha's death made the newspapers.[15]

Americans grieved a bird once killed in huge numbers for pleasure and left to rot in the fields. It was a change of social consciousness that helped rouse interest in the fate of other unprotected creatures. Lists of "saved children" joined those kept for "redeemed dogs," and new organizations, such as the New York Society for the Prevention of Cruelty to Children, emerged.[16] The development was logical. Progressivism demanded that the strong help the weak, primarily through improving society. Where better to begin than with children, even if that meant that the state had to become a substitute parent?

That idea moved American society into unfamiliar terrain. The use of private philanthropies as proxies cut a trail. By 1910, over 250 organizations passionately attacked "cruelists" – usually a child's own parents.[17] Like their counterparts in animal protection, members in these societies were typically from "the better class of citizens."[18] Both groups identified the "brutal poor" as the ones most likely to beat a child or whip a horse.[19]

---

[13] For further discussion of Victorian Romanticism, see James Turner, *Reckoning with the Beast: Animals, Pain, and Humanity in the Victorian Mind* (Baltimore, 1980).

[14] For instance, two of the early twentieth century's most fervent and effective environmental conservationists, Theodore Roosevelt and Gifford Pinchot, were both raised in families that included leaders of "anticruelty" crusades.

[15] Martha's death marked the first time in history when scientists recorded – to the hour – when a species became extinct. The publicity about her death marked a kind of watershed in American consciousness of man's impact on other species and on the environment. For more discussion of Martha's fame, see Errol Fuller, *Extinct Birds* (Ithaca, NY, 2000).

[16] Elbridge Gerry, "The Relations of the Society for the Prevention of Cruelty to Child-Saving Work," *Proceedings of the National Conference of Charities and Correction* (Boston, 1882): 13034. The New York Society, chartered in 1874, was the nation's first.

[17] "Child rescue" was the most commonly stated of missions, and gross physical abuse by parents or relatives, the most pressing problem identified by the movement. See American Humane Association, *Thirty-Third Annual Report of the American Humane Association* (New York, 1910), 34–36.

[18] Roswell McCrea, *The Humane Movement*, 3.

[19] *Ibid.*, 142.

However, there was a crucial difference between animal and child protection groups. The former depended on members' dues, while the latter did not. Although both philanthropic and government officials consciously downplayed their relationships, private child protection was, from the beginning, semipublic. Almost one half of the budgets of the nation's most prominent child saving societies, those in New York, Massachusetts, and Pennsylvania, came from municipal subsidies. In fact, city authorities often paid twice – for investigation and rescue services, then through reimbursement of fines levied against persons convicted of cruelty.[20] Interestingly, fines for maltreatment of children were generally less steep than those magistrates' courts imposed for cruelty to animals. In 1908 a survey by the American Humane Association recorded 26,015 convictions involving adults who injured children. Fines paid averaged $2 per case, contrasted to $7 when charges involved animals.[21] However, courts rarely returned the larger fines to the coffers of the societies that initiated the cases.

In the late twentieth century, tensions between children's rights to protection, parents' rights to discipline offspring, and states' duties to both groups made debates about child abuse minefields of controversy. But between 1900 and 1925, challenges to new roles played by governments were muted. Not many realized the extent to which private children's aid societies were allies of the state. Moreover, the objects of scrutiny rarely could effectively protest the actions of private societies commonly known to the urban poor as the "Cruelty."

Most societies were urban, and most chastised the "irresponsible poor."[22] The Board of Directors of the Worcester branch of the Massachusetts Society for the Prevention of Cruelty to Children repeated a typical charge when it argued that "It would be impossible for the normal parent to conceive of the ease and willingness with which some fathers and mothers give up their children, expecting, even hoping, that they will never see them again."[23]

Impoverished arrivals had difficulty challenging such patronizing stereotypes, just as they found the rules of the juvenile courts bewildering. Significantly, however, residents of poor city neighborhoods themselves often solicited the help of the Cruelty and regarded society officials with both fear and approval. A working-class family might resent a society official's visit, but a wife afraid of a vicious husband who beat her and the children or a

---

[20] For discussions of the financial organization of charitable child helping and anticruelty societies, see William Letchworth, *History of Child Saving in the United States* (New York, 1926), 95–130.

[21] McCrea, *The Humane Movement*, 23. See also: *Annual Report of the Washington (DC) Humane Society* (Washington, DC, 1908), 12–20.

[22] Worcester, 6.

[23] *Ibid.*

CASE NO. 25,745 ON THE SOCIETY BLOTTER : ANNIE WOLFF, AGED SEVEN YEARS, AS SHE
WAS DRIVEN FORTH BY HER CRUEL STEP-MOTHER, BEATEN AND STARVED, WITH HER
ARMS TIED UPON HER BACK ; AND AS SHE APPEARED AFTER SIX MONTHS IN THE SOCIE-
TY'S CARE.

PHOTO 2.1   Worcester Branch of the Massachusetts Society for Prevention of Cruelty
to Children, *Second Annual Report* (Boston, 1912), 2.

concerned neighbor who heard screams from an adjoining courtyard was just as likely to file a report and ask for intervention.[24]

Indeed, early-twentieth-century child rescue was part of a larger phenomenon that sought to relocate the children of many of the more than twenty million immigrants who crowded the nation's fast-growing cities.[25] Most of the hundreds of thousands of youngsters sent west on "orphan trains" were certainly not alone in the world, despite publicity that painted them as friendless "tiny waifs and strays." The majority had at least one living parent, and probably half were adolescents, many eager volunteers. Aid societies that wanted to be seen as saviors of the helpless, not employment agencies, deemphasized the fact that many of their "large boys and girls" were, by the standards of their era, certainly on the verge of adulthood, clearly capable of full-time labor.

However, the romantic vision propelling the trains also spurred the growth of anticruelty societies. City dwellers who championed what they thought to be rural values created both phenomena. Some children went to loving homes. Many ended up working long hours for their room and board. Uncounted numbers of older youngsters thwarted these adult plans. They demanded real wages or simply walked away.[26]

Reformers judged what would be best for "orphans" through the prism of the norms of their own class and culture and often unfairly conflated cruelty and poverty. Were the "filthy" parents condemned by the Massachusetts Society for the Prevention of Cruelty to Children abusive because they "foolishly procrastinated" in seeking treatment of their daughter's neck abscess? Or were they, more likely, unaware that free care was available at the philanthropy's clinic?[27]

---

[24] This is a point made by the historian LeRoy Ashby, *Endangered Children: Dependency, Neglect, and Abuse in American History* (New York, 1997), 59–61. Ashby's more nuanced argument challenges one made in Elizabeth Pleck's earlier, pioneering book on domestic violence. Pleck focused on poor people's fear that anti-cruelty societies would take away "children who were spanked too hard." Elizabeth Pleck, *Domestic Tyranny: The Making of American Social Policy Against Family Violence from Colonial Times to the Present* (New York, 1987), 76.

[25] During these years the percentage of foreign-born in the American population ranged from 11 to 15 percent, though that figure was much higher in the nation's biggest cities. For a good overview of patterns in immigration, see Roger Daniels and Otis Graham, *Debating American Immigration, 1882–Present* (Lanham, MD, 2001), 6–29.

[26] Contemporary estimates put between 150,000 and 400,000 youthful passengers on the trains. The huge disparity reflects the highly unregulated nature of the venture. For further discussion of the "orphan trains" phenomenon, see Marilyn Irvin Holt, *The Orphan Trains: Placing Out in America* (Lincoln, NE, 1992); A. Blake Brophy, *Foundlings on the Frontier: Racial and Religious Conflict in Arizona Territory, 1904–1905* (Tucson, AZ, 1972); Linda Gordon, *The Great Arizona Orphan Abduction* (Cambridge, MA, 1999); Stephen O'Connor, *Orphan Trains: The Story of Charles Loring Brace and the Children He Saved and Failed* (New York, 2001); Clay Gish, "Rescuing the 'Waifs and Strays' of the City: The Western Emigration Program of the Children's Aid Society," *Journal of Social History* (1999): 121–41.

[27] Worcester, 5.

Nonetheless, court records and charity society reports detailed horrors: children beaten, stabbed in the eyes with scissors, thrown from third story windows.[28] Poverty imposed high levels of stress, and surely some adults behaved unforgivably. Had levels of abuse risen dramatically when compared to earlier ages? Was the problem most common among the poor and relatively absent from the homes of privileged families? Reliable records to answer these questions for the years 1900–1920 just don't exist.

Child abuse at some level plagued the early twentieth century. No doubt it continued. However, after the mid-1920s, attention to the problem as a public policy matter virtually ended.[29] The appearance of child abuse as an issue had many causes: romantic concern for helpless creatures, Darwinianism, the growth of alliances between anticruelty philanthropies and city governments, and worries about the "ignorant" immigrant poor.

Two major factors hastened its disappearance as a social concern. Abused children were a dramatic symbol of the dangers high levels of immigration posed. After 1924, quota restrictions imposed by the National Origins Act caused percentages of new arrivals to the nation's urban areas to stagnate, then decline.[30] Concomitantly, anticruelty philanthropies broadened their concerns and accepted the "scientific" ideas about charity promoted by men such as John D. Rockefeller, Sr. Rescuing a child was well and good, but even better would be the correction of conditions that caused abuse in the first place. As prevention became a watchword, interest in child rescue faded.[31]

---

[28] For a representative litany, see *25th to 31st Reports of the Pennsylvania Society for the Prevention of Cruelty to Children* (Philadelphia, 1901–1909).

[29] After 1925, the number of court cases involving adults charged with cruelty to children declined significantly. By 1933, most adults who were prosecuted under early-twentieth-century municipal and state anticruelty statutes were actually charged with nonsupport, not any kind of specified injury, of a child. In the bleak times of the Great Depression, nonsupport was not a voluntary choice, but a fearful reality, for many parents. For discussion of statistics covering classification of neglect offenses, see *Dependent and Neglected Children: A Report of the Committee on the Socially Handicapped, Dependency, and Neglect* (Homer Folks, Chairman, J. Prentice Murphy, Vice Chairman), Published Proceedings of the White House Conference on Child Health and Protection (New York, 1933), 386–92.

[30] Some analysts who discuss the history of child abuse as a political issue blame the financial and social turmoil of the Great Depression, which pushed a great number of more compelling problems onto policy makers' agendas. For an instance of this sort of argument, see Barbara Nelson, *Making an Issue of Child Abuse: Political Agenda Setting for Social Problems* (Chicago, 1984), 10–11. However, this explanation does not jibe chronologically with the rapid decline of interest and decrease of influence of child protection societies in the mid-1920s. Immigration restriction does.

[31] The historian LeRoy Ashby sees the influence of Freudianism, which encouraged social workers to regard reports of abuse as children's fantasies, as important to the decline of child abuse as a political issue. Ashby, *Endangered Children*, 118–19. However, Geoffrey Steere argues that while 1920s popular culture embraced all sorts of misconceived forms of Freudianism – everyone talked about the Id, though few understood exactly what they were saying – among psychological and social work professionals, Freudianism did not really take

The "Rediscovery" of Child Abuse

Why, then, did the issue resurface spectacularly decades later during the 1960s? Medical innovations, a socially activist reform climate, and bureaucratic survival strategies all helped spur the reemergence of child abuse and neglect as a public policy issue.

In the early twentieth century, parents and caretakers accused of cruelty frequently countered that an accident caused a child's shattered jaw or broken arm. Since most injuries occurred out of public sight, and most relatives did not confess guilt, evidence of child abuse was difficult to obtain. By mid-century, however, X-rays proved what parents denied.

In 1962, the *Journal of the American Medical Association (JAMA)* published the results of a pathbreaking nationwide survey that labeled nonaccidental injuries of children "the battered child syndrome." The Denver pediatrician Dr. C. Henry Kempe and his coauthors reported that most adults claimed a child had suffered an accident. Only a tiny fraction of "sociopaths" said, "Yeah, Johnny would not stop crying, so I hit him. So what?" Since the majority of injured children were infants under the age of one, even physicians found it hard to believe that parents were to blame. But Kempe urged, "The bones tell the story." Radiologic examination of a child's skeleton often revealed healing lesions or unusual patterns of fractures in long bones that almost never occurred in genuine accidents. While some abusers were severely mentally ill, most were "normal" people with insufficient control of aggressive tendencies. Attempts to counsel most abusers were "far from successful." Children returned to their homes were "likely to be assaulted again."[32]

Although the article's theses were frightening, its language was not. Kempe carefully instructed the physicians who read *JAMA* how to recognize the characteristics of residual external cortical thickening – bone irregularities he identified as tell-tale markers of child abuse.[33] Had it remained in this form, the study would likely have been of interest only to pediatric specialists.

Instead, in a climate roiled by social crusades, a technical medical survey became a cause célèbre. Newspaper and magazine editors rarely included the

---

hold until the 1930s, a decade after the decline of child abuse as a public policy concern. Geoffrey Steere, "Freudianism and Child Rearing in the 1920s," *American Quarterly*, 20 (1968): 759–67.

[32] C. Henry Kempe, Frederick Silverman, Brandt Steele, William Doregemueller, and Henry Silver, "The Battered Child Syndrome," *Journal of the American Medical Association* 181 (1962): 17–24. The article concluded that "significant" numbers of American children were abused, though, notably it offered no data other than the few hundred cases reported from its seventy-one sample hospitals. Elizabeth Pleck confirms Kempe's observation that pediatricians had great difficulty believing that the parents of their small patients could be so abusive. Radiologists, by contrast, were more objective observers. Freqently they had never met the parents or other relatives. Pleck, *Domestic Tyranny*, 167.

[33] *Ibid.*, 21–23.

JAMA on their lists of required reading, but almost all watched the AP wire. Kempe, brilliantly, persuaded the American Medical Association (AMA) to issue a press release with a title that caught Associate Press summarizers' attention: "Parental Abuse Looms in Childhood Deaths." Within weeks, Kempe's findings were refashioned for a much wider audience.

As had an earlier generation during the Progressive era, millions of Americans again opened daily newspapers and weekly mass-circulation magazines such as *Time, The Saturday Evening Post,* and *Life* to read shocking stories about savage assaults on children by their own parents. They learned that every hour of every day, somewhere in the United States, children were being beaten senseless, burned with cigarettes and matches, scarred with boiling oil, tied to poles, locked in closets, even buried alive.[34]

The almost-instantaneous publicity turned a new medical nomenclature into a household word. That alone might have been enough to propel legislative efforts to prevent "battered child syndrome." However, organizational survival strategies coupled with an activist social climate also encouraged governments to take greater responsibility to protect children.

The American Humane Association (AHA) was a doughty surviver, by the 1950s one of the few national private philanthropies left with a mission to prevent cruelty to children.[35] Vincent De Francis, the tough-talking New Yorker who headed the AHA's Children Division, decided to give the issue, and not coincidentally his organization, renewed visibility. He commissioned the first-ever comprehensive survey of the availability of children's protective services in the United States. Published in 1956, the AHA report condemned a "woefully inadequate" system that intervened only when abuse was "too gross for communities to tolerate."[36] Social workers, De Francis fumed, "...are more comfortable serving a middle class clientele with the ability to pay a fee."[37]

De Francis, a lawyer himself, wanted a legal solution to the problem. He found allies among similarly angry members of the United States Children's Bureau, especially after 1962, when the Humane Association cooperated

---

[34] Barbara Nelson provides an excellent summary of mass-media reaction to the Kempe article, *Making an Issue of Child Abuse*, 56–63.

[35] Child rescue societies disappeared, but animal protection just got more popular during the century, an interesting comment on the "Century of the Child." At the end of the century the Humane Society of the United States had seven million members and was just one of dozens of such protection groups (http://www.hsus.org/ace/12552). For an overview, see Harold Guither, *Animal Rights: History and Scope of a Radical Social Movement* (Carbondale, IL, 1998).

[36] Vincent De Francis, still an AHA leader, provided extensive testimony that included a review of the 1956 report's conclusions when he appeared before Walter Mondale's Senate Subcommittee on Children and Youth in 1973. See "Testimony of Vincent De Francis," Hearings, Abuse, 1973, 472. The AHA report itself is Vincent De Francis, *Child Protective Services in the United States: Reporting a Nationwide Survey* (Denver, 1956).

[37] *Ibid.*, 469.

with Children's Bureau staffers to produce a second survey that described 662 case studies of child abuse, spread across forty-eight states. These incidents involved the kind of terrible stories that sold front pages: children with gouged-out eyes, children drowned in bathtubs, children tortured with whips, or set on fire with cigarette lighters. The leaders of both the Children's Bureau and the Humane Association, like most Americans, recoiled from such information and sincerely worried that institutional responses to child abuse lacked sufficient coherence, commitment, and cash. But they also were members of organizations facing oblivion unless they found a popular cause to champion.

The Children's Bureau had always been small. Even at its height during the 1940s, its professional and support staff numbered no more than 250 individuals. Nonetheless, since 1912 it had reported directly to the Secretary of Labor.[38] That changed in 1947. Secretary of Labor Frances Perkins, the first female Cabinet appointee, unwittingly spurred a war with the Eightieth "Meat-Axe" Congress that badly bruised her Department. Perkins, a Holyoke-educated blue-blood, and a highly effective former Industrial Commissioner, was one of the large group of New York State reformers Franklin Roosevelt brought to Washington. Despite Perkins' qualifications, union leaders violently opposed a woman as Labor's head. Some even kept their initial vow never to speak to her.

Perkins, for her part, did not make peace with a constituency used to her predecessors: backslapping good old boys who often convened meetings with AFL and CIO officials in the capital's bars. The self-righteous Perkins proved easy prey for rumor-mongering campaigns, which included totally false charges that she was a bigamously married, practicing Communist. By the end of 1947 the Department of Labor had lost almost 50 percent of its budget and many of its agencies and bureaus. The Children's Bureau ended up in the new Federal Security Administration, where, rather than reporting directly to a high federal official, it was one of many divisions in a non-Cabinet-level agency. Moved again in 1968, late in the Johnson Administration, to the Welfare Administration of the Department of Health, Education, and Welfare, a new Department fast-becoming-mammoth, the Bureau finally lost any real independence. After 1969, in the wake of yet another round of reorganizations conducted by Robert Finch, it was part of HEW's newly formed Office of Child Development. The Nixon Administration created this new flowchart to gut the Great Society's Office of Economic Opportunity (OEO).[39] The Children's

---

[38] Labor did not emerge as a separate Cabinet-level department until 1913, and the Children's Bureau transferred to Labor from the Department of Labor and Commerce.

[39] For discussions of the reorganizations that slashed the Labor Department and of the fate of the Children's Bureau in the 1950s and 1960s, see Judith Sealander, *As Minority Becomes Majority: Federal Reaction to the Phenomenon of Women in the Work Force, 1920–63* (Lexington,

Bureau, almost as an afterthought, lost control of most of its former functions.[40]

Therefore, in the early 1960s, when the Children's Bureau allied with the Humane Association, two organizations almost down for the count staggered up from the mat as champions of child abuse prevention. The Children's Bureau successfully lobbied high-ups within HEW for a special appropriation to research and distribute a model child abuse law.

First published in 1963, the Children's Bureau proposal was very influential, in part because Children's Bureau staffers learned lessons from the furor surrounding the identification of "battered child syndrome" and released accessible versions of the report to the press.[41] Arguing that children were "more than ever vulnerable" to danger within their own homes, the Bureau emphasized a premise that had, at least implicitly, motivated its small staff of reform-minded members since the Progressive era: the creation of optimal conditions for the country's children demanded government intervention. When their own parents and caretakers injured them, children needed the state to act as their protector. What could be more obvious? Legislatures in all fifty states quickly agreed. Within a brief, four-year period, between 1963 and 1967, every state passed some kind of child abuse reporting statute, and most directly copied Children's Bureau language. No politician wanted to come out against prevention of child abuse, especially during a decade of increased attention to social justice and civil rights.

Child Abuse Legislation: Part One

If youth accused of crimes had rights, how could any great society deny totally innocent children that most basic of rights, safety from physical injury? State reporting laws readily accepted the Children's Bureau's premise: mandatory reporting of known and suspected cases of child abuse could help alleviate the "evil."[42]

First passed by California in 1963 and finally by Hawaii in 1967, the fifty state abuse reporting laws shared many similarities. The primary duty

---

KY, 1988), 133–37; Gilbert Steiner, *The Children's Cause* (Washington, DC, 1976), 37–40; Barbara Nelson, *Making an Issue of Child Abuse*, 37–50.

[40] In the decades after its near-execution in 1947, the Labor Department revived, largely through regaining authority over workmen's compensation. But, arguably, among Cabinet-level departments it became a late-twentieth-century backwater, as functions once controlled by Labor devolved to HEW, then HEW's successor, Health and Human Services, as well as to other federal agencies.

[41] U.S. Department of Health, Education, and Welfare, Welfare Administration, United States Children's Bureau, "The Abused Child: Principles and Suggested Language for Legislation on Reporting of the Physically Abused Child" (Washington, DC, 1963).

[42] U.S. Children's Bureau, "The Abused Child," 3. The word appeared in the Children's Bureau model law and was widely copied.

to report verified or suspected child abuse rested with physicians and other medical personnel. Some states extended mandatory reporting of abuse to social workers, teachers, pharmacists, and dentists. In all but three states, these professionals received immunity from civil or criminal lawsuits provided they reported in good faith and participated fully in all subsequent judicial proceedings. Failure to report carried criminal penalties, including fines and prison terms. In addition to demanding that certain people provide information, almost all states created "hot-line" systems that enabled anyone, anonymously, to phone in charges.

Most laws established vague guidelines mandating that cases of intentional physical mistreatment be reported and cited four categories of suspicious injuries: (1) a very young child with a severe injury; (2) a child with multiple injuries; (3) a child with many scars; and (4) a child with injuries that could not plausibly have been caused in the manner described by parents or caretakers.[43]

By requiring notification of nonaccidental physical injuries, reporting statutes applied an old legal concept, *res ipsa loquitur.* Meaning "the thing speaks for itself," the doctrine recognized the ability of an injury alone, in the absence of reasonable explanation, to condemn. But while invoking established legal theory, reporting legislation also waived two very traditional principles underpinning rules of evidence: physician-patient and husband-wife privilege. Physicians could not invoke doctor-patient confidentiality. One spouse familiar with alleged abuse had to testify in court against the other, if both were not charged.[44]

Reporting laws certainly condemned abusive parents and caretakers, but were children saved? Debate raged for the rest of the century, but one development was obvious. The rate of incidence of reported cases of child mistreatment increased tremendously. That outcome was totally unanticipated. No state coupled reporting legislation with meaningful budgetary increases for agencies that handled child protection. Predictably, though no one predicted it, the latter were soon overwhelmed.

---

[43] A complete, annotated summary of child abuse and neglect reporting laws can be found in U.S. Department of Health, Education, and Welfare, Administration for Children, Youth, and Families, National Center on Child Abuse and Neglect, United States Children's Bureau, "Child Abuse and Neglect: State Reporting Laws" (Washington, DC, 1978). A few states required reporting child abuse to a public child welfare agency in addition to law enforcement. States that required that the larger group of professionals listed report included: Alabama, Arkansas, Alaska, California, Illinois, Indiana, Iowa, Maryland, Minnesota, Mississippi, Montana, Nevada, New Mexico, New York, North Carolina, and Wisconsin. Tennessee included undertakers and coroners on the list. Minnesota, Oregon, and Wisconsin did not grant immunity to the professionals they required to report known or suspected child abuse.

[44] For discussions of the application of *res ipsa loquitur* doctrine, see Vincent De Francis and Carroll Lucht, *Child Abuse Legislation in the 1970s* (Denver, 1974), 184–86; For a discussion of the waiver of privileges against testimony that child abuse reporting laws enacted, see Thomas, "Child Abuse and Neglect," 333.

Florida was typical. In 1965, state protective services reported only six-teen cases of child abuse statewide. By 1971, the number had risen to 250. In 1972, officials initiated a television and radio campaign that described the provisions of the state's reporting law. Reported incidents increased to fourteen thousand. The next year, Florida inaugurated a statewide "hot-line" program, with a single toll-free number. Alleged incidents ballooned within twelve months to twenty-eight thousand. However, the number of child wel-fare and protective service workers employed in Florida remained almost static after 1970.[45]

State after state faced similar dilemmas. Swamped by thousands of calls to hot-lines, staffers often put phones on answering machines, or took down information, only to add it to an impossibly high pile of uninvestigated cases. A journalist's exposé revealed that fully one third of the people who dialed New York State's hot-line in Albany in 1979 never got through. And the New York system was better funded than most.[46]

In theory, state child protective service (CPS) workers were empathetic, skilled professionals, who constantly weighed three difficult-to-reconcile in-terests: those of the state, parents, and children. Yet, in common with pro-bation officers in the juvenile courts, protective service employees usually failed to meet the high standards social science theory demanded. Instead, child protection was one of the most poorly paid of all government jobs. Toll booth collectors and entry-level clerks earned higher wages. In 1970, a full-time protective services employee's annual salary averaged less than $13,000. For the rest of the century, this low wage, in real dollar terms, rose only slightly.[47] The Children's Bureau repeated the hiring advice it had given for juvenile court probation officers. A degree in social work was a neces-sary credential.[48] Few employees of either the courts or protective services possessed one.

A stressed-out high school graduate working in cramped quarters was the person who really picked up the phone at a hot-line. She often had to supply her own pens and paper and share space with from two to four other workers . . . if she was lucky. In Florida, a 1972 review of conditions at public protective services agencies revealed that caseworkers in several cities had

---

[45] Statement of Brian Fraser, Staff Attorney for the National Center for the Prevention of Child Abuse, Hearing, Prevention, 83.

[46] For discussion of the ways hot-lines actually worked in their first fifteen years of existence see "Testimony of Joseph Pisani, Chairman, New York State Temporary Commission on Child Welfare," Oversight Hearings on Title 1 – Child Abuse Prevention and Treatment and Adoption Reform Act of 1978 before the Subcommittee on Select Education of the Com-mittee on Education and Labor, House of Representatives, Ninety-Sixth Congress, Second Session (Washington, DC, 1981): 296–97 (hereafter Hearing, Title 1).

[47] For discussion of the poor pay for CPS workers see Richard Wexler, *Wounded Innocents: The Real Victims of the War Against Child Abuse* (Buffalo, NY, 1990), 231–33.

[48] U.S. Children's Bureau, "The Abused Child," 4.

no desks, file cabinets, or bookshelves. Supervisors told them to keep their paperwork on the back seats of their cars.

Like her counterparts in the juvenile court, a frustrated CPS employee was likely looking for another job. Throughout the country turnover rates were, unsurprisingly, phenomenal, averaging over 60 percent annually. In big cities, the rates were even higher. In 1970, 80 percent of Miami's CPS workers quit within twelve months. In other cities a third to one half of caseworker positions were vacant, and the remaining personnel each handled from sixty to one hundred cases.[49]

As if these problems weren't overwhelming enough, the threat of lawsuits further complicated procedures in large numbers of protective services agencies. Lawyers entered the juvenile courts in large numbers in the 1970s. They also made their presence felt at child welfare bureaus. Fearing class action suits filed on the behalf of clients or their relatives, agencies insisted that caseworkers investigate all charges filed – even those that appeared frivolous.[50] Afraid that a case they rejected might turn later into a headline, most agencies abandoned efforts to screen. But, inundated with far more reports than they could possibly investigate, they simultaneously adopted haphazard first-come, first-serve approaches that gave highest priority to avoidance of litigation.

Too often child protective services didn't protect children most at risk of severe injury or even death. "Imagine," said the sociologist Douglas Besharov, "a 911 system that cannot distinguish between life-threatening crises and littering. That is the condition of child abuse hot-lines."[51] Lela Costin, whose texts on child welfare practices were required reading in schools of social work, denounced child abuse reporting laws as a policy that increased "demand for an as-yet-to-be-identified service."[52] In 1974, two Democratic politicians with presidential ambitions, Senator Walter Mondale

---

[49] For an overview of the problems in state and local level child protective services, see "Testimony of Joanne Johnson-Hershman, Assistant Director of Social Workers, St. Lukes Hospital, New York City," Reauthorization of the Child Abuse Prevention and Treatment Act, Hearing before the Subcommittee on Select Education of the Committee on Education and Labor, House of Representatives, One Hundredth Congress, First Session, Hearing Held in New York City (Washington, DC, 1987) (hereafter Hearing, Reauthorization).

[50] Beginning in the 1970s judges in many jurisdictions also required that children involved in abuse investigations have attorneys. Most were court-appointed, and lawyers' fees added to agency costs. See "Statements of Brian Fraser, Staff Attorney, National Center for the Prevention and Treatment of Child Abuse and Neglect, Denver, Colorado," Hearing, Prevention, 92–94.

[51] Testimony of Douglas Besharov, "Child Abuse and Neglect in America: The Problem and the Response," Hearing before the Select Committee on Children, Youth, and Families, House of Representatives, One Hundreth Congress, First Session (Washington, DC, 1987): 43 (hereafter Hearing, Problem and Response).

[52] Costin, Karger, and Stoesz, *The Politics of Child Abuse*, 116.

of Minnesota and Colorado Representative Patricia Schroeder, sponsored the first of three important pieces of federal legislation that sought to sort out the mess.

Child Abuse Legislation: Part Two

In the next twenty years, federal involvement in child protection increased. National politicians now set the standards for activities traditionally entirely under state and local control. The 1974 Child Abuse Prevention and Treatment Act (CAPTA), the 1980 Adoption Assistance and Child Welfare Act, and the Family Preservation and Support initiative of the Omnibus Budget Reconciliation Act of 1993 all provided states and localities with detailed guidelines. None solved the problem of child abuse and neglect.

Amended several times, CAPTA was the centerpiece of federal efforts to exercise leadership. Reflecting trends at the state level, the 1974 Act defined "abuse and neglect" more broadly than had the first wave of state reporting laws, which emphasized intentional physical injuries. Now the term included mental injury, sexual abuse, or negligent treatment as well. CAPTA's central purpose, in the Act's various incarnations, remained consistent: to spur research about child abuse and neglect and to establish a national information clearinghouse about programs that prevented, identified, or treated the problem.[53]

As reported incidents of child abuse jumped during the 1970s, hundreds of thousands of American children entered already overburdened foster care systems. By 1980, in a tenfold increase during just one decade, some 510,000 were in foster homes, and officials estimated that about 70 percent had been removed from their parents or other relatives because of abuse allegations. Once in foster care, kids stayed longer than they had prior to the 1960s. Rather than being an emergency arrangement, a foster home, or more likely,

---

[53] For the complete text of the original 1974 Act, see *United States Statutes at Large: Containing the Laws and Concurrent Resolutions Enacted During the Second Session of the Ninety-Third Congress of the United States of America, 1974*, 88:1, Public Laws 93-246 through 93-446 (Washington, DC, 1976): 4–8. CAPTA was PL 93-247. For the text of later amendments and reauthorization statutes, see Improving the Well-Being of Abused and Neglected Children, Hearing before the Committee on Labor and Human Resources, United States Senate, One Hundred Fourth Congress, Second Session (Washington, DC 1996): 4–10 (Hereafter, Hearing, Neglected Children). See also: U.S. Department of Health and Human Human Services, Administration for Children and Families, National Center on Child Abuse and Neglect, *Child Abuse Prevention and Treatment Act, As Amended* (Washington, DC, 1997). The Child Abuse Prevention and Treatment Act was rewritten in the Child Abuse Prevention, Adoption, and Family Services Act of 1988. It was further amended by the Child Abuse Prevention Challenge Grants Reauthorization Act of 1989 and the Drug Free School Amendments of 1989. In 1996, a series of major amendments to CAPTA established the goal of improving the timeliness of decisions about permanent homes for abused children removed from parents or other relatives.

a series of foster homes, shaped the experience of growing up for increasingly large numbers of American youngsters.

The Adoption Assistance and Child Welfare Act of 1980 emphasized "permanency planning" and provided financial incentives to states and localities to reorganize their foster care systems. It promised a bonus to states that implemented comprehensive inventories of all children in foster care, established procedures so that each child in foster care had his or her case reviewed every six months, and created programs that reunited children with parents or other family members.[54]

Spurred by the more than $420 million in federal grants the act made available between 1980 and 1985, states and localities pared their foster care rolls; by 1985 total numbers had decreased substantially, to an estimated 275,000.[55] Then, disturbingly, the progress reversed. By 1993, some 420,000 youngsters swelled states' foster-care statistics. The family preservation and support provisions of the 1993 Omnibus Budget Reconciliation Act sought to stem the tide, by establishing a $930 million capped entitlement spread over a five year period to help states either return children to their own families or release them from foster care for permanent adoptions.[56]

By 1998 the money was gone, but the numbers of children in foster care rose, and an estimated 80 percent were abused. For these kids, foster care, all too often, was a trap. Hundreds of thousands grew up, shifting from one temporary home to another. In 1996, some 659,000 American youngsters were foster children for at least part of the year. Only twenty thousand were adopted during the same twelve-month period.[57]

At the end of the century, after four decades of sustained efforts at every level of government, child abuse and neglect seemed a more dire problem than ever. Experts testified that homicide as a cause of children's death in the western world was "almost uniquely" a U.S. phenomenon and that in the United States murder was the leading cause of death from injury before the age of one.[58] The pediatrician Vincent Fontana, Head of New York City's Child Abuse Prevention Services, warned that abused youngsters grew up

---

[54] For a summary of the Act's provisions, see "Continuing Crisis in Foster Care: Issues and Problems," Hearing before the Select Committee on Children, Youth, and Families, House of Representatives, One Hundredth Congress, First Session (Washington, DC, 1987), 1–3 (hereafter Hearing, Foster).

[55] *Ibid.*, 19.

[56] For discussion of these provisions, see "Statement of Olivia Golden, Assistant Secretary for Children and Families, Health and Human Services," Hearing, Neglected Children, 4–7.

[57] *Ibid.*, 4.

[58] The statistics came from a 1992 survey done by the National Center for the Prevention of Child Abuse (NCPCA) and were cited by Representative Patricia Schroeder in 1992, Hearing, New Demands, 4. According to the NCPCA, among boys aged one to four, the homicide rate in the U.S. of 2.6 deaths per one thousand children was more than twice the highest rate in Europe: 1.2 in Belgium.

to "assault, rob, murder." They became "juvenile suicides, the young drug addicts, the alcoholics."[59] Other experts challenged these statistics and these predictions, although with little optimism, and said no one could reliably answer how many such adult survivors of child abuse existed.[60]

Undeniably, however, allegations of abuse spurted after the adoption of reporting laws in the 1960s. Some 150,000 incidents nationwide in 1963 rose to 1.9 million by 1980, and then to over three million by 1996, a twentyfold increase. Had enormously more parents and caretakers begun mistreating the children for whom they were responsible? No one knew for sure, but it seemed highly unlikely.

By the end of the century, state programs to prevent child abuse were in disarray everywhere, despite an estimated $11 billion spent annually on child protection services at local, state, and federal levels. Seemingly everyone, from parents, to protective service staff members, to pediatricians, to politicians, was angry. The Republican Senator Mike DeWine of Ohio, father of eight children and a longtime supporter of increased funding for protective services, asked, "What in the world are we doing?"[61] It was a good question. An answer demands examination of definitions – what *was* child abuse, and who *were* its perpetrators and victims? It also requires analysis of the actual impact of permanency planning and reporting laws.

Policy, Social Science, and Child Abuse

As the history of juvenile justice demonstrated, social science theory significantly influenced public policy in the twentieth century, but policy makers were selectively attentive to social scientists. In the early twentieth century, child rescue societies confidently assumed that physical mistreatment of children was a phenomenon linked with impoverished immigrant neighborhoods. The only children needing saving belonged to the families of brutal, ignorant newcomers. That fact helped make the intrusion of the state into questions of child care and parental discipline acceptable.

But, by the 1970s, a curious reversal had occurred. It was no longer politically correct to connect poverty, ethnicity, and child abuse. In the early twentieth century, it would have been politically impossible to define child abuse as a phenomenon that cut across all social, racial, and economic lines.

---

[59] "Statements of Dr. Vincent Fontana," Hearing, Reauthorization, 7.

[60] As the sociologist Thomas Holmes noted in 1995, although an enormous literature on treatment options for survivors of childhood abuse existed, little research clearly demonstrated the effectiveness of any particular treatment model and no universally accepted statistics quantified how many adult survivors of abuse needed help. Thomas Holmes, "History of Child Abuse: A Key Variable in Client Response to Short-Term Treatment," *Families in Society: The Journal of Contemporary Human Service* 76 (1995): 357–58.

[61] "Statement of Senator DeWine," Hearing, Neglected Children, 31.

By the late twentieth century, it was politically impossible not to.[62] Social scientists risked professional abuse when they tied child abuse to problems of race or class. However, empirical studies pointed repeatedly to a generalization that prejudiced earlier generations regarded as a given: low income was a very powerful predictor of rates of physical injury to children by parents or caregivers.[63] And race seemed to matter as well.

Created by an amendment to CAPTA in 1988, the U.S. Advisory Board on Child Abuse and Neglect brought together fifteen nationally respected pediatricians, academic social scientists, and state welfare officials. In its annual reports, the Board repeatedly noted a disturbing, if mystifying, statistic. African-American families were dramatically overrepresented in fatal abuse and neglect deaths, at rates three times more than any other ethnic group. At the end of the century, Native Americans had higher poverty rates than did blacks, and nearly one in every three Hispanic families was poor, but neither group appeared to include significantly increased rates of severe abuse injuries and fatalities.[64]

Two studies by private children's advocacy groups also found that African-American children were disproportionately represented among child abuse deaths. Although neither the U.S. Advisory Board nor the latter two organizations, the National Committee for the Prevention of Child Abuse (NCPCA) and the Children's Defense Fund, could provide adequate explanations, they all collected strikingly similar data. Nonetheless, by 1986, most organizations' response to a puzzle that suggested severe physical abuse might be linked to race, was self-defeating, if understandable. Starting with the NCPCA, they stopped amassing data on the race and ethnicity of child fatalities.[65]

Not hearing politically awkward social science conclusions was, by then, an established tradition. Testifying before Walter Mondale's Senate

---

[62] Early-twentieth-century child savers rarely questioned assumptions about the greater prevalence of violence among the poor and recently arrived. Elizabeth Pleck notes that, by the late twentieth century, a "myth of classlessness" conformed to the medicalization of child abuse as a "battering" syndrome. Elizabeth Pleck, *Domestic Tyranny*, 172.

[63] For good summaries of this research, see Peter Pecora, James Whittaker, and Anthony Maluccio, *The Child Welfare Challenge* (New York, 1992); Leroy Pelton, "The Myth of Classlessness," in Leroy Pelton, Ed., *The Social Context of Child Abuse and Neglect* (New York, 1981); Leroy Pelton, "Child Abuse and Neglect: The Myth of Classlessness," *American Journal of Orthopsychiatry* 48 (1978): 600–8. Costin, Karger, and Stoesz, *The Politics of Child Abuse*, 142–59.

[64] Department of Health and Human Services, *A Nation's Shame*, 25. The Denver-based National Center for the Prevention of Child Abuse and Neglect was established in 1972, founded by concerned medical personnel, while lawyers (most famously Hillary Clinton) and children's advocates with social work backgrounds established the Children's Defense Fund.

[65] Howard Karger and David Stoesz note this development, in *American Social Welfare Policy* (New York, 1990), 240–50.

Subcommittee on Children and Youth in 1973, Brandeis University sociologist Dr. David Gil noted that:

"While physical abuse of children is known to occur in all strata of our society, the incidence rate seems significantly higher among deprived and discriminated-against segments of the population."
At this point, Mondale interrupted: "Would you yield there? Would you not say that the incidence of child abuse is found as well in the families of middle class parents?"
Dr. Gil: "Definitely so."
Senator Mondale: "You may go into some of the finest communities from an economic standpoint and find child abuse as you would in the ghettos of this country."
Dr. Gil: "Definitely so. However, as I have said on another occasion, the factors that lead to abuse among the well-to-do are the same that also lead to abuse among the poor. The poor, in addition, have many other factors.... Middle class families are spared the more devastating daily tensions and pressures of life in poverty. They tend to have fewer children, more living space, and more options to relax, at times, without their children."
Senator Mondale's response? "This is not a poverty problem. This is a national problem."[66]

In the late twentieth century, as had always been true, the lives of the poor were more open to public scrutiny than were those of the economically privileged. Abused children who turned up at inner-city hospital emergency rooms were more likely to be reported than were those whose parents took them to private physicians. Nonetheless, to discount the importance of poverty and race in child abuse was to deny the overwhelming preponderance of evidence collected by the pediatricians and social scientists who identified the "battered child syndrome" in the first place.

If policy makers shied away from volatile questions of race and class, they also avoided another troubling social science conclusion, one that first appeared in C. Henry Kempe's famous article, to be repeated by two generations of psychologists, sociologists, and pediatricians. While some child abusers were indeed seriously mentally ill, most were not. The idea that someone who was not medically diagnosed as abnormal could still hurt defenseless children was difficult to accept. That murdering or battering adults were not fringe cases, exceptions to the rule that parents were naturally loving, required confrontations with cultural norms few wanted to make. But, repeatedly, social scientists suggested that, taken to an extreme, otherwise normal American styles of childrearing could easily lead to abuse. The United States was a country where people generally did not interfere even when parents scolded, slapped, and punched children in public. And most physical abuse occurred behind closed doors.

[66] "Testimony and Comments of Dr. David Gil and Senator Walter Mondale," Hearing, Abuse, 1973, 17, 31.

Instead of confronting difficult issues involving race, poverty, or even the nature of American culture, late-twentieth-century child abuse policy repeated a different mantra: child abuse knew no boundaries. It occurred everywhere and was a growing problem. Perpetrators needed psychological help. Victims needed psychological help. Each group also needed plenty of lawyers.

Reliable data on the incidence of child abuse did not exist in 1970, nor in 2000. But during those thirty years, figures verified another development: the rapid growth of the child abuse industry. Poor people didn't hire private attorneys to litigate charges filed against those who had sexually abused them as children; they didn't enter therapy programs for victims or join self-help groups for "recovering" perpetrators. They didn't have the money. But tens of thousands of middle-class Americans did, especially when the media reported as fact unverifiable claims that one in three adult women and one in five men in the country were victims of childhood sexual abuse.[67] By defining child abuse as a medicalized, classless condition, governments at all levels encouraged this trend, one further abetted by expanded categories of abuse and neglect.

By mid-century, the X-ray proved what physicians and nurses had long suspected – that many childhood injuries were not accidental. But no widely accepted tool emerged to measure the new terms included in most state and federal child protection statutes. What constituted sexual, emotional, or educational abuse was often anyone's guess. Rape of a young child by a parent was obviously sexual abuse, but where did hugging stop and "fondling" begin, especially if "unnatural touching" was not confined to genital contact? Where did a parent's right to reprove stop and emotional abuse begin? And what, indeed, was "educational abuse"?

In the absence of agreed-on standards, definitions spanned the gamut. A popular manual distributed by American Humane Association included among examples of "emotional" abuse "any behavior" by parents or other caretakers that "lowered self-esteem in a child" or failed to "individualize" children.[68] Did that make almost all American parents, at one time or another, child abusers?

---

[67] For discussions of these estimates, see Billie Wright Dziech and Charles Schudson, *On Trial*, 50–55. The fact that millions of adults might not remember such abuse, some therapists said, only meant that they had repressed exceedingly painful memories. Indeed the "Recovered Memory" movement was a bonanza for attorneys and therapists in the 1980s and 1990s, though many doubted its efficacy. Elizabeth Loftus, "The Reality of Repressed Memories," *American Psychologist* 48 (1993): 518–37; Lela, Karger, and Stoesz, *The Politics of Child Abuse in America*, 15–40; Douglas Besharov, "Unfounded Allegations – A New Child Abuse Problem," *Public Interest* 83 (1986): 25–29.

[68] Most efforts to create guidelines floundered, and vagueness dominated all attempts. The AHA guidelines were typical. See American Humane Association, *Definitions of Child Abuse* (Denver, 1988), 3, 6.

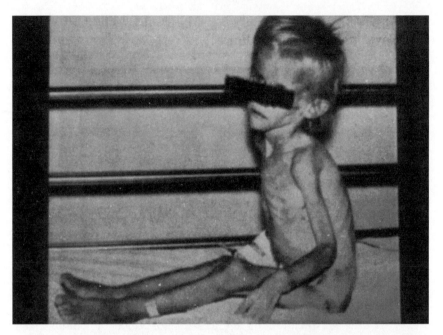

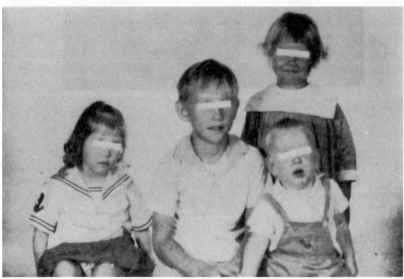

PHOTOS 2.1 AND 2.2   Hearings, Child Abuse Prevention, 1973 (complete citation in endnotes). Held in Denver, these congressional hearings featured testimony from noted pediatrician Dr. C. Henry Kempe, who provided slides, two copies of which are here reproduced from Congressional documents. Photos 2.1 and 2.2 show photographs of children from the same family, to illustrate Kempe's point that sometimes one child (2.1) would be horribly abused (in this case intentionally starved) – while the other children (2.2) appeared to be cared for in a normal fashion and showed no signs of abuse.

Congress passed the Child Abuse Prevention and Treatment Act in 1974 and created the National Center on Child Abuse and Neglect (NCCAN) to get to the bottom of such basic questions. In the next quarter-century, that did not happen.[69] In fact, Center reports reinforced a notion which social scientists had challenged since the 1960s: that women were the primary abusers of children. Since the 1870s child savers had portrayed the "evil stepmother" as prime villain. Inadvertently, the Center continued that tradition.

In 1873, the Mary Ellen Wilson case encouraged the New York Society for the Prevention of Cruelty to Animals to found a sister chapter to fight the mistreatment of children. For years, an Irish immigrant stepmother, Mrs. Thomas Connally, beat the little girl almost daily with a rawhide whip, and Mary Ellen's wan face and blood-stained dress became relics, brilliantly manipulated by Elbridge Gerry, the wealthy New York attorney who put Mrs. Connally in prison.[70] Gerry realized the potential of the face of an abused child in a late-nineteenth-century culture quickly being reshaped by mass-manufactured images.

In the mid-nineteenth century, photography was in its infancy. Heavy tripods, fragile glass plate negatives, and an absence of timed shutters made cameras expensive, best suited to studio work. Within a few decades, however, cameras were smaller, cheaper, and used readily available celluloid film. George Eastman made a fortune with his Kodaks, which turned ordinary citizens into photographers.

People not only took pictures; they expected them: in urban newspapers grown thick with advertisements, in the hefty Sears-Roebuck catalogues that arrived at millions of country homes, in the dozens of new "illustrateds" – glossy magazines with mass circulations that featured big headlines and color photography. Dramatic improvements in technology transformed printing, allowed urban dailies to grow in size, while diminishing in price, and made a huge industry of "dime" novels. Halftone photoengraving, a process that reprinted photographs quickly and cheaply, made realistic images a new staple of American life.[71]

Mary Ellen Wilson was one of the first children to become a symbol at the birth of a new age in which Americans expected information to contain

---

[69] For representative listings of the types of grants the NCCAN supported, see Hearings, Title 1, 28–70; "Child Abuse and Neglect and Child Sexual Abuse Programs," Hearing before a Subcommittee of the Committee on Government Operations. House of Representatives, Ninety-Ninth Congress, Second Session (Washington, DC, 1986), 8–30 (hereafter Hearing, Abuse, 1986).

[70] For the best analysis of the Mary Ellen case, see Lela Costin, "Unraveling the Mary Ellen Legend: Origins of the 'Cruelty' Movement," *Social Service Review*, 65 (1991): 203–23.

[71] For the rise of photography and the emergence of American visual culture, see Reese Jenkins, *Images and Enterprise: Technology and the American Photographic Industry* (Baltimore, 1975); Robert Taft, *Photography and the American Scene: A Social History, 1839–1880* (New York, 1964); Amy Kaplan, *The Social Construction of American Realism* (Chicago, 1988).

"true-life" graphic pictures. Readers of New York newspapers raptly absorbed the copiously illustrated details of her rescue and followed the trial of her "evil" stepmother through installment after installment. Years later, her story still sparked interest. Cruelty officials featured her photograph as a happy young woman in her twenties in later fundraising campaigns.

Walter Mondale never acknowledged the "Mary Ellen" case. Perhaps he'd never heard of it. Nonetheless, in 1973, exactly one hundred years later, he invoked the same set of visual images Gerry had used so effectively. He opened hearings on his landmark child abuse bill by noting, "Only ten days ago the stepmother of nine-year-old Donna Stern of Cedar Grove, Maryland, was found guilty of the pre-meditated murder and torture of the child."[72]

Donna had been beaten repeatedly with a rawhide whip before she was killed. Both the Mary Ellen Wilson and Donna Stern cases were revolting. Linked by the same grisly details, but separated by one hundred years, both implicitly emphasized the same idea: women posed the most danger to children. Indeed, more than 50 percent of reported cases of child abuse involved mothers or stepmothers. But when false charges and relatively minor physical injuries were eliminated, fathers and, even more important, boyfriends emerged in study after study as the ones most likely to rape, inflict grievous harm, or even kill.[73] But mothers and other female caretakers who hurt children tapped a deeper social aversion.[74] From the 1970s through the end of the century and at local, state, and federal levels of governments, prevention programs focused on "one to one" support for "the moms."[75] Yet, "moms" were *not* the perpetrators of most rapes or life-threatening physical abuse; fathers and boyfriends were. That was true in a country where, by the year 2000, single parents, 90 percent of whom were women, headed one third of American families. Live-in boyfriends, visiting boyfriends, estranged and former husbands were a danger to growing numbers of children, while policies continued to target women.[76]

---

[72] "Statement of Senator Walter Mondale," Hearing, Abuse, 1973, 1.

[73] Such studies spanned the quarter century of federal involvement in child abuse prevention. For a summary, see R. L. Helgar, S. J. Zuravin, and J. G. Orme, "Factors Predicting Severity of Physical Child Abuse Injury: A Review of the Literature," *Journal of Interpersonal Violence* 9 (1994): 170–83.

[74] In 1994 the United States Department of Justice released a report, *Murder in Families* (Washington, DC), which demonstrated that conviction rates for mothers and fathers prosecuted for murder of their own children were different. Juries convicted women at notably higher rates.

[75] For a typical program see the report on "Proud Parents" – demonstration projects in eight different cities funded jointly through state and federal monies: See "Testimony of Bulinda Hereford," "Proud Parents" Program Director, Hearing, Abuse, 1986, 7–11.

[76] The number of out of wedlock births skyrocketed between 1950 and 2000 – 141,000 in 1950; 770,000 in 1984; 1,210,000 in 1998. For discussion of the economic and social problems this caused, among them the presence in single parent female headed families of boyfriends not biologically related to the children, see David Ellwood, "Anti–Poverty Policy for Families

If programs unfairly saw "the moms" as the greatest source of serious danger to children, they also misidentified the ages of children most likely at risk. Public funds paid for huge numbers of workshops, radio announcements, and pamphlets that encouraged grade schoolers to tell teachers or school counselors about "scary hitting" or "bad touching." However, since the 1960s, specialists in child abuse agreed, although their conclusion was one so unsettling that even fellow professionals wished it away: the most severely abused were children younger than three. As Dr. Margaret McHugh, the pediatrician who headed Bellevue Hospital's Child Protection Team in New York City, explained, " Doctors, especially younger doctors, want to believe that parents only beat older children. I have to keep telling them, no; they beat babies."[77]

Oddly enough, Americans seemed more willing to believe themselves a nation of sexual perverts than a society that injured and killed infants. Critics charged that figures on child abuse and neglect underestimated the numbers of children who were maimed or murdered by abusive caretakers, while simultaneously overestimating cases of sexual abuse.

By the 1990s many states kept databases on children reported to be abused or neglected, but only if the child did *not* die. The truth about murder of infants and small children remained essentially unknown even after more than two decades of government subsidies to promote research into causes and cures for child abuse. In 1993 the respected flagship journal of the Academy of American Pediatricians estimated that 85 percent of childhood deaths from abuse and neglect were misidentified.[78]

Child abuse policy failed to thwart child murder. The crime was, admittedly, extremely difficult to prove. Babies and toddlers, especially those who lived in families without permanent addresses or strong community connections, were not likely to be missed. Birth and death registers did not track very well across jurisdictional lines. Children killed by shaking, dehydration, suffocation, or bruising to inner body organs might, indeed, have died accidentally.

In 1981, Jerome Miller, president of the nonprofit advocacy group, National Center on Institutions and Alternatives, commented worriedly about actions needed to keep children physically safe. "It seems to me," he said, "that prevention [of physical abuse] is more often outside the expertise of the helping professions. It seems to me that prevention has to do with adequate employment, adequate nutrition, and wider family support

---

in the Next Century: From Welfare to Work – and Worries," *Journal of Economic Perspectives*, 14 (2000): 187–98.

77 Margaret McHugh, quoted in Department of Health and Human Services, *A Nation's Shame*, 51.

78 The most common misidentification was to label an abuse death an accident. P. McClain, J. Sacks, and R. Frohlke, "Estimates of Fatal Child Abuse and Neglect, United States, 1979 through 1988," *Pediatrics*, 91 (1993): 3338–43.

systems."[79] He was right, but implementation of his suggestions required public policy to pay closest attention to physical child abuse as a social ill connected to poverty.

It did not. Instead, from the 1970s through the end of the century, expanded legal definitions that included emotional maltreatment and sexual abuse helped to reshape child abuse as a middle-class problem. In many jurisdictions "sexual abuse" exploded traditional criminal categories of genital rape or forced fellatio and included vaguely defined acts such as "improper touching." But, sexual and emotional abuse were even more difficult to identify than was physical abuse.[80]

Nonetheless, by the 1980s, sexual abuse of children was big news and big business. Self-help books for adult victims of childhood sexual abuse were bestsellers, and therapists counseled that most people who had been sexually assaulted as children probably had deeply repressed, bitter memories. An inability to enjoy any kind of physical intimacy, or, conversely, a compulsion to have sex with many partners, a habit of wearing too many clothes, or too few, taking too many risks, or not enough – all could be signs that an adult was unconsciously suppressing childhood sexual abuse. Readers learned that perhaps as many as sixty million American adults had been sexually victimized by trusted caregivers during their childhoods.[81]

Such guesses were never substantiated, but they provoked widespread alarm and a great deal of litigation. Since statutes of limitations forbade criminal charges for most alleged acts that occurred decades in the past, thousands of adults instead filed civil suits for financial damages against their own parents. As clinics and centers specializing in hypnosis and "memory regression" therapy flourished, celebrities joined the crusade.

In the wake of massive publicity, governments championed the cause as well. When Mrs. Barbara Sinatra testified before Congress in 1992, she thanked not only her husband Frank, but the members of Connecticut Senator Christopher Dodd's Subcommittee on Children, Family, Drugs, and Alcoholism, for supporting the Barbara Sinatra Children's Center. Located in Rancho Mirage, California, one of the country's most affluent communities, the Center supplied intensive psychotherapy to the victims and families of childhood sexual abuse, which was, said Mrs. Sinatra, a "national emergency."[82] Was it? No one really knew.

The agendas of the child abuse industry and a political unwillingness to confront physical abuse as strongly connected to poverty distorted late-

---

[79] "Testimony of Jerome Miller," Hearing, Title 1, 307.

[80] Lela Costin, Howard Jacob Karger, and David Stoesz, *The Politics of Child Abuse*, 23–27.

[81] For typical examples of the self-help literature that flooded the market in the 1980s and early 1990s, see Ellen Bass and Laura David, *The Courage to Heal: A Guide for Women Survivors of Child Abuse* (New York, 1988); Sue Blume, *Secret Survivors: Uncovering Incest and its Aftermath in Women* (New York, 1990).

[82] "Testimony of Barbara Sinatra," Hearing, Reauthorization, 1991, 16.

twentieth-century child abuse policy. Bureacratic turf wars further complicated effective action. Sharon Harrell, a welfare official working for the
Washington, DC, city government, got it right when she said, "No cop or
social worker, on their own hook, wants to start an investigation that might
lead to screaming headlines the next day."[83] Moreover, child protection and
law enforcement agencies vied to blame each other for poor performance
whenever a truly awful case emerged.

At the federal level, during years when both Republican and Democratic
administrations promised to shrink the size of the federal government, the
National Center for Child Abuse and Neglect had little chance to thrive. It
did not become a national clearinghouse for research. Instead it doled out
questionable "demonstration" grants to favored self-help groups and funded
conferences where the child abuse nomenklatura gathered. The American
Psychological Association charged it with "being drastically out of touch,"
an accusation confirmed in several witheringly negative performance evaluations filed by the General Accounting Office.[84]

Child abuse prevention, indeed the Department of Health and Human
Services itself, became a dead-end appointment by the mid-1980s, with relatively high positions given as political favors. Challenged by Democratic
Representative Ted Weiss of New York, Dodie Livingston, President
Reagan's Commissioner for the Administration of Children, Youth, and Families, could not recite much of a resume. What was her "professional and
academic background relating to children, youth, and families?" "Well,"
said Livingston, "I've done a great deal of volunteer work with young people over my adult life, and...I've done a great deal of work in political
campaigns."[85]

Bill Clinton entered the White House pledging to improve the lives of
all American children. However, by 1996, major revisions in federal welfare policy raised doubts about what kind of leadership of children's policy
Washington would exercise.[86] Besides, by the 1990s, state action against
child abuse was no longer such a popular cause. Child abuse reporting laws
had provoked a backlash.

Who Are the Victims Here?

The negative response to child abuse reporting laws was inevitable. By the
early 1990s, groups such as VOCAL, an organization of self-described "Victims of Child Abuse Laws," had chapters in all fifty states. More than ten

[83] "Testimony of Sharon Harrell," Hearing, Title 1, 330.
[84] See "Testimony of Dr. J. Lawrence Aber, on behalf of the American Psychological Association," Hearing, Abuse, 1986, 44–51 (quotation on 49).
[85] "Testimony of Dodie Livingston," Hearing, Abuse, 1986, 96.
[86] Chapter 3 explores the impact and implications of the 1996 "End to Welfare as We Know
It."

thousand dues-paying members claimed that too many innocent people were caught in dragnets meant to snare abusers.

They were right. Reporting laws in every state defined child abuse vaguely, established hot-lines that permitted anonymity, and granted immunity to all callers. As overworked, poorly trained staff members at children's protective services wearily fielded calls, abuses of child abuse systems multiplied. Lacking clear directives, even well-meaning individuals were on their own. Vengeful people found ample room for mischief, and "child abuse" became a staple charge in late-twentieth-century divorce courts.

Neighbors phoned to report that a child down the street wore too many "hand-me-down sweaters"; that the furniture in a youngster's bedroom was "too rickety"; that "everyone next door screams all the time." Reports like these became a kind of white noise, since most states, fearing lawsuits, required that all calls be investigated. Without adequate screening guidelines, state protective services floundered, and the barrage of reports made situations that posed serious, perhaps even life threatening, danger to a child harder to discern.[87]

Poorly worded guidelines meant that truancy from school, juvenile delinquency, or ordinary family fights could prompt child abuse charges. Anyone could be an accuser; anyone could be an abuser. Critics charged that over half of all calls to hot-lines were unfounded.[88] Since, by the mid-1980s, more than two million reports of child maltreatment poured in to local, county, and state protection agencies annually, the victims of defective child abuse policy also included hundreds of thousands of blameless adults, who, during the last three decades of the century, opened their doors to a child protective service worker and the beginning of a long nightmare. No one knew how many families were thrown into chaos by false charges. Anecdotal evidence, however, suggested a big problem.

In 1992 a grand jury convened in San Diego County, California, conducted interviews with over 250 social workers, therapists, judges, physicians, and families. It issued a thick report concluding that the child protection system in the county was "... out of control, with few checks, and little balance. Services ... cannot distinguish real abuse from fabrication, and neglect from poverty."[89] The grand jury reviewed three hundred cases and decided that

---

[87] Quotations from: "Prepared Statement of Dr. Richard Krugman, Director of the Henry Kempe Center for the Prevention and Treatment of Child Abuse and Neglect," Hearing, Problem and Response, 13–21; For further analysis of how hotlines were actually used, see Mary Pride, *The Child Abuse Industry* (Westchester, IL, 1986).

[88] Richard Wexler, *Wounded Innocents*, 86–88. Even the NCCAN admitted that the rate of false reports was too high, although it was unwilling to estimate a percentage.

[89] This report was summarized in Michael Compitello, "Parental Rights and Family Integrity: Forgotten Victims in the Battle Against Child Abuse," *Pace Law Review* 18 (1997): 144–6.

83 percent needed reevaluation. Moreover, it estimated that 60 percent of all charges involved innocent families.[90]

On the other side of the country, the Fowlers of Plattsburgh, New York, personalized these kinds of statistics. On the evening of March 8, 1993, Reverend and Mrs. Frank Fowler and two of their children, Frank and Ligia, ages eleven and six, were on their way to choir practice. Frank Jr., unhappy about being forced to go to church with his family instead of being allowed to go to a basketball game, pounded his father's seat back and refused to buckle his safety belt. After telling his son repeatedly to "cut it out," Reverend Fowler stopped the car and opened the door to the back seat. A furious Frank Jr. bolted out, kicking and screaming. An equally angry Reverend Fowler slapped him in the face. After the melee ended, everyone quieted down and proceeded to choir practice.

As almost all parents knew, even journeys to church sometimes seem like drives to Hell. The incident would have ended there, with a chastened Frank Fowler Jr. reluctantly singing hymns, had not a school nurse overheard one of the boy's friends recount that Frank told him, "My father beat me up." She called the twenty-four-hour toll-free hot-line maintained by the New York State Central Register of Child Abuse and Mistreatment.

The call generated a report to New York's Clinton County Department of Social Services. On April 22, caseworkers descended on two different public schools, removed Frank, Ligia, and their younger sister, who had not been present in the car, and held all three in a locked room. Despite the fact that none accused their father of abuse, Clinton County law enforcement officers went to the elder Fowler's church, arrested the minister as an alleged child abuser, and took him away. After extended litigation, the Fowlers won. All abuse charges against Frank Sr. were dropped, but the family's finances and reputation were in shreds.[91]

So, too, were child protection programs across the country. Few had effectively solved the thorny dilemma mistreatment of children posed: how to provide government agencies with sufficient leeway to deal with real threats to children, without harming innocent families or unnecessarily violating family privacy.

Indeed, the sensational McMartin Preschool trials symbolized for millions of Americans child abuse policy in tatters. In February 1984, affluent Manhattan Beach, California, in suburban Los Angeles, recoiled from startling news. Virginia McMartin, the owner of the town's "best" day care center, her daughter, Peggy Buckey, and grandson, Ray Buckey, as well as four other teachers, had been charged with two hundred and nine counts of sexual abuse of forty children, ranging in age from two to five years old. Six years and $16 million later, the first McMartin trial ended with acquittals

[90] *Ibid.*
[91] *Ibid.*, 135–37. See also: *Fowler v. Robinson*, 94 – CV – 836, 1996 WL 67994 a l (NDNY).

of six defendants. A retrial on thirteen deadlocked counts against the one remaining defendant, Ray Buckey, resulted in a hung jury.

In the interval, the country watched with pained fascination as a parade of five- and six-year-olds, most of whom had not been at the preschool since they were two or three, took the stand to tell their stories – of trap doors and tunnels – of "secret" rooms and forced anal sex – of "naked movies" filmed on airplanes – of trips to cemeteries where teachers hacked up human corpses with kitchen knives – of rabbits butchered at snack time – of school rooms dripping with blood.

Investigators tore up all the floors in Virginia McMartin's school. They used sonar equipment to search for tunnels. They scoured flight plans filed with area airports, and they found nothing. Ray Buckey spent five years in jail before raising bail. His mother, Peggy Buckey, jailed for two years, emptied her bank account and deeded her house and car as partial payment to her lawyers.[92]

The Buckeys were, in the end, free, bankrupt, and emotionally stripped of all dignity. None of the questions their trials raised were answered. With research on the actual functioning of memory and fantasy in the minds of young children itself still in its infancy, controversy raged in the academic community about the truth of the children's charges. Social scientists investigating juvenile crime debated whether very young children could form criminal intent. Here, could they be false victims, coached by therapists? Might they even be knowing liars?

Immediately after the announcement of the final verdict, Los Angeles County Supervisor Mike Antonovich proclaimed that frightened children had been denied justice. Others charged that southern California was lost in a frenzy of "molestationmania." What else could explain the fact that during the trials one California newspaper announced a contest with prizes for the reader who turned in the most child molesters.[93] As Senator DeWine asked, "What in the world are we doing?"

Did child abuse policy prevent child abuse? That was debatable. But child abuse policy clearly provoked a widespread backlash against state attempts to protect children from domestic mistreatment. Between 1984 and 1994 hundreds of thousands of citizens signed petitions demanding that "parents' rights" amendments be added to state constitutions so that parents would be legally assured "inalienable" rights to control the upbringing, education, values, and discipline of their children.[94] By 1995, a proposed federal bill,

---

[92] For an extensive summary of the trials, see Paul Eberle and Shirley Eberle, *The Abuse of Innocence*, 37–357.

[93] Eberle and Eberle, *The Politics of Child Abuse*, 129–30.

[94] For an analysis of this religiously endorsed grassroots movement, which spread across the country in the mid-1990s, see Linda Lane, "The Parental Rights Movement," *University of Colorado Law Review* 69 (1998): 825–32.

enthusiastically backed by religiously conservative organizations, echoed the language of such documents.

Charging that governments engaged in "systemic violation of parents' rights," two Republicans, Senator Charles Grassley of Iowa and Representative Steve Largent of Oklahoma, cosponsored the Parental Rights and Responsibilities Act. The legislation established a new four-part legal test under which police or public children's protective services had to prove a "compelling need" existed before either could investigate charges of child abuse. In essence, the bill reinserted "probable cause" into child mistreatment cases, since most reporting laws exempted law enforcement and public social workers from traditional search and seizure rules.

The Parental Rights and Responsibilities Act stopped those "infringements" on the sanctity of the home.[95] And it went further. According to an enthusiastic Florida Representative Charles Canady, the bill "helps to ensure that Government will recognize parental authority."[96] "Rights of parents" included, but were not limited to: directing the education of the child, making health care decisions, unless those decisions resulted in a danger to the life of the child, disciplining the child, including reasonable corporal discipline, and directing the religious teaching of the child.[97]

In a bitterly divided, deeply partisan Congress, responses to the Parental Rights and Responsibilities Act cleaved along party lines. Liberal politicians, led by Massachusetts Representative Barney Frank, joined organizations traditionally in the Democrats' camp, such as the Children's Defense Fund and the National Education Association. Calling it "... nothing more than the child abuser's bill of rights," opponents of the bill noted that it never defined "education" and "reasonable corporal punishment." Would the proposal "strap a six-hundred-pound gorilla to the back of every public school teacher in the country" and pave the way for a flood of lawsuits from parents who didn't like the way their children were being taught? Would child abusers be able to challenge state reporting laws on the grounds that they were exercising reasonable corporal discipline?[98] Democrats managed to stall the proposal in committee, but the battle did not end. In 2000, conservative Republicans marked the beginning of a new century by ceremonially reintroducing a slightly revised version of Largent's original bill.

---

[95] "Parental Rights and Responsibilities Act of 1995," Hearing before the Subcommittee on the Constitution of the Committee on the Judiciary, House of Representatives, One Hundred Fourth Congress, First Session, "Statement of Representative Charles Canady" (Washington, DC, 1997), 1 (hereafter Hearing, Parental Rights).

[96] *Ibid.*

[97] For the full text of the bill, see *Ibid.*, 4–9.

[98] For summaries of opposition points see "Get Off! Congress Is Considering Legislation That Would Strap a 600 Pound Gorilla to the Back of Every Public School Teacher in the Country," *NEA Today* (1996): 22; Randy Burton, "Nothing More Than the Child Abuser's Bill of Rights," *Houston Chronicle*, March 26, 1996.

Indeed, despite all the end-of-the-millennium Republican rhetoric about government attacks on the fundamental rights of parents, since 1980 state attempts to rescue children emphasized "family reunification." Both the left and the right embraced social science theories that advocated family preservation. After all, the Adoption Assistance and Child Welfare Act of 1980, so widely copied at the state level, marked a legislative victory for liberal Democrats and the influential Children's Defense Fund.

However, between 1980 and 2000, more abused children than ever ended up for longer periods of time in foster care. Painful ironies marked late-twentieth-century child abuse policy. Some youngsters returned too quickly to dangerous homes; "family preservation" erected absurdly high legal barriers to termination of parental rights; far too many children languished in inadequate foster care.

"The Greatest Contributor to Abuse and Neglect of Children Is the State Itself"

In 1974 Joseph Pisani, a powerful member of the New York State Senate and a long-time children's advocate, lobbied successfully for funding for a Commission on Child Welfare that he eventually headed. Under Pisani's energetic leadership, the Commission spent five years traveling the state, inspecting hundreds of agencies, eventually interviewing thousands of people – from runaway kids in temporary shelters, to foster care mothers, to child protection service employees. In 1980, results in hand, Pisani announced a disturbing verdict: "I feel it is necessary to make a very sad . . . statement. . . . The greatest contributor to the abuse and neglect of children is the State itself."[99] In New York, neither "family reunification" nor foster care worked. In the world of ideas, sensitive, highly motivated psychologists and social workers employed by public child protection services reached out to abusive parents, themselves likely to be little older than teenagers, while simultaneously keeping a close eye on the kids.[100] In the world as it really existed, Senator Pisani's Commission created better training manuals for New York State protective service workers, only to find them "useless." Too many employees were "functionally illiterate," and could not read them.[101]

This kind of conflict between theory and reality reverberated throughout the country. Policy emphasized the importance of rehabilitating dysfunctional families, so that abused children could return to live with kin. Help that enabled children to grow up safely with their own struggling,

---

[99] "Testimony of Joseph Pisani," Hearing, Title 1, 297.
[100] For a summary of the psychological theory underpinning "family reunification" policies, see Jacqueline Parker, "Dissolving Family Relations: Termination of Parent-Chid Relations – An Overview," *University of Dayton Law Review* 11 (1986): 573–78.
[101] "Testimony of Joseph Pisani," Hearing, Title 1, 301.

young parents was a terrific idea. It was also expensive and rarely fully implemented. Peter Digre, Director of the Los Angeles Department of Children and Family Services, produced a plan for a model program for family reunification for his city that included twenty-three separate support services.

Although few politicians wanted to link abuse by race or class, Digre, an experienced social worker, knew that children in the most physical danger lived in extremely poor, often minority, households, where one or both young parents were drug or alcohol dependent. Therefore, Digre included everything from free substance abuse rehabilitation, to emergency cash assistance, to mental health services, to transportation, to day care, in his plan. Moreover, he cautioned how important it was that social workers "constantly see the kids" – visiting at-risk families a minimum of eight, and up to sixteen times, every month. Predictably, Digre's family preservation system was a wishlist that the Los Angeles municipal budget did not fully accommodate, although the city had better-developed services than did most others.[102]

For the last two decades of the century some one thousand to twelve hundred American children died annually at the hands of their parents or caretakers. Each year about half of these murders occurred *after* the family came to the attention of one or more public child welfare agencies.[103] In the case of particularly brutal killings, when children were mutilated, or starved, or boiled alive, the details led the news and riveted a disgusted public. Politicians pounded tables and demanded in-depth investigations. Shortly, however, all the outrage died – until the next time.

With rare exceptions, local police and child protective workers were neither brutal nor uncaring. They were overwhelmed. The Adoption Assistance and Child Welfare Act of 1980, the model for similar legislation at state and local levels throughout the country, promoted a fiction: that it was possible to neatly balance family preservation and child safety. Without greatly more money than jurisdictions were willing to spend, it wasn't.

Instead of giving them resources, public policies imposed additional duties on hopelessly overburdened public protective services workers. Section 384-b of the Family Court Act of New York, amended in 1981 to parallel federal law, mandated that the state's first obligation was to reunite the biological parent with the child. In order to do that the social worker had to be "cognizant of the problems that the biological parent faces which frustrate the return of the child." For example, if the "biological mother has a drinking problem, the case worker should be giving case counseling and referring the mother to alcohol abuse facilities. It is not enough for the caseworker to inform the mother that she has a problem and must solve it. The caseworker

---

[102] "Testimony of Peter Digre," Hearing, Neglected Children, 34.
[103] "Statement of Richard Gelles, Director, Family Violence Research Program, University of Rhode Island," Hearing, Neglected Children, 10.

should make detailed referrals and, if necessary, accompany the mother to the first or second meeting."[104]

By including such requirements New York State legislators indulged a dream world. They were not alone. Such language did not mean that workers with huge numbers of assigned cases actually complied, but the terminology did force them to consign children to ever-longer stays in foster care. Only after the passage of a full year could most agencies begin considering releasing a child for adoption, even if parents or relatives could not or would not take him back.

By 1980, two decades after its rediscovery as a social problem, child abuse was intimately linked with fosterage. Removed from dangerous relatives, far too many children were then abused by strangers. Though the actual number of children in foster homes fluctuated constantly, the yearly averages of numbers over whom governments temporarily assumed legal custody rose after 1985. Family reunification wanted to make the foster home an obsolete public institution. Instead, it grew. In 1988, 343,000 American children were in a foster home at least part of the year. By 1996, that number had mushroomed to more than 659,000.[105]

In all states, foster systems strained at the seams, while, everywhere, shortages of qualified foster parents reached critical levels. By the 1980s, both parents in an average American family worked. That changed demographic profile meant that fewer couples had the time to consider taking in a child, especially one who needed a lot of attention. Through the end of the century, the demands placed on foster parents became more onerous. Children entering state care were far more likely to be emotionally and physically traumatized. The people taking care of them needed to be alert and able. In general, they were not. By 1993, the mean age of American foster mothers was fifty-two, fathers fifty-eight. In most homes, neither foster parent was employed, and in three quarters, one or both adults was too sick to look for another job.[106] This was not exactly an ideal safe haven for any child, much less a frightened, confused, abused one.

Reimbursement rates for foster care stagnated. Few localities paid more than $14 per day, even in the 1990s. That sum barely covered necessities, much less treats or toys. Foster parents complained of persistent problems getting medical care for children and reported that caseworkers ignored

[104] The Family Court Act of New York provides the case study used to advise attorneys, social workers, and others of their responsibilities under the law in Joseph Carrieri, *Child Abuse, Neglect, and the Foster Care System: Effective Social Work and the Legal System and the Attorney's Role and Responsibilities* (New York, 1995), 122–25.

[105] "Testimony of Assistant Secretary Olivia Golden," Hearing, Neglected Children, 1.

[106] Susan Zuravin, Mary Benedict, and Mark Somerfield, "Child Maltreatment in Family Foster Care," *American Journal of Orthopsychiatry*, 63 (1993): 589–96.

their questions. No wonder that the exodus of fostering adults turned into a stampede.[107]

But children themselves were not free to leave. In 1995, the Child Welfare Research Center at the University of California estimated that over one third of all newborn infants entering foster care were neither adopted nor reunified with family members after four years. On average, children in the Center's sample endured more than two home placements per year. Released from the system at age eighteen, fully independent, but with no family, no money, and, usually, a woefully inadequate education, half of the study group left foster care for a life of homelessness on the streets.[108]

Advocacy groups for children joined forces with personal injury lawyers to try to force change in public foster care, taking advantage of court rulings that substantially altered the law of class action. Individual claims for children abused by foster parents had almost always been settled behind closed doors for small amounts. That changed in the 1990s, as lawyers sued child welfare bureaucrats, and throughout the country, more than one hundred state and county departments of child and family welfare operated under court-ordered consent decrees. Typically, these suits demanded reform of policies and conditions in public programs, not monetary damages. They certainly turned judges into *de facto* public welfare executives who issued orders with the consent of litigants.

Consent decrees entangled courts in the internal workings of child abuse prevention systems. Often bulky documents of a hundred pages or more, decrees held bureaucrats in civil contempt if they did not comply with all requirements, which ranged from hiring additional hundreds of employees in child protective services, as the Connecticut Department of Children and Families was forced to do in 1999, to tartly mandating that anytime an abused child had to sit in a chair overnight in New York City awaiting disposition of his case, the official responsible had to spend the next night there as well.[109]

---

[107] *Ibid.* See also "No Place to Call Home: Discarded Children in America." A Report, Together with Additional and Dissenting Views, of the Select Committee on Children, Youth, and Families, United States House of Representatives, One Hundred First Congress, First Session (Washington, DC, 1989), 24–80 (hereafter Report, Discarded Children).

[108] Peter Digre summarized the 1995 report's conclusions in "Testimony of Peter Digre," Hearing, Neglected Children, 24–25.

[109] Court orders regulating caseloads demanded that Connecticut's Department of Children and Families hire 146 social workers and 84 support workers, at a cost of $20.5 million. The consent decree in New York City also forbade the city from keeping homeless families overnight in welfare while officials searched for temporary shelter. For these and other cases, see Tamia Perry, "In the Interest of Justice: The Impact of Court-Ordered Reform on the City of New York," *New York Law School Review* 42 (1998): 1239–45; "State Finds It Must Hire More Social Workers," *New York Times*, June 18, 1999; "Legislature Attacks

The cases provided no shortcut solution to child abuse policy dilemmas. Such litigation was time consuming and expensive. Public agencies often constructed high hurdles when defense lawyers demanded confidential records needed to prove a case. It took sixteen years of increasingly acrimonious litigation before the Jackson County Division of Family Services in Kansas City agreed to a consent order outlining measures to reform child welfare, including children's protective services.[110] In hundreds of other cities, the century ended, but there was no end in sight for lawsuits that kept everyone in and out of courtrooms for decades. As one critic noted, there had to be a better way to fix dysfunctional children's protective services than to "litigate them into a state of Bosnian exhaustion."[111] Was there?

Solutions?

Around the country, a number of states and local communities developed protective services programs that promised better solutions. Following the passage of the Adoption Assistance and Child Welfare Act in 1980 the state of Maryland created "Intensive Family Services" (IFS). A social worker and a parent aide, helped by a team of psychologists, worked intensively for three months with families where an adult had been charged with child abuse. IFS caseworkers had "flexible dollars" to use as they saw fit – for everything from emergency help with the rent, to bus tokens, to day care. Families received phone numbers that connected them to a hot-line that actually worked, as trained therapists talked distraught adults through a moment of rage or despair.

Comprehensive, but quite short-term, state intervention–centered IFS strategy. It worked. A study done in 1989 showed that in families that received ninety days or less of in-depth IFS help, three out of four abused children remained in their own homes or with relatives.

The national rate of removal of children into foster care was almost the mirror image of Maryland's IFS success. By the late 1980s, more than 60 percent of children involved in abuse cases ended up placed out-of-home. The Maryland initiative not only kept families together more frequently, it

Child Abuse Broadly," *Chicago Sun-Times*, April 24, 1994; Ruben Castaneda, "D. C. Moving Too Slowly on 262 Child Neglect Cases, Report Says," *Washington Post*, October 27, 1992. For informative overviews of the late-twentieth-century impact of consent decrees, see Judith Resnick, "Judging Consent," *University of Chicago Legal Forum* 45 (1987): 43–48; Abraham Chayes, "The Role of the Judge in Public Law Litigation," *Harvard Law Review* 89 (1976): 1281–99; Lloyd Anderson, "Implementation of Consent Decrees in Structural Reform Litigation," *University of Illinois Law Review* (1986): 725–34.

110 Ellen Borgersen and Stephen Shapiro, "*G. L. v Stangler v. Stangler*: A Case Study of Court-Ordered Child Welfare Reform," *Journal of Dispute Resolution* 2 (1997): 189–213.

111 Ibid., 190.

was cost efficient, at least in the long run. By keeping thousands of kids out of the foster care, over a decade's time it probably saved Maryland taxpayers more than $6 million. A half-dozen statewide programs similar to that inaugurated in Maryland dotted the country.[112]

Statistically they were rare, however. Even in the cities and states which tried them, they remained pilot programs for decades. Short term, they were very costly, and the end-of-the-century mood in the country was not one that accommodated increased spending on social services.

A nationwide solution to the problem of child abuse demanded that rhetoric be cooled and that careful research be conducted. By the 1990s, more than thirty years had passed since several prominent pediatricians identified "battered child syndrome." The problem of child abuse supported wholly new therapeutic and legal subspecialties, but nobody produced widely accepted statistics about its extent.

For decades certain unverified assumptions were endlessly repeated, giving them the gloss of truth: abused children grew up to abuse their own offspring; high percentages of adult prisoners and juvenile delinquents had been mistreated by parents or relatives; children who'd experienced physical or emotional harm when young were permanently injured. However, the few social scientists who actually conducted longitudinal studies of child abuse victims argued that the effects of child abuse on adult behaviors were far from clear.[113]

Choruses of alarm, however, drowned social scientists' calls for careful study. Liberals shouted that child abuse was an "out of control epidemic," a "spreading disease," "the root of everything we are afraid of in our society."[114] Bigger budgets and greater government intervention were imperative. Conservatives countered that, under the guise of preventing child abuse, the state willfully invaded the privacy of the home. Child abuse policy, indeed, was "just the tip of the iceberg. . . . Government mandated bedtimes for children just passed in Durham County, North Carolina!"[115] The state should abandon most of its attempts to supervise parental decisions about proper discipline.

---

[112] For discussion of IFS in Maryland as well as comparable programs in Washington state, Vermont, New Hampshire, and New Orleans, see Report, Discarded Children, 90–98.

[113] As late as the 1990s there had still been very little empirical research done on connections between child abuse and later adult dysfunction, though policy (and politicians) almost universally made anecdotal connections. The few social scientists who did twenty- and thirty-year-long term studies reported varied results. Some suggested that abused children became adults who faced greater risks of serious depression or alcoholism. Others thought that perhaps a majority of child abuse victims did not demonstrate signs of long term harm. Lela Costin, Howard Jacob Karger, and David Stoesz summarize this research in *The Politics of Child Abuse*, 30–33.

[114] "Testimony of Dr. Vincent Fontana," Hearing, Reauthorization, 43.

[115] "Prepared Statement of Representative Steve Largent," Hearing, Parental Rights, 18.

On each side the sensationalized rhetoric shed far more heat than light. The numbers of victims of the child abuse "epidemic" and the nature of the "disease's" symptoms varied from speaker to speaker. And, although Oklahoma's Steve Largent vividly suggested that if little North Carolinians weren't in their beds at nine at night, the Durham County Department of Social Services would spirit them away, in fact, the Department's "bed-time" rules were voluntary guidelines distributed for grade schoolers in conjunction with the local PTA.[116]

But the politics of child abuse had always been the politics of emotion, beginning with the New York Society for the Prevention of Cruelty to Children's masterful exploitation of the "little Mary Ellen" case. In 1973, Dr. Annette Heiser, a pediatrician at the George Washington University Medical Center and a specialist in child abuse, brought slides with her when she testified before Senator Mondale's Subcommittee on Children and Youth: pictures of babies whose feet had been plunged into boiling water and who needed skin grafts to live, pictures of a young boy whose father had burned his palms to the bone with a cigarette lighter, pictures of an emaciated, intentionally starved, infant. Understandably, when the lights finally came up, a shaken Mondale erupted, "This is the most nauseating, offensive thing I have ever seen.... After this (my bill) is going to be stronger than I had originally planned, because there is no sense.... going into sterile debate about federal, state and local."[117]

Mondale's anger was real. Who wouldn't have shared it? But there should have been a serious debate about "federal, state, and local." Instead, from city council rooms to the floor of the Senate, outrage fueled policy. It encouraged the quick passage of child abuse reporting laws and spurred a plethora of policies to stop the "epidemic." Agencies needed to coordinate their efforts; legislatures needed to provide adequate funding to the bureaucracies to which they gave so many new assignments. They did not do so. Instead most shuffled through versions of the "Pontius Pilate" routine – a dance whose steps juvenile court administrators knew well.

Although by mid-century it had become unfashionable to say so, child abuse *was* connected to poverty, ethnicity, and race. And throughout the twentieth century there were always more poor children than there were abused ones, even though statistics for both categories perpetually stirred intense debate. Americans liked to think they belonged to a society that would not tolerate child abuse nor limit a child's chances because of the

---

[116] Julia White, "DSS Parenting Standards Guidelines Only, Not Rules," Durham (North Carolina) *Herald-Sun*, October 10, 1995. Most of Largent's lists of government intrusions into the sanctity of family life, like the bedtime story, turned out to be exaggerations. For text of Largent's speech, see Hearing, Parental Rights, 18–22.

[117] "Statements of Senator Walter Mondale," Hearing, Abuse, 1973, 149–50.

economic misfortune of his parents. Neither belief was true. State responses to child mistreatment, however well-meaning, made truly heinous physical abuse harder to find. And, despite a dramatic growth in welfare systems meant to provide financial assistance to "dependent" youngsters, children replaced the elderly in the twentieth century as America's poorest group of citizens.

3

"Illusory Promises"

State Aid to Poor Children

In 1996, the U.S. Congress abolished the Aid to Families of Dependent Children program begun in 1935 as a provision of the landmark Social Security Act. Some quickly predicted that the "end of welfare" would also reduce child abuse. Patrick Murphy, Public Guardian of Cook County, Illinois, could not contain his enthusiasm. American welfare systems, he confidently predicted, would no longer send an "illusory promise" to "inexperienced girls that they and their children would be supported for the rest of their lives."[1] That promise had encouraged too many poor women to bear and then abuse too many children. As had many before him, Murphy placed undue blame for child abuse on single mothers.

Moreover, at century's end, the welfare revolution was only four years old, and massive reductions in numbers of recipients coincided with record prosperity. Certainly no one yet could make more than anecdotal connections between changes in state aid to dependent children and incidence of child abuse. But a larger conclusion could be made. Most promises of government aid to impoverished young Americans involved illusions – overconfidence in the generosity of public benefits or unwarranted faith that a twentieth-century woman without an adult partner could usually escape poverty through paid labor.

If twentieth-century portraits of juvenile criminals were exaggerated, and profiles of abused children misidentified, the poor child disappeared into the shadows. Debates about policies purportedly designed to help economically disadvantaged children focused, instead, on the morality, marital status, and employability of their mothers. If discussions about the philosophy of the juvenile court invoked images of the state as "surrogate father" for children in trouble, debates about aid to poor youngsters did not. Instead, they

---

[1] Patrick Murphy, "A Trap of Welfare and Child Abuse," *New York Times*, August 11, 2000. The Cook County Public Guardian's office annually acted as guardian *ad litem* for over thirty thousand abused and neglected children.

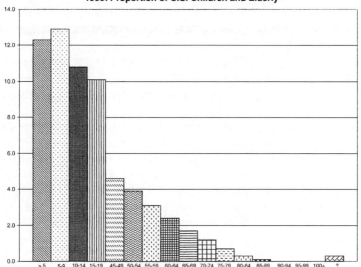

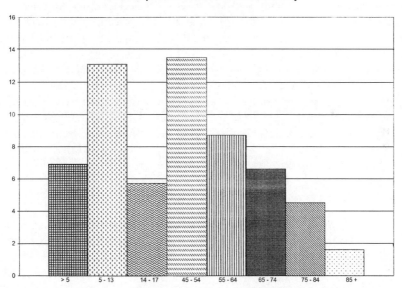

FIGURE 3.1   The demographics of childhood and senescence in twentieth-century America. Source: Statistics used to create graphs from U.S. Department of Commerce, Bureau of the Census, Census of 1910, General Population Characteristics, Census of 2000, General Population Characteristics.

revolved around choosing the poor women for whom a government bureau would act as "surrogate husband."[2]

An examination of twentieth-century government programs for poor children and their families demonstrates the importance of culturally and racially coded definitions of poor mothers' worthiness. It also illustrates the ways that age trumped youth, regardless of gender. The promises that produced concrete economic gains and redistributed wealth were made to the old.

This chapter begins with an overview of the changing realities of poverty in America from the mid-nineteenth to the late twentieth century. Then, within this frame, it examines the abandonment of the orphanage and the rise of supervised outdoor relief. It explores the impact of the precedent-breaking establishment of federal guidelines for aid to dependent children during the New Deal and situates the "welfare explosion" of the 1960s and early 1970s within the context of an increasingly racialized debate about aid to the poor.[3]

The Changing Face of Poverty in America

The most important fact about poverty in twentieth-century America is its absolute disappearance. Perhaps as many as 40 percent of city dwellers in turn-of-the-century America faced periodic, but desperate, want. They leased small rooms in fetid tenements and owned almost nothing, not even handed-down furniture or flimsy bedding. That, too, was rented. Everyone, including children, drank cheap coffee and survived on oatmeal, or cornbread soaked in grease, or bowls of boiled potatoes. Poor youngsters rarely wore anything but made-over adult clothing. "Store bought" toys or sweets were, for most, unimagined luxuries. Both children and adults were frequently sick, and, even if unhealthy, all labored. Young children tended infant siblings, did piece work, ran errands, peddled newspapers in the streets, swiped the odd piece of coal for the stove at home. Adolescents' contributions to household survival were crucial.[4]

---

[2] The historian Susan Pedersen used the phrase to label programs of British aid to servicemen's wives during World War I, but it appropriately describes American public policy decisions about aid to dependent children. Susan Pedersen, "Gender, Welfare, and Citizenship in Britain During the Great War," *American Historical Review* 95 (1990): 985.

[3] The phrase "welfare explosion" is historian James Patterson's. But since the appearance of the first edition of his influential *America's Struggle Against Poverty* in 1981 it has become a generic phrase, rarely attributed to its proper author. This chapter's page citations are from the 1994, rather than the 1981, edition of the book. James Patterson, *America's Struggle Against Poverty, 1900–1994* (Cambridge, MA, 1994).

[4] For discussions of life among the impoverished and working classes of both urban and rural America in the period 1890–1920, see David Danbom, *Born in the Country: A History of Rural America* (Baltimore, 1995); Michael Katz, Ed., The *"Underclass" Debate: Views from*

At the onset of the Great Depression the respected National Bureau of Economic Research, a statistical clearinghouse funded by Rockefeller philanthropy, concluded that there was "... no certainty that a male wage earner can earn enough to support a family even if steadily employed. When hazards of unemployment, illness, and accident are taken into account, all hope of so doing vanishes. Saving for old age is an impossibility."[5]

By these standards, at the end of the century far fewer Americans were poor. Officials from the Social Security Administration estimated that the number of the impoverished decreased from 30 percent of the total population in 1939, to 22 percent in 1959, to 13 percent in 1999.[6] Post–World War II prosperity enabled the vast majority of married workers to raise their families above absolute poverty lines, generally defined by thresholds set at three times the cost of a minimally nutritious diet.[7] With the old buoyed

---

History (Princeton, 1993); Ewa Morawska, *For Bread with Butter: Life-Worlds of East Central Europeans in Johnstown, Pennsylvania, 1890–1940* (New York, 1985); Peter Mandler, Ed., *The Uses of Charity: The Poor on Relief in the Nineteenth Century Metropolis* (Philadelphia, 1990); Michael Katz, *Poverty and Policy in American History* (New York, 1983), 17–134. Most analysts of early-twentieth-century poverty suggest that an urban family with three children that earned between $500 to $800 annually fit into the extremely broad base of the working poor in America between 1900 and 1925. Poor in rural areas operated with far less money, sometimes even no money, as farmers or sharecroppers subsisting in largely barter-based economies.

[5] Report of the Bureau of Economic Research, summarized in *White House Conference on Child Health and Protection, Preliminary Commitee Reports* (New York, 1930), 533–36.

[6] Economists add an important caveat to this generalization, however. Most estimates of decreases in twentieth-century poverty rates measure *mobility*. In the twentieth century, greatly more Americans moved from lower to higher deciles of wealth distribution. However, economists also measure *persistence* when examining historic changes in standards of living. Most of those who "left poverty" in the twentieth century did not go too far. Richard Steckel and Jayanthi Krishnan's longitudinal examination of income found that those jumping over the poverty line – moving out of the first decile – generally remained in the second decile. In the mid-nineteenth century, economists suggest that the persistence rate for poverty was much greater, but the smaller numbers of people who managed to move beyond the first decile, on average, moved much farther up wealth scales. Over 40 percent made it to the fifth decile. Nearly 9 percent made it to the top 20 percent of income distribution – giving some credence to the era's fascination with Horatio Alger's success stories. See Richard Steckel and Jayanthi Krishnan, "Wealth Mobility in America: the View from the National Longitudinal Survey," Working Paper 4137: National Bureau of Economic Research (Cambridge, MA, 1992), 4–5.

[7] For discussions of changing definitions of and debates about official poverty lines, see James Patterson, *America's Struggle Against Poverty, 1900–1994*, 57–81; Alice O'Connor, *Poverty Knowledge: Social Science, Social Policy, and the Poor in Twentieth Century U.S. History* (Princeton, 2001), 183–85. Quantifying poverty-level income was maddeningly difficult, even if analysts used only reported money received and in-kind benefits. The twentieth-century poor, likely, had always managed to conceal some sources of support from private charities or government bureaucrats. In the late 1990s, the sociologists Kathryn Edin and Laura Lein's research on how low-income "welfare" and low-wage mothers really got by suggested that, in addition to cash welfare, food stamps, SSI, and income from legitimately reported jobs, most also worked – off

by federal retirement pensions, Medicare, and Supplemental Social Security, those left behind were more likely to be members of the nation's growing percentage of female-headed households.

In the 1990s a poor child ate meat regularly, even if the entree was greasy hamburger, owned toys and commercially made children's clothing, even if neither was new, and lived in a dwelling equipped with radios, televisions, and a host of other consumer items, despite the fact that they, too, were often secondhand. And, as had been true for most of American history, more children suffered periodic poverty than perpetual want. In the early twentieth century, a father's desertion or death frequently caused a family's fortunes to spiral downward. But relatives sometimes rallied; a priest helped; a mother remarried or found work. Things often got a little better, at least for a while. In later decades, a divorce, a job loss, or an unexpected pregnancy outside of marriage had the same impact, and then, too, bad circumstances frequently improved.[8]

Nonetheless, the percentage of poor Americans under the age of eighteen remained stubbornly static between 1950 and 1990, at one in five, improving slightly during the 1990s economic boom. Even then, the percentage of impoverished children exceeded poverty rates for the population. Critics argued that rising dollar minimums allowed those classified as impoverished to live more comfortably, especially since official estimates rarely incorporated the cash value of in-kind benefits widely available after 1965, such as food stamps and free Medicaid-subsidized health care.[9] That was certainly true. It also begged an important question. Why was American public policy more generous to one group of dependent citizens than to another? A commitment to the young was, by its nature, a finite one. A commitment to the old was,

the books, under false names, or obtained money illegally: drugs, prostitution, traffic in stolen goods. They also constructed networks of friends and family members who periodically helped them. Only *one* woman among Lein and Edin's study population of 214 mothers met all her expenses with welfare benefits alone. Kathryn Edin and Laura Lein, *Making Ends Meet: How Single Mothers Survive Welfare and Low Wage Work* (New York, 1997), 20–45.

[8] For that reason, economists attacked the "snapshot" approach of counting the number of children below the poverty line at a given moment in time as, simultaneously, an underestimate of the number of children likely to experience hard times at some point before they reached adulthood and an overestimate, if interpreted to suggest that the child counted remained impoverished for years. But few longitudinal studies of childhood poverty have ever been attempted. For discussions of how poverty is "counted," see Althea Huston, Ed., *Children in Poverty: Child Development and Public Policy* (Cambridge, UK, 1991).

[9] "Poverty Guidelines for Families of Specified Size," *Social Security Bulletin Annual Statistical Supplements, 2000* (Washington, DC, 2000). Poverty guidelines, adjusted in real dollars, *did* get more generous, especially after 1965. For instance, guidelines issued in December 1965 specified a poverty line of $2,440 annually for a family of three. The guideline increased to $5,010 by April 1980 and to $11,250 by February 2000. Poverty rates for the nation's population at large dropped to a century-low measurement of 7 percent in 1999, while the percentage of children in poverty hovered at 16 percent.

in contrast, open-ended, especially as the number of American "old old" – those over age eighty-five – grew rapidly after 1950.

In 1900, just under seventy-five million people lived in the United States. One hundred years later, the country had grown to more than 275 million. Throughout this time, the percentage of its residents under the age of eighteen remained relatively stable, usually around 25 percent, except during the Baby Boom years, between 1942 and 1960, when that figure reached almost 40 percent. At the millenium Americans still imagined themselves a youthful people, but in fact the striking demographic development of the twentieth century was an increase in the numbers of the country's aged.

In 1900, relatively few Americans, slightly more than 4 percent, reached what public policy later enshrined as a chronological benchmark. By the late 1990s, 15 percent were sixty-five or older. In a few popular retirement states, such as Florida, the proportion of those who were "old" – over sixty-five – matched those who were "young" – under eighteen. Both figures composed about 20 percent of the total population. That was an historic first.[10]

Americans agreed that the care of the aged was a public duty and convinced themselves, wrongly, that elderly recipients deserved government checks earned through workplace contributions. A system that gave the old unprecedented retirement and health benefits that far exceeded their individual payroll deductions was firmly in place.

Despite rhetoric that sanctified motherhood and sentimentalized children, in truth, twentieth-century Americans always thought poor mothers should undertake paid work whenever feasible and provided systems of meager benefits that compelled them to do so. When, briefly, public policies during the 1960s and 1970s challenged that judgment, they provoked furious opposition and could not be sustained.

An emphasis on the importance of paid work made discussion of what needy children "deserved" difficult. If age formed one pillar of twentieth-century U.S. welfare state promises, connections, however fragmentary, to paid employment provided another. Nonworking wives and children of workers increasingly received work-related "entitlements" – as did those who could prove that they were too disabled to work. And an American cultural veneration of paid work paralleled in self-contradictory fashion a growing acceptance of leisure for adults. During the last forty years of the twentieth century, the average age of retirement for men fell dramatically.

---

[10] For discussions of these demographics, see Organization for Economic Cooperation and Development, Social Policy Study 20, *Aging in the OECD Countries: A Critical Policy Challenge* (Washington, DC, 1996); United States Social Security Administration, *Social Security Bulletin, Annual Statistical Supplement, 1998* (Washington, DC, 1998); United States Bureau of the Census, *Population Projections in the United States by Age, Sex, Race, and Hispanic Origins: 1995–2050: Current Population Report P25-1130* (Washington, DC, 1996).

For the first time in history, male workers in the United States looked forward to spending a third or more of their lives as retirees.

The emergence of retirement as a socially acceptable phenomenon was one of the most significant markers of late-twentieth-century life throughout the developed world. Until World War II, most workers remained on the job until their deaths, unless thwarted by incapacitating illness or injury. Indeed, until the 1960s, the very word "retirement" retained much of its old nineteenth-century negative meaning – when people used it to designate disposal of obsolete objects. A torn buggy whip, left forgotten for years, might eventually be "retired" to a dustbin. Even prosperous people did not retire.[11]

A status of "useless" retirement might link them to the average poor person, an old man who lacked a job or the support of offspring. As late as 1900 his image would have been familiar to citizens of earlier eras. Adult children in all centuries preferred to take in their indigent, aged mothers. A toothless codger who shambled through the country's streets and slept under its bridges epitomized poverty in 1900. By 2000, that had long since changed. After 1960 a young child, with minorities, especially African Americans and Latinos, proportionally overrepresented, typified poverty. An examination of state aid to dependent children over the century helps explain why that occurred. The story begins with an analysis of the end of the orphanage and the return of "supervised" outdoor relief.

The Orphanage, Scientific Philanthropy, and the City

States did not begin spending money to help the poor in the twentieth century. Indeed, along with punishment of lawbreakers, charity to the indigent was one of the oldest of public duties. Colonial and early-nineteenth-century American towns felt responsible for their sick and poor, though relief took many forms and was often given in kind. A desperate family might receive a basket of food, a load of firewood, help rebuilding a house lost to fire. Sometimes officials distributed cash payments, although few cities or counties codified rules for exact amounts. Most places strictly applied the principle of "settlement." Needy strangers not only needed not apply; they were usually chased out of town. This highly decentralized, locally controlled system was generally known as outdoor relief.[12]

---

[11] The emergence during the 1950s of positive attitutudes toward retirement was not confined to the United States but changed the ways millions of people lived throughout the developed world. See Peter Peterson, *Gray Dawn: How the Coming Age Wave Will Transform America and the World* (New York, 1999), 127–204; Jonathan Gruber and David Wise, *Social Security Programs and Retirement Around the World* (Washington, DC, 1988); Craig Karpel, *The Retirement Myth* (New York, 1995); Carolyn Weaver, *How Not to Reform Social Security* (Washington, DC, 1998).

[12] For nineteenth-century charity practices, see Paul Boyer, *Urban Masses and the Moral Order in America, 1820–1920* (Cambridge, MA, 1978).

Outdoor relief, critics argued, worked in an agricultural society where people in communities all knew each other. It failed to meet the needs of cities with millions of new foreign born residents. Rapid urbanization demanded "indoor relief" – the institutionalization of recipients of charity – for financial and ideological reasons. Faced with the demand that they enter workhouses or asylums, applicants might think twice. If quickly growing cities sought to cope with escalating costs, "scientific" philanthropies embraced indoor relief for different reasons.[13] For assistance to be of benefit, it had to be accompanied by strict supervision. Operating under this philosophy, the orphanage became an increasingly important institution after 1870, finally declining during the 1930s. But only those unable to work deserved help. That included the old, the mentally ill, the blind and deaf, and young children.

The residents of orphanages in the early twentieth century were rarely children without living parents, as the term came to be understood decades later. Rather, they were usually "half" orphans – those whose fathers had died or abandoned the family. Domestic service provided one of the few real job opportunities for the wives and widows left behind, but most employers preferred live-in maids, nannies, and cooks. Few allowed servants to bring their own children along. In such circumstances, late-nineteenth- and early-twentieth-century orphanages provided temporary room and board for the children a woman could not keep. In most cases, neither the orphanage nor the mother expected the child to stay more than several months; neither side attempted to break contact.[14]

Between 1870 and 1910, cities, counties, and private charities united to build a network of institutions for dependents. The dozens of orphanages that dotted every American big city were frequently cooperatively run enterprises, as were workhouses, municipal lodging homes, and many free hospitals. A few states created "children's homes." Ohio, for example, required that each of its counties establish a publicly funded orphanage. In 1923, the country's orphanage population peaked, when 142,971 youngsters, almost all of them under the age of nine, spent at

---

[13] For case studies of the growth of indoor relief, see Joan Gittens, *Poor Relations: The Children of the State in Illinois, 1818–1990* (Urbana, 1994); Barry Kaplan, "Reformers and Charity: The Abolition of Public Outdoor Relief in New York City," *Social Science Review* 52 (1978): 202–14.

[14] For example, Michael Katz's examination of the inmates of institutions in New York State in 1880 found that fewer than 20 percent of resident children had actually lost both their parents. The vast majority were separated from mothers whose jobs or illnesses prevented them from keeping them. Another 20 percent had a living father as well as a living mother, though the father was usually a long-absent figure from his family. Katz, *Poverty and Policy*, 151–56. Census Department figures back up Katz's case study. See United States Department of Commerce, Bureau of the Census, *Children Under Institutional Care and in Foster Homes, 1933* (Washington, DC, 1935), 55–110.

PHOTO 3.1 United States Children's Bureau, Anna Louise Strong, "Child Welfare Exhibits: Types and Preparations" (Washington, DC, 1915). The caption reads, "Wall panel from the exhibit of the Children's Bureau showing the use of cartoons."

least part of the year in one of the country's estimated one thousand institutions.[15]

By the mid-1930s, the severity of the economic crisis swamped orphanages, along with all sorts of other charity institutions with roots in the late nineteenth century. All had been more expensive, per person, than traditional outdoor relief. Economics, not ideology, doomed the orphanage as a solution to state care for poor children. But social science ideology also played a role in its demise. The pioneer generation of psychologists, sociologists, and college-trained social workers which built the juvenile court helped dismantle the orphanage. Instead, they championed "mothers' pensions" – which returned outdoor relief, but as state aid governed by the standards of social work.

The Mothers' Pensions and Poor Children

Between 1911 and 1921 forty of the country's forty-eight states passed loosely drawn "mothers' pensions" laws that provided public cash payments to allow poor mothers to raise their young children at home. By 1930, all but two states enacted bills endorsing them. The pension movement coexisted with the orphanage, and in any given year during these decades the numbers of poor children housed in an orphanage rivaled those whose mothers received state aid explicitly conceived in opposition to the institution.

Frederick Almy, the fiery General Secretary of the Buffalo, New York, Charity Organization Society, expressed scientific philanthropy's view of outdoor relief when he thundered, "To the imagination of the poor, the public treasury is inexhaustible and their right. They will draw upon it without thrift, as they dare not do with private charity."[16]

Almy's worries were unfounded. At the pension movement's height in early 1930 about ninety thousand women received payments that, per month, averaged $20 – less than the amount the care of just one child typically cost on orphanage. During years when most social workers calculated that an annual income of at least $700 was necessary for a family of four to live in minimal comfort, pensions paid far less.[17]

Mothers' pensions were definitely not pensions. Instead, under the guise of support of worthy poor widows, the bills state legislatures rushed to pass opened the door again to outdoor relief. Edward Devine, contributing editor

---

[15] Those older than that age were usually "placed out" by private charities or city officials in approved homes. The orphan trains were part of the larger phenomenon of "placing out." For further discussion of children in orphanages between 1900 and 1935 as well as the various approaches states took, see Matthew Crenson, *Building the Invisible Orphanage: a Prehistory of the American Welfare System* (Cambridge, MA, 1998), 42–60.

[16] "Remarks of Frederick Almy," *Proceedings of the National Conference of Charities and Corrections* (New York, 1912), 478.

[17] The best overview of the actual operation of the pension systems can be found in United States Children's Bureau, "Mother's Aid," Publication 220 (Washington, DC, 1933).

of the social work bible, the *Survey*, was right: pensions were "re-vamped and, in the long run, unworkable, public outdoor relief."[18]

In the end, the Depression crushed both orphanages and mothers' pensions. But pensions were never a workable solution to childhood poverty because the same politicians who eagerly endorsed cash payments for mothers were far less willing actually to provide much money. At no time were more than a tiny fraction of potentially eligible poor families covered. Probably no more than one fifth of 1 percent of America's impoverished children were helped.

The first wave of laws passed between 1911 and 1915 generally limited aid to children of widows, but by the end of the 1920s the wording of many pension statutes widened and allowed families where fathers were absent due to divorce, desertion, or imprisonment to apply for assistance. No pension statute barred African Americans from application, although some demanded proof of citizenship, and a few even required evidence of fluency in English. All pension laws demanded documentation of indigence. Generally, the possession of more than $50 rendered a family ineligible, although some states raised higher hurdles and asked applicants to provide affidavits explaining why relatives could not offer financial assistance. Almost all stipulated that the children in the home be under the age of fourteen, and most ended help when a mother had at least one teenager able to obtain a work certificate.

Pension advocates noted approvingly that mothers expected to be independent as soon as their youngsters found full-time work. They produced letters such as one written by a Chicago widow with four youngsters who explained that she no longer needed assistance because, "Helen now has a very nice position and is getting along well.... Frank will soon be able to do something."[19]

Theoretically, pensions could have alleviated the material distress of a large group of non-working-age dependent children in families with a single female head. In reality, respectable native-born white widows with at least two children under the age of ten were, overwhelmingly, the only recipients. And, everywhere but in just nine of the country's major cities pensions remained a legislative fiction. In Arkansas and Mississippi the laws were entirely meaningless. Not a single woman in either place received a penny. None was ever authorized.[20] The 1930 White House Conference on Child

---

[18] Edward Devine, "Pensions for Mothers," *Survey*, 30 (1913): 457.

[19] The letter – whose sender was not identified – was written in 1926 and delivered to the Juvenile Court of Cook County, the administrator of the Cook County, Illinois, mothers' aid law. United States Children's Bureau, Mary Bogue, "Administration of Mothers' Aid," Publication 184 (Washington, DC, 1928), 5.

[20] *Ibid.*, 37–153. For further discussion of varieties of eligibility requirements, see U.S. Children's Bureau, Edith Abbott and Sophonisba Breckinridge, "The Administration of Aid-to-Mothers Law in Illinois," Legal Series 7, Publication 82 (Washington, DC, 1921), 11–19.

Health and Protection acknowledged this situation when it resolved that: "Mother's aid should be everywhere available in fact as well as in theory."[21]

Each state pension law differed, sometimes slightly, sometimes significantly. Most authorized some form of cost-sharing between states, counties, and cities and established systems for review of applicants and distributions of funds. The administrative structures varied, but many reflected Progressive era advocacy of consolidated bureaucracies. Almost everywhere, even in places where states left decisions about mothers' pensions up to new juvenile courts, county boards of welfare emerged as advisory panels.

Relatively unstudied by scholars of Progressivism, the county emerged as a notably more important governmental unit during the early twentieth century. The administration of mothers' pensions gave "good government" reformers an entering wedge to create centralized welfare authority within counties, even though, usually, the new welfare boards had almost no money to spend and few clearly specified duties. Like the pensions that justified their existence, these county welfare agencies were often hopelessly underfunded, but they were forerunners of a future when few social policies remained truly local.

For instance, in 1924, soon after it too enacted a mothers' pension, the state legislature of South Dakota mandated that a welfare board be formed in each of the state's forty-two counties. Two appointees, who served without compensation, joined a county judge and the county superintendent of schools, the latter a new position. In South Dakota social workers paid by private charities dominated most county boards. In its first report to the legislature, a commission created to review the new system estimated that the innovation cost South Dakotans the grand annual sum of $769.86 in increased paperwork costs.[22]

So – outdoor relief returned, but with several twists. It was no longer – as it had always been historically – thoroughly localized. Moreover, the supervision exercised was "professionalized" through the language of social work, not dictated by patronage or individual community mores. That said, mothers' pensions reflected continuity, as well as a break with established poor law. Indeed, indoor relief marked the real – but eventually repudiated – change.

Food, fuel, or money given outright formed the core of state responses to poverty since ancient times, with women and children the primary recipients of alms. Did the middle- and upper-class women who belonged to groups like the General Federation of Women's Clubs, which endorsed pensions, really want to "embrace" needy women as "sisters," ... "in the same moral

---

[21] *White House Conference on Child Health and Protection, Preliminary Committee Reports*, 536.
[22] U.S. Children's Bureau, Emma Lundberg, "The County as a Unit For an Organized Program of Child Caring and Protective Work," Publication 169 (Washington, DC, 1929), 18–19.

universe as themselves?"[23] If the phrase indicates highly abstract applause for sisterhood, then all these women belonged to the same "moral universe." Otherwise, they were worlds apart. Mary Richmond, the Baltimore Charity Organization Society head and Russell Sage Foundation officer, saw the situation more clearly than have most scholars. "Donors," she said, would be willing to give money to a mother – "whose hard work doesn't supply enough for children. A similar appeal for a hard working father will be scrutinized – and denied."[24]

The idea that turn-of-the-century America embraced an emerging "paternalist" state favoring men needs qualification.[25] Certainly workmen's compensation and other kinds of state benefits overwhelmingly helped males. Nonetheless, a society that congratulated itself – excessively at that – for helping worthy mothers would have thought "fathers' pensions" ridiculous. And men who were needy, but unattached or unemployed, received nothing but hatred. An army that probably enlisted hundreds of thousands of unemployed vagrants criss-crossed the country seeking work. States responded with "tramp acts," not pensions.

New Jersey made it a crime to be a man without visible means of support. Ohio said a man without written proof of a fixed address could be sent to prison. Police enforced these laws irregularly, but enforce them they did, especially when landowners needed extra field hands during harvest seasons, since most statutes required that "tramps" pay for the costs of their incarceration through contract labor.[26]

States that passed mothers' pensions also stiffened criminal penalties against "home slackers" – men who deserted or failed to provide for their families. Tellingly, relatively meager pension payments went to widows. A

[23] The sociologist Theda Skocopol makes this argument in *Protecting Soldiers and Mothers: The Political Origins of Social Policy in the United States* (Cambridge, MA, 1992), 479.

[24] Mary Richmond, "Women's Work," *Charity Organization Bulletin* – "Printed but Not Published – For the Confidential Use of the Charity Organization Societies by the Russell Sage Department" 3 (1912): 202. Copies of these "printed, but not published" editions of the *Charity Organization Bulletin* are in the Publications Pamplet File, Records of the Russell Sage Foundation (hereafter RSF), RAC.

[25] The literature on "maternalist" versus "paternalist" welfare states is large. Generally, maternalist states provided direct state services to mothers and encouraged fertility in the face of declining birth rates. Paternalist states demanded that women and children depend on the income of a husband. For an introduction to this literature, see Robyn Muncy, *Creating a Female Dominion in American Reform, 1890–1935* (New York, 1991); Gwendolyn Mink, *The Wages of Motherhood: Inequality in the Welfare State, 1917–1942* (Ithaca, NY, 1995); Seth Koven and Sonya Michel, Eds., *Mothers of a New World: Maternalist Politics and the Origins of Welfare States* (New York, 1993); Nancy Hewitt and Suzanne Lebsock, Eds., *Visible Women: New Essays on American Activism* (Urbana, 1993).

[26] For an excellent investigation of the "tramp laws," see Eric Monkkonen, *Walking to Work: Tramps in America: 1790–1935* (Lincoln, NE, 1984).

deserted wife usually learned that she should call her errant husband before a court of equity to force him to meet his obligations. This was true even if the man in question was nowhere to be found or jobless. State governance systems look less unfairly male-friendly in the light of statutes that threw out-of-work husbands into county jails.[27]

Mothers' pensions – linked to criminalization of a husband's nonsupport of dependents – reflected outdoor relief's guiding principle: alms should never be sufficient for comfort, lest they promote sloth. And indeed, as the Children's Bureau realized, mothers' aid was "cheap care of children."[28] So it was – especially since only a tiny fraction of those whose poverty might have made them eligible under the vague guidelines that typified almost all pensions ever received anything. True, about half of the pension laws forbade recipients to take outside paid work, but none provided enough money to allow families to live adequately on state benefits alone. None prevented a woman from doing piece work, laundry, or other supplemental wage labor inside her dwelling. Significantly, most laws refused pensions to a woman with only one child, unless she could prove, as the Illinois law put it, "that she is unable to do normally hard work."[29] The pensions were always meant as financial supplements. Nevertheless, their declarations that poverty alone should never remove a child from his home echoed a new social science emphasis on the importance of a stable home to children's development.

"Scientific" philanthropy promoted the orphanage as one of many institutions where unfortunates could be isolated. A successor generation of charity workers, much-influenced by the new professions of psychology and social work, thought that the "modern basis" for care of impoverished children

---

[27] For analysis linking state efforts to stiffen criminalization of male non-support of wives and children with the mothers' pensions, see Michael Willrich, "'Home Slackers': Men, the State, and Welfare in Modern America," *The Journal of American History* 87 (2000): 460–87.

[28] A national conference in 1919 on child welfare organized by the Children's Bureau did not precisely denounce mothers' aid, but it did say that "cheap care of children . . . is unworthy of a strong community." U.S. Children's Bureau, "Standards of Child Welfare: A Report of the Children's Bureau Conference, 1919," Conference Series 1, Publication 60 (Washington, DC, 1919), 341.

[29] U.S. Children's Bureau, "The Administration of Aid-to-Mothers Law in Illinois," 15. Those who have used the pension movement as evidence of state acknowledgment of the unique social value of services provided by mothers have paid too much attention to the rhetoric of advocates and too little to the actual wording of the many different pension laws. Even statutes that sought to limit outside paid work assumed that the state aid would be only a supplement, and many actively encouraged women to seek outside sources of money. Scholars who have condemned the pensions as "laws that boomeranged on the intentions of their original supporters" because they ended up "prohibiting (recipients) from doing better-paid, full-time work" are notably vague about just what sort of work that might have been – especially when the recipients were almost always young, uneducated, widows with at least two – and often quite a few more – babies and toddlers underfoot and no alternative systems of child care readily available. Quotation from Skocpol, *Protecting Soldiers and Mothers*, 476.

was in their own homes.[30] In fact, institutions, once lauded as providing a better environment than "unfit" destitute parents could ever achieve, were dangerous, especially to infants and children under age six, precisely the group most likely to spend time in an orphanage. They suffered "arrested development traits."[31]

President Theodore Roosevelt, in a brilliant display of "Bully Pulpit" politics, highlighted the new attitude in 1909 – by acting as voluble chair of a White House Conference on the Care of Dependent Children. Roosevelt's concern for children's causes was long-standing. Indeed, it ran in the family. Roosevelt's father, Theodore Sr., was a prominent member of the New York Society for the Prevention of Cruelty to Children and gave large sums as well to orphanages and children's hospitals. Presaging his son's showmanship, he once gave a reception at his 57th Street mansion, invited Mrs. Astor and the rest of the city's A list, and, at a crucial moment, threw back the doors to his opulent dining room to reveal a group of big-eyed waifs, some with crutches, others lying on cots, all palpably poor. Not surprisingly, donations poured from the pockets of the assembled wealthy.[32]

With Theodore Roosevelt Jr. visibly in charge, the 1909 White House Conference was equally successful. The three Conference vice chairs, Judge Julian Mack, of the Chicago Juvenile Court, Homer Folks, then Secretary of the New York Charities Aid Association, and Thomas Mulry, president of the St. Vincent De Paul Society, all agreed: "Long standing prejudices in favor of the orphanage" had to be abandoned. Instead, ". . . destitute children should live a life as nearly as possible like the life of other children in the community."[33]

Between 1909 and 1930, government agencies regularly echoed this new idea. The Children's Bureau repeatedly endorsed it.[34] In 1930, Herbert

---

[30] "Report by Hastings Hart on the Care of Dependent Children: The Conclusions of the White House Conference – Ten years After," in U.S. Children's Bureau, "Standards of Child Welfare," 343. Hart, the former superintendent of the Illinois Children's Home, a state-funded orphanage, epitomized the shift in opinion. By 1909, he had accepted the Russell Sage Foundation's invitation to head a new "Child-Helping Department." In that capacity, he was a major advocate of juvenile courts as well as the new philosophy that poor children should stay at home – even if that required supplemented public aid.

[31] William Goldfarb summarizes these early-twentieth-century psychological assessments of institutional children in "The Effects of Early Institutional Care of Adolescent Personality," in Sandra Scarr-Salapetek and Philip Salapetek, Eds., *Socialization* (Columbus, OH, 1987), 66–73.

[32] David McCullough tells the story in *Mornings on Horseback* (New York, 1981), 138–39.

[33] "Summary of Resolutions of the White House Conference – Report by Hastings Hart": 342. Matthew Crenson also credits much of the push to organize the Conference to James West, the National Child Rescue League official whom Theodore Dreiser, editor of the popular woman's magazine, *The Delineator*, hired. *Building the Invisible Orphanage*, 11–17.

[34] For a summary of Children's Bureau conferences and pamphets emphasizing the theme, see U.S. Children's Bureau, "Standards of Child Welfare," 11–31.

Hoover, former president of the American Child Health Association, again lent Oval Office imprimatur to a much more ambitious undertaking than had occurred in 1909. Then, about two hundred juvenile court judges, social workers, charity society officials, and other "child-savers" gathered in the East Wing. By 1930, more than 340 experts joined forces just to plan for a conference attended by over two thousand delegates, meeting in auditoriums all over the capital.

Hoover embraced wholeheartedly the scientific study of social problems. Not surprisingly, his White House Conference on Child Health and Protection tackled a wide gamut of subjects. For over a year prior to meeting in Washington, task forces of specialists investigated the status of children's medical care, nutrition, and education, as well as many other topics.[35] However, with the national economy in free-fall, conference attendees devoted particular attention to the problems of poverty in childhood.

As had its predecessor in 1909, the 1930 White House Conference endorsed "public home relief" for poor children. It also noted that "large" numbers of families eligible under law to receive such aid did not. "Despite mothers' aid," the Conference summary report concluded, "public home relief is still the 'no man's land' of public welfare." Federal help was needed to negotiate the territory.[36] Hoover's doomed presidency ended before such a map appeared in the form of Title IV, an initially little-noticed feature of one of the most important laws of the twentieth century, the Social Security Act of 1935.

ADC to AFDC to the Welfare Mess

Social Security's Aid to Dependent Children program (ADC) outlined in Title IV changed the nature of state responses to childhood poverty by initiating federal-state cost sharing and cooperation. It also, unwittingly, spurred such intense dislike that, over time, it symbolized, in many Americans' minds, classic misuse of public funds. Herbert Hoover's White House Conference resolved that "The needs of children born out of wedlock for good care are the same as those of other children."[37] Franklin Rosevelt's historic Social Security Act put that principle into practice. However, it was a policy change that never won genuine public acceptance.

[35] Major sectional divisions for Conference discussion included: prenatal care, child growth and development, medical care of children, milk production and control, communicable diseases, parent education, preschool education, vocational education for children and adolescents, recreation and physical education, the physically and mentally handicapped child, and the dependent child. For an overview of Conference task forces and organization, see *White House Conference on Child Health and Protection: Preliminary Committee Reports*, vii–20.

[36] *Ibid.*, 505.

[37] *Ibid.*, 537.

AFDC Participation as a Percentage of the U.S. Population 1936-1996

Spending on Supports for Low-Income Workers 1974-1996 (in constant 1996 dollars)

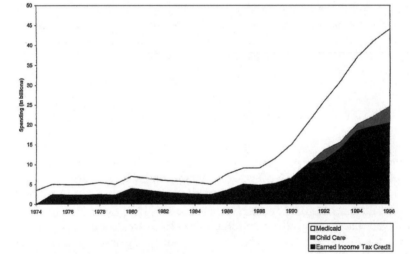

□ Medicaid
■ Child Care
■ Earned Income Tax Credit

FIGURE 3.2   Welfare trends. Source: Statistics used to create these graphics depicting AFDC participation, and other spending supports for low-income families from U.S. Department of Health and Human Services, http://www.acf.dhhs.gov/news/stats.

benefits to parents, widows, and children of the workers who contributed to the system through payroll taxes. After 1939 "deserving" widows, the mainstay of mothers' pensions, and the justification for ADC, became "entitled" recipients of survivors' benefits. They disappeared from ADC rolls.[49] Moreover, even though large numbers of states found ways to limit minority participation, from the outset the proportions of African-American beneficiaries of ADC was five times that for mothers' pensions.[50]

ADC *did* have a little-remembered, if indirect, federal antecedent. Between 1917 and 1921 hundreds of thousands of black women were among the more than two million American wives who received War Risk Insurance payments from the U.S. Treasury Department – deducted as a subsidized percentage of their husbands' pay, so that military duty would not cause families financial distress. The response was immediate. When southern communities learned that U.S. Treasury checks enabled poor black women to stay home and avoid field labor, many responded with harsh "work or fight" ordinances that threatened jail time for any able bodied adult who could not supply written proof of employment. Of course, nobody expected married white women to comply.[51]

Openly avowed racial prejudice was not confined to southern small towns, or small-minded conservatives. In 1935, the year of Title IV's initial authorization, former Secretary of War Newton Baker wrote to Carnegie Corporation President Frederick Keppel. He was "amazed" at " ... the courage of white people in this country who received the slaves from the slave ships and undertook to make useful laborers of them. How many [other] white civilizations would have dared to receive so many wild savages, who were practically uncaged animals, and spread them around over their farms in contact with their own families?"[52]

During an era when many whites felt similarly free to express such open contempt, what is truly noteworthy about the implementation of Title IV is the fact that, by 1939, 17 percent of ADC households were African American, well above the proportion of 11 percent of blacks within the national population. Between 1940 and 1962, when amendments to Title IV renamed ADC to emphasize its support for entire families, welfare rolls grew slowly,

---

[49] Title I (old-age) and Title II (unemployment insurance) remained the heart of Social Security with Title III (limited aid to the blind and physically handicapped children) and Title IV (ADC) far less important. Only after 1972, when Supplemental Security Income greatly expanded federal grant in aid programs for the aged, blind, and disabled, did Title III become vastly more important and costly. Title IV turned into the "welfare mess."

[50] Nancy Cauthen and Edwin Amenta, "Not for Widows Only: Institutional Politics and the Formative Years of Aid to Dependent Children," *American Sociological Review* 61 (1996): 444–45.

[51] For further discussion of this program, see K. Walter Hickel, "War, Region, and Social Welfare: Federal Aid to Servicemen's Dependents in the South, 1917–1921," *Journal of American History* 87 (2001): 1362–96.

[52] Baker, quoted in Ellen Lagemann, *The Politics of Knowledge: The Carnegie Corporation, Philanthropy, and Public Policy* (Middletown, CT, 1990), 128.

but steadily, especially in the Northeast and Midwest, where more generous state payment schedules echoed these regions' earlier embrace of mothers' pensions. By 1960, almost three million children received Title IV cash payments. The 1939 amendments that greatly broadened old-age assistance also increased the federal share of revenue matching with states to one half of the total amount. By 1960, that meant that states could receive up to $32 for a first child, and up to $23 for a second child.

Grace Abbott eloquently voiced the needs of struggling white widows in her appeal to Congress to include aid to poor children within Social Security. But such women ceased to be important recipients a mere three years after Social Security's inauguration. Instead, divorced, deserted, or, increasingly, never-married women enrolled.[53] And in numbers dramatically higher than their proportions in the population, these women were African Americans. By 1960, the numbers of black and white children receiving ADC converged. Welfare rolls listed about a million and a half African-American children and an equivalent number of whites. That figure still totaled only about 6 percent of the country's estimated fifty million children. Nonetheless, that was a big enough group and a big enough cost to garner negative comment, especially as black children were overrepresented.[54]

Like the juvenile court and child abuse reporting laws, federalized welfare was an idea supported by reformers who favored the establishment of centralized governments, in which trained experts acted as important sources of counsel. No popular groundswell demanded these changes, and, in fact welfare administration, governed as were delinquency and abuse procedures by social science doctrines, espoused ideas ordinary Americans did not accept.

Even when they touted motherhood and the importance of home life, Americans never really included families in which husbands were absent or unable to earn a good living among those where wives and children could cluster at the hearth. Outdoor relief recognized that impoverished women with children too young yet to enter the labor force full time might require temporary assistance in cash or in kind. But only those with roots in a particular community and lives judged to be morally blameless deserved

---

[53] The rates of illegitimacy in the country began rising well before the 1960s. Between 1940 and 1960 the illegitimacy rate among whites went from 3.6 births per thousand to 9 per thousand. The rates among blacks increased from 35.6 per thousand to 98.3 per thousand. *United States Bureau of the Census, Historical Statistics of the United States: Colonial Times to 1970* (Washington, DC, 1971), Series B-28, 50–52. For further discussion of the changing composition of ADC rolls, see Steven Teles, *Whose Welfare? AFDC and Elite Politics* (Lawrence, KS, 1996), 20–26; Bobbie Green Turner, *Federal/State Aid to Dependent Children Program and Its Benefits to Black Children in America, 1935–1985* (New York, 1993), 71–127.

[54] County welfare departments created to administer the pensions finally gained paid employees, and new state-wide welfare departments emerged to administer ADC under federal guidelines. See U.S. Children's Bureau, "Child Welfare Legislation," Publication 236 (Washington, DC, 1938), 27–53.

assistance, and the aid was never meant to prevent poverty – only to ease its worst pain. In that sense, the supervised and limited nature of mothers' pensions connected public policy to popular attitudes. However, ADC, from its inception, did not. By the 1960s, when the welfare rolls exploded during a decade of astonishing growth, the seeds sown for a late-twentieth-century legislative rebellion were already flourishing.

Between 1949 and 1951, one of the nation's biggest-selling mass circulation magazines, *The Saturday Evening Post*, featured a long-running series on "relief chislers." Investigative reporter Paul Molloy traveled around the country interviewing welfare mothers and "discovered" that most were "grafters," "irresponsible," "probably criminals," or "prostitutes." The "young woman" who unlocked the door to a "decrepit, dirty apartment" in Tulsa, Oklahoma, "wore jeans and a man's suit coat. She was naked beneath it." Her three children were illegitimate. She wasn't entirely sure who the fathers were, but, in any event, she couldn't get [them] "to take no blood [paternity] test." Molloy fervently condemned "unwed baby breeders" as "racketeers" who stole honest taxpayers' money. "Put the children in orphanages," he urged, and send their mothers to jail.

Readers enthusiastically agreed and responded with fury to Molloy's stories of promiscuous women whom ADC allowed to be "professional paupers." They didn't want to give "a red cent" to anyone who gave birth outside of marriage, especially when she likely had "a lazy man" lying around in bed in a back room living off her welfare check.[55]

No reputable survey ever verified the *Post*'s anecdotal suggestions that ADC mothers were part-time prostitutes, with fancy men on the side. But since 1935 ADC had given money to never-married women, a practice state and local officials avoided. As the program became ever more generous, if judged by the narrow standards of outdoor relief, local officials expressed strident outrage. Margaret Lamm, Tulsa, Oklahoma's, County Attorney, condemned ADC for: "...paying women to add to the population of miserable, illegitimate children. [ADC] doesn't eliminate want. It compounds it. It raises new generations of twisted, subnormal people bred in the foulest environments."[56]

Less than twenty years after its expansion into a federal cost-sharing initiative "welfare" was already a program everyone loved to hate. It provided poor relief to the undeserving – only because "liberal social workers originated a strange new language – a sort of mumbo jumbo double-talk, which includes such mysterious terms as 'dynamic passivity.'"[57]

[55] Paul Molloy, "The Relief Chislers Are Stealing Us Blind," *Saturday Evening Post* 224 (1951): 142–44.

[56] Quoted in *Ibid.*, 143.

[57] Rufus Jarman, "Detroit Cracks Down on Relief Chislers," *The Saturday Evening Post* 222 (1949): 122.

Social scientists did not discuss "dynamic passivity." They assessed the "dynamnics" of "cultures of poverty," which encouraged the poor to be passive. The fact that Rufus Jarman, another *Saturday Evening Post* contributor, misquoted the phrase illustrated a larger truth, one already demonstrated by the histories of juvenile justice and child abuse law: the policy impact of pervasive misunderstanding of social science theory.

As the number of mothers employed full time away from home surged, a social science philosophy that emphasized the cultural roots of poverty supported expanded state aid to a growing group of never-married-mothers, to enable them to stay at home with their children. That turned several traditional attitudes about public obligations to poor children upside down, and the welfare mess eventually prompted a legislatively led revolution.

The "Welfare Explosion" and the Revolt Against Welfare

By 1960, about one quarter of women receiving ADC had never wed the fathers of their children. That figure approached one half for black recipients.[58] Early-twentieth-century reformers condemned the "dangerous classes" but never considered those who drank, shunned work, or despised thrift to be average.[59] In the cold analysis of eugenics such "shiftless" people deserved nothing. Indeed, the state had a different obligation: to keep the "unfit" from multiplying, through mandatory sterilization, if necessary. Had they believed, as did a later group of reformers and social scientists in post–World War II America, that poverty was in large part a product of cultural deviancy, Progressives would never have supported spending a single dime on a mothers' pension.

However, "culture" as an explanation for poverty won adherents among professionals, if not among average Americans. "Tangles of pathology" trapped poor families.[60] They lived for the moment, vented emotions improperly, wasted chances.[61] By 1962, liberal politicians allied with public

---

[58] Charts with these figures were introduced into his testimony by Secretary of Health, Education, and Welfare Abraham Ribicoff in 1961. Testimony of Abraham Ribicoff, "Temporary Unemployment Compensation and Aid to Dependent Children of Unemployed Parents," Hearings before the Committee on Ways and Means, House of Representatives, Eighty-Seventh Congress, First Session (Washington, DC, 1961), 96–97 (hereafter Hearing, Temporary Unemployment).

[59] Charles Loring Brace, New York-based leader of the orphan trains movement, first popularized the phrase in the late nineteenth century. Charles Loring Brace, *The Dangerous Classes of New York and Twenty Four Years Work Among Them* (New York, 1872).

[60] Daniel Patrick Moynihan infamously used the phrase in the Moynihan Report, but he borrowed it from existing social science literature. Alice O'Connor, *Poverty Knowledge*, 204.

[61] For a good review of the impact of "culture of poverty" social science thinking, see *Ibid.*, 153–231. Important works presenting the argument include Lee Rainwater, *Behind Ghetto Walls: Black Families in a Federal Slum* (Chicago, 1970); Oscar Lewis, *The Children of Sanchez*

welfare bureaucrats enacted key principles of "culture of poverty" theory into revisions of Title IV. Together with several important Supreme Court decisions that overturned states' abilities to limit welfare applications, these changes produced the "welfare explosion."

The new name used by the 1962 amendments was important. Children grew up and left, but *families* could remain perpetually dependent. Aid to Families with Dependent Children emphasized the need for social work's "rehabilitative" intervention. A program for needy children metamorphosed into one which sought to cure the "pathologies" of poverty and provide services to whole families: resident unemployed adult men, as well as women and children, with federal financial participation for noncash benefits authorized at a 75-percent rate. In the early twentieth century America's first degreed-sociologists proclaimed juvenile delinquency a disease. By the 1960s, child abuse and poverty had become similarly medicalized, and all these "ailments" required professional intervention.

The 1962 AFDC amendments included "provision for the training and further education of personnel employed or preparing for employment in public welfare programs."[62] Aid for impoverished children now contained grants to the country's professional schools which trained psychologists, therapists, sociologists, and social workers. Winifred Bell, a professor at the influential Columbia University School of Social Work, defended the proposed changes: "We do not save money by hiring tenth graders to build missiles, nor can we save families by hiring untrained persons to do the family counseling."[63]

President John Kennedy correctly labeled the amendments "... the most far-reaching revision of our public welfare program since it was enacted in 1935."[64] He did not note that the idea that the public should subsidize social work training so that "disturbed" young, unmarried mothers and "disoriented, out-of-work" fathers could remain together to receive job-training and counseling services – at state expense – would have dumbfounded an earlier generation of experts.[65] The 1962 amendments that made a program for dependent children a much-enlarged system for dysfunctional families

(New York, 1961); Kenneth Clark, *Dark Ghetto: Dilemmas of Social Power* (New York, 1965); Abram Kardiner and Lionel Ovesey, *The Mark of Oppression* (New York, 1951).

[62] Public Welfare Amendments of 1962 (Public Law 87–543), United States Statutes at Large (Washington, DC, 1962): 185.

[63] Testimony of Winifred Bell, "The Public Assistance Act Amendments," Hearings before the Committee on Ways and Means, House of Representatives, Eighty-Seventh Congress, First Session (Washington, DC, 1961): 410.

[64] John Kennedy, quoted in James Patterson, *America's Struggle Against Poverty*, 131.

[65] "Testimony of Loula Dunn, Director, American Public Welfare Association," Hearings, Temporary Unemployment, 220–21. The American Public Welfare Association, founded in 1936, came into its own in the 1960s – as the national organization representing the burgeoning field of public welfare. Its membership included most of the leaders of state and local welfare departments.

reflected emergent social science philosophy and the growing influence of public welfare bureaucrats. In no way did it reflect grassroots attitudes toward the poor.

The "Kennedy Amendments" should be called the Cohen Clauses. Wilbur Cohen, the seasoned Washington insider and University of Wisconsin–trained economist whom Frances Perkins had first employed thirty years earlier, assembled a coalition of public welfare advocates and social work professionals. Together, they transformed liberal poverty culture ideology into law. Cohen won the support of friendly legislators for hearings on Aid to Dependent Children just when Ways and Means, the powerful Committee in charge of Social Security appropriations, was mightily distracted by debates over Kennedy's proposed large tax cuts. Social workers packed the Ways and Means Hearing room in 1961, but the seats that were empty were the important ones – those of many committee members.[66]

The 1962 AFDC amendments were not mandatory. No Title IV programs ever were, and states could ignore the lure of 75 percent matching federal funds for rehabilitative services or for grants to families with resident, unemployed fathers. About half did. Nonetheless, a pattern was in place. "Welfare" enshrined tenets of social science which directly challenged entrenched beliefs about the "deserving" and "undeserving" poor. When asked to justify the growing federal role in expanded programs of aid to the poor, Kennedy's Secretary of Health, Education, and Welfare Abraham Ribicoff explained, "I think the national conscience is a little more sensitive than the local consciences about people who are in trouble."[67] "National sensitivity," however, was a figment of Abraham Ribicoff's imagination – confined to an elite dominated by social sciences professionals and sympathetic jurists.

Several Supreme Court decisions validated Ribicoff's hope of greater "sensitivity" at the federal level, although the policies endorsed eventually diverged so sharply from generally accepted beliefs that they provoked a major Congressional rebellion – as, similarly, had the Supreme Court's reinterpretations of juvenile justice.[68]

---

[66] Patterson, *America's Struggle Against Poverty*, 116–153; Edward Berkowitz, *Mr. Social Security: the Life of Wilbur J. Cohen* (Lawrence, KS, 1995).

[67] "Testimony of Abraham Ribicoff," Hearing, Temporary Unemployment: 101.

[68] Steven Teles and James Patterson persuasively argue that the welfare explosion was a top-down revolution. In contrast, sociologists Francis Fox Piven and Richard Cloward emphasize the influence of poor people's groups, such as the National Welfare Rights Organization (NWRO) which, not coincidentally, the latter two university-based sociologists helped to organize in 1967. But by that date, the key legislative changes and Supreme Court decisions were already in place, and Steven Gillon notes that the success of NWRO depended very significantly on legal aid lawyers, another elite group. Legal Aid became part of public social welfare bureaucracies in 1965. Congress authorized the Legal Services Program as a division within the Office of Economic Opportunity. Steven Gillon, *"That's Not What We Meant*

Until 1962, Title IV granted aid only to female heads of households and their children. About one half of all states followed South Carolina's initiative and adopted morals tests that included "suitable home" and "man-in-house" provisions denying ADC to the "unfit." The language could have been taken directly from any number of mothers' pensions statutes. In the 1940s and 1950s, the workers from state welfare bureaus who burst into bedrooms on midnight raids to see if a woman was sleeping alone or who checked closets, looking for a man's clothing, reenacted scenarios early-twentieth-century charity associations endorsed. But legal doctrines in the due-process era no longer allowed the intrusions early-twentieth-century aid workers unquestioningly accepted.

Of course, the poor themselves hated these violations of their privacy. Early-twentieth-century immigrants in the nation's cities often dreaded visits from the "Cruelty." Mid-century impoverished families despised the "Welfare." In his *Autobiography*, Malcolm X remembered the searing shame he felt when the "Welfare" showed up uninvited at his house, looking at his mother and at him as if "we were not people.... just *things.*"[69]

King v. Smith challenged the state's right to make the kind of moral judgments about AFDC families that caused Malcolm X such rage. Alabama's AFDC program, like many others, forbade "cohabitation" – defined as "continuing sexual relations" between a female recipient and a man to whom she was not married. Mrs. Sylvester Smith and her four children, ages fourteen, twelve, eleven, and nine, lived in Dallas County, Alabama. Between 1963 and 1966 the family received AFDC benefits for the three children born before Mrs. Smith's husband's death and for the nine-year-old born from a liaison with a boyfriend Mrs. Smith never married. In 1966, a neighbor reported that Mrs. Smith, who worked four days a week as a night-shift cook, was having sex with a new boyfriend, Ben Williams, in "broad daylight on her back screen porch." Welfare officials promptly cut the Smith family loose. The Smiths, like the Gaults, received free ACLU counsel, and their case eventually reached the Supreme Court in 1968.

In his majority opinion, Justice William O. Douglas declared, "Congress has determined that immorality and illegitimacy should be dealt with through rehabilitative measures rather than measures that punish dependent children.... Federal public welfare policy now rests on a basis considerably more sophisticated and enlightened than under the 'worthy person' concept of earlier times."[70]

To Do": *Reform and Its Unintended Consequences in Twentieth Century America* (New York, 2000), 69–72. Francis Fox Piven and Richard Cloward's most important book on the topic is *Regulating the Poor: The Functions of Public Welfare* (New York, 1971).

[69] Malcolm X, with Alex Haley, *The Autobiography of Malcolm X* (New York, 1964).

[70] *King, Commissioner, Department of Pensions and Security, Et Al., v. Smith, Et Al.*, Supreme Court of the United States, 392 U.S. 309, S. CT 2128, 1968, at 4, 15.

Welfare now was a due process right. Faced with a denial of benefits, welfare recipients and applicants could demand an attorney, provided with public funds, to represent them at a "fair hearing" – where they could cross-examine welfare officials and other witnesses.[71] The stage was set for the "welfare explosion."

Appointed officials in courts and administrative agencies, not elected legislatures, said welfare was an entitlement. A transformed program grew enormously. In a single decade's time, between 1968 and 1978, welfare rolls increased by an amazing 300 percent, while the nation's population grew only 19 percent. The three million children and parents on AFDC in 1960 increased to 4.3 million by 1965, to 6.1 million in 1969, to 10.8 million by 1974, and to over 13 million by 1978.

By the mid-1970s, this hugely increased number of recipients typically received in-kind benefits as well as cash. Those eligible for AFDC were also automatically enrolled in the national program of free medical assistance for the poor created in 1965. In addition to Medicaid cards, AFDC families also got food stamps and often lived in the high-rise public housing complexes that became a much-maligned symbol of Great Society mistakes. Poorly designed and badly maintained, most were havens for crime, not decent homes, but they did provide many women and children with a chance to live independently.[72]

Like the beneficiaries of mother's pensions, AFDC families had at least two children under age ten and a young female head, and like their predecessors, they lived in a big city. By 1980, one in five AFDC families resided in Chicago, Detroit, Houston, Los Angeles, New York, or Philadelphia.[73] There the similarities ended. AFDC mothers were not widows; they were not "respectable"; more than one half were either black or Hispanic; and the vast majority had never married the fathers of their children. Indeed, between the 1950s and the early 1970s the rates of illegitimacy among AFDC children

---

[71] The crucial case that guaranteed welfare recipients right to counsel and cross-examination was *Goldberg v. Kelley*, U.S. 254; 90 S. CT 1011; 1970. Other important due process cases include: *Dandridge v. Williams* 397 U.S. 471; *Shapiro v. Thompson* 395 U.S. 618. Steven Teles argues that these Court decisions acted to divert the attention of poverty professionals away from the need to mobilize any kind of broad-based support for the idea that welfare was an entitled right. Teles, *Whose Welfare?*, 117.

[72] For overviews of welfare spending during this decade, see Patterson, *America's Struggle Against Poverty*, 143–200; Robert Stevens and Rosemary Stevens, *Welfare Medicine in America: A Case Study of Medicaid* (New York, 1974); Morris Janowitz, *Social Control of the Welfare State* (Chicago, 1976); Michael Katz, *The Undeserving Poor: From the War on Poverty to the War on Welfare* (New York, 1989).

[73] Interestingly, Winifred Bell estimated that the vast majority of mothers' pension recipients lived in just nine American cities: Boston, Philadelphia, Cleveland, Chicago, Detroit, Los Angeles, Milwaukee, New York, and Detroit – all, with the single exception of Houston, cities where AFDC families concentrated decades later. Winifred Bell, *Aid to Dependent Children* (New York, 1965), 13.

grew, and mothers got even younger. When the program began in 1935, mothers were generally in their mid-thirties. By 1980, their ages had dropped considerably, and an AFDC recipient was usually under age twenty-six, with two children age five or younger.[74]

As early as 1965, Henry Wise, chair of the New York State Senate's Committee on Public Welfare, stormed, "A start must be made to administer welfare in the interest of the general public, not social worker theorists. Despite the howls of the pros, [my] constituents know that social work dogma is hogwash. Ask any taxi driver, cop, factory worker, or stenographer."[75]

Cops, taxi drivers, and stenographers did routinely tell pollsters that they agreed with Senator Wise. They thought that AFDC had created a lazy class of "welfare queens" who preferred life on the dole to work. They blamed the program for contributing to illegitimacy and family breakups. They agreed that blacks moved to northern and western cities just to get on welfare.

They were wrong on all counts. Peer-reviewed research never confirmed that women got pregnant to increase their welfare checks or that more generous benefits made particular cities and states "welfare magnets." Moreover, most AFDC recipients were on welfare for fewer than two years.[76]

There *was* a federal policy that directly contributed to the historic internal migration that sent America's black population between 1942 and 1965 to the cities: the New Deal's Agricultural Adjustment Act, which gave landlords the cash money they needed to buy tractors and evict tenants.[77] The truth didn't matter. Americans believed that welfare promoted indolence, encouraged immorality, and gave undue help to African Americans.

---

[74] For discussion of changing demographic trends among AFDC recipients, see "Welfare: Reform or Replacement?" Hearing before Subcommittee on Social Security and Family Policy of the Committee on Finance, United States Senate, One Hundredth Congress, First Session (Washington, DC, 1987): 20–21 (hereafter, Hearing, Replacement).

[75] Testimony of Henry Wise, "Social Security," Hearings before the Committee on Finance, United States Senate, Eighty-Ninth Congress, First Session (Washington, DC, 1965): 448–49 (hereafter Hearing, Social Security).

[76] Since the typical welfare recipient was a young woman under the age of twenty-six, and millions of teenagers with children received benefits, AFDC did allow separate living quarters for very young families who might otherwise have stayed with parents or other relatives. The 1971 Brooke Amendment, sponsored by then–Massachusetts Senator Edward Brooke, provided for separate dependents' allowances for each child under the age of eighteen for use in calculating "adjusted" rent, meaning that the more dependents, the lower the rent, and the larger the unit. See Paul Messenger, "Public Housing Perversity: A View From the Trenches," *Public Interest* 108 (1992): 132–43; Robert Moffitt, "Incentive Effects of the U.S. Welfare System: A Review," *Journal of Economic Literature* 30 (1992): 1–61.

[77] For an examination of the impact of the AAA, see Gilbert Fite, *Cotton Fields No More: Southern Agriculture, 1865–1980* (Lexington, KY, 1984), 140–60.

Not Welfare but "Workfare"

The 1962 Title IV amendments assumed that the problems of the poor were much more than economic. Every AFDC family needed a "social service" plan. Because the federal government paid 75 percent of costs for services, including caseworkers' salaries and administrative overhead, states had a substantial incentive to expand their welfare bureaucracies. But little evidence emerged during the next twenty years that the panoply of counseling and training "services" prepared welfare mothers for work.

In 1965, officials of the American Public Welfare Association warned, "A few AFDC families can become independent very soon. Many others will not achieve self-support before their children are grown. Others may not achieve financial independence within this generation."[78] If welfare administrators found this scenario acceptable, politicians did not. Ronald Reagan campaigned for Governor of California promising to separate "welfare cheats" from the "truly needy." He brought the same message with him to Washington.[79] Between 1980 and 1988 Congress endorsed his pledge to cut welfare caseloads dramatically.

In 1996 pundits and public alike thought that welfare had been revolutionalized. It had, but only after more than fifteen years of incremental change. Although the trend did not register in the popular imagination, which continued to see AFDC as a program spinning out of control, welfare enrollments remained flat from 1978 through the early 1980s, then dropped. By the end of Ronald Reagan's second term, caseloads were smaller by almost a third. Between 1983 and 1988, an average of five hundred thousand women and children left welfare monthly. In 1978, 40 percent of all female-headed families in the country participated in AFDC – a percentage that included an estimated one in eight American children. Ten years later, the proportions had fallen noticeably. Fewer than one in three families headed by a woman alone received welfare.[80] This did not happen by accident.

---

[78] American Association of Public Welfare, "The AFDC Mother is 97% Better than the Public Thinks!" submitted in evidence, Hearing, Social Security, 293.

[79] For discussion of Reagan's anti-welfare programs in California, many of which were implemented nationally between 1980 and 1988, see David Keefe, "Governor Reagan, Welfare Reform, and AFDC Fertility," *Social Service Review* 57 (1982): 234–53.

[80] For discussion of these changes, see Dorothy Miller, "AFDC: Mapping a Strategy for Tomorrow," *Social Service Review* 57 (1983): 599–613; Mildred Rein, "Work in Welfare: Past Failures and Future Strategies," *Social Service Review* 56 (1982): 211–29; Fred Englander and John Kane, "Reagan's Welfare Reforms: Were the Program Savings Realized?" *Policy Studies Review* 11 (1992): 3–23; Becky Glass, "Child Support Enforcement: An Implementation Analysis," *Social Service Review* 64 (1990): 543–58; Robert Moffitt and Douglas Wolf, "The Effects of the 1981 Omnibus Budget Reconcilation Act on Welfare Recipients and Work Incentives," *Social Service Review*, 61 (1987): 247–60; Peter Szanton, "The Remarkable 'Quango': Knowledge, Politics, and Welfare Reform," *Journal of Policy Analysis and*

Ronald Reagan's anecdotes were famous, and the 1980 campaign featured several of his favorites about "welfare queens": the woman in Chicago who claimed nonexistent children; the chisler in Boston who used three different names to get three different checks. That these "misuses of your money" were rarely fully substantiated mattered little. Nonelected policy makers, not ordinary Americans, endorsed welfare as a due process right. The president was a master storyteller who tapped simmering public anger about the welfare explosion.

In 1980, with bipartisan support, Congress passed the Omnibus Budget Reconciliation Act (OBRA). The bill encouraged states to devise experimental "demonstration projects" designed to get welfare recipients to work. It also capped federal matches for eligibility for AFDC at 150 percent of the need standard established by a state and standardized reimbursements for work expenses. Previously, an AFDC recipient who held a job could deduct any "reasonable" costs such as payroll taxes, child care, transportation, and work uniforms before calculating gross income for eligibility.[81] In 1984, the Deficit Reduction Act tightened federal standards even further, raising the AFDC gross income limit from 150 percent to 185 percent of a state's need standard, while also requiring that all income of both parents, as well as any money earned by resident children, be counted when determining AFDC eligibility.[82]

In the 1986 mid-term elections, the Democrats regained control of the Senate, and New York's Daniel Patrick Moynihan had a chance to answer the critics who for two decades had excoriated the 1965 Moynihan Report – in which the then–Assistant Secretary of Labor worried about the "deterioration of the Negro family." In the turbulent 1960s, Moynihan's planning document won instant notoriety, even though it presented no new ideas but, rather, was the author's colorful distillation of then-current social-science thinking about the culture of poverty.[83]

As the new Chair of the Senate Subcommittee on Social Security and Family Policy of the Committee on Finance, Moynihan drafted another bill, the last in the triad that shaped welfare reform during the 1980s. Titled the Family Support Act, Moynihan's measure required fathers to pay court-ordered child support and told custodial parents, almost always mothers, to register for "Job Opportunity and Basic Skills" programs that provided education,

---

Management 10 (1991): 590–603; Catherine Chilman, "Welfare Reform or Revision: The Family Support Act of 1988," *Social Service Review* 66 (1992): 349–78.

[81] For detailed discussion of OBRA's provisions see "Report by the U.S. General Accounting Office: An Evaluation of the 1981 AFDC Changes, Final Report" (Washington, DC, 1985), 13–34.

[82] *Ibid.*, 14.

[83] For analysis of the controversies the Report spurred, see Lee Rainwater and William Yancey, Eds., *The Moynihan Report and the Politics of Controversy* (Cambridge, MA, 1967).

job training, and work-experience. It also required states that participated in AFDC to extend benefits to families where both parents were present. As early as 1962, that had been a voluntary option, which slightly under one half of states incorporated into welfare administrative regulations and which almost none actually implemented.[84]

Indisputably, 1980s welfare reform cut costs. The nonpartisan federal General Accounting Office calculated that OBRA's restrictions alone saved the federal government $93 million monthly.[85] During the decade, almost all recipients dropped from rolls belonged to the estimated 15 percent of AFDC mothers who earned paychecks. Most worked full time, at minimum-wage jobs that exceeded the new 185 percent standards but still left family income below the poverty line. Hundreds of thousands of other welfare mothers went to classes, engaged in mandatory job searches, and did their "workfare" time – which usually meant showing up for low-skill municipal-services jobs – such as passing out food trays at public hospitals. Despite the fact that the law now made them eligible, very few men participated. Typically, they had never shared a home with the mothers of their children, or had long since left.

"Workfare" job training provided few clear paths to jobs, and most AFDC recipients managed to avoid it. Moreover, a distressingly large percentage, one in four, of all welfare beneficiaries stayed on AFDC rolls for at least ten years – although not necessarily ten years running.[86] It began to seem that the only way to get women off welfare was to end welfare.

Why indeed should some mothers receive state aid that enabled them to stay home when, by the mid-1980s, 72 percent of all Americans mothers worked outside the home, even if their children were similarly young? Early-twentieth-century Americans had always expected an impoverished mother to work, even if she needed public help until her children grew old enough to bring home wages. But the "welfare explosion" of the 1960s and early 1970s coincided with a work explosion among married women. The labor force participation rate of single women changed only slightly between 1960 and 2000. Wives, then wives who were also mothers, led the huge increases in late-twentieth-century female work.[87]

---

[84] Generally, the number of "workfare" hours required equaled the number of hours recipients' welfare benefits would have earned at the minimum wage, although some states chose lower ceilings. For discussion of the major provisions of the Family Support Act, see Hearing, Replacement, 9–22.

[85] General Accounting Office, "1981 AFDC Changes, Final Report": iii.

[86] Robert Moffitt, "Incentive Effects of the U.S. Welfare System," 22–26; Greg Duncan and Saul Hoffman, "Welfare Benefits, Economic Opportunities, and Out-of-Wedlock Births Among Black Teenage Girls," *Demography* 27 (1990): 519–35; Saul Hoffman and Greg Duncan, "A Comparison of Choice-Based Multinomial and Nested Logit Models: The Structure and Welfare Use Decisions of Divorced and Separated Women," *Journal of Human Resources* 23 (1988): 550–62.

[87] By 1960 about 60 percent of American single women were already working full time, a percentage that increased to 70 percent by 1995. Those left were either students or old

By the 1990s, American middle-class married women were also on the job, even if they had babies or toddlers. Intellectual justifications of AFDC as an entitlement had never been widely embraced. Most people never thought a poor woman had a "right" to demand the state subsidize her decision to stay home with young children. By the 1990s, few thought that any adult younger than age 65 had a "right" to opt out of paid work. In 1996 a system long under attack ended.

The "End of Welfare as We Know It"

In 1988 a Republican president worked with a Democratically controlled Senate to pass the Family Support Act. In 1996 a Democratic president signed into law a bill crafted by Republican lawmakers. The Personal Responsibility and Work Opportunity Reconciliation Act (PRA) abolished Title IV of the Social Security Act, replacing it with a block grant program controlled by states called "Temporary Assistance for Needy Families" (TANF). The language of these grants broke sharply with a sixty-year-old trend that federalized standards for aid to impoverished children. States could establish their own eligibility criteria and were no longer categorically required to provide assistance to anyone.

PRA terminated all welfare recipients within two years, placed a five-year lifetime limit on the receipt of benefits, and narrowed children's eligibility for Supplemental Social Security. Begun in 1972, the program established a minimum monthly income stipend for the aged, blind, and disabled. By tightening definitions of behavioral and learning disabilities, the "End of Welfare" also ended benefits for almost two hundred thousand Americans under the age of eighteen.[88]

The impact of this sweeping change was stunning. Within four years, the nation's welfare rolls dropped by 49 percent, and analysts projected annual fiscal savings to taxpayers of over $54 billion. Almost half of the estimated 7.5 million children in four million households still receiving AFDC in 1996 no longer received public cash allotments. Florida Representative E. Clay Shaw, the primary author of the legislation, declared that August 22, 1996, was "...independence day for all those trapped in the system...which has corrupted their souls and stolen their futures."[89]

The futures of millions of people certainly changed. Throughout the country, the job title "welfare caseworker" disappeared. Instead, clients met

women who had retired. For statistics discussing changing employment patterns for women, see Hearing, Replacement, 22–24.

[88] Personal Responsibility and Work Opportunity Reconciliation Act, Public Law No. 104–193, 110 *United States Statutes at Large* (Washington, DC, 1996).

[89] Clay Shaw, quoted in John Collins, "Developments in Policy: Welfare Reform," *Yale Law and Policy Review* 16 (1997): 221.

with "work assessment specialists" at "work opportunity offices."[90] Within two years, caseloads nationally plummeted by almost one half; in certain states and regions, the reductions were much greater. Wisconsin, a state that had taken advantage of OBRA's incentives to experiment with "workfare" demonstrations, boasted an 80 percent drop.[91] In August 2000, Schuyler County, Illinois, on the state's prairie west of Springfield, announced that it was entirely "welfare-free." For more than a year not a single person among the county's seventy-five hundred residents had received a penny of welfare.[92] "It was scary," admitted Karen DeMoss, who'd spent twelve years as an AFDC mother, before learning that her benefits would end in 1999. Within six months she'd landed a job as a cook with a wedding catering service and claimed, "Now my boys are proud of me. I cook for three hundred people."[93] Karen DeMoss was not alone. Newspapers brimmed with tales like hers. Politicians regularly invited a former welfare mom to sit in the front rows when they gave major addresses.

Wisconsin Governor Tommy Thompson asked Michelle Crawford to take a turn herself at the podium. She was a star performer – whose speech to a packed Wisconsin state legislature probably exceeded Thompson's fondest dreams. When she'd had her first baby in 1979, Crawford was a high school dropout, unemployed, unwed, and nineteen years old. For the next two decades she'd been chronically dependent on welfare. In 1998 she stood before the assembled politicians to describe a new life as a machine operator at a plastics factory. Pointing to her three youngest kids sitting in the gallery, she ended, "Now I tell them this is what happens when you do your homework.... Thank you, Jesus. Oh, thank you, Jesus."[94] Half of Crawford's audience was in tears, and, eyes brimming, Tommy Thompson rushed to hug his success story.

Was welfare reform a success? It was certainly a transformative policy change. At AFDC's peak, in the late 1970s, the nation spent an estimated $244 billion annually on cash allotments and more than three times that much on in-kind benefits. By the end of the century, analysts guessed that figure might have been reduced to less than $80 billion countrywide. Those kinds of financial savings left states with an odd problem: a windfall many struggled to spend. Wisconsin used its block grants to establish new state-funded child care programs, offered poor women door-to-door rides to mandatory motivation classes, and rewarded women who'd

---

[90] Steven Hayward, "The Shocking Success of Welfare Reform," *Policy Review* 4 (1998): 6.

[91] Greg Duncan and Jeanne Brooks-Gunn, "Welfare's New Rules: A Pox on Children," *Issues in Science and Technology*, 14 (1998): 68–69.

[92] Robert Pear, "How One County Cleared the Welfare Rolls," *New York Times*, August 14, 2000.

[93] *Ibid.*

[94] Jason DeParle, "A Bold Effort Leaves Much Unchanged for Wisconsin's Poor," *New York Times*, December 30, 1999.

held a first job after welfare for more than a year with low-interest car loans.[95]

Block grants left states awash in money in the late 1990s, but most former AFDC families were still desperately poor. During boom years, those on the economic bottom slid down even further. After a year in the work force only about a third of previous beneficiaries earned more money than they had received on welfare. Only a quarter rose above the poverty line. In 1999, just four percent managed to make at least $19,000 annually. Moreover, about 20 percent of former welfare recipients vanished from the rolls but did not resurface as employees. They apparently were without either welfare or work, though few states kept accurate track of their actual circumstances.[96]

Supporters of welfare reform argued that a change so momentous would necessarily leave some behind – but that even those who obtained minimum wage jobs would be better off than if they remained on welfare, especially if they took advantage of Earned Income Tax Credits. Congress created the tax credits in 1972 to reduce income and Social Security payroll tax deductions for low-income workers. In 1996, a worker with two children who earned $15,000 a year, the figure often estimated as the average full time entry-level salary of a former welfare recipient taking her first step away from dependence, got $2,800 back in earned income tax credits if she claimed them.[97]

Rosy pictures were easy to draw during the dazzlingly good times of the late 1990s; even the giddiest of optimists acknowledged that the real test of welfare reform would be a recession. Since 1965, AFDC families also had received Medicaid and Food Stamps. That changed in 1996, but nowhere in PRA was there a requirement that those let loose from welfare be denied Medicaid and supplemental food programs.

In some areas, however, new rules made application procedures for these benefits strangely onerous. California, New York, and twenty-seven other states asked if applicants owned a burial plot. Nebraska inquired, had they ever been paid to give blood? Hawaii demanded garage-sales receipts, South Dakota detailed statements about any bingo winnings. All counted against a family's food allotment. Some states distributed thirty-six-page application forms. The shortest, Florida's, still exceeded seven. All listed stiff fines and up to twenty-year-long prison terms as penalties for incorrect answers.[98]

[95] Jason DeParle, "States Struggle to Use Windfall Born of Shifts in Welfare Law," *New York Times*, August 29, 1999.

[96] DeParle, "A Bold Effort."

[97] Michael Graetz, *The U.S. Income Tax: What It Is, How It Got That Way, and Where Do We Go from Here?* (New York, 1999), 34–35, 57; Jack Meyer, "Assessing Welfare Reform: Work Pays," *Public Interest*, 136 (1999): 113–20.

[98] Nina Bernstein, "Burial Plots, Bingo, and Blood in Quest for Food Stamps," *New York Times*, August 12, 2000.

At least twelve million people left welfare between 1996 and 2000. Studies suggested that significant numbers did not get supplemental food, though most qualified as extremely low-income Americans. Perhaps one out of four former welfare families became uninsured as well. In some states, computers automatically cut off Medicaid for people leaving welfare, and state employees were not told to inform former Medicaid beneficiaries to reapply.[99]

In 1997, to much fanfare, Congress passed the Children's Health Insurance Program, which provided more than $4 billion to help families with too much income to qualify for Medicaid and too little to afford private health insurance for their children. Yet, three years later, almost one half of the money remained unspent. Some states argued that their benefit systems already covered most low-income children. Others, however, made little effort to publicize the new program.[100] In 1999, an estimated eleven million poor children were without health insurance, up from about nine million in 1996.

And, even during record prosperity, homelessness rose. A twenty-five-city survey by the U.S. Council of Mayors discovered a 17-percent increase in homelessness in 1999 – the highest percentage rate increase in one year since 1980. Almost all of the new homeless were women and young children. Overburdened administrators in New York City, with one of the nation's sharpest increases in housing costs, imposed a "one-night only" rule, assigned families beds a night at a time, and shuttled people from shelter to shelter. Many of those carrying their life's belongings in paper shopping bags from one place to the next were young women who had jobs – and at least three children. But full time work at the minimum wage allowed such a mother to pay, at a maximum, about $700 monthly rent. Such apartments, at least ones that accepted an adult with three kids in tow, were hard to find in New York City and its suburbs.[101]

The Promises of Poverty Policy

The prospects of poor children in the 1990s depended, just as they always had, on whether they had support from an able-bodied father. That had

---

[99] Robert Pear, "Study Links Medicaid Drop to Welfare Changes," *New York Times*, May 14, 1999.

[100] The states of Texas and California created two of the most cumbersome application systems, and together, they had the dubious distinction of claiming about one third of all the nation's eleven million poor uninsured children. See Robert Pear, "Forty States Forfeit U.S. Insurance Aid for Poor Children," *New York Times*, September 24, 2000. See also: "Implementation of the State Children's Health Insurance Program," Hearing Before Committee on Finance, United States Senate, One Hundred Sixth Congress, First Session (Washington, DC, 1999).

[101] Nina Bernstein, "Shelter Population Reaches Highest Level Since 1980s," *New York Times*, February 8, 2001.

perpetually been more important than whether their mothers moved from reliance on minimal state aid to dependence on inadequate wages.[102]

Critics of the 1996 policy changes angrily charged that "Without welfare, mothers who work inside the home are deprived of equal citizenship."[103] They warned that "a war against poor women is a war against all women."[104] They said that the Personal Responsibility and Work Opportunity Act reached ". . . new depths in the commodification of women by mandating employment."[105] Outside of academe, few found such arguments plausible.

The "brutality" of the 1996 Act's sanctions against non-marital child rearing wasn't an example of "Republican . . . patriarchal(ism)."[106] Americans had never endorsed helping child rearing outside of wedlock, especially if the children's mothers were poor. Of the two welfare "revolutions" – the first – engineered through court rulings and bureaucratic orders during the 1960s – was the one without popular backing. It expanded aid to mothers society judged "undeserving," even though it did not lift most from poverty. The outcry was inevitable.

Americans venerated work, and the majority of American children who were not poor at the end of the century had two working parents. Middle class life required the paychecks of two adults. By the 1990s, most American mothers were employed full time even when their offspring were infants. Analysts suggested that, over time, full time work might blur income inequality between genders. With fewer family supports than existed in Europe, American mothers maintained more continuous labor force participation, accruing promotions, higher incomes, and retirement benefits. In 1995, American single women in their twenties earned 98 percent of men's wages, while, on average, all female wage earners earned 77 percent of male earnings. Perhaps soon, mothers would catch up, some economists suggested, since lower labor force participation of mothers in childbearing years largely explained income differentials between men and women.

---

[102] The landmark 1996 welfare reforms came up for renewal in 2002. Leaders of the National Governors' Association demanded that, in view of economic downturns, the PRA's insistence on work requirements be eased, but President George W. Bush formally recommended that they be increased and that states be pushed even harder to meet them. After six years of major policy change, clearly no consensus at all had been reached on how to proceed at the beginning of the twenty-first century. See Robert Pear, "Relaxing of Welfare's Work Rule Sought," *New York Times*, February 24, 2002; Robert Pear, "Bush's Plan on Welfare Law Increases Work Requirement," *New York Times*, February 26, 2002.

[103] Gwendolyn Mink, "The Lady and The Tramp (II): Feminist Welfare Politics, Poor Single Mothers, and the Challenge of Welfare Justice," *Feminist Studies* 24 (1998): 58.

[104] Eva Feder Kittay, "Dependency, Equality, and Welfare," *Feminist Studies* 24 (1998): 41.

[105] Sonya Michel, "Childcare and Welfare (In)justice," *Feminist Studies* 24 (1998): 51.

[106] Gwendolyn Mink, "Aren't Poor Single Mothers Women? Feminists, Welfare Reform, and Welfare Justice," in Ruth Brandwein, Ed., *Battered Women, Children, and Welfare Reform* (New York, 1999), 177.

In Sweden, famous for family-friendly policies that helped mothers to balance work and maternity by granting paid maternity leaves and universal children's allowances, women earned less than one half the wages of their male counterparts. Government policies made work and family life easier for mothers of young children but had long-term negative consequences for mothers' careers.[107]

Paid labor was the only way to advance economically in America – and throughout the Western world. But putting people to work was only one goal of the Personal Responsibility and Work Opportunity Act. Its other aim was to reduce the numbers of American children born outside of marriage. Mothers had to identify the fathers of their children to get benefits. Mothers under the age of eighteen had to live at home or in an approved adult-supervised setting. Fathers who did not pay court-ordered child support were supposed to lose their driver's licenses. States that managed to substantially diminish their illegitimate birthrates received $20 million annual "bonuses."

However, the "End of Welfare" did not seem to be doing much to end illegitimacy. No one had ever been able to prove that women got pregnant to get welfare. They certainly did not get pregnant, either, in the hopes of becoming poor. But between 1960 and 2000 more and more women had children without ever marrying the fathers. That trend cut across all races and classes.

In 1960, the rate of unwed births for black women aged fifteen to forty-four was nine times higher than for whites; in 1980, four times as high. By 1990, unwed births among white women had increased so dramatically that the percentage of difference between the races was just twice as high. "Just" twice, however, still meant that the number of black female-headed households tripled between 1960 and 1995.[108]

As the welfare rolls emptied, blacks and Latinas remained in highly dispro-portionate numbers. In 1998, an estimated 30 percent of those left on welfare were white, 37 percent African American, and 33 percent Latina. Dominated by minorities, welfare became even more of an urban phenomenon. Big city slums had always housed most welfare recipients. Now few lived anywhere else. In Wisconsin, 85 percent of everyone left on welfare lived in Milwaukee. One out of two recipients of cash aid in Pennsylvania lived in Philadelphia.

Since the Social Security Act of 1935 made ADC aid available to them, minority recipients had always been poorer than whites and less likely to marry. They were, on average, less well educated and had larger families.[109] Would growing racial imbalances make state aid to the impoverished even

---

[107] These kinds of figures were true for most northern European and Nordic countries with "family friendly" workplaces and policies. Sandra Scarr, "American Child Care Today," *The American Psychologist* 53 (1998): 100.

[108] Stoesz, "Unraveling Welfare Reform," 54–56.

[109] Jason DeParle, "Shrinking Welfare Rolls Leave Record High Share of Minorities," *New York Times*, July 27, 1998.

more unpopular? If applicants were diligent but couldn't find work, would welfare again become more generous? The twentieth century's history of aid to the young poor didn't provide much hope of that. The one group raised spectacularly by state policy from poverty was old.

In 1900, those over sixty-five were a small percentage of the country's population, but those unable to work or rely on adult children were typically destitute. As recently as 1970, the U.S. median age was only twenty-eight, but the nation was aging rapidly. By 2000, Americans under the age of thirty were a minority. By 2030, demographers predicted, more than one half of all the country's adults would be fifty years old or older. Beginning in the 1930s, elders organized, and, by 2000, were one of the country's most powerful interest groups. The American Association of Retired Persons alone had over 33 million members and an annual operating budget topping five billion dollars. In 1950 about 40 percent of all elderly Americans lived below official poverty lines. After 1972, Social Security's Supplemental Security Income program guaranteed the aged a minimum income.[110] At the end of the century, less than 3 percent of the nation's old lived in striking poverty.

Those left behind were mothers and children. In the last twenty-five years of the century, one half of the country's female-headed families were poor. The divorce rate dropped slightly after 1980, and birth rates steadily declined. What increased was the proportion of births to unmarried women. Fertility behavior had not changed, but attitudes about marriage certainly had. Once considered shameful by almost everyone, a birth out of wedlock was no longer a "dreadful social stigma."[111] It some quarters it was even celebrated.[112] By the year 2000, single parents, 90 percent of whom were

---

[110] SSI was an outgrowth of debates about negative income taxes. In 1969, Richard Nixon proposed his Family Assistance Plan (FAP), which would have given all Americans with children a guaranteed minimum income. Nixon's FAP proposal did not apply to single people or families without children. In any event it was soundly defeated, but the idea that certain groups deserved a government-guaranteed income floor persisted. See Patterson, *America's Struggle Against Poverty*, 185–98.

[111] The Children's Bureau used the phrase in 1941 – arguing that a woman's "dread" would help ensure that illegitimacy rates remained relatively low, even among the poor and ill-educated. United States Children's Bureau, Mary Ruth Colby, "Problems and Procedures in Adoption," Publication 262 (Washington, DC, 1941), 10. Birth rates for all American women, high income and impoverished, white and minority, declined between 1969 and 2000. The only factor which kept the nation from falling below zero population growth rates was an increasing percentage of residents who were newcomers, after immigration laws liberalized in 1965. Moffitt, "Incentive Effects of the U.S. Welfare System," 27–29.

[112] Some groups of feminists argued that a woman's reproductive choice was an essential right, and that society should support a "woman's right to choose motherhood" even if the woman could not provide economically for the child. Mink, "Feminists and Welfare Reform," 176.

women, headed one third of all American families, and greater numbers of those mothers had never married. Statistically, they were much poorer than their divorced counterparts.[113] Americans wanted parents to take care of their own children, even in the face of the reality that in a large number of American households one parent provided little emotional or financial support.

Patrick Murphy, the Cook County Public Guardian, said, "No one listened to Pat Moynihan in 1966 when he asked what was ... going to happen when kids were having kids without the benefit of fathers. ... You can run a (welfare system) from Washington. You can run it from Springfield. You can run it from L.A. You can run it from Mogadishu."[114]

Nothing would make a difference if poor women kept trying to raise children alone. To the extent that welfare had ever convinced such individuals to raise a family, it certainly was an "illusory promise." But so was the notion that the country's most impoverished just needed to get busy and find husbands.

Charge for charge, crime for crime, the juvenile justice system arrested and jailed an overwhelmingly disproportionate percentage of minority males. So too did adult courts. By the early 1990s, it was not uncommon for half of all young African-American males from an inner city neighborhood to be in prison, on probation, or awaiting bail.[115] That certainly limited the pool of marriageable men.[116]

---

[113] Between 1950 and 2000 the number of out of marriage births went from: 141,000 in 1950, to 770,000 in 1984, to 1,210,000 in 1998. Never-married mothers were, on average, younger than divorced mothers, with much less education. About half of never-married mothers in the last quarter of the twentieth century did not graduate from high school, while three quarters of divorced women had a high school degree or better. Many never-married mothers had their first babies between ages 15 and 20 and had never worked full time before that birth, limiting their work experience options as mothers. See David Ellwood, "Anti-Poverty Policy for Families in the Next Century: From Welfare to Work – And Worries," *Journal of Economic Perspectives* 14 (2000): 187–98; Douglas Besharov and Alison Quin, "Not All Female-Headed Families Are Created Equal," *Public Interest* 89 (1987): 48–56; James Alm and Leslie Whittington, "Income Taxes and the Marriage Decision," *Applied Economics* 27 (1995): 25–31; Steven Ruggles, "The Effects of AFDC on American Family Structure, 1940–1990," *Journal of Family History* 22 (1997): 307–26.

[114] Testimony of Patrick Murphy, "Child Welfare Programs," Hearing before the Subcommittee on Oversight of the Committee on Ways and Means, House of Representatives, One Hundred Fourth Congress, First Session (Washington, DC, 1995), 85 (hereafter Hearing, Child Welfare).

[115] Stoesz, "Unraveling Welfare Reform," 54.

[116] Congressman Clay Shaw argued in 1998, "Now I am aware that there are many ... who think that getting government involved in promoting marriage is foolish. ... But if government policy can contribute to creating single parent families, it seems reasonable to conclude that government policy can also contribute to the demise of single parent families." Opening Statement of E. Clay Shaw, "Fatherhood and Welfare Reform," Hearing before the Subcommittee on Human Resources of the Committee on Ways and Means, House of

Throughout the twentieth century, children stood a better chance of escaping poverty if their parents were married and living under the same roof. However, the late-twentieth-century's conservative promotion of marriage faced odd hurdles. The same Congress that passed the Personal Responsibility and Work Opportunity Act of 1996 left unaltered a significant marriage penalty in the Earned Income Tax Credit. A woman with two children earning a poverty-level annual income of $11,000 could gain a $3,600 tax "refund," even if she paid no taxes. If she met a man who also had two children, and who also earned $11,000 or less, he too could take home $3,600 in tax credits. But if the two married, they would likely lose over $5,000 in tax benefits.[117]

No evidence supported the notion that "marriage penalties," however much they flew in the face of "family values" rhetoric, actually deterred very many people from marrying. In poor households, just hanging on took highest priority. It always had. Aid for dependent children always focused on the "suitability" of mothers and insufficiently acknowedged the kinds of struggles a poor family faced.[118]

Representatives, One Hundred Fifth Congress, Second Session (Washington, DC, 1998): 5 (hereafter Hearing, Fatherhood). Shaw's comments reflected commonly shared beliefs, but no reliable study conclusively linked increases in unwed parenthood and the growth of AFDC. In mid-century Ingrid Bergman had to flee the country in disgrace when she bore out of wedlock twins. By century's end, tabloids ran stories about the glamorous exploits of the legions of Hollywood stars who chose to be single moms – role models for young women who could never achieve such a life, especially as wage gaps between the country's richest and poorest widened in the last 25 years of the twentieth century.

[117] The EITC was a partial implementation of Richard Nixon's defeated idea of providing all impoverished and working poor Americans with a guaranteed minimum income. However, significantly, the EITC affected only those people who had earned *some* income, not those without jobs. In 1997 the Earned Income Tax Credits provided a poor family with two children a 40 percent credit of earnings up to a maximum of $3,656. Above $11,930 in income, the credit began to phase out based on a percentage of 21 cents on the dollar and ended completely at a maximum income of $29,290. But the marriage penalty which affected the Earned Income Tax Credit affected huge numbers of married people. Most Americans who married paid more in federal taxes; by the mid-1990s those with high incomes taxed at the 28 percent rate generally paid about $15,000 yearly. Graetz, *The U.S. Income Tax*, 29–34.

[118] Its champions argued that, among other benefits, welfare reform would provide greater numbers of poor children with two parent homes. Six years after the passage of the Personal Responsibility and Work Opportunity Act, debate about actual results raged, but some suggested that just the opposite might have begun to happen, especially to impoverished black children living in urban slums. Rather than two parents, they had "no parents." A Harvard case study published in 2002 estimated that the share of poor children living in households without their parents present rose for all groups, but especially dramatically for African-American city youngsters, more than doubling since 1996 – from 7 percent to more than 16 percent. One researcher guessed that at least two hundred thousand more black, urban children lived with neither parent and argued that significant percentages were children of former welfare mothers who, in order to hold jobs, gave up children to fosterage

Michelle Crawford was illustrative. Her triumphant speech to dazzled Wisconsin legislators blurred a difficult life. Crawford *had* married her boyfriend, Donald Crawford. After an extended bout with unemployment, he found a job as a night maintenance man. With their two incomes coming to a fraction more than $16,000 annually, the couple no longer qualified for Food Stamps. Often, they ran out of milk. Crawford worried constantly about her oldest son, a nineteen-year-old imprisoned for selling cocaine. Tensions spurred frequent, noisy quarrels with her husband, and neighbors sometimes called the police. Crawford's three younger children complained that she was no longer ever around. "She doesn't want to cook – she says she's too tired and stuff," said fourteen-year-old Lorenzo. "She says, 'Leave me alone.' She acts mean," complained eleven-year-old Lavita.[119] In the 1990s, most exhausted working mothers heard similar taunts from their own children, although fewer had mothers and grandmothers who'd also had to juggle jobs and childrearing. Michelle Crawford was black. Her sisters in previous generations had led a century-long trend that increased employment among mothers.

Had she lived during the first half of the twentieth century, Michelle Crawford would have expected Lorenzo, and perhaps Lavita, too, to work and contribute wages to the household. Crawford's oldest boy would have certainly been considered an adult, although an adult son in prison would have provided no more help in the early twentieth century than he did at its end. But a historic transition occurred between 1900 and 2000. By the time Michelle Crawford fought to make a new postwelfare life for herself and her children, all able-bodied adults under the age of sixty-five were supposed to work. Children were not. Twentieth-century efforts to regulate child labor, however, posed complicated dilemmas.

---

or left them with other relatives. In the twentieth century, child abuse policy inadvertently contributed to rising percentages of American children in foster care. Would the twenty-first see even higher statistics as welfare reform swelled the ranks of youngsters in some form of state-sponsored fosterage, either with strangers or non-parental relatives? For a summary of research cited above, see Nina Bernstein, "Side Effect of Welfare Law: The No Parent Family," *New York Times*, July 29, 2002.

[119] Ellwood, "Anti-Poverty Policy," 189.

PART TWO

CHILDREN'S WORK

4

"Inducting into Adulthood"

State Reactions to the Labor of Children and Adolescents

"Child saving" united Progressivism's otherwise vaguely connected reform agenda. Innovations from city manager government to the secret ballot supposedly made America better for the young. Not surprisingly, then, advocates of genuinely child-specific issues often cooperated, and crowd-pleasing speakers – Homer Folks, Julian Mack, and most of all, Ben Lindsey – constituted an informal child-savers' Chautauqua. From one stage they promoted the ideals of the juvenile court. Standing on another they solicited contributions for an anticruelty philanthropy. At a different meeting, they denounced child labor. Sometimes one stem-winding appeal mentioned all three.

Ben Lindsey's expansive personality magnified two central traits of early-twentieth-century reform: its buoyant embrace of many causes and its apocalyptic sense of crisis. Without the juvenile court, he declaimed, "struggling humanity" would be crushed. Similarly, Denver's juvenile court judge warned that unless the state intervened, the "cancer" of child labor would "destroy the American democratic experiment."[1]

A generation of attentive Progressives accepted Lindsey's challenge, and by 1930, every state in the union regulated the paid work of children. Most extended their lists of prohibited occupations, imposed greater restrictions on night work, and demanded that youngsters complete the fifth grade before working during school hours.[2] In 1938, the United States Congress passed the Fair Labor Standards Act (FLSA), for the next sixty years the benchmark for state and federal regulation of child labor. Its child labor provisions barred youths under the age of seventeen from "hazardous" work and banned from

---

[1] Ben Lindsey, Edwin Markham, and George Creel, *Children in Bondage* (New York, 1914), 315. This book contains separate sections, identified by author.

[2] Ellen Nathalie Mathews, *Child Labor: Report of the Subcommittee on Child Labor, White House Conference on Child Health and Protection, Section Three: Education and Training, Committee on Vocational Guidance and Labor* (New York, 1932), 29–32.

interstate trade any products of mines or factories which employed underage laborers.[3] In ensuing decades governments further limited the ages, hours, and circumstances in which children could accept paid jobs, but by the 1930s expanded state supervision of youthful work was firmly established and itself exemplified another public policy – an extension of the chronological limits of childhood. Having restricted the work of "children" earlier eras considered to be adults, governments assumed an ironic obligation – one also in place by the 1930s – the creation of subsidized jobs and work training opportunities for teenagers, especially those trapped by economic and social circumstances over which they had no control. The New Deal's Civilian Conservation Corps, Franklin Roosevelt's personal pet project, transformed millions of unemployed adolescent boys into "soil soldiers."[4]

This chapter examines the impact of these two agendas, as government took on a new duty: "inducting" youth into the work life of adulthood.[5] The effort had decidedly mixed results. The CCC was the exception that proved the rule. Twentieth-century public policy failed to prohibit unsuitable labor by children or to promote effective work training. Again, as with regulations meant to stop child abuse, the politics of emotion shaped child labor law.

The Politics of Emotion and the Realities of Child Labor: A Twentieth-Century Overview

In 1900, an estimated two and a half million children, one in every six between the ages of ten and sixteen, worked a ten-hour day, six days a

---

[3] Orme Wheelock Phelps, *The Legislative Background of the Fair Labor Standards Act: A Study of the Growth of National Sentiment in Favor of Governmental Regulation of Wages, Hours, and Child Labor* (Chicago, 1939), 9.

[4] Most government work programs, at local, state, or federal levels, were relatively short-lived or focused on "young adults" – not teenagers. That explains this chapter's choice of two programs, the Civilian Conservation Corps and the Jobs Corps, for in-depth analysis. The first existed for almost a decade, the other for forty years. Other programs not examined in this chapter include the New Deal's National Youth Administration, which provided part-time jobs for students. But most NYA recipients were over the age of twenty; a significant percentage were even older gradaute students in their thirties. Since the 1960s, a great number of programs came and went. The Manpower Development and Training Act of 1962, the Youth Conservation Corps of 1972, Title VIII and Title IV, Part a the Comprehensive Employment and Training Act of 1973, the Youth Employment Demonstrations Projects Act of 1977, and the Youth Act of 1980 did not focus on teenagers but rather defined "youth" to include young adults under age thirty, and most participants were in their twenties. The only long-term major federal projects which consistently dealt with a population with an average age of eighteen or younger were the CCC and the Job Corps. For discussions of federal government work programs, see Richard Reiman, *The New Deal and Youth: Ideas and Ideals in a Depression Decade* (Athens, GA, 1992); Paul Bullock, *Youth Training and Employment – From New Deal to New Federalism* (Los Angeles, 1985).

[5] The phrase is University of Chicago president Charles Judd's. Charles Judd, "The Induction of Young People into Adulthood," *The School Review* 58 (1940): 188.

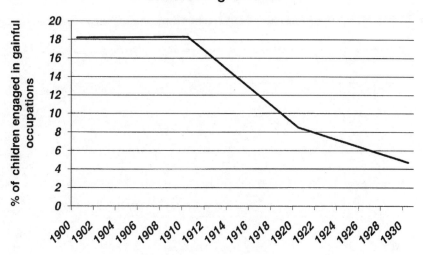

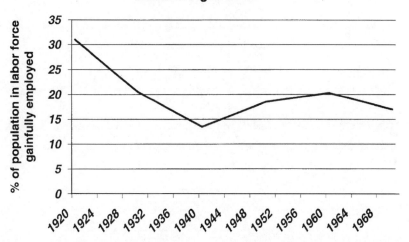

*Note: In 1940 the United States Census changed the terminology of categorizing child workers. Before 1940, the term gainfully employed was used. After 1940, the term labor force replaced gainful employment.

FIGURE 4.1   Patterns in child labor. Source: Statistics used to create graphs from: U.S. Department of Commerce, Bureau of Census, *Census of 1904, Population, Vol. 4; Census of 1920, Population, Vol. 4; Census of 1930, Population, Vol. 5; Census of 1940, Population, Vol. 3; Census of 1950, 1A-21–119, Population; Census of Population: 1960; Census of Population: 1970; Census of Population: 1980, Characteristics of the Population; Statistical Abstract of the United States, 1990; Statistical Abstract of the United States, 1999;* Bureau of Labor Statistics, http://146.142.4.24/cgi-bin/surveymost.

Note that there were problems incurred creating a composite graph to represent child labor, 1900–2000.

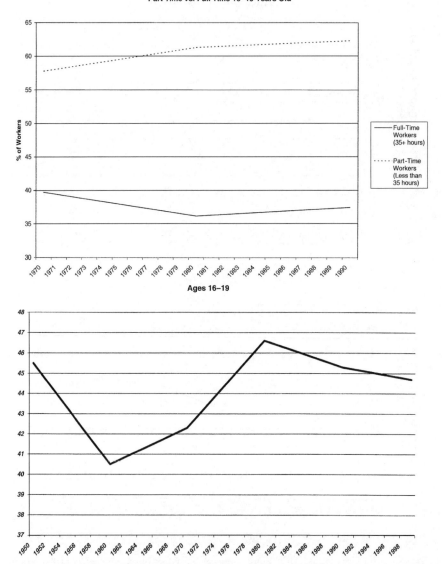

FIGURE 4.1 (*continued*) There is no way to prepare a meaningful comparative graph of all American child labor for the twentieth century. From 1990 to 1930 the Census defined "child labor" as full-time work done by ten- to fifteen-year-olds, and no child younger than age ten was ever officially counted between 1900 and 2000. From 1940 to 1970 Census statistics included both full- and part-time work by those age fourteen to seventeen, but no younger. Between 1970 and 2000, the Census counted part- and full-time workers between age sixteen and nineteen, but no younger. Before 1940, these "child" workers would have been generally considered to be adults. Moreover, seasonal agricultural work, a major source of labor for children, was also a kind of job state and federal occupational censuses routinely miscalculated throughout the century.

week.[6] By the 1990s, that kind of work week had largely disappeared, except for adult professionals.[7] "Underage employees" were not in coal mines, textile mills, lumber yards, or in most of the other kinds of dangerous workplaces that caused Progressive outrage.

Children, however, were still at work. The United States led the industrialized world in the numbers of hours its adolescents spent at paid labor. The average kid in an American high school worked twenty-five hours per week, with millions employed during school terms in excess of the federal standard of a maximum of eighteen hours per week for fifteen-year-olds and twenty-eight hours per week for those aged sixteen to eighteen. In the early twentieth century, a child most commonly worked in the fields. By the 1990s, he or she served food rather than harvested it and worked part, rather than full, time.[8]

This summary, however, incorporates a great deal of guesswork. Given its seasonality, irregularity, and frequent invisibility, twentieth-century child labor was maddeningly difficult to document. Commentators relied on anecdote or case study, not accurate statistics. Even defining child labor proved difficult. United States occupational censuses never counted children under the age of ten. Federal, state, and local definitions of "adult," "youth," and "child" were never uniform. and each changed over time. An early-twentieth-century "adult" could be, in different jurisdictions, fourteen, fifteen, or sixteen. By mid-century, the age of "adulthood," at least in terms of occupational eligibility, crept upward, but still varied. It could be "seventeen," "eighteen," "nineteen," or even older. Two adolescents employed at identical jobs in different states, or different counties, or even different cities, easily faced variances in workplace regulations. That was true in 1900 – and in 2000.

Controversies were not limited to disagreements about the ages of workers labeled children. Did children have to be paid by someone other than a parent to be included in statistics? The answer depended on the date of the occupational census.[9] Doubtless, great numbers of young workers never

---

[6] Katharine Dupre Lumpkin and Dorothy Wolff Douglas, *Child Workers in America* (New York, 1937), 10–12, 152–56.

[7] The work week was shorter, at least for those *under* eighteen. It lengthened for large numbers of adults, particularly professionals. Juliette Schor, *The Overworked American: The Unexpected Decline of Leisure* (New York, 1991), 1–63.

[8] See Jerald Bachman, "Premature Affluence: Do High School Students Earn Too Much?" *Economic Outlook USA* 10 (1983): 64–67; L. D. Steinberg and S. M. Dornbusch, "Negative Correlates of Part-Time Employment During Adolescence: Replication and Elaboration," *Developmental Psychology* 27 (1991): 304–13; Julian Barling and C. A. Loughlin, "Teenagers' Part Time Employment and Their Work-Related Attitudes and Aspirations," *Journal of Organizational Behavior* 19 (1998): 197–207.

[9] Bryna Fraser, et al., *Minor Laws of Major Importance: A Guide to Federal and Child State Labor Laws*, Office of Education Research and Improvement, U.S. Department of Education (Washington, DC, 1994), 2–21.

showed up in official records. For much of the century, census takers tallied jobs in January and April, ensuring undercounting of participation by children in agriculture. Even if children were not seasonal farm laborers, they routinely faded into statistical shadows. Prominent New York "child saver" Edward Clopper inquired skeptically in 1914, "Are we to believe there is only one bootblack in the city of Niagara Falls? If so, he must be sadly overworked."[10] Indeed, in 1914, or in any year, working children were likely to be missed.

Employers, parents, even children themselves, often had a vested interest in disguising child labor. Documents could be forged; ages could be stretched; most commonly, children could just melt away, though the need to make kids scramble for a back door was never very pressing. In 1990 Connecticut's Senator Christopher Dodd produced documents suggesting that the U.S. Labor Department's enforcement divisions spent less than 2 percent of their resources on efforts to uncover illegal child laborers. Commented Dodd, "That's not what you'd call a juggernaut of a police force."[11] It never had been.[12]

For much of the twentieth century, opponents of child labor neglected to note the economic fragility of working-class families. In 1914, Jane Haas displayed a common attitude at a convention of the National Child Labor Committee. The NCLC was one of the era's most famous reform coalitions, linking the settlement house movement, municipal reform campaigns, and factory safety groups.[13] Haas triumphantly reported to delegates from these constituencies that in her home town of Dayton, Ohio, "little, infirm shopgirls" no longer toiled at night. When asked when working people

---

[10] Edward Clopper, "The Extent of Child Labor Officially Measured," *Child Labor Bulletin* 3 (1914): 32.

[11] Christopher Dodd, "Statements of Senator Dodd," Joint Hearings before the Subcommittee on Labor and Subcommittee on Children, Family, Drugs, and Alcoholism of the Committee on Labor and Human Resources, United States Senate, One Hundred Second Congress, First Session (Washington, DC, 1991): 82 (hereafter Hearing, Child Labor Amendments, 1991).

[12] For discussions of collection of child labor statistics, see W. E. Halperin, *Children Who Work: Challenges for the Twenty-First Century* (Washington, DC, 1991); Julian Barling and E. Kevin Kelloway, Eds., *Young Workers: Varieties of Experience* (Washington, DC, 1999); General Accounting Office, *Child Labor Characteristics of Working Children: Briefing Report to Congressional Requestors* (Washington, DC, 1991).

[13] Though it is an overly romantic treatment, Walter Trattner's *Crusade for the Children: A History of the National Child Labor Committee and Child Labor Reform in America* (New York, 1970), remains the standard organizational history. In the year 2000 the NCLC survived, just four years short of its 100th birthday, but its mission had changed dramatically. Funded primarily by Burger King, it worked with businesses to advertise job opportunities for teenagers. In 2001, when Burger King was acquired by another corporation, it ceased to give NCLC $600,000 annually. By 2002, the NCLC faced bankruptcy and sold its remaining Lewis Hine negatives to a private collector. Sarah Boxer, "Organization Sells a Legacy of Hine Photos," *New York Times*, April 16, 2002.

would do their shopping she dismissively replied, "When the circus comes to town...they find time to go....If they can do this during the daytime, they can go shopping."[14]

Progressives often assumed that poor people could just find a way, whether to do shopping or to do without the work of their children. Their projections of working-class family economic needs rarely acknowledged the truth: children of unskilled laborers in the early twentieth century provided between one third to one half of an entire family's income.[15] Even when they admitted family need, reformers often demanded that youngsters cease work, without offering another solution. Ben Lindsey agreed that without child labor, "Three fourths of the families of New York cannot provide the necessaries." "But," he railed, "whatever the need of the family, cannibalistic living on the child should never be permitted."[16]

Writing during the Great Depression, the economists Katharine Lumpkin and Dorothy Douglas provided more dispassionate analysis. The family economy of the working class was a "puny dike." Working-class families had "little choice" but to put to work "all members, including children."[17] After World War II, "all members" ceased to work full time, as wives substituted outside pay checks for the work they had done within their homes.[18] Most "child" labor in the last half of the twentieth century was in fact part-time work done by older adolescents, as Utah Senator Orrin Hatch reiterated in 1991, "We are *not* talking about child labor. It is teenage labor."[19]

Late-twentieth-century opponents of child labor demanded greater state restrictions. Defenders just as vehemently denied their utility. Each side assumed that public policy had an impact on children in the workplace. It did.

---

[14] Jane Haas, Report of the Eighth Session, "Proceedings of the Tenth Annual Conference of the National Child Labor Committee, New Orleans, Louisiana, March 15–18," *Child Labor Bulletin*, 3 (1914): 191.

[15] This was a conclusion regularly repeated by early-twentieth-century economists' living standards surveys. For examples: Lee Frankel, *Report of the Special Committee on Standards of Living in Albany, New York* (New York, 1907); Robert Chapin, *Works on the Standards of Living Among Workingmen's Families* (New York, 1909).

[16] Lindsey, Markham, and Creel, *Children in Bondage*, 230.

[17] Katharine Dupre Lumpkin and Dorothy Wolff Douglas, *Child Workers in America*, 172, 180.

[18] Working-class married women, prior to the mid-twentieth century, often contributed "paid" labor: by taking in washing, doing piece work, running a boarding house, and in many other ways, *but* within their households, not at outside jobs. The Women's Bureau of the U.S. Labor Department noted this trend long before it became a subject of scholarly interest. United States Women's Bureau, "Women's Occupations Through Seven Decades," *Bulletin 218* (Washington, DC, 1951).

[19] Orrin Hatch, "Statement of Minority Views," Report of the Committee on Labor and Human Resources on Child Labor Amendments, S. 600, Report 102–380 (Washington, DC, 1992): 31 (hereafter Report, S. 600).

But important changes in the nature of the American economy, which in turn transformed paid work roles for married women, were the really meaningful engines moving child labor force participation. The disjunction between child labor law and actual child labor was a longstanding one.

Early Child Labor Law

State attempts to control the work of youngsters began in 1813, when Connecticut required employers of children in textile mills to provide classes in reading. In 1836, Massachusetts demanded that all its factory children go to school for three months annually. By the end of the nineteenth century, most states regulated child labor. Seldom enforced, these measures forbade children, usually defined as persons ages ten to fourteen, from working more than ten hours per day or sixty hours per week. None regulated agricultural labor, which occupied the vast majority of nineteenth-century Americans and their children.[20]

In the early twentieth century, Progressives agreed: additional restriction was needed. However, this top-down reform movement championed "uplift – by a large class of people who expect to go to Heaven by repenting of other people's sins." When former Colorado governor Charles Thomas made this charge in 1925, he captured an aspect of Progressivism to which child labor law made a powerful appeal.[21]

Child labor committees, as had anticruelty societies, traced the origins of a problem to a class of adults to which they did not belong. Of course, great numbers of the same reformers belonged to both groups, and both realized the gut-wrenching appeal of visual images of haggard, misused children. Lewis Hine's pictures of exhausted boys sorting coal with bleeding fingers, or of thin, young girls standing on boxes to reach spindles, famously personalized the issue. The compelling photos of the staff photographer of the National Child Labor Committee joined images of little Mary Ellen Wilson as icons of American shame.[22]

Such portraits tugged heart strings, as did the "Child Labor Sundays" routinely observed in Protestant churches. In the place of the usual sermon,

[20] For a summary of these and other laws, see Statement of the Department of Labor, Office of the Assistant Secretary, "Child Labor Amendment to the Constitution," Hearings Before a Subcommittee of the Committee on the Judiciary, United States Senate, Sixty-Seventh Congress, Fourth Session (Washington, DC, 1923): 14–17.

[21] Charles Thomas, "Debate on the Proposed Twentieth Amendment," National Child Labor Committee, Publication 326 (New York, 1925), 39 (hereafter NCLC, 326).

[22] Hine's fame has only grown, as his photographs have become staples in high school and college texts. The cottage industry of scholarly analysis of Hine is overwhelmingly positive, even sentimental. For a sample: George Dimock, "Children of the Mills: Re-reading Lewis Hine's Child Labour Photographs," *The Oxford Art Journal* 16 (1993): 37–54; F. N. Boney, "Little Laborers: Children in Georgia's Textile Mills," *Georgia Historical Quarterly* 7 (1986): 518–27. For examples of Hine's photography, see Photo 4.1.

ACCIDENTS

LAD FELL TO DEATH IN BIG COAL CHUTE

Dennis McKee Dead and Arthur Allbracher Had Leg Burned In the Lee Mines.

"Children are not equipped by experience to care for themselves in modern industry"

AND SO THEY PAY

WITH A MAIMED LIFE

Three times as many industrial accidents occur to children as to adults

EMPLOYMENT OF CHILDREN IS DUE TO

IGNORANCE
GREED   OF INDUSTRY AND PARENTS
NECESSITY

ARE ANY OF THESE REASONS WORTH A CHILD'S LIFE?

PHOTO 4.1   National Child Labor Committee, "High Cost of Child Labor, A Birdseye View of This National Problem," Pamphlet 234 (New York, 1914).

congregations performed playlets. One of the most popular, "Is It Nothing to All Ye?" featured "child workers" – "heads bent and weary...coming, coming, coming, while their mothers weep." The NCLC script suggested that these "holy innocents" wear "little white shirts belted at the waist," and, "if their mothers allow it," go barefoot.[23] Right there in church their own children embodied the Victorian ideal of unblemished childhood, and whole congregations of adults lined up to sign pledges to fight child labor.

Such tactics allowed a generation of Protestant Progressives to enjoy a trip to moral higher ground. Meanwhile, the codes themselves prompted little public opposition. Why? Paralleling their nineteenth-century counterparts, most local and state child labor laws in effect between 1900 and 1916 regulated work done by a small minority of American children.

Most controlled labor in mines, mills, and factories and barred girls from "dangerous" jobs, particularly in textiles. The ten-hour day and the sixty-hour week ceded to a new standard: the nine-hour day and fifty-four-hour week. These laws convinced many Americans that major strides had been made. However, most exempted street selling, domestic service, and agricultural labor: the jobs children actually held.

Educational minimums varied, though most labor laws demanded that a child worker be able to read a paragraph written in English. "Employment certificates" were common, although they, too, differed from region to region. Most required that a child seeking employment present proof of age. Finally, in contrast to their nineteenth-century predecessors, almost all early-twentieth-century child labor laws provided some kind of inspection system, giving school principals, health officials, labor departments, local police, or even, in three states, "any citizen" access to work sites to uncover evidence of violations.[24]

Decrying this welter of different laws, child labor reformers demanded that the federal government impose uniformity. Between 1916 and 1922, two federal laws sought to close interstate commerce to the products of "oppressive" child labor.[25] Congress passed both bills during a maelstrom of wartime activity, and the U.S. Supreme Court promptly ruled each, in turn, to be unconstitutional. Twenty years passed before a different Supreme Court accepted increased federal regulatory authority over child labor.

---

[23] This playlet went through several editions and was performed, though with less frequency, through the 1930s. Marion Wefer, "Suggested Devotional Service and Script: 'Is It Nothing to All Ye?'" National Child Labor Committee (New York, 1937), 7–13.

[24] For discussions of child labor legislation during this period, see Miriam Loughran, *The Historical Development of Child Labor Legislation in the United States* (Washington, DC, 1921); United States Children's Bureau, "Child Labor: Facts and Figures," Publication 197 (Washington, DC, 1934); Charles Gibbons and Chester Stansbury, *Administration of Child Labor Law in Ohio* (New York, 1931).

[25] In 1907, Senator Albert Beveridge of Indiana spoke for four straight days in impassioned defense of a bill that very broadly banned "the employment of children in factories and mines." Beveridge's proposal never had a chance. Grace Abbott, "Federal Regulation of Child Labor," *Social Service Review* 13 (1939): 409–10.

Federal Standards for Child Labor, 1916–1922

In 1916, Senator Robert Owen of Oklahoma and Representative Edward Keating of Colorado, both leading Democratic Progressives, introduced a bill banning from interstate commerce the products of American mines or

WHEN A FELLER NEEDS A FRIEND

By permission of Briggs, New York Tribune.

PHOTO 4.2   National Child Labor Committee, "New Standards in Child Protection," *American Child* 1 (1919): Frontispiece.

quarries that employed children under the age of sixteen and of factories with child workers under the age of fourteen. Moreover, no child between fourteen and sixteen years old could work after seven at night or before six in the morning.

During the summer of 1916, in a supercharged political atmosphere over-heated by impending Congressional elections, as well as war in Europe, Keating-Owen was one of the few measures that won bipartisan support. Republicans favored the bill, aware that prominent northern textile mill own-ers, fearing southern competition, favored uniform regulation of child labor. When southern Democrats wavered, Woodrow Wilson personally traveled to the Capitol and called in chits.[26]

The Keating-Owen Bill easily passed with little discussion. The problems faced by the 5 percent or fewer of child laborers employed by mines and mills were not uppermost in the minds of either the public or politicians. One crisis after another dominated the news in 1916: defense readiness, maintenance of neutrality, German submarine attacks, the threat of a nationwide railroad strike. Only one national organization, the NCLC, cared fervently about child labor reform, and Woodrow Wilson was more than willing to gain its support by publicly twisting a few fellow-Democrats' arms. In a time of national distraction, Republicans and Democrats both were willing to play, if briefly, the politics of emotion. The Children's Bureau, beloved by reformers, but tiny and politically weak, received authorization to administer Keating-Owen and sufficient funds to put fifteen new federal child labor inspectors on its payroll.[27]

If Congressmen were willing to stand up for an emotionally appealing issue, the members of the United States Supreme Court were not. Three days before the Keating-Owen Act went into effect, Roland Dagenhart, an employee of Fidelity Manufacturing, a cotton mill in Charlotte, N.C., and the father of two sons, Rueuben and John, who worked alongside him, brought suit against William Hammer, the United States District Attorney in the western district of North Carolina. A coalition of southern mill owners persuaded Dagenhart to front for them and challenged Keating-Owen as an

---

[26] For contemporary accounts of the political deal-making, see J. M. Leake, "Four Years of Congress," *American Political Science Review* 11 (1917): 258–83; A. J. McKelway, "Passing the Federal Child Labor Law," *Child Labor Bulletin* 5 (1916): 91–93.

[27] During the war years the Children's Bureau employed between 135 and 150 persons, including clerks and temporary employees. The inspectors authorized by Keating-Owen were to "work with" state and local counterparts, but, nonetheless, supervised child labor violations nation-wide. Even at its high point, during the late New Deal and World War II, the Children's Bureau entire staff never numbered more than 260 individuals. For discussions of the history of the Children's Bureau during the Teens through the Forties, see Kriste Lindenmeyer, "*A Right to Childhood: The U.S. Children's Bureau and Child Welfare* (Urbana, IL, 1997); United States Children's Bureau, "The Children's Bureau: Yesterday, Today, and Tomorrow" (Washington, DC, 1937); Edith Abbott, "Grace Abbott: A Sister's Memories," *The Social Service Review*, 13 (1939): 351–407.

unconstitutional Congressional exercise of power.[28] In 1918, the Supreme Court agreed.

The defense argued that Congress had already passed, and the Court had already upheld, a variety of restraints on trade in interstate commerce, including traffic in impure food and drugs, prostitutes, lottery tickets, even margarine.[29] If the Supreme Court was willing to protect the interests of the dairy industry, surely far more important were the rights of exploited children? The High Court disagreed.

Mr. Justice Day, delivering the majority opinion, declared that Congress did have regulatory power to protect "the channels of commerce" from "the demoralization of lotteries, the debasement of obscene literature, the contagion of diseased cattle, or the systematic...debauchery of women." However, Congress could not use the Commerce Clause to control "unfair trade." Therefore, it had no right to ban child-made goods from interstate commerce.[30] No mention was made of margarine.

Outraged supporters of Keating-Owen immediately reintroduced the bill, as Title XII of the Revenue Act of 1918. Title XII levied a 10 percent tax on the annual net profits of any industry that employed children in violation of the provisions outlined in the original 1916 law. Supporters sought another way to skin the cat, arguing that if Congress could not control onerous child labor through its power to regulate interstate trade, then it could tax it out of existence. In 1918, a federal tax on certain products produced by child labor was a minor footnote to far more momentous debates about greatly increased federal control of a wartime economy. Title XII passed with little comment.

Once again, proponents of the measure, widely known as the Child Labor Tax Act, argued legal precedent. The Supreme Court accepted a heavy federal tax on white phosphorus to deter manufacturers from using the substance in matches. It already sanctioned taxes on cotton futures contracts, foreign-built yachts, and dealers in opium.[31] Opponents quickly sued, and once again, in 1922, the Supreme Court declared a federal attempt to regulate child labor in mines and industry unconstitutional.

In overturning Title XII in 1922, the High Court conceded that "This is not the first time...that taxes have been imposed for other than fiscal purposes." However, Title XII was a "privilege" tax. If manufacturers were willing to pay a levy on their goods, they were then free to employ

---

[28] Arden Lea, "Cotton Textiles and the Federal Child Labor Act of 1916," *Labor History* 16 (1975): 485–94.

[29] Donna Wood, *Strategic Uses of Public Policy: Business and Government in the Progressive Era* (New York, 1986), 154–64.

[30] *William Hammer, United States Attorney for the Western District of North Carolina v. Dagenhart Et Al.*, No. 7041 Supreme Court of the United States, 247 U.S. 251; 38 S. CT 529; 1918.

[31] Thomas Parkinson, "Constitutionality of a Federal Child Labor Law," National Child Labor Committee, Pamphlet 250 (New York, 1916), 10–11.

underaged children, even for night work. That, the Court decreed, was unconstitutional.[32]

Supporters of both the Keating-Owen Act and Title XII drew wrenching portraits of young child workers "broken in spirit and old before their time."[33] These youngsters did exist. Nonetheless, when child labor reformers orated against the "shame of the two million," they rarely mentioned to their audiences that eight of every ten American children worked in fields, not factories. Neither Keating-Owen, Title XII, nor any state measures controlled child labor in agriculture. Furious child savers reacted to two successive Court defeats with a drive to give the U.S. Congress explicit power to regulate child labor.

The Child Labor Amendment

Passed by Congress and sent to the states in 1924, the Child Labor Amendment featured simple wording and complex possibilities. It read: "That Congress shall have the power to limit, regulate, and prohibit the labor of persons under eighteen years of age."[34] Between 1924 and 1933, only nine states ratified, while most voted the amendment down or threw procedural hurdles in the way of plans for special constitutional conventions. However, unusually, Congress attached no time limits to the Child Labor Amendment. In the 1930s, during a time of unsubstantiated, but general, public belief that children "stole" adult jobs, interest in the amendment revived. By January of 1938, twenty-eight states ratified the proposal, but supporters never gained the required three-quarters' approval.[35] Two phenomena, U.S. participation in World War I and victory for woman suffrage, helped spin the U.S. Congress to pass an amendment that exceeded popularly accepted parameters for state action.

The Great War sparked a revolutionary increase in federal power – to tax, to control vital resources, to stipulate profit margins, and to draft millions

---

[32] *J. W. Bailey, Collector of Internal Revenue for the District of North Carolina v. Drexel Furniture Company*, 657 Supreme Court of the United States 259 U.S. 20; 42 S. CT 449; 1922.

[33] Emily Van Vorst, *The Cry of the Children: A Study of Child Labor* (New York, 1908), 18.

[34] Hearings on the Proposed Child Labor Amendment before the Committee on the Judiciary, House of Representatives, Sixty-Eighth Congress, First Session (Washington, DC, 1924): 5 (hereafter Hearing, Amendment, 1924).

[35] Historian David Kyvig notes that the idea that constitutional amendments necessarily should be ratified within a relatively limited time span was an innovation of the twentieth century. David Kyvig, *Explicit and Authentic Acts: Amending the U.S. Constitution, 1776–1995* (Lawrence, KS, 1996): 468. Scholarly commentary on the defeat of the Child Labor Amendment has focused on the activities of organized opponents – such as the Catholic Church, the American Farm Bureau, or the American Bar Association. Almost no attention has been paid to the fact that the amendment really did pose challenges to parental power. See Richard Sherman, "The Rejection of the Child Labor Amendment," *Mid-America* 45 (1963): 3–17; Thomas Greene, "The Catholic Committee for the Ratification of the Child Labor Amendment, 1935–1937: Origin and Limits," *The Catholic Historical Review* 74 (1988): 248–69.

of citizens as soldiers.[36] Women did not go abroad to fight but were crucial to Home Front mobilization. Gratitude for female contributions to the war effort played a role in the passage of the Nineteenth Amendment, which finally granted women the vote in 1920. Congressmen were persuaded that this group of newly enfranchised citizens wanted uniform protections for child laborers, especially when leaders of the women's divisions of both the Democratic and Republican Parties warned them to "beware of the women's vote if the child labor amendment is not passed."[37]

By the end of the decade, the reality of woman suffrage began to sink in; women voted with, not in opposition to, their male relatives. Nonetheless, for a few years at least, the specter of millions of women demanding a socially activist federal agenda proved powerful, in Washington, if not throughout the nation.

In 1924, within months of the Child Labor Amendment's swift success in Congress, Massachusetts legislators took a step no other state copied, but, that, nonetheless, had important repercussions. They declared that their decision on the proposed Twentieth Amendment would be governed by the wishes of the electorate. Massachusetts' voters, by more than three to one, soundly defeated it.[38] Startled by this decisive setback, supporters of the amendment waffled.

People will try to tell you, Owen Lovejoy said, that this amendment will mean, "No girl under eighteen would be able to wash dishes and no boy could crank up the family Ford." The president of the National Child Labor Committee countered, "Nothing could be further from the truth."[39] The Twentieth Amendment, if ratified, would simply protect American children. In fact, their own words indicated that advocates of the Child Labor Amendment wanted a more intrusive role for government than the public supported. Owen Lovejoy, in consultation with allies in Congress and among the child-saving movement, crafted the language of the proposed Twentieth Amendment. The use of the word "labor" instead of "employment" was no accident. It targeted the family wage system. As Lovejoy argued, "Children who work in New York City tenements are not 'employed.' They only 'help' mother."[40]

Moreover, the amendment's designation of the age of eighteen reflected a reform agenda far ahead of even official understandings of child labor. Federal occupational censuses listed workers aged sixteen or older as adults.

---

[36] For discussions on the war's impact on federal Congressional and Executive authority, see David Kennedy, *Over Here: The First World War and American Society* (New York, 1980); Ronald Schaffer, *America in the Great War: The Rise of the War Welfare State* (New York, 1991).

[37] "Testimony of Harriet Upton, Vice President, National Executive Committee, Republican Party," Hearing, Amendment, 1924, 69.

[38] NCLC, 326, 35.

[39] *Ibid.*, 27.

[40] *Ibid.*, 33.

PHOTO 4.3   Grace Abbott, "A Time to Ratify," *Collier's* 99 (1937): 86. Reproduction of pro–child labor amendment poster.

Labor codes in many states and localities counted only those under fifteen as child laborers. To most Americans in the 1920s, the idea that the federal government could potentially "limit," "regulate," or even "prohibit" the work of all sixteen- and seventeen-year-olds was an incredible assertion of government power. It was.

A book published two years before Congressional passage of the Twentieth Amendment by New York attorney and NCLC stalwart, Raymond Fuller, revealed the NCLC's real agenda. "Child labor legislation," he said, "properly has no place of ending." He continued, "As childhood merges little by little into manhood, so child labor legislation should be joined without break to labor legislation for adults."[41]

Child labor advocates tried to convince Americans that the Twentieth Amendment would simply authorize the U.S. Congress to write a uniform child labor code. But opponents were right; the proposal was the creation of reformers who wanted a more powerful federal government. Fuller and fellow members of the NCLC Executive Board supported the Child Labor Amendment. They also wanted strengthened workers' compensation, a national system of unemployment insurance, federal occupational health and safety laws, uniform provision of cash relief to widows with children, and government-sponsored health insurance. In important ways, the Child Labor Amendment was the most radical proposal of all.[42]

Supporters of the amendment tried to dismiss as totally foolish charges that it interfered with the rights of parents. Nonetheless, for decades, child savers had shown contempt for parents who allowed their children to work. As Owen Lovejoy said in his presidential speech to the Fifth Annual Meeting of the National Child Labor Committee, "If the parent . . . is unable to provide the protection needed, then the state is bound to enter and become the parent of that child."[43]

The vague language of the Child Labor Amendment convinced many Americans that a government official just well might show up to supervise their children's chores. Newspapers throughout the country gleefully encouraged the fear. Publishers worried the proposal threatened traditional child labor law exemptions for newsboys and orchestrated biting, witty attacks. Millions of Americans picked up their morning papers and laughed at cartoons in which bored teenagers staring at wall posters were dismayed to see that, while the "Twentieth Amendment" banned child labor, the "Twenty-First Amendment" demanded that "all jellybeans and flappers do some work."[44]

---

[41] Fuller, *Child Labor and the Constitution*, 195.

[42] For a summary of this reform agenda, see Florence Kelley, "The Child Breadwinner and the Dependent Parent," *Child Labor Bulletin* 1 (1912): 1–15. Kelley was a member of the NCLC Board.

[43] Owen Lovejoy, "Some Unsettled Questions about Child Labor," Proceedings of the Fifth Annual Conference of the National Child Labor Committee, Chicago, Illinois, January 21–23, 1909 (New York, 1909): 58.

[44] In contrast to the already cited outpouring of work on Lewis Hine, scholars have virtually ignored the equally compelling (and much funnier) visual images opponents of stricter child labor laws utilized. For examples of widely reprinted anti–Child Labor Amendment cartoons, see Photos 4.4 and 4.5.

UNDER THE TWENTIETH AMENDMENT

—Ireland in the Columbus *Dispatch.*

PHOTOS 4.4 AND 4.5 "Why the Child Labor Amendment Failed," *Literary Digest* 85 (1925), 11. These two images are copies of anti–Child Labor Amendment newspaper cartoons.

After 1933, legislatures in nineteen hard-hit Midwest and East Coast states joined those that had already passed the Child Labor Amendment, but with the exception of the disastrous statewide referendum held in Massachusetts in 1924, it was never put to popular vote, nor was there ever any genuine grassroots ground swell supporting ratification. When asked by pollsters, Americans condemned all "job stealers" – though they tended to view the labor of married women as a greater threat.[45]

Ordinary citizens paid little attention to the legislative jousting over the Child Labor Amendment or to the debates in Congress about the merits of the child labor provisions of the Fair Labor Standards Act. However, the latter became the template for child labor law for half a century, while the

---

[45] The work of women and children did not significantly compete with that done by adult males. See Lois Scharf's *To Work and To Wed: Female Employment, Feminism, and the Great Depression* (Westport, CT, 1980).

HOW ABOUT THE TWENTY-FIRST AMENDMENT?

—Knott in the Dallas *News.*

PHOTOS 4.4 AND 4.5 *(continued)*

former quietly died. Unlike the proposed Child Labor Amendment, the FLSA was not "drastic."[46]

"Fair Breaks" for Children? The New Deal and Youth Work Initiatives

Nonetheless, fear of competition from child workers dominated Congressional debate about provisions restricting child labor in the 1938 Fair Labor Standards Act. The FLSA reproduced almost verbatim the Keating-Owen Act of 1916. Provisions of the FSLA specifically exempted child actors as well as children working in agriculture when not legally required to attend school. Moreover, the act made no mention of children working as messengers, street

[46] Representative George Graham was right that the Child Labor Amendment was potentially a "drastic" step that could greatly restrict state-level jurisdiction. "Minority Report on the Child Labor Amendment," Committee on the Judiciary, United States Congress, House of Representatives, Sixty-Eighth Congress, Second Session, No. 395 (Washington, DC 1924): 8 (hereafter Report 395).

sellers, or domestic servants, or for industries that did not ship goods out of state.[47] Neither had Keating-Owen. In 1918, the Supreme Court declared the latter bill unconstitutional. In 1941, it approved its doppelganger and openly repudiated *Hammer v. Dagenhart*. What had happened? In three words: the New Deal.

By 1941, Franklin Roosevelt succeeded in appointing several High Court judges favorable to increased federal regulatory authority. The FSLA was the model for child labor law for the rest of the century. Just as consequential, however, was another New Deal initiative – the Civilian Conservation Corps, which dwarfed in scale all subsequent efforts and established a new public policy agenda. Government might well prohibit unsuitable paid work done by children, but it should promote work training and, if necessary, provide subsidized jobs for certain categories of disadvantaged teenagers.

Both objectives required unprecedented levels of state oversight of the employment of the young. The publicity given the Child Labor Amendment campaign had an unexpected consequence. Even though its supporters eventually abandoned the effort, their proposed Twentieth Amendment dramatically extended definitions of child work to include the labor of all under the age of eighteen. And that concept, if not the Child Labor Amendment itself, gradually began to take root, especially as the Civilian Conservation Corps, one of the New Deal's most popular programs, repeatedly emphasized the ways it was helping "boys." Hundreds of thousands of these "boys" *were* under the age of eighteen, but most were over the age of sixteen – until the 1930s, the chronological threshold for adulthood most American labor laws accepted.

The Soil Soldiers

Between 1930 and 1933, in warm, well-lit legislative chambers, politicians debated whether the nation should further restrict the work of its adolescents through constitutional amendment. For teenagers who were out of school, out of work, and in many cases, out of a home, the issue was not a constitutional abstraction. Probably at least three hundred thousand kids, mostly boys, were jobless tramps: jumping freight cars, cadging food, sheltering in woods. Vastly more stayed put, but as frustrated, hungry, unemployed sons.

Within days of his inaugural, on March 21, 1933, Roosevelt asked Congress to approve an emergency work program to conserve both the nation's natural environment and its youth. A "civilian construction corps" could "take a vast army of unemployed . . . out into healthful surroundings" to replant the country's forests, improve its soil, and refurbish its parks.[48]

---

[47] Phelps, *The Legislative Background of the Fair Labor Standards Act*, 9.
[48] Franklin Roosevelt, *The Public Papers and Addresses of Franklin Roosevelt, Volume Two, The Year of Crisis: 1933* (New York, 1938), 80.

Unable to finish high school

Their allotment checks help support dependents

They stayed in the CCC for 2 years

They were sent to camps far from home

PHOTO 4.6 Federal Security Agency, Civilian Conservation Corps, "The CCC at Work: A Story of 2,500,000 Young Men" (Washington, DC, 1941), reproduction of a CCC recruiting poster.

Roosevelt shared the family passion for conservation. As a student at Harvard, he enthusiastically supported his professor William James's idea that, as an alternative to army service, the nation encourage boys to work as "soil soldiers." So, for Roosevelt at least, the CCC was an old idea. For many in the rest of the nation, however, implementation was astonishingly rapid. On March 30, Congress approved the President's plan. Within three weeks the CCC was operational.

Roosevelt's ambitious scheme demanded interdepartmental cooperation on a huge scale, since the Departments of Interior, Agriculture, Labor, and War ran the new CCC jointly. Labor, in concert with state and local relief officials, identified eligible candidates. Interior and Agriculture, working with their counterparts at state levels, planned projects, which the Army supervised. A relatively small, separate administrative staff headed by a presidential appointee coordinated all activities.

Selection of recruits began on April 7. Camp Roosevelt, located on national forest land in northern Virginia, officially opened on April 17. On April 16, two hundred teenagers made the trip down from Washington, DC, in World War I–vintage open-bed Army trucks. In pouring rain, they set up tents in the dark. Promptly at six the next morning, wet to the skin, they began chopping trees. The CCC had begun, right on time.

Between April 17 and the July 1 deadline imposed by Roosevelt himself, the CCC achieved its initial objectives. Over 275,000 young men arrived at some 1,300 camp sites throughout the country. The Regular Army called back to service almost its entire force of reserve officers to supervise this massive mobilization. It also unearthed surplus equipment – much of it left over from the Great War. For the first six months, hundreds of thousands of recruits lived in canvas tents moldy from years of storage while they built wooden barracks and began work.

Surprised by the speed with which the president acted, organized labor offered only brief resistance to a CCC in which enrollees earned only a dollar a day. Indeed, unions knew that young workers posed little real threat in the depths of the Depression, and recruits all came from families on relief. Moreover, Labor Department officials took pains to reassure unions that CCC work would not compete with private industry. Instead of "pay" recruits received a "cash allowance" of $30 – $25 of which they sent home to their families. When Roosevelt appointed prominent labor leader Robert Fechner, Vice President of the International Order of Machinists, to head the CCC, organized labor's doubts vanished.

Fechner was an inspired choice. Like most of the millions of boys who would become his charges, he had been born poor and never finished high school. Blunt, and "ugly as a potato bug," he identified with a generation growing to adulthood during hard times.[49] Crucially, War, Labor, Agriculture, and Interior all regarded him, correctly, as an honest broker. For the

---

[49] The description comes from Leslie Lacy's *The Soil Soldiers* – a lively collection of letters, oral interviews, and stories about the CCC in which many former Cs praised Fechner's leadership. *The Soil Soldiers: The Civilian Conservation Corps in the Great Depression* (Radnor, PA, 1976), 16–17. The CCC called its recruits "enrollees." Most called themselves Cs.

next nine years the CCC remained one of the New Deal's best-loved ideas. Only a few socialists grumbled that its existence was one more sign of the steady militarization of American society.[50]

At its height in 1935 the CCC operated 2,652 camps – where slightly over five hundred thousand recruits worked on a great variety of conservation projects. By the time the program ended in 1942 almost three million Americans had spent time in the CCC. Despite age limits which varied through the course of the history of the Corps, the average CCC boy was always a teenager.[51] He had just turned eighteen, came from a poor

---

[50] The CCC has received relatively less scholarly attention than have many other New Deal administrative agencies. Few book-length national studies exist, though there is an interesting, growing literature of specialized state-by-state histories, a good example of which is: Richard Melzer's *Coming of Age in the Great Depression: The Civilian Conservation Corps Experience in New Mexico, 1933–1942* (Las Cruces, 2000). The standard work remains John Salmond, *The Civilian Conservation Corps 1933–1942: A New Deal Case Study* (Chapel Hill, 1967). Good books on New Deal labor policy which include discussion of the CCC include Stanley Vittoz, *New Deal Labor Policy and the American Industrial Economy* (Chapel Hill, 1987); Steve Fraser and Gary Gerstle, Eds., *The Rise and Fall of the New Deal Order* (Princeton, 1989). Much book-length work on the CCC remains relatively inaccessible in the form of unpublished dissertations. Among those worth seeking out are: Michael Sherraden, "The Civilian Conservation Corps: Effectiveness of the Camps" (PhD Dissertation, University of Michigan, 1979); John Saalberg, "Roosevelt, Fechner, and the CCC: A Study in Executive Leadership," (PhD Dissertation, Cornell University, 1962). The majority of short article-length works on the CCC appear in state historical society journals and present laudatory, narrative accounts of CCC work in particular states. Typical are: Kenneth Hendrickson,"The Civilian Conservation Corps in South Dakota," *South Dakota History* 11 (1980): 1–20; Harold Carew, "A Fair Deal Wins – A Foul Deal Loses," *California History* 62 (1983): 172–4; Billy Hinson, "The Civilian Conservation Corps in Mobile County, Alabama," *Alabama Review* 45 (1992): 243–56; David Draves, "The Civilian Conservation Corps in New Hampshire," *Historical New Hampshire* 43 (1988): 89–119. In contrast to scholarship, memoirs by former Cs and their supervisors are legion. Among the best are: Charles Humberger, "The Civilian Conservation Corps in Nebraska: Memoirs of Company 762," *Nebraska History* 75 (1994): 292–300; Frederick Johnson, "The Civilian Conservation Corps: A New Deal for Youth," *Minnesota History* 48 (1983):295–302; David Rouse, "Pages from My Past: The Civilian Conservation Corps," *Wisconsin Magazine of History* 71 (1988): 205–16; Donald Jackson, "They Were Hungry, Poor, and They Built to Last," *Smithsonian* 25 (1994): 66–70, 72, 74, 76, 78; Frank Knox, "The CCC: Shaper of Destinies," *Pacific Northwesterner* 36 (1992): 17–26; Robert Ermentrout, *Forgotten Men: The Civilian Conservation Corps* (Smithtown, NY, 1982); Albert Jernberg, *My Brush Monkeys – A Narrative of the CCC* (New York, 1941); Ray Hoyt, *We Can Take It: A Short Story of the CCC* (NY, 1935); Glenn Howell, *CCC Boys Remember* (Medford, OR, 1976); Leslie Lacy, *The Soil Soldiers – The Civilian Conservation Corps in the Great Depression* (Radnor, PA, 1976); Chester Nolte, *Civilian Conservation Corps: The Way We Remember* (Paducah, KY, 1990).

[51] In 1933, the CCC accepted male recruits between the ages of eighteen and twenty-five – provided they could do manual labor and were unmarried. After 1935, the CCC extended its age limits; males age seventeen to twenty-eight could apply. At all times, however, Cs were overwhelmingly teenagers. After 1939, when the American economy began to improve, offering more jobs for men in their twenties, the average age of a recruit actually dropped – to seventeen. By then, however, the program was winding down, and enrollments were far

family, and had four brothers and sisters. He left school after the eighth grade, read at a sixth-grade level, and had failed to find a full-time job. His health was fairly good, although he was very significantly underweight. He was slightly more likely to be a rural boy, although 40 percent of his fellows came from the country's big cities. Overwhelmingly, he was a native-born white. Notably, however, blacks comprised about 10 percent of Corps members, roughly equivalent to their proportions within the national population. Most seriously underrepresented were children of newly arrived immigrants.[52]

Officially, no boy under the age of seventeen qualified, but anecdotal evidence abounds in memoirs of kids much younger sneaking in. Underage Cs remembered borrowing a brother's birth certificate or inking a different date in the family Bible. A number of camp commanders told tales of kids "obviously under enrollment age" who woke them up in the middle of the night sobbing with homesickness.[53] Given the incomplete nature of birth registration in America in the 1930s, such accounts ring true.

---

below the 1935 peak. About 10 percent of the slots in the program were reserved – allotted to World War I veterans of any age, provided they were on relief rolls, and Native Americans. There were separate camps for the former group, and no camps for the latter. Most Army commanders who wrote memoirs of their experiences in the CCC thought the small number of veterans' camps were far less successful. Robert Ermentrout, who commanded camps in several states, perceptively noted that the veteran issue was a "hot potato." Camp commanders were quietly made to know that if veterans ignored fire drills, or shirked work in bad weather, or, against CCC rules, brought alcohol into camp, they were to be humored as out-of-work adults, not the typical "boys" for which the program was designed. And isolated camps in rural areas kept these veterans from "any concerted ideas of another march to Washington or some equally futile nuisance action." See *Forgotten Men*, 15–19. Tribal CCCs did reclamation work as well, but on their own reservations. Official accounts by CCC officials agreed with Ermentrout that avoidance of "another Bonus Army" was a consideration when allowing veterans special consideration. See J. J. McEntee, Director, Civilian Conservation Corps, *Federal Security Agency: Final Report of the Director of the Civilian Conservation Corps,* April 1933–June 1942, Typescript, Report M-2125, 50–55 (hereafter Final Report, McEntee). Records of the Civilian Conservation Corps, Record Group 115, National Archives (hereafter CCC, NA).

[52] The American Youth Commission, a nonpartisan private group established in 1935 to investigate the problems of American young people and chaired by General Electric's Owen Young, did many of the best surveys of CCC youth. See American Youth Commission, "Report on the CCC, August 1940." Records of the General Education Board, Series 1, Sub-series 3, Box 557, Folder 5956 (hereafter GEB), RAC. Douglas Abrams has argued that Fechner, a Southerner, demanded that all CCC camps be segregated and that whites supervise all black camps "Irony of Reform: North Carolina Blacks and the New Deal," *North Carolina Historical Review* 66 (1989): 167. Most camps, and all in the South, were segregated, but there were 71 integrated camps in northern states, worth noting, given the pervasive segregation within American society in the 1930s. It happened rarely, but in at least one instance, reported by Albert Jernberg, a U.S. Army Captain who ran two integrated camps, a black enrollee became a leader of a white boys' crew. See Alberg Jernberg, *My Brush Monkeys*, 104–6.

[53] For a typical example, see Albert Jernberg, *My Brush Monkeys*, 198–9.

Indeed, even official CCC reports acknowledged that the age and physical fitness requirements were not rigidly followed. J. J. McEntee, another machinist who followed his close friend to Washington and then succeeded him as head of the CCC after Robert Fechner's unexpected death in 1939, admitted that "Face to face with acute distress, many an Army doctor examining...an ill fed specimen...who did not meet requirements...passed him anyhow. The doctors simply said, in effect, 'That poor kid is starving; he needs food.'"[54]

Between 1933 and 1942, by the hundreds of thousands, such hungry boys boarded trains, trucks, or buses bound for Army-run orientation centers, where they stripped for physical examinations, sat to have abscessed teeth pulled, and stood in lines for clothing – for most: denim work pants, shirts, jackets, and a single set of Army-issue surplus World War I woolens for a dress uniform. Most recruits hated the old-fashioned puttee-style pants, musty after fifteen years in moth balls. A thriving after-hours trade enriched Cs who knew how to alter clothing, although the Corps looked askance at the common practice of cutting bed blankets into strips to widen the legs.[55] Thus equipped, new recruits left in groups for their work camps.[56]

After the program's first six months, when the majority of enrollees lived in soggy tent colonies, CCC camps assumed a uniform appearance – regardless of the kind of work the recruits did. Each housed two hundred boys, divided into ten-person squads. Ten wooden barracks slept twenty apiece and centered the camp. In all but the most remote locations, camps had running water and electricity, shower buildings, latrines, and mess halls. All provided separate quarters to the two camp officers – usually a captain or a first lieutenant, assisted by a second lieutenant. The ten to twelve LEMs, or "Local Experienced Men," who trained CCC boys for their tasks, usually were married and lived in the nearest town.

Every year tens of thousands of Cs fought forest fires or worked in mobile units established to aid victims of natural disasters, such as the great floods that inundated the Ohio River valley in 1936. For these recruits, the workday had no set timetable. Everyone else followed a strict routine. Up at six in the morning, Cs ate breakfast, reported to the tool shed, then departed camp in groups to work an eight-hour day. Enrollees received three hot meals, unless their work took them some distance from camp, in which case mess cooks

---

[54] Final Report, McEntee, 17.

[55] *Ibid.*, 27–28.

[56] Army surplus was the rule for items used by the CCC until at least 1938, when, for the first time, most recruits could be outfitted in new CCC forest green uniforms. The surplus extended well beyond moth-balled clothing. Robert Ermentrout reported that the Army "issued with relief" its remaining stocks of canned salmon to his camp, all dated 1917. He looked the other way when the cooks threw the stuff out. *Forgotten Men*, 23.

provided sack lunches.[57] From 6 to 9 P. M., an enrollee's time was his own. After 1936, most camps offered evening courses in English grammar, but attendance was voluntary.[58] Promptly at ten every night, all lights went out.

In 1939 CCC officials argued that the Corps should be made permanent. "At least twenty years" of land and water reclamation projects remained to be done.[59] Instead, the vast majority of the Cs entered the military in 1942. Nonetheless, the CCC's history was important – an overwhelmingly successful effort that provided clear lessons later public work programs for similarly disadvantaged youth rarely heeded.

The Lessons of the CCC:
One: Have Clear Goals

The Civilian Conservation Corps had three clear goals: environmental conservation, unemployment relief, and, after 1940, military preparedness. It met them all. As a terrible drought compounded misery, and choking dust storms emptied the Great Plains, scientists at the Department of Agriculture warned that a third of the country's tillable top soil had blown or washed away.[60] The CCC left the country a vastly improved natural resources balance sheet. Work planned by the Department of Agriculture emphasized reforestation, improvement of national and state park lands, soil conservation, drainage, and insect control. Trees planted by Cs reclaimed over two and one half million acres of bare, completely unproductive land. Tens of thousands of miles of roads and graded trails made the national and state forests and parks accessible, as did thousands of bridges. Campgrounds, cabins, showers, picnic shelters, swimming pools, and scenic overlooks provided inexpensive vacation destinations for millions of Americans for the rest of the century. Two hundred wildlife refuges helped prevent the extinction of the buffalo, big horn sheep, and over forty species of migrating birds. Levees, windbreaks, dams, contour plowing, and swamp drainage returned millions of acres of soil to fertility. The Department of Agriculture controlled about

[57] Many memoirs emphasize the routine – maintained in all sorts of weather. See, for instance, Johnson, "Civilian Conservation Corps," 295–99.

[58] This policy, however, was often dependent on the teaching skills and enthusiasm of those assigned the chore. Alfred Oliver and Harold Dudley, *This New America: The Spirit of the Civilian Conservation Corps* (New York, 1937), 6–7.

[59] For discussion of this effort, see Calvin Gower, "A Continuing Public Youth Work Program: The Drive for a Permanent Civilian Conservation Corps," *Environmental Review* 5 (1981): 39–51. The Corps did not officially take the name "Civilian Conservation Corps" until 1937, even though everyone called it that from the beginning. Rather, Congress biannually authorized funding for "Emergency Conservation Work."

[60] For discussion of the environmental problems facing the country during the 1930s, see Roderick Nash, Ed., *The American Environment: Readings in the History of Conservation* (Reading, PA, 1968).

80 percent of CCC projects – Interior the rest. Cs who worked under the direction of Interior repaired historic buildings, mapped archeological sites, constructed fish hatcheries, and improved millions of acres of overused range land.[61]

Almost three million unemployed boys led immensely productive lives in the CCC. Without it, they faced nothing but hunger and idleness. The fact that the government paid for their room and board relieved millions of families of the burden of their care. Indeed, the Cs turned the tables and sent over $700 million home, stretching unemployment relief by helping to support an average of four family members apiece.[62]

Finally, quietly in 1937, and openly after 1940, the CCC prepared for combat. As war loomed in Europe, the Army, initially a reluctant participant in the experiment, realized the value of the camps as training grounds for its officer corps. It rotated as many reserve officers as possible through a twelve-to-eighteen month cycle as a camp commander. By the time of the Japanese attack on Pearl Harbor, over sixty thousand captains and first lieutenants had spent at least a year learning firsthand how to lead young men. After 1940, promising enrollees were excused from half a day's regular work to receive training in fields the Army deemed critical to war readiness. Thousands learned how to be radio operators, tank drivers, or signalmen. With the declaration of war, the vast majority of soil soldiers, most of whom had put on weight and muscle and who, by definition, were of draft age and unmarried, became real soldiers. They began their service wearing World War I uniforms. Millions ended it as World War II GIs.

Fittingly, the two machinists who headed the CCC insisted that the Corps only do jobs that genuinely needed doing with proper tools. In December 1941, the CCC owned the largest fleet of motorized equipment in the world. With the declaration of war, the military immediately inherited over forty thousand well-maintained pieces of heavy machinery: cargo trucks, pickups, dump trucks, tractors, snow plows. Indeed, CCC officials privately groused at talk of the miraculous speed with which the nation mobilized. As far as they were concerned, they had been preparing for years.[63]

Personnel directors told CCC officials that good work habits, self-reliance, basic literacy, and good personal appearance mattered more than specific

[61] Agriculture's National Forest Service used CCC labor in 148 national forests covering 99 million acres of land. It also supervised reforestation projects on over eight million acres of state-owned land; the CCC built 3,600 bridges, 711 fire lookout towers, and more than 40,000 miles of roads and trails. It planted almost three billion tree seedlings and stocked more than 2,000 CCC-made lakes and ponds with 150 million fish. The National Monuments and Historic Buildings' Surveys were also CCC accomplishments. See *Final Report*, McEntee, 43–68.

[62] *Ibid.*, 34–35.

[63] *Ibid*, 76–80.

technical knowledge.[64] That, too, fit into the CCC's clear goals. Recruits with meager writing ability received sheets of paper and orders to send letters home. Illiterates could use an X for their names, witnessed by a company commander, only for a few months. After that, most camps demanded that each C personally sign a payroll book. From there, many enrollees progressed to captions under comics or simple stories in dime novels, available free at camp libraries; if they made it through a thriller or a western, most were hooked.

Tens of thousands of Cs came from homes without electricity or running water. The Corps demanded that they wash regularly, keep their hair cut short, and, if they could manage to grow a beard, shave. It also emphasized practice in social interaction. Most camp commanders festooned the walls of mess and recreation rooms with homilies: "Are You Good Company?" "Have You Bettered Yourself Today by Improving Your English?" "Did You Pay Your Way Today?"[65]

In 1942, J. J. McEntee predicted that CCC enrollees had learned work attitudes that would later make them "star employees in many lines of endeavor."[66] It seems he was right. Economists who studied the lifetime job histories for CCC recruits discovered remarkable success. Robert Severson, for example, provided the Social Security Administration with a random sample of one hundred names from CCC rolls, and the agency agreed to disclose earnings data without giving identifying information on any one individual. Twenty years after their initial enrollments, these CCC veterans occupied notably higher-income groups than did members of the general population. That in itself was incredible, as the typical C was badly educated and very poor. The CCC provided unemployment relief and preserved natural resources on a massive scale. It also might have achieved social and economic compound-interest: greater lifetime earnings for a huge group of out-of-luck American teenagers.[67] Clear goals helped make that possible, as did the other important lesson taught by CCC success.[68]

---

[64] *Ibid.*, 80–81.

[65] "Suggestions for Individual Development and Guidance in CCC Camps," Pamphlet Series III: Personality Guidance Scripts, Contributions to Education, Office of Education, Second Corps Area, Governors Island, New York, February 1936, Pamphlet Files, CCC, NA.

[66] Final Report, McEntee, 61.

[67] Robert Severson, "The Civilian Conservation Corps: A Workfare Solution," *Research in Economic History* 1982 (Supplement 2): 121–26. Of course the Cs were mature men at an advantageous time – the post–World War II boom years, but then, so were all the other American men in their age cohort.

[68] A failed attempt to include girls illustrates the perils of vague goals. Made possible by Eleanor Roosevelt's personal intervention, Camp Tera in New York State's Bear Mountain State Park was for adolescent girls. Mrs. Roosevelt had a fine idea: to have CCC girls work in greenhouses preparing saplings. That would have linked Camp Tera with a CCC mission, while deferring to an American public not ready to send its daughters into the woods. However, Camp Tera failed. About eighty girls spent an aimless summer doing embroidery;

The Lessons of the CCC:
Two: Maintain Discipline

The CCC established a national network of camps each housing no more than two hundred boys. Even before their arrival at a work site, Cs viewed themselves as members of teams. They left orientation centers in groups, ate in groups, worked in groups. Peer pressure combined with Army-style discipline to produce order and promote hard work.

Critics worried that the camp experiment would produce an American "Hitler Youth Corps."[69] It did not. Cs came from impoverished, often broken, homes, filled with quarrelling, exhausted adults, hunger, and despair. Most had experienced years of imposed idleness before their enlistments. The discipline imposed by the Corps promoted the good work habits most had never been asked to develop.

CCC camps contained no guardhouses. If a homesick youth violated his oath to remain in the Corps for at least six months, no military police fanned the countryside searching for him. Instead, the C received a "dishonorable" discharge.[70] A handful of adults who could not imprison succeeded by encouraging a peer culture that viewed leaving without permission as "yellow-bellied" and that shunned enrollees who did not carry their fair share.

The Army managed the Corps, but it remained civilian. Before 1940, few camps practiced military drill. In most, the commander preferred to be called "Mr.," not "Sir."[71] Small camps in often-isolated areas encouraged camaraderie among otherwise highly diverse groups of boys from all parts of the country. So, too, did work in groups. Commanders did not censor camp newspapers. But great numbers warned new recruits, as did one produced by Company 2775, Camp SP/3, near Mandan, North Dakota, that "Gold-bricking on the WPA seems to have become a national pass-time. [*sic*] We do not want that here."[72]

---

the camp never even met its quota of two hundred. For the story of Camp Tera, see Alexander Rodriguez, *Civilian Conservation Corps: Concept to Mobilization* (San Jose, CA, 1992), 76–82.

[69] Samuel Harby, *A Study of Education in the Civilian Conservation Corps Camps of the Second Corps Area* (New York, 1938), 20–22.

[70] Anyone who found a full-time job before the end of his six-months' term was congratulated and given an "honorable" discharge, as were Cs with family emergencies that demanded their presence back home. Most commanders, however, wrote to relatives urging them not to report any trouble at home that might encourage desertion, unless the need for a recruit was unavoidable.

[71] This was a fact official CCC literature encouraged. It maintained a "Script Exchange Service" for camps that wanted to put on skits and plays. In one, "Mightly Poorly," a recalcitrant kid from Appalachia learns that he better "Cut out the Sergeant stuff. This is no army. My name is Voss. MR. VOSS to you." Script Exchange Service Files, Department of Interior Typescripts, Script 5, CCC, NA.

[72] Quoted in Kenneth Hendrickson, "Relief for Youth: The Civilian Conservation Corps and the National Youth Administration in North Dakota," *North Dakota History* 48 (1981): 20.

Law and order did not always prevail. A camp commander and several other adults died in a botched payroll robbery led by four enrollees at an Oklahoma camp. Constant dust storms completely unnerved the Cs working to prevent further soil erosion in western Kansas, and the entire camp refused to leave barracks. Wisely, CCC officials shut down the operation and transferred everyone to other locations. Nonetheless, given the enormous number of adolescent males involved, the program was remarkably well run.[73]

Technically, the CCC could not accept anyone with a criminal record. It fudged that rule by allowing boys given probation by a juvenile court to enlist, but most had gotten into trouble for relatively minor offenses. Nonetheless, tens of thousands of Cs had come to the Corps from the hard streets of big cities, or, even rougher, hobo camps. The Depression had not allowed very many to remain innocent children. The CCC worked because Army discipline and Army psychology worked. In 1938 case workers from the Western Reverse University interviewed 272 Cleveland boys. Their memories of service were fresh; indeed, many were still enrollees. Interestingly, however, their reports of life in the Corps confirmed the highly positive reminiscences written decades later by dozens of memoirists. Most were fiercely loyal to their work brigades and proud that they'd managed to live up to the CCC motto: "We Can Take It."[74]

Lessons Ignored: The Job Corps

In striking contrast to the CCC, Job Corps did not have clear goals but rather tolerated conflicting agendas and high levels of corruption. It failed to maintain discipline and did not provide most enrollees with basic employability skills. Ironically, however, Job Corps emerged from a Congressional campaign begun in 1959 to make the CCC permanent. Led by Minnesota Senator Hubert Humphrey, the effort floundered. Cold War America focused on Soviet aggression, not soil erosion. During years when the national GNP soared, Humphrey promoted his program as a chance to save "trees, land, and boys."[75] In 1964 Vice President-elect Humphrey watched silently as Lyndon Johnson stole his bill and reshaped it. As did the CCC, but unlike the majority of other twentieth-century public work training initiatives, Job Corps targeted teenagers, not young adults. In no other major way, however, did Job Corps parallel its New Deal predecessor. An unworthy successor, it failed to practice the lessons taught by the CCC.

---

[73] Ermentrout, *Forgotten Men*, 26–27.

[74] Helen Walker, *The CCC Through the Eyes of 272 Boys: A Summary of a Group Study of the Reactions of 272 Cleveland Boys to Their Experiences in the Civilian Conservation Corps* (Cleveland, OH, 1938).

[75] Hubert Humphrey, "A Plan to Save Trees, Land, and Boys," *Harpers* (1959): 53–57.

Johnson drafted Kennedy in-law and former Peace Corps director Sargent Shriver to head a task force on solutions to poverty and directed him to pay particular attention to unemployed youth. The CCC model soon surfaced in the form of a proposal to include residential training camps supervised by the Army in the omnibus Economic Opportunity Act of 1964. Political realities promptly killed the idea. With the war in Vietnam growing and opposition starting to surface, the Administration had no wish to hand critics a volatile issue.

Instead, almost by default, the private, for-profit sector administered Job Corps. John Rubel, an executive with Litton Industries and a member of Shriver's poverty task force advisory group, dashed off a memo urging that the fight against poverty be contracted out. In general, that did not happen. Most of the other initiatives included in the elephantine Economic Opportunity Act remained clearly under the control of the Labor Department or the new Office of Economic Opportunity, with Sargent Shriver as its first head. The Job Corps, in contrast, long before the concept became fashionable in the 1980s, operated as a privatized program.[76]

Job Corps became a government conduit to private business. As an agency within the Office of Economic Opportunity, its primary responsibility was supervision of the companies that actually ran most Corps residential centers. The Interior Department operated a few rural programs, but a dozen or more independent contractors, companies such as Litton Industries, Xerox, Burroughs, Westinghouse, and Manpower Training Corporation, administered the vast majority of Job Corp facilities. During its first thirty years, the number of Job Corps centers hovered at just over one hundred, and the number of teenagers annually enrolled in the program averaged forty-five thousand, a figure that increased to just under sixty thousand in

---

[76] For review of the climate surrounding the creation of the Job Corps, see Paul Combs, "Job Corps to 1973" (EdD Dissertation, Virginia Polytechnic Institute, 1985), 64–104. Combs provides a thorough, though disappointingly nonanalytic, review of Job Corps' first ten years. For a program nearing its fourth decade by the end of the century, there is remarkably little unbiased historical scholarship about Job Corps. Much writing about the program remains intensely polemical, produced by former staff members, who loved or hated the Corps. Typical of the former: Christopher Weeks, *Job Corps: Dollars and Dropouts* (Boston, 1967), and of the latter: Alfred Richards, *Over a Million Kids Sold – On What? The Job Corps Story* (Owings Mills, MD, 1992). Sociologists have written most of the scholarly analyses of the Corps. Many are quasi-memoirs, since many authors were consultants hired by the Department of Labor to assess the Job Corps. Typical of this genre is Sar Levitan and Benjamin Johnston, *The Job Corps: A Social Experiment That Works* (Baltimore, 1975). Scholars without axes to grind have produced more insightful, though usually article-length, work. Much of this literature uses Job Corps as a case study that tests the effectiveness of a social science theory. For instance, Jill Quadagno and Catherine Fobes examine the Corps as a model of the ways the "welfare states culturally reproduce gender roles." See "The Welfare State and the Cultural Reproduction of Gender: Making Good Boys and Girls in the Job Corps," *Social Problems* 42 (1995): 171–90.

the 1990s. There was no standard Job Corps site, though the dominant model was a large facility able to house between twelve hundred and fifteen hundred recruits. About 30 percent of Job Corp centers were much smaller – built along CCC lines to house from two hundred to five hundred teenagers.

As an agency of the OEO, the Job Corps removed "at-risk" youth from bad environments, giving them a new chance to learn in a place far removed from home. As it had with the juvenile courts, child protective services, and aid to dependent children, social science theory played a critical role in structuring Job Corps.

In 1960, Columbia University sociologists Richard Cloward and Lloyd Ohlin published a widely discussed book, *Delinquency and Opportunity*. "Opportunity theory" argued that teenagers became delinquents when they had no chance to achieve socially approved goals legitimately. Impoverished black kids from inner-city ghettoes were perfectly normal. Like other adolescents, they wanted nice clothes, cars, and part time jobs. However, their environments were deviant. Lacking the channels and minimal skills that allowed suburban white youngsters to find after-school work, such kids stole what they needed. Their surroundings were to blame.[77]

Job Corps provided an "alternative" opportunity, away from a poisoned neighborhood. Kids from the Bronx or South L.A. ended up in Clearfield, Utah, or Breckinridge, Kentucky. The Nixon Administration called Job Corps an excessively costly "country club for juvenile delinquents" and tried to abolish it.[78] However, Corps defenders had strong bipartisan support in Congress. Job Corps did not die, although the Nixon Administration's massive internal bureaucratic restructuring transferred it to the Labor Department's Manpower Administration.

In 1993, the Clinton Administration's "50-50 Plan" proposed to expand the Corps by 50 percent – increasing the number of centers from 113 to 163 and the number of teenagers enrolled to 122,000 annually. A Republican-controlled Congress said "no," but declined, once again, to dismantle the program. Instead, in 1998 the number of centers remained at around one hundred, as had been true throughout the Corps' history. Between 1964 and 1999 about 1.8 million disadvantaged kids spent time in the Job Corps.[79]

---

[77] Richard Cloward and Lloyd Ohlin, *Delinquency and Opportunity: A Theory of Delinquent Gangs* (New York, 1960).

[78] "Testimony of Augustus Hawkins, former chair, Committee on Education and Labor," Hearing on the Job Corps 50–50 Plan Before the Subcommittee on Employment Opportunities of the Committee on Education and Labor, House of Representatives, One Hundred Second Congress, First Session (Washington, DC, 1991): 8 (hereafter Hearing, 50–50). Hawkins, a defender of the Corps, recalled that the phrase had been in use by detractors since the Nixon years.

[79] For summaries of this history, see Hearing on Job Corps Oversight Before the Subcommittee on Employment Opportunities of the Committee on Education and Labor, House of Representatives, Ninety-Ninth Congress, Second Session, April 22, 1986 (Washington,

As was true for the CCC, the average Job Corps recruit was an eighteen-year-old male, an unemployed school dropout who read at barely the sixth-grade level. Like a C, he received a token amount as a monthly cash subsidy – an initial figure of $40 per month that escalated to around $100 a month by the 1990s, but unlike their predecessors, Job Corps trainees kept their cash. They were not required to send most of it home to relatives on relief. Moreover, the average Corpsman was black, not white, and came from a big, inner-city neighborhood.

Additionally, unlike the CCC, the Job Corps welcomed girls. Indeed, formidable Oregon Congresswoman Edith Green used her position on the House Committee on Education and Labor to insert a requirement in the 1964 bill that one out of every three Job Corps members be female. However, only in the mid-1990s, after the Corps amended its rules to allow single mothers admittance, were Green's guidelines met. The adolescent girl in the Corps paralleled the profile of her male counterpart: eighteen, black, a school-dropout, barely literate.[80]

As did members of the CCC, Job Corps teens lived away from home, but, unlike Cs, they did not really have jobs. Their "employment" consisted of taking classes. That meant that, unlike the routine at a CCC camp, Job Corps students were not members of groups, especially since Corps training philosophy emphasized individualized learning. Enrollees ideally participated in vocational training in the morning, followed by an afternoon's attendance at remedial English and math classes. However, an illiterate might spend his entire time in the Corps learning to read, while skills training could occupy an entire day's time for someone with a better basic education. While Job Corps literature mentioned over a hundred "skill clusters," the actual training available varied greatly from center to center. In many, choices came down to four or five trades – chief among them: office work, health care assistance, food-service preparation, and heavy equipment operation.[81] This system ignored the CCC's emphasis on clear goals.

DC, 1986) (hereafter Hearing, 1986); Joseph Pichler, "The Job Corps in Transition," *Industrial and Labor Relations Review* 25 (1972): 336–54; Daniel Saks and Ralph Smith, "Youth with Poor Job Prospects," *Education and Urban Society* 14 (1981): 15–32; Lynn Olson, "Great Society-Era Jobs Program Gets a Boost in 1993," *Education Week,* 12 (1993): 21–23; Mary Ann Zehr, "Job Corps Successes Were Overstated, GAO Audit Finds," *Education Week,* 18 (1998): 16.

80 The Corps also paid trainees "readjustment" expenses, for up to six months after he or she left the Corps. For a review of characteristics of Job Corps recruits, see "Testimony of Andrew Cainion, Director, Frenchburg Job Corps," Hearing, 50–50; see also: Robert LaLonde, "The Promise of Public Sector-Sponsored Training Programs," *Journal of Economic Perspectives* 9 (1995): 149–68.

81 For discussion of Corps teaching philosophies, see "Statements of Al Androlewicz, Vice President, RCA Service Company; Bernie Diamond, Vice President, Management and Training Corporation; Dave Maranville, Center Director, Los Angeles Job Corps Center; Roger Semerad, Assistant Secretary of Labor, Employment and Training Administration," 32–52, Hearing, 1986.

In contrast to the CCC, the history of the Job Corps provides one example after another of agendas in conflict. For decades its defenders orated impressively, as did Illinois Senator Paul Simon, that "there is absolutely nothing more important to the future of this nation than how we prepare our youth for future employment and productive citizenship."[82] The Corps effectively prepared for neither. Instead, a private contract system almost guaranteed that it would, as Randall Godinet, an inspector for the California State Department of Labor, charged, "lose focus of what it is all about. . . . Somewhere along the line what it could do for at-risk youth shifted to how much [*sic*] salaries the management was going to make."[83]

A program meant to teach impoverished high school dropouts employment skills spent, on average, less than 17 percent of its budget annually on vocational training. Job Corps consistently claimed over 90 percent of the kids "trained" by its program were "placed." For decades supporters crowed, "Sure it's expensive, but it's so enormously successful."[84] Was it?

An answer demands analysis of the Corps' definitions of "training" and "placement." Throughout its history, the Corps rarely required that a recruit accomplish all the duties and tasks associated with a vocational program in order to be listed as a "completer."[85] To compound problems, few Corps sites rigorously supervised class attendance, though learning a trade was supposed to be an enlistee's "job." Gerald Peterson, a former assistant inspector general at Labor, was only one of dozens of other ex-officials who

---

[82] "Prepared Statement of Senator Simon," Hearing on Youth Training Before the Subcommittee on Employment and Productivity of the Committee on Labor and Human Resources, United States Senate, One Hundred Second Congress, Second Session, December 11, 1992 (Washington, DC): 1 (hereafter Hearing, Youth Training).

[83] "Testimony of Randall Godinet," Hearings on Job Corps Oversight, Performance Accountability and the Incidence of Violence at Job Corps Sites Before the Committee on Labor and Human Resources, United States Senate, One Hundred Fourth Congress, First Session (Washington, DC, 1995): 36–37 (hereafter Hearing, Violence).

[84] The phrase was California Representative Matt Martinez's, but it or a variation could have been said by many dozens of supporters. "Statement of Chairman Martinez," 1, Hearing, 1986.

[85] For a review of GAO reports that issued highly negative assessments of Job Corps reporting practices, see Report of the Comptroller General of the United States, *Job Corps' Eligibility and Performance Standards Have Serious Problems,* Document HRD-79-60 (Washingon, DC, 1979); United States General Accounting Office, *Job Corps High Costs and Mixed Results Raise Questions About Programs' Effectiveness,* Document 95–180 (Washington, DC, 1995); United States General Accounting Office, *Job Corps: Need for Better Enrollment Guidance and Improved Placement Measures,* Document 98–1 (Washington, DC, 1997); United States General Accounting Office, *Job Corps: Where Participants Are Recruited, Trained, and Placed in Jobs,* Document 96–140 (Washington, DC, 1996); United States General Accounting Office, Transcript of Testimony Before the Subcommittee on Human Resources, Committee on Government Reform and Oversight, House of Representatives, *Job Corps Performance Data Overstate Program Success,* Document 98–218 (Washington, DC, 1998). (Hereafter, these GAO reports will be cited by their report numbers.)

claimed that the Corps never established "decent standards for classroom attendance." He and fellow field investigators found that " . . . the kids are just not there."[86] Absentee rates ranging from 33 to 70 percent were common. Nobody paid any attention to Gerald Peterson's complaints.

If Job Corps obfuscated about "training," it created a near-fictional standard for "placement." It took credit for a placement that occurred up to a year after a youth left a site, whether or not the job was connected in any way to training. Part-time or temporary employment counted as a placement. Finally, all kinds of activities other than work at a job counted as a successful placement. A youth who returned to school or who entered the Army was "placed." Many Job Corps centers counted a mere statement of intention to continue education or go into the military as placement and did not follow through to see if either actually occurred. Some listed girls who left the Corps for marriage as "placed," prompting one astonished critic to ask, "How can you consider marriage a positive placement unless the Job Corps arranged it?"[87]

Worst of all, the Corps allowed its independent contractors to compute placement statistics – a system begging to be corrupted, since contracts were numbers-driven, and placements earned bonuses. At no time during its history did Job Corps skeptically scrutinize the figures contractors mailed to Washington. However, independent pollsters and auditors did. In 1969, Senator Gaylord Nelson, chair of the Senate's Subcommittee on Employment, Manpower, and Poverty, hired Louis Harris – whose polling firm conducted interviews at 1,139 firms that had employed "placed" recruits. Over a quarter reported that kids hired from the Corps lasted at their jobs for fewer than six weeks. However, since the Corps counted even one day's employment as a "placement," that did not matter.[88]

A well-publicized Senate hearing exposing such chicanery did not end it. Statistical trickery characterized Job Corps reporting for the ensuing three decades. In 1998 the General Accounting Office tried to find the trainees listed as "vocationally connected successes" by five Job Corps sites. A participant who had finished an "office skills cluster" and was said to be working as a "sales consultant" turned out to be discarding bad tomatoes at a cannery. A kid listed as a welder turned out to be an airport baggage handler. Indeed, the GAO concluded, after discovering hundreds of other misstated "successes," that Job Corps placements were wildly inflated. Perhaps

---

[86] "Testimony of Gerald Peterson" 33–34, Hearing, Violence.

[87] GAO, Document HRD – 79–60: 15–29. The use of marriage as placement was common through the early 1970s. The quotation occurred during a question and answer session with Job Corps officials led by Republican Senator Winston Prouty during 1969 oversight hearings on the Job Corps. For further discussion, see Pichler, "The Job Corps in Transition," 342–43.

[88] For a more complete review of the findings of the Harris poll, see Pichler, "The Job Corps Transition," 339–43.

somewhere between 8 and 14 percent of enrollees actually found relevant full time jobs within a year of leaving the program.[89]

Even if judged by its own vaguely defined goal of "individualized training" the Job Corps was an abysmal failure. Yet, pork-barrel politics, conveniently tied to an increasingly cynical use of "opportunity theory," kept Job Corps from dying a deserved death in 1969. A system that provided almost unlimited opportunities for overbilling was a magnet for private industry. The real goal of Job Corps became profit statements in a company's bottom line. By the 1980s, facing mounting criticism for its failure to meet its vocational training objectives, Corps supporters invented a new goal: crime prevention. Nationally syndicated columnist Carl Rowan claimed it as a given, as did dozens of other Corps defenders: "The Job Corps helps desperately at-risk children avoid the lockups."[90] Did it? No one really knew.

In 1995, Vermont Senator Jim Jeffords launched a letter-writing campaign and inundated the Labor Department with requests to produce data proving that Job Corps enrollees were less likely to be incarcerated. "I would appreciate the information," he said.[91] Nobody produced it, because it didn't exist.

The idea that a teenager with a job or job skills was less likely to get in trouble certainly appealed to common sense. However, social scientists challenged the connection between unemployment and youth crime. By the end of the 1990s, several case studies suggested that, compared to nonemployed kids, adolescents with jobs smoked more marijuana, drank more beer, and were more likely to have participated in a theft.[92]

The criminologists who made these assertions used national population samples that included large percentages of middle-class kids. If, indeed, employment did promote delinquency in a much more heterogeneous adolescent group, was it plausible that the typical Job Corps teen was immune? Indeed, throughout the program's history, a high percentage of Corps enrollees already *were* criminals. From the 1960s through the 1990s about one half possessed arrest sheets. Critics charged that there wasn't that much difference between a bed at a Corps site and a bed in prison.[93] The violence

---

[89] Zehr, "Job Corps' Successes Were Overstated," 16.

[90] Carl Rowan, "Invest in the Job Corps, Not Prisons, for America's Youth," *Chicago Sun-Times*, May 3, 1991.

[91] "Testimony of Senator Jeffords," 123, Hearing, Violence.

[92] Matthew Ploeger, "Youth Employment and Delinquency: Reconsidering a Problematic Relationship," *Criminology* 35 (1997): 659–75.

[93] The sociologist John Pandiani has argued that the CCC also had an "invisible" crime control agenda, indeed that it was the "Crime Control Corps." Officials did comment in a vague way about the trouble hungry and idle boys might generate, but crime control in the CCC was explicit only for one group – the 8 percent of Cs who were unemployed former veterans *and* adults. Analysts conflate the quite openly stated desire to prevent other "Bonus Army" public relations disasters with crime control, never a truly important goal of the CCC.

and crime that plagued the program illustrate the Corps' inability to absorb the CCC's lessons about the importance of discipline.

If CCC camps were generally orderly, Job Corp centers were often chaotic. Since significant percentages of enrollees came to Job Corps after serving time for aggravated assault, felony theft, rape, or use of concealed weapons, the need for a clear system of discipline was even more important than it had been in the 1930s. The CCC provided a workable example: small rural camps where boys worked closely in teams. Instead, the typical Job Corps site was large and housed more than one thousand kids. Contractors didn't bid on small camps with two hundred or fewer residents. They were not as profitable.

In 1995, Kansas Senator Nancy Kassebaum began a major investigation of violence within the Job Corps and charged that for decades the Corps "had tolerated unacceptable behavior in the interest of keeping up the numbers."[94] It had. Contractors who recruited, administered, and "placed" Job Corps students all worked with systems that paid bonuses: for beating recruitment quotas; for retaining enrollees past thirty days; for making a placement. No administrator had any incentive to get rid of troublemakers, although Job Corps rules demanded that anyone charged with crimes be released to the relevant justice system. Instead, he had every reason to focus obsessively on "OBS" – the "on board strength" numbers that, in many cases, determined salaries.[95]

CCC camp commanders were Army officers serving tours of duty. In contrast, the dropout rates among Job Corps administrators were almost as high as those among their students. Many took on work for which they had little preparation and were, as a staff nurse at a site in Edison, New Jersey, complained, "just totally unaware of the reality of the situation."

There, she reported, a new regional director told her earnestly that his "main priority is to stop smoking on centers." He meant tobacco. Region Two of the Job Corps, which included Edison, was notorious for pervasive drug use. Who could have been surprised? At least one third of Corps recruits there had arrest records that included drug charges.[96]

John Pandiana, "The Crime Control Corps: An Invisible New Deal Program," *British Journal of Sociology* 33 (1982): 348–58. When contemporaries talked about possible intangible benefits for the average CCC recruit, they tended to view the experience in larger terms than just prevention of crime. For instance, the Rockefeller-backed General Education Board provided funds to prepare simply written grammar and other textbooks CCC boys could use. The GEB hoped that "The CCC educational program can prevent the development of a proletarian element which might serve as the nucleus of some anti-democratic force-group." "Interview with Kenneth Holland, New England Area Educational Adviser, CCC Camps, Boston," GEB, Series 1, Sub-series 3, Box 558, Folder 5969, RAC.

[94] "Opening Statement of Senator Kassebaum," 2, Hearing, Violence.
[95] "Testimony of Shirley Sakos, Acting Health Services Manager, Edison Job Corps Center, Edison, NJ," 22–23, Hearing, Violence.
[96] *Ibid.*, 34–36.

Region Two's manager was not the only Job Corps manager with no idea how to control sites where drug use, beatings, rapes, theft, even murders, occurred. In 1994 the Labor Department admitted that twenty-five Job Corps sites had "histories of excessive violence."[97] That number, one fourth of all Job Corps centers, was probably too low. In many places, "the kids ruled."[98]

Disgruntled former Job Corps trainees told of "blanket parties," in which eight to ten kids threw a blanket over a sleeping newcomer and "then took turns punching you and kicking you. The blanket is so you cannot identify who is doing the punching and kicking." They alleged that gangs controlled many places and made it easy to obtain drugs and guns.[99] Law enforcement officers backed up their stories.

Ron Stallworth, head of the Utah Division of Criminal Investigation, argued that the Management and Training Corporation actively thwarted his unit's efforts to probe gang activity at its Clearfield, Utah, operation. The assistant district attorney of Chavez County, New Mexico, threatened to arrest center administrators at the Roswell Job Corps Center when they failed to notify the police of a rape and instead allowed the alleged perpetrator to resign and leave the state.[100] Intent on "a polished image" private contractors practiced a policy of downplaying problems of violence and gang activity at their facilities.[101]

Was Job Corps violence tolerated not just to maintain profit margins but also to avoid the potentially explosive issue of race? Did Congress and the Department of Labor sedulously look the other way? Were politicians unwilling to charge that a program whose participants overwhelmingly were deprived black teenagers tolerated crime? For forty years, few wanted to discuss these questions. Dr. Robert Belfon was a notable exception. A pediatric dentist, he agreed in 1986 to join the Edison, N.J., Job Corps Center as a contracted dental services provider. He did so because, "As a forty-six-year-old African-American male who was raised in the Bronx in a housing project, and a former gang member, I . . . saw myself as a role model, as I assumed the other staff members and administrators undoubtedly were. Well, I was wrong."[102]

Instead, Belfon encountered staff members, black as well as white, who doubted that impoverished inner-city black kids would ever amount to much under any circumstances. The Job Corps, Belton charged, was a "ghetto

---

[97] "Statement of Gerald Peterson," 18, Hearing, Violence.

[98] "Testimony of Fred Freeman," 11, Hearing, Violence.

[99] *Ibid.*, 7.

[100] "Testimony of Ron Stallworth," 24–26, "Testimony of John McKay, 122–23, Hearing, Violence.

[101] "Testimony of Ron Stallworth," 25, Hearing, Violence.

[102] "Testimony of Robert Belfon," 119, Hearing, Violence.

dumping ground." Its primary purpose was "to keep the numbers up so that government checks kept coming in."[103]

Stung by all the bad publicity, between 1995 and 1997 the Labor Department promised reforms. For the first time it asked enrollees to sign a pledge "of personal commitment" to stay in Job Corps for at least thirty days. Moreover, it abandoned its long-standing refusal to allow students' lockers to be searched.[104] These simple steps should not have taken four decades to achieve. All CCC enrollees took a solemn oath. Each knew the word "deserter" would go on his record if he failed to abide by it. Every CCC camp commander had the right to search the possessions of a boy suspected of theft.

The CCC cost the nation one half billion dollars, an astonishing amount at the time and equivalent in 1994 constant dollars to about five billion dollars. The total expense of Job Corps was harder to calculate, given the program's fuzzy accounting. Nonetheless, it probably cost American tax payers in excess of forty billion 1994 dollars.[105] The money spent on the CCC was a good investment, both in terms of benefit to the nation and to millions of Cs. The huge sums poured into the Job Corps were wasted. The Job Corps ignored the CCC's lessons. In similar fashion, post–World War II labor regulation failed to remedy the obvious defects of a half-century of child labor law. Regulations continued to be inconsistent, poorly enforced measures.

"What Difference Does it Make?"
Child Labor Regulation in the Late Twentieth Century

The Fair Labor Standards Act greatly influenced child labor law at state and local levels, where its language reappeared for the rest of the century. A 1949 amendment to the Act banned children from farm work during school hours when schools were in session, even if states granted parents or employers harvest exemptions. In 1974, another amendment said that an agricultural operation covered by FLSA minimum wage regulations could no longer hire children under the age of twelve. Younger children could only work on farms owned by their parents that exclusively employed family members.

Although these amendments were the first significant federal effort to regulate farm work done by children, the FLSA never covered the activities of any youngsters working in agriculture outside of school hours or the work

---

[103] *Ibid.*, 120.

[104] "Statement of Mary Silva, Director, Job Corps," Hearing on Innovations in Youth Job Training, Before the Subcommittee on Employment and Training of the Committee on Labor and Human Resources, United States Senate, One Hundred Fifth Congress, First Session (Washington, DC, 1997), 8–11 (hereafter Hearing, Innovation).

[105] For adjusted real dollar calculations of the cost of the Job Corps over time, see LaLonde, "The Promise of Public Sector-Sponsored Training Programs," 150–53.

of children holding retail and service sector jobs that made no deliveries across state lines. Nor did most state and municipal codes. Newspaper carriers and child actors retained their exempt status. As the century ended, a few other categories of child workers joined them. In 1986, for instance, deferring to the wood products industry, Congress excluded all homeworkers engaged in the making of wreaths composed principally of natural holly or pine from all provisions of the Fair Labor Standards Act.[106] Municipal ordinances and state laws broadly copied FLSA precedent. What difference did it make?

In 1908, a "social doyenne" assured the muckraking journalist Emily Van Vorst that mills in Anniston, Alabama, "civilized our ignorant" hill children. If that were so, Van Vorst inquired, why did Alabama pass a law in 1903 prohibiting the employment of children under the age of twelve in factories? "'What difference does it make?'" her informant responded, "'Why not? There are no inspectors, no school laws, no truant officers.'"[107] The phrase "why not" characterized state regulation of child labor in 1908 and for the rest of the century, though jurisdictional inconsistencies often left honest employers confused.

Jackie Trujillo began his career as a teenage carhop at a Kentucky Fried Chicken outlet and was, by 1991, President of Kentucky Fried Chicken's management umbrella, Harman Corporation. He voiced the views of many food industry executives: "All...the discrepancies leave an operator open to unexpected charges of noncompliance. Let me give you some examples: Federal law: fourteen- and fifteen-year-olds can work until 7 P.M. on a school night; Minnesota law: fourteen- and fifteen-year-olds can work until 9 P.M.; Maryland law: fourteen- and fifteen-year-olds can work until 8 P.M.; Kansas law; fourteen- and fifteen-year-olds can work until 10 P.M."[108]

Trujillo condemned a system he described as a regulatory nightmare: great variance in definitions of night work, differences in times of day at which child workers could begin work or had to clock out; Friday nights designated as allowable "weekend" hours in some states, banned in others. Indeed,

---

[106] The categories of excluded youngsters remained relatively stable over the decades, but the numbers of jobs defined as hazardous expanded. By the 1990s, the Labor Department had declared seventeen occupations to be hazardous and off limits to anyone under age eighteen. The 17 were: (1) manufacturing and storing explosives; (2) driving a commercial motor vehicle; (3) coal mining; (4) logging and sawmilling; (5) work with power-driven woodworking machinery; (6) any job that involved exposure to radioactivity; (7) work with power-driven hoists; (8) work with power-driven metal punches; (9) all other mining, other than coal mining; (10) slaughtering or meat-packing; (11) work with power-driven bakery machinery; (12) work with power-driven paper-product machinery; (13) work involving the manufacture of brick or tile; (14) work with any power-driven circular or band saws; (15) wrecking or demolition; (16) roofing; (17) any work involving earth excavation. Bryan Fraser et al., *Minor Laws of Major Importance*, 4–7.

[107] Van Vorst, *Cry of the Children*, 20–22.

[108] Jackie Trujillo, 75–76, Hearing, Child Labor Amendment, 1991.

Trujillo alleged, 90 percent of all child labor violations in the restaurant industry were hours-related infractions. Who, he implied, could wonder?[109]

Child labor laws were not only regionally inconsistent, they were haphazardly enforced. In the early twentieth century, an undeveloped state structure imposed barriers to effective administration. For example, by 1913, all states had some form of employment certificate system requiring proof of a child's age, but only eight paired certificate statutes with effective, mandatory birth registration.[110] Indeed, through the 1940s, children in many parts of the country often got working papers based on the testimony of their parents, or, even, their own recollections of their ages.[111]

At the end of the century, the collection of birth information was compulsory in all states, and most Americans possessed a birth certificate. Nonetheless, few working children had to fear an inspector's demand to show it. Overworked, underpaid labor investigators still struggled with impossible assignments, as did similarly beleaguered child welfare bureaucrats who worked as juvenile court probation officers or as child protective service caseworkers.

In 1974, California inspector Seward Young was one of only eighteen labor law inspectors for the entire state of California. Working out of Fresno, Young policed violations of 215 different labor laws and supervised 396 farm labor contractors in a six-county region that included two dozen cities and towns. He admitted that he really had no time to search for children working illegally.[112] If state enforcement was lax, federal was rarely better. The United States Labor Department's Wages and Hours Division spent little time on investigations of child labor law violations.[113] Even had state and federal government officials increased the heat, the chances of their making much impact would have been muted by another long-term reality: violators of child labor law paid laughably small fines. By the 1990s, employers faced maximum fines of $10,000 for each proven instance of noncompliance with child labor provisions of the FLSA. States and localities, in turn, increased their penalties. The amounts sounded daunting: thousands of dollars for each infraction of law. It meant nothing. The risk of getting caught was miniscule, and the tiny number of violators governments prosecuted still generally paid

---

[109] *Ibid.*

[110] Julia Lathrop, "The Federal Children's Bureau," *Child Labor Bulletin* 11 (1913): 56–57.

[111] By 1933, all states had established some kind of birth registration system, but adequate monitoring of physicians, midwives, and hospitals took time to establish. Truly universal systems of American birth registration only existed in the last half of the twentieth century. Earl Davis, *Birth Certificates: A Digest of the Laws and Regulations of Various States* (New York, 1942); United States Department of Health, Education, and Welfare, *First Things and Last: The Story of Birth and Death Certificates* (Washington, DC, 1960).

[112] Ronald Taylor, "If You Are Lucky and Get Hired, Avoid the Dangers of Exploitation," *Los Angeles Times*, June 23, 1974.

[113] "GAO Estimates of Illegal Work by Children," Report, S. 600, 6–7.

a pittance, usually from $50 to $200.[114] Moreover, as restaurant industry executives constantly pointed out, most child labor law fines concerned the relatively trivial offenses of legitimate businesses: a harried manager who let a fifteen-year-old fast-food server work past seven at night.

Truly abusive work situations involving hundreds of thousands of youngsters eluded sanction. The 1965 Hart-Celler Act liberalized American immigration policy, yet not all who wanted to come could. Millions arrived in the country illegally, especially from Latin America, sparking significant increases in under-age banned labor, especially in textiles.[115] The sweatshop thrived, as did "ghost" child work done in family groups. In such situations, violations of the ages or hours provisions of state or federal child labor law were the least of an employer's sins, or worries.

"Sweatshops" could be literal – a worker's shabby apartment piled to the ceiling with shirts to finish, an ill-lit warehouse in a run-down industrial district – or figurative – bosses who employed gangs of children as candy sellers, crew leaders who paid migrant families an illegally low single sum in cash at harvest time. Many times, "sweatshops" violated dozens of laws: tax codes, workers' compensation, Social Security, occupational and environment safety rules. Legitimate businesses overburdened meager state inspection systems; these enterprises defeated them. A labor investigator for the state of New York could "only guess" how many "thousands of children are hunched over machines, sewing clothes with labels that read, 'Made in America.'" The actual numbers, he predicted, were probably "amazing."[116]

Celia Barragan gave such child labor a face. She came to the United States from Mexico in 1974, along with her parents, two sisters, and a brother. Her mother worked from dawn until after midnight seven days a week finishing blouses and skirts. Everyone else helped. Celia's father sewed garments on a second machine at night when he returned from his job at a grocery, and, when they came home from school, all the children in the family pitched in, often until one or two in the morning – turning clothes inside out, making corners in collars, or cutting threads. When deadlines threatened, all the kids stayed home from school to work with their parents. Celia's father and mother knew about the existence of minimum wage and overtime laws. However, they cheated on their records rather than anger a boss they feared and received about $100 a week, from which a jobber regularly deducted for "sloppy" sewing. From the time she was six years old until she left home,

---

[114] "GAO Summary," Report, S. 600, 2–9.

[115] For a review of post-1965 American immigration policy, see Reed Veda, "The Changing Face of Post-1965 Immigration," in David Jacobson, Ed., *The Immigration Reader: America in a Multidisciplinary Perspective* (Oxford, England, 1998), 72–91.

[116] "Testimony of Hugh McDaid, New York State Department of Labor," 25–26, Hearing, Child Labor Amendments, 1991.

Celia Barragan's life centered on a cramped Los Angeles living room choked with lint. Testifying before Congressional hearings held in 1990 on industrial homework in the women's apparel manufacture, Barragan accurately noted, "This will not change unless you have a government inspector stationed in every home that does homework."[117]

Government inspectors were not in homes. They were largely absent from fields as well. Few kids were in the nation's grain, corn, or soybean crops. There, insecticides, herbicides, and sophisticated machinery transformed agricultural practice. However, in areas where hand harvesting prevailed, children were still present.

Much of this labor fit persistent images of farming as wholesome outdoor work done by rural youths during the summer or at harvest time for extra cash. However, once kids of any age were in the fields, there was no knowing what kinds of work they actually did. State and federal labor codes forbade anyone under the age of eighteen from operating commercial vehicles or power-driven machinery. Nonetheless, an estimated 10 percent of fatal tractor accidents in 1990 involved a child under the age of fourteen. Anecdotal evidence suggested that young kids did not just pick berries, beans, and tomatoes. They laid irrigation pipe and drove cultivators. Children too small to reach the pedals stood up in wheel-wells to operate tractors.[118]

State and federal laws also excluded children from agricultural work when school was in session. In the early twentieth century, when most school terms spanned fewer than five months, planting and harvest seasons rarely conflicted with school hours. Decades later, when school years averaged nine months everywhere, agricultural districts often declared official holidays during peak work seasons. For most children, that meant a few weeks off. For migrant kids, however, who traveled west to east, harvesting fruit in Oregon, tomatoes and cucumbers in Ohio, then potatoes in Maine, the consequences were far more serious. Thousands effectively had no access to public schooling, since they moved for six to nine months of the year from one school harvest holiday to another.[119]

---

[117] "Testimony of Celia Barragan," Hearings on S. 2548, Before the Subcommittee on Children, Family, Drugs, and Alcoholism of the Committee on Labor and Human Resources, United States Senate, One Hundredth Congress, Second Session (Washington, DC 1990), 102–08 (hereafter Hearing, Child Labor Act of 1990.)

[118] Accurate data on work-related injuries and illnesses incurred by children were largely non-existent in the late twentieth century and had never been systematically collected. For discussions on the hazards of farm labor by children, see *Ibid.*; also: "Testimony of Linda Golodner, Executive Director, National Consumers' League," 51–67, Hearing, Child Labor Act of 1990; J. A. Swanson, M. I. Sachs, K. A. Dahlgren, and S. J. Tinguely, "Accidental Farm Injuries to Children," *American Journal of the Diseases of Children* 141 (1987): 1276–79.

[119] Chaya Piotrkowski and Joanne Carrubba, "Child Labor and Exploitation," in Barling and Kelloway, *Young Workers*, 129–56.

Public Policy and Youthful Employment: Lessons Learned?

The market, not state regulation, shaped twentieth-century child labor. American manufacturing mechanized, then automated. Increasingly valuable equipment dominated precious floor space. Owners did not want expensive capital investments damaged by incompetent workers. Even before the outbreak of World War II, this phenomenon greatly reduced the appeal of child workers in many industries.

Economic change pushed children out; it also lured adult women in, not just to factories, but also to growing white and pink collar sectors. The replacement of full-time child labor with full-time female work was a century's long process.[120] During the 1960s, when, for the first time, a majority of adult American women worked forty or more hours per week, another market emerged for children. Adults shunned this "secondary sector" work in service and retail fields. They didn't want jobs characterized by low wages, irregular shifts, weekend hours, little or no fringe benefits, and few opportunities for advancement. But teenagers searching for after school and weekend jobs found a perfect fit. Kids rarely viewed filling paper cups with french fries as the first step to a career; they didn't care that such work didn't lead to promotions. They didn't stick with one job, anyway. Employers made their peace with very high teenage turnover rates. Most of the work could be taught very quickly, and fickle young employees also were nonunionized workers.[121]

Those wringing their hands over the negative impact of such "child labor" were more likely to be academic sociologists, not parents or labor leaders. Tacitly acknowledging that fears of competition from child labor were exaggerated, unions continued their historic, but largely unenthusiastic, support for child labor laws. Children were low-wage, minimally skilled, highly impermanent workers and offered labor unions little challenge. They didn't provide much inducement to attempt organization drives, either.

The AFL-CIO dutifully opposed Oregon Senator Bob Packwood's unsuccessful effort in 1975 to overturn the 1974 FLSA amendment that prohibited children under age twelve working in agriculture. Far more indicative, however, of general union indifference to child labor law was the testimony of ten-year-old Deena Killion of Oregon City, Oregon. She declared, "This law that keeps me from picking strawberries is wrong. Last spring I was signed

---

[120] Carolyn Moehling, "State Child Labor Laws and the Decline of Child Labor," *Explorations in Economic History*, 36 (1999): 72–106; Martin Brown, Jens Christiansen, and Peter Philips, "The Decline of Child Labor in the U.S. Fruit and Vegetable Canning Industry: Law or Economics?" *Business History Review* 66 (1992): 723–70; Maurine Greenwald, "Women and Pennsylvania Working-Class History," *Pennsylvania History* 63 (1996): 78–95.

[121] For a good review of this new secondary market, see David Stern and Dorothy Eichorn, Eds., *Adolescence and Work: Influences of Social Structure, Labor Markets and Culture* (New York, 1989).

up, but my dad said I couldn't [pick] because of the law. I was really mad." Packwood interjected, "Just for the record – Is your dad Dean Killion?"[122] Dean Killion was the head of the AFL-CIO in Oregon, as Packwood well knew, and, by 1976, Deena could join thousands of other under-twelve kids in the berry fields. A court-ordered injunction made the FLSA amendment meaningless in her state. Neither Dean Killion nor any other major union official protested.

If unions were quiescent, so were parents. Poll after poll revealed that the latter group had no objections to the comparatively long hours their kids spent at work, despite the fact that a number of late-twentieth-century analysts plausibly connected an adolescent work week of more than fifteen hours to lower grades in high school, greater school absenteeism, and student unwillingness to sign up for tough courses.[123] While Americans thought child labor in sweatshops was a national disgrace, they exerted no meaningful pressure on politicians to do anything concrete about it. Finally, they, like generations before, continued to believe that farm work was healthy, even though the American Academy of Pediatrics declared it to be the most dangerous occupation in America.[124]

Public policy restricting child labor maintained a century's consistency. It didn't work. Public policy that provided job training for economically deprived adolescent youth often failed to emulate the CCC's success. The oldest jobs training program in twentieth-century American history, Job Corps, certainly did not profit from the CCC's example. By the end of the century, however, dozens of smaller-scale initiatives learned its lessons well. This book's emphasis on overviews of large issues does not permit close assessment of all of these efforts. However, three examples, the California Conservation Corps, Youth-Build Boston, and Texas YouthWorks, illustrate the ways that successful government work-for-youth projects at state and local levels applied the lessons of Franklin Roosevelt's Civilian Conservation Corps.

The California Conservation Corps carefully studied its national predecessor. Begun by Governor Jerry Brown in 1977, it revived the idea of simultaneously saving natural resources and the lives of poor kids. To join this West Coast CCC, one had to be between the ages of eighteen and twenty-three and a resident of California. Successful candidates worked forty hours a week for minimum wage and signed a written oath that read: "The CCC

---

[122] "Testimony of Deena Killion," Hearings on the Provisions of the Fair Labor Standards Act Against Exploitation of Child Labor in Agriculature, Ninety-Third Congress, Second Session, in Portland, Oregon (Washington, DC 1974), 40 (hereafter Hearing, Portland).

[123] The results of surveys conducted by the International Mathematics and Science Survey in the late 1990s that came to these conclusions are summarized in Richard Rothstein, "When After-School Jobs Lead to Poor Performance in School," *New York Times*, October 31, 2001.

[124] American Academy of Pediatrics, Committee on Environmental Health, "The Hazards of Child Labor," *Pediatrics* (1995): 95.

is a WORK program. You will do dirty, back breaking work; and no one will thank you for it. You must accept supervision."[125]

The typical California C was an unemployed teenager – at the program's beginning a nineteen-year-old male. By the 1990s, almost half of the participants were girls. Indeed, the latter were better bets, more likely to make it through an identically rigorous orientation than were boys. Although two thirds of California Cs had high school diplomas, most read at below a seventh-grade level. Dropout rates averaged around 10 percent, far below those experienced by Job Corps.

Like the Depression-era national CCC, California's program emphasized small residential camps. Unlike the original, camps were not sex-segregated. Girls and boys slept in separate dormitories, but in every other respect the program was gender-blind. Girls got no breaks in work assignments. They wore a uniform identical to the boys: high boots, tan pants, cotton work shirts, and a hard hat. Enrollees rose at six in the morning and spent exhausting days clearing streams, constructing parks, and restoring historical landmarks. After communal suppers, each had to write at least a page a day in a journal, turned in to crew leaders. Everybody was back in bed with mandatory lights out at ten o'clock.

The California Corps enrolled about two thousand young people annually. Most stayed for a full six-months' stint, even though they could have earned more money, with far less trouble, flipping burgers. Just as had the original Cs, they thrived on disciplined, hard work that produced tangible results. Adolescents in Roosevelt's CCC boasted, "We Can Take It." The California Cs motto, "Hard Work, Low Pay, Miserable Conditions," enshrined the same spirit. More applicants than the program could accommodate always vied for its relatively small number of positions.[126]

At century's end, the California CCC was a venerable government program, more than twenty years old. The two other initiatives used as examples here were much younger, but they, too, had learned the CCC's lessons. Begun in 1990, Youth-Build Boston was a cooperative venture, supported by the City of Boston, the United Way, building trades unions, and grants from the National Affordable Housing Act. Teenage high school dropouts renovated abandoned buildings as low cost homes for the poor. The program worked closely with carpenters' and electricians' unions, which agreed to take enrolled kids on as apprentices. In striking contrast to the Job Corps, Youth-Build Boston retained over 70 percent of its enrollees for a full year of on-the-job training. Eighty-five percent of Youth-Build kids never missed

---

[125] Quoted in Thomas Bass, "A Reborn CCC Shapes Young Lives with an Old Idea," *Smithsonian*, 14 (1981): 59.

[126] *Ibid.*, 56–65; See also: United States General Accounting Office, *Training Strategies: Preparing Noncollege Youth for Employment in the United States* (Washington, DC, 1990).

a day of work, and almost all graduates went on to well paid jobs in the construction industry.[127]

Before joining up with Youth-Build Boston John James was a drug dealer, gang member, and high school dropout. His family considered him a "worthless kid." When a cousin in Youth-Build persuaded him to come for an interview he reluctantly agreed. Then, he got caught up learning the trade of carpentry: "At first they [friends in the neighborhood] laughed at me wearing my tools, coming home dirty. Now they respect me."[128]

Like Youth-Build Boston, Texas YouthWorks taught through real jobs. Administered by the Texas Department of Housing, it too was relatively new, begun in the late 1980s. It also focused on training teens for construction trades by building subsidized housing for the poor. Like the Cs, these kids improved their own lives and helped others. Many discovered that they liked the feelings of responsibility and power that provided.

Monroe Madison, raised by a single mother on welfare, was a juvenile court veteran, a convicted thief and drug dealer. When a judge promised an early release from yet another incarceration if sixteen-year-old Madison joined up with Texas YouthWorks, he "didn't care" but was "just looking to do less time." But Madison, like many of the several hundred other criminal kids lucky enough to be pushed into the program, turned his life around. By age eighteen, he was well on his way to becoming a licensed, union carpenter. More important, he was proud that his crew "built the best houses in Austin." "It's not like we have gone and made a hamburger and somebody ate it.... We can go back forty years from now, and our house will still be standing there, and I can take my kids by that house, and say, 'This is what I did.'"[129]

Forty years after he helped build Minnesota's Whitewater State Park, CCC enrollee Frederick Johnson still enjoyed taking family members to "his" park. He loved seeing children swim in "his" lake and walk "his" trails.[130] He could still say, "This is what I did." Tens of thousands of other aging Cs felt the same way.

Government work-training programs that nourished that kind of pride succeeded and were examples of lessons learned, even if not absorbed directly from CCC examples. However, millions of American youngsters felt alienated from, rather than proud of, their public schools. They did not boast, "This is what I did," when asked about a school day.

---

[127] "Testimony of Jackie Gelb, Executive Director, Youth-Build Boston," 31–32, Hearing, Youth Training.

[128] "Testimony of John James," 35, Hearing, Youth Training.

[129] "Testimony of Monroe Madison," 27–28, Hearing, Innovations.

[130] Frederick Johnson, "The Civilian Conservation Corps," 302.

PART THREE

CHILDREN'S EDUCATION

5

"Laying Down Principles in the Dark"

The Consequences of Compulsory Secondary Education

Early-twentieth-century Progressives wanted to excise the "cancer" of child labor in part because they thought that adolescents should be in classrooms, not at work. As Philander Claxton, U.S. Commissioner of Education, explained, "We cannot educate children . . . for a democratic government in an age like ours, if we have them in school only through the years of childhood and previous to adolescence."[1]

The nineteenth century's common school movement advocated public education of children. Twentieth-century education policy required that adolescents attend high school, transforming an institution previously meant for a tiny elite. Less than 7 percent of all seventeen-year-olds in the country were high school graduates in 1900. By 1940, almost half were.[2] The percentages of American youth earning a high school degree steadily increased before stalling in the mid-1970s at a little over eight out of ten.[3] That was a

---

[1] P. P. Claxton, "A Substitute for Child Labor," *Child Labor Bulletin* 2 (1913): 6

[2] The significance of the great increase in the number of teenagers served by secondary public schools becomes clearer when high school enrollments are compared with population data for youth fourteen to seventeen years of age. While high school enrollments doubled during every decade between 1890 and 1940, the increases in the numbers and percentages of the nation's population between fourteen and seventeen were far more modest. A nation with 5,300,000 residents of that age in 1890 included 9,340,000 in 1940 – a rate of increase dwarfed by those for high school enrollments. See *Report of the First Commission on Life Adjustment Education for Youth*, Bulletin 1951:3, United States Office of Education, *Vitalizing Secondary Education* (Washington, DC, 1951), 4–6.

[3] Educators and government agencies sometimes challenged that 80 percent figure. Those who believed that recipients of general educational development (GED) or other high school equivalency certificates, often earned many years after dates of school leaving, should be included in American high school graduation rates argued that high school graduation rates, by the 1990s, were closer to 90 percent. Because this chapter examines the consequences of compulsory attendance rules only, and not the consequences of the creation of post–high school remediation programs, it will use the former percentage. For discussion of high school graduation rates in

policy success, with unexpected consequences. Extended schooling changed the daily lives of a majority of adolescents. However, generations of educators and politicians debated how and what to teach the millions of kids now forced to stay in school for most of their childhoods. In 1923, analysts at the U.S. Office of Education concluded wearily that much of the time they were "laying down principles in the dark."[4] That continued to be true throughout the century.

Nonetheless, acceptance of the idea that a prolonged period of education should be mandatory was enormously important. It was the key to the development of at least a minimally shared sense of American identity in a nation uniquely willing to make citizenship a personal choice. This chapter surveys the origins and organization of the early twentieth century's hugely bigger school systems and analyzes cycles of curriculum reform. It also assesses the reactions of teachers and students to education policies that altered the experience of growing up. To understand the impact of extended, state-sponsored public education requires, first, a review of common school precedents and examination of reasons why many turn-of-the-century leaders were convinced that education could "no longer be the province of the home."

"No Longer the Province of the Home": The Move for Compulsory Education of Adolescents

New England pioneered public regulation of children's education, as well as paid labor. In 1852, Massachusetts required all resident children between the ages of seven and fourteen to attend a public school for at least twelve weeks a year. Gradually, especially in the Northeast and Midwest, other states copied the precedent. Almost everywhere the focus was on basic training of young children.[5] Indeed, in 1873 the Massachusetts legislature revised its landmark statute and no longer demanded school attendance after the age of twelve. In classrooms that emphasized recitation and often included children of all ages, adolescents threw order into disarray. Terms sometimes ended abruptly when older boys smashed schoolroom windows, broke up furniture, set fires, or assaulted teachers.[6]

---

the twentieth century, see: U.S. National Center for Education Statistics, *Digest of Education Statistics 1992* (Washington, DC, 1992), 108–10.

[4] United States Office of Education, *Summary Report on Apprentice Education in the United States* (Washington, DC, 1923), 13.

[5] For a summary of the mandatory schooling legislation that created the nineteenth century common school, see Michael Katz, *A History of Compulsory Education Laws* (Bloomington, IN, 1976), 1–15.

[6] Maris Vinovskis, David Angus, and Jeffrey Mirel summarize Horace Mann's estimates that ten percent of school terms in mid–nineteenth-century Massachusetts ended prematurely because of older boys' vandalism or physical attacks on teachers, even though, as they note, nineteenth-century New England schools were generally divided into "summer" sessions, for quite young

As a new century began in 1900, high percentages of American children attended elementary schools. Still, only about one half of those who entered first grade went further than the sixth. Barely one in three completed the typical eight-year grammar school course. Fewer than one in five went on to high school, and of that number five out of six failed to graduate. Citizens and state legislatures certainly resisted the principle that the property of all should be taxed to educate the children of all. Tuition fees and voluntary contributions continued to provide substantial portions of school budgets in many parts of the country through the turn of the century. In the South, even this kind of "public" schooling was unavailable for many children, regardless of race.[7]

An urban elite led the drive for expanded public education, just as it had the movement to restrict employment of the young and to expand state agencies to supervise children's welfare. Compulsory high school was a policy change that epitomized Progressivism's boundless love of big ideas and fear of imminent doom. Jane Addams warned, "Until educators take hold of the situation, the rest of the community is powerless."[8] The "situation" to which Hull House's founder referred was the survival of democracy in America. Clearly another top-down reform, tax-supported mandatory secondary schooling nonetheless reflected deeper national unease about the civic costs of modernization.

During decades when the average American ceased to live in a rural area, and when cities' concentrated populations became richly, but for many disturbingly, polyglot, ordinary citizens accepted a new notion – that decisions about the education of teenagers could "no longer be the province of the home."[9]

children, taught by an adolescent female, and "winter" sessions, where a man or an adult woman thought to be able to handle discipline of older adolescents was in charge. Maris Vinovskis, David Angus, and Jeffrey Mirel, "Historical Development of Age Stratification in Schools," in Maris Vinovskis, *Education, Society and Opportunity: A Historical Perspective on Persistent Issues* (New Haven, 1995), 174–76. For other discussions of nineteenth-century compulsory education legislation and the common school, see Joseph Kett, "School Leaving: Dead End or Detour?" in Diane Ravitch and Maris Vinovskis, *Learning from the Past: What History Teaches Us About School Reform* (Baltimore, 1995), 265–71; Carl Kaestle and Maris Vinovskis, *Education and Social Change in Ninteenth Century Massachusetts* (Cambridge, 1980); Michael Katz, *A History of Compulsory Education Laws*, 14–21.

[7] In the nineteenth century a typical school system paired an eight-year elementary school curriculum with a four-year high school course attended by a tiny percentage of a community's children. Junior high schools remained atypical innovations until the 1920s. In many rural areas, public education ended at the elementary level, and even moderately large cities of 50,000 to 80,000 residents had only one high school. Everett Lord, "Child Labor and the Public Schools," National Child Labor Committee, Pamphlet 93 (New York, 1909), 5–7; Hollis Caswell, "The Great Reappraisal of Public Education," *Teachers College Record* 54 (1952): 12–22.

[8] Jane Addams, *The Spirit of Youth and the City Streets* (New York, 1915), 110.

[9] Lord, "Child Labor and the Public Schools," 4.

PHOTO 5.1   The caption reads "A consolidated school in Indiana." From Edward Clopper, *Rural Child Welfare: An Inquiry by the National Child Labor Committee: Based upon Conditions in West Virginia, Kentucky, and Indiana* (New York, 1922).

Opponents of child labor condemned "lazy" native-born fathers as villains who preferred to put their offspring to work rather than give them a chance to gain the skills necessary for citizenship. If American-born parents were a cause of worry, crowds of immigrants in urban areas prophesied catastrophe.[10] At no time between 1890 and 1920 did the incidence of the foreign born within the national population top 15 percent. Nonetheless, contemporaries viewed the millions lured by industrial America's prosperity as a kind of tidal wave that threatened to obliterate American social and political traditions.[11]

---

[10] The "lazy and too proud" man who willfully refused to allow his children education was a staple of literature demanding tougher compulsory education laws, just as it was for that decrying child labor. For a typical example, see Harriet Comstock, "The Whitest Gift of All," *Child Labor Bulletin* 3 (1914): 7–12. In this story little Maria Maud has a "turrible" desire for learning, but her father refuses to allow her to go to school, and in her "southern hills" state, laws did not exist to challenge him.

[11] The historian Roger Daniels wryly notes that scholars of all stripes have continued to use "hydraulic metaphors" favored by the Progressives. Almost inevitably, early-twentieth-century immigration to the United States becomes metaphorically a "flood," an "inundation," a "torrent," "a stream," implying overwhelming natural force and potential danger, as well as a profound sense of "otherness." Roger Daniels and Otis Graham, *Debating American Immigration, 1882-Present* (Lanham, MD, 2001), 6–7.

PHOTO 5.2   The caption reads, "A typical rural school, note lack of playground space." From Edward Clopper, *Rural Child Welfare: An Inquiry by the National Child Labor Committee: Based upon Conditions in West Virginia, Kentucky, and Indian* (New York, 1922).

And percentages of newcomers in the country's big cities *were* much higher. In Cleveland, for instance, a comprehensive population survey commissioned by business leaders revealed the "damaging" news that the city had become "one of the most foreign in the United States." In 1916, one out of three Clevelanders was not native-born. Two thirds of the city's children between the ages of six and seventeen had parents who did not speak English. "Even worse," the latter were "indifferent to the privileges and duties of American citizenship." Compared to 1900, proportionally far fewer of Cleveland's immigrants took out naturalization papers. The social and political assimilation "of the great mass of aliens in the city," the report concluded, "is proceeding at a steadily decreasing pace."[12]

Throughout the country, people shared the concerns expressed by Cleveland's leaders. The threat of the country's "foreign" cities, in which over one third of resident male adults were nonvoting noncitizens, worried many, even in the nation's rural areas, the final destination for just a fraction of arrivals. Throughout the country, elected officials speechified

[12] Herbert Miller, *The Cleveland Education Survey: The School and the Immigrant* (Cleveland, OH, 1916), 11–26.

about perils posed by "hordes of prolific immigrants which pour upon our shores," even if they hailed from landlocked states with no shores at all.[13]

Immigrants were the same "prolific" people whose children urban anti-cruelty societies thought most in danger. How could anyone expect these newcomers to instill acceptable civic values? Worried state legislatures responded by passing mandatory education laws. By 1918, when Mississippi became the last state in the nation to enact such a statute, trends that distinguished twentieth-century compulsory education from its nineteenth-century antecedents were already apparent.[14]

Legislation usually established much longer periods of schooling per year for children between the ages of six and sixteen. Moreover, most statutes established enforcement mechanisms, requiring school districts to employ attendance officers and keep truancy records.[15] A few months a year of attendance at a common school from the ages of six to twelve no longer typified the average American child's formal education. The public high school, funded by local property taxes, had arrived. During the first two decades of the twentieth century, a new one opened, on average, every single day.[16]

In general, American courts at all levels accepted forced attendance, and private schools had to prove they provided an education comparable to one a child received in a public school. Governments were the ultimate arbiter of what education for children between the ages of six and sixteen would be.

Pierce v. Hill Military Academy established the legal precedent that prevailed for the rest of the century. Hill Military Academy joined the Catholic Society of Sisters to challenge a 1922 Oregon law that required all the state's children to attend a public school. When the case finally reached the U.S. Supreme Court, the appellees won. However, the Court emphasized that it raised "...no question concerning the power of the State reasonably to regulate

---

[13] The speech quoted here was given in 1903 before the Kentucky legislature and ended with a plea to educate the "American stock" of which Kentucky was so proud, in order to "balance" immigration. For a collection of such speeches, see "A Rare Type of Oratory," *Berea Quarterly* 7 (1903): 26–32, The Berea College Archives, Berea, Kentucky.

[14] For a summary of early-twentieth-century mandatory education statutes, see Kern Alexander and K. Forbis Jordan, *Legal Aspects of Educational Choice: Compulsory Attendance and Student Assignment* (Topeka, KS, 1973).

[15] Interestingly, once in place by 1920, compulsory education laws changed relatively little for the rest of the century. The mean legal age for leaving school remained sixteen in most states. The one state (Delaware) that compelled attendance until age seventeen and the five (Idaho, Ohio, Oklahoma, Nevada, and Utah) which required it until age eighteen had already done so by 1920. Southern states were the last to adopt compulsory education, and they remained, except for a few urban areas, the states with the fewest numbers of days per year of required schooling and the greatest number of exemptions.

[16] Katz, *A History of Compulsory Education*, 23.

all schools...and to require that all children of proper age attend some school."[17]

So, courts validated policies prolonging mandatory, publicly supervised education. But the new high schools were not like the old. Unlike their predecessors, the former promised to train for citizenship, not for college. That demands further examination of the goals underpinning reformers' demands for extended public education.

The Cardinal Principles

At the end of the nineteenth century, about 10 percent of American teenagers spent some time in a high school. Although fewer than 4 percent went on to college, all studied a curriculum that emphasized Latin, Greek, and mathematics. Prestigious urban high schools offered courses in physics, anatomy, chemistry, and astronomy as well.[18] Mass secondary education introduced striking curricular change. The mission of the new high school was not to teach anatomy – but to instill American values.

In 1918 an influential report published by the U.S. Office of Education summarized this dramatically new goal. *The Report of the Commission on the Reorganization of Secondary Education*, commonly called *The Cardinal Principles* after its subtitle, signaled the birth of an interesting alliance that thrived for decades.[19] Federal officials working with big city school administrators and education professors from a few leading universities successfully promoted curriculums that emphasized the importance of social values, not information.

Property owners everywhere were forced to support the new mass high school, but coalitions such as the one that produced the *Cardinal Principles* shaped what happened inside its walls. The U.S. Congress established a Cabinet-level federal Department of Education only in 1979. However, it authorized a federal agency with a mandate to promote public education in 1866. For almost a century, the United States Office of Education was a tiny branch of the United States Department of Interior. Its miniscule budgets might have doomed it to total irrelevance. However, a series of aggressive

---

[17] *Pierce, Governor of Oregon, Et Al., v. Hill Military Academy.* Supreme Court of the United States, 268 U.S. 510; 45 S. CT 571; 1925. This Supreme Court case is also sometimes called *Pierce v. Society of Sisters*, since the Society of Sisters, which administered religious schools throughout the state, was a co-litigant.

[18] For discussions of curriculum at end-of-the-century high schools, see Edward Krug, *The Shaping of the American High School* (New York, 1964), 1–127; David Labaree, *The Making of an American High School: The Credentials Market and The Central High School of Philadelphia, 1838–1939* (New Haven, 1988), 64–133.

[19] *Report of the Commission on the Reorganization of Secondary Education: Cardinal Principles of Secondary Education*, Bulletin 1918: 35, United States Bureau of Education, Department of the Interior (Washington, DC, 1918).

commissioners remade their unpromising positions. They became brokers, bringing together university professors, school superintendents, and leaders of the National Education Association, the organization most interested in promoting the professionalization of teaching.[20] The results of these meetings bore the stamp of federal approval and appeared as government bulletins. They were, in fact, the collective judgments of a triumvirate: policy makers in a weak federal agency acting in concert with influential university-based educational theorists and deal-making urban school officials.[21] As did Children's Bureau leaders, commissioners of the Office of Education cleverly allied with private organizations that helped them issue "public" bulletins that would have otherwise not have been discussed, perhaps never have even been published.

The Cardinal Principles was just such a document. It was preeminently the creation of reformers, who, taking their name from the larger movement of the same name, called themselves Progressive educators. As did most other Progressives, the drafters of the *Principles* thought education was the key to national improvement. Indeed, the new public high school would bind together a civic culture in grave danger. To accomplish such a feat, schools had to become "laboratories for citizens." Public education should not simply prepare children from all kinds of ethnic, class, and religious backgrounds for life in a democracy, it should *be* democratic. Whether poor or rich, native-born or immigrant, youngsters could learn from each other, as well as their teachers, especially if they "learned by doing."[22] That necessitated a radical

---

[20] The National Education Association began in 1857 in Philadelphia as the National Teachers' Association. It remained small and uninfluential, however, until the late nineteenth century when it took a new name, the National Education Association, and championed increased government support for public education. For information about the history of the NEA, see Allan West, *The National Education Association: The Power Base for Education* (New York, 1980).

[21] Professors affiliated with Columbia University's Teachers' College were an especially influential force in this alliance. There is no good history of the Bureau/Office of Education that links it with the much more visible role played by the federal government in shaping education policy after World War II. Stephen Sniegoski has written a brief, nonanalytic, history that includes the creation of the Office of Education. Stephen Sniegoski, *The Department of Education* (New York, 1988). Between 1870 and 1929 Congress reduced the already meager budget of the Office of Education and demoted it to the status of a bureau within Interior. In 1929, it resumed its original name. In 1953, the Office of Education became part of the new Department of Health, Education, and Welfare, with a dramatically increased budget and new duties. For excellent discussions of the enlarged federal role in education policy after 1945, see Diane Ravitch, *The Troubled Crusade: American Education, 1945–1980* (New York, 1983); Hugh Graham, *The Uncertain Triumph: Federal Education Policy in the Kennedy and Johnson Years* (Chapel Hill, 1984); Ravitch and Vinovskis, *Learning from the Past.*

[22] The conjoined ideas that schools would be democratically run "laboratories" where children "learned by doing" were two of John Dewey's most famous dictums, best expressed in *Democracy and Education: An Introduction to the Philosophy of Education* (New York, 1916),

departure from traditional high school curriculums. Rather than study about Greek government, students should investigate their own. Rather than memorize facts, they should examine current problems. Above all, they should be taught that, collectively, they had the power to improve society.

Clarence Kingsley, a mathematics teacher from Brooklyn, epitomized Progressive era alliance building. When the NEA and the Office of Education created a commission to study secondary education curriculums, he became its energetic chair. A fervent advocate of the fledgling National Education Association's drive to make teaching a credentialed occupation, Kingsley soon caught the eye of David Snedden, one of Columbia's first doctorates in education. When Snedden returned to his alma mater after a stint as Massachusetts Commissioner of Education to introduce sociology of education courses at Teacher' College, Kingsley became an eager acolyte.[23]

Convinced by Kingsley that educators could shape students' social values, not just impart knowledge, the Commission on the Reorganization of Secondary Education promoted a new goal for high school education, one that wholeheartedly embraced Progressive education: "The school is the one agency that may be controlled consciously by our democracy for the purpose of unifying its people."[24] In order to create "bonds of common understanding" schools should promote: the development of healthy physical habits and ethical behavior, "worthy" use of leisure time, love of home, "command of fundamental processes," an appreciation of "vocation," and an understanding of civics. These goals constituted the seven "cardinal" principles.[25]

Overwhelmingly, they emphasized nonacademic ambitions. Only one, "command of fundamental processes," suggested that mastery of subject content was an important purpose of secondary education. Instead high schools should forge ties of trust among fellow citizens.

Mandatory public schooling, to a striking degree, did achieve this goal. Immigration caused a great deal of exaggerated fear. Nonetheless, even between 1924 and 1965, the United States remained a country that allowed millions of newcomers entry, in percentages far higher than did any other

---

ix–xi. Through the 1930s Dewey remained one of the best-known advocates of Progressive education.

[23] For further information about the Kingsley-Snedden relationship, see Herbert Kliebard, *The Struggle for the American Curriculum, 1893–1958* (New York, 1995), 96–98.

[24] *The Cardinal Principles*, 22.

[25] *Ibid.*, 11–14. *Cardinal Principles* defined the goal of "vocation" in group, rather than individual, terms. For additional analysis of the *Principles*, see Patricia Albjerg Graham, "Assimilation, Adjustment, and Access: An Antiquarian View of American Education," in Diane Ravitch and Maris Vinovskis, *Learning from the Past*, 10–16; William Wraga, *Democracy's High School: The Comprehensive High School and Educational Reform in the United States* (New York, 1994), 3–30.

developed country.[26] And, in contrast to all its industrial rivals, it always defined citizenship as a matter of birthright *and* choice. Efforts to deny immigrants a right to future citizenship, while numerous, failed. Most were potential fellow Americans, not permanent "guest" workers. Indeed, one of Progressivism's biggest worries was that too *few* arrivals embraced the rights and responsibilities of citizenship.

Multicultural societies can dissolve. The Progressives understood that. They also knew representative democracy was a legacy of a particular type of eighteenth-century European thought, not shared by all societies that sent immigrants in great numbers after 1880. The Progressives thought schools could institutionalize civic culture and help unite an increasingly diverse population. Extended compulsory education partially accomplished that goal. Struggles to make America a society whose laws and practices did not discriminate by race, gender, national origin, even disability, marked the twentieth century. Would they have occurred had mass access to publicly funded education not preceded them? That question demands proving a negative, and, therefore, cannot easily be answered. However, those who denounced the academic achievements of public high schools failed to remember, if they had ever known, that their creators did not particularly care about the best ways to improve reading skills or teach math. The idea behind the *Cardinal Principles* was more ambitious – to use education to broaden the nation's civic consciousness and to encourage egalitarianism. To the extent that that happened, mandatory secondary education not only reshaped childhood; it remade American society.

The prominent educational theorist John Dewey wanted American public schools to become "microcosms of democracy." In fact, the CCC camps best realized Dewey's vision. African-American youths became Cs in numbers proportional to their presence in the national population. Some camps were integrated, and, in a handful, black adolescents were leaders of mixed-race teams. Although underrepresented, hundreds of thousands of the sons of recent immigrants became "soil soldiers." Big-city kids routinely bunked with boys who had never before left the farm. Millions certainly "learned by doing." Memoir after memoir written by former Cs recounted an author's transformative realization that someone from another ethnic group, a distant region of the country, or even a different race, could be a friend.

There is no evidence that the two tough-minded machinists who ran the CCC studied John Dewey, or any other academic. Neither Robert Fechner nor J. J. McEntee was a big reader – of anything, much less educational

---

[26] Between 1925 and 1965 more than 48 million immigrants came to the United States and a higher percentage of these newcomers stayed and eventually became citizens than did those who arrived between 1870 and 1920. United States Bureau of the Census, *Statistical Abstract of the United States, 1999* (Washington, DC, 2000).

theory. However, they did create genuine laboratories for democracy that turned millions of deprived Depression-era adolescents into productive, proud citizens. They did it by bringing boys together and making them work in groups.

Mandatory adolescent education's legacy is enormous. No other American social policy affected so many people, for so many years. Nonetheless, public high schools did not fully implement the *Cardinal Principles'* vision of education that tied together the nation's young through use of a common curriculum that emphasized training for citizenship. *The Cardinal Principles* was the product of a highly segregated age. Its paeans to unity did not include African Americans. Not until the 1960s did the country abandon racially prejudiced separate schooling for black children and change immigration policies that banned Asians from the country, much less the nation's schools.[27]

After 1965, as public schools finally opened to the children of Indian, Pakistani, Chinese, and other Asian immigrants, members of these fast-expanding segments within the American population did not remain residentially isolated to the same extent as did blacks. Despite the abolition of formally segregated education, black kids continued to go to school primarily with other blacks. That was not as true for Asians, whose record of economic and social assimilation provided a back-handed compliment to a Progressive educators' dream that, blinded by race prejudice, failed – but only to meet its own high mark of civic integration of all segments of American society.[28]

That is not to suggest that those not forcibly segregated received equal treatment. Expanded schooling soon embraced categorizations promoted by the new social science of psychology that separated students by quantifying their supposed intelligence. The CCC did not utilize intelligence testing. The public schools did. Early-twentieth-century school leaders' enthusiasm for this controversial innovation altered the history of public education in America. Public schools employed much of Progressive education's rhetoric about democracy and education, and that mattered. America did not shatter, as did many other twentieth-century societies, torn by bloody conflicts

---

[27] The topic of segregation/desegregation of American public education is an important one, with a rich literature. Good overviews include: Richard Fossey, Ed., *Race, The Courts, and Equal Education: The Limits and the Law* (New York, 1998); Jennifer Hochschild, *The New American Dilemma: Liberal Democracy and School Desegregation* (New Haven, 1984); Gary Orfield and Susan Eaton, *Dismantling Desegregation: The Quiet Reversal of Brown v. Board of Education* (New York, 1996); Jeffrey Raffel, *Historical Dictionary of School Segregation and Desegregation: The American Experience* (Westport, CT, 1998).

[28] For more discussion of easing of anti-Asian immigration restrictions and Asian assimilation, see Roger Daniels, *The Politics of Prejudice: The Anti-Japanese Movement in California and the Struggle for Japanese Exclusion* (Berkeley, 3rd ed., 1999); Timothy Hatton and Jeffrey Williamson, *The Age of Mass Migration: Causes and Economic Impact* (New York, 1998).

between ethnic groups twisted by hate. But intelligence testing guaranteed that public secondary education would fail to achieve its own exuberant goal.[29]

The Triumph of Intelligence Testing in American Schools

Between 1900 and 1918, a small cohort of psychologists with PhDs from American universities struggled for legitimacy. Few members of the general public knew the profession even existed, much less what its practitioners did. The regular physicians who controlled health care rarely treated psychologists as equal colleagues. Few followed the latter group's largely sectarian arguments about human mentality or emotional growth. Nor was the idea that intelligence was quantifiable widely accepted.

In fact, when the French psychologist Alfred Binet tried to study intelligence during the first decade of the twentieth century, he turned to old-fashioned nineteenth-century craniometry and took out calipers to measure skulls. However, Binet soon abandoned the work, regarding all his results as hopelessly inconclusive. Instead, he invented "mental testing." The ability to reason, not physical characteristics, such as the width of the skull or the speed of blinking, demonstrated intelligence. In 1904, Binet persuaded the French government to allow him to develop a set of procedures to identify "feeble-minded" children who would not succeed in regular classrooms. By 1906, he had created a battery of tasks, calculated to determine a child's ability to reason. Youngsters copied drawings, judged which of two objects was heavier, and repeated sentences verbatim, proceeding to progressively harder tasks until they could no longer complete any instructions successfully. The age at which a child failed to perform was his "mental age." When the tester divided this mental age by the subject's chronological age, then multiplied by one hundred, he created an "intelligence quotient."[30]

The IQ was born, but initially few noted the appearance of a calculation that would affect the lives of millions of American schoolchildren and

---

[29] Patricia Albjerg Graham notes that public school leaders often used John Dewey's writings as a kind of bible. "But like the *Bible*, *Democracy and Education* was rarely read in full and was suitable for constant reinterpretation." "Assimilation, Adjustment, and Access: An Antiquarian View of American Education," in Ravitch and Vinovskis, *Lessons from the Past*, 14. For further discussion of what she condemns as the "excessive quantification" of American education, see Ellen Lagemann's excellent *An Elusive Science: The Troubling History of Education Research* (Chicago, 2000).

[30] For discussions of Binet's work, see Stephen Jay Gould, *The Mismeasure of Man* (New York, 1981), 146–58; Leonard Ayres, "The Binet-Simon Measuring Scale for Intelligence: Some Criticisms and Suggestions," *Psychological Clinic* 5 (1911): 187–96; Paul David Chapman, *Schools as Sorters: Lewis Terman, Applied Psychology, and the Intelligence Testing Movement, 1890–1930* (New York, 1988), 19–36; John Burnham, "Psychology, Psychiatry, and the Progressive Movement," *American Quarterly* 12 (1960): 457–65; Paula Fass, "The IQ: A Cultural and Historical Framework," *American Journal of Education* 88 (1980): 431–58.

permanently change the way Americans thought about ability and education. After all, rankings of French schoolchildren did not resonate with the
general American public. However, mass testing of men summoned for the
draft in 1917 and 1918 did.

Robert Yerkes, a Harvard professor and president of the infant American
Psychological Association, scored a coup of immense consequence when he
persuaded Secretary of War Newton D. Baker to test recruits to eliminate the
"mentally unfit." The Binet test required an examiner to spend three hours
with each individual child, recording responses to a great number of tasks and
questions. Yerkes knew that such a system would never work when utilized
on a vast scale. Instead, he and Stanford University colleague Lewis Terman
created a simplified system of two tests that could be administered to large
groups – Alpha, for those who read English, and Beta, for those who didn't.

Cultural and class biases riddled the exams. Better-educated recruits were
far more likely to successfully complete the verbal analogies that the Alpha
tests emphasized. Expected to work rapidly and timed by stopwatches, they
raced through lists of words to choose whether "butter, rain, cold, cotton,
or water," most resembled "ivory, snow, and milk." Even the nonverbal
Beta tests demanded comprehension of cultural cues many poorly educated
natives and a majority of new immigrants did not possess. A Beta recruit's
fate rested in his ability, for instance, to assemble a picture puzzle of the
American flag, with the proper number of stars and stripes.[31]

Army testing certainly imprinted intelligence testing on the American
mind. But it did not establish its permanence. Illinois Senator Lawrence
Sherman joined many other politicians in ridiculing supposed psychological technique during openly hostile Congressional hearings held in late
1918. Yerkes and fellow testers had to sit and hear themselves mocked as
" ... psychologists with X-ray vision (who) drop different colored handker-
chiefs on a table, spill a half-pint of navy beans, ask you in sepulchral tones
what disease Sir Walter Raleigh died of, and demand the number of legumes
without counting."[32]

Indeed, at war's end, the military promptly disbanded the program. Army
Brass hated the tests, thought they posed threats to chain of command,
and successfully lobbied the War Department to abandon the experiment.

---

[31] For a scholarly summary of the Army testing, see Daniel Kevles, "Testing the Army's
Intelligence: Psychologists and the Military in World War I," *Journal of American History*
55 (1968): 565–81. Yerkes himself wrote extensively about the program. See Robert Yerkes
and Clarence Yoakum, Eds., *Army Mental Tests* (New York, 1920); Robert Yerkes, "Psychology in Relation to War," *Psychological Review* 25 (1918): 85–115; Robert Yerkes, "Report
of the Psychology Committee of the National Research Council," *Psychological Review* 26
(1919): 83–149.

[32] Senator Lawrence Sherman (Republican of Illinois) quoted in JoAnne Brown, *The Definition
of a Profession: The Authority of Metaphor in the History of Intelligence Testing, 1890–1930*
(Princeton, 1992), 114.

Moreover, American business executives, after an initial flurry of enthusiasm, quickly discovered that workers in factories and offices resented IQ tests – especially if they were part of interviews for employment.

Only one group of American leaders, superintendents of schools, enthusiastically accepted intelligence testing, guaranteeing that the kind of schooling millions of children received rested on decisions about their mental abilities. Even when words popularized by the tests, such as "idiot, moron, and imbecile," ceased to have psychological significance, they remained as invectives, and Americans continually sought to be "normal."[33]

Prejudice blinded the authors of the *Cardinal Principles* to the importance of including young African Americans. But race alone proved insufficient for swamped school superintendents seeking sorting devices. Intelligence tests provided many more to those struggling to organize the new mass systems of American public education.

The job of superintendent itself was a by-product of the explosive growth of the high school. At the turn of the century, when 70 percent of Americans still lived in rural areas, hundreds of thousands of local school boards presided over relatively simple school systems in which one-room schoolhouses were still common. Members of these boards were more likely to be farmers or local businessmen than professional educators. In major cities, school boards were huge and highly political, typically composed of hundreds of members, all elected by wards. A seat on such a board was valued spoil distributed by municipal patronage systems, since each person belonged to one or more subcommittees – which squabbled over everything from the price of paint to the choice of textbooks.

The same Progressives who engineered extended mandatory schooling revolutionalized this system during the first two decades of the twentieth century. In many states, charters from state legislatures allowed them to reorganize public education without popular vote. Everywhere, the watchword was consolidation. Previously independent school populations merged. Per capita spending on public education increased sixfold, and even in the countryside, professionals began to run systems that suddenly seemed too complicated for amateurs.[34]

---

[33] *Ibid.*, 58–117. Some state asylums used the term "idiot" in the nineteenth century, but it was not common in usage until after the advent of the IQ tests, nor did the term in the nineteenth century indicate a specific numerical deficiency of intelligence, as it did in the twentieth-century tests. Nineteenth-century terms for those deemed to be of low intelligence were not necessarily kinder, but they derived from popular culture: "fool," "simpleton," and "dim-wit" were the three most prevalent.

[34] For discussions of the transformation of school systems between 1900 and 1925, see David Tyack, *One Best System* (Cambridge, MA, 1974), 66–88; David Tyack and Elizabeth Hansot, *Managers of Virtue: Public School Leadership in America, 1820–1980* (New York, 1982); Paul Boyer, *Urban Masses and Moral Order* (Cambridge, MA, 1978); 123–134; Michael Kirst, "School Board: Evolution of an American Institution," *American School Board Journal*, Special

Especially in extremely overcrowded urban school districts, intelligence testing provided a vehicle that classified students by ability. No longer needed by the Army, Lewis Terman relentlessly promoted a revised Stanford-Binet battery of examinations for use in the public schools. By 1925, almost 90 percent of urban school districts used some form of intelligence testing, and urban systems employed staffs of full time psychologists.[35]

By the time the enthusiasm for testing peaked in 1930, many districts employed a panoply of mental examinations.[36] Schoolchildren took speed tests that draftees in 1918 would have found familiar: naming four synonyms for "red" in one minute; counting backward, finding the missing element in a picture. They also faced many more examinations, some of which greatly blurred the line between tests of intelligence and judgments about character. The "Will-Profile Test" purportedly measured children's "will-to-do" – the ability to stick to a task even when distracted – by demanding that they write the same word repeatedly. Psychologists studied the resultant handwriting samples and scored the test-takers for such personality characteristics as "perseverance," "self-assurance" and "self-inhibition."[37]

The "Liao Test" attempted to judge "trustworthiness and moral worth." It presented students with a statement, underneath which were placed five reasons for its truth. The statements were verbal minefields; only one answer was a "morally good" one. For example, appended to the phrase: "It is wrong not to work" were the following five explanations: "(1) Idle people are called lazy; (2) Idle people earn no money; (3) Idle people are discontented; (4) Idle

---

Issue (1991): 11–15; Michael Kirst, "Who's in Charge? Federal, State, and Local Control," in Diane Ravitch and Maris Vinovskis, *Learning from the Past*, 30–34. In proportional terms increases in public spending on schools during the first half of the twentieth century greatly exceeded those since 1950, and the greatest spurts in school expenditures came between 1900 and 1929. Since 1960, the major increases in state spending were for prisons, health care, and hospitals.

[35] Paul David Chapman, *Schools as Sorters*, 3; Paul David Chapman, "Schools as Sorters: Testing and Tracking in California, 1910–1925," *Journal of Social History* 14 (1981): 701–17; United States Children's Bureau, "Vocational Guidance and Junior Placement: Twelve Cities in the United States," Bureau Publication 149 (Washington, DC, 1925), 93–275.

[36] If a first generation of psychologists helped institutionalize the tests, a second altered them in significant ways. Binary distinctions based on innate qualities, for example, a child was an "idiot" or he wasn't, and that was that, declined in favor. Intelligence tests continued, but they were notably more subtle – even the use of the term "ability groupings" indicates that. Categorizations – "superior," "moron," "imbecile" – fell out of favor, as psychologists embraced a more environmental view of aspects of intelligence and began to question whether intelligence was fixed. See Hamilton Cravens, "Child Saving in the Age of Professionalism, 1915–1930," in Joseph Hawes and Ray Hiner, Eds., *American Childhood* (Westport, CT, 1985), 415–88.

[37] "Self–inhibition" was a "clear" characteristic of intelligent people. Descriptions of the test can be found in Guy Montrose Whipple, Ed., *Intelligence Tests and Their Uses: The Nature, History and General Principles of Intelligence Testing and the Administrative Use of Intelligence Tests*, Twenty-First Yearbook of the National Society for the Study of Education (Bloomington, IL, 1923), 39.

people live on the work of others; (5) Good men tell us we should work."[38]
Pity the poor child who did not choose the correct answer: number four.
His or her school records would include the notation: "doubtful intellectual
honesty."[39] As the psychologist Edwin Baring admitted in 1923, "Intelligence
as a measurable capacity must at the start be defined as the capacity to do
well in an intelligence test."[40] At least he was being intellectually honest.
Rarely were his colleagues as forthright.

After the 1930s, fewer school systems openly tested for intelligence. Instead, they examined for "ability" and organized students into "ability
groupings." The change meant little, even if softer words replaced the early-
twentieth-century's stark divisions into "defectives," "inferiors," "normals,"
and "superiors." "Superior" children continued to be white, native-born,
and relatively privileged. School psychologists remained a fixture of
American public education, and American kids continued to be tested. In
the early twentieth century, high percentages of the children of the poor
and recent immigrants scored in "subnormal" ranges. After the 1960s,
when American public schools finally began to desegregate, so did black
youngsters.

Despite a rising tide of criticism of testing's cultural, racial, class, and
gender biases, it remained "the bread and butter" of an influential group
of public school specialists.[41] Indeed, the numbers and percentages of psychologists employed by the nation's public schools steadily increased during
the last three decades of the century. During years of retrenchment, school
psychology was still a growth area. [42]

Indeed, the one half of high school students who were college bound
took more intelligence tests than ever. In 1948, the nonprofit corporation,
the Educational Testing Service (ETS), opened for business in Princeton,
New Jersey. In the decades to follow, dozens of other examinations joined
its first test battery, the Scholastic Achievement Test (SAT). Although ETS

---

[38] *Ibid.*, 40–41.
[39] *Ibid.*, 41. Another example of the bewildering quality of the Liao Test, which allowed for
    no deviation from the one "right" answer. Statement: "A kind word is better than a harsh
    word." Explanations: 1. A harsh word makes others unhappy. 2. A harsh word makes us
    disliked. 3. President Roosevelt said, "Speak Softly." 4. A harsh word is generally a hasty
    word. 5. Kind people succeed in life.
    (The child with "good moral judgment" was supposed to pick answer one.)
[40] Edwin Baring, "Intelligence as the Tests Test It," *The New Republic* 35 (1923): 35.
[41] For an interesting series of interviews conducted with school psychologists in the 1980s,
    see Carl Milofsky, *Testers and Testing: The Sociology of School Psychology* (New Brunswick,
    1989), quotation: 22. Psychologists Milofsky interviewed argued that, while they often had
    doubts about the validity of their results, without ability testing they would lose legitimacy
    and probably their jobs.
[42] J. M Heffron, "Intelligence Testing and Its Pitfalls: The Making of an American Tradition,"
    History of Education Quarterly, 31 (1991): 82–88.

took great pains to say otherwise, in fact the SAT was an IQ test.[43] Like all its predecessors, it best measured language fluency. And the notion that intelligence bore racial and ethnic tags persisted. In 1994, Rutgers University president Francis Lawrence created a firestorm when he let slip his view that few blacks had the "genetic, hereditary background" to earn high SAT scores.[44]

Indeed, American schoolchildren remained "the most thoroughly IQ tested in the world."[45] The consequences were enormous. The really extraordinary increases in U.S. high school attendance occurred in the early twentieth century, far ahead of parallel surges in other highly industrialized countries in Europe and Asia. There, substantial opportunities for publicly funded education past the elementary level came only after World War II. In some countries, American-style free schools for everyone never arrived.[46]

But mass access did not mean shared curriculums, as *The Cardinal Principles* had insisted it should. By the time most adolescents left the eighth grade, they had long since been divided into groups, ostensibly ranked by intelligence. In 1922, for instance, the Pittsburgh schools tested all first graders and assigned "defectives," "subnormals," and "low-grade normals" to special classrooms. After another round of group intelligence testing in the eighth grade, all pupils with poor scores were urged to take vocational courses.[47]

To a greater or lesser degree most American school systems followed Pittsburgh's model for much of the rest of the century. In 1919 Lewis Terman reassured that "inferiors were ... not necessarily undesirable members of

---

[43] For a provocative examination of the history of the SATs and the continuing importance of intelligence testing in American life, see Nicholas Lemann, *The Big Test: The Secret History of the American Meritocracy* (New York, 2000). Lemann focuses on the SAT's use as a sorting device for elite universities and on testing between 1945 and 1999. Thus, he misdates the importance of intelligence testing, writ large, to public policy. He says, for instance, that IQ testing was born of an "absolute mid-century faith in rationality" (quotation: 262). By the time Lemann begins his story the first great wave of intelligence testing in public schools had already peaked.

[44] Francis Lawrence quoted in Nicholas Lemann, "The Great Sorting," *Atlantic Monthly* 276 (1995): 88.

[45] *Ibid.* And as the century ended, controversies over IQ and its meanings continued unabated. Despite decades of experiments that suggested that racial, gender, or ethnic intellectual differences had less to do with heredity, and more to do with environmental advantage, notions of intelligence by group persisted. A 1990 poll of members of the American Psychological Association revealed that a majority of respondents believed black-white IQ difference to be a product of both genetic and environmental variation, compared to only fifteen percent who felt the difference to be due entirely to environmental variation. Asa Hilliard, "What Good Is This Thing Called Intelligence and Why Bother to Measure It?" *Journal of Black Psychology* 20 (1994): 430–44. (Results of poll: 438.)

[46] For discussions of the different approaches to high school training in other developed countries, see Patricia Albjerg Graham, *S.O.S: Sustain Our Schools* (New York, 1992), 22–23.

[47] United States Children's Bureau, "Vocational Guidance and Junior Placement," 288–93.

society."[48] But academic training for anyone who tested at or below 80 IQ was "just so much dead waste."[49] School leaders accepted his judgment. As a result, government-supported education originally meant to improve the skills of adults and already employed adolescents entered the high school curriculum.

Vocationalizing the School: 1920–1999

In 1906, Governor Hoke Smith of Georgia embarked on a national tour to promote one of his favorite causes – the improvement of life in rural America. What the country's farmers really needed, his stump speech said, was training in scientific agriculture.[50] County extension agents told Smith that the traditional southern diet of salt pork, corn meal, and molasses could be made much healthier if only farmers learned to cultivate cow peas. The lowly cow pea was not only nutritious; it enriched soil with nitrogen, the costliest ingredient in commercial fertilizers. A farmer who set aside acreage for cow peas would soon enjoy enriched soil good enough for profitable crops of wheat and cotton, as well as fodder for a cow or two.[51]

Hoke Smith and fellow believers thought that this kind of "vocational education" could transform a farmer's life. In 1911, Smith, as Georgia's new junior senator, took his crusade to Washington, DC, where he met Charles Prosser, the first secretary of the just-established National Society for the Promotion of Industrial Education. In Prosser, Smith found a ghostwriter with an even larger vision of vocational education's role in America. Prosser was largely responsible for the wording of both the Smith-Lever Act of 1914, which provided federal aid for agricultural extension work and the

---

[48] Lewis Terman, *The Intelligence of Schoolchildren* (New York, 1919), 133. The book enjoyed several reprintings and was a staple item on the shelves of school superintendents and principals in the 1920s. It is tempting to indulge in a little armchair psychological assessment of Terman himself. Born the twelfth of fourteen siblings in a struggling Indiana farm family, Terman was the family's only child to attend high school. After years spent teaching in rural Indiana one-room schools, Terman made an improbable leap. By dint of a cheeky letter writing campaign, he convinced G. Stanley Hall to mentor him to study for a PhD in psychology at Clark University. Would a six-year-old Lewis Terman have had the cultural background to have even tested "normal"? For biographical information on Terman, see JoAnne Brown, *The Definition of a Profession*, 68–71; Robert Church, "Educational Psychology and Social Reform in the Progressive Era," *History of Education Quarterly* 11 (1971): 390–405.

[49] Terman, *The Intelligence of Schoolchildren*, 288.

[50] William Camp, "Smith, Hughes, Page, and Prosser," *Agricultural Education Magazine* 10 (1987): 5–7.

[51] Hoke Smith and other early-twentieth-century champions of vocational education were much influenced by A. C. True, Director of the Office of Experiment Stations at the U.S. Department of Agriculture. For discussion of True's impact and the origins of vocational training, see "Memorandum of Interview, January 22, 1903," Records of the General Education Board (hereafter GEB), Series 1, Sub-series 5. Box 716, Folder 7385, RAC.

Smith-Hughes Act of 1917, which increased federal support for vocational education. The latter earmarked at least one third of federal aid for the establishment and support of "continuation schools." Any full-time worker between the ages of fourteen and eighteen could attend these schools, which Prosser imagined primarily as night-time institutions, where, two or three evenings a week, students took courses meant to improve workplace skills or basic literacy.[52]

For the next thirty years, Charles Prosser tirelessly championed publicly sponsored vocational education. But state departments of education and local school districts never really accepted his idea of job-based training. In dozens of angry books, Prosser railed that vocational education was the "deserted child" of public education.[53] He would have been more accurate had he said, "kidnapped."

As the CCC and Job Corps demonstrated, and as Charles Prosser always said, there was no substitute for training on a real job. Practice in a classroom was a bad imitation. Ironically, compulsory education statutes thwarted truly effective vocational education. By 1920, a majority of states lengthened their school years and demanded full time attendance of all youngsters between the ages of six and sixteen. Although some codes accepted forms of "cooperative" education and gave academic credit for time spent during the week at a job, none embraced Prosser's model of a full time adolescent worker who was an occasional student. By the 1930s, the night continuation school for irregular students had metamorphosed into a five-days-a-week vocational "track" or, often, an entirely separate vocational high school that required regular daily attendance.

By the 1990s, nobody dared used the phrase "schools for inferiors" anymore, but budgets told the hard truth. For the 60 percent of American youngsters who matriculated, college became a transition between school and work. It even opened a road to success for the 30 percent of college entrants who actually were graduated. The education of this top one third was far more heavily subsidized, beginning in the junior high.[54] The vocational high school, with half or more of secondary students, was an underfunded

---

[52] For discussion of Prosser's influential as the author of Smith-Hughes, see John Gadell, "Charles Allen Prosser: His Work in Vocational and General Education" (PhD Dissertation, Washington University, 1972).

[53] Charles Prosser, *Have We Kept the Faith? America at the Crossroads in Education* (New York, 1929), 328. Prosser was a prolific author. Among his many books that repeated the theme, and sometimes the phrase, were: Charles Prosser, *Vocational Education in a Democracy* (New York, 1925); Charles Prosser, *Evening Industrial Schools* (Chicago, 1951); Charles Prosser and James Lincoln, *The Employer, The Employee, and the Job* (Omaha, 1940); Charles Prosser and Ronald Palmer, *Practice Book on Selecting an Occupation* (Bloomington, IL, 1936).

[54] For discussion of the relative levels of local, state, and federal subsidy for training of college-bound and non-college-bound youth, see Stephen Hamilton, *Apprenticeship for Adulthood* (New York, 1990), 5–19.

dead end. For many, such schools were holding pens, from which enrollees escaped after their sixteenth birthdays.

Specialized vocational high schools that trained intensively for one group of occupations were a proud tradition in some of the nation's largest cities. In these schools, teenagers prepared for specific careers. Some, such as New York City's celebrated High School for the Performing Arts, boasted impressive rosters of successful alumni. But the typical vocational high school in America was far different. School systems in America consolidated in the 1920s, but localities never ceded complete control. Outside of large metropolitan areas, most secondary vocational education programs trained students for a wide variety of jobs. Local superintendents resisted the creation of specialized, but centralized, vocational training open to students on a regional basis.[55]

Instead, "vo-tech" students usually stayed at home, attending a school in their own towns. Often the oldest, most nondescript building among a district's plant, the typical vocational high school was a two-story brick rectangle that lacked amenities common to its academic track counterpart. It rarely had an auditorium or a gym. It almost never offered its students a wide variety of extracurricular programs. A school band or football team was an oddity.

Between the 1930s and the 1990s, vocational curriculums changed little. Students generally spent one half of their days taking academic courses: English, social studies, or math. Fulfilling Lewis Terman's expectations with a vengeance, such classes emphasized rote repetition. In 1990, one critic charged that the average American graduate of a vocational high school read at the fifth-grade level.[56]

The afternoons at a "vo-tech" were devoted to "shop." Typically, students rotated through training in at least three different career paths, learning relatively little from any. Most training facilities were poorly equipped, most machines outdated. Students learned plumbing with the wrong tools and practiced TV repair on black and white sets. The computers they programmed were obsolete models. Auto shops were notoriously subject to unsolved burglaries.[57]

The kids themselves knew they were wasting their time. A survey in 1988 concluded that fewer than one half of vocational students thought they

---

[55] For decades, university-based vocational education specialists urged the adoption of such a model – with only one institution in a region or state providing training for a particular group of careers. The costs for such an idea, as well as the loss of local control, made a majority of school superintendents oppose it. See Charles Benson and Anette Lareau, "The Uneasy Place of Vocational Education," *Education and Urban Society* 15 (1982): 104–21.

[56] Hamilton, *Apprenticeship for Adulthood*, 95.

[57] *Ibid.*, 94–101.

would actually work in their field of training.[58] They were right. Most skilled nonprofessional workers in the United States learned on the job. Employers preferred to train their own workers but wanted applicants who were quick studies. As CCC Director J. J. McEntee knew, that meant they wanted to hire people with general skills. They wanted applicants who knew how to dress for work, how to interact with bosses and co-workers, and how to read and write. By isolating non-college-bound students, in whose ranks the poor and minority groups were always overrepresented, and then expecting less of them, vocational education actually worsened their chances of acquiring these essentials.

In striking contrast to many European countries, apprenticeship in the twentieth-century United States was an adult phenomenon. In Great Britain, France, and Germany craft apprentices were typically teenagers. In the United States, since the end of World War II, when businesses and unions gave preference to returning veterans, they were young adults. By the 1990s, in fact, they were over the age of twenty-six. Although the United States Occupational Census listed more than eight hundred jobs that recognized apprenticeship training, in fact, only a handful of building trades unions systematically employed the system. Even there, most American plumbers, carpenters, and masons reported that they learned their crafts informally, neither in a vocational school nor in an apprenticeship but, rather, by virtue of family contacts or chance encounters.[59] Tellingly, white collar work provided better on-the-job training than did the trades for which many vocational schools supposedly prepared their students.

Compulsory education law allied with applied psychology condemned millions of American teenagers to several years of meaningless schooling. Lewis Terman was a notorious fretter, a near-sighted, nervous man who neither physically nor emotionally fit his fellow eugenicists' descriptions of a classic "superior." Throughout his life, he kept meticulous count of colleagues who slighted him and wondered endlessly whether he would leave a legacy.[60] He certainly did, although not the one he envisioned. For much of the twentieth century, American high school education offered the "vocationalized" curriculum he urged for all but for the mentally elite. The country was not the better for it.

Applied psychology's influence over American education policy did not end with an enduring division of schoolchildren into "subnormals,"

[58] *Ibid.*, 95.
[59] Beatrice Reubens, Ed., *Youth at Work: An International Survey* (Totowa, NJ, 1983); Robert Glover, *Apprenticeship Lessons from Abroad* (Columbus, OH, 1985); E. Kevin Kelloway, "Preemployment Predictors of Union Attitudes: Replication and Extension," *Journal of Applied Psychology* 79 (1994): 631–34; J. A. Klerman and L. A. Karoly, "Young Men and the Transition to Stable Employment," *Monthly Labor Review* 117 (1994): 31–48.
[60] Brown, *The Definition of a Profession*, 68–69.

"normals," and "superiors." Between the 1940s and the 1960s, schools first meant as laboratories of democracy promoted another goal: school was for personal adjustment.

Life Adjustment Education

Once again a U.S. Commissioner of Education forged ties with university theorists and state education bureaucrats and engineered an improbable policy coup. In 1918, the *Cardinal Principles* urged that schools mold future citizens. Between 1944 and 1955, the still-small U.S. Office of Education blessed another widely influential new set of goals for American education, and, led by Commissioner John Studebaker, the Office vigorously promoted "life adjustment education." Even though critics damned the movement from its inception, only in the 1980s did a sufficiently strong backlash develop to engender another round of recommendations for policy change.

Between 1944 and 1948 many of the movers and shakers in American education circles were on the road – attending a series of conferences on the problems facing American schools. Offices in state education departments, school superintendents' headquarters, and certainly at Teachers' College, emptied as their occupants converged on Chicago, Sacramento, Birmingham, and New York City to discuss education policy and the American high school. They even managed to include a week of hand-wringing and relaxation at a luxury resort in Cheyenne, Wyoming.

One well-known attendee was a now-elderly Charles Prosser. In his last years, the father of publicly financed vocational education essentially abandoned it. Instead, he urged fellow conferees to emphasize "life adjustment" for the "majority" of students of secondary school age for whom neither college preparatory offerings nor vocational training had been effective. Having inadvertently spawned one bad education policy, now Prosser intentionally initiated another.[61]

What did life-adjustment education propose? Its creators concluded that "at no time" in American history had so many of the country's adolescents been "so badly adjusted to life."[62] An entire generation of "nervous" teenagers were unprepared to assume their full responsibilities as family members.[63] The "keystone" to a revised secondary school curriculum was "psychological guidance – personal assistance to individual boys and girls with *all sorts* of personal problems."[64]

---

[61] For a review of these rounds of conferences, see "Life Adjustment Education for Every Youth," U.S. Office of Education, Bulletin 17-291 (Washington, DC, 1948), 14–20.

[62] *Ibid.*, 46.

[63] *Ibid.*, 69.

[64] *Ibid.*, 56. Emphasis in original.

"Life Adjustment Education for Every Youth," the U.S. Office of Education report that summarized the conferences of 1944–1948, created a mythical school district called "Farmville." In the ideal world of Farmville, teachers no longer prepared lesson plans alone. Rather, they worked with their students to create "fun" education. The Farmville Community High School adopted a new creed, with five dogmas: "(1) Less emphasis will be placed upon learning for marks and more on learning that is interesting; (2) Opportunities will be provided for cooperative group projects; (3) Use of awards and artificial recognition will be discouraged; (4) Teachers will no longer rely on fear and compulsion; (5) Pupils will participate in a wide variety of co-educational activities to establish relationships which will lead to intelligent selection of mates and to living happily with them."[65]

State departments of education had never really accepted Charles Prosser's ideas about vocational education, but they leaped to embrace his plans for life-adjustment. The National Commission on Life Adjustment Education, established in 1948, ostensibly was the creation of the U.S. Office of Education. However, John Studebaker had no money. Instead, he lobbied the heads of every state education department to provide funding and suggestions for commission membership. The vast majority did, and *Education for Life Adjustment*, like its predecessor, *Cardinal Principles*, represented the received wisdom of the country's most influential school superintendents, leaders of professional teachers' organizations, and state education department heads. As such, its recommendations carried weight and altered public high school curriculums around the country.[66]

Life educators emphasized process and discussion, not information.[67] Teachers of all subjects were to search for "personal" relevance. English instructors should assign literature that "illustrates the strengths and weaknesses of our group processes."[68] Dryden, Pope, Poe, and Cooper were

[65] *Ibid.*, 54.

[66] *Education for Life Adjustment: Its Meaning and Implementation*: Report of the National Commission on Life Adjustment Education for Every Youth (New York, 1950). The Commission's first report had a supplement, "Secondary Education for Life Adjustment of American Youth," Report of the National Commission on Life Education for Every Youth (New York, 1952).

[67] An extended period of home room could accommodate such discussions, as well as the showing of social guidance movies. Such films, when not a feature of home room, became commonplace in health classes. At least in some form, most school districts in the country embraced the educational movie as a new tool for life adjustment. The author, educated in rural Arkansas, remembers countless showings of "Soapy the Germ Fighter" and the classic "Cindy Goes to a Party." Perhaps these two films exhausted a poor district's budget? More affluent systems had more than three thousand social hygiene films from which to choose. For a discussion of the use of these films in life adjustment classrooms, see Ken Smith, *Mental Hygiene: Classroom Films, 1945–1970* (New York, 1999).

[68] "Secondary Education," 210.

out. Shakespeare stayed, but on probation. A teacher might introduce "Macbeth," but should "conclude the Macbeth unit" by asking students to write short stories "into which they projected a situation of unfairness which they had known in their own lives."[69]

Learning "some" of the world's history was desirable, but a teacher should choose "countries, areas, trends, and concepts that have the greatest utility for the world of today, recognizing that this means eliminating many things."[70] One "thing" not eliminated was home room.[71] Instead, around the country it was extended so that pupils could discuss "important personal problems." Sample topics? "(1) How can I become more popular?; (2) Am I normal?; (3) Is God a person?; (4) What causes pimples?"[72] Life educators loved such lists but never acknowledged the weirdly disproportionate nature of the questions.[73]

In the new order of life adjustment education the goals of "development of self-reliance," "safety education," "health education," and "promotion of confidence" ranked much higher than did "instruction in English grammar" or "training in mathematical processes."[74] Of course, the *Cardinal Principles* had not emphasized the importance of specific academic training, either. They outlined the crucial role the schools should play in creating civic-minded citizens who knew right from wrong. The *Cardinal Principles* wanted high school graduates to be worthy. Life adjustment education wanted them to be happy.

Opponents thought these kinds of priorities cheated American children: "The men who drafted our Constitution were not trained for the task by 'field trips' to the mayor's office and the county jail."[75] However, since they were not generally members of the education establishment, their angry disapproval only gradually gained general attention. Meanwhile, the movement had an impact. In 1987 Diane Ravitch and Chester Finn, then codirectors of the Educational Excellence Network, an organization created to lobby for greater academic content in public education, published the results of a nationwide survey of history and literature teaching in secondary schools.

---

[69] *Education for Life Adjustment*, 106.

[70] *Ibid.*, 124.

[71] Smith, *Mental Hygiene*, 1–36.

[72] "Secondary Education," 81–82.

[73] Critics, however, had a field day. The historian Arthur Bestor argued, "No incidental disclaimer could save me from the charge of disordered thinking if I offered the following as an inventory of my possessions: 1) library 2) sauce pan 3) umbrella 4) furniture 5) fountain pen 6) house and lot 7) doormat 8) automobile 9) clothing 10) lawnmower." *Educational Wastelands: The Retreat from Learning in Our Public Schools* (Urbana, IL, 1953), 87.

[74] *Ibid.*, 449.

[75] Bestor, *Educational Wastelands*, 64.

They asked the question, "What Do Our Seventeen Year Olds Know?" and answered, "appallingly little."[76]

Until the 1940s, kids on academic tracks studied history every year from kindergarten through twelfth grade. By the late 1980s, few states required more than one year of history instruction, even for their elite students. Often history was no longer even taught as a separate course, but instead was part of a "social studies" or "community living" unit. Not surprisingly, eleventh graders had only a vague grasp of which European nations explored and settled different parts of North America, had never heard of the *Federalist Papers*, were only fuzzily aware of the causes of the Civil War, and were unable to answer whether the Soviet Union in 1944 was allied with or opposed to Nazi Germany. They had seen a video of "Macbeth" but had not read the play and had never heard of T. S. Eliot or Homer.[77] Ravitch and Finn concluded that something was "gravely awry." American high school students were not "stupid," but they *were* "ignorant of important things that (they) should know."[78] These worried conclusions echoed those of an influential 1983 report whose title summarized its conclusions. The nation was "at risk" because the nation's schools were failing their students.[79]

The Standards Movement

The National Commission on Excellence in Education issued *A Nation at Risk* as its final report. Chaired by Secretary of Education William Bennett, the Commission concluded that a "rising tide of mediocrity" threatened to engulf the country.[80] The only way to make it to higher ground was to restore academic content to American public schooling. *A Nation at Risk* recommended that all high school graduates complete a curriculum that included, at a minimum, four years of English grammar and literature, three years of mathematics, three years of science, three years of social studies, and one half year of computer science.[81]

---

[76] Diane Ravitch and Chester Finn, *What Do Our Seventeen Year Olds Know?* (New York, 1987). The National Endowment for the Humanities funded the survey.

[77] *Ibid.*, 53–120. By the late 1980s, high school teachers too had an increasingly vague grasp of historical information, as state certification requirements gave more emphasis to pedagogy courses taught by university schools of education and less to content courses taught by other colleges. An increasingly smaller knowledge base characterized teachers, as well as students. By the 1990s, nationally, almost one half of teachers of social science units did not major or minor in a specific subject, like history. That was even more true of subjects with serious teacher shortages, especially math and science.

[78] *Ibid.*, 200–201.

[79] National Commission on Excellence in Education, *A Nation At Risk* (Washington, DC, 1983).

[80] *Ibid.*, 5.

[81] *Ibid.*, 17–18.

Politicians around the country enthusiastically accepted this call for tougher academic standards in high schools. It was a rare state governor who did not organize news conferences, appoint blue-ribbon panels, and promise to improve the quality of public education. Indeed, some governors, such as Tennessee's Lamar Alexander and Arkansas' Bill Clinton, made the issue the centerpiece of their policy agendas.[82] The air was thick with demands for a return to a time when all American adolescents could date the American Revolution and recite Homer. In fact, such a time had never existed. The early-twentieth-century laws that created the high school as a mass institution demanded attendance, not academic achievement, and the *Cardinal Principles* emphasized the inculcation of civic consciousness. There had never been an era when a majority of American teenagers completed a tough, academic curriculum.[83] Calls for a "return" to rigor suffused the late-twentieth-century standards movement. The goal itself was new.

Between 1983 and the 1997, however, standards-based education policy was overwhelmingly popular. In 1994 Congress approved the establishment of a new federal agency, The National Education Standards and Improvement Council, to encourage state development of "content standards," "performance standards," and "opportunity-to-learn" standards. By 1997, every state but Iowa imposed new regimes of standardized testing of academic content at regular intervals. A high school senior would not get a sheepskin without demonstrating an acceptable level of competence in math, science, and English. In the space of a decade "standards" education captured policy makers' imaginations everywhere.

By 1999, many were having second thoughts. Wisconsin was the first of several states to repeal a law that demanded that every student pass a standardized test in math and English grammar as a condition of high school graduation. When 91 percent of Arizona high school sophomores flunked a new statewide math test, the Arizona State Board of Education met in emergency session and agreed to cancel further testing indefinitely. In 1998, the Virginia Board of Education adopted new rules that obligated schools, as a condition of accreditation, to show that at least 70 percent of their students met state testing requirements by 2007. One year later, it abandoned the effort. In December 1999, only seven percent of the state's schools passed muster. Faced with the possibility of denying accreditation to the remaining 93 percent, the Board blinked. Instead, it established a considerably watered-down rule. Schools should "show progress." After Los Angeles school administrators calculated that they would have to hold back more

---

[82] For discussion of the responses to *A Nation at Risk*, see Diane Ravitch, "Standards in American Education," in Diane Ravitch and Maris Vinovskis, *Learning from the Past*, 180–85.

[83] Patricia Albjerg Graham makes this point persuasively in *S.O.S.: Sustain Our Schools*, 16–17.

than one half of the city's tenth and eleventh graders if they ended "social" promotion through the grades, they waffled and announced that the whole issue needed further thought.[84] In 1989, before the testing bandwagon really picked up steam, the sociologist Jackson Toby sardonically warned that its unexpected consequence might well be "twenty-seven-year-olds huddled in high school classrooms because they cannot yet multiply two-digit numbers."[85] A decade later, policy makers everywhere faced that prospect and beat a retreat.

In 1999, investigators in New York City unearthed evidence of the country's most widespread effort to cheat on standards tests. The thirty-two schools, dozens of teachers, and two principals indicted were "probably only the tip of the iceberg." Teachers who erased mistakes, flashed kids palm cards, or in some cases simply passed out mimeographed copies of answer sheets, claimed that they were only following their bosses' tacit – but well-understood – demands.[86] If the kind of cheating unearthed in New York City was indeed common in other parts of the country, yet great numbers of high school students still failed to pass tests, the standards movement faced high hurdles.[87]

The century began with a new policy expectation – that adolescents stay in school longer. It ended with little agreement about what they should be doing there. Critics charged that, "after decades of endless gold stars, happy faces, and inflated grades" American parents were not ready for a "reality check about how much our schools are really teaching."[88] Middle-class parents did fret about the "excessive pressure" their children faced, but opposition to standards-based education created odd alliances between suburban soccer moms and residents of inner-city slums, as minority groups argued that blacks and Hispanics failed the tests at disproportionately higher rates and that graduation testing was a "sad blow for civil rights."[89]

---

[84] Jacques Steinberg, "Academic Standards Eased as a Fear of Failure Spread," *New York Times*, December 3, 1999.

[85] Jackson Toby, "Coercion or Choice?" *Public Interest* 96 (1989): 133.

[86] Anemona Hartocollis, "Liar, Liar, Pants on Fire," *New York Times*, December 12, 1999.

[87] As the critic Richard Rothstein noted, "passing" or "failing" a standardized test in the 1990s was often less straightforward than it seemed. Most states set up panels to evaluate questions and establish minimums for "passing." However, the level of difficulty of test questions varied greatly from state to state, as did the percentage of right answers needed to succeed. Some states set the mark as low as 50 percent, while others established a much higher ratio of wrong to right – 70 percent or higher. Students judged as "lacking reading competence" in one district, or one state, might pass easily in another, and experts debated exactly what "reading and math competence" meant, even what "competence" meant. Richard Rothstein, "In Standardized Tests, Standards Vary," *New York Times*, July 18, 2001.

[88] Charles Sykes, "Soccer Moms v. Standardized Tests," *New York Times*, December 6, 1999.

[89] Numerous challenges to standardized testing clogged the courts. In Texas, for instance, a

When education officials in many states rejected substitutes for standard-ized tests, vocational high schools around the country began, quite liter-ally, to close up shop. Some systems eliminated vocational education al-together. Others further restricted the variety of trades for which training was available. However, few realized the implicit promise of the standards movement: that all students would graduate with competence in academic subjects. Chuck Merten, who taught plumbing at New York City's Edison Vocational High until 1999, when the program disappeared, said, "You go along, not paying attention to the aches and pains, and then you wake up one day, and you say, 'Oh, my God. I am really sick.' That's where we are."[90]

If standards education signaled a decline in the "vocational track" it also indirectly challenged another early-twentieth-century education pol-icy: the idea that public school curriculums should be the model for all education. If schools could not meet standards, why shouldn't pupils de-camp? In the 1980s and 1990s many school districts established taxpayer-financed voucher programs that paid tuition at private schools. Since a majority of these institutions were parochial, vouchers raised controver-sial issues about separation of church and state. Judicial rulings promised no quick solutions. Some courts upheld plans that allowed taxpayer money to defray certain costs of attendance at private, religious schools. Others called vouchers unconstitutional "government-sponsored religious indoctrination."[91]

The 1924 *Pierce* decision guaranteed parents the right to enroll offspring in publicly accredited private schools. But the end-of-the-century debates about choice were different. They raised basic questions about the future and value of compulsory public education. Some feared that vouchers would siphon essential resources and the best students from the public schools. Others charged that they would push public education to improve or die. Students, they argued, must be allowed to vote with their feet.[92]

In truth, significant percentages always had. That raises a final question that an assessment of the impact of compulsory education policy should consider. How did students and teachers respond?

federal judge ruled a statewide graduation test constitutional but critics vowed to appeal, arguing that testing placed minority students at extreme disadvantage because they usu-ally attended schools with fewer resources. Jim Yardley, "Texas Graduation Test Ruled Constitutional," *New York Times*, January 8, 2000.

[90] Quoted in Sarah Kershaw, "Schools Turning from Teaching the Trades," *New York Times*, June 22, 2000.

[91] "Voucher System Unconstitutional in Ohio, Judge Says," *New York Times*, December 21, 1999.

[92] For discussions of late-twentieth-century debates about school choice, see Paul Peterson, "The New Politics of Choice," in Diane Ravitch and Maris Vinovskis, *Learning from the Past*, 215–40; Clifford Cobb, *Responsive Schools, Renewed Communities* (San Francisco, 1992).

How Teachers Taught; What Students Thought

A review of compulsory education reveals it, overwhelmingly, to be top-down policy making, shaped by cadres of school administrators and their allies who rarely spent much time consulting teachers, parents, or children themselves. Authorities who spent their days outside classrooms made most of the important decisions affecting what went on inside them. They determined how many and which students should be in class. They established standards for promotion or expulsion. They determined the length of the school day and year. They chose the textbooks. They demanded standardized tests or abandoned them. They determined a teacher's courses and reviewed her lesson plans. They bought the furniture and lights.

Teachers, in contrast, decided whether students could talk, stand up, or work in groups. They emphasized certain parts of their assigned subject matter. They sometimes chose from an array of instructional materials: would students see a video? use a computer? read the first story or the second?[93] Clearly, the match-up was uneven.

Nonetheless, any analysis of policy making should note the flexibility that usually marks implementation. That certainly was true for compulsory education. In a century marked by the rise of the public high school and periodic tidal changes in preferred curriculums, there was considerable continuity in how teachers taught.

Most teachers were relative beginners at school systems in flux from top to bottom. If the dedicated teacher who spent a lifetime in one classroom was not completely mythical, she was certainly a statistical rarity, and always had been. Half of all beginning teachers left the profession altogether at the end of their fifth years.[94] At the top, American school superintendents came and went with startling rapidity. By the 1990s average job tenure for the head of an urban school system was two years.[95] In the year 2000, the country faced a severe educator shortage. The last generation of women with professional options limited to teaching, nursing, and a few other fields retired, without ready replacements in sight, and over two million available teaching jobs remained unfilled.

Most of the nation's 120,000 public school principals began working in education in the early 1970s. Their median age was fifty. In the 1990s, they retired in droves. Robbe Brook, a superintent of schools in central Vermont, noted that districts wanted principals to "... have a legal background and a business sense, to know children and child development [theory], plus statistics, accounting, and certainly, technology."[96] It was a tough bill to fill,

[93] Larry Cuban makes this point in his excellent *How Teachers Taught: Constancy and Change in American Classrooms, 1890–1990* (New York, 1993), 263.

[94] *Ibid.*

[95] Graham, *S.O.S.: Sustain Our Schools*, 38.

[96] Quoted in Jacques Steinberg, "Nation's Schools Struggling to Find Enough Principals," *New York Times*, September 3, 2000.

especially since persons with such impressive talents could usually command much higher salaries in another occupation.

That reality necessarily colored the way any educational innovation moved from plan to practice. Newcomers just learning the ropes filled the teachers' lounge, the principal's office, and the superintendent's suite. Teachers' and administrators' faces changed, but their genders remained relatively constant. At the end of the century, as at its beginning, most public school teachers were still poorly paid, inadequately trained women and most administrators still men, although the latter group was less uniformly male.[97]

In 1900, a teacher typically expected her students to enter and exit her classroom in unison and to spend most of their time sitting at desks bolted to the floor. Except for periods devoted to student recitation, teachers did most of the talking. Despite vocationalism's emphasis on practical training or life-adjustment's emphasis on group activities, that, in large part, remained the way teachers taught. Behind their classroom doors, they continued to do most of the talking, lecturing, explaining, and demonstrating, while students primarily listened and watched.

By the 1990s, desks were rarely attached in fixed positions, and students did not march to classes. Relationships between students and teachers were decidedly more informal. Much had changed, but more had stayed the same. And in most schools throughout the country teachers, many of them quite inexperienced, struggled to master the accouterments of policy – the texts and tests and lesson plans assigned them. Selective implementation was inevitable.

There was probably an even larger gap between what teachers said and what students heard, although few education specialists tried to examine

---

[97] In the 1990s, when the nation faced significant shortages of teachers, especially in mathematics and science, the salary gap between teachers and other professionals of the same age and with the same level of education only grew, and salary disparities increased with additional training. For example, the average salaries for master's degree recipients outside of teaching increased by $17,500 from 1994 to 1998, while the average salary of teachers with master's degrees rose by less than $200. While administrators talked about the need to improve teacher training, only nine states required middle school teachers to pass tests in the subjects they taught. All the rest required "skills tests." In 1999, despite a decade of standards rhetoric, thirty-six states allowed teachers who had failed such tests to be hired anyway. Jacques Steinberg, "Salary Gap Still Plaguing Teachers," *New York Times*, January 13, 2000. At the end of the century, an international study compared 30 member nations of the Organization for Economic Cooperation and Development. The organization, based in Paris, concluded that U.S. teachers in the 1990s earned less relative to national income than their counterparts in many industrialized countries, yet spent many more hours in front of a classroom. As a percentage of average per capita income, teachers throughout Europe, in Australia, and in South Korea earned better average salaries and enjoyed greater respect. And in terms of pay relative to national average incomes, the U.S. fell even further behind its developed-nation counterparts in the 1990s. For a summary of the report, see Jodi Wilgoren, "Education Study Finds U.S. Falling Short," *New York Times*, June 13, 2001.

critically students' perspectives.[98] Clearly, however, formal schooling was only one source of training in a media-drenched twentieth-century United States. American children in the years before World War I grew up with the halftone photograph. Those who were youngsters at mid-century, as Miriam Van Waters lamented, were addicted to radio and the movies. By the end of the century, the United States, with 5 percent of the earth's population, managed to consume more than one half of all the world's advertising.[99]

Politicians and education leaders fought curriculum wars for decades. They spent less time discussing the growing role of corporate advertising not only outside schools, but right within them. Between 1970 and 2000 growing numbers of financially strapped public systems accepted company offers to provide worksheets, exercise plans, even texts, to use in school, not to speak of "news" television channels, which also carried ads. In the 1970s and 1980s, the Washington, DC, schools used health materials provided by the Kellogg Corporation. No one should have been surprised that Kellogg's pamphlets and filmstrips touted the virtues of eating cereal in the morning, although most nutritionists thought a kid might just as well down a couple of candy bars as consume a bowl of sugar-laden, ready-to-eat breakfast food.[100]

Students watched television in home room, then they went home for another dose. By the 1990s, the average American child had spent over twenty thousand hours in front of the box, and only eleven thousand in a classroom by the time he or she graduated from high school.[101] Kids weren't just watching television or exploring the Internet away from school. The Progressives' hope that the classroom would replace a paid job was only partially realized. In the last three decades of the century, significantly greater percentages of American adolescents worked than did their counterparts in any other developed country. They also did proportionally far less homework.[102] Any analyst who imagined that formal learning in classrooms was the only, or even the formative, influence on American children had some explaining to do. Nonetheless, twentieth-century education policy demanded that all youngsters between the ages of six and sixteen spend many of their daytime hours in school. Longitudinal studies that examine exactly what sorts

---

[98] David Cohen, "A Revolution in One Classroom," *Educational Evaluation and Policy Analysis* 12 (1990): 327–46.

[99] Joan Dye Gussow, "Who Pays the Piper?" *Teachers' College Record* 81 (1980): 449.

[100] *Ibid.*, 455–58.

[101] Stephen Kline, *Out of the Garden: Toys, TV, and Children's Culture in the Age of Marketing* (New York, 1993), 17.

[102] Given differences in labor statistics calculations, these numbers were always controversial, but a general estimate was that 70 percent of children in the U.S. between the ages of fifteen and nineteen worked, at least part time, contrasted to a number closer to about 30 percent for most European youngsters in the same age cohort, and about 20 percent for Japan and South Korea. Wilgoren, "Education Study Finds U.S. Falling Short," June 13, 2001.

of uses students made of this mandated activity are rare. We know more about what policy makers wanted, and what teachers taught, than we do about how American children actually utilized the institution of school. Students, however, did make one clear statement. Throughout the century, a percentage of them dropped out.

The incidence of truancy was always contested, and guesses ranged wildly. Even after the 1980s, when the school census was a universal bureaucratic routine, estimates varied. Some studies found that fewer than two percent of students who should have been in school had, in fact, left. Others publicized rates as alarmingly high as 30 percent.[103]

Until mid-century, school administrators did not really regard the dropout as a problem. They were too overwhelmed by the numbers crowding into their schools to worry very much about those who left. While most state compulsory education laws required attendance at school until the age of sixteen, most also allowed exemptions for children fourteen or over with valid working papers. No law demanded high school graduation. And nobody spent much energy reviewing work permits or looking for absentees.

State laws demanded that school systems establish procedures for recording attendance, but until the mid-twentieth century few made more than token efforts. Revealingly, a set of guidelines issued by the New York State Department of Education in 1935 noted that "Taking the school census is no job for anyone who is illiterate."[104] Only at the end of World War II did official attention focus on nonattenders. During the war, with significant percentages of the nation's eighteen- and nineteen-year-olds off in the service, younger teenagers found ample opportunities for paid work. At least two million additional adolescents entered the labor force.[105]

Six months after V-E Day, the proportion of adolescents enrolled in school was still lower than it had been in 1940. Worried that a teenage workforce might compete for jobs with returning veterans, policy makers tried to get large numbers from both groups to return to school – the veterans off to

---

[103] The huge discrepencies often came when figures collected by the National Center for Educational Statistics were misinterpreted. The Center distributed three different measures – event dropout rates, comparing the number of students at the beginning and end of a twelve month period; cohort dropout rates – the experiences of a single group of students; and status dropout rates – a composite of event rates summed over several years. See Joseph Kett, "School Leaving: Dead End or Detour?" 267.

[104] Walter Deffenbaugh and Ward Keesecker, "Compulsory School Attendance Laws and Their Administration," Bulletin 1935:4, United States Office of Education (Washington, DC, 1935), 30.

[105] For discussions of the surge in child labor during the war, see Ella Merritt and Floy Hendricks, "Trends of Child Labor, 1940–1944," *Monthly Labor Review* 60 (1945): 756–75; Gertrude Folks Zimand, "Child Workers in Wartime," Publication 386, The National Child Labor Committee (New York, 1942).

college or trade schools on GI loans, the teenagers back inside high schools –
in systems that enforced their truancy laws.[106]

Mandatory attendance laws remained as they had been written in the
early twentieth century, with school-leaving legal after age sixteen. But increasingly the dropout was defined not as an absent "underage" teenager.
Instead, he or she was anyone who failed to finish high school.

In the 1950s, dropouts emerged as a danger to society. Early-twentieth-
century educators assumed, generally correctly, that "school leavers" needed
to go to work. Their mid-century counterparts thought school leavers were
"social misfits ... with an emotional block."[107] The fact that most dropouts
still said they left school to find jobs meant nothing. They gave such answers, according to George Smith, Superintendent of Schools in Hollywood,
California, only to "save face."[108] They really failed to finish school, because
"they have never been satisfied with anything, and have never have [*sic*] had
any success in life."[109]

An early-twentieth-century education official would have been glad to
see the backs of such pariahs. But if school was for social adjustment, then
dropouts were the lost sheep most worth saving. For the rest of the century,
local, state, and federal governments spent tens of millions of dollars on
efforts to coax the unwilling to stay in school. Programs such as Job Corps
sought to provide a safety net for those who left anyway.

But not everyone accepted the idea that a dropout would soon be a jail
bird, despite the overwhelming popularity of the notion among policy makers. Nor did all analysts judge school leaving to be a ticket to oblivion.[110]
In the late twentieth century, most professional work demanded at least a
college degree. Luck and ambition, much more than a high school certificate,
determined success at all other sorts of enterprises.[111]

Policy recommendations about school attendance ran the gamut. Some
school boards began openly to discuss the problems caused by "stay-ins."

---

[106] Joseph Kett notes the worries at the end of the war about potentially disruptive conflicts between teenage workers and demobilized veterans, "School Leaving: Dead End or Detour?"
278–79.

[107] "Why Do Boys and Girls Drop Out of School and What Can We Do About It?" Work
Conference on Life Adjustment Education, Chicago, Illinois, January 24–27, 1950, Report
of Representatives of School Systems in Cities of More Than 200,000 Population, Circular
269, United States Office of Education (Washington, DC, 1950), 19–20.

[108] George Smith, quoted in *Ibid.*, 20.

[109] *Ibid.*, 21.

[110] There was one very troubling exception to this generalization. Black male high school dropouts did end up in prison in remarkably high numbers. In 1998 29 percent of the nation's
black male high school dropouts were employed. Far more, 41 percent, were in prison. Peter
Kilborn, "Ex Convicts Straining U.S. Labor Force," *New York Times*, March 15, 2001.

[111] Graham Lower and Harvey Krahn, "Reconceptualizing Youth Unemployment," in Julian
Barling and E. Kevin Kelloway, *Young Workers: Varieties of Experience* (Washington, DC,
1999), 201–33.

Some formulated expulsion policies for teenagers who came to school – only to engage in a range of misbehaviors – from carrying weapons to sleeping in home room. Indeed, during the 1990s high school detentions, suspensions, and permanent expulsion rates exploded, jumping tenfold between 1995 and 1999 alone.[112]

But paralleling this phenomenon was another. If schools were throwing record numbers of students out, they also were beefing up truancy enforcement. Around the country, public school administrators teamed up with prosecutors and threatened parents of children who chronically skipped school with fines and jail time. And, unlike early-twentieth-century officials, they meant it. Parents in several states found themselves serving from sixty to ninety days in the slammer when they failed to heed repeated warnings to get their kids to school. Some districts tried another approach, one many prosecutors claimed to be even more effective.

Truants learned that their parents were "sentenced" to school, required to sit next to their child all day in each class. Michael Godwin, district attorney of Escambia County, Alabama, explained, "The kids don't care that their parents go to jail, but they do not want a parent in the classroom. That strikes fear in their hearts."[113] The half-dozen states that followed West Virginia's 1986 example did something even more terrifying. They created "no-pass, no-drive" laws that withheld car keys from school dropouts.[114]

At the least, the messages sent were mixed. Some even suggested that the creators of early-twentieth-century compulsory education were right all along. There was no good reason for teenagers to stay in school past the age of sixteen. Bard College president Leon Botstein thought that elementary school should begin at the age of four and end at the sixth grade. The junior high should be abolished, to be replaced by four additional years of mandatory secondary education beginning with the seventh grade. Most American kids would be out of high school well before they reached their sixteenth birthdays.

"Adults," said Botstein, should "face the fact that they don't like adolescents, and that they have used high school to isolate (them) away from both the idealized innocence of childhood and the more accountable world of adulthood."[115] But the attempt wasn't working. In a culture that allowed children omnipresent exposure via computers, films, and television to life's raw realities, the worst thing possible for American kids was to force them

[112] Dirk Johnson, "Schools Are Cracking Down on Misconduct," *New York Times*, December 1, 1999.

[113] Robyn Meredith, "Truants' Parents Face Crackdown Across the U.S.," *New York Times*, December 6, 1999.

[114] Toby, "Coercion or Choice?" 135–36.

[115] Leon Botstein, "Let Teenagers Try Adulthood," *New York Times*, May 17, 1999.

to spend a few more years "sitting in a lunchroom with only their peers."[116] Botstein was one of a growing group of critics who challenged the twelve-year model for American public education, although others who also wanted students to complete high school before the age of sixteen called for additional changes in secondary education – the abandonment of the traditional long summer vacation or a lengthened school day that began at six in the morning and did not end until six at night.[117]

Interestingly, Botstein's call for public schooling to begin at the age of four had many supporters. While unsure about the content and value of compulsory education, Americans supported public programs of formal education for children at ever-younger ages. By the 1990s, politicians of many stripes made campaign pledges to introduce universal, tax-supported preschool. An idea abandoned in the mid-nineteenth century as a bad one returned with a vengeance: public education of "infants."

---

[116] *Ibid.*
[117] Daniel Mitchell and John Clapp, *Legal Constraints on Teenage Employment: A New Look at Child Labor and School Leaving Laws* (Los Angeles, 1979), 154–56.

6

The Return of the Infant School

Twentieth-Century Preschool Education

Both the high school and the preschool were nineteenth-century innovations. However, only after 1900 did either institution affect the lives of millions of American youngsters.[1] Early-twentieth-century American leaders thought expanded secondary education was crucial to democracy's survival. By the 1990s, many also supported public training of children aged two to five as "central to the future of American childhood."[2]

That claim stirred controversy but also illustrated another chain of connections between social science theory and social policy. Politicians who said that the early years were absolutely vital to child development repeated, although often in distorted ways, ideas first promoted by psychologists. Moreover, as had youth training programs, early childhood education initiatives failed to learn lessons from their predecessors, perhaps because few remembered that any existed.[3]

---

[1] This chapter defines "preschool" broadly: education for youngsters under the age of six, the age when most early-twentieth-century compulsory education laws demanded that American children begin mandatory attendance at a state-sponsored or state-approved school. However, for most of the century kindergartens were for four and five year olds, while nursery schools were for children under the age of four. When a specific type of "preschool" is discussed in these pages, that distinction will be noted. It is also true, however, that there was no absolutely uniform age cut-offs. The WPA "nursery" schools analyzed in this chapter enrolled many children older than three, and some "kindergartens" accepted children younger than four or older than five.

[2] Senator Edward Kennedy of Massachusetts made this statement about Head Start, in the context of remarks about the importance of early childhood education for all American youngsters. See Opening Statement of Senator Edward Kennedy, "Partners in Creating a 21st Century Head Start," Hearing before the Committee on Labor and Human Resources, United States Senate, One Hundred Third Congress, First Session (Washington, DC, 1994): 1 (hereafter Hearing, 21st Century).

[3] In 1998, for instance, Representative Christopher Shays welcomed Early Head Start as a program that, "For the *first* time joins the science of child development with the art of parenting." Neither he nor any other supporters of the new Head Start sibling seemed to realize that it

222

This chapter's analysis of twentieth-century educational policy for children under the age of six surveys the legacies of the 1921 Sheppard-Towner Maternity and Child Protection Act and the Works Progress Administration's (WPA) nursery schools, reviews the pivotal importance of the Head Start program and assesses a late-twentieth-century middle-class embrace of preschools. But early childhood education had nineteenth- and early-twentieth-century origins that, first, require a brief examination.

The Infant Schools

In the early nineteenth century, public officials, especially in New England, promoted "infant schools." Worried that Irish and German newcomers neglected the proper moral training of their children, Massachusetts, for instance, required towns of more than fifty families to establish classes for very young children, usually taught by respectable widows who otherwise might have needed alms. In such schools, which in 1840 enrolled an estimated 40 percent of the state's three-year-olds, toddlers learned to avoid "wickedness" – chiefly the sin of drinking.[4]

Infant schools sought to transform tiny children into the teachers of their own elders. Instructors proudly reported that their charges scolded fathers who reached for rum or mothers who danced on Sundays. The image of an innocent child saving a degenerate parent was central to Victorian Romanticism, but it could not trump another, the idea that children belonged at home with their mothers. By mid-century, the country's small minority of college-trained physicians turned against formal training of babies and toddlers. Small children's muscles and nerves easily tired, and the full-day sessions of infant schools imposed excessive strain. Indeed, insanity in adulthood might be their bitter long-term legacy.[5] By the time the Civil War

---

reinvented without acknowledgment the Sheppard-Towner Maternity and Child Protection Act of 1921. Statement of Representative Christopher Shays, "Early Head Start: Goals and Challenges," Hearing before the Subcommittee on Human Resources of the Committee on Government Reform and Oversight, House of Representatives, One Hundred Fifth Congress, Second Session (Washington, DC, 1998): 3 (hereafter Hearing, Early Head Start).

4 Even in Massachusetts, the state which most enthusiastically championed infant schools, ages varied. Most schools accepted children between age eighteen months and age five, though the great majority of children in attendance clustered in the middle of that range. Barbara Beatty, *Preschool Education in America: The Culture of Young Children From the Colonial Era to the Present* (New Haven, 1995), 23–27.

5 For discussions of the decline of the infant schools, see Caroline Winterer, "Avoiding a Hothouse System of Education: Nineteenth Century Early Childhood Education from the Infant Schools to the Kindergarten," *History of Education Quarterly* 32 (1992): 290–94; Maris Vinovskis and Dean May, "A Ray of Millennial Light: Early Education and Social Reform in the Infant School Movement in Massachusetts, 1826–1840," in Maris Vinovskis, *Education, Society, and Economic Opportunity*, 34–37. Vinovskis and May argue that the well-educated female reformers who helped found the schools in Massachusetts paid much closer attention

divided the country, physicians had won their war against infant schools. Most closed.[6]

Even when the German kindergarten movement gained American adherents after 1870, medical ideas about protecting young children from too much stimulation prevailed. Most among the fewer than 2 percent of the country's youngsters who attended were at least aged five and stayed away from home for no more than three hours, spent in supervised play, not stern moral instruction. Late-nineteenth-century kindergartens wore a Janus face. Some were charitable institutions, intended as cultural enrichment for poor children. Others enrolled the offspring of privileged mothers.

Complicating the picture was the presence of "day nurseries," philanthropies, which, as had the Cruelty, concentrated in cities in the Midwest and along the East Coast. Most founders of such nurseries did not view them as schools, but instead as safe, affordable places for working mothers to leave their young children.[7] However, the differences between caring for toddlers and teaching them remained unresolved. Moreover, no clear standard existed in the nineteenth – or twentieth – century for the ages of children suited to "nursery" or "kindergarten" training. Some kindergartens took children up to age seven, others accepted those as young as three. Nursery schools varied, too, both in goals and in ages of children enrolled. There was one constant: turn-of-the-century preschools were private. That fact did not signal ebbing interest in early childhood education. Indeed, early-twentieth-century child development specialists promoted such training as absolutely crucial. However, they focused on the need to educate small children by properly training their parents.

Parent Education and the Sheppard-Towner Act

Early-twentieth-century behavioral psychologists talked about the need to educate all parents, but mothers – bad mothers – earned their gimlet gaze. The pioneering child psychologist G. Stanley Hall approved of the kindergarten movement's emphasis on play. He and fellow Instinct theorists argued that until about the age of eight children should be left to develop as nature intended, unhindered by formal training. The discipline of child psychology was still itself an infant when John Watson, Edward Thorndike, and other Behaviorists attacked Hall's ideas and split the profession into warring camps. If Hall and his followers championed nature as the key to human

---

to physicians' attacks on infant schools than did the general public and withdrew their social and financial support.

[6] Barbara Beatty, *Preschool Education in America*, 101–03.

[7] For discussion of the nineteenth-century day nursery movement, see Sonya Michel, *Children's Interests/Mothers' Rights: The Shaping of American Child Care Policy* (New Haven, 1999), 51–59.

growth, their rivals argued that nurture was all-important, especially during the first five years, when a child's personality was uniquely plastic. By the onset of World War I, Behaviorism was in ascendance, and its concern about the inadequacies of American parenting won attention.[8]

John Watson, volatile and ambitious, soon abandoned the maternity wards of the Johns Hopkins University hospital, where he had been observing babies with the help of funding from the Laura Spelman Rockefeller Memorial.[9] Instead, between 1914 and 1928, he spent much of his time on the road, warning that "mother-love" was "dangerous."[10]

Icily dedicating his influential *Psychological Care of Infant and Child* to the "first mother who brings up a happy child," John Watson warned that "... once a child's character has been spoiled by bad handling – which can be done in a few days – who can say the damage is ever repaired?"[11] America's "overkissed" toddlers were on the road to ruin, and their mothers were to blame.[12]

Like psychologists, the social workers, home economists, and nutritionists at the United States Children's Bureau also were first-generation members of new professions. All were emergent specialties with amorphous identities in the early twentieth century. Behaviorism provided each with cachet and sent the urgent message that supervision of parents was vital to national well-being. Parent training was the subtext that linked a number of early-twentieth-century "child saving" campaigns. Juvenile courts were to act as "kindly fathers," when the real thing proved inadequate. "Lazy" fathers unwisely sent their sons and daughters into the mills. The "cruelists" anticruelty organizations attacked were usually a child's own parents. The

---

[8] For discussions of the early history of American child psychology, see Daniel Wilson, *Science, Community, and the Transformation of American Philosophy, 1860–1930* (Chicago, 1990); Keith Benson, Jane Maienschein, and Ronald Rainger, Eds., *The American Expansion of Biology* (New Brunswick, NJ, 1991); Hamilton Cravens, *Before Head Start: The Iowa Station and America's Children* (Chapel Hill, 1993); Milton Senn, *Insights on the Child Development Movement in the United States* (Chicago, 1975); Frank Kessel, Marc Bornstein, and Arnold Sameroff, Eds., *Contemporary Constructions of the Child: Essays in Honor of William Kessen* (Hillsdale, NJ, 1991).

[9] John D. Rockefeller Sr. created the Memorial in 1918 with a bequest of $74 million as a tribute to his late wife. For discussion of its patronage of the new field of child psychology, see Judith Sealander, *Private Wealth and Public Life, Foundation Philanthropy and the Re-Shaping of American Social Policy from the Progressive Era to the New Deal* (Baltimore, 1997), 79–100.

[10] "Mother-Love, Is it Dangerous?" was the title of Watson's stump speech. For a transcript, see "Conference on the Nursery School, April 22–23, 1927, at the Hotel Majestic, New York City," Remarks of Dr. John B. Watson, Records of the Laura Spelman Rockefeller Memorial (hereafter LSRM), Series 3.5, Box 31, Folder 330, RAC. Among Watson's best-known books were: *Psychological Care of Infant and Child* (New York, 1928); *Behaviorism* (New York, 1924); *The Ways of Behaviorism* (New York, 1928).

[11] Watson, *Psychological Care of Infant and Child*, x, 3.

[12] Ibid., 71.

Sheppard-Towner Act reiterated this unease about parental competence but focused its attention on females.

In late 1921, the United States Congress passed the Sheppard-Towner Maternity and Child Protection Act and charged the Children's Bureau with its administration.[13] Julia Lathrop, the politically savvy Chicago social worker who was the Bureau's first chief, masterminded the campaign that led to the bill's passage, just as she earlier engineered support for passage of the Keating-Owen Bill and the Child Labor Tax Act.

Since the Bureau's creation in 1912, Lathrop tirelessly promoted an especially emotionally charged cause: the need to reduce high American infant mortality rates. She and her small professional staff circulated reports annually that condemned a nation unwilling to curb "preventable" deaths of babies.[14] Beginning in 1919 the Bureau began publishing a "Maternal Mortality Thermometer," graphically depicting a list of sixteen developed countries, with the United States ranking below all but two in maternal and early childhood death rates.[15] Editors at the reform-minded journal *Survey* reprinted the Bureau's graphic regularly.[16]

The same year that the maternal mortality thermometers first appeared, a bipartisan team, Republican Representative Horace Towner of Iowa and Democratic Senator Morris Sheppard of Texas, introduced a bill to promote "the welfare and hygiene of maternity and infancy."[17] Sheppard and Towner, strong supporters of Prohibition, child labor restrictions, and the Children's Bureau itself, proposed a federal-state cooperative effort in which a federal panel, composed of the Surgeon-General, the Commissioner of Education, and the head of the Children's Bureau, supervised state boards of infant and maternal hygiene.

In 1919 Congress ignored the Sheppard-Towner bill. The Treaty of Versailles dominated discussion. Caught up in titanic struggles about America's role in a postwar world, politicians wrangled over the wording of the peace treaty President Woodrow Wilson brought home from France. By 1921, much had changed. Wilson was an exhausted, embittered former president, and the nation's interests turned inward, spurred by the victory of two

---

[13] For good overviews of the Act, see Kriste Lindenmeyer, *"A Right to Childhood": The U.S. Children's Bureau and Child Welfare* (Urbana, 1997), 76–107; Robyn Muncy, *Creating a Female Dominion in American Reform, 1890–1935* (New York, 1991), 93–123; Kristine Seifert, "An Exemplar of Primary Prevention in Social Work: The Sheppard-Towner Act of 1921," *Social Work in Health Care* 9 (1983): 87–102.

[14] See, for instance, the Bureau's compiled *Annual Reports* for the years 1914–1921, United States Children's Bureau, *Annual Reports* (Washington, DC, 1913–1922).

[15] For an example of these graphics, see United States Children's Bureau, "Save the Youngest: Seven Charts on Maternal and Infant Mortality, with Explanatory Comments," Publication 61 (Washington, DC, 1919).

[16] "Passage of the Maternity Bill," *The Survey* 47 (1921): 357–58. For a reproduction of one of the "Maternal Mortality Thermometers, see Photo 6.1.

[17] United States Senate, *Congressional Record*, Sixty-Sixth Congress, First Session, 1919: 6314.

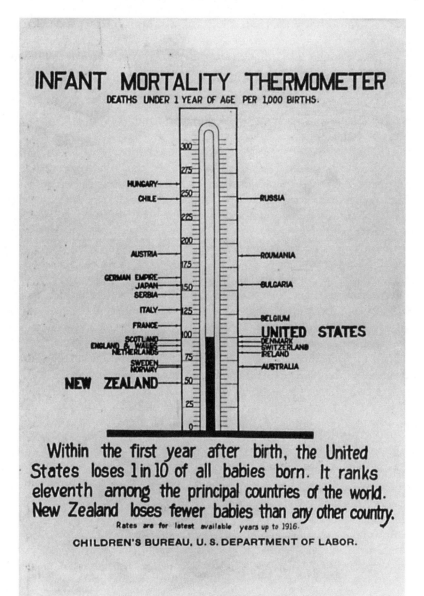

PHOTO 6.1   United States Children's Bureau, "Save the Youngest: Seven Charts on Maternal and Infant Mortality, With Explanatory Comment," *Children's Year Follow-up Series*, 2, Publication 61 (Washington, DC, 1920), Chart 1.

reform amendments to the United States Constitution, one banning alcohol, the other granting the vote to women. Uncertain about the ultimate impact of either, politicians wooed the "women's vote," convinced, at least temporarily, that it really existed. In this climate, a reintroduced maternity protection bill sailed to easy victory, just as did the Child Labor Amendment.[18]

Ironically, Republican Representative Alice Robertson of Oklahoma, the only female member of Congress in 1921, led the fight against Sheppard-Towner. Robertson, a fierce antisuffragist, excoriated the Children's Bureau's mortality thermometers as misleading "sob sister stuff." In a country where only twenty-three of forty-eight states required that births and deaths be registered, who really knew how many of America's youngest children died? "The number of babies the American Congress is murdering every year varies from 100,000 to 300,000, but then, as long as you are killing babies, why not kill a' plenty?"[19]

Robertson's sarcasm won few over, especially since, as supporters of Sheppard-Towner noted, the funds allocated were "a drop in the bucket."[20] Congress appropriated a total of $1,240,000 annually, a $5,000 minimum to go to each state, with an additional $5,000, if matched by state spending. Participating counties received, at most, a few hundred dollars a year to launch new programs. Like the mothers' pensions state legislators simultaneously rushed to approve, this, too, was "child-saving" on the cheap.

The Children's Bureau always described Sheppard-Towner as a "logical extension of the American principle of providing free public education," in part to counter opposition from physicians worried about intrusion onto their turf, in part out of firm belief that much information about the care and training of infants and young children was not necessarily medical.[21] Members of the wholly outnumbered group in Congress which tried to defeat Sheppard-Towner certainly found "socialized" medicine anathema.[22] Indeed, some thought that federally sponsored maternal education alone "...pushed the doors of American homes...wide open...to the parlor Bolshevists, boisterous birth controlists and voluntary parenthood priestesses" the Children's Bureau harbored.[23]

Bureau professionals did not promote Bolshevism, birth control, or, even, boisterous behavior. However, they did fervently champion Behaviorism's dictate that, from the moment of birth, parents had to be disciplined teachers

---

[18] The vote was 75 for 6 against in the Senate; 279 for 39 against in the House.

[19] Statement of Representative Robertson, United States House of Representatives, *Congressional Record*, Sixty-Seventh Congress, First Session, 1921: 7980.

[20] *Ibid.*, Statement of Representative Lea, 7988.

[21] United States Children's Bureau, "The Promotion of the Welfare and Hygiene of Maternity and Infancy," Publication 186 (Washington, DC, 1928), 4.

[22] Representative Caleb Layton of Delaware, a physician, worried publicly that "a cloud of amateurs" would be teaching lessons best left to trained doctors. *Ibid.*, 7928.

[23] Statement of Samuel Winslow, *Ibid.*, 8013.

of their own children. Programs varied within and among states, though in most regions efforts concentrated on giving information to new parents in small towns and isolated rural areas. Only Massachusetts refused to partici-pate.[24] While male physicians connected to state health departments directed Sheppard-Towner work in most states, the effort's most typical "teacher" was a female nurse.

During the program's seven-year lifetime an annual average of 750 nurses worked around the country as home visitors, talking one-on-one each year to over eight hundred thousand mothers with newborns and toddlers. About the same number of social workers and nurses worked part time as "conference" organizers. In each case, Sheppard-Towner funds paid a portion of their salaries, with the rest supplied by state or county public health services. Driving "health cars" loaded with films, charts, posters, and pamphlets, these women circled town squares, using bullhorns to urge people to come to a school gymnasium, the town hall, a room at a library, even, on occa-sion, a ballfield or a playground. There they used blankets, sheets, sometimes the odd overcoat, to create temporary examination rooms. Nurses inspected mothers and babies and urged the parent of any child suspected to be ill to take her to a physician, but medical care was ancillary to Sheppard-Towner workers' main mission. Whether inside a makeshift cubical, at someone's kitchen table, or in front of a crowd in a city park, they told their over-whelmingly female audiences how to promote the "normal" development of very young children.[25]

They preached from a Behaviorist's canon that sanctified "habit forma-tion." Babies at three weeks could learn to take food at regular hours by-the-clock and to be satisfied when fed only at those times. Mothers had to be "invariably firm" about feeding, and everything else, since a touchstone of successful parenting was "constant discipline." It protected a child from the formation of bad habits and taught "...him fundamental lessons of self-denial."[26]

The years of early childhood were formative, a time when proper train-ing by parents "stamped the permanent pattern of [a child's] mind and

---

[24] Massachusetts played an interesting role in childhood policy, as an innovator of child labor law and compulsory education campaigns in the mid-nineteenth century, then, as a bitter opponent of federalized child labor law and health care initiatives in the early twentieth century. It produced several important (all female) antisuffragists. At the same time it was also the state that provided the most generous funding for its mothers' pensions. Policymaking in Massachusetts provides a good example of one of this book's themes: federalism has remained a powerful ideological principle throughout the twentieth century, and its advocates were by no means only southerners or interested only in racial issues.

[25] United States Children's Bureau, "The Promotion of the Welfare and Hygiene of Maternity and Infancy," 10–13.

[26] United States Children's Bureau, "Child Care: The Preschool Age," Care of Children Series 3, Publication 30 (Washington, DC, 1918), 47.

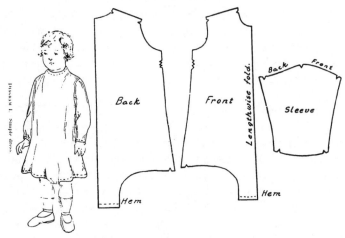

PHOTO 6.2   United States Children's Bureau, "Child Care: The Pre-School Age," *Care of Children Series 3, Publication 30* (Washington, DC, 1918), 31. Reproduction of a pattern for a toddler's playsuit later included in materials distributed by Shepphard-Towner "nurse educators."

character."[27] Children's Bureau *Bulletins* emphasized that "parents were a child's first and most important teachers." It was a durable slogan, used by generations of policy makers, many of whom doubtless did not know its source.

Viewing mothers as babies' first teachers, the Sheppard-Towner program dispensed all sorts of useful advice – along with Behaviorism's sterner messages about the dangers of excessive maternal indulgence. Home visitors gave inexperienced, young women paper patterns for inexpensive play smocks for toddlers; they left drawings of the proper way small feet should fit in shoes; they shared instructions for learning games using homemade wooden blocks.[28] Why did Congress kill such a program in 1929?

Most scholars have emphasized organized medicine's adamant opposition, but that provides an insufficient explanation. Sheppard-Towner's home visitors did not openly challenge physicians' authority. They urged that parents immunize their children against smallpox and diphtheria, but they did not bring needles and antitoxin serums in their bags. In fact, other than making rudimentary physical inspections of pregnant women, new mothers, and young children, Sheppard-Towner "nurse-teachers" always deferred to physicians.

Certainly the American Medical Association wanted Sheppard-Towner abolished, arguing that advice about care of mothers and young children

[27] *Ibid.*
[28] *Ibid.*, 40–43. For an example of these kinds of Bureau patterns, see Photo 6.2.

was a state and local, not a federal, function. Nonetheless, the majority of American physicians did not belong to the AMA.[29] The story of Sheppard-Towner's repeal is more complex. The 1921 bill authorized funding for only five years. By 1927, the AMA was not the only national organization which denounced federally supervised health care education. As the Child Labor Amendment stalled at the state level, fear of the "women's vote" vanished. Indeed, the Child Labor Amendment, condemned from Catholic pulpits as an unwarranted assertion of government control over parents' choices, may have encouraged national Catholic leaders to change their minds about Sheppard-Towner. Father John O'Grady, Secretary of the National Conference of Catholic Charities, originally favored the initiative. By 1927, however, he had decided that, like the proposed Twentieth Amendment, Sheppard-Towner threatened to put public officials in control of American childrearing.[30]

Proponents of both the Child Labor Amendment and the Sheppard-Towner Act wanted a dramatically increased federal role in social policy making. Facing the specter of millions of women voting them out of office, cowed Congressmen sent the Child Labor Amendment to the states and authorized Sheppard-Towner. By 1927, the amendment floundered, as did Sheppard-Towner. Influential state governors such as Democrats Albert Ritchie of Maryland and Al Smith of New York argued that the federal/state cost sharing arrangement embodied in Sheppard-Towner was unwise. The promotion of health, the training of preschool children, and the control of child labor were, and should remain, the domain of state and local governments.[31]

Confronting growing opposition, Morris Sheppard compromised. His reappropriation bill provided funding for only two years.[32] Sheppard and his supporters thought that well before June of 1929, they could regroup and get the votes necessary for another reauthorization. They misjudged the opposition. With no support from President Herbert Hoover, the Sheppard-Towner Maternity and Infancy Protection Act died.

[29] Kriste Lindenmeyer notes that some pediatricians initially broke ranks with other doctors and supported Sheppard-Towner's passage in 1921, but she does not record their change of heart after 1926, as the educational materials distributed by the program vigorously promoted breastfeeding as absolutely the best form of nutrition for children during their first year of life and threatened the authority of the fledgling specialty of pediatrics, whose practitioners often advocated formula feeding. Kriste Lindenmeyer, "*A Right to Childhood*," 85–86; for discussion of pediatricians' championship of bottle feeding, see Rima Apple, *Mothers and Medicine: A Social History of Infant Feeding, 1890–1950* (Madison, 1987).

[30] For a summary of reasons for Catholic opposition, see "Uncle Sam in the Nursery," *America* 36 (1927): 368–72.

[31] United States Senate, *Congressional Record*, Sixty-Ninth Congress, Second Session (1927): 1583–85.

[32] *Ibid.*, 1584.

Hoover, as a former president of the American Child Health Association, was a seasoned supporter of public health education. However, in the spring of 1929, he decided to rethink Sheppard-Towner. It fell victim to his ambitious plans for a thorough reorganization of the federal bureaucracy. The president wanted his Secretary of Interior, Ray Lyman Wilbur, to act as a kind of "super" Cabinet official on domestic policy, just as Hoover himself had earlier done at Commerce under Presidents Harding and Coolidge. Wilbur, a prominent physician, had always opposed Sheppard-Towner, and, like Hoover, was no friend of the Children's Bureau.

No small point: in the 1920s Herbert Hoover and Grace Abbott were two of the country's most famous "child savers." Like the larger alliance they represented, they epitomized odd fellowship. Personally, they despised each another. Grace Abbott's accession to the leadership of the Children's Bureau, as replacement for Julia Lathrop, only strengthened Hoover's resolve to gut his enemy's agency and give the U.S. Public Health Service authority over children's health.[33] He did not do so, but primarily because, after the great crash of the stock market in October 1929, reorganization of minor federal agencies no longer was a major administration priority.[34]

What did Sheppard-Towner accomplish? Even supporters were hard-pressed to cite precise achievements. The work varied from state to state, even county to county. Apart from statistics that totaled the numbers of home visits made or "health cars" on the road, no state rigorously evaluated Sheppard-Towner's impact. The program, after all, provided a miniscule fraction of the sums spent on health education in the early twentieth century. In the 1920s, the American infant mortality rate dropped, though maternal deaths associated with pregnancy did not.[35] In fact, they rose, before beginning a long-term decline in the 1940s. At most, the Sheppard-Towner Act

---

[33] Grace Abbott thought that Hoover was a charlatan, who pretended to be a friend of children. She was too harsh, but there was some truth to her charges. Privately she always called Hoover the *"great, great humanitarian,"* meaning just the opposite. For the story of Hoover's unsuccessful attempts to strip the Children's Bureau, see Judith Sealander, *Private Wealth and Public Life: Foundation Philanthropy and the Reshaping of American Social Policy, from the Progressive Era Through the New Deal* (Baltimore, 1997), 154–59.

[34] Efforts to take away many of the Children's Bureau's functions continued through 1930, however, and the Hoover White House Conference on Child Health and Protection included a real cat fight among supporters and opponents of the Children's Bureau. Hoover underestimated the redoubtable Grace Abbott, but Abbott was also fortunate that Hoover was mightily distracted in 1930.

[35] Many public health experts credited some of the reduction in infant mortality during the 1920s to rapidly growing acceptance of pasteurization of milk. As the prominent Yale public health physician C. E. A. Winslow remarked, "It is an easy matter for a germ to get by a (city milk) inspector, but to escape being cooked at the gates of the city is quite another proposition." "Pasteurization *v.* Milk Inspection in New York," typscript, C. E. A. Winslow Papers (hereafter Winslow), Record Group 749, Box 33, Folder 21, Yale University Archives, New Haven, CT (hereafter Yale).

provided a few federal dollars and national sanction to aid an important public health crusade that was overwhelmingly a local one, led not from Washington but from the offices of municipal public health physicians.[36] Sheppard-Towner's defeat was not so much a victory for the AMA as it was a signal of Congressional satisfaction with that political arrangement.

Finally, were the mothers who received counsel from Sheppard-Towner's visitors "educated" in accordance with the Children's Bureau's wishes? There is no clear answer to that question. Not even selective surveys exist. However, one body of evidence hints at the ways mothers may have used the parent education offered them. Over the years, thousands sent letters to the Children's Bureau, expressing gratitude for specific, practical advice – how to bathe a baby, when to express breast milk, what to feed for lunch.[37] If mothers also followed Behaviorism's habit formation techniques, so important to Children's Bureau advisors, they did not mention it.

During the 1920s many urban middle-class women enthusiastically joined "child-study" clubs, and collectively plunged into nerve-wracking discussions of proper ways to suppress their toddler's "autoerotic" thumb-sucking. They learned that letting a two-year-old take a toy to bed indulged a "sloppy habit" and encouraged future adult selfishness. They followed John Watson's advice to strap infants at the age of eight months to toilet seats and leave them alone until the babies produced results.[38] They kept elaborate charts of kisses stingily given.[39]

However, it is doubtful that the rural, working-class mothers Sheppard-Towner's champions thought most in need of Behaviorism's lessons took them much to heart. After all, only the prosperous could afford the kind of infant care John Watson demanded. He and other Behaviorists specified physical child care arrangements totally out of reach of the average family. How many homes were big enough to give each child *and* his maid a separate room in which to sleep?[40]

---

[36] This is a point made by numerous historians of public health and medicine. See Richard Meckel, *Save the Babies: American Public Health Reform and the Prevention of Infant Mortality, 1850–1929* (Baltimore, 1990); Nancy Tomes, *The Gospel of Germs*; Georgina Feldberg, *Disease and Class: Tuberculosis and the Shaping of Modern North American Society* (New Brunswick, NJ, 1995).

[37] Molly Ladd-Taylor has edited a representative sample of these letters written between the years 1915 and 1932. See Molly Ladd-Taylor, Ed., *Raising a Baby the Government Way: Mothers' Letters to the Children's Bureau* (New Brunswick, NJ, 1986). The entire group of letters can be found in the Records of the Children's Bureau, National Archives, Suitland, Maryland.

[38] John Watson, *Psychological Care of Infant and Child*, 94–123.

[39] For the child-study movement in the 1920s, see Julia Grant, *Raising Baby by the Book: The Education of American Mothers* (New Haven, CT, 1998), 39–70.

[40] Separate sleeping rooms for each child in the family were, for John Watson, crucial to proper training. John Watson, *Psychological Care of Infant and Child*, 120.

After Sheppard-Towner's defeat, state sponsorship of efforts to train the country's youngest children and their parents was distinctly a low-priority issue. The fact that the WPA justified several thousand "emergency" nursery schools as relief work for unemployed teachers illustrates that fact.

The WPA Emergency Nursery Schools

By the summer of 1933, tens of thousands of teachers joined the ranks of America's jobless. Many local districts cut school terms, often to a few months, while others shuttered a percentage of their buildings. One out of four teachers still clinging to a job made less than $700 a year.[41] When Harry Hopkins joined Franklin Roosevelt's New Deal, he did not forget his past as an activist for the National Child Labor Committee and other causes. Soon after accepting leadership of federal relief efforts as head of the Federal Emergency Relief Administration (FERA), he telephoned Mary Dabney Davis, a specialist in primary education within the U.S. Office of Education, to ask how the new FERA could help young children. A scheme to establish nursery schools using relief funds emerged from this conversation.[42]

In 1933, fewer than five hundred nursery schools existed in the entire country. They were overwhelmingly the creation of the same urban middle class that flocked to child study classes. Indeed, they responded to Behaviorism's edicts about the perils of "mother-love." Almost all of the two- and three-year-olds who attended these private institutions had nonworking mothers who heeded child development specialists' urgent command to give their toddlers a daily period of physical separation. Many of these women had servants to help them with child care duties and definitely viewed these nurseries as schools, not babysitters.

These privileged young kids lived in a totally different world than did the tens of thousands of working-class toddlers left in city-run or charitable "day nurseries." Day nurseries were often overcrowded, grim places, crammed with cribs, tired attendants, and crying children. Their creators did not want the working-class mothers who used them to leave their homes but, rather, saw out-of-home labor as a last resort, an alternative to badly paid piece work, prostitution, or outright begging. Ironically, the middle-class matron who sent her child to a private nursery school very well might have employed a nanny forced to send her own youngsters to a day nursery.[43]

[41] Grace Langdon and Isabel Robinson, "The Nursery School Program: Record of Program Operation and Accomplishment: 1933–43," Records of the Works Projects Administration, Record Group 69, Unpublished Reports of the Division of Service Projects, 120–26, National Archives, Washington, DC (hereafter Nursery Schools).

[42] *Ibid.*, 3–10.

[43] Sonya Michel, *Children's Interests/Mother's Rights: The Shaping of America's Child Care Policy* (New Haven, CT, 1999), 57–92. Michel concludes that in 1923, 613 municipal day nurseries across the country accommodated over twenty-three thousand poor infants and toddlers.

Day nurseries had inmates, often confined with little to do for ten or more hours per day. In contrast, nursery schools for affluent families were bright and cheerful places, full of musical instruments and books, ringed with gardens and playgrounds. These nursery schools had students – who spent a morning or afternoon singing, painting, modeling clay, and digging in the dirt, all under the close supervision of teachers eager to maximize their potentials.

Between 1933 and 1942, the federal nursery school program sought to imitate this latter model. First under the FERA, then its successor, the WPA emergency nursery schools were consciously defined as *schools*, reflecting the significant influence of the U.S. Office of Education, though the programs were never jointly run. Public school buildings housed the great majority of them, and local school districts usually paid for rent and utilities. Until America's entrance into World War II erased the need for government-sponsored work relief, the FERA/WPA nursery schools provided jobs for out-of-work teachers, as well as nurses, cooks, and janitors. Peaking at the beginning with almost three thousand schools and sixty-four thousand children in 1934, the schools gradually dwindled in numbers and enrollments, to some twelve hundred in January of 1942, enrolling thirty-five thousand kids.[44] Grace Langdon, the former private nursery school teacher who directed the FERA/WPA effort, wanted the federal nursery schools to set a "high standard" that would demonstrate, at emergency's end, the need for universal public preschools.[45]

That goal proved unreachable. In place of the well-heeled parents and privileged toddlers who populated pre-Depression private nursery schools, both the employees and students of the federal schools were members of families on relief. Only a fraction of the teachers had any kind of previous experience with young children. As emergency nursery school instructors, they faced mixed classes of twenty to thirty physically and emotionally stressed children aged two to six. A 1935 WPA survey of four thousand enrolled children revealed that most were severely underweight and suffered from a variety of untreated ailments. Their teachers judged fewer than 9 percent of them to be physically "robust." As their fathers lost work, and their families struggled to find cheaper housing, they typically slept three to a bed with their siblings.[46]

Peaking at eight hundred in 1931, day nurseries declined during the 1930s – as cities and charities reeled under the onslaught of the Depression.

[44] Nursery Schools, 11–12.

[45] Grace Langdon, "The Facts About Nursery Schools," Transcript of speech delivered to the National Council on Childhood Education, Atlantic City, NJ, February 25, 1935, GEB, Series 1, Sub-series 3, Box 379, Folder 3975, RAC.

[46] *Ibid.*

Under such conditions, Behaviorism's recommendation that toddlers needed rooms of their own was preposterous. Nonetheless, nursery school administrators argued that the program was not solely a work-relief project for unemployed teachers. It could develop "definite habits of play, eating, sleeping, and self-control...not easily built up in the average home."[47] Moreover, since parents were children's "first teachers" the schools could help mothers "gain a better understanding of children's varying needs."[48] Within psychological circles, Behaviorism's hold was slipping, but it retained fervent disciples at the U.S. Office of Education, which sent training pamphlets over to the WPA suggesting that in their after-duty hours nursery school teachers might consider making home visits to scold the parents of any non-toilet-trained two-year-old.[49]

At least some of the schools were successes. In New York City, Jessie Stanton, Director of the municipally sponsored Cooperative School for Student Teachers, established an effective training program. With help from Columbia's Teachers' College, she ran weekend workshops, where educators, psychologists, physicians, and other specialists in the emerging field of early childhood development gave advice to WPA teachers about appropriate activities. The indefatigable Stanton convinced volunteers to paint all the classrooms in eleven unused school basements. Lions, tigers, and rabbits roamed on formerly chipped grey walls. Other good Samaritans built child-size swings and contributed warm sweaters. Teachers welcomed mothers and gently coached them in ways to be better "mother-teachers." One harried woman who admitted that at home her child "just gets slapped from chair to chair" learned how to control her emotions and channel those of her offspring. Another, who spent days watching the whole class, was surprised to learn that "little children have to do things slowly."[50]

Such published stories were encouraging, but unpublished government documents suggested that Stanton's experience was not typical. Most nursery schools were in small towns and rural areas, far from Teachers' College. Memoranda that circulated between the U.S. Office of Education and WPA officials suggested that in many areas the hot, nutritionally balanced lunch children were supposed to receive rarely materialized. Cooks often struggled to make meals with surplus foodstuffs from the Department of Agriculture and served toddlers plates of mashed turnips. Sometimes everybody did

---

[47] United States Office of Education and the National Advisory Committee on Emergency Nursery Schools, Bulletin of Information for the Emergency Nursery Schools, "Administration and Program," Bulletin 1 (Washington, DC, 1934), 10.

[48] *Ibid.*, 31.

[49] *Ibid.*, 30.

[50] Jessie Stanton, "Emergency Nursery Schools in New York City," *Childhood Education* 11 (1934): 78–79.

without.[51] Many rural schools had no indoor toilets, sinks, or even faucets for running water.[52]

In 1936, the psychologist George Stoddard was one of the country's preeminent child development researchers, a leader in a still-small professional subculture. As director of the Iowa Child Welfare Research Station, he had a nationally recognized platform.[53] A supporter of the WPA nursery schools, he predicted that they were an exciting step into a "new frontier." Nursery education would soon grow into a "tremendous" publicly sponsored enterprise. Through a combination of "inertia and ignorance" the nation, he lamented, "consistently deprived children at a time when they were too young to protest." That, however, was about to change. "At the preschool level, we have a million potential consumers of new social and material goods."[54]

Stoddard was a prophet, but not in his own time. As the nation girded for war and shut down its last federally sponsored nursery schools, government interest in preschool education faded. Thirty years passed before Project Head Start revived public promotion of "infant" education. For the rest of the century, however, the national focus on the educational needs of the very young and their parents finally was, as Stoddard predicted, "tremendous."

Social Science and the Emergence of Project Head Start: The 1960s

Lyndon Johnson's attack on poverty renewed long-dormant interest in government sponsorship of early childhood education.[55] Once again, applied

---

[51] "Emergency Nursery School Report," copy, February 12, 1934, GEB, Series 1, Sub-series 3, Box 378, Folder 3952, RAC.

[52] Report of Isabel Robinson, State Supervisor of Emergency Nursery Schools, Iowa, March 10, 1936, GEB, Series 1, Sub-series 3, Box 378, Folder 3953, RAC.

[53] The Iowa Station received both state funding and generous support from the Laura Spelman Rockefeller Memorial. In the 1920s and 1930s it was one of the country's most prestigious centers, promoting a variety of research efforts in the new field. See Hamilton Cravens, *Before Head Start*, 73–184.

[54] George Stoddard, "The Nursery School as an Economic Enterprise," *School and Society* 43 (1936): 3.

[55] Of course, another war preceded Johnson's on poverty. In 1941 the U.S. Congress passed the Lanham Act to provide funding to help "war-impact" areas adjust. After 1943, during the last two years of World War II, Lanham funding helped establish 3,100 child care centers, usually connected to defense plants, serving around 129,000 children annually, less than ten percent of all children who needed care. These centers, however, followed a day-nursery model, and, importantly, were not free. Most charged from fifty to seventy-five cents per day. The average mother employed by defense industries spent far less than that sum and left her young children with friends, relatives, or neighbors. The minority who took children to commercial day nurseries chose ones which cost less than did the Lanham centers. Interestingly, in striking contrast to Head Start's clientele, almost no black children attended Lanham centers. Sadie Ginsberg, who organized two model Lanham centers in Portland, Oregon, for

social science theory encouraged education of toddlers and their parents. Unlike early-twentieth-century initiatives, however, Project Head Start began with a bang, and only got bigger. By 1998, over sixteen million impoverished children and their families had participated for at least the length of a summer, at a cost to taxpayers of over $35 billion.[56] Despite a long history of fiscal mismanagement and questionable results, Head Start, like Job Corps, remained politically invulnerable. It had, champions boasted, "a proven record of success...and was universally recognized as a program that worked."[57] Since neither of these statements was true, why were they constantly repeated? The answer to that question demands an exploration of Head Start's early history.

On January 8, 1964, President Lyndon Johnson delivered his first State of the Union address, one of the greatest speeches of his career. In it, he pledged an "unconditional" war on poverty, hunger, illiteracy, and joblessness.[58] In only four years, Lyndon Johnson, beaten by a war in Vietnam he could not win, retired to Texas in disgrace, no longer able to lead a nation with a much-altered sense of what was politically possible. But in 1964, Congress enthusiastically accepted Johnson's challenge and authorized the creation of the Office of Economic Opportunity. The OEO operated out of the White House, and was neither part of the Department of Labor nor of Health, Education, and Welfare. New and unbeholden to entrenched bureaucracy, the OEO demanded that the poor exercise "maximum feasible

Kaiser Shipbuilding, noted that (unfounded) rumors circulated in the black community that the all-white staff liked to beat black children. "The Child Care Center Chronicle: An Interview with Sadie Ginsberg," in James Hymes, Ed., *Early Childhood Education: Living History Interviews, Book Two* (Carmel, CA, 1978), 49. For additional analysis of the Lanham program, see William Tuttle, "Rosie the Riveter and Her Latchkey Children: What Americans Can Learn about Child Care from the Second World War," *Child Welfare* 74 (1995): 92–114; Susan Hartmann, *The Home Front and Beyond: American Women in the 1940s* (Boston, 1982), 170–85.

[56] Report from the Senate Committee on Labor and Human Resources, 105–256, Human Services Reauthorization Act of 1998 (Washington, DC, 1998): 3–5 (hereafter, Report 105–256). The original title for Head Start further emphasized the tie to Job Corps. It was "Kiddy Corps." Sargent Shriver was smart enough to kill the name. See Laura Dittmann, "Project Head Start Becomes a Long-Distance Runner," *Young Children* 35/6 (1980): 3.

[57] Prepared statement of Sarah Greene, Executive Director, National Head Start Association, "New Challenges for Head Start," Hearing before the Subcommittee on Children, Family, Drugs, and Alcoholism of the Committee on Labor and Human Resources, United States Senate, One Hundred Third Congress, First Session (Washington, DC, 1993): 59 (hereafter Hearing, New Challenges).

[58] With this speech Johnson made his own a federal initiative begun by President John Kennedy. In December 1962, Kennedy asked a key economic adviser, Walter Heller, to draft proposals to attack poverty in America. However, the War on Poverty only took concrete form under Johnson. Peter Marris and Martin Rein, *Dilemmas of Social Reform, Poverty and Community Action in the United States* (Chicago, 1982), 245–46.

participation." The "community action program" rapidly emerged as key to OEO philosophy, the vehicle that would allow federal officials and local communities to bypass traditional power structures.

Not surprisingly, Sargent Shriver, Johnson's hand-picked choice to head OEO, soon discovered that traditional power structures were not thrilled with the arrangement. Rather than taking the bait of federal dollars, cities and counties around the country, especially in the South, rejected the community action program concept outright. Shriver faced an embarrassing dilemma. He had far more money in his budget than he had takers. Confronted with this unusual crisis, Sargent Shriver had a brainstorm: children could be the wedge used to create support for community action. Who could object to giving disadvantaged youngsters aged three to five a "head start," so that by the time they reached first grade they had the same skills as middle-class youngsters.[59] Shriver convened a panel of experts, led by Johns Hopkins University pediatrician Robert Cooke. Most of the thirteen members of Cooke's committee were fellow physicians or child psychologists, and their justifications for a program of early childhood intervention relied heavily upon ideas promoted in the 1950s and 1960s by developmental psychologists and sociologists.

In 1992, Edward Zigler, the feisty Yale University child psychologist who, more than anyone else, made the study of Head Start an academic cottage industry, admitted that the term "cultural deprivation" was a misnomer. "How could anyone be deprived of a culture? All one could be deprived of was the culture that someone else thought should be the norm." But in 1965, cultural deprivation theory justified many Great Society initiatives, including Job Corps and Head Start.[60]

Impoverished adolescents, enmeshed in a deficient environment marked by weak family structures, illegitimacy, an inability to delay gratification, and apathetic despair, deserved an "opportunity" to escape to a Job Corps site far from home. However, more important was the need for a program

---

[59] For discussion of Shriver's focus on children's issues, see Kathryn Kuntz, "A Lost Legacy: Head Start's Origin in Community Action," in Jeanne Ellsworth and Lynda Ames, *Critical Perspectives on Project Head Start, Revisioning the Hope and the Challenge* (Albany, NY, 1998), 1–48.

[60] Edward Zigler and Susan Muenchow, *Head Start: The Inside Story of America's Most Successful Education Experiment* (New York, 1992), 21. The subtitle of this book accurately reflects the Alice in Wonderland quality of much of the literature about Head Start. The memoir emphasizes mismanagement, unsuccessful attempts at quality control, inability to discover what really happened in local centers, and other failures. Zigler co-wrote or co-edited numerous books about Head Start, which he headed during the Nixon Administration. In addition to the above, see Edward Zigler and Sally Styfco, Eds., *Head Start and Beyond: A National Plan for Extended Childhood Intervention* (New Haven, 1993); Edward Zigler and Jeanette Valentine, Eds., *Project Head Start: A Legacy of the War on Poverty* (New York, 1979); Edward Zigler, Sharon Kagan, and Edgar Klugman, Eds., *Children, Families, and Government: Perspectives on American Social Policy* (Cambridge, MA, 1983).

that broke "cycles of poverty" even earlier, before a child dropped out of school or decided to break the law.

Children born to poverty too often lived in "barren" environments bereft of "wonder-provoking" experiences.[61] This was all the more distressing because young children were at risk of life-long failure if they did not receive proper care and training. The beginning years, between birth and the age of five, were the time when permanent foundations for a child's self-worth, self-respect, ability to learn, and will to achieve were laid. Disaster beckoned for those left behind.

Indeed, even intelligence hung in the balance. Beginning in the 1950s, an influential group of researchers led by the child psychologists Benjamin Bloom and J. McVicker Hunt challenged their early-twentieth-century's predecessors' belief that IQ was fixed at birth. In the 1960s, Hunt, a professor at the University of Illinois, achieved an academic's daydream – "vindication" after decades of collegial scorn. Indeed, he gloated, fellow university psychologists no longer "picked to pieces" his theories about "wandering IQ." "As recently as World War II," Hunt continued, his work had "been considered a stupid waste of time and effort." By the early 1960s, he was the toast of Washington, invited to consult by both the Kennedy and Johnson administrations. Among those showering approval was Sargent Shriver of the OEO.[62]

Strongly influenced by the child psychologists Erik Erickson and Arnold Gesell, not John Watson, Hunt and his colleagues argued that the first years of a child's life were all-important. Babies and toddlers needed a great deal of adult warmth as they moved through various stages of development. If not exactly a return to G. Stanley Hall, these new notions repudiated Behaviorism. Kissing toddlers was "in" again.[63]

Moreover, Hunt and Bloom counseled that carefully controlled stimulation was important to children's mental, physical, and emotional growth. Behaviorists thought that actions, but not intelligence, could be molded. Hunt suggested that IQ itself could be significantly manipulated, especially

---

[61] For a typical cultural deprivation analysis, see Wallace Ramsey, "Head Start and First Grade Reading," in Jerome Hellmuth, Ed., *The Disadvantaged Child: Head Start and Early Intervention, Volume* 2 (Seattle, 1968), 291–92. For astute assessment of cultural deprivation theory's place within Great Society thinking, see Alice O'Connor, *Poverty Knowledge,* 197–237.

[62] J. McVicker Hunt, "The Psychological Basis For Using Preschool Enrichment As an Antidote for Cultural Deprivation," in Jermone Hellmuth, Ed., *The Disadvantaged Child: Head Start and Early Intervention, Volume* 1 (Seattle, 1967), 257.

[63] By the 1990s many psychologists condemned Gesellian psychology as overly simplistic. However, Gesell's categorizations: "three as conforming, four as lively; three as assentive, four as assertive" influenced American popular culture, as parents tried to determine whether their young children were developing "normally." For discussion of Gesell's influence, see Grant, *Raising Baby by the Book,* 208–18.

between birth and the age of four.[64] Match an OEO director desperate to give away money with optimistic predictions about the intellectual malleability of young children, who could be made smarter through improved environments, and Project Head Start's quick, largely unexamined, growth was inevitable.

Robert Cooke's planning committee recommended that OEO sponsor a small pilot program during the summer of 1965. It also warned that Hunt's ideas about toddlers' IQ were controversial. Starting very cautiously was vital. Perhaps some two thousand children in carefully monitored situations? Sargent Shriver dismissed the suggestion out-of-hand. Project Head Start began, not with a few regional experiments, but as a national effort involving one hundred thousand kids, and costing $18 million. Influenced by Lady Bird Johnson, whom Shriver sagely recruited to serve as honorary chair of Head Start, Lyndon Johnson became personally involved in the new program's planning phase. Within three months, a controlled effort to test the validity of a social science theory about poor children's intellectual development, involving at most two thousand youngsters, grew enormously. By May 1965, the original budget request of $18 million rose to $50 million, and, by summer's end, over half a million children had already enrolled for eight-week-long "enrichment" classes. Indeed, three months before the first Head Start center even opened, the Johnson Administration set aside an additional $150 million to make Head Start a year-round program in 1966.

Lady Bird Johnson announced that she would launch Head Start with a White House tea. Weeks before the event, the party became a "must-have" invitation, and on the day itself everyone from Italian bombshell Gina Lollobrigida to the ubiquitous Ed Zigler crowded into the East and Red Rooms. Mrs. Johnson announced that, for the first time in American history, government would reach out to "young children lost in a gray world of neglect," children so deprived by a low-income environment that "they don't know their own first names."

Zigler may indeed, as he remembered, have "cringed" at these statements, since he and almost every other child development specialist knew that children aged three or four who wouldn't say their names usually were just shy. The act signaled refusal, not inability. But if Zigler cringed, he made sure not to do so in sight of Lady Bird Johnson.[65]

---

[64] Of course Watson too thought these years were important, not to elevate intelligence (which he thought impossible) but because without habit formation training children would become tyrants. Bloom, even more than Hunt, was an advocate of the idea that intellectual growth was extremely rapid in the first four years of life. Benjamin Bloom, *Stability and Change in Human Characteristics* (New York, 1964).

[65] Zigler's memoir, *Head Start*, tells this story. It is worth reading and is full of lively, if self-serving, detail, 24–25.

Awash in money and told to generate and process over five hundred thousand applications in a matter of a few weeks, Zigler and other members of the Cooke planning committee hunkered down in inadequate quarters in Washington, DC's, crumbling Colonial Hotel. With no time to buy file cabinets, they stacked paperwork in bathtubs in empty rooms.[66] Jule Sugarman, another influential child psychologist on the planning committee, who, like Zigler, alternated careers in academia and at Head Start for the next several decades, got his marching orders straight from Sargent Shriver: "I want to prove this program is valuable. I'd like to say how many IQ points are gained for every dollar invested." Ten IQ points per six-week session, Shriver suggested, would not be a bad first goal.[67]

Thus, Project Head Start began, with carelessly spent money, hype, and dependence on unproven social science theory. For the next thirty-five years, these three characteristics dogged a program already burdened by the long shadow of maximum feasible participation. Sargent Shriver thought that community action initiatives that helped disadvantaged children would be politically irresistible. In the long term, he was right. In the short run, the idea blew up in his face.

OEO guidelines promoted Head Start as a comprehensive early childhood education program meant for youngsters aged three to five and their parents. Its broad objectives included improving children's physical and emotional health and their conceptual and verbal skills, increasing "constructive" bonds between parents and their children, and teaching parents how to be good "first teachers."[68] "Community action programs" received preference as organizers of this ambitious agenda. Only in localities where no community action agency existed could school boards, local welfare departments, or private charitable groups apply to run Head Start centers.[69] All administrators of Head Start, moreover, had to establish a "policy council" composed of parents of children enrolled in the program, and each council was to have genuine power: the right to choose a center's director and hire its teachers and staff, the authority to oversee its budget, and the chance to plan activities. This was classic maximum feasible participation.[70]

---

[66] Testimony of Edward Zigler, 23, Hearing, 21st Century.

[67] Sargent Shriver, quoted in Zigler, *Head Start*, 26.

[68] Community Action Programs, Office of Economic Opportunity, "Statement of Purpose" (Washington, DC, 1966), 3–4.

[69] *Ibid.*, 7–8.

[70] The "community action" idea had its origins in private philanthropic initiatives, most importantly the "Grey Area" and "Mobilization for Youth" projects funded by the Ford Foundation between 1960 and 1963, which relied on Lloyd Ohlin's "opportunity theory." "Grey areas" were the deteriorating impoverished neighborhoods between downtowns and suburbs in big cities, and the Ford Foundation sought ways to help residents organize to improve their own communities. Robert Kennedy's aide, David Hackett, became interested in Ohlin's work with the Foundation and invited the sociologist to become a consultant at Justice, to help develop programs to combat juvenile delinquency. For further discussion of the

In the summer of 1965, in rural Mississippi, it exploded. Dr. Tom Levin, New Yorker, psychoanalyst, and committed civil rights reformer, traveled south as the founding director of the Child Development Group of Mississippi (CDGM). Under his energetic leadership, eighty-four Head Start centers opened by July, despite the active opposition of state government. When school superintendents, health departments, and mayors refused use of buildings, parents used tents for classes. When local police lay in wait, ticketing cars of Head Start parents for usually fanciful traffic violations, the parents stopped driving and walked.[71]

In 1964, the social activist Aaron Wildavsky, worried about the ramifications of community action, wrote a "recipe" for violence: "Have middle-class civil servants...use lower-class Negroes as a battering ram against the existing local political systems...then chastise local politicians for not cooperating with those out to do them in."[72]

By August, dozens of crosses left to burn in yards of Head Start families, shots fired into classrooms, cars forced off roads, even buildings burned to the ground, provided ample evidence of the validity of Wildavsky's prediction. Sargent Shriver sent letters to Tom Levin condemning the "disgraceful" violence, expressing gratitude that no one had died, and promising continued support.[73] He did not mean it. Quietly, he authorized a stalling action – first delaying funding for CDGM, then, by 1966, transferring most Head Start programs to the more moderate Mississippi Action for Progress.

The conflicts between Head Start activists and local authorities were most horrific in Mississippi, but parallel stories reverberated across the country. Moreover, internal controversies about what kind of education Head Start should promote complicated struggles, and issues of race and class caused bitter fights. In Mississippi, for instance, Levin urged centers to create their own "books" – usually mimeographed or hand-copied collections of the children's own stories. At the Mt. Peel, Mississippi, Child Development Center "Pond" was read aloud:

I BEEN SWIMMING
UP IN THE POND
FRANCES AND ME

    origins of "community action," see Peter Marris and Martin Rein, *Dilemmas of Social Reform*, 14–26.

[71] Tom Levin's account of the summer of 1965 and its aftermath can be found in Tom Levin, "Preschool Education and the Communities of the Poor," Jerome Hellmuth, Ed., *The Disadvantaged Child, Volume 1*, 351–90. For another account, again from the point of view of a CDGM leader, see Polly Greenberg, *The Devil Has Slippery Shoes: A Biased Biography of the Child Development Group of Mississippi* (New York, 1969).

[72] Aaron Wildavsky, quoted in Daniel P. Moynihan, *Maximum Feasible Misunderstanding: Community Action in the War on Poverty* (New York, 1969), iv.

[73] For a collection of these letters, see OEO Files, Folder 3, "Child Development Group of Mississippi," Sargent Shriver Papers, The John F. Kennedy Presidential Library, Boston, Massachusetts.

FOUND TREE TOAD AROUND THE TREE
I DIDN'T GET SCARED
IF TOAD FROG HOP UP ON YOU
AND WET ON YOU
HE MAKE A BIG BLISTER ON YOUR FEET
CAT FISH HAS A MOUTH
LIKE A BIG SMILE[74]

In 1965, stories like "Pond" provoked raging battles between middle-class black teachers and poor black parents. The former demanded that only literature in standard English be used. The latter shouted them down as "Uncle Toms." By the end of the summer, many of the teachers were gone, replaced by parent volunteers.

The confrontations were inevitable, given the rhetoric of community action and the legacies of state-sponsored parent education. Lady Bird Johnson's speech at the White House reception inaugurating Head Start unwittingly echoed those given by previous generations of "child-savers" intent on spreading middle-class values. The "lost" children of America had to be "led back to the human family.... Some have never seen a book." Mrs. Johnson assumed that poor parents, once informed of the necessity of reading to a young child, would be gratefully reformed. But, as a black mother of thirteen scornfully told Tom Levin, "Books is stuffed with white-man lies."[75]

Head Start Rebuked: The Westinghouse Study

Social science theories that suggested an enriched environment boosted toddlers' IQs justified Head Start's creation and encouraged its swift growth. When a group of prominent social scientists drawn from the private Westinghouse Learning Corporation and state-run Ohio University doubted that such results had been achieved, controversy erupted.

Jule Sugarman and Ed Zigler, Head Start's first and second directors, knew that measuring cognitive gains among very young children was risky business and that tests of disadvantaged children were the hardest of all to analyze. When asked, for instance, "What is a gown?" did a poor child reply, "I don't know" because he had never heard the word "gown," even though he could perhaps identify the garment in question by sight? Did he respond, "I don't know," as did a great number of all three- and four-year-olds, because he tired easily of question-and-answer sessions and wanted this particular one to end? Did he say, "I don't know" because the test administrator was a frightening grown-up, likely of another race? The two child psychologists knew that, particularly with young children, refusing to

---

[74] Levin, "Preschool Education," 361.
[75] *Ibid.*, 357.

accept an "I don't know" answer often produced the correct response after a second try. They knew that dramatic IQ point "gains" occurred, simply if the tester manipulated the order of the questions or praised a child.[76]

Nonetheless, as Head Start catapulted from pilot project to practically every politician's pet program, they kept quiet. The idea that early childhood intervention produced intelligence spurts was too popular. The Westinghouse investigation challenged that idea. The report itself was a by-product of Defense Secretary Robert McNamara's efforts to restructure accountability in the Army. McNamara's idea that quantitative analysis should play a crucial role in decision making spread quickly throughout the federal bureaucracy between 1964 and 1968.[77] Using McNamara's example at Defense, Bureau of the Budget–commissioned studies became popular. The Westinghouse Study was one such analysis.

By 1969, however, a repudiated Lyndon Johnson was back in Texas, and Robert McNamara was on his way to the World Bank. Ongoing, independent performance reviews soon fell out of favor. But the Nixon Administration, an enemy of OEO and no friend of Head Start, leaked the Westinghouse Study's conclusion that children's minimal gains in cognitive and emotional development soon faded.[78]

For the next several years, academics furiously debated the strengths and weaknesses of the Westinghouse Study. Charges and countercharges flew. Social scientists scheduled conferences to debate the review's sampling techniques and use of control populations. They fired off articles to academic journals. Some concluded that, while not flawless, the report was accurate.[79] Others thought that Head Start *did* benefit disadvantaged children but was not sufficiently comprehensive. We must be prepared, intoned the educational psychologist Charles Hill, to "remove (poor) infants from the home."[80] Of course, before taking such a drastic course of action, Hill demanded "more research to validate our instructional assumptions."[81]

In the end all the heated exchanges between insiders meant little. The national press paid almost no attention to the first national comparative review of Head Start's impact.[82] Richard Nixon achieved his larger ambition,

---

[76] These are Zigler's own examples. Edward Zigler, *Head Start*, 58.

[77] Walter Williams and John Evans, "The Politics of Evaluation: The Case of Head Start," *Annals of the American Academy of Political and Social Science* 385 (1969): 118–32.

[78] Zigler, *Head Start*, 61–81.

[79] See, for instance, Victor Cicirelli, John Evans, and Jeffrey Schiller, "The Impact of Head Start: A Reply to the Report Analysis," *Harvard Educational Review* 40 (1970): 105–29.

[80] Charles Hill, "Head Start: A Problem of Assumptions," *Education* 92 (1972): 92. In the 1970s, Hill's ideas spurred furious debate among social scientists. However, remember that the orphan trains, which *did* send hundreds of thousands of children far away from their homes, were seen as state-of-the-art social science in the early twentieth century.

[81] *Ibid.*

[82] Jeanne Ellsworth, "Inspiring Delusions: Reflections on Head Start's Enduring Popularity," in Jeanne Ellsworth and Lynda Ames, *Critical Perspectives*, 328–29.

emasculating OEO by shifting many of its programs, among them Head Start, now supervised by the Department of Health, Education, and Welfare's new Office of Child Development.

Social Science and the Maintenance of Head Start, 1970–2000

By the time Nixon's successor, Gerald Ford, killed OEO outright in 1974, Head Start was a battle-hardened bureaucratic survivor. It was an "education" program that sucessfully thwarted efforts by President Jimmy Carter to transfer it to his new Department of Education. Its documents repeatedly referred to enrolled children as "caseloads," but the program escaped a massive Congressional restructuring of federal welfare programs in 1996. A constantly moving target, Head Start just kept growing. By 1998, it operated over 16,000 centers, enrolled an average of 830,000 children yearly, and cost more than $4 billion annually.[83]

How had that happened? In part, Head Start flourished because, for almost a quarter century, few examined its actual impact. Once the furor over the Westinghouse analysis died, Head Start's examiners were friends of the court. Most belonged, in the Ed Zigler tradition, to the legions of educational and developmental psychologists who evaluated a program with which they had some kind of affiliation.

Interestingly, despite the fact that between 1970 and 1995 the federal government spent tens of millions of dollars on hundreds of Head Start studies, little analysis of what went on behind the doors of an actual Head Start center occurred.[84] Harvard University educational psychologist Sheldon White a consultant for the Westinghouse Study, noted, "When one listens ... to people talking about their preschool programs, it is very hard to tell whether two people who talk alike or differently *actually run* their programs alike or differently."[85]

Investigations of Head Start did little to examine how programs were "actually run." Rather, studies became forums, as Charles Hill had urged,

---

[83] For discussion of the successful effort by the Children's Defense Fund and its allies to halt "an outrageous" transfer of Head Start to the control of the Department of Education, see Robin McDonald, "Head Start in Jeopardy," *Reporter* (1978): 8–10; for "caseload" references and 1998 statistics, see Report 105–256, 3–7.

[84] As was the case with Job Corps, figures that clearly outlined exactly how annual appropriations were spent were difficult to locate. Head Start, as an agency of HEW, then of its successor, Health and Human Services, repeatedly received warnings from GAO to remedy what one highly critical report called "poor recordkeeping." Little happened, and at both the federal and local levels, funds regularly went missing. See Report to the Congress of the United States, Comptroller General, "Head Start: Fund Distribution Formula Needs Revision and Management Controls Need Improvement," HRD-81-83 (Washington, DC, 1981), 62.

[85] Sheldon White, "The National Impact Study of Head Start," in Jerome Hellmuth, Ed., *The Disadvantaged Child: Compensatory Education, A National Debate, Volume 3* (New York, 1970), 167.

for discussions about "validation of instructional assumptions." In 1998, Vermont's Senator Jim Jeffords, the same man who vainly demanded accountability from Job Corps, "looked forward" to convening "the expert panel of researchers and reviewing their recommendations on the best approach to carry out the research initiative [on Head Start.]"[86] By then, a quarter-century's worth of expert panels had worn a deep path between their universities and the capital, but as Mary Jo Bane, Assistant Secretary for Children and Families at Health and Human Services, admitted, "We have not had over the years the kind of research that all of us would like – to be able to look very carefully at the program."[87] So: What kind of research did occur? Studies of Head Start were studies in how to assess studies, useful to social scientists embroiled in lively controversies about the processes by which very young children learn.

Most researchers took groups of twenty to fifty Head Start children and parents, paired them with comparable numbers of non–Head Start children and parents, and examined everybody away from the centers, usually on university campuses. Both parents and children took batteries of tests that measured emotional adjustment, language ability improvement, and listening skills. The results were almost always mixed. A review commissioned by Health and Human Services of over two hundred such Head Start studies contained dozens of pages of "Yes – But," "Maybe," and "Perhaps" answers to such questions as: "Does parental education produce changes in parental childrearing practices?" "Does Head Start have positive effects on children's social development?" "Do Head Start children perform better on test orientation measures than their peers?"[88]

After concluding that no clear benefits to either Head Start children or their parents were immediately apparent, Head Start researchers then moved quickly to judgments about the significance of testing. Was variation at the $p < .05$ level reportable? Should testers employ "type-I error probability scales" or use several separate "t-tests"? Should a null hypothesis require two or three estimates of variation?[89] These questions were important, especially to the burgeoning fields of developmental, behavioral, and educational

---

[86] Prepared Statement of Senator James Jeffords, Report 105–256, 41–42.

[87] Testimony of Assistant Secretary Bane, "The Administration Proposal for Head Start Reauthorization," Joint Hearing before the Subcommittee on Children, Family, Drugs, and Alcoholism of the Committee on Labor and Human Resources, and the Subcommittee on Human Resources of the Committee on Education and Labor, House of Representatives, United States Senate, One Hundred Third Congress, Second Session, February 10, 1994 (Washington, DC, 1994): 22 (hereafter Joint Hearing).

[88] Office of Program Development, Administration for Children, Youth, and Families, Office of Development Services, Department of Health and Human Services, "A Review of Head Start Research Since 1970 and An Annotated Bibliography of the Head Start Research Since 1965," 105-81-C026 (Washington, DC, 1983), 10–17.

[89] For one example, easily multiplied by hundreds of others, see Colleen Bee, "A Longitudinal Study to Determine If Head Start Has Lasting Effects on School Achievement," (EdD Dissertation, University of South Dakota, 1981), 35–41.

psychology, but incomprehensible to the general public and the average politician. By 1999, over a thousand studies of Head Start had appeared; the program had provided research subjects for two generations of social scientists, not to speak of dissertation topics for hundreds of educators and psychologists. Outside of academic circles, or outside of the Beltway, nobody read them.

As early as the 1970s, Head Start supporters began to discuss the program's goals more vaguely. Promises of quick IQ spurts had helped the measure breeze through Congress, but with little clear evidence of any lasting cognitive or social skills improvements, Head Start metamorphosed yet again. It helped improve a child's health, not just his intelligence.

It had always been a program that supposedly provided a wide range of services. But Head Start officials, like those at Job Corps, always turned a blind eye to sloppy bookkeeping and rarely produced concrete proof of the delivery of noneducational services, such as dental care. The fact that, by the 1990s, a number of legal services programs for the poor sued nonprofit Head Start contractors, charging that they had taken hundreds of thousands of dollars in federal money, but had failed to deliver any nutritional, dental, or medical services at all, suggested serious problems.[90]

Head Start, predictably, again mutated. Now it was a program that "enhanced the self-esteem of poor children."[91] Ironically, amid the welter of controversy about testing, social scientists had generally agreed about one question. When asked, "Does improved self-esteem relate to achievement?" they said, with rare unanimity, "No."[92]

Most social scientists looked at sample populations. Amazingly, the smaller number who examined institutional organization justified Head Start's potential through the use of results obtained from publicly supported preschools for disadvantaged youngsters *not* connected to the program. The Perry Preschool in Ypsilanti, Michigan, was a perennial favorite. However, the Perry project was a small-scale experiment jointly funded by the city of Ypsilanti and its neighbor, the University of Michigan. In Ypsilanti, Ann Arbor–based researchers closely followed 123 youngsters, from the age of three to the age of twenty-eight, and concluded that early childhood education had a positive impact. The impoverished toddlers from the Perry Preschool became young adults who graduated from high school, delayed marriage, and stayed out of jail.[93] Using such evidence, champions for Head

---

[90] For an account of these legal services' actions, see Jan Stokely, "Working with Head Start: Profile in Community Building," *Clearinghouse Review* 28 (1994): 257–62.

[91] Sadie Grimmett and Aline Garrettt, "A Review of Evaluations of Project Head Start," *Journal of Negro Education* 58 (1989):30.

[92] See "A Review of Head Start Research Since 1970": 10.

[93] Testimony of David Weikart, President, High/Scope Educational Research Foundation, Ypsilanti, Michigan, "The Future of Head Start," Hearing before the Subcommittee on Education and Health, Joint Economic Committee, Congress of the United States, One Hundred First Congress, Second Session (Washington, DC, 1990): 49–52 (hereafter Hearing, Future).

Start argued that the program saved at least $6 for every $1 invested.[94] It was the same monetary logic used to justify Job Corps, with financial gains measured in unprovable future reductions in crime.[95] But, at least in the case of Job Corps, the evidence offered *came* from a Job Corps site.[96]

By the 1980s, Head Start's many Congressional supporters relied less and less on any kind of study. Rather, they invited "successes" to testify. Terrible recordkeeping obscured the exact numbers of Head Start parents who also had been Head Start employees, but the program always estimated that at least 35 percent of its workers were parents. Therefore, over the decades, probably well over four million held Head Start jobs, most as janitors, bus drivers, cooks, and aides. Only a few thousand ever became center directors or administrators. A handful of parents from this latter group trooped to Washington to tell their stories. With such huge numbers involved, there was little reason to doubt that some parents "put down drugs and picked up Head Start."[97]

However, the tales had a curiously coached quality. Why did Diane Herbert, a Head Start parent from Woburn, Massachusetts, repeat that phrase when she spoke, first before the House Committee on Education and Labor and then before the Senate Committee on Labor and Human Resources?[98] Did the Head Start program really "awaken" Michael Hunter "... as a preschooler to know that my dreams of a better life could be achieved through the boundaries of the laws of society"?[99] No question: Herbert and Hunter were successes. A former drug addict, she was a

---

[94] The idea of huge "savings" in human capital had always been a constant in Head Start rhetoric. Indeed, as early as 1965, Lyndon Johnson had said, "This program this year means that thirty million man-years, the combined lifespan of these youngsters, will be spent productively and rewardingly, rather than wasted in tax-supported institutions or in welfare-supported lethargy." *Public Papers of the Presidents of the United States*, Lyndon B. Johnson, Book One, January 1 to May 31, 1965 (Washington, DC, 1966), 259.

[95] "Prepared Statement of Frank Doyle, Senior Vice President, General Electric Corporation," *Ibid.*, 10. Indeed, even in the very different Perry school, where teachers were affiliated with the University of Michigan and where children received years of concentrated follow-up attention, which never occurred at a typical Head Start center, the success rates were not astonishing. For instance, 18 percent of Perry's preschool graduates were on welfare at age 28, versus 32 percent for the non-preschool control group. 31 percent had at least one arrest, versus 51 percent for the control group. "Testimony of David Weikart," 50, Hearing, Future.

[96] In 1996, the Roundtable on Head Start Research, under the auspices of the National Research Council and the Institute of Medicine, concluded that, after 30 years, "There is (still) no broad consensus regarding the parameters of an appropriate control group for a study of Head Start's effects." Deborah Phillips and Natasha Cabrera, Eds., *Beyond the Blueprint: Directions for Research on Head Start's Families* (Washington, DC, 1996), 10.

[97] "Testimony of Diane Herbert," 13, Joint Hearing.

[98] *Ibid.*; see also "Testimony of Diane Herbert," 14, Hearing, 21st Century.

[99] "Testimony of Michael Hunter," 31, Joint Hearing.

community college graduate planning to attend law school.[100] Hunter was a cop with the city of New Haven, Connecticut.[101]

These examples were heart warming but typified nothing. Only in the late 1990s did the reality of Head Start begin to emerge. It was a mismanaged program whose clients overwhelmingly were poor African Americans and Latinos, in percentages far beyond their numbers within the poverty population. The program had become an entitlement that helped control minorities socially and politically. Whether significant numbers of parents received education or very many youngsters got a "head start" was questionable.

The Reality of Head Start

Head Start planners never resolved the inherent contradictions in goals that spoke of parent empowerment and practices that demanded remedial education – of both parents and their kids. Given the program's emphasis on local control, centers varied enormously. Some served as few as forty children and had a small staff of two teachers, several teacher's aides, perhaps a part-time nurse. Others enrolled two to three hundred children and had staffs of thirty to forty. But whatever the arrangement, observers noted high levels of tension between parents, aides, and teachers. The former two groups were often highly intermingled. OEO guidelines demanded that parents be given preference whenever possible for all Head Start positions. In most, the cooks, janitors, and aides were also the students' parents. Teachers and directors of Head Start programs complained that parents were disruptive, or unqualified. Indeed, in order to maximize employment of poor parents, OEO's guidelines substituted the phrase "reasonable potential" for "demonstrated competence." Teacher's aides who could not meet the thirty words-per-minute minimum were indeed hired as typists. Teacher's aides who could not type were hired as typists.[102] Teachers told observers that they could accomplish more if parents weren't around. Parents, in turn, reported that teachers were "cold."[103]

The glossy full-color brochures Head Start administrators distributed by the hundreds of thousands featured appealing faces of adorable tykes happily engaged in learning colors, distinguishing shapes, and enlarging their

---

[100] "Testimony of Diane Herbert," 15, Hearing, 21st Century.

[101] "Testimony of Michael Hunter," 30, Joint Hearing.

[102] Qualifications were relaxed for most jobs, or very vaguely defined. That would remain true throughout the history of Head Start. For a review of the ways in which OEO pressure led to lowered standards, especially for hiring of parents as aides, see Joseph Caliguri, "Will Parents Take Over Head Start Programs?" *Urban Education* 5 (1970): 54–64.

[103] Office of Child Development, Department of Health, Education, and Welfare, Laura Dittmann and Others, "A Study of Selected Children in Head Start Planned Variation, 1969–1970," First Year Report: 3–5 "Case Studies of Children," Office of Child Development: DHEW (Washington, DC, 1971), 2–25.

vocabularies. The thick, unprinted, typed reports sent in by evaluation teams told a different story. Observers were struck by the fact that at many centers the same finger paintings were hanging on the walls in January – and in May.[104] Everywhere, they encountered teachers, who, lacking anything else, used tools and materials intended for first graders.[105] Were poor children getting a "head start"? A number of observers entertained serious doubts. Those from strong families appeared happy and well-adjusted at the centers. Those from families in trouble were in trouble at the centers – "sullen," "prone to fighting," "starving for adult warmth that they rarely get . . . at home or in the school situation."[106]

Reprising his role as watchdog of Job Corps, Jim Jeffords inundated the Head Start bureaucracy with demands for clear, verifiable accounting of how money was spent, not just "some fuzzy feeling that things are going well."[107] Moreover, another group of social scientists, anthropologists employing participant-observer techniques, started to make tentative forays into actual Head Start centers.[108] They reported that a "fuzzy" feeling that things were just fine was rarely justified.

In 1965, poor black children from inner-city slums were seven times more likely than were comparably disadvantaged white kids to attend sessions at a Head Start center. Deprived black youngsters from rural areas were four times more likely to be Head Start recruits.[109] Even if, as some suggested, 40 percent of American black children were impoverished, the percentages of disadvantaged black youngsters in Head Start were always disproportionately high, during decades when analysts guessed that the program helped fewer than 20 percent of all eligible children.

Race and class were rarely openly mentioned, but they quietly dominated the politics of Head Start. With about half of its directors African-American men and women, the program employed far more black professionals than did most other government educational or welfare outreach efforts. But black and Latino representation in employees' roles was most striking within the centers themselves.

---

[104] *Ibid.*, 36.

[105] Office of Economic Opportunity, "Project Head Start at Work: Report of a Survey Study of 335 Project Head Start Centers, Summer, 1965" (Washington, DC, 1966), 30.

[106] Laura Dittmann and Others, "Study of Selected Children," 19–23.

[107] He made this request of Head Start supervisor Mary Jo Bane of Health and Human Services. "Comments of Senator Jeffords," 22, Joint Hearings.

[108] The anthropologist Peggy Sissel, who spent a year in daily attendance at a Head Start center, reported that she faced intense pressure from other colleagues not to publish her study. They argued that her highly negative findings would endanger the program's continuance. The bureaucratic and academic worlds treated Head Start, she charged, with "structured silence." Peggy Sissel, *Staff, Parents, and Politics in Head Start: A Case Study in Unequal Power, Knowledge, and Material Resources* (New York, 2000), 10.

[109] James Coleman and Others, *Equality of Educational Opportunity* (Washington, DC, 1966), 491–92.

Information about on-ground operations remained maddeningly anecdotal. In 1993, despite the fact that funding renewal supposedly depended on their completion, only 314 (17 percent) of the personnel surveys mailed to 1800 Head Start centers were returned to headquarters at the Administration for Children, Youth, and Families in Health and Human Services, the successor agency to HEW's Office of Child Development.[110] The centers that responded, however, provided a disturbing portrait. Since 1970, the average Head Start program served at least two hundred children and employed fifty staff members. It also operated multiple centers, often at significant distances apart. Yet, only one in ten program directors possessed formal training in management techniques. Most had bachelor's degrees in education, with no background in preparing budgets or supervising personnel.[111]

At the centers themselves, significantly, teachers did *not* have education degrees. Most were just high school graduates. Head Start had never required that teachers earn college degrees with preschool specialization. Rather, it encouraged the acquisition of a "child development associates" credential, earned after completion of an eight-week training course. Even that could be waived.[112] There were not, and had never been, any requirements for the position of teacher's aide. Moreover, except at administrative levels, Head Start jobs were poorly paid. In the 1990s, full time Head Start teachers earned less than $17,000 a year, and teacher's aide's positions for a nine month school term paid less than $8,000 annually. For many, Head Start was a "holding tank" until they could find a "real job."[113] Not surprisingly, Head Start centers historically faced perpetual staffing crises – with annual job turnover ranging from 40 to over 60 percent.[114] Outside of the medical professions, few adults whose jobs centered on children earned good livings in twentieth century America. Head Start workers were no exception.

The anthropologist Peggy Sissel's year at the "Downtown Center" confirmed this statistical picture of low wages, administrative disorganization, and constant turnover. Many staffers there doubled up on jobs, while crucial positions, such as center nurse or dietician, went unfilled.[115] Far from being a warm, safe place where young children learned social and cognitive skills, and parents received child care training, "Downtown" center seethed with

[110] "Background Survey," "New Challenges to Head Start," Hearing before the Subcommittee on Children, Families, Drugs, and Alcoholism of the Committee on Labor and Human Resources, United States Senate, One Hundred Third Congress, First Session (Washington, DC, 1993): 59 (hereafter Hearing, New Challenges).

[111] *Ibid.*, 80–82.

[112] "Staff Qualifications for Head Start," Report 105–256, 28–29.

[113] "Remarks of Senator (Christopher) Dodd," 49, Joint Hearings.

[114] "Statement of Sandra Waddell, Director, North Shore Community Action Program, Inc., Beverly, MA" 64–65, Hearing, Future.

[115] Sissel, *Staff, Parents, and Politics*, 89–92. In the "Middletown" tradition of granting anonymity to respondents, Sissel changed the names of the center and people she studied.

controversies, evoking the conflicts between parents and professional staff that marred the Child Development Group of Mississippi's first Head Start summer.

Housed in a rundown building that had once been a Catholic school, the "Downtown" center was a filthy, depressing place, where the stench from overflowing toilets filled the hallways, where cold styrofoam cups of coffee gathered mold for days, and where flies buzzed around unmopped, spilled milk in the children's lunchroom. Parents and administrators distrusted each other, miscommunicating through the high barriers imposed by class.

The "Education Coordinator" urged "Downtown Center's" Head Start mothers to make grocery shopping a "learning experience," where kids improved their abilities to "count, sort, and weigh." The mothers knew all too well that only someone from the middle class would create such a "lesson." They did their best to leave kids at home with relatives or neighbors. They knew all about the inevitable struggles that youngsters' efforts to grab foods that were too expensive caused.[116]

Parent-led "policy councils" supposedly hired education coordinators and all other staff members. In reality, parent involvement was rarely substantive, and parents almost never controlled programs, much less professional hiring decisions. That die had been cast decades earlier when parent-run programs like the MCDG gradually lost their funding.

At the "Sandy Hills" center, the anthropologists Roslyn Mickelson and Mary Klenz transcribed the exchanges in one policy meeting:

President: All right. We'll have our center reports. Western Bradley?
Parent 2: Nothin' happen'n.
President: Fulbright Center?
Parent 5: Fulbright doesn't have a report.
President: Franklin Street?
Parent 7: We talking about, us, rafflin' off tickets and sell for a dolla.
President: Lewis Street?
Parent 8: No report.[117]

If typical, the meeting was hardly a ringing endorsement for parent education or for Head Start's organizational health. Yet, as the century ended the program expanded yet again, with the creation of Project Early Head Start, to provide educational opportunities for poor women and their babies and toddlers before age three. Congress authorized an appropriation of $21 billion to fund Head Start and its new partner through the year 2003.[118] Another program, Healthy Start, emphasized community-based approaches to infant mortality reduction and focused on health education for pregnant

---

[116] *Ibid.*, 112–13.
[117] Rosyln Mickelson and Mary Klenz, "Parent Involvement in a Rural Head Start," in Jeanne Ellsworth and Lynda Ames, *Critical Perspectives*, 124–25.
[118] "Estimated Effects on Authorizations of Appropriations," Report 105–256, 44–45.

women. Nobody acknowledged the precedent of Sheppard-Towner. Perhaps nobody remembered it.

In 1969, the much-reviled Westinghouse Study argued that early childhood intervention programs optimally should begin prenatally, with education and medical help for the mother, followed by a program of "infant education" for the next three years.[119] Despite a lack of consensus among pediatricians, psychologists, and other early childhood specialists about the "critical" nature of the first three years, Early Head Start and Healthy Start supporters accepted the theory wholeheartedly, if in somewhat distorted fashion. Democratic Senator Christopher Dodd of Connecticut, an enthusiastic supporter of the new initiatives, said, "There are one thousand trillion electrical connections that occur in the thirty-six months from the day that a child is born. And if you do not have those electrical connections made, they are lost forever. Unfortunately, they are lost forever."[120]

Once again, the federal government, in cooperation with state and local authorities, sent out experts to contact the mothers of infants and toddlers. This new generation of "home visitors" broadly defined the term – even including female residents of the Connecticut state prison system. Just because they were inmates did not mean that they couldn't learn how to be a "child's first teacher."[121] Sheppard-Towner and Healthy Start utilized only a fraction of state funds spent to enhance the educational and health prospects of the country's youngest. But, bracketing the early and late twentieth century, they were the two public initiatives that did the most good, at relatively little cost.[122]

As the century ended, policy makers continued to praise Head Start and its growing brood of related programs, although they often repeated

---

[119] Westinghouse Learning Corporation, Ohio University, *The Impact of Head Start: An Evaluation of the Effects of Head Start on Children's Cognitive and Affective Development*, Presented to the Office of Economic Opportunity, Pursuant to Contract B89-4536 (Washington, DC, 1969), 255.

[120] "Remarks of Senator Dodd," 15–16, Hearing, Early Head Start.

[121] "Prepared Statement of Dona Ditrio, Norwalk (CT) Economic Opportunity Now, Inc., *Ibid.*, 70–74. In Early Head Start's first year of operation, 1995, over 22,000 parents of children ages 0–3 were contacted, largely through home visits or through invitations to attend Early Head Start workshops and clinics. Sheppard-Towner had risen from the dead, though no one seemed to realize it.

[122] Initial evaluations suggested that Healthy Start was worth the investment. For discussions of Healthy Start, see Karen Raykovich, Embry Howell, Marie McCormick, and Barbara Devaney, "Evaluating the Healthy Start Program," *Evaluation and the Health Professions* 19 (1996): 342–51; Embry Howell, Barbara Devaney, Marie McCormick, and Karen Raykovich, "Back to the Future: Community Involvement in the Healthy Start Program," *Journal of Health Politics, Policy, and Law*, 23 (1998): 291–317. Interestingly, the authors of the latter publication chose "Back to the Future" as a title. But "back" involved making comparison between Healthy Start and community action programs initiated by the War on Poverty. No reference occurs to the federal initiative that *was* far closer in objectives than any of the War on Poverty examples used: Sheppard-Towner.

jumbled versions of child development theory that no psychologist ever promoted. Witness Attorney General Janet Reno's testimony to Congress in 1998 in support of extending Head Start. Conflating Freudian, Gesellian, and Ericksonian ideas, and muddling in a little Hunt to boot, she said, "Zero to three is the most formative time in a person's life. That's the time a child develops a conscience. What good are all the prisons eighteen years from now, if that child doesn't learn to have a conscience? Fifty percent of all learned human response is learned in the first year of life."[123]

Reno's garbled testimony reflected an interesting development: the spread of formal training of children of all classes at ever-younger ages. In 1966, an initial assessment of Head Start predicted that it would "modify the country's entire educational system." That did not occur, but another prophecy in the report proved true: "Public education will take hold at a much earlier age than six."[124] That, in the end, was Head Start's most significant legacy.

The Legacies of Head Start

The creators of Head Start envisioned a program to improve the health, social, and cognitive skills of disadvantaged youngsters, so that they could catch up with their more fortunate peers by the time they entered first grade. Between 1965 and 2000, Head Start was a hardy survivor, though doubts soon surfaced about the degree to which its varying goals had been achieved. However, there was no mistaking another trend in American public education. Great numbers of middle- and upper-class parents decided that, if preschool was good for the poor, it would be even better for their own children.

In 1928, just before the Great Crash, about one third of America's cities provided public kindergartens. These urban kindergartens responded to the same pressures that led philanthropists to establish free day nurseries: the need for safe places for working class mothers' infants.[125] Most metropolitan systems that introduced preschooling in the 1920s accepted private charitable subsidies. The majority of compulsory education statutes expressly forbade spending tax dollars for programs meant for children younger than six years old.[126] But after 1930, philanthropies confronted sharp declines

---

[123] "Testimony of Attorney-General Janet Reno, 48, Hearing, 21st Century.

[124] "Project Head Start at Work," 35. The report also accurately predicted that, for the rest of the century, "Child development specialists will enjoy a great vogue": 34.

[125] For discussions of the early twentieth century free kindergarten movement, see Barbara Beatty, *Preschool Education in America*, 72–101; Ann Taylor Allen, "'Let Us Live With Our Children': Kindergarten Movements in Germany and the United States, 1840–1914," *History of Education Quarterly*, 28 (1988): 23–48.

[126] United States Department of Interior, Office of Education, "Kindergarten-Primary Education: A Statistical and Graphic Study," Bulletin 30 (Washington, DC, 1930), 3. Many states did not begin to modify these statutes to allow expenditures on programs for children younger than age six until the 1960s.

in donations and abandoned their support of the public early childhood education.

As late as the 1960s, the public kindergarten remained an anomaly. Even when prosperity returned in the 1940s, few systems, even in urban areas, revived kindergartens. Indeed, between the years 1942 and 1965, fewer children proportionally attended any kind of formally organized preschool than had been the case in 1929.[127] In 1965, Head Start's inaugural year, about 10 percent of the nation's youngsters between the ages of two and five were enrolled in either a nursery school or a kindergarten.

In the next thirty-five years, preschool education boomed. By 1999, almost every school district in the country provided free public kindergarten classes. Over 85 percent of the nation's five-year-olds attended, and when figures included children in private kindergartens as well, more than 97 percent of American five-year-olds were at school. If the benchmark age for public education by the end of the century definitely dropped below age six, it was on its way below five as well. By 1999, almost one half of all the country's three- and four-year-olds attended a public preschool program for at least part of the day.[128] Never before in the nation's history had so many of the very young been called students.

Head Start was billed as a "whole-child" program, but sold as a way to boost IQ. That idea, controversial within medical and psychological communities, took hold of the popular consciousness. In the late twentieth century, "Everyone (wanted) to raise the smartest kid in America, rather than the best adjusted, happiest kid."[129]

Specialists continued vigorously to question definitions of "learning" among very young children. Most thought, at the least, "learning" and "development" were conflated for those under age six. By the 1990s a large number of psychologists, in a distant echo of their nineteenth century colleagues, the physicians who killed the "infant schools," worried that young children could not take the pressure of excessive schooling. Rather, their "learning" should focus on relatively unstructured play and exploration. Math, reading, and violin lessons could wait. Indeed, they were a form of "miseducation."[130]

---

[127] In no state did more than ten percent of three and four year olds attend such a school. In some of the country's more rural states public kindergartens virtually disappeared in the 1950s. See Kentucky Department of Education, "Pre-Elementary Education in Kentucky: Trends and Description of Status" (Frankfort, KY, 1966), 6–9.

[128] For a review of the state of kindergarten education in 2000, see United States Department of Education, Office of Educational Research and Improvement, "America's Kindergartens: Statistical Analysis Report" (Washington, DC, 2000).

[129] Phillip Piccigigallo, "Preschool: Head Start or Hard Push?" *Social Policy* 19 (1988): 46.

[130] This is the thesis of the child psychologist David Elkind's book, *Mis-education: Preschoolers at Risk* (New York, 1989), a theme updated in his edited volume, David Elkind, Ed., *Perspectives on Early Childhood Education: Growing with Young Children Toward the 21st Century* (New York, 1991).

Echoing these concerns, the American Medical Association reported as "troubling" research that indicated that the number of preschoolers taking stimulants, antidepressants, and other psychiatric drugs rose drastically from 1991 to 1995. The diagnosis of U.S. children under the age of six suffering from attention deficit hyperactivity disorder and depression more than doubled in the 1990s, even though physicians were unsure about how to establish criteria for either problem in children so young. Some asked publicly if normal three-, four-, and five-year-olds, when confined too long in classrooms, weren't being mislabeled with attention disorders and inappropriately drugged?[131]

But, for once, public policy did not follow expert advice. Books that misstated scientific discoveries about IQ were wildly popular. Glen Dolman's *How to Teach Your Baby to Read* sold over two million copies in the 1980s before going into second and third editions. Parents who bought it learned that, "A four-year-old who has not learned to read may be irreversibly damaged. A three-year-old learns (to read) quicker than a four, and a ... less-than-one learns quicker than a one-year-old."[132] The long shadow of Lewis Terman hung heavy – as parents worried whether eight-month-old infants who showed little interest in the dictionary were "subnormal." And reading was the least of it. Parents could buy a host of other titles: *How to Have a Smarter Baby*; *Teach Your Baby Math*; *Raising Brighter Children*.[133] In 1996, the journalist Ron Kotulak told new parents that they had better learn how to push "the right biological buttons" in their babies' brains. Failure to do so could stunt IQ permanently.[134] Caught up in the hoopla, in 1998 Georgia's Governor Zell Miller promised a free classical music CD to each of the state's newborns. There was not a minute to waste, since, as he said, "No one doubts that listening to music, especially at a very early age, affects the spatial-temporal reasoning that underlies math, engineering, and chess."[135]

Add to these cultural pressures to produce superbabies increasing numbers of two-income families with infants and toddlers, and the growth of public preschool was a foregone conclusion. By the 1990s, both parents in the average American married couple with children under the age of six worked outside the home. In response, kindergartens became universal, then, full-day programs. Nursery schools became "prekindergartens." And, since after a century of effort, educators had not yet agreed what kinds of curriculums

---

[131] Erica Goode, "Sharp Rise Found in Psychiatric Drugs for the Very Young," *New York Times*, February 23, 2000. Dr. Steven Hyman, Director of the National Institute of Mental Health, said that he was "more than shocked" by the JAMA survey's revelation of dramatic increases in the use for children as young as two of antidepressant drugs such as Prozac, which had been tested only for adults.

[132] Glen Dolman, quoted in Piccigigallo, "Preschool: Head Start or Hard Push?" 46.

[133] *Ibid.*, 45.

[134] Ron Kotulak, *Inside the Brain: Revolutionary Discoveries of How the Mind Works* (Kansas City, 1996), 49.

[135] Zell Miller, quoted in Bruer, *The Myth of the First Three Years*, 62.

best suited their youngest students, many school districts gave assignments usually reserved for first grade.

In the 1960s, Ed Zigler was one of the country's best known advocates of preschool education for poor four- and five-year-olds. By the 1990s, he had become a widely quoted champion of preschool for all, urging that the "public school of the twenty-first century" had to begin at the age of four.[136] The nation was well on its way to that objective, although it was clear that one of the six goals established by President George Bush and the nation's governors at their 1989 Education Summit had not been reached. By the year 2000, *not* all children in America started school "ready to learn."[137]

But they no longer started school at the age of six. If twentieth-century education policy extended formal training for both teenagers and toddlers, it also accomplished something else worth examining with care. It deinstitutionalized handicapped children and "mainstreamed" them in the public schools.

[136] Edward Zigler, quoted in Ernest Boyer, *Ready to Learn: A Mandate for the Nation* (The Carnegie Foundation for the Advancement of Teaching, Princeton, 1991), 57.

[137] For a good review of the 1989 goals and of late-century approaches to school readiness, see Maris Vinovskis, "School Readiness and Early Childhood Education," in Maris Vinovskis and Diane Ravitch, Eds., *Learning From the Past: What History Teaches Us about School Reform* (Baltimore, 1995), 243–65.

7

Public Education of Disabled Children

"Rewriting One of the Saddest Chapters"

The twentieth-century public high school and preschool greatly altered the landscape of American education, lengthening at both chronological ends the years when children were in school. However, the most dramatic change in public education policy was not determined by a child's age, but by the existence of a disability.[1]

With the exception of facilities for the blind and deaf, always a miniscule percentage of the general population, state-run institutions for the disabled in the early twentieth century housed far more adults than children and saw their purpose as custodial, not educational.[2] Compulsory education's

---

[1] Throughout the century, terms used to indicate people with handicaps were not generally age-differentiated, but they certainly reflected social attitudes. As public policy became more humane, so too did labels. The early twentieth century's "defectives" and "deformed" became "crippled," then "handicapped," and, by the 1930s, the latter word reflected the idea that fate had dealt such persons an unfair blow. By the 1970s the terms "handicapped" and "disabled" were used interchangeably, though some made a distinction – using "disability" to mean physical or psychological impairment, "handicap" to refer to the limitations that the disability caused. By the 1990s, most advocates preferred the term "people with disabilities" to "handicapped persons" and the two phrases ceased to connote that earlier semantic difference. This chapter notes phrases that came to bear heavy emotional baggage in later generations in quotation marks. It does not employ a phrase used in the 1990s – the highly politicized term, "differently abled," used almost exclusively by disability rights advocates.

[2] The percentages of totally blind and deaf people within American society have always been quite small, a fraction of one percent for both groups combined. Indeed, twentieth century medical advances contributed to declining percentages. For discussions of the education of blind and deaf children in nineteenth and early twentieth century institutions, see Frances Koestler, *The Unseen Minority: A Social History of Blindness in America* (New York, 1976), 1–43; Margret Winzer, *The History of Special Education: From Isolation to Integration* (Washington, DC, 1993), 83–140. While experts agreed that the incidence of complete blindness and deafness was relatively rare, they never agreed upon standardized definitions for visual or hearing impairment, and estimates for the extent of those disabilities always varied dramatically, especially in the mid-to-late twentieth century when speech, language, and hearing impairments emerged as types of learning disabilities.

demand that children between the ages of six and sixteen go to school did not apply to those with handicaps. Most children with physical or mental impairments stayed home, condemned by the cruel language of eugenics as "human waste."[3]

Within this context, the changes in the second half of the twentieth century in rules governing education of the handicapped were astonishing. Senator Edward Kennedy rightly called them an effort to "rewrite one of the saddest chapters in American education."[4] No longer scorned, youngsters with disabilities were guaranteed a chance for "special" education, and they, alone among all groups of schoolchildren, could assert detailed substantive and due process rights, should such education be denied. This chapter examines the multifaceted origins and complex consequences of this transformative policy change. Regulations that remedied historic mistreatment also led to huge increases in vaguely defined categories of youthful disability. They prompted misuse by middle-class parents, who hired attorneys and threatened suits if their disabled children did not receive a particular kind of "individualized" training. Conflicts about special education swamped courts and drove school systems to the brink of bankruptcy. The price paid to correct injustice, in the end, was unduly heavy. No other group of policies better illustrates the high aspirations and serious failures of the "Century of the Child."

This chapter examines education of the disabled young, first, by framing the subject with examination of the legacies of earlier public responses to "cripples" and the "feeble-minded." It dissects the factors which, by midcentury, collectively forced significant changes in law and practice, and finally, assesses the momentous consequences set in motion by the passage of the Education of All Handicapped Children Act in 1975.

A summary of nineteenth- and early-twentieth-century initiatives to educate the disabled requires, first, that the eras be divided. In important ways, the Progressive era was a time of retreat.

The Nineteeth-Century Reform Impulse

Efforts to improve the lot of the disabled in America exemplified an antebellum northern culture that, before the Civil War's carnage, dreamed of a society victorious over a host of human ills. Prison reform, equality for women, and better treatment for the unfortunate were only a few

---

[3] Thomas Bess, "Sterilization," *Bulletin of the Iowa Board of Control* 4 (1923): 183.

[4] Statement of Senator Edward Kennedy, "Education for All Handicapped Children, 1973–74" Hearings before the Subcommittee on the Handicapped of the Committee on Labor and Public Welfare, United States Senate, Ninety-Third Congress, First Session, May 7, 1973, Part One, Boston: 341 (hereafter Hearing, Handicapped, 1973–74, Part One).

PHOTO 7.1   Edith Reeves, *Care and Education of Crippled Children in the United States* (New York, 1914), 49. The caption notes that this bus, which transported hand-icapped children to "special education" classes in New York City, was provided cooperatively, with the city Board of Education and the Association for the Aid of Crippled Children splitting the cost.

causes championed during decades when some even thought human nature perfectible and utopian communities realistic.[5]

By 1900, some forty asylums for blind children flourished, as did al-most an equal number for the deaf. A few were free, state-supported, and open to all who applied, but the majority operated as private philanthropies that charged fees to parents of resident youngsters, as did "homes" for the mentally ill and impaired. All of these institutions excluded small children. Inmates at schools for the blind and deaf were almost always older than twelve, and most other nineteenth-century facilities admitted only adults.[6]

---

[5] Thomas Gallaudet and Samuel Howe epitomized the range of nineteenth century reformism. Gallaudet gave up the pulpit to crusade against slavery, then, after the Civil War, worked to establish schools for the deaf and was active as well in crusades for temperance and against prostitution. Howe sought a better world, not just a redeemed America, and fought in the Greek war for independence, went to prison in Germany for aiding Polish revolutionaries, and, at home, founded asylums for the blind. See Margret Winzer, *The History of Special Education*, 104–08; Laura Richards, *Samuel Gridley Howe* (New York, 1935).

[6] Few nineteenth-century institutions for the mentally ill or impaired accepted any inmates under the age of sixteen. Between 1857, when the Ohio legislature provided funding for the Ohio Asylum for Idiotic and Imbecilic Youth, and 1900, fourteen states opened institutions for children and young adults under age twenty-five. However, even in this minority of states, these institutions housed only several hundred of the estimated population of many thousands of eligible mentally retarded, and many charged fees working class and poor parents could not afford. And inmate "youths" were generally in their mid-teens. Care for children under

The nineteenth-century asylum demanded hard work. Many schools for the deaf specialized in shoe-making; those for the blind emphasized basket-making for girls, chair-caning for boys, and sold items produced to supplement tuition and charitable donations. These schools expected inmate labor, but they were not isolated workhouses. The nineteenth-century reformers who built them fervently wanted to train blind and deaf teenagers to communicate with the outside world. Indeed, "wars of the dots" raged over the relative merits of the five different systems of tactile type printing invented between 1820 and 1876. Deaf educators debated the relative advantages of signing and lip reading.[7]

However, an intense nineteenth-century interest in better techniques for teaching the blind and the deaf did not extend widely to those with other disabilities. We don't know exactly how many American children were handicapped in the nineteenth century. No reliable figures exist. Probably most remained at home, if families could afford their care. Overwhelmingly, any education they received was private, but at least nineteenth-century reformers vigorously challenged the idea that "afflicted" children were a social danger or a sign of parental sin.[8] As a new century began, such youngsters became, once again, a menace.

The Early Twentieth Century and Changing Ideas About Disability

In the first two decades of the twentieth century, popular and expert views of handicapped individuals changed, and different language usage indicated renewed harshness. Children once called "afflicted" now were "defectives," blamed for many of society's problems. The ascendance of eugenics was only one reason for the shift, although its emphasis on "fit" and

the age of fourteen was extremely uncommon, in an era when most regarded fourteen as a benchmark birthday after which it was appropriate to begin full time work and many adult responsibilities. W. E. Fernald, "Care of the Feeble-Minded," *Proceedings of the National Conference of Charities and Corrections* 31 (1904): 3–6.

[7] For discussion of the "war of the dots," see Frances Koestler, *The Unseen Minority*, 37–40. For patterns in deaf education, see B. A. Crouch, "Alienation and the Mid-Nineteenth Century American Deaf Community," *American Annals of the Deaf*, 131 (1986): 322–24. For a good overview see also: John Fliedman and William Roth, *The Unexpected Minority: Handicapped Children in America* (New York, 1980). Throughout the nineteenth century, and lingering into the twentieth, were strongly stated beliefs that the blind were more educable than the deaf, whose disability was often, incorrectly, linked with low intelligence.

[8] Schools for the blind and deaf were the best-organized of nineteenth century charities that helped educate disabled children, but even in these institutions, officials estimated that their small physical plants, which generally could accommodate two hundred or fewer, added to the costs of tuition, and prevented 70 percent or more of those eligible in their areas from attending. For reviews of nineteenth century treatment of the unfortunate, including disabled children, see Michael Grossberg, *Governing the Hearth: Law and the Family in Nineteenth Century America* (Chapel Hill, 1985); Gerald Grob, *The Mad Among Us: A History of the Care of America's Mentally Ill* (Cambridge, MA, 1994).

"unfit" was powerfully influential, especially among the elite, and particularly among school leaders who embraced IQ testing as further evidence of the importance of heredity as a force in shaping society.[9] Many eugenicists wanted to restrict immigration, but, ironically, huge influxes of newcomers encouraged the movement's derision of the handicapped native-born. Millions of able-bodied young foreigners provided employers with an ample labor supply, just at a time when rapid mechanization diminished the value of the handcrafted products impaired youths were still taught to make.

Eugenicists thought the state should pay attention to disability – in order to contain "inferior germ plasm."[10] Industrialization abetted this pitiless ideology. As assembly lines produced shoe soles by the thousands or mechanically caned chairs, disabled people seemed less employable than ever, especially since the passage of workers' compensation laws discouraged industries from hiring those judged more likely to be involved in an accident.[11]

By the 1920s, public policy demanded that the handicapped be isolated, or eliminated, not trained. Laws required that victims of tuberculosis, syphilis, and epilepsy be institutionalized. More than twenty states authorized the sterilization of the "feeble-minded," rapists, alcoholics, prostitutes, and members of "self-abusing classes." Politicians around the country called for revisions in marriage laws to ensure that the blind and deaf could not wed before the age of forty-five.[12] The U.S. Supreme Court declared

---

[9] Daniel Kevles has argued that the American version of eugenics was more "negative" than was its British counterpart. British eugenics leaders thought that "selective breeding" could accelerate social progress; Americans championed it as a way to staunch further decline. Daniel Kevles, *In the Name of Eugenics: Genetics and the Uses of Human Heredity* (New York, 1985), 50–65.

[10] Bess, "Sterilization," 183.

[11] In the nineteenth century workers who suffered accidents often filed suits against employers, but a legal principle generally called the "fellow servant" rule prevailed. Employees asking employers for compensation bore the burden of proving that their own carelessness did not cause any job-related injury. Between 1890 and 1908 the majority of states established new laws which substituted public commissions for courts as adjudicators of injury claims. However, employers won cases much more frequently than did claimants. Nonetheless, by the early twentieth century they were on notice that they too bore responsibility for dangers in the workplace. Many responded by more careful screening of potential hires. An employee injured more than once might have a better chance of convincing a state workers' compensation board that an employer had not exercised enough effort to make a workplace as safe as possible. For further discussion of the origins of workers' compensation, see Edward Berkowitz, *Disabled Policy: America's Programs for the Handicapped* (Cambridge, MA, 1987), 16–24.

[12] A lack of sufficient bureaucratic capacity kept many of these sterilization laws from being efficiently enforced. For additional discussion of eugenics' impact on attitudes toward and treatment of the disabled, see Phillip Safford and Elizabeth Safford, *A History of Childhood and Disability* (New York, 1996), 62–100. In a twist on eugenics, Alexander Graham Bell,

"feeble-minded" individuals to be an "antisocial, shiftless, and worthless" class.[13]

In this hard climate, pessimism about the worth of educating the disabled prevailed. Institutions for the deaf and blind deemphasized training, and states constructed huge hospitals as holding pens for the thousands of mentally ill or retarded people the age dismissed as: "menaces to society and... a blot on civilization."[14] However, the vast majority of handicapped people in these much-expanded state facilities were adults. Indeed, between 1915 and the early 1960s, most parents with a disabled child had little reason to fear the knock of a state official coming to commit a son or daughter.[15] They also knew that the truant officer would not come calling.

Most children with severe impairments stayed home – "excused" from compulsory education. Those with milder problems sometimes ended up in separate classrooms. Restricted to big metropolitan areas, these programs went by various names: "ungraded" school, "crippled classes," or "special education."[16] In many cases, administrators justified such an arrangement as

who always thought of himself as a teacher of the deaf first and inventor of the telephone second, and who married a deaf woman, tirelessly crusaded for laws that banned marriages of two deaf people. See Alexander Graham Bell, *Graphical Studies of the Marriages of the Deaf in America* (Washington, DC, 1917). For general discussions of eugenics' impact on American social and political life, see Wendy Kline, *Building a Better Race: Gender, Sexuality, and Eugenics From the Turn of the Century to the Baby Boom* (Los Angeles, 2001); Garland Allen, "The Misuse of Biological Hierarchies: The American Eugenics Movement, 1900–1940," *History and Philosophy of the Life Sciences* 5 (1984): 105–28; David Barker, "The Biology of Stupidity: Genetics, Eugenics, and Mental Deficiency in the Inter-War Years," *British Journal for the History of Science* 22 (1989): 347–85; Carl Degler, *In Search of Human Nature: The Decline and Revival of Darwinism in American Social Thought* (New York, 1991); Edward Larson, *Sex, Race, and Science: Eugenics in the Deep South* (Baltimore, 1995).

[13] "Deposition of Harry Laughlin," in Harry Laughlin, *The Legal Status of Eugenical Sterilization: History and Analysis of Litigation Under the Virginia Sterilization Statute, Supplement to the Annual Report of the Municipal Court of Chicago, 1929* (Chicago, 1930), 17. In 1927, the U.S. Supreme Court, in an opinion read by Mr. Justice Holmes, upheld the constitutionality of this Virginia law demanding sterilization of "morons," imbeciles," and "epileptics" in the case of *Carrie Buck v. J. H. Bell*: No. 292.

[14] Quotation from a statement made in 1915 by Dr. Clara Hayes, staff doctor at the Illinois Peoria State Mental Hospital, in Joan Gittens, *Poor Relations: The Children of the State in Illinois, 1818–1990* (Urbana, 1994), 188.

[15] United States Children's Bureau "Families of Mongoloid Children," Publication 401-1963, Department of Health, Education, and Welfare (Washington, DC, 1963), 28–30.

[16] The phrase "special education" appeared in the 1880s but was used interchangeably with these others. By 1931, forty of the sixty-eight American cities with populations exceeding 100,000 had established such separate programs. In big cities like New York or Philadelphia, in an average year, seven to eight thousand children between the ages of six and sixteen enrolled in classes for the "defective" or "backward." Another two thousand, on average, were students in classes for the physically "crippled." See Irving Hendrick and Donald Macmillan, "Modifying the Public School Curriculum to Accommodate Mentally Retarded Students: Los Angeles in the 1920s," *Southern California Quarterly* 70 (1988): 401–2.

a benefit to their other students, since it separated "normal" children from their "abnormal" peers. Under such regimes, "crippled" children, whose physical problems stemmed from injury or illness, were in turn often isolated from "backward," "defective," or "feeble-minded" youngsters, whose inherited mental or physical impairments Progressives judged to be more socially threatening.

Courts agreed with school superintendents' decisions to isolate "fit" from "unfit." In 1919, the Wisconsin Supreme Court upheld the expulsion of William Beattie, a congenitally blind student whom teachers praised as highly intelligent. Because the child's small town did not have the resources to provide a separate classroom, he had to leave. His very presence produced "...a depressing and nauseating effect on teachers and school children." The best advice judges could give to Beattie's distraught parents was to try to enroll their son in the state's one hopelessly overcrowded school for the blind.[17]

Had William Beattie suffered from tuberculosis, rather than blindness, and lived in Boston, he would have been luckier. There, in cooperation with private philanthropy, the city constructed a special school for young TB patients in 1912. The building had a tile roof, containing an ingenious system of movable skylights, and one brick wall; the other three sides boasted vast sliding glass partitions. Except during bitter winter storms, children benefited from one commonly prescribed therapy: constant exposure to fresh air.[18] New York City schools, again allied with private charities, provided barges floating on the Hudson for young students with tuberculosis and paid a handsome annual bonus of $100 to teachers assigned there.[19] But children suffering from the dreaded "White Plague" belonged to the less socially dangerous category of those "crippled" by illness.

Among the first Americans to win a PhD in sociology, Henry Abt concluded that such treatment of physically "crippled" children strengthened the "social health" of communities and the "psychological health" of the children themselves. A system that provided disabled youngsters with "companions of their own age, similarly handicapped," prevented the development of "mental peculiarity."[20]

---

[17] 169 Wis. 231, 172 N. W. 153. Joseph Clair also discusses this case in "Urban Education and the Exceptional Child: A Legal Analysis," *The Journal of Negro Education*, 17 (1973): 353.

[18] Edith Reeves, *Care and Education of Crippled Children in the United States* (New York, 1914), 54.

[19] Despite the extra money, the assignment was not a coveted one, given the danger of exposure to tuberculosis. The most important private charity in New York City aiding the public schools was the Association for the Aid of Crippled Children, but several dozen other charities contributed as well. The Russell Sage Foundation paid the salaries of ten additional teachers in 1910, for instance, so that classes for the disabled could be kept to a maximum of twenty students. *Ibid.*, 56–57.

[20] Abt was a member of Cornell University's first graduate PhD class in sociology. Henry Abt, *The Care, Cure and Education of the Crippled Child* (New York, 1924), 5.

Abt thought that such segregation protected "crippleds'" mental health. Overwhelmingly, however, the concern of the urban school leaders who created early-twentieth-century special education was the health of their systems, not the progress of individual handicapped children. Indeed, through mid-century the "ungraded" classroom was also a place of exile for disruptive students. "Repeated failures" and "naughty boys" dominated classrooms which were primarily punishment halls.[21]

Early-twentieth-century school systems grew enormously but found few spaces for impaired children. In fact, new procedures systematically identified and rejected them. Rules like those imposed by the Los Angeles Superintendent of Schools in 1922 were common in urban districts. L.A.'s children underwent their first round of IQ testing in the second grade. Those who ranked at fifty or below were classified as "imbeciles" or "morons." A high proportion of the children of Mexican immigrants tested at these levels and were usually expelled as ineducable.[22]

Those who *did* get assignments to special classrooms received, as Lewis Terman advised, basic vocational training. Despite the fact that schools for the blind had long since despaired of finding profitable markets for such products, New York City's ungraded classes continued to teach boys chair caning. Girls learned to clean, so that they could be "of some usefulness in the homes of their parents after they leave."[23]

Indicative of their status, ungraded classes met in basements, or on the oldest, unrenovated floors of a building. To ensure their near-total segregation, principals often scheduled children assigned there to come to school an hour late, leave an hour early, and go outside for recess at different times than did regular pupils.[24]

Students in small towns and rural areas usually did not get even this meager chance for a public education. Indeed, from the early twentieth century through the mid-1970s, perhaps as many as two thirds of all children in America with physical and mental impairments received inadequate schooling. In 1950, the U.S. Congress provided extra funding for Social Security's Title III programs that aided "crippled" children. Before then, most states restricted their cost-sharing Title III programs to blind youngsters. With

[21] Quotation from Elizabeth Farrell, a teacher of "special" classes in New York City in 1908, in Phillip Safford and Elizabeth Safford, *A History of Childhood and Disability*, 245. For a discussion of the nature of early twentieth century special classrooms as places where teachers sent children they could not control or thought did not fit, see James Yesseldyke, Robert Algozzine, and Janet Graden, "Declaring Students Eligible for Learning Disability Service: Why Bother with the Data?" *Learning Disabilities Quarterly* 5 (1982): 37–44.

[22] Irving Hendrick and Donald Macmillan, "Modifying the Public School Curriculum," 402–03.

[23] Reeves, *Care and Education of Crippled Children*, 80–81.

[24] For a discussion on the physical isolation of special education classrooms well into the 1940s, see K. C. Coveney, "The Growth of Special Classes in the City of Boston," *The Training School Bulletin* 39 (1942): 57–60.

more ample financial support, some began to expand categories of disability and encourage schools to enroll the handicapped. In 1948, the nation's school systems included an estimated 378,000 youngsters with disabilities. By 1966, perhaps as many as two million were public school students.[25]

Those increases, however, still left most handicapped children outside public school doors, though statements about total numbers of disabled American youngsters remained guesses, dependent on varying definitions.[26] In 1975, when President Gerald Ford reluctantly signed the Education of All Handicapped Children Act (EHCA), advocates claimed that there were more than eight million handicapped children in America and that most were denied access to schooling from which they could benefit.

The EHCA revolutionized decades of neglect. It demanded that "all handicapped children between the ages of three and eighteen have available to them . . . a free and appropriate education." Handicapped children also had a right to nondiscriminatory testing, evaluation, and placement procedures, individually tailored to each one's particular circumstances, the right to be educated in the "least restricted environment" available, and the right to challenge school decisions.[27] These substantive rights to free, appropriate education and procedural rights to formal due-process hearings were unique.

EHCA transformed special education. It would no longer be hidden down a dark hallway, starved for resources, and characterized as an unlucky dead-end for teachers. Rather, it would be compensatory education, redistributing resources to a previously neglected population.

The new policy came via federal directive, at a time when a U.S. Department of Education did not yet exist, and certainly when a great number of policy makers thought the federal role in setting mandates for the public schools should remain limited. Indiana Representative John Brademas, Chair of the House Select Subcommittee on Education and an outspoken advocate for the rights of the disabled, acknowledged that " . . . the unsuspecting might believe that the responsibility for educating handicapped children is a mandate that has been imposed by the government of the United States while people's backs were turned."[28] During the next quarter-century, many

---

[25] Defining disability remained a fiercely controversial issue for the rest of the century. The figures quoted are estimates using sample populations derived from state education statistics. For further discussion of problems with estimating numbers and categories of disabled children in America, see Samuel Kirk, *Educating Exceptional Children* (Boston, 1972), 4–5.

[26] That remained true for the rest of the century. As definitions of disability expanded, especially to include the fuzzy categories of learning problems, controversies about the numbers and percentages of the disabled in American schools worsened, particularly since so much more was at stake after the passage of EHCA.

[27] Pub. L. No. 94-142, 89 Stat. 773. (1975) (codified at 20 U.S. C./1400-1461), 1976.

[28] Statement of Representative Brademas, "Education of All Handicapped Children Act," Hearings before the Subcommittee on Select Education of the Committee on Education and Labor, House of Representatives, Ninety-Fifth Congress, First Session (Washington, DC, 1977): 101 (hereafter Hearing, Select Education).

stunned school administrators wondered what had hit them, and, indeed, talked gloomily about policy crafted in Washington while their backs were turned. In reality, though, the seeds of the special education revolution had been growing in plain sight for quite some time.

Untangling the causes of the policy upheaval that the Education of All Handicapped Children Act embodied reveals that many factors nourished a movement to provide educational equity for the handicapped young, chief among them: advances in medicine, post–World War II social activism, pressure from organized lobbies, and, finally, a push to deinstitutionalize the disabled and further centralize the schools.

Medical "Miracles"

The appearance of infantile paralysis as a new epidemic disease in the early twentieth century provoked an all-out campaign to find a cure, since polio respected no barriers of color or class and struck seemingly at random. Thousands of middle- and upper-class families experienced its terrors, which for many included the need to care for a young, disabled survivor.

The first terrible polio summer occurred in 1916, when more than twenty-seven thousand Americans, most of them young, contracted the disease. With help from the Rockefeller Foundation, New York City officials created the Committee on After-Care of Infantile Paralysis Cases and hired the sociologist Henry Wright to survey "cripples" to learn the extent of the problem. Presenting his report in 1919, Wright concluded that polio was the most important cause of disability within the city's jurisdiction.

In notable contrast to previous eras, when workplace accidents involving adults accounted for one half of all cases, by 1919 almost 70 percent of the thirty-six thousand physically disabilities Wright uncovered in door-to-door canvassing stemmed from diseases contracted during childhood. The "crippling period of life" was now stacked against the young, and Henry Wright worried, "very few cripples attend high school."[29] Anticipating a shift in attitudes still several decades in the future, Wright thought that, "Education is more important...for cripples than for a normal child. If a normal child is not educated, he can at least perform manual labor.... Many cripples can perform little or no physical labor, but are unrestricted in work requiring intelligence...and can render as good service as a bookkeeper, stenographer, typist, and in various other occupations, as a person who is not handicapped."[30]

At least for some, polio's grip relaxed previously rigid attitudes about treatment of the disabled. Henry Wright judged New York City's provisions for handicapped education to be adequate until he personally visited

[29] Henry Wright, *Survey of Cripples in New York City* (New York, 1919), 11.
[30] *Ibid.*, 12.

crumbling buildings in which, defying common sense, children encumbered by heavy crutches and braces labored up steep stairs to their second floor classrooms. Those who lacked the strength stayed at home. That was, a shocked Wright charged, "insupportable."[31]

Politicians agreed. By 1924, nine states, led by Ohio, passed laws that specifically provided for the education of "physically crippled" children. Twenty to forty children crowded into the typical early-twentieth-century ungraded classroom, and those with physical disabilities jostled for attention with a high percentage of healthy "troublemakers." Imitating New York City's system of cash bonuses given to teachers of tubercular children, the Ohio legislature provided the princely supplement of $300 annually per "physically crippled" pupil to school districts, demanding in return that such classes include no more than five students and provide training in academic subjects, if the students were capable.[32] In contrast to New York City, however, where private philanthropy provided the teacher subsidy, Ohio's new law authorized that the additional sum come from taxpayer dollars.

The phrase "physically crippled" became a proxy for the after-effects of polio, which few wanted to chalk up to the sufferer's innate inferiority. Then, the vaccine revolution that the conquest of polio set in motion encouraged a climate, not just of selective legislative support, but of more general optimism about the place of the handicapped within American society.[33] Who knew what cures lay just over the horizon? By the late 1950s, polio was on the wane, as were scarlet fever, rheumatic fever, tuberculosis, and childhood blindness.

Since the early twentieth century, the best-trained physicians had known that an application of silver nitrate to the eyes of a newborn infected in the womb with gonorrhea could prevent congenital blindness. By the 1940s, the practice was widespread. Better remedies for trachoma, the highly infectious ailment that reduced vision and sometimes blinded, became affordable. These two medical breakthroughs eliminated the causes of an estimated one third of all lost sight in children under the age of fifteen.

Inventions like the electrocardiograph made it possible for physicians to detect childhood heart malfunction much earlier. And simpler devices, like smaller hearing aids and cheaper prescription eyeglasses, allowed significant numbers of children who might have failed in school just because they could not read a blackboard or hear a teacher to live normal lives.

---

[31] *Ibid.*, 62–63.

[32] The seven other states were: Michigan, Wisconsin, Minnesota, Missouri, New Jersey, New York, and Oregon. Abt, *The Care, Cure, and Education of the Crippled Child*, 32–33.

[33] Chapter 9 emphasizes polio's importance for public policy about mandatory immunization of children.

An arsenal of new sulfa drugs and antibiotics promised other victories to come.[34]

Finally, psychologists challenged decades-old assumptions about children with learning difficulties. Teachers had long used the term "word blindness" to describe the problems of students who mistook the letter "b" for "d" or read the word "saw" as "was," but they still viewed children able to get through only a page or two before becoming distracted as willfully bad. New research urged such attitudes be abandoned.[35] In 1963, the University of Illinois psychologist Samuel Kirk first called these problems "learning disabilities" and argued they were often manifestations of brain malfunctions or injuries.[36]

As early as the 1930s, particularly in discussions of polio, the word "handicapped" had gradually begun to replace "crippled." "Handicapped," like "learning disability," clearly suggested an unfair external burden that deserved sympathy, not shunning. A child with a "handicap" was not a danger to society, but rather an individual to whom life had given extraordinary burdens, ones that society should try to ease. If medical advances helped encourage changed attitudes, so, too, did post–World War II social activism that emphasized the idea that those previously stigmatized should be helped, not hated.

Post–World War II Social Activism

At war's end, reformers demanded equal treatment for many whom justice had long ignored and argued that equal, not equivalent, access to public education was vital. In 1954, famously, the United States Supreme Court agreed. *Brown v. Board of Education* declared that "[Public education] . . . is a right that must be provided to all on equal terms."[37]

The civil rights struggle began with the schools. So did efforts to desegregate America. But as black children began, finally, to walk through

---

[34] The use of electrocardiograms and electroencephalograms to probe head injuries and malfunctions of the brain became increasingly common after 1946. During the 1940s obstetricians also began to monitor the newly discovered Rh factor in pregnant women, aware that Rh iso-immunization could cause mental retardation and other problems when an Rh-negative mother gave birth to an Rh-positive child. For discussions of medical progress during the 1940s and 1950s, see Harry Dowling, *Fighting Infection: Conquests of the Twentieth Century* (Cambridge, MA, 1977); Frank Ryan, *Forgotten Plague: How the Battle Against Tuberculosis Was Won and Lost* (Boston, 1992).

[35] Barry Franklin discusses the research that led to new interpretations of childhood learning disorders in *From "Backwardness" to "At-Risk": Childhood Learning Difficulties and the Contradictions of School Reform* (Albany, NY, 1994), 61–70.

[36] Samuel Kirk and Winifred Kirk, *Psycholinguistic Learning Disablities: Diagnosis and Remediation* (Urbana, 1971).

[37] 347 U.S. 463 (1954) at 493–94.

the front doors of schools attended by whites, administrators and teachers sought ways to impose "de-facto" separation. IQ testing, once again, came in handy as a tool to isolate and organize. But unlike several generations of new immigrants and poor whites whose children the exams labeled intellectually inferior, African Americans seized the impetus provided by civil rights litigation to protest. In 1967, civil rights advocates won a notable victory in *Hobson v. Hansen.*[38]

The Washington, DC, schools, like the majority of other urban systems in the country, had "ungraded" classes, where teachers sent children with "low potential," "low IQ scores," or "behavior difficulties." DC school administrators called their program "Basic Track." It was a new name under which the old rules of early-twentieth-century special education remained in force, with one difference: the presence of black children in a comprehensive public school system.

Hobson v. Hansen found that an unreasonably disproportionate number of minority children ended up in "Basic Track." To remedy the inequity, it declared that teachers could no longer unilaterally send "difficult" or "slow" students to separate classrooms. They had to request a formal individual psychological evaluation to corroborate findings from an IQ test and had to prove that the student did indeed have behavioral or learning problems.[39]

Throughout the 1960s, civil rights lawyers elaborated the idea that education was a fundamental right, on which others rested. For instance, real exercise of freedom of speech depended on an individual's ability to talk knowledgeably. Soon, using precedents established by the continuing battle to achieve racial equality in America, attorneys for the handicapped filed their own briefs.

---

[38] This volume does not tackle the issues of gender and race separately as it studies the "Century of the Child" but rather recognizes the categories as immensely important ones to integrate into a variety of discussions. For those who wish to read in more detail about the rise and (at least legal) fall of segregated education, see Paula Fass, *Outside In: Minorities and the Transformation of American Education* (New York, 1989); Hugh Davis Graham, *The Uncertain Triumph*; Jeffrey Mirel, *The Rise and Fall of an Urban School System: Detroit, 1907–1981* (Ann Arbor, 1993); Diane Ravitch, *The Troubled Crusade*; John Rury and Frank Cassell, Eds., *Seeds of Crisis: Public Schooling in Milwaukee Since 1920* (Madison, WI, 1993). This list is meant as an introduction to the topic, and is by no means complete.

[39] *Hobson v. Hansen*, 269 F. Supp. 401 D. C. (1967); Joseph Tropea discusses this case in "Bureaucratic Order and Special Children: Urban Schools, 1950s–1960s," *History of Education Quarterly* 27 (1987): 339–61. Tropea argues that placements of minorities with "behavior problems" replaced placements of those with putatively "low intelligence," that DC teachers soon came to call the "Request for Personality Investigation Form" the "Get Rid of the Kid" form (345), and that minority enrollment in special education remained suspiciously high. The situation in Washington, DC, was by no means unique. In many school districts up to 80 percent of students labeled as mildly retarded were African Americans or members of other ethnic minorities. See J. Mercer, *Labeling the Mentally Retarded* (Berkeley, 1973), 2–60.

A Trail of Court Challenges

Eugenics' embrace of survival of the fittest demoted the nineteenth-century "afflicted" to the netherworld of early-twentieth-century "deformed inferiority."[40] Post–World War II rights crusades demanded that such severe views be themselves cast aside. Handicapped youngsters were no longer to be kept hidden by shamed families and stigmatized by school and society. Instead, they deserved the "same basic services" as all other children.[41]

By 1970, more than twenty states' departments of education faced lawsuits alleging that they denied disabled children the equal education *Brown v. Board of Education* mandated. Plaintiffs claimed that the handicapped, like African Americans, constituted a "suspect class" and were persons who had been subjected to a long history of purposefully unequal treatment, and, thus, deserved an extra measure of protection within the political process.[42] At first, justices hearing such cases were skeptical. Did the Constitution's equal protection clause apply to the disabled as well as to African Americans?

In 1971, a federal district court in Philadelphia said: Yes; it did. In a settlement to a class action suit brought by the Pennsylvania Association of Retarded Citizens (PARC), the state of Pennsylvania signed a consent decree that abolished a state law relieving state schools of responsibility to enroll "uneducable" children. Since almost all compulsory education laws contained such language, *PARC v. Commonwealth of Pennsylvania* was a thunderclap heard by education officials everywhere.[43] According to one exuberant litigant, "*PARC* printed the bumper stickers for disability rights."[44]

Just a year after *PARC*, the same federal district court that banned the Washington, DC, school system's use of "Basic Track" as a dumping ground for minority students took the district again to task. Just because the city's school system bled red ink was not reason enough for it to refuse to establish programs for disabled children that satisfied *Brown*'s equal-terms language.[45]

So, even before the active intervention of the U.S. Congress, legal battles and landmark rulings in state and federal district courts frontally assaulted old assumptions about the educational rights of youngsters with disabilities.

---

[40] (Punctuation in transcript) Printed transcript, Proceedings of the Conference on Education and the Exceptional Child, November, 1949, Harrisburg, Pennsylvania (Harrisburg, 1949), 29. Attendees at the conference, called by Pennsylvania Governor James Duff, specifically denounced the use of such phrases.

[41] *Ibid.*

[42] For discussion of debates about the legal uses of the "suspect class" category, see Dennis Haggerty and Edward Sacks, "Education of the Handicapped: Towards a Definition of an Appropriate Education," *Temple Law Quarterly* 50 (1977): 527–35.

[43] *Pennsylvania Association for Retarded Children* (PARC) *v. Commonwealth of Pennsylvania,* 334 F. Supp. 1257 (E. D. Pa. 1971) and 343 F. Supp. 279 (E. D. Pa., 1972).

[44] Quoted in Maggie Hume, *A Mandate to Educate: The Law and Handicapped Children* (Alexandria, VA, 1987), 14.

[45] *Mills v. Board of Education of the District of Columbia,* 348 F. Supp. 866 (D. D. C., 1972).

Not only should they have access to public education, the courts seemed to say, but states had a duty to locate such children and provide suitable teaching environments.

The Power of Parents and Others

By the early 1970s, well over three thousand organized parents' groups demanded improved educational opportunities for their offspring. Many amplified their impact by forming interconnected regional and national alliances. Together with the several hundred nonprofit organizations that crusaded against a wide variety of disabling conditions and diseases, and in concert with groups formed by teachers, psychologists, and others involved in special education, they formed an immensely effective lobby.[46]

Disability knew no barriers of class, status, or race. Of course it never had, but until the mid-twentieth century ashamed, well-to-do parents of handicapped offspring generally quietly kept their youngsters at home. They certainly did not take to the streets demanding public policy change. While the national obsession with polio was not the only cause of changed attitudes, it played an important role.

In 1916, audiences around the country flocked to free matinee screenings of a silent movie provided by the Rockefeller Institute: *Fighting Infantile Paralysis*. Interestingly, the most heroic figures in the battle were not medical researchers but dedicated mothers who cared for their bedridden youngsters. By 1940, the vigilant women captured by the Rockefeller Institute's lens had become sexy. Starlet Nancy Davis, later to become Mrs. Ronald Reagan, played the female lead in *The Crippler*, a popular film about a shy, small town girl who became a volunteer for the Foundation for Infantile Paralysis. In 1916, screen mothers of polio victims were proud fighters; by 1940, they were positively noble.[47]

Moreover, the nation did not have to look to fictional heroes, since a polio survivor occupied the Oval Office, and, during World War II, the nation's leader was not the only disabled citizen working for victory. Sudden

---

[46] Within five years of the passage of EHCA, membership in the Council for Exceptional Children, in which teachers of special education predominated, increased significantly. John Pittenger and Peter Kuriloff, "Educating the Handicapped: Reforming a Radical Law," *Public Interest* 66 (1982): 74–76.

[47] Naomi Rogers, *Dirt and Disease: Polio Before FDR* (New Brunswick, NJ, 1990), 52, 171. Women charitable volunteers and philanthropic leaders, such as Dorothy Dix, had long been staples in inspirational literature. Dix's twentieth century successors appeared in film strips and movie newsreels, but they were generally portrayed in sensible shoes. Eleanor Roosevelt was the most prominent of such figures in the 1930s and 1940s. Millions of Americans adored the First Lady, but few thought she gave Betty Grable any competition. Much has been written about another First Lady, Mrs. Ronald Reagan, but to the author's knowledge, no one has ever described her as a Hollywood icon of changed attitudes in the 1940s about disability. She was.

demands for labor improved the job prospects for many groups, including the handicapped. Many states reported that between a third and one half of physically impaired individuals on waiting lists for vocational training programs had removed their names. The reason: they had secured well-paying jobs on their own. Disabled teenagers joined the surge into the workforce.

State labor officials everywhere winked at wholesale violations of the Fair Labor Standards Act as youngsters took all sorts of jobs, and the public cheered the exploits of teenagers who, despite a handicap, did their bit. In 1937, polio struck Richard Jones, leaving him with a severe, permanent limp. Then, in 1941, the Japanese struck Pearl Harbor, killing his father. When the seventeen-year-old son of one of the war's first American victims canceled surgery on his left foot to take a defense job surveying sites for new air strips in Honolulu, his decision made the newspapers, and the public applauded true grit.[48]

Richard Jones became a hero, symbol of a society that no longer so harshly stigmatized disability. By the 1960s, evidencing the changing social mood, Vice President Hubert Humphrey urged photographers to snap pictures of him hugging a granddaughter with Down's Syndrome.[49] Many thousands of other articulate, powerful, and influential people with handicapped relatives joined Hubert Humphrey and decided to speak out. Copying lessons learned from blacks, feminists, and college students opposed to the war in Vietnam, parents became protestors.

A widely distributed booklet compiled by the Chicago-based Coordinating Council for Handicapped Children argued that services for the disabled had too long remained a "rock-bottom" government priority because parents "had never really used their power."[50] The Council told its members to feel free to contact psychologists, social workers, school superintendents, and pediatricians, but warned that these professionals were often "nondoers" – too busy to become fully involved and too worried about "militancy." "Too much" leadership from experts would invariably lead a parents' group to "death's door."[51]

Instead, parents should stay in control and be angrily visible – everywhere. When conducting sit-in demonstrations at government offices, they should be "... prepared to spend the day. Bring the children. All of them. Do not

---

[48] *Ibid.*, 80. See also: Blue Network Transcripts: Radio Scripts, 1942, "Children in Wartime," Records of the Children's Bureau, Record Group 86, National Archives, Washington, DC and Suitland, MD.

[49] James Cremins describes Humphrey's important role in urging more humane treatment of the handicapped in *Legal and Political Issues in Special Education* (Springfield, IL, 1983), 12–20.

[50] Charlotte Des Jardins, *How to Organize an Effective Parent Group and Move Bureaucracies* (Chicago, 1971), preface.

[51] *Ibid.*, 14.

stop them from making noise.... Come with sleeping bags, camp stoves, pots and pans."⁵²

Across the country many thousands of parents complied. Since a great majority of these protestors were solid citizens – law-abiding, middle-class, white, *and* registered voters – politicians noticed. The idea of arresting a mom with whom he might have shared brunch at the country club, but who now was lying rolled in a blanket blocking his office door, must have given many a mayor pause.

Moreover parents' groups formed crucial alliances with organizations of disabled adults as well as with the growing number of nonprofits formed to seek cures for particular diseases. Advocates claimed that somewhere between twenty-five and thirty million Americans were involved in the fight to gain disability rights. Objective observers discounted such numbers and suggested, more plausibly, that no more than five to seven million of the country's citizens were active lobbyists for disability causes.⁵³ Nonetheless, even this smaller statistic guaranteed influence, especially since the disability rights movement benefited from two other phenomena that further accelerated demands for a new educational policy for the handicapped: deinstitutionalization of the mentally ill and additional centralization of school districts.

Deinstitutionalization and Centralization

The reform climate spawned by postwar social activism demanded justice not merely for those able to shout in the streets, but, gradually, also for those too young or too powerless to speak effectively for themselves. In the mid-1960s, the nation learned about abuses suffered by inmates in state institutions.

Since the early-twentieth-century public asylums had primarily housed mentally ill or senile adults, though, in keeping with the nineteenth-century belief that those with mental disabilities remained "children" all their lives, few states segregated by age.⁵⁴ While their locations were not secret, most

---

⁵² *Ibid.*, 24, 29.

⁵³ Memberships often overlapped, of course, one of the prime reasons that figures totaling numbers of active disability rights campaigners so conflicted. Parents with a child who suffered cerebral palsy might donate money and time to United Cerebral Palsy, but also to several other groups. Parents with children who had conditions that tended to be inherited, like deafness, were often advocates, both for themselves and for their offspring. Since no reliable cross-checking system existed, such patterns of multiple memberships had a geometric effect on numerical estimates. Hearing, Handicapped 1973–74, Part One, also: Oversight of Public Law 94-142, Hearings before the Subcommittee on Select Education of the Committee on Education and Labor, House of Representatives, Ninety-Sixth Congress, First Session (Washington, DC, 1979), Appendix Material to Part One (hereafter Hearing, Appendix Material).

⁵⁴ Hospitals or homes for those with physical disabilities that required long-term care were more often private or cooperative ventures organized by municipal governments in concert with

state institutions discouraged visits, even by relatives. Most were in hard-to-reach rural areas. As if that were not impediment enough, few allowed regular contact. In bold letters directly under its name, the Illinois Asylum for the Insane, on farmland in the western part of the state, insisted: "NO VISITING ON SUNDAYS" – the only day family members would usually have free to take a long train ride there.[55] A system created during an era when the disabled were openly called "worthless" operated for decades on the principle that it was best for everyone if those who were institutionalized were ignored.

In 1966, *Look* magazine turned a blazing spotlight on care in facilities long left in the shadows of national consciousness. Fred Kaplan used concealed cameras to shoot pictures that made millions of readers recoil in horror: attendants using high power hoses to wash down five old men cowering against a cement wall, a bathroom where excrement coated the floor and flies swarmed near the ceiling, patients tied spread-eagle to filthy beds, crying children locked into five foot by three foot "therapy" cages.[56]

Other disturbing stories followed. In 1972, New York State faced a class action suit filed against supervisors at Willowbrook, a public institution on Staten Island for mentally handicapped children and adults. The testimony presented by the plaintiffs was overwhelming. One hundred percent of the residents of Willowbrook contracted hepatitis within six months of

---

private philanthropy. In 1965 the Children's Bureau estimated that during most prior decades of the twentieth century between ten and sixteen percent of those residing in state-financed institutions were children, from one quarter to one third of the adult rate. The Bureau included prisons and jails in its survey, overwhelmingly adult, thus skewing the figures, but balancing that was its inclusion of orphanages, training schools for juvenile delinquents, and reformatories, all institutions for children. Probably children were a distinct minority, no more than a quarter of most mental hospitals' populations. United States Children's Bureau, "America's Children and Youth in Institutions: A Demographic Analysis" (Washington, DC, 1965), 1–14.

[55] Joan Gittens, *Poor Relations*, 190.

[56] For discussion of the impact of the *Look* exposé, see Douglas Biklen, "The Case for De-institutionalization," *Social Policy* 10 (1979): 49–50. Dr. Burton Blatt, the chief author of the *Look* story, expanded his findings into a widely read book, *Christmas in Purgatory* (New York, 1966). This chapter's focus does not allow sustained discussion of the policy impact of post-1960 deinstitutionalization of the adult mentally ill. The historian Gerald Grob has persuasively argued, however, that it was not a disaster, as many advocates of the mentally ill have claimed. For two insightful reviews of the subject, see Gerald Grob, "Deinstitutionaliza-tion: The Illusion of Policy," *Journal of Policy History* 9 (1997): 48–73; Edward Berkowitz, "A Historical Preface to the Americans with Disabilities Act," *Journal of Policy History* 6 (1994): 98–119. Berkowitz echoes other historians who have noted that the peak of social welfare spending came during the Nixon Administration, not during Johnson's War on Poverty. And Berkowitz also argues that, since it did not pose fundamental threats to the social system of any region, nor did it pit one political party against another (prominent disability advocates included both Republicans and Democrats), disability rights were a natural cause for the post-1968 period.

entering the facility. Half suffered from pneumonia. Pus-filled sores caused by innumerable roach bites covered faces and hands. Worse news was to come. Willowbook was not just a squalid hellhole, but also a biomedical laboratory, using nonconsenting human subjects. Without asking permission from any families, officials there conducted research experiments, including one that sought to "stimulate" selected patients by soaking their clothing with undiluted ammonia. In the light of such evidence, no one was surprised to hear that the children incarcerated at Willowbrook received no education at all.[57] Under court order, Willowbrook closed.

By the mid-1970s, a phenomenon that had begun slowly in the 1940s was fully apparent: the abandonment of the huge state institutions created by early-twentieth-century policy makers eager to isolate those with mental and physical impairments. One by one, they emptied, sending their populations, including their relatively small numbers of children, back to the communities from which they came.

Not every state hospital was a snake pit. Nonetheless, the unbearable photographs from Willowbrook became a searing symbol of the need to do something about the mistreatment of the disabled. In the nineteenth century, reformers seeking more humane care for the insane published etchings of scenes in municipal poorhouses. Drawings of children wearing leather collars and tied like dogs to posts galvanized calls for action. Photographs of skinny kids at Willowbrook huddled in wire cages had the same effect.

Moreover, while the care of the nation's retarded and mentally ill decentralized, school systems did just the opposite and further centralized. Both phenomena made the disabled more visible. As late as the 1940s, many states had twelve thousand or more school districts. Such numbers hid handicapped children. After all, the "ungraded" classroom existed only in early-twentieth-century big cities. In much of rural America, a few, obviously ungraded, one room schools lingered, and many more provided only one classroom for each different age group. Few allowed seriously disabled children to attend. Post–World War II America continued to expand the size of school districts, especially in rural areas, and shrink that of school boards. One unanticipated effect of that development was to make the plight of disabled children more apparent.[58] When each school district was relatively small, officials could individually discourage parents from seeking schooling for widely scattered numbers of disabled kids. Consolidated districts meant consolidated numbers of students – including those with handicaps.

Together, all of these factors acted as potent impetus for an education policy that no longer spurned handicapped children.

[57] For discussions of the terrible conditions at Willowbrook and at other institutions, see Burton Blatt, Ed., *Souls in Extremis: An Anthology on Victims and Victimizers* (Boston, 1973).

[58] Michael Kirst, "School Board: Evolution of an American Institution," *American School Board Journal*, Special Issue (1991): 11–15.

The Education of All Handicapped Children Act (Public Law 94-142)

Since 1963, when President John Kennedy signed the Community Mental Health Centers Act, which provided subsidies for the construction of smaller facilities for the mentally retarded, federal funding encouraged better treatment of the disabled. In 1966, Congress amended the Elementary and Secondary Education Act of 1965 to give monetary incentives to states that trained teachers of the handicapped at public universities. In 1970, the Education of the Handicapped Act provided additional grant money for special education teacher training.[59]

These initiatives were waves. The Education of All Handicapped Children Act of 1975, which remained the benchmark legislation governing the subject for the rest of the century, was a tsunami.[60] As did other post–World War II education initiatives, including Head Start, EHCA channeled aid to states, but, by giving handicapped children very specific legal rights, it raised uniquely thorny questions about the nature and limits of federalism.

EHCA allocated funds to states to supplement spending on educational services for handicapped youngsters. In order to qualify, states had to guarantee that all handicapped children had the right to a "free, appropriate" education, which included "related" nonmedical services necessary to such an education. They also had to create plans to find and evaluate all eligible children, who included: "the mentally retarded, hard of hearing, deaf, speech impaired, visually handicapped, emotionally disturbed, orthopedically impaired, or other health impaired children, or children with specific learning disabilities."[61]

A multidisciplinary team consisting of teachers, administrators, social workers, and psychologists had to assess each student's needs and write an "individualized education plan" (IEP) for him, which parents could review. Once all participants agreed on a course of education, the child had to be placed in the "least restrictive environment" (LRE) commensurate with his

[59] Charles Weldon, Lynne White, and Betty Wilson, "A Modern Wilderness: The Law of Education for the Handicapped," *Mercer Law Review* 34 (1983): 1045–54. The 1970 Education of the Handicapped Act, in addition, created a federal Bureau of Education for the Handicapped that preceded the establishment of a federal Department of Education. For a detailed analysis of the 1970 Act, see "Education of the Handicapped Act," Report 95-268, House of Representatives, Ninety-Fifth Congress (Washington, DC, 1977).

[60] To avoid an alphabet soup of initials, this chapter refers both to the Education of All Handicapped Children Act and to its inclusion as Part B of the Individuals with Disabilities Education Act after 1990, when IDEA superseded the 1975 legislation, as EHCA, acknowledging the revisions made by IDEA when appropriate. Much scholarly discussion of EHCA and IDEA conflates the two bills, without clearly acknowledging that IDEA replaced EHCA in 1990, but did not change the original legislation in a major way. IDEA did, however, demand "transition planning" for sixteen-year-olds. For a review of the impact of "transition planning," see Katharine Furney, Susan Hasazi, and Lizanne DeStefano, "Transition Policies, Practices, and Promises: Lessons from Three States," *Exceptional Children*, 63 (1997): 343–57.

[61] Pub. L. No. 94-142, 89 Stat. 773. (1975) (codified at 20 U.S. C./1400–1461) (1976).

or her IEP. If participants in IEP conferences could not agree, either side had a right to demand a formal due process hearing. If it failed to resolve the dispute, EHCA allowed for suit in federal district court.[62]

In May 1977, two years after the passage of the Education for All Handicapped Children Act, President Jimmy Carter hosted the first White House conference devoted solely to the problems of handicapped Americans. Challenging age-old prejudices, conference participants endorsed a ringing position statement: "We reject the attitude that compels handicapped people to conform to criteria of acceptance based upon bigotry and ignorance."[63]

If the worth of a society rests in part on the degree of humanity it exhibits toward its weakest members, then the Education for All Handicapped Children Act was a turning point – an apology from late-twentieth-century America for the indifference of earlier generations. However, acknowledgments of past wrongdoing are rarely cost-free. The price for a radically different education policy for disabled children was a heavy one and threatened the stability of public school systems already under attack.

Special education raised tough questions entirely unresolved at century's end. How could schools reconcile edicts to educate the handicapped "individually" with practices that educated all other children by age and group? Did students' rights to procedural due process force school districts to throw too many resources into a "bottomless pit" of attorneys' fees?[64] When did "education" stop and "medical" treatment begin? Despite a goal of educating *all* handicapped children, were minorities and the poor still being short-changed? How could school districts cope with the staggering costs of special education?

An Appropriate Education?

The Education of All Handicapped Children Act demanded that each child with special needs be provided an "appropriate" education in the "least restrictive environment" possible. It did not require "mainstreaming" into regular public school classrooms. In fact, the term was never used.

Rather, EHCA gave handicapped students a right "regular" ones never possessed – to an "individualized education plan." Of course, the idea that every American child should be educated in ways that maximized his individual talents was a goal many applauded. But it also was unattainable in the vast majority of American school districts, which, since the creation of the mass high school in the early twentieth century, categorized kids in groups.

---

[62] *Ibid.*

[63] Conference Position Statement quoted in David Pfeiffer and Michael Giampietro, "Government Policy Toward Handicapped Individuals: The White House Conference on Handicapped Individuals," *Policy Studies Journal* 6 (1977): 96.

[64] Dave Dagley, "Feeding a Bottomless Pit: Attorneys' Fees for Special Education," *School Business Affairs*, 59 (1993): 5.

After 1975, handicapped children, but no others, had a legal right to an IEP. Not only that, they had a right to an IEP created by a "multidisciplinary" team of professionals. The EHCA's language was vague. Beyond requiring that the education offered be "appropriate" and that those who created an individual plan be from different disciplines, and that parents be involved, it offered little guidance. Over the next quarter-century, fights over what was indeed "appropriate" became fierce, and they were battles, as California Representative George Miller accurately predicted, most effectively waged by the "most sophisticated" parents.[65]

Middle- and upper-class couples with the financial ability in the late twentieth century to include that increasing rarity, a spouse who stayed home full time to care for children, were the most active participants in the creation of individualized education for their disabled kids. University of Wisconsin education professor Lynn Doyle discovered that working-class and poor parents found the whole IEP consultation process bewildering. "Mrs. R," for instance, an unemployed single mother, had not responded to three certified letters inviting her to review an IEP for "Mae," her six-year-old daughter. When Doyle asked why, "Mrs. R," a high school dropout, pointed in despair to a pile of carefully saved paperwork, all of which mystified her.[66]

The IEP conference itself could be intimidating, even to parents blessed with far more education than "Mrs. R." Most districts implemented EHCA's requirement that decisions be made by a "multidisciplinary" team by including a school psychologist, a school administrator, and at least one teacher. Those able to decipher educational and medical terminology were best able to comprehend the decisions of these assembled "experts."[67] As one confused parent explained, "They talk so fast, with so many numbers, you need someone with you to know what they're saying."[68]

Parents who did understand the often-complicated rules imposed by school districts, and who had the time and energy, often disputed IEPs, and the "someone" who came with them was an attorney. Within ten years of passage of EHCA, special education had become the second most litigated issue in American courts.[69]

---

[65] Miller noted that in talks with hundreds of people in his district, only parents with significant amounts of education and, often, the financial ability to allow one spouse to care for children full time were able to devote the "time, energy, and effort to successfully fight public school systems." Hearings, Appendix Material, 30.

[66] Lynn Doyle, "Multiple Perspectives: A Narrative of Special Education Alternatives," *International Journal of Educational Reform* 4 (1995): 452–54.

[67] Willam Clune and Mark Van Pelt, "A Political Method of Evaluating the Education for All Handicapped Children Act of 1975 and the Several Gaps of Gap Analysis," *Law and Contemporary Problems*, 48 (1985): 30–35.

[68] Kevin Hill, "Legal Conflicts in Special Education," *ONU Monographs' Abstracts* 30 (1988): 2.

[69] The first category included procedural issues, such as burden of proof, standing, and statutes of limitation. Melinda Maloney and Brian Shenker, "The Continuing Evolution of

"Legalized" Education

Suits ran a wide gamut, from disputes about whether IEPs truly provided appropriate education to questions about the constitutional duty of schools to protect students from harm inflicted by disabled students. Due process hearings quickly evolved from informal procedures to quasi-judicial ones. Said one school official, "The only thing we're missing is a robe for the hearing officer."[70] Overwhelmingly, those who challenged schools' special education decisions were middle-class or wealthy parents, even after Congress made it possible for plaintiffs to recover all or some of their legal expenses. Only the prosperous were financially able to shoulder the costs of litigation and then wait months or years for reimbursement.

School districts had always retained counsel. Now, many began to give preference to administrators with legal backgrounds who could understand the thick bulletins regularly distributed by the U.S. Department of Education outlining "criteria for evaluating the due process procedural safeguards provisions" of Public Law 94-142.[71]

Parents were sure that school districts had a huge advantage; in turn administrators bemoaned the crushing burden of litigation.[72] The actual amount of school revenue diverted to pay attorneys' fees was hard to determine, since judges often sealed financial information. Nonetheless, the decisions themselves were open to scrutiny. Neither parents nor school districts emerged clearly victorious. Each won about half the time.[73]

One change was clear. Worried about the very real possibility of lawsuits, administrators responsible for special education demanded ever more elaborate records. In many districts special education teachers spent more

Special Education Law, 1978–1995: Individuals with Disabilities Education Law Report 12" (Danvers, MA, 1995), 1. This became especially true after 1986, when Congress amended EHCA to include reimbursement to plaintiffs for attorneys' fees. See Barry Winnick, "Congress, *Smith. v. Robinson*, and the Myth of Attorney Representation in Special Education Hearings; Is Attorney Representation Desirable?" *Syracuse Law Review* 37 (1987): 1161–77.

[70] Maloney and Shenker, "The Continuing Evolution of Special Education Law": 1.

[71] Educators and attorneys often used a convenient shorthand and referred to the Education of All Handicapped Children Act as "Law 94" or "PL 94-142," its code number in statutory classifications. Between 1976 and 1978 the Office of Education and then after 1979, the Department of Education, regularly issued bulletins advising school districts about due process procedural rights. These bulletins, generally written by lawyers, were usually best understood by lawyers. See, for example, "Due Process Procedural Safeguards," The United States Office of Education, Division of Innovation and Development, Bureau of Eucation for the Handicapped, 121a501 (Washington, DC, 1979).

[72] Dagley, "Feeding a Bottomless Pit," 5–6.

[73] Melinda Maloney and Brian Shenker analyzed more than 1,200 judicial decisions rendered from 1978 to 1995 and found that schools won 54.3 percent of cases, parents won 45.7 percent of cases: "The Continuing Evolution of Special Education Law": iii.

than two hours daily filling out required paperwork.[74] Superintendents, concerned that principals could not keep abreast of all the regulations, separated special education teachers, establishing a regional coordinator as their supervisor. Although a large number of analysts agreed that a dynamic principal able to inspire teachers was important to any school's success, more and more principals found that some of the teachers in their buildings did not report to them.[75]

If special education teachers acted independently of normal procedures, so, too, did their pupils. Discipline of disabled students became a complicated issue, ensnared in legal red tape. Courts generally ruled that use of disciplinary measures, such as study hall or time-outs, could only be used when consistent with a student's IEP. In addition, disabled children could not be suspended from school for more than ten consecutive days, without a prior determination that the misconduct was in no way related to the student's disability. A series of shorter suspensions could constitute a change of placement – grounds for a lawsuit.[76] In the 1980s and 1990s, as increasing numbers of children with behavior disorders were defined as "learning disabled," that posed big problems.

On November 6, 1980, "John Doe," aged seventeen and a student in a special education class at a San Francisco high school, tried to strangle a fellow student. Pulled off by adults, "John Doe" continued to scream and kick wildly, shattering the glass in several window panes. "Doe's" school recommended that the adolescent be suspended indefinitely.

In 1981 "John Doe's" parents filed suit in federal district court in California against the San Francisco Unified School District, demanding monetary damages and a revocation of the suspension. By 1988, the case worked its way to the United States Supreme Court, which found for the plaintiffs in *Honig v. Doe*.[77] Although granting that Congress, in passing the Education of All Handicapped Children Act, did not intend to deprive school authorities of their traditional right to provide a safe school environment, the High Court nonetheless ruled that no school could suspend a handicapped child for dangerously disruptive behavior, if that conduct was in some way related to the child's disability. Instead, a school district could only petition for an expedited due process hearing to review a child's education program.

---

[74] Edward Moscovitch, *Special Education: Good Intentions Gone Awry* (Boston, 1993), 86.

[75] *Ibid.*, 84–86.

[76] Thomas Hehir, Director, Office of Special Education Programs, United States Department of Education, OSEP Memorandum 95-16, "Questions and Answers on Disciplining Students with Disabilities" (Washington, DC 1995), 1–23.

[77] *Honig v. Doe*, 108 S. CT 592 (1988). For discussion of the implications of the case, see Christopher Baxter, "The 'Dangerousness' Exception," *Rutgers Law Journal* 20 (1989): 561–78.

In the 1990s, as reports of school shootings transfixed worried Americans, localities, states, and the federal government passed a variety of laws banning firearms from school grounds and buildings, with immediate expulsion a common punishment for any violation. However, courts ruled that, while the federal Gun-Free Schools Act and its state and local companions did apply to students with disabilities, they had to be implemented in accordance with students' individualized education plans. Therefore, a "group of persons knowledgeable about the student" had to determine that the bringing of a firearm to school was *not in any way* a manifestation of the student's disability.[78] That proved difficult to do.

If a disabled student with a gun was hard to expel, so, too, was one who peddled drugs. In *School Board v. Malone*, a judge in the federal Fourth District ruled that an adolescent with a learning disability caught selling amphetamines to two nonhandicapped students could not be expelled, as was school policy for all students found dealing on school property.[79]

Dismayed school officials contended that these rulings made "mainstreaming" children with behavior disorders enormously difficult. Theoretically, kids could be punished for misconduct, but not for their disabilities. In practice, teachers had trouble making the distinction. When were they allowed to discipline a special education pupil who screamed in class, pulled another child's hair, or laughed uncontrollably? When could punishment for misbehavior provoke a lawsuit? Administrators asked, were handicapped children being sent the wrong message about social expectations once they left their classrooms? Would they come to believe that their emotional or physical problems made inappropriate behavior acceptable?[80]

In 1975, the U.S. Congress declared that all of the country's handicapped youngsters must learn in the "least restrictive environment" possible. By the 1990s, more and more schools, worried that they could neither expel special education children nor control them in regular classrooms, began assigning greater percentages of disabled students to separate classrooms. Sometimes such students remained listed as "mainstreamed" but they were only "mainstreamed" for lunch or "mainstreamed" for home room.[81]

That did not mean, however, that late-twentieth-century special education had returned, *de facto*, to an earlier generation's ungraded classes. The latter had been grudgingly created by a relatively small number of urban school systems intent on protecting "normal" students from exposure to their "inferiors." Hidden away, the ungraded class was an underfunded, neglected

---

[78] Hehir, "Questions and Answers," 35–36.

[79] 762 F 2d. 1210 (4th Cir. 1985).

[80] Caryn Gelbman, "Suspensions and Expulsions under the Education of All Handicapped Children Act: Victory for Handicapped Children or Defeat for School Officials?" *Journal of Urban and Contemporary Law* 36 (1989): 137–65.

[81] Moscovitch, *Special Education: Good Intentions Gone Awry*, 88–89.

place, and administrators certainly could remove any student thought to be excessively disruptive. In the late twentieth century, those options were far less available. Instead, the numbers of special education classrooms increased. The more students enrolled in these programs, the less money there was for everybody else. Indeed, the staggering cost of special education was the worst problem it posed.

"Going Bankrupt"

Before the passage of the Education of All Handicapped Children Act, parents who wanted better public school educations for their children had one avenue. They joined with others. They passed school levies or elected local and county officials who pledged to increase school budgets. Their activism benefited not just their own children but also those of their neighbors, even if the neighbors in question were indifferent. But, at the end of the twentieth century, a curious reversal occurred. When energetic parents of disabled children hired lawyers and threatened school districts with suits, their efforts did not generally help other children in the community, especially since many disputes involved parental demands that public schools pay for private schooling. Instead, special education students and regular students were financially opposed.

In 1975, Congressional supporters of EHCA had no real idea how many handicapped children the bill might aid. An advocacy group, the American Association for the Retarded, claimed that eight million schoolage Americans, or about 10 percent of the population of kids between the ages of six and seventeen, were handicapped. However, the Association's numbers were controversial. Estimates during floor debate about the percentages of American children who might be covered by the Act's provisions ranged from 4 percent to 38 percent.[82]

For the rest of the century, states failed to agree on uniform definitions of disability, and no one created what every school administrator wanted: a national data system to use in analysis of excess expenditure needed to educate handicapped children.[83] But everyone thought that costs were disastrously high.

---

[82] For discussions of the bases for these estimates, see David Kirp, William Buss, and Peter Kuriloff, "Legal Reform of Special Education: Empirical Studies and Procedural Proposals," *California Law Review* 62 (1974): 40–51.

[83] For the last quarter of the century officials at various levels could not resolve the problems first outlined in 1975. They could not agree on a standard definition of disability, and therefore could not even estimate how many children would likely be eligible for services. Nor could they find legally unchallengeable ways to separate services for handicapped students from those offered to students who also received special services and may have been in special education classes for other reasons – such as pregnancy. See A. Stafford Metz, Nelson Ford, and Leslie Silverman, "Study of Excess Costs of Educating Handicapped Pupils," Report NCES 72-223, Department of Health, Education, and Welfare (Washington, DC, 1975), 18–25.

In 1974, as the Senate debated passage of EHCA, Senator Jennings Randolph of West Virginia, a ranking member of the Senate's Committee on Labor and Public Welfare, circulated a questionnaire outlining the proposed law to directors of state education departments. The response from Ohio was typical: "Ohio will go broke."[84]

Indeed legislation to promote the educational rights of disabled children proved to be a classic exercise in which lawmakers reaped the political favors associated with providing new services without really paying for them.[85] No state education department challenged the implementation of EHCA. In fact, a handful of states, led by Massachusetts, passed laws that strengthened its provisions. Massachusetts required that public education for the handicapped do everything possible to "maximize" potential, a promise not made in a legally binding way to any other category of students. By the early 1990s, there were several handicapped students in public schools in Massachusetts, each of whose *individual* annual educational costs exceeded $100,000.[86]

The threat of financially punishing lawsuits deterred less generous states from ignoring the guidelines EHCA mandated, even though at no time during the period between 1975 and 2000 did the federal government ever fund more than 8 percent of the extra costs incurred nationwide by special education. As had always been the case, public education remained a local financial burden, although increasingly one shaped by federal and state guidelines.

The legal disputes that overwhelmed court systems in the late twentieth century focused on definitions of appropriate education and centered on costs. In 1982, the U.S. Supreme Court ruled that an appropriate education was one that provided "some clear benefit."

Everyone agreed that Amy Rowley was a bright little girl who was earning "A"s at the Furnace Woods Elementary School in Peekskill, New York. Amy was severely hearing impaired but an excellent lip reader. The Peekskill school system provided the grade schooler with a powerful, wireless hearing aid that amplified conversations and improved her residual hearing. Her parents, however, argued that their daughter needed a full-time sign language interpreter. The Supreme Court disagreed, arguing that Amy's high grades indicated that she was certainly receiving "some benefit" from her public education. Her school district was not required to pay the salary of an interpreter assigned solely to Amy.[87] The *Rowley* decision suggested

[84] See "Survey of States Regarding Proposed Legislation," Education of All Handicapped Children Act, 1975, Hearings before the Subcommittee on the Handicapped of the Committee on Labor and Public Welfare, United States Senate, Ninety-Fourth Congress, First Session (Washington, DC, 1975): 79 (hereafter Hearing, Education, 1975).

[85] Edward Moscovitch makes this point in *Special Education: Good Intentions Gone Awry*, 203–05.

[86] *Ibid.*, 224–25.

[87] *Board of Education of Hendrick Hudson Central School District v. Rowley*, 458 U.S. 176 (1982). For discussions of the Rowley case, see Cathy Broadwell and John Walden, "Free 'Appropriate' Education," after *Rowley:* An Analysis of Recent Court Decisions," *Journal of Law*

a modest definition of "appropriate" education: it should provide "some benefit." However, for the rest of the century, school districts and parents battled over the latter phrase. Judgments, some rendered by the Supreme Court itself, challenged *Rowley*'s precedent.

Courts had difficulty defining the parameters of appropriate education and an even harder time distinguishing between necessary "related" services and medical care. Several key decisions determined that, as long as care could be provided by nonmedical personnel, school districts had to pay. In 1982, the U.S. Supreme Court denied Amy Rowley an interpreter, but in 1999 the same body ordered the Cedar Rapids, Iowa, schools to provide a full-time aide to Garrett Frey, a sixteen-year-old whose injuries in a car accident left him a paraplegic. In this instance, the Court decided that without such assistance, Garrett could not attend school, since he needed someone to turn pages for him, move him from class to class, feed him, clean his ventilator tubes, and change his catheters.[88]

In 1975, Congressional supporters assumed that, by mandating the education of all disabled children in the "least restrictive environment" possible, they would encourage more integration of the handicapped into public school classrooms.[89] Ironically, however, many parents wanted their children removed from regular classrooms and enrolled in special schools. Indeed, a significant number of late-century cases involved demands by parents that their children receive around-the-clock care, provided for by a school district.

In the nineteenth and early twentieth centuries most institutions, whether private or public, required that parents either pay at least part of the costs of their child's care or document their indigence. Often a disabled person entered an asylum only when a parent died, or when a family crisis upended other arrangements. The aftermath of the passage of EHCA changed this long-standing expectation, since the Act required that education of disabled children not only be appropriate, but that it be free.

By the 1990s analysts had a term for a new phenomenon – parents who moved from state to state seeking the best possible private education for their disabled children – at state expense. They were "special-care migrants."[90]

---

and Education 17 (1988): 35–53; John Kibbler, "The Education of the Handicapped Act: The Floor of Opportunity," *Journal of Juvenile Law,* 12 (1991): 26–34; Elizabeth Hardy, "The Education for All Handicapped Children Act: What Is a 'Free, Appropriate' Education?" *Wayne Law Review* 29 (1983): 1285–1300.

[88] Linda Greenhouse, "Court Says Schools Must Pay for Needs of Disabled Pupils," *New York Times,* March 14, 1999.

[89] The majority of special education students did receive educational services in public schools; however, the estimated 3 to 6 percent in most states who attended private day or residential programs incurred huge costs: from $25,000 to $100,000 *per student.* For figures, see ETS Policy Information Center, *The Education Reform Decade* (Princeton, NJ, 1990).

[90] Iver Peterson, "High Rewards and High Costs as States Draw Autistic Pupils," *New York Times,* May 6, 2000.

In close touch with each other through membership in associations and over the Internet, some parents of children with severe handicaps, such as autism, searched diligently for areas in the country with the best private facilities. New Jersey had special allure, close to New York City's world-class medical facilities and home to highly ranked private centers for the study and treatment of the condition. Between 1991 and 1997 total school enrollment in New Jersey grew by 11 percent, and the state's number of disabled students increased by 14 percent. Strikingly, however, the numbers of autistic children schooled at New Jersey's expense rose enormously – by more than sevenfold. A very significant number of these kids never set foot in a public classroom. Their parents immediately put them in a private school, and then petitioned the state for reimbursement of costs.[91]

Only a comparative handful of autistic children could get into premier programs, such as Princeton University's Child Development Institute, and they tended to be the offspring of savvy, affluent parents. By the mid-1990s, many such people moved to New Jersey specifically to seek education for their children. After extensively researching educational possibilities for his autistic son, Sam, Dr. Rob Mandel relocated his Indiana medical practice to West Windsor, New Jersey. The state paid Sam's $46,024 annual fees at the Princeton Institute. The boy, according to his parents, was making "spectacular progress." Other families, some of whom had moved to New Jersey from as far away as India or Australia, were similarly pleased. However, frustrated school officials reeled, as a "Volvo brigade" of well-to-do moms and dads sideswiped their budgets.[92]

In 1997, a survey of educational spending during the previous twenty-five years revealed that school districts that, in the early 1970s, devoted under 4 percent of their budgets to special education were, by 1996, spending about a quarter. Meanwhile, funding for regular education declined from 80 percent of the education dollar to under half of it.[93] Schools cut programs in music, art, and, particularly, physical education, to attack shortfalls, but there was no getting around the fact that a minority of American schoolchildren were being given financial priority, at the expense of the majority.

Convinced that a veto would be overturned, President Ford signed EHCA, but he made clear his dislike for the legislation, arguing that, financially, Congress promised far more than it could deliver. Ford doubted that federal funds in the amounts needed would ever materialize.[94] They didn't.

---

[91] *Ibid.*

[92] *Ibid.* See also John Crafton, "Putting the Brakes on 'Squeaky Wheel' Politics," *School Business Affairs*, 63 (1997): 14–16.

[93] Crafton, "Putting the Brakes on 'Squeaky Wheel' Politics," 15.

[94] Roberta Weiner and Maggie Hume, *And Education for All: Public Policy and Handicapped Children* (Alexandria, VA, 1987), 15–16.

In 1975, almost nobody anticipated how enormously the numbers of children covered by the Education of All Handicapped Children Act would grow in the next twenty-five years. By the 1980s, already over 15 percent of children in many school districts were enrolled in special education, a percentage that rose to about 20 percent by the end of the century.[95] Most belonged to two amorphous categories: "learning disabled" and "developmentally disabled," the phrase that gradually replaced "mentally retarded." California schools in 1982 enrolled 203 blind or deaf students, 7,298 with physical impairments, and 190,727 described as "learning disabled."[96] Such skewed figures were typical in all states and only grew. The education scholar Edward Moscovitch argued, "The problems of many children included [in special education] may be indistinguishable from the problems of children not receiving special services."[97] He was right.

Throughout the twentieth century, localities funded America's public schools. By the 1980s, voters in many places rebelled, endorsing initiatives that limited their governments' ability to raise property taxes. The costs of special education were rarely specifically cited, but a general dissatisfaction with the state of public education certainly was. Parents did not sit at school administrators' sides, but they saw the results of special education's financial demands: larger class sizes, minimal raises for teachers, sports programs available only to children whose parents paid for uniforms.

Special education's price included less effective teaching as well. About half of all children in its programs attended regular classrooms for most of the day. As the numbers of special education kids burgeoned, so did the disruptions in an average teacher's day. When children with learning or other disabilities spent the bulk of their days in regular classrooms, they were, to use educators' jargon, routinely "pulled out." A "pull-out" could be for a speech therapy session, a meeting with a visiting psychologist, a small reading class. The traveling specialists employed by school districts usually set up schedules for students without coordinating timetables with teachers. A teacher with several special education children could anticipate that, about every twenty minutes, a child would enter or leave her

---

[95] As had always been the case throughout the century, children with disabilities received more services in urban school districts than they did in rural areas. See "Hearings Held in Bozeman, Montana, on August 27, 1985," Reauthorization of the Discretionary Programs under the Education of the Handicapped Act, Hearings before the Subcommittee on Select Education of the Committee on Education and Labor, House of Representatives, Ninety-Ninth Congress, First Session (Washington DC, 1986): 1–74 (hereafter Hearing, Reauthorization).

[96] "The Number of Children Served Under Public Law 89-313 and Public Law 94-142, By Handicapping Condition, During School Year: 1981–82," *Ibid.*, 408.

[97] Edward Moscovitch, *Special Education: Good Intentions Gone Awry*, 7. For similar arguments, see Bob Audette and Bob Algozzine, "Re-Inventing Government? Let's Re-Invent Special Education," *Journal of Learning Disabilities* 30 (1997): 378–83.

classroom. Just keeping track of who covered what material became a logistical nightmare, as did the constant need to reestablish class attention after an interruption.

A special education teacher who ran a small tutoring session for dyslexic students might "pull out" kids from many classrooms. She and the other teachers involved would rarely have a chance to organize work together, however. In most schools, paperwork documenting compliance with IEPs consumed whatever planning time special education teachers had.[98]

In fact, all teachers ended up doing much more recordkeeping. They learned that "precision" teaching was the only way to comply with "individualized" education. If two targets in a child's IEP, for example, included increasing his ability to say consonant sounds and decreasing the number of times he talked out of turn, a regular classroom teacher had to keep a tally on a pad of paper of each time the student blurted out a comment inappropriately. She might note that "Paul 'talked out' twenty-three times on Monday, thirty-six times on Tues . . . and so on." Not only would such counts have to be made each day, but a teacher had to note how many times all the other pupils in her class also interrupted her or other students, in order to figure out a goal for "Paul" to try to meet.[99]

Teachers were not the only exhausted school personnel. "Administrative schizophrenia" faced principals and superintendents. In essence, they ran two school systems simultaneously, one based on individualized education, the other on standardized requirements. The Education of All Handicapped Children Act and its successor, the Individuals with Disabilities Education Act, had two principal goals: the integration of handicapped children into regular classrooms and individually tailored education for the disabled. These two purposes, while both laudable, were in conflict.[100]

Finally, despite its immense costs, special education still failed a significant number of children. University of Washington education professor Eugene Edgar argued that "more than" 25 percent of kids enrolled in such classes dropped out before completing high school, though he was unsure whether "they dropped out or were elbowed out."[101] A longitudinal study published in 1991 argued that the number was much higher, and that about one in two disabled students aided by EHCA dropped out of high school before graduating. The report, the first to attempt a long-term assessment of the kinds of lives a national sample of secondary students with disabilities led after they left school, came to troubling conclusions. Two years after leaving school, less than 15 percent had acquired any postsecondary schooling; 30 percent

[98] Moscovitch, *Special Education: Good Intentions Gone Awry*, 90–91.
[99] Tom Lovitt, *Precision Teaching* (Seattle, WA, 1975), 62–65.
[100] Kevin Hill summarizes this argument in "Legal Conflicts in Special Education," 3.
[101] "Statement of Eugene Edgar," 136 Hearings, Reauthorization.

had never held a paid job; one in three of the "behaviorally disabled" had been arrested.[102]

Of course, definitions of failure can be as controversial as those for disability itself. As late as 1970, most schools in the country tolerated prejudice. Sue Ellen Walbridge, born with spina bifida, had to accept the edict of her school librarian in small-town Rutland, Vermont, and send her mother to check out books. Sue Ellen's crutches "made too much noise."[103]

By the end of the century, the noise made by Sue Ellen's angry mother and millions of others caused public schools to end this and hundreds of other practices.[104] But, as the disability rights movement became a potent political lobby, it skewed education policy in an unfair way. Advocates counseled parents of children with handicaps "never" to tolerate "excuses of no money."[105] But, in fact, sometimes school districts really did have empty pockets. And public school systems that typically spent more than twice as much on a disabled youngster as they did on any other student went beyond remedying historical injustice. They had become inequitable. Special education was a case of "good intentions gone awry."[106] So, too, were efforts to regulate the play, exercise, diets, and general fitness of American youth.

---

[102] Mary Wagner, Lynn Newman, Ronald D'Amico, E. Deborah Jay, Paul Butler-Natlin, Camille Marder, and Robert Cox, *Youth with Disabilities: How Are They Doing? The First Comprehensive Report from the National Longitudinal Transition Study of Special Education Students* (Menlo Park, CA, 1991), 1–20.

[103] "Testimony of Mrs. Richard Walbridge," Part One, 400, Hearings, Handicapped, 1973–74.

[104] Evidence, however, was mixed about changes in attitudes about the handicapped. Some analysts argued that "mainstreaming" did not necessarily lead to more favorable feelings about disabled students among either teachers or other students. Teachers hated all the extra paperwork and sometimes admitted that they found themselves earnestly wishing they had no handicapped students in their classes. One social scientist did a series of experiments with young children and discovered that four-year-olds began to reject drawings of disabled youngsters, regardless of whether they had such students as classmates in preschool classrooms. In about equal numbers children responded that they did not want to sit next to a child drawn as sitting in a wheelchair, but, rather, preferred to sit next to one drawn in a regular chair. They said this when they had actually encountered a real child in a wheelchair and when they had not. It appeared that more than daily exposure was going to be needed to end prejudice. Moreover, levels of education were not necessarily a marker for enlightened attitudes. Another experiment found that Americans with college degrees had some of the least favorable attitudes toward persons with learning disabilities of any group tested. For reviews of such studies, see Reginald Jones, Ed., *Attitudes and Attitude Change in Special Education: Theory and Practice* (New York, 1984), 7–12, 190–93.

[105] Statement of David Bartley, Speaker, Massachusetts House of Representatives, Part One, 347, Hearing, Handicapped, 1973–74.

[106] This is both title and thesis of Moscovitch's *Special Education: Good Intentions Gone Awry.*

PART FOUR

CHILDREN'S HEALTH

8

"Shaped Up" by the State

Government Attempts to Improve Children's Diets, Exercise Regimes, and Physical Fitness

When the Indiana State Conference of Charities and Correction held its thirtieth meeting in Muncie in October of 1921, all area schoolteachers received a Monday afternoon off, to enable attendance at roundtables on "planning exercise assignments," "playground planning," and "proper feeding for children's weight gain." The state's governor, the superintendent of public instruction for Indiana, social workers, volunteers from juvenile court committees, representatives of anticruelty societies, members of mothers' pension selection committees, politicians, and several hundred teachers crowded into Muncie's largest auditorium.[1]

In 1900, the idea that they needed a paid play supervisor would have astonished the counterparts of most of the state and local officials gathered in Muncie. The thought that it was a public duty to supervise the nutrition of children would not have occurred to them. Scales in classroooms so that "malnourished" children could be weighed on a weekly basis? Tax-supported playgrounds? Amazing.

Nonetheless, another expansion of state responsibility took firm root in the twentieth century. The United States embraced the physical training and proper nutrition of its young as public policy. Periodically, informed that its progeny were unable to defend the country against the Hun, or the Nazis, or the worldwide Communist threat, the nation went into a collective tailspin, and politicians appropriated more money for nutrition education, supplementary feeding programs, and mandatory physical training and testing.

The billions in tax dollars spent to promote nutrition, exercise, and "the science of play" did not pay many dividends.[2] Once again, muddled versions

---

[1] Royal Agne, "Roundtable Conversations," Proceedings of the Thirtieth State Conference of Charities and Correction, Muncie, Indiana, October 22–25, 1921 (Indianapolis, 1922), 138–40.

[2] The phrase was first introduced by Clarence Rainwater, a University of Chicago sociologist who in the 1920s convinced Chicago municipal officials to hire "recreation scientists" to

of social science theory justified public policies, whose primary achievement was to encourage the growth of several new professions, among them physical education and nutrition science. American kids themselves just grew fatter and flabbier.

This chapter tracks these developments through an examination of the early twentieth century's "pure milk" and "planned play" campaigns, assessment of the impact of subsidized school lunch, and analysis of the history of public school physical education and "youth fitness" standards. America's attention to childhood fitness issues first focused on malnourished babies and bad milk.

The Pure Milk Movement

The "Infant Mortality Thermometers" the U.S. Children's Bureau used to win support for the Sheppard-Towner Act got attention because they reflected widespread national concern with high American infant mortality rates. In 1900, an estimated 15 percent of all babies died before they reached their first birthday. In large cities and in the impoverished rural South, the toll reached as high as one in three. Early-twentieth-century pediatricians thought improper infant feeding contributed to the "slaughter."[3]

Some physicians had long suspected that cows' milk spread communicable diseases, and by the late nineteenth century the microscope banished any remaining doubts that unclean milk contained dangerous bacteria. If infant mortality was a scourge, and if babies needed safe supplements to their mothers' own milk, then pure milk had to become a priority.[4]

In many areas "swill dairies" kept from five hundred to over a thousand cows closely huddled together head-to-tail in filthy pens. Unable to move, the animals drank gallons of brewery mash, an extremely cheap feed that kept them barely alive, but still able to produce thin, blue "slop" milk, sold after the addition of chalk turned its color acceptably white.[5] Even when milch cows were not fed swill, farmers routinely confined them for months at a time in windowless, rarely cleaned barns. Often sick, the animals infected those who drank their milk with tuberculosis, scarlet fever, typhoid, and infantile diarrhea, a great killer of the very young.[6]

create a playground and recreation program for the city and Cook County. Clarence Rainwater, *The Play Movement in the United States* (New York, 1922), 331.

[3] Richard Meckel, *Save the Babies: American Public Health Reform and the Prevention of Infant Mortality, 1850–1929* (Baltimore, 1990), 1–3.

[4] Leonard Wilson, "The Historical Riddle of Milk-Borne Scarlet Fever," *Bulletin of the History of Medicine* 60 (1986): 321–42.

[5] For a description of swill dairies, see Norman Shaftel, "A History of the Purification of Milk in New York, Or: How Now, Brown Cow," *New York State Journal of Medicine* 58 (1958): 911–28.

[6] Thomas Pegram, "Public Health and Progressive Dairying in Illinois," *Agricultural History* 65 (1991): 36–38.

Reformers agreed: supplemental cows' milk was a crucial food for infants and had to be made safer. Many thought that, in the long run, "scientific" dairying would solve the problem of tainted milk. The "milk depots" that became a common sight in several hundred U.S. cities supplied a more immediate solution. Often operated as cooperative ventures between city governments and private charities, they supplied poor mothers with free or cheap milk.

In a few dozen of the nation's largest cities, these distribution centers operated year-round. In most, they were a summer-time phenomenon, housed in storefronts, park pavilions, or free-standing canvas tests. During months when the infant death rate soared, depots gave away milk by the bottle or glass.[7] All proclaimed that they provided only pure milk, but defining purity provoked controversy.

A majority of depots provided certified milk. Such milk was raw but produced on dairy farms that submitted to semiannual veterinary inspections of all cows for tuberculosis and other diseases, daily bacteriological testing of milk, and monthly examinations by physicians of all dairy workers. The milk itself had to contain no colorings or preservatives. By 1906, thirty-six city governments created "Milk Commissions," usually attached to public health departments, to oversee certification. By 1918, hundreds of others followed the example.

Advocates of this form of raw, but thoroughly tested, milk jousted with champions of pasteurized milk. Invented by French chemist Louis Pasteur, pasteurization heated liquids to a temperature of 145°F for twenty minutes, then cooled them rapidly. The process was common in Europe, but little American milk was heat-treated to destroy bacteria before 1900, and the first pasteurizers were large urban dairies that hoped to prolong shelf life. Most used pasteurization secretly, and the public, long accustomed to adulteration by milk producers, initially regarded the process as another industry attempt to disguise spoiled milk.

Pasteurized milk only gradually became accepted as an ideal food for infants and toddlers. The majority of the early-twentieth-century's municipal milk committees might have continued to support pasteurized milk's rival longer, had the certification movement not collapsed because of the insuperable weight of its own internal problems. Certified milk was greatly more expensive, out of the financial reach of all but the wealthy unless given away at milk depots. During years when milk sold for about five cents a quart, most certified milk cost twenty cents. Moreover, the vaunted inspection system had major flaws.

---

[7] Some sold milk on sliding scales, determined by customers' ability to pay, though the majority of milk distributed was free. Julie Miller, "To Stop the Slaughter of the Babies: Nathan Strauss and the Drive for Pasteurized Milk," *New York History* 74 (1993): 167–93.

Most urban milk committees expected the physicians and veterinarians who examined cows and dairy employees to do so as volunteers. Needless to say, even those willing to donate time to the cause could not give this unpaid work a high priority. At a time when at least one third of American milch cows carried transmittable bovine tuberculosis, serious infections were overlooked.[8]

The pure milk movement faded after 1918, as pasteurization solved some of the most serious problems of tainted supplemental milk fed to infants. Advocates claimed that clean milk saved the lives of millions of American babies, but they had little proof. Only a fraction of the nation's urban infants consumed milk obtained from depots. Most depots dispensed only a day's supply of milk at a time, requiring regular users to make time-consuming trips to get it. Few followed up on the progress of infants fed clean milk or advised adult caregivers about proper refrigeration. Such instructions would have been impossible to follow in the average city tenement, anyway. Reformers shifted their attention from debates about procedures to guarantee milk purity to focus on the need to educate mothers about proper infant care. Pasteurization had won, even though raw milk continued to be widely available in rural areas and small towns through the 1930s. By the 1920s, high infant mortality rates began to decline, although larger scale efforts by municipal public health officials to construct water reservoirs, sewage plants, and effective garbage disposal systems contributed more than did "pure" milk to this development.[9]

With the milk war won, the Great War spurred another, its battle plans coordinated by local governments intent on defeating perceived weakness among the country's young. By the time the Depression forced most to cut their budgets, almost a thousand American cities added "youth recreation" to their rosters of municipal services and collectively spent over $50 million annually for swimming lessons, ballfields, basketball tournaments, and a host of other "organized play" activities for children and teenagers.[10] But to understand how play became "municipalized" first requires a discussion of why Progressive era charities decided it should be "planned."

[8] For discussion of the pasteurization/certification controversies, see James Giblin, *Milk: The Fight for Purity* (New York, 1986). See also: Correspondence between Paul Taylor and C. E. A. Winslow, Winslow, Record Group 749, Box 33, Folder 20, Yale.

[9] For a good review of early-twentieth-century public health and hygiene crusades, see John Duffy, *The Sanitarians: A History of American Public Health* (Urbana, 1990).

[10] "Report on Playground Activities," undated, The Records of the Laura Spelman Rockefeller Memorial (hereafter LSRM), Series 3, Subseries 4, Box 18, Folder 192, RAC.

Psychology, "Planned Play," and the Playground Movement

Despite the legacies of a Puritan work ethic and the rigors of an agricultural life that left little free time, colonial Americans certainly played. However, children and adults frequently enjoyed the same amusements. Games such as "Snap the Whip" or "Blindman's Buff" were not age-specific. The "snapper" at the end of a joined line of ice skaters might be five years old, or fifty. In either case, his job was the same – to skate suddenly away. If games a later age would define as childish were enjoyed by all, so, too, were pastimes the twentieth century restricted to adults. Only in the mid-nineteenth century did most states require taverns to exclude young boys.[11]

The world of children and adults diverged more sharply after the 1820s. For the first time, holidays such as Christmas became occasions for wealthy adults to shower their offspring with costly manufactured toys, usually imported from Germany: Noah's Arks, china dolls, plush monkeys, and, a big favorite, boxes of true-to-life spun sugar cockroaches.[12] But the vast majority of American children couldn't begin to dream of such extravagances. They made their own toys, and they made their own games.

Boys' play was often rowdy. "Stray Goose," for instance, gave one child a half-mile head start, but as he ran from a pack of other boys, the "goose" had to cry out "stray goose" every time he changed direction. Once the others caught him, the "goose" often ended up completely buried under a few feet of dirt, with a straw to use to breathe. Girls' games, especially in rural areas, were not necessarily more sedate. In nineteenth-century Wyoming, girls enjoyed flushing gophers out of their holes, then branding them with lengths of red-hot baling wire.[13]

In 1880, nobody, except the gophers, cared. Child's play was not the concern of adults, much less government. By 1910, however, popularized versions of psychological theories declared that play was a necessary part of child development, and adults had to guide it.[14] Most of the leaders of

---

[11] For discussions of play and toys in the colonial period and early nineteenth century, see Karin Calvert, *Children in the House: The Material Culture of Early Childhood, 1600–1900* (Boston, 1992); Kathryn Grover, Ed., *Hard at Play: Leisure in America, 1840–1940* (Amherst, MA, 1992).

[12] For a fascinating account of the substitution of age for class in the nineteenth century celebration of Christmas, see Stephen Nissenbaum, *The Battle for Christmas* (New York, 1997).

[13] See Bernard Mergen, "Children's Play in American Autobiographies, 1820–1914," 175–177; Andrew Gulliford, "Fox and Geese in the Schoolyard: Play and America's Country Schools, 1870–1940," 196. Both in Glover, Ed., *Hard at Play.*

[14] For discussions of early child psychology's responses to the question of play, see Dorothy Ross, *Stanley Hall: The Psychologist and the Prophet* (New York, 1972); Carl Degler, *In Search of Human Nature: The Decline and Revival of Darwinism in American Social Thought* (New York, 1991); Douglas Candland, *Feral Children and Clever Animals: Reflections on Human Nature* (New York, 1993); JoAnne Brown, *The Definition of a Profession.* For a highly opinionated

the playground movement were not psychologists themselves and felt no need to choose between Instinct Theory or Behaviorism. They haphazardly embraced both. Children traveled in immutable stages along a developmental path, as followers of G. Stanley Hall insisted; they also were empty vessels ready to be filled, as Behaviorists argued. However, to an even greater degree than did the psychologists whose ideas they skewed, playground advocates thought that organized recreation was crucial to the development of minds and morals, not just muscles.

Luther Gulick, a New York City physician and first president of the Playground and Recreation Association of America (PRAA), worried that children had lost their "play instinct." Joseph Lee, the Boston philanthropist and the Association's second president, echoed his predecessor: the children he observed on travels around the country did not know how to play.

Yet, Lee recounted a walking inspection of New York City's Upper East Side interrupted, near-lethally, by a tin can used for a football.[15] Luther Gulick, the same man who was sure children had forgotten how to play, admitted city boys' rules for craps differed from block to block.[16] Play organizers did not really believe that children were unable to invent their own games. They worried that children misused free time. The idea that children *had* free time meshed seamlessly, although in often-unacknowledged ways, with contemporary efforts to restrict child labor and compel school.

"Planned play," in common with many other child-saving measures, addressed concerns about social and political disorder in cities overflowing with immigrants, most of whom were young men and boys. The idea that playgrounds could supplement compulsory education and also help "school for citizenship" appealed to several of the early twentieth century's most prominent philanthropists, particularly Olivia Sage, whose foundation promoted organized recreation relentlessly.[17] By 1915, the country had some 3,000 supervised playgrounds, all but a handful the donations of private charities. But philanthropic leaders thought that would soon change. The Russell Sage Foundation's Department of Recreation optimistically concluded that Americans were ready to consider adult-planned and adult-supervised children's play a "public problem... (and will) call upon local government for appropriate communal action."[18]

In fact, that prediction proved accurate, but not because mayors and state legislators decided to champion the philosophy of play. Cities that spent taxes to build municipally sponsored playgrounds for younger children and

first-person review of the field, see G. Stanley Hall, *Life and Confessions of a Psychologist* (New York, 1923).

[15] Joseph Lee, "Play and Congestion," *Charities and the Commons* (1908): 43–45.

[16] Luther Gulick, *A Philosophy of Play* (Boston, 1920), 238.

[17] Joseph Lee, "Play as a School of the Citizen," *Charities and the Commons* (1907): 486.

[18] Michael Davis, "The Exploitation of Pleasure: A Study of Commercial Recreations in New York City," Pamphlet File, RSF, 45, RAC.

tennis courts, playing fields, and other amenities for their older siblings, would likely have remained the exception to the rule had not a much more compelling event intervened: American entrance into World War I.[19] The fact that the Army disqualified over one third of all young men called up for the draft as physically unfit prompted public support for planned play. The Great War accomplished in less than a year what the playground movement had failed to achieve in two decades: widespread public sponsorship of organized play.

World War I: Government Embrace of Physical Training

Indeed, the almost two million men who *did* past muster were recruited into planned recreation, as well as the Army. In many ways they represented the highly diverse, urban populations that so worried philanthropists searching for vehicles of assimilation. One in five draftees was foreign-born. Over half had at least one nonnative parent. They arrived at training camps speaking fifty different languages. And they were overwhelming young – most just on the cusp of adult life. The first draft registration included men aged twenty-one to thirty; additional call-ups extended the age limits from eighteen to forty-five years. However, marriage and occupational exemptions meant that the average American Doughboy was in his early twenties. Hundreds of thousands were still teenagers.[20]

Raymond Fosdick, a key adviser to John D. Rockefeller Jr., took leave from the Rockefeller family philanthropies to devote attention full time to his work as chair of the Commission on Training Camp Activities. Fosdick, an early convert to the virtues of planned play, was determined that the young men the nation sent to France would carry with them not just the newly invented safety razor but the safety of higher moral standards learned through organized recreation. Over the initial objections of the War Department, Fosdick banned liquor, routed prostitutes, and persuaded officials in most of the 120 towns that bordered camps to bar troops from taverns. The Russell Sage Foundation shut down all other recreational planning activities and sent its experts to Fosdick. Every training camp soon had a full array of organized play – folk dancing with girls from neighboring towns, boxing matches, baseball teams, basketball tournaments.[21]

---

[19] As late as 1914, only 55 American cities provided any tax support for supervised play for children. Clarence Rainwater, *The Play Movement in the United States*, 21.

[20] For discussions of draft legislation and implementation, see David Kennedy, *Over Here: The First World War and American Society* (New York, 1980), 144–68; John Whiteclay Chambers, *To Raise an Army: The Draft Comes to Modern America* (New York, 1987), 153–260. For discussion of athletics in the Army during the war, see Steven Pope, "An Army of Athletes: Playing Fields, Battlefields, and the American Military Sporting Experience, 1890–1920," *Journal of Military History* 59 (1995): 35–56.

[21] Raymond Fosdick, "The Commission on Training Camp Activities," *Proceedings of the Academy of Political Science* 7 (1917–18): 164–70. The attempt to keep the troops

Even before these men returned from Europe, the Society of Directors of Physical Education sprang into action. The group was small, several dozen playground and recreation supervisors, but the chance was big. Led by Oberlin College professor Charles Savage, the Society lobbied relentlessly. Every state legislature and thousands of city councils received pamphlets that warned, "We must admit that the war found this country totally unprepared.... The army organization seems to have been *inconceivably* ignorant of the values of physical education."[22] City governments by the hundreds responded. With the image of millions of young men physically too weak to defend their country still fresh, municipalities all over the country rushed to include planned recreation.

The "Home Rule" movement prompted two decades of creative political ferment at the local level and played an important role in creating institutionalized recreation. Reinventions of city governments remade public conceptions of localities, as the city itself became a far more important element in American life. In 1900, two thirds of the American population lived in villages or on farms. In most states, even the average town was small – with two thousand or fewer people. A ten-minute walk in any direction from its center would end in open woods or fields. By the onset of the Depression, that had changed significantly. Only a third of the country's people lived in rural areas. As the nation rapidly urbanized, its growing cities flexed their muscles and extended their responsibilities.[23] Within two years of the Armistice that brought America's basketball-playing soldiers home, over five hundred cities "municipalized" recreation for their young. By the end of the 1920s, almost twenty thousand recreation specialists were city employees.[24]

Recreational facilities meant for children expanded dramatically in the country's largest cities. By 1922, Chicago had seventy-six baseball diamonds, fifteen skating rinks, twenty-five playgrounds, and 250 tennis courts. Use of any was free. In addition to these kinds of amenities, Los Angeles maintained a camp for children in the nearby San Bernardino Mountains. Kids could

---

occupied with wholesome activities and protected from sin continued even after the AEF reached France. The French were astonished by the vehement American rejection of their offer to establish medically inspected brothels for American soldiers.

[22] Speech transcript, Charles Savage, "Lessons from the War for Physical Education," reprinted in *American Physical Education Review* 24 (1919): 189. (Emphasis in original.)

[23] For discussion of the early-twentieth-century revolution in city government systems, see Kenneth Fox, *Better City Government: Innovation in American Urban Politics, 1850–1937* (Philadelphia, 1977); Raymond Fragnoli, *The Transformation of Reform: Progressivism in Detroit – and After, 1912–1933* (New York, 1982); Bradley Rice, *Progressive Cities: Commission Government in America, 1901–1920* (Austin, TX, 1977); Judith Sealander, *Grand Plans: Business Progressivism and Social Change in Ohio's Miami Valley, 1890–1929* (Lexington, KY, 1988).

[24] "When Bob Came Home: The Story of an American City in 1927," Pamphlet File, LSRM, RAC.

go there for two weeks for $7.50 – a cost that included transportation, food, and housing in cabins with electric lights.[25]

These kinds of elaborate programs only existed in urban areas. In America's small towns, the gospel of planned play was not so enthusiastically embraced. Olive Pepper, whose teacher training at the University of Wisconsin included preparation for "child recreational supervision," returned to her home town of Allensville, Kentucky, population 305, brimming with ideas. She organized group gymnastics for twelve girls – "about the entire female population of our high school" – and tried to persuade local farmers to buy sports equipment for all the village children. As she groused to an old teacher: "Whew!! For the most part they listen as though they were hypnotized, and I think I am scoring. Then when I finish they come to long enough to murmur, 'And now Olive, just what is it you have been doing?' The first five times that happened I felt the need for two strong men and a stretcher."[26]

Nonetheless, "Youth Recreation" emerged as another new profession. By 1925, Olive Pepper's alma mater was just one of dozens of universities and colleges that offered courses in "Playground Management" and "Symbolism in Play."[27] And graduates with such training frequently became city workers.

Municipal recreation's progress from crisis-driven response to the presence of a generation of unfit draft defectives to entrenchment within local bureaucracies was swift. Stalled during the 1930s, when cities across the country curtailed expenses, fired employees, and closed "frills" like playgrounds, planned play nonetheless remained legitimate public policy. Interestingly, however, when the wartime employment boom enabled local governments to reopen their playing fields and community centers in the 1940s, many focused less intently on programs exclusively for children. The complaint of an eighteen-year-old girl responding to a questionnaire distributed by the American Council on Education summarized the change. "Here the community center might better be called 'reducing center.' Who wants to go up to the gym and see a lot of fat old married women doing calisthenics?"[28]

If tax-supported physical training conducted by city governments worried about the fitness of children had already seen its heyday, another fitness program, this time concentrated on nutrition, was just getting under way.

---

[25] *Ibid.*, 30–39. During the 1920s most economists calculated $700 per year as the amount necessary for a family of four to live above the poverty line. As such, the cost of the Los Angeles camp, about one percent of even a relatively poor family's yearly budget, was not beyond the means of many working-class families.

[26] Olive Pepper to T. E. Rivers, January 25, 1924, RSF, Series 3 Subseries 4, Box 16, Folder 176, RAC.

[27] University of Wisconsin Training Courses: in Educational Pamphlet 27, *The Playground Movement in America and Its Relation to Public Education* (London, 2d ed., 1923), 38–39.

[28] C. Gilbert Wrenn and D. L. Harley, *Time on Their Hands: A Report on Leisure, Recreation, and Young People* (Washington, DC, 1941), 11.

The Supplemental School Lunch

Early-twentieth-century reformers built milk depots. By the onset of the Depression, however, it was very clear that infants were not the only malnourished American children. In 1927, as administrator of the Sheppard-Towner Act, the Children's Bureau gathered statistics on the weight of children ages two to eight. Scales went into "health cars" already crammed with films, posters, and pamphlets. Around the country Children's Bureau investigators, aided by local public health officials, totaled numbers and concluded worriedly that, if their sample populations were representative, between one fourth to one third of American children weighed far too little, relative to height and age.[29]

The WPA Nursery program confirmed the concern and concluded that almost all of the youngsters under its care were far too thin. Every child in the WPA program was supposed to receive a hot lunch daily, although that goal was incompletely realized. Nursery school students were not the only undernourished children the federal government tried to feed. Public Law 320, passed in 1935, allowed the Department of Agriculture to distribute surplus commodities to eligible recipients, including educational institutions. Between 1935 and 1942 an estimated five million schoolchildren annually ate federally subsidized lunches at school, although most paid between a nickel and ten cents to do so.[30] The three million older adolescent boys who joined the CCC provided yet another demonstration of nutritional problems among the young. Almost all were seriously underweight.

When the U.S. Senate considered reestablishing subsidies for school lunches in 1944, the initiative proved popular. Since the Great War, the physical unfitness of the young periodically provoked alarm. By the 1940s, as nutrition science became a better defined specialty, Americans learned that inadequate diets contributed to that lack of fitness. Publicly sponsored feeding was not just for babies, nor an additional beneficial result of Depression era work relief. Between 1942 and 1945 the military once again rejected over one out of three draftees, most because they could not meet the Army minimum weight of 105 pounds, had lost the majority of their natural teeth, or suffered from severe vision problems. Many physicians thought that all three problems stemmed from defective diets.

During the war, the American economy roared back to life, and plentiful meals reappeared on dinner tables, although rationing meant that Americans did not consume many pound cakes or thick steaks. Ironically,

---

[29] United States Children's Bureau, "What Is Malnutrition," Children's Year Follow-Up Series 1, Publication 59 (Washington, DC, 1927), 5–16.

[30] Testimony of Sidney Hall, "School Lunch and Milk Programs": Hearings before a Subcommittee of the Committee of Agriculture and Forestry, United States Senate, Seventy-Eighth Congress, Second Session (Washington, DC, 1944): 5 (hereafter Hearing, Agriculture and Forestry).

restrictions on meat, butter, and sugar probably made the country's diet healthier than ever, as people consumed more fruit, fiber, and vegetables – even discovering items such as eggplant, previously confined to city ethnic neighborhoods.[31]

Concern for the fitness of the nation's youth did not disappear at war's end, especially since feeding children nicely answered another public problem, the disposal of record levels of surplus commodities. The National School Lunch Act of 1946 authorized the U.S. Department of Agriculture to administer the program, to "safeguard the health of the nation's children and encourage the domestic consumption of nutritious agricultural commodities." For the rest of the century, School Lunch embraced those two, not necessarily compatible, goals and proved perennially popular in Washington. Who wanted to attack a program that supplemented the inadequate diets of poor youngsters and provided a well-balanced hot noontime meal to everybody else, at nominal cost?[32]

However, School Lunch's supporters, in common with Head Start's, credited achievements they could not prove. In many districts, school administrators tried to make feeding children a federally subsidized meal a profit-making enterprise, something the School Lunch Act never endorsed. Little incentive existed to expand the lists of children who received a free lunch. Critics profiled the casual cruelty of school superintendents who, rather than trying to find more poor, malnourished children to feed, required those unable to afford lunch to sit in hallways or on the other side of cafeterias, hungrily watching their more prosperous classmates eat.[33] A balanced budget, not a balanced meal for all, took highest priority.

The Type A School Lunch reflected long-established fears among dieticians and politicians that significant numbers of American children were unfit because they were underweight, even if local superintendents often stymied delivery of calories to the children most in need. Each lunch sought to increase calcium and calorie intakes by containing at least two ounces of meat, two

---

[31] Indeed, Harvey Levenstein titles his chapter on American eating habits during World War II, "Oh What a Healthy War," in Harvey Levenstein, *Paradox of Plenty: A Social History of Eating in America* (New York, 1993), 64–79.

[32] For a review of the language of the original School Lunch Act and its most important amendments through 1970, see "A Program of Nutrition Education for Children as Part of the National School Lunch and Child Nutrition Programs," Hearings before the General Subcommittee on Education of the Committee on Education and Labor, House of Representatives, Ninety-Third Congress, First Session (Washington, DC, 1973): 180–86 (hereafter Hearing, Nutrition Education for Children).

[33] Journalist Charles Remsberg went to Appalachia to investigate stories of abuses within the program and reported these stories in "School Without Lunch," *Everyman's Guide to Federal Programs Impact! Reports* 1 (1969): 1–22. Remsberg also claimed politicians told poor parents their children "might" get a chance to eat a School Lunch if they "voted right."

PHOTO 8.1 United States Office of Education, Arthur Steinhaus, "More Firepower for Health Education," *Bulletin 1945: 2* (Washington, DC, 1945), 35.

servings of vegetables, bread with butter, and a half pint of whole milk. In 1977, however, a benchmark report signaled new concerns about the fitness and food consumption habits of American children. "Dietary Goals of the United States" cautioned that Americans of all ages and income groups were eating too much, not too little, and that everyone should cut back on fat and reduce sugar consumption.[34] A School Lunch tray loaded with butter, milk, and meat guaranteed obesity, not health.

Nutritionists at Agriculture convinced Congress to authorize a revised School Lunch plan that emphasized the consumption of more fiber and less fat, but the American Dietetic Association guessed that less than 5 percent of the nation's school districts served meals that fully satisfied the new guidelines.[35] The continuing debates about School Lunch distracted attention from the reality that, at no time, had the program reached more than one half of American schoolchildren. Even in the districts that participated, children increasingly chose their own foods, rejecting government menus to select candy, pop, hot dogs, and pizza from machines or fast food outlets on school premises. Strapped administrators used royalties paid by vendors to fill budget gaps. In fact, at century's end, candy was king in American public schools. In 2000, a federal Government Accounting Office spot check discovered that nineteen out of nineteen schools visited relied on chocolate bar fundraisers to help pay for extras such as field trips, athletic uniforms, or school assemblies.[36]

Before World War II, significant percentages of American children were unfit because they were too thin. In the decades after 1945 increasing numbers were unfit because they were too fat. In a society in which, by the end of the century, one in three kids lived in a single-parent home, and where most mothers worked, School Lunch was a minor nutritional offender. Some dieticians suggested that one third or more of an average child's calories came from between-meal eating, especially of chips and the sweets increasing numbers of schoolkids sold to qualify for extracurricular activities.

As noshing replaced meals, highly competitive snack food manufacturers defied the "Dietary Goals." In the 1990s, many "super-sized" their products, dramatically increasing portion quantities. Compounding that development was another. To improve taste, food companies made many items, such as potato chips, far more caloric by adding sweeteners, even as they, accurately, promoted them as "low fat" foods.[37] Beginning in the 1980s, great numbers of producers substituted much-cheaper corn syrup for sugar. Many American children consumed as much as one quarter of their daily calories in the form of fructose, as thousands of new kinds of corn syrup–drenched prepared foods appeared on grocery shelves. A few dieticians began to worry publicly

---

[34] For discussion of the impact of the "Dietary Goals" see H. O. Kunkel, "Interests and Values in the Recommended Dietary Allowances and Nutritional Guidelines for Americans," *Publications of the Center for Biotechnology Policy and Ethics*, CBPE 95–9 (College Station, TX, 1995).

[35] Mary Story, Marcia Hayes, and Barbara Kalina, "Availability of Foods in High Schools: Is There Cause for Concern?" *Journal of the American Dietetic Association* 96 (1996): 123–24.

[36] The results of the GAO investigation are summarized in Richard Rothstein, "Schools' Chosen Cure for Money Ills: A Sugar Pill," *New York Times*, August 21, 2002.

[37] "Snacks Putting on Calories," *New York Times*, April 24, 2001.

that millions of overweight youngsters ate too many carbohydrates, principally in the form of corn-based sweeteners, not too much fat. Preliminary research suggested that fructose from corn might metabolize differently in the human body than did other sweeteners, elevating triglyceride and promoting obesity.[38]

By the end of the century the original fat-laden School Lunch of the 1940s seemed poised to return to favor. However, the young ignored it, whatever its composition, ate throughout the day along with their elders, and, especially after 1985, gained too much weight at ever-younger ages. Childhood malnourishment had generally become a problem linked to consumption of too much of the wrong foods, not having enough to eat.

Which foods were "right" provoked furor. In 1998, a class action suit filed against the U.S. Departments of Agriculture and Health and Human Services demanded that milk be eliminated from federal nutritional guidelines, alleging that it encouraged significant increases in food allergies, anemia, and diabetes among the young.[39] If a super-size, fructose-filled soft drink was bad, might milk be worse? The century began with public officials' search for proper methods to purify children's milk supplies. It ended with public officials in the dock, charged with serving children milk.

Connections between food and fitness were hotly disputed. One fact was clear: American children just got fatter and fatter – not just because their diets were dangerous; they also exercised less. That demands a review of efforts to increase childhood fitness through mandatory exercise.

You Can't Graduate Without Passing PE

World War I's "draft defectives" crisis prompted city officials to support youth recreation and Children's Bureau dieticians to survey "the underweight" problem among the country's children. It also convinced alarmed state legislatures to redesign school curriculums to include mandatory physical training. Between 1915 and 1919 all but a few states passed laws compelling compulsory military drill for every boy attending a public high school.[40]

---

[38] Historically, American producers used glucose from sugar cane or sugar beets to sweeten foods. For a succinct summary of this research, see Michael Pollan, "When a Crop Becomes King," *New York Times*, July 19, 2002. For further discussion of late-twentieth-century genetic alternation of plants, see Michael Pollan, *Botany of Desire: A Plant's Eye View of the World* (New York, 2001).

[39] Adrienne Coles, "Milk Lawsuit Leaving Some with Bad Taste," *Education Week*, 19 (2000): 15–16.

[40] Thomas Storey and Willard Small, "Recent State Legislation for Physical Education," Department of the Interior, Bureau of Education, Bulletin 1918:40 (Washington, DC, 1919), 7–15.

Before the war, no states and few school districts paid any attention to the physical education of public school students. In scattered cities with many ethnic Germans some schools developed "turnverein": the gymnastics drills common in the old homeland.[41] After the Great War, continuing anti-German sentiment banished any idea of using a "Hun model" for public school PE. But states did not retreat from the physical training they demanded of boys. Instead, during the 1920s and 1930s, they expanded physical education requirements to include girls, and state legislators made sure that games, not German-style gymnastics, centered curriculums.

Basketball, invented in the 1890s by Luther Gulick and one of his proteges, James Naismith, was quintessentially all-American and high on the list. Indeed, the existence of lists of specific requirements was a new kind of state assertion of authority over formerly autonomous school districts. Now, in many states, laws specified the length and content of physical education lessons and provided bounties for school districts that exceeded daily or weekly minimums.

The Smith-Lever Act of 1914 gave federal subsidies to school districts with vocational education programs, but in no public school system were all students on a vocational track. PE was the harbinger of a different educational model: state-mandated curricular minimums.[42] School districts would no longer be independent political entities. By 1930, all but five states required their public schools to provide some kind of physical education training as a requirement of graduation.[43] Despite this fact, the Army rejected a comparably high percentage of recruits as physically unfit during World War II. Predictably, states responded to this "fearfully frightening crisis" by boosting mandatory PE requirements yet again.[44]

---

[41] Emmett Rice, "The American Turners," *The Journal of Health and Physical Education* 5 (1934): 3–6. In Cincinnati and elsewhere where "turning" was popular, the programs were usually at a teacher's option and substituted for recess.

[42] Virginia was typical of this trend. The State of Virginia's "Third Annual Report of Physical Education" noted, "Counties and cities are increasingly relying upon the State Department (of Education) to employ or recommend qualified physical educators. About fifty percent of present personnel of physical education in the public schools have been engaged or recommended by the State Department.... (This practice) reduced the possibility of having to withdraw state financial aid in case of lack of qualifications." "Third Annual Report," typed copy, July 1922–July 1923, 6, LSRM, Series 3.9, Box 105, Folder 1059, RAC.

[43] Most required daily thirty minute sessions of physical education in elementary schools, with varying, but reduced, requirements for high schools. Some allowed health education to be substituted. James Rogers, "State Wide Trends in School Hygiene and Physical Education," United States Department of Interior, Bureau of Education, Pamphlet 5 (Washington, DC, 1934), 4–9.

[44] Charles Forsythe, "What We Have Learned about Physical Fitness," *Athletic Journal* 25/26 (1945): 18–26 (quotation, 18); John Lucas, "War and Physical Preparedness: E. D. A. History, 1940–49," *Journal of Physical Education, Recreation, and Dance*, 56 (1985).

By 1942, it had been over two decades since most states first demanded that public elementary and high schools include physical training for all enrolled students, but in the twenty years that separated World War I and World War II, neither the problems of "underfeeding" nor of "undertraining" significant numbers of America's young boys had been solved.

Physical education in the schools did not meet its goal. The idea, always vague, that adult-supervised PE encouraged morality and good citizenship was inherently unprovable. However, it was easy to check to see if it taught large-muscle motor skills. The failure was obvious. Lieutenant Commander Charles Forsythe, who resigned his position as state director of high school athletics in Michigan to take charge of the Navy's physical training programs, rediscovered a nation whose young males couldn't manage sit-ups or push-ups, collapsed during the sixty-yard dash, and, worse yet from the Navy's perspective, did not swim.[45] His recruits, Forsythe wearily concluded, had "not the faintest idea" how to keep fit. All mandatory public school PE had given them was "an almost unholy hate of so-called physical training."[46]

In fact, from its inception, physical education in the public schools was a neglected stepchild of the far more popular athletics programs Charles Forsythe supervised in civilian life. If a PE teacher were not also a winning coach, he or she ranked at the very bottom of most schools' pecking orders. "Gym" instructors frequently were told to arrive early and leave later than other teachers, so that they could supervise school safety patrols, or even substitute for janitors and open the building. By mid-century, it was common practice in many districts to give "real" teachers a free "preparation" period during the school day, while physical education teachers supervised study halls or conducted driver's education classes.[47]

By the 1990s, few elementary or middle schools had regular PE teachers. Instead, their districts hired itinerant instructors, who alternated days at three to eight schools, teaching fifty or more children at a time. When they reached secondary school, kids who weren't members of athletic teams rarely exercised. After their sophomore year, typically they could "elect" to take PE, and fewer than one in four did. Their lack of enthusiasm was justified. The "3 Rs" of PE teaching were: "record the roll, roll out the ball, and read the paper."

One survey estimated that in an average American high school physical education class of forty-five-minutes' duration, students performed a motor

---

[45] Forsythe, "What We Have Learned about Physical Fitness," 24. One in three white, and eight out of ten black, recruits to the Navy had never swum. Forsythe's figures, moreover, dealt only with the men *actually inducted* into the Navy, which, obviously, placed priority on swimming. Only a tiny minority of men drafted into the Army could swim.

[46] *Ibid.*

[47] Mary O'Sullivan, "Failing Gym Is Like Failing Lunch or Recess: Two Beginning Teachers' Struggle for Legitimacy," *Journal of Teaching in Physical Education* 8 (1989): 227–43.

skill for a grand total of two and one half minutes. Precious little occupied the other forty-two and one half minutes of class time. Students stood in lines while the roll was called. They stood in lines waiting to throw a ball. They heard the game rules repeated. They undressed and dressed. Professors from schools of education fanned out across the country, distributing "cognitive-meaning surveys" and conducting "phenomenological in-depth interviews" to learn why students were "alienated" from gym class.[48] Of course, the answer was obvious.[49]

Several state legislatures tried to rescind their PE laws. New Jersey's Governor Thomas Kean said, "Let's abolish the state mandate and let parents and children choose between dodge ball and Dickens, relay races and relativity."[50] That did not happen. In a few wealthy school districts the storms of criticism produced results. Some adopted the "All Children Totally Involved Exercising" (ACTIVE) program introduced by the Oakhurst, New Jersey, school district. In a typical ACTIVE gym a dozen or so children engaged in as many different activities. A few pumped away on stationary bicycles. Others lifted weights. Two or three skipped rope. One was off in a corner doing breathing exercises. The kids on the stationary bicycles needed to lose some pounds. The girl practicing breath control had asthma. A high proportion of children met an individual fitness goal – be it weight loss or increased cardiopulmonary strength. This kind of school PE worked. It was also enormously expensive and very uncommon.[51]

Between 1987 and 1999 the U.S. Congress passed several resolutions encouraging states to mandate daily physical education. Only one state, Illinois, rose to the challenge.[52] Nonetheless, most retained minimal physical education requirements. By the late 1990s, an average American public school

---

[48] For a classic from this genre – complete with charts, diagrams, and dotted-line graphs that track the "physical education alienation–non-alienation model in the physical education setting" – see Teresa Carlson, "We Hate Gym: Student Alienation from Physical Education," *Journal of Teaching in Physical Education* 14 (1995): 467–77.

[49] Throughout the last two decades of the century physical education's professional journals brimmed with discussions that rarely identified the real problem: justified student boredom. For a sampling: Artie Kamiya, "Today's High School Physical Education," *Clearing House* 58 (1984): 92–94; Paul Paese, "Improving Secondary School Physical Education," *Physical Educator*, 40 (1983): 60–63; George Graham, "Physical Education in U.S. Schools, K–12," *Journal of Physical Education, Recreation, and Dance* 61 (1990): 35–9; David Griffey, "Trouble for Sure: A Crisis – Perhaps? Secondary School Physical Education Today," *Journal of Physical Education, Recreation, and Dance* 58 (1987): 19–26; Sandra Stroot, "Contemporary Crisis or Emerging Reform: A Review of Secondary School Physical Education," *Journal of Teaching in Physical Education* 13 (1994): 333–41; Murray Mitchell and Ruth Earls, "A Profile of State Requirements for Physical Education, K–12," *Physical Educator* 44 (1987): 337–43.

[50] Quoted in Graham, "Physical Education in U.S. Schools," 35.

[51] Dorothy Siegel, "Breaking with Traditional Physical Education," *American Education* 14 (1978): 30–4.

[52] "Program Aims to Counter Lack of Physical Fitness," *New York Times*, August 3, 1999.

student had to complete 150 hours of physical education instruction over the span of thirteen years, from kindergarten through the senior year of high school, fewer than twelve hours per year – hardly overwhelming, especially when students spent many of those hours on other activities. A little semisecret kept physical education a state requirement. School principals and teachers' unions loved PE and lobbied to keep it. In the words of an unusually candid school principal: PE was a "sort of slush fund."[53] It justified a contract for a football or basketball coach, who might then teach few or no regular physical education classes. It gave school administrators a handy block of time to use for pep rallies or school assemblies. It gave the "real" teachers their treasured "class planning and preparation" hour free. PE's fiercest supporters were in the teachers' lounge – not on the playing fields.

Among America's prosperous, the idea that adults should organize and supervise children's play did not die. If anything, affluent parents by the 1990s were in hyperdrive – lining up classes for their children in everything from soccer to kickboxing to ballet. But, significantly, they paid out of pocket, and these activities took place away from schools.[54] Sports increasingly disappeared from public school curriculums, but not just because American families were willing to pay for private lessons. Two other factors complicated the PE requirement: lawsuits against PE teachers and school systems, and the passage of Title IX of the Educational Amendments Act of 1972 – a measure denying federal funds to any school district that practiced gender discrimination.

Suing PE

By the late 1980s, when special education litigation became a consuming concern, charges that insufficient care had been taken to safeguard students in PE classes only exacerbated school districts' legal problems.[55] One administrator offered increasingly common counsel in a memo to PE teachers. They should "increase their non-interactive preparation time."[56] Such advice willfully ignored the huge amount of "non-interactive" time already wasted in gym classes, but it did reflect the impact made by a looming threat of lawsuits.

Prior to mid-century, negligence cases brought by parents against school districts were rare. Until the 1970s, the few that occurred involved claims

---

[53] Quoted in Mitchell and Earls, "A Profile of State Requirements," 338.

[54] "For Some Children, It's an After-School Pressure Cooker," *New York Times*, August 3, 1999.

[55] Important: special education remained the gorilla in the room; in the 1980s and 1990s all other cases, including PE litigation, paled in proportion.

[56] Quotation in Robin Chambers, "Legal and Practical Issues for Grouping Students in Physical Education Classes," *Physical Educator* 45 (1988): 180.

of gross lack of responsibility. In 1944 the parents of Gerald De Gooyer took their charges against the Highmore, South Dakota, school district to the state's Supreme Court. Athletes at Highmore High won their letter sweaters only after they'd undergone an initiation ceremony, usually held in the basement of the town's Catholic church. But in May 1941, carpenters were at work repairing the building's basement, and Maurice Gardner, Highmore High's athletic coach, received permission to hold the ritual at the school gym. Gardner was present as each blindfolded initiate was brought in. Stripped of all clothing but underwear, each was made to lie on the gym floor on top of a pile of electric wires. Other boys poured jars of salted water over each candidate's naked chest, while simultaneously plugging the wires into an electric light socket. The shock killed Gerald De Gooyer. The Supreme Court of South Dakota held the Highmore schools and coach Gardner negligent and awarded damages to the grieving parents.[57]

To say that Coach Gardner was outrageously irresponsible would be an understatement. However, by the late twentieth century, charges against PE teachers and coaches were not so clear-cut. No one agreed where instruction ended and negligence began. In 1973, Carol Grant was a twelve-year-old student in the Lake Oswego, Oregon, school district. Toni Berke, her PE teacher, told Carol and several other girls to return a gymnastics springboard to its storage place in an alcove off to the side of the gym. Rather than follow Berke's explicit orders to tip the springboard up on its side against a wall, Carol and her buddies dared each other to jump. Carol struck her head against the alcove's low ceiling, breaking two bones in her face. Her mother sued, and the Circuit Court of Clackamas County, Oregon, agreed that Toni Berke had not given her students sufficiently in-depth instruction about the dangers of improper use of gymnastics equipment.[58] No guidelines for what would be suitably "in-depth" existed.

Between 1970 and 1990 lawsuits involving public school physical educators increased tremendously. Surveys estimated that one in every thirty American schoolchildren got hurt during the 1990 school year. Most injuries were relatively minor, and no proof existed that PE was any more dangerous than it had ever been. The figure of one injury in thirty had been tossed around school administrators' offices for decades. Children were not having more accidents, but their parents were more likely to sue. Moreover, courts no longer routinely granted public school teachers immunity from liability as government employees.

[57] This case has been summarized in Larry Berryhill, "A History of Law Suits in Physical Education, Intramurals, and Interscholastics in the Western United States: Implications and Consequences," EdD Thesis, Brigham Young University, 1976, 87–90. For additional information, see *DeGooyer v. Harkness*, 13 NW 2nd, 815, Supreme Court of South Dakota, 1944.

[58] *Ibid.*, 194–97.

At the end of the century, the legal maneuvering was byzantine. In 1986, officials of the Burlington City, North Carolina, school district settled out of court and paid an undisclosed amount to the parents of Lori Brown, a Burlington City grade schooler. The child had tripped and sprained a wrist while following her PE teacher's command to run a race backward. Expert witnesses for the Browns contended that if running backward were to be justified as a speed event, a teacher exercising proper caution had to ascertain the "anxiety level" that competition produced in each participant. If, on the other hand, running backward were a motor skill, noncompetitive exercise, the teacher needed "pre-knowledge of the individual skill levels" of each child in class.[59] Little wonder that gym teachers took the roll and retreated to the bleachers, or that school boards bartered PE hours for "preparation time" to keep teachers' unions happy. When students showed up for PE in street dress or complained that an exercise was too hard, increasingly nervous PE teachers often did nothing.[60]

Moreover, gender entered the mix as another cause of lawsuits. The world of state-mandated public school physical education in the late twentieth century was one that, since 1972, was supposed to be gender-neutral.

The Curious Consequences of Title IX

Title IX demanded that boys and girls receive equal opportunities to experience the full range of activities offered by physical education. Ironically, women physical educators, not men, and certainly not members of the general public, first relegated girls to less demanding play and "girls' rules," separate-sex physical education.

Girls' basketball provides a case in point. Both girls and boys loved the new game. Not surprisingly, variations soon appeared in a sport still without universally accepted rules. A team might have five players, or seven, or nine. Definitions of fouls differed, as did out-of-bounds rules. Nonetheless, region, not gender, determined the differences.[61]

---

[59] Kate Barrett, "Running Backwards in a Relay Race: Brown v. Burlington City Board of Education," *Journal of Physical Education, Recreation, and Dance* 61 (1990): 33–35.

[60] By the 1990s, the problem of students simply refusing to "dress out" had become a significant one, about which physical educators fretted in their journals. The student–teacher relationship had obviously changed from the days when a war-time survey conducted by the U.S. Office of Education in 1945 discovered that at the very top of the list of "our youth's worst worries" was "fear of incurring disapproval of teachers." "Loss of friends and family members in battle" and "war's uncertainties" ranked, respectively, third and thirteenth. Arthur Steinhaus, "More Firepower for Health Education," Federal Security Agency, U.S. Office of Education, Bulletin 1945, 2 (Washington, DC, 1945), 8.

[61] Richard Swanson and Betty Spears, *History of Sport and Physical Education in the United States* (Madison, 1995), 209–40.

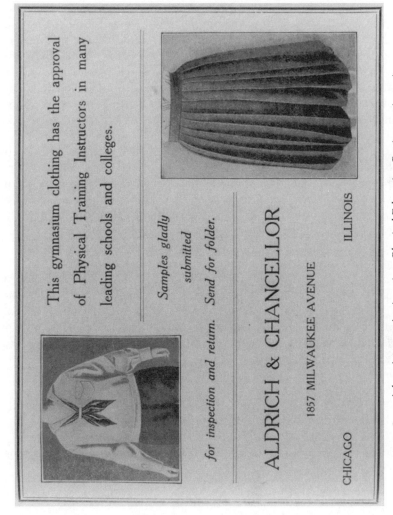

This gymnasium clothing has the approval of Physical Training Instructors in many leading schools and colleges.

Samples gladly submitted for inspection and return. Send for folder.

ALDRICH & CHANCELLOR

1857 MILWAUKEE AVENUE

CHICAGO   ILLINOIS

PHOTO 8.2   Advertisement in *American Physical Education Review* 24 (1924): 133.

Writers predicted happily that girls who played basketball would mature into "vigorous" women. Basketball was "athletic dessert" – perfect for girls. Those who learned to love the quick pace of the game would not grow into sour matrons who spent their free time planning revenge when "Mrs. Jones snubbed you."[62]

By the early 1920s, girls' basketball teams were a craze in many parts of the country. Particularly popular in the South and the Midwest, they often outdrew boys. In testament to that fact, the Boy Scouts of Indiana in 1922 and 1923 set up their Eskimo Pie concessions exclusively at girls' games. The decision was purely financial; their take was better than when boys were on the courts. In many cities and towns merchants raised money to pay the travel expenses of a community's favorite team. Girls' regional and tristate tournaments drew sell-out crowds of tens of thousands of spectators. Winners came home in triumph – to parades, free dinners at restaurants, and considerable local glory.[63]

By 1930, high-energy, exciting girls' basketball was gone, replaced by "girls' rules" basketball, with restricted passing, restricted dribbling, restricted court lines. Girls' basketball did not die a natural death. The female leaders of the recently established Women's Division of the National Amateur Athletic Federation (AAF), in concert with the United States Bureau of Education, killed it.[64] AAF leaders convinced school boards and state legislatures around the country to ban tournament play for girls and women and to forbid girls energetic versions of basketball and other popular team games. In 1924, the Women's Division cautioned, "The fact remains that, as a group, girls cannot safely follow boys' programs. Even if, at the time, no ill effects are evident, we cannot be sure that harm has not been done. It is only when children begin to come, or ought to begin to come, that many women find that they are having to pay a heavy price for a very temporary period of . . . athletic glory."[65]

Only two years earlier, the National Amateur Athletic Federation advocated "athletic glory" for both genders. The organization was itself a product of the World War I "draft defectives" crisis, begun in 1921 with the

---

[62] Alice Fallows, "Basketball: A Builder-up of Vigorous Women," *Good Housekeeping* 34 (1902): 198.

[63] James Rogers, "Athletics for Women," Department of Interior, Bureau of Education, Physical Education Pamphlet Series, 4 (Washington, DC, 1924), 1–5; Helen Coops, "Sports for Women," *American Physical Education Review* 31 (1926): 1086–89.

[64] A reminder about the confusing name changes within the Office/Bureau/then again Office of Education. Congress created the *Office* of Education in 1866. Between 1870 and 1929 it demoted an already tiny agency to the status of a *Bureau*, then in late 1929 restored the title of U.S. *Office* of Education. In 1976 the United States *Department* of Education superseded the Office of Education.

[65] Report of Lillian Schoedler, Typescript, December 29, 1924, LSRM, Series 3, Sub-series 4, Box 14, Folder 156, RAC.

encouragement of the War Department. Never again, it vowed, would the country be caught short. Instead, strong, skilled young American athletes would be the envy of the world. However, when the AAF sent a girls' track team to the 1922 Paris Olympic Games, controversy erupted.[66]

The opposition came from the horrified female professional physical educators who ran the Women's Division, not from the organization's male leadership. Helen Coops, a professor of physical education for women at the University of Cincinnati, summarized their view: the "athletics craze" had to end – at least for girls.[67] The evidence could be found in hundreds of towns all over the country that talented girl athletes had no problem whatsoever mixing it up in combative, exhilarating games that won them the devotion of adoring fans. In a perverse acknowledgment of this fact, the U.S. Bureau of Education, persuaded by the Women's Division, issued an official report reproving athletics for girls that began, "Girls have taken whole-heartedly to the athletic field.... But we should be deeply concerned as to how far (they) should go."[68]

What motivated the stand taken by the Women's Division? After all, most of its members were coaches or physical education directors at universities or high schools. Their suicidal efforts to refuse girls the right to play by gender-free rules in highly competitive sports guaranteed these women a lifetime of meager budgets and minimal status at their own institutions. The only explanation is one replayed continually in history – ideas matter, even when they thwart the believer's own economic best interest – and the leaders of the Women's Division of the AAF were fervent disciples of the philosophy of play. Planned play had, at best, ambiguous, and, at worst, addled-brained, opinions about the virtues of exercise for women. Luther Gulick intoned, "Women do not enjoy competition the way men do. Even in adults, the possession of the fighting instinct is one of the differentiations between men and women.... There is a spontaneous dog fight. Men gather around it; no women will be found there."[69]

Girls' basketball had been the dogfight, proving earnest protestations of female delicacy to be lies. The next two generations of American girls would get no chance to prove their daring at publicly sponsored athletics. Instead of competition, they were instructed to play cooperatively. The "girls' play day" became an institution in school systems around the country. Football or basketball occupied boys; girls got together for "posture parades." A Children's Bureau recreation handbook helpfully suggested that adolescent

[66] Eline Borries, *The History and Functions of the National Section on Women's Athletics* (Baltimore, 1941), 9–11.

[67] Helen Coops, "Outstanding Problems of Girls' Athletics," *American Physical Education Review* 31 (1926): 846.

[68] Rogers, "Athletics for Women," 1.

[69] Gulick, *A Philosophy of Play*, 84.

girls would "get a great deal of fun" out of a "kitchen band" – playing with forks, saucers tapped on the edge by wooden pencils, and oatmeal boxes filled with beans.[70]

At least theoretically, President Richard Nixon changed all that in 1972 when he signed the Educational Amendments Act. Title IX of that law demanded that any institution receiving federal aid adopt gender-neutral educational policies. The biggest impact, of course, was on traditionally gender-segregated classes. Schools that once sent girls to Home Economics to sew aprons and boys to Shop to craft birdhouses abolished these courses or merged them awkwardly into "family living units." But since PE was still a state-mandated graduation requirement, the sponsors of Title IX thought the amendment would finally give girls equal programmatic opportunities, as well as equal use of facilities and equipment.

Mixed results, not clear achievement of that goal, marked the twentieth century history of Title IX. The law intended that boys and girls get equal chances. A minority of suburban school districts provided them, and girls and boys enthusiastically played on coed golf and swimming teams. Title IX regulations allowed for sex separation during participation in "contact" sports, although instruction in the game was to occur in groups that included both girls and boys. So, finally, girls' basketball, without restrictive "girls' rules," returned to school gyms. Moreover, girls' soccer, field hockey, and volleyball joined basketball.

However, that good news did not extend to most American schools. Some continued sex-segregated programs and channeled more money to boys' athletics – in defiance of the law. Others practiced "paper" compliance. Boys' and girls' names appeared together on a class roster, but a surprise visitor to a gym found sex-segregated groups. Schools that previously hired women to teach PE to the girls and men to coach the boys frequently retained the male teacher to coach both genders. Male coaches for girls' teams became common. A woman who trained boys' teams remained an exception. Some school districts decided that Title IX's enumerations posed too many social and legal challenges. Rather than integrate sexes or provide for separate, but equally funded, girls' contact-sports teams, they eliminated these activities for everybody.[71]

---

[70] Helen Smith and Helen Coops, *Play Days: Their Organization and Correlation with a Program of Physical Education and Health* (New York, 1928); United States Children's Bureau, "Handbook for Recreation," Bureau Publication 231 (Washington, DC, 1959), 120–21. At least one school in America implemented the idea, since the author vividly recalls being force-marched around a field in 1959 – while playing a partially filled Coke bottle as a member of a misnamed "girls' fun orchestra."

[71] Patricia L. Geadelmann, "Coed Physical Education: For Better or Worse?" *NASSP Bulletin* 65 (1981): 91–5; Pat Griffin, "Coed Physical Education: Problems and Promises," *Journal of Physical Education, Recreation, and Dance* 55 (1984): 36–37; Linda Bain, "Implementing Title IX: Concerns of Undergraduate Physical Education Majors," *Journal of Physical Education*

Title IX's impact on schools went beyond physical education and sports. By the end of the 1990s, a dramatic growth of lawsuits was an unexpected consequence of banning gender-bias in public education. The phrase "sexual harassment" does not appear anywhere in Title IX. Those who drafted the measure wanted girls to get their fair share of athletic budgets. Ironically, Title IX opened a gateway to a new world of harrassment litigation. Most measures forbidding sexual harassment focused on adult workplaces. However, Title IX explictly barred any kind of gender-biased behavior in school districts that received federal funds. Any "non-gender-neutral" interaction between teachers and students or among students themselves was illegal. Courts began hearing cases that argued sexual slurs scrawled on bathroom stalls, comments muttered in the lunchroom, or taunts in class violated a school's pledge to provide a gender neutral learning environment.

In 1999, the United States Supreme Court ruled in *Davis v. Monroe County Board of Education* that Title IX required schools to intervene energetically when one student complained of sexual harassment by another. LaShonda Davis, a Georgia fifth-grader, complained repeatedly to her teacher that the boy sitting next to her kept up a steady, and highly explicit, sexual patter, describing what he wanted to do with her, while leering in her direction, a doorstop stuffed in his pants. For three months, LaShonda's teacher refused to move the girl. The boy, identified as GF in the suit, was not punished. When LaShonda's parents discovered that their daughter had written a suicide note, they decided to take matters into their own hands and sued the school district. The case eventually reached the Supreme Court, where puzzled High Court Justices pondered the meaning of sexual harassment suits involving relatively young children. Justice Anthony Kennedy argued vehemently that schools had enough trouble just teaching kids to read and write and that the term "sexual harassment" properly could be applied only to the behavior of adults at workplaces, but in a five to four ruling the High Court decided for Lashonda.[72]

Confusion about *Davis v. Monroe County* reigned. American schools were on notice that they should ensure that no student suffered sexually connected insults or degrading remarks. Even administrators who regarded that as a worthy objective were often unsure how to implement it.

---

and Recreation 50 (1979): 77–78; Mary Hoferek, "At the Crossroads: Merger or __ ?" *Quest* 32 (1980): 95–96. Equal opportunity did not mean equal physical capacities, however. At the end of the century schools with sports programs coped with some troubling news – with consequences for gender-blind sports policy. It began to appear that girls who engaged in very active physical contact sports suffered proportionally greater numbers of (and more severe) knee injuries than did boys.

[72] Kennedy's argument summarized in Cynthia Gorney, "Teaching Johnny the Appropriate Way to Flirt," *New York Times Magazine*, June 13, 1999: 44.

The "Weakling" Child: And State Standards for Physical Fitness

Implementation of "fitness standards" was an equally fraught subject, even though, of all the state interventions meant to promote general childhood fitness investigated here, standards remained the most consistently promoted. Also consistent were the disappointing results.

Between 1919 and 1929, hundreds of city youth recreation programs urged urban kids to join team sports, then inserted a catch. Before a boy could pitch a baseball or a girl guard a center, he or she had to meet minimum fitness standards. The tests most often used demanded that boys, by a third try, be able to do nine pull-ups, perform the sixty-yard dash in under eight seconds, and run a one-hundred-yard dash in under fourteen seconds. Girls, with two chances, had to make three basketball free throw goals in under two minutes and walk a twenty-four-foot elevated beam with a bean bag on their heads.[73] Children who passed won a prize – a small bronze medal or a cloth badge to sew on a shirt. More important, they got the right to participate in a sport they loved playing, a strong incentive to succeed. Had so many cities not been forced to cancel sports activities during the lean years of the Depression, their regimes of fitness testing might have helped produce a better group of recruits for the Army and Navy during World War II. School physical education programs conducted during the 1930s certainly didn't.

The real cause of so much continued "unfitness" was economic. During the Depression millions of children not only lost their chances to play on city baseball teams, they also lived in families struggling to put any kind of meal on the table. Before 1950, a "weakling" child was usually a severely underweight one. City playgrounds joined schools in the 1920s and set up scales. A verdict of 10 percent or more below an ideal weight-to-height ratio disqualified a child from further fitness testing as well as sports. Municipal recreation directors sometimes pinned a "weight tag" to the clothing of excessively thin children with instructions telling parents to give their wearers' extra servings of milk and meat. They did not tell impoverished families how to get the money to buy such items, and the common playground practice of posting every child's name and weight probably discouraged many cities' neediest and most "unfit" kids from even venturing inside.[74]

By mid-century, definitions changed. Increasingly, "unfit" kids were chubby, not thin, a progression that led to what some called an "epidemic" of childhood obesity by century's end. The country had barely had enough time to digest the dire news about World War II draft washouts, before two physicians at the Bellevue Medical Center in New York City, working with

---

[73] Clarence Rainwater, *The Play Movement in the United States*, 250–51.
[74] "The Goals of Playgrounds," 1924, Report Prepared for the Playground and Recreation Association of America, LSRM, Series 3.1, Box 1, Folder 9, RAC.

another at New York's Columbia-Presbyterian Hospital, announced that America's grade-school children were also serious "fitness failures."

Between 1948 and 1954, Drs. Hans Kraus, Ruth Hirschland, and Sonja Weber repeatedly tested sample populations of four thousand American, Austrian, and Italian children. Fifty-eight percent of the American kids could not even do the "level one," or easiest, leg and trunk exercises, while 92 percent of the Austrian and Italian children passed, despite the fact that the latter groups lived in the ruins of two defeated Axis powers. A majority of the Americans could not perform a sit-up, with hands behind their necks and legs held straight by a partner. Nor could they put their feet together, keep their knees unbent, and lean down to touch the floor with their fingertips.[75] Kraus blamed the highly mechanized luxury of postwar U.S. life. The European children did not use cars, schoolbuses, or elevators. Instead, they walked miles every day. American grade schoolers, in contrast, had "automobile legs."[76]

The reports got immediate attention. President Dwight Eisenhower appointed a Council on Youth Fitness and told its prominent members, including the baseball great Stan Musial, to recommend ways to improve fitness levels for America's children. However, after rounds of picture taking and a few obligatory meetings in Washington, attended by a minority of the appointees, Eisenhower's advisers faded from view.

Youth fitness returned to the national policy agenda when John F. Kennedy made it a campaign issue in 1960. Kennedy was a natural for such a crusade. While Eisenhower enjoyed a leisurely game of golf, and Mamie kept indoors, most members of the entire Kennedy clan were manic sports enthusiasts. Kennedy looked terrific when photographed, as he allowed himself to be, bare-chested at the beach. The nation's young, Kennedy proclaimed, were "soft."[77]

Once elected, the country's new president continued to push for fitness. He posed for a color spread in the pages of *Sports Illustrated* – running barefoot on the beach at Hyannisport – standing at the tiller of his sloop, *Victura*.[78] He revived the moribund President's Council on Youth Fitness. This time the requisite sports hero was football legend Bud Wilkinson. Kennedy ordered the Department of Health, Education, and Welfare to make the physical fitness of America's children a "top priority." He appeared on television

---

[75] Hans Kraus and Ruth Hirshland, "Minimum Muscular Fitness Tests in School Children," *The Research Quarterly of the American Association for Health, Physical Education, and Recreation*, 25 (1954): 178–89.

[76] *Ibid.*, 183.

[77] John F. Kennedy, "The Soft American," *Sports Illustrated* 13 (1960): 15.

[78] *Ibid.*, 18–22. The Kennedy family was indeed one that relished vigorous sports, but the supposed athleticism John Kennedy himself displayed to the American people hid a personal history of constant pain and serious ailments, including osteoarthritis and Addison's disease.

to urge every American child to participate in fifty-mile hikes.[79] Given the apparent fact that the nation's grade schoolers couldn't manage a single sit-up, perhaps the president should have aimed lower? Despite all the publicity, his "Youth Fitness Initiative" went nowhere. It did, however, give Kennedy a chance to showcase the handsome members of his large, extended family in shorts, t-shirts, and body-hugging swim suits.

John F. Kennedy's Fitness Council accomplished little, but a tradition was established. For the next three decades each of his successors appointed their own youth fitness advisers. These councils primarily provided an excuse for physical educators and government bureaucrats to gather for conferences at which, in lugubrious tones, they announced the sad results of the latest study – American children were not meeting fitness goals.[80]

In fact, the establishment of "President's Councils" was actively counterproductive. Most followed Kennedy's precedent and gave awards only to youngsters who ranked above the 85th percentile on fitness tests, an achievement precious few kids managed. Only a handful of thirteen-year-old girls, for instance, could do forty sit-ups in under sixty seconds – the standard for scoring in a typical test's top 15 percent. The system overcompensated the already gifted.[81]

But fitness norms remained popular. They gave politicians regular opportunities to look alarmed before the cameras. President Bill Clinton unwittingly underscored the illusory quality of White House support for childhood fitness when he announced his choice of a presidential youth fitness adviser: Arnold Schwarzenegger – a man best known for movie roles in which he pretended to be athletic.[82]

In 1980 the U.S. Department of Health and Human Services (HHS) announced its "health objectives for 1990." Among them: that 90 percent of American children between the ages of ten and seventeen would participate regularly in vigorous exercise that significantly increased their cardiorespiratory fitness. Instead, probably less than one in two American youngsters exercised at all, much less engaged in the kinds of strenuous activities that

---

[79] *Ibid.* See also John F. Kennedy, "The Vigor We Need," *Sports Illustrated* 17 (1962): 12–15.

[80] Ash Hayes, "Youth Physical Fitness Hearings: An Interim Report from the President's Council on Physical Fitness and Sport," *Journal of Physical Education, Recreation, and Dance* 55 (1984): 29–32; Peter Vidmar, "The Role of the Federal Government in Promoting Health Through the Schools: Report from the President's Council on Fitness and Sport," *The Journal of School Health* 62(1992): 129–30; Kerry White, "Fitness Council Battles Diminishing Profile," *Education Week* 16 (1997): 21–23.

[81] This is an argument made by Kenneth Fox and Stuart Biddle, "The Use of Fitness Tests: Educational and Psychological Considerations," *Journal of Physical Education, Recreation, and Dance*, 59 (1988): 50.

[82] By the time Schwarzenegger accepted his appointment, his career as a body builder was decades in his past. Body building was the only sport with which he had ever been publicly identified, and Schwarzenegger acknowledged that he, like almost all champions, was once a heavy user of steroids, though, of course, he told boys not to follow his own example.

increased cardiorespiratory strength. HHS bureaucrats retrenched and announced their next set of goals – for "Healthy America 2000." Interestingly,
this time, they lowered their fitness expectations for children. By the year
2000, they hoped 75 percent of kids between the ages of six and seventeen
were engaged in regular, vigorous exercise that promoted cardiorespiratory
fitness.[83]

Instead, the fitness gap grew. Affluent, unmarried twenty- and thirty-year-
olds patronized the country's booming exercise clubs, which became dating
meccas. Children and their parents were not flattening their abs. Specialists
in nutrition and physical education had long known that the single greatest
predictor for a lean, muscular kid was the presence in the house of a lean,
muscular mother or father. End of the century surveys revealed that some
60 percent of people with children between the ages of four and seventeen
never exercised at all. About 20 percent exercised on an irregular basis. Less
than eight in a hundred practiced what officials at HHS preached as optimal
behavior: thirty minutes of daily, strenuous exercise. Even that pathetic statistic was probably exaggerated, since surveys relied on self-reporting.[84] Late-
twentieth-century Americans married, divorced, remarried, started families,
broke up families, reconstituted families, and, typically, all the adults in a
household held outside jobs. American parents were pooped, and their children had not "shaped up." Or had they? "Shaping up" was a phrase that
entered American slang in the 1880s, when cattlemen used it to refer to
fattening up stock for slaughter.[85]

A Last Look: From the Playground Movement to the End of Recess

At the beginning of the twentieth century, private philanthropy preached
the children's playground as community salvation; schools and city governments heard the call and got religion. By the end of the 1990s, many had
abandoned faith. Public schools in increasing numbers saw no need for playgrounds. American children became students at ever-younger ages, but they
had no time for physical activity. "The notion that kindergarten is a place
where kids come and play is an anachronism," scolded Karen Lang, deputy
superintendent of schools for Greenwich, Connecticut. Worried about

---

[83] Public Health Service, U.S. Department of Health and Human Services, *The 1990 Health Ob-
jectives: A Midcourse Review* (Washington, DC, 1986), 230–37; National Center for Chronic
Disease Prevention and Health Promotion, Centers for Disease Control and Prevention,
"Guidelines for School and Community Programs To Promote Life-Long Physical Activity
Among Young People," *Journal of School Health* 67 (1997): 204–05.

[84] James Ross and Russell Pate, "The National Children and Youth Fitness Study II: A Summary
of Findings," *Journal of Physical Education, Recreation, and Dance* 58 (1987): 51–57.

[85] Donald Mrozek, "Sport in American Life: From National Health to Personal Fulfillment,
1890–1940," in Kathryn Grover, Ed., *Fitness in American Culture: Images of Health, Sport,
and the Body, 1830–1940* (Amherst, MA, 1989), 37.

guaranteeing success on the fourth-grade standardized competence tests all Connecticut students took, the Greenwich school board demanded that kindergartners concentrate on learning to "make valid inferences about characters, using supporting details."[86]

If kindergartners were inferring, first graders certainly didn't have time for the playground. Atlanta's (Georgia) Cleveland Avenue Elementary School epitomized the trend. A sparkling brick structure built in 1996, it had neither gym nor playground. "We are intent on improving academic performance," snapped Benjamin Canada, Atlanta's superintendent of schools. "You don't do that by having kids hanging on monkey bars."[87] When a reporter asked a small girl whether she missed recess, she looked at him blankly and replied, "What's recess?"[88] Poor Luther Gulick spun in his grave.

While the battle to "shape up" American children through dietary advice, government food programs, and required exercise failed, another state policy meant to improve children's health was a stunning success, albeit with complicated consequences.

---

[86] Kate Zernike, "No Time for Napping: Kindergartens Make Play Academic," *New York Times*, October 23, 2000.
[87] Quoted in "Many Schools Putting an End to Child's Play," *New York Times*, April 7, 1998.
[88] *Ibid.*

9

Mandatory Medicine

Twentieth-Century Childhood Immunization

American children in the late twentieth century were still malnourished and physically unfit. But a group portrait of their general health contained one stunningly positive change: a greatly lessened threat from infectious and contagious illness.[1] In 1900, sixteen out of every one hundred American children died from disease before reaching the age of five. Through the 1920s, more than fifteen thousand youngsters annually suffered agonized deaths from diphtheria alone. Their rasping gasps as they fought for breath were a familiar, and terrifying, sound, as was the high-pitched wail that gave pertussis its common name, whooping cough.[2]

By the end of the century, vaccines defeated diphtheria, pertussis, and many other childhood enemies. In 1999, no American child died of diphtheria. All fifty states required that children be immunized against seven preventable diseases, and an estimated 97 percent of American schoolchildren received vaccinations against diphtheria, tetanus, pertussis, polio, measles, mumps, and rubella (German measles) by the time they began the first grade.[3]

---

[1] Physicians distinguish between contagious diseases – that require transmission through direct contact – and infectious diseases – that can be passed through indirect contact, via airborne particles, for instance.

[2] Susan Ellenberg and Robert Chen, "The Complicated Task of Monitoring Vaccine Safety," *Public Health Reports* 6 (1997): 10–12; S. L. Plotkin and S. A. Plotkin, *A Short History of Vaccination* (Philadelphia, 1994), 1–24; "Childhood Immunizations," A Report Prepared by the Subcommittee on Health and the Environment of the Committee on Energy and Commerce, U.S. House of Representatives (Washington, DC, 1986): 1–7 (hereafter Immunizations).

[3] A few states did not require immunization against tetanus and pertussis, but the differences in regulation were largely meaningless, since almost all American children received the required immunization against diphtheria in the form of a series of five shots that combined three vaccines – against the former disease as well as against tetanus and pertussis. Commonly called DTP vaccine, the sequence called for three DTP shots in the first year of life, a fourth shot around 15 months, and a fifth booster shot usually given between the fifth and sixth birthdays. See U.S. Department of Health and Human Services and Centers for Disease Control, *Parents' Guide to Childhood Immunization* (Atlanta, 1990), 1–8.

After 1985, new vaccines to protect against other childhood infectious diseases appeared. One prevented Haemophilus influenza type b (Hib) – which, despite its confusing name, was not a flu virus but a bacterium that could cause meningitis, epiglottitis, croup, pneumonia, and severe infections of the heart and soft tissues. Others protected against the Varicella virus (chicken pox) and Hepatitis strains A and B. In 1998, the Food and Drug Administration (FDA) approved a vaccine against yet another childhood illness, rotavirus, a diarrheal disease that annually sickened an estimated 3.5 million American babies. Vaccines to thwart other diseases of the young were in the pipeline.[4]

At first glance, then, American governments, through compelling vaccination of children, participated in a great medical victory. However, furor, not triumphant self-congratulation, marked end-of-the-century discussion about mandatory immunization. Enraged parents charged government agencies with massive cover-ups of the injuries to their children vaccines caused. Hundreds of product liability cases clogged the courts. By 1996, only two of what had formerly been more than a dozen American companies in the business of producing vaccines against childhood illnesses remained, with one the sole producer of five of the seven vaccines that laws required as a condition of entrance to school. Prices for all childhood vaccines were stunningly higher.[5]

Vaccination itself, one of the unqualified successes of twentieth-century American public health practice, faced a popular backlash. Advocacy groups demanded that parents be given the federally guaranteed right to enroll their

---

[4] As of 1999, in keeping with recommendations from the Centers for Disease Control, the most common new vaccine additions, generally required before entrance into pre-school or kindergarten, were those for Hepatitis B and for Hib. See Hilary Korprowski and Michael Oldstone, Eds., *Microbe Hunters, Then and Now* (Bloomington, IL, 1996), 1–62; Centers for Disease Control, "Recommended Childhood Immunization Schedules: United States," *Morbidity and Mortality Weekly Report* 45 (1996): 635–38.

[5] The two companies were the dominant player, Merck, Sharp, and Dohme, and Wyeth-Ayerst Labs, the latter a product of end-of-the-century mega-mergers in the drug industry. Wyeth-Ayerst joined the formerly independent Wyeth Labs with Lederle Labs, a long-time producer of children's vaccines, and both were subsidiaries of American Home Products Corporation. When, in 1996, the Centers for Disease Control recommended a major change in U.S. practices for vaccination against polio – that two doses of killed virus injectable (Salk) vaccine be followed by two doses of live oral (Sabin) vaccine, not a single American company had produced the older, killed Salk virus vaccine for over a decade, and very few physicians' offices or public health clinics possessed it. David Wood and Neal Halfon, "The Impact of the Vaccine for Children's Program on Child Immunization Delivery," *Archives of Pediatric and Adolescent Medicine* 150 (1996): 577–79; "Polio Vaccination Recommendations Changed in the U.S.," *Antiviral Agents Bulletin* 9 (1996): 9; "O'Connell v. Shalala, 1st Circuit Affirms Denial of Compensation Under Vaccine Act," *Pharmaceutical Litigation Reporter* (1996): 11299. In 1962 parents paid around $5 for a complete set of compulsory immunizations. By 1996, compulsory immunization cost more than $500 for a full set of treatments, a hugely higher cost, even in real dollar terms.

children as students without vaccinations. Less than a year after its licensure, the Centers for Disease Control (CDC) withdrew approval of rotavirus vaccine. "No one," said CDC spokesperson Barbara Reynolds, "should be giving rotavirus vaccine to anyone." It caused intussusception when given to babies.[6] Its quick retraction sadly symbolized a changed national mood, as news stories defined intussusception and described the terrible pain infants suffered when a section of the bowel suddenly telescoped into another part of the bowel.

Childhood vaccination was a public health triumph that became a victim of its own success. That requires examination of the central roles played by smallpox and polio in the creation of mandatory immunization policy. It also demands analysis of a product-liability revolution in American jurisprudence and assessment of the impact of the federal government's emergence as dominant purchaser of childhood vaccine supplies.

Smallpox: Act One

Ironically, neither smallpox nor polio, the two diseases that spurred compulsory immunization in America, was a major killer of children in the twentieth century. Diphtheria, whooping cough, and other respiratory illnesses ended the lives of far more of the nation's young.

Smallpox probably emerged in epidemic form in human populations tens of thousands of years ago, and, until the twentieth century, killed more people than any other infectious disease. Far larger than most other viruses, it is particularly dangerous – highly stable outside its human host and capable of causing outbreaks for extremely long periods of time.

Smallpox is a nightmarish disease. Aching muscles quickly give way to spiking fevers. Tens of thousands of blisters appear, swell, then grow together, sealing eyes, obliterating facial features, bursting to bathe the bloated victim's body in oozing pus. Historically, those who survived smallpox often spent the rest of their lives blinded or terribly scarred. Child survivors were frequently stunted, never growing taller than they had been at the disease's onset.

Smallpox remained a major health threat through the eighteenth century. Even among populations long exposed to it, one third to one half of its victims died. Edward Jenner's development of a smallpox vaccine in 1796 revolutionized the treatment of the disease in the West. It worked, as do all vaccines, by stimulating the body's immune system to produce antibodies.

---

[6] Quoted in "U.S. in a Push to Bar Vaccine Given Infants," *New York Times*, July 16, 1999; Lawrence Altman, "Vaccine for Infant Diarrhea Is Withdrawn as Health Risk," *New York Times*, October 16, 1999. By September 1999, the CDC documented more than one hundred cases of severe intussusception in infants given the vaccine and recommended that the risk was too great to continue its use.

By the end of the nineteenth century, the practice of vaccination, although rarely compulsory, was sufficiently widespread to weaken smallpox's danger.[7] In the United States, it was no longer the horrific killer of previous centuries. Rather, its symptoms mimicked those of its cousin, chicken pox, and twentieth-century American smallpox victims rarely died. Not even all that many sickened from the disease. The smallpox epidemics of the early twentieth century never rivaled the toll taken by tuberculosis. But the fear of the pox's dangers outlived its mutation into a milder disease. Most Americans exaggerated its deadliness and prevalence.[8]

Diphtheria, not smallpox, was the dread killer that stalked young children in the early twentieth century. Moreover, it was a disease for which a relatively effective treatment existed. In the early 1890s, scientists in Berlin discovered that horses injected with heat-killed broth cultures of diphtheria could survive repeated inoculations with the live bacilli. Fluid serum extracted from the animals' blood provided a high degree of protection to humans. An injection of this substance, generally called antitoxin, did not provide complete immunity, but only about one in eight exposed individuals developed symptoms. After 1895 diphtheria antitoxin preparations were available in the United States.[9]

In the decades between 1900 and 1950, smallpox killed few American children. It killed few Americans – period. Diphtheria, by contrast, struck hundreds of thousands of children annually. One in ten, in an average year, died horribly, clawing for air, unable to swallow, suffocated by mucus.[10] But the opponents and advocates of vaccination in the early twentieth century did not debate the need to compel diphtheria serum therapy. Rather, their frequently fierce struggles involved smallpox vaccine.

That fact illustrates smallpox's remaining iconic power. Moreover, it demonstrates the era's very incomplete acceptance of research science and

---

[7] The scientific language describes the phenomenon as "herd immunity." Even if not everyone in a population receives innoculation, at a certain point everybody benefits. The achievement of herd immunity was a major argument made by proponents of childhood innoculation throughout much of the twentieth century.

[8] Philip Frana, "Smallpox: Local Epidemics and the Iowa State Board of Health, 1880–1900," *Annals of Iowa*, 54 (1995): 87–117; John Duffy, "School Vaccination: The Precursor to School Medical Inspection," *Journal of the History of Medicine and Allied Sciences* 30 (1978): 344–55. For a case study of public health approaches to smallpox outbreaks in one American city in the late nineteenth and early twentieth centuries, see Judith Walzer Leavitt, *The Healthiest City: Milwaukee and the Politics of Health Reform* (Princeton, 1982).

[9] Institute of Medicine, Division of Health Promotion and Disease Prevention, *Vaccine Supply and Innovation* (Washington, DC, 1985), 15–17.

[10] Even if a child survived this terrifying stage of diphtheria, other dangers lurked. Between one to two months after the initial symptoms appeared, toxins secreted by the diphtheria virus sometimes caused death from sudden cardiac arrest. Antitoxin treatments usually prevented this secondary development.

the germ theory of disease.[11] At the turn of the century, aspiring American physicians who wanted to learn the newest medical theories and techniques still studied in Europe. The average physician's income was modest, as was his knowledge. The country's many medical schools were almost all small for-profit operations owned by the faculty.[12]

The rise to dominance of mainstream allopathic medicine can be charted in the gradual increase of acceptance of compulsory smallpox vaccination of elementary schoolchildren. Since children were not uniquely vulnerable to smallpox, the child-vaccination battles of the late nineteenth and early twentieth centuries served as proxies for a larger fight – what function, if any, should the state play in regulating medical treatment?

One answer persisted through the 1950s, as the refusal of Congress to reauthorize the Sheppard-Towner Act demonstrated: the federal government's role should be minimal. Health regulations should be left to states and localities. In 1813, the U.S. Congress passed the Vaccine Act, giving the president the right to appoint a special agent responsible for guaranteeing the purity of smallpox vaccine. Within a few years, it thought better of the effort and repealed the measure, declaring that vaccine regulation should be left to local officials.[13]

Eighty years later, in 1902, the St. Louis Health Department accidentally prepared a batch of tainted diphtheria antitoxin, which killed thirteen children. The incident made the national newspapers, and the "St. Louis Innocents" helped persuade Congress to reenter the field of biologics regulation. The Virus Anti-Toxin Act of 1902 expanded the powers of the Public Health Service, originally established in 1798 to provide medical care for the nation's merchant seamen.[14]

---

[11] Popular acceptance of the germ theory of disease was not automatic. The nineteenth-century belief that explained disease in terms of environmental dangers like filthy water and rotting garbage or as chemical reactions between the body and natural elements did not disappear overnight. For insightful discussions of the popularization of the germ theory in early-twentieth-century America, see Roger Cooter and Stephen Pumfrey, "Separate Spheres and Public Places: Reflections on the History of Science Popularization and Science in Popular Culture," *History of Science* 32 (1994): 237–67; Nancy Tomes, *The Gospel of Germs*; Martin Melosi, *Garbage in the Cities: Refuse, Reform and the Environment, 1880–1980* (College Station, TX, 1981).

[12] For discussions of the state of American medicine, see John S. Haller, *American Medicine in Transition, 1840–1910* (Urbana, 1981); James Burrow, *Organized Medicine in the Progressive Era* (Baltimore, 1977).

[13] P. B. Hutt, "Investigations and Reports Respecting FDA Regulations of New Drugs," *Clinical Pharmacology* 33 (1983): 537–42.

[14] The name, United States Public Health Service, only came into use in 1912, however. Between 1798 and 1902 the agency was called the United States Marine and Hospital Service. Between 1902 and 1912 it was called the United States Marine Hospital and Public Health Service. For a history of the early decades of the Public Health Service, see Ralph Williams, *The United States Public Health Service, 1798–1950* (Washington, DC, 1951).

The Service theoretically controlled dozens of hospitals, spread around the country. In reality, the hospitals were largely autonomous, funded by voluntary deductions from the wages of the sailors who used them. The authority of the Service's new Hygienic Laboratory, in like fashion, was primarily fictive. Its licensing regulations applied only to vaccines and antitoxins sold abroad or across state lines, which excluded most preparations used in the country. Only in 1955, when Congress merged the Hygienic Laboratory with the new and far-better-funded Division of Biologics Standards of the National Institutes of Health (NIH), did federal regulation assume genuine importance.[15]

Until World War II, a political debate about a medical treatment for children usually occurred on the floor of a state legislature, within the chambers of a city council, or in a public health commissioner's office, and it often became heated when the subject was smallpox vaccination.

Indeed, the logic of immunization invited distrust, especially in an age when bacilli and viruses were mysterious, little-understood by researchers, much less the general public. Vaccines are not drugs; they are biologics – dead or weakened forms of an apparently invisible organism, given to a healthy person to provoke immunity to their full fury. To many physicians, especially homeopaths, no government board or agency could ever certify such a substance as pure. Instead, they were "pure poison." J. M. Peebles, a California homeopath, raged, "Think of it! Parents! Pure pus-rottenness – think of it! Calf lymph from calves' filthy sores put into the arms of innocent schoolchildren. Beastly calf brutality thrust into our children's budding humanity."[16] The "people" he warned, once they learned that vaccination caused many cases of blood-poisoning in children, would soon "turn out of office" the "vile ... smallpox scare promoters" who had convinced

[15] Victoria Harden, *Inventing the NIH: Federal Biomedical Research Policy, 1887–1937* (Baltimore, 1986), 161–75.

[16] J. M. Peebles, *Vaccination: A Curse and a Menace to Personal Liberty, With Statistics Showing Its Dangers and Criminality* (New York, 1902), 129. Seemingly unaware of the challenges predecessors such as Peebles made a century earlier, medical professionals once again contested the safety of smallpox vaccinations, in the wake of President George W. Bush's announcement in December 2002, of a two-part federal plan to innoculate, on a voluntary basis, more than ten million Americans, beginning with 500,000 health care workers. Responding to worries about possible use of weaponized smallpox by terrorists or enemy states, Bush's decision to reinstitute smallpox vaccination emphasized the importance of innoculating adults who would be in the front lines should germ warfare come to American soil: physicians, nurses, firefighters, and police. The plan, however, met strong resistance. As its first phase began, hundreds of hospitals and thousands of medical personnel, citing the risks of dangerous side effects, refused to participate. And many experts urged that smallpox vaccine not be offered to any American children, at least before an attack happened. See Donald McNeil, "Citing Dangers, Experts Warn Against Vaccinating Children," *New York Times*, December 13, 2002; Donald McNeil, "Many Balk at Smallpox Vaccination," *New York Times*, February 7, 2003.

legislatures, city councils, or school boards to require vaccination of schoolchildren.[17]

In fact, Peebles was half right. Between 1900 and 1930, more cities, counties, and states repealed statutes demanding mandatory smallpox immunization as a condition of school attendance than passed them, despite the fact that both federal and state courts consistently held that vaccination was a proper exercise of a state's police powers.[18] Newspapers around the country reflected the highly emotional quality of the controversy. In 1902, when San Diego repealed its municipal ordinance requiring schoolchildren be vaccinated, an editorial in the *Sun* crowed: "Persons with families, proposing to spend the winter in southern California, sending their children to the public schools, should avoid Los Angeles as they would a den of vipers, and go on down to San Diego, where parents are not now compelled by school boards to have their children's blood poisoned with cow-pox virus."[19]

In 1900, eleven of the then forty-five states mandated compulsory vaccination against smallpox as a condition of school entrance. Thirty years later, that small number was even smaller. Four states – Arizona, Minnesota, North Dakota, and Utah – repealed vaccination requirements by referendum vote, and in their stead passed laws declaring that no minor child could be subjected to compulsory vaccination.

The few states remaining with vaccination laws on the books included widely varying punishments for parents or guardians who refused to allow a child to be vaccinated. Fines ranged from $10 to $2,000 and jail terms from not more than thirty days to not less than one year. The disparities meant little, since no state with vaccination laws vigorously enforced them. Nor did a single state authorize supplemental funds to enable school districts to verify children's vaccination records.[20] Lack of money certainly was a deterrent to systematic enforcement; so, too, was public confusion.

Even a few public health officials weighed in as opponents. In 1925, Dr. William King, Indiana's Health Commissioner, declared, "I know

---

[17] *Ibid.*, 90.

[18] For influential cases argued before the United States and state Supreme Courts, see *Jacobson v. Massachusetts* 70: Supreme Court of the United States, 197 U.S. 11; 25th S. CT 358, 1905; *Rosalyn Zucht, Et Al. v. W. A. King, Et Al.* 319 Supreme Court of the United States 257 U.S. 650; 42 S. CT 53; 1921; *W. D. French v. F. P. Davidson, Et Al.*, 1427 Supreme Court of California, Department Two 143 Cal. 658; 77 P. 663; 1904; *Clifton Hagler Et Al. v. R. H. Larner Et Al.*, 12167 Supreme Court of Illinois 284 Ill. 547; 120 N. E. 575, 1918.

[19] Quoted in Peebles, *Vaccination, A Curse*, 157.

[20] For discussion of vaccination laws from 1900 to 1942, see Kristine Severyn, "Jacobson *v.* Massachusetts: Its Impact on Informed Consent and Vaccine Policy," *The Journal of Law and Pharmacy* 5 (1995): 248–56; New York Academy of Medicine, Committee on Public Health Relations, James Miller, Chairman, *Preventive Medicine in Modern Practice* (New York, 1942), 127–35.

of nothing that causes more useless antagonism and trouble to (health departments) than the more or less grandstand orders ... requiring vaccination of schoolchildren."[21]

By 1942, many proprietary medical schools had disappeared; medical standards had risen; the AMA was no longer an organization of the elite few; and a majority of physicians accepted smallpox vaccination as good preventive medicine.[22] Most state and county medical societies concurred with the recommendations of the New York Academy of Medicine that children be immunized against smallpox at two months, with required booster shots when they began school.

Nonetheless, public resistance persisted. Only ten states required compulsory smallpox immunization.[23] A decade later, that number inched up to twelve. Then, between 1958 and 1965, in a rush, all fifty states passed laws demanding that schoolchildren produce proof of vaccination against smallpox as well as other diseases.[24] The appearance of a vaccine that prevented polio caused a policy earthquake. Dr. Jonas Salk's famous breakthrough in 1954 finally made mandatory vaccination popular.

---

[21] William King, "Comments," *Public Health Bulletin* 149, United States Public Health Service (Washington, DC, 1925), 53.

[22] Howard Markel (both a pediatrician and a historian) argues that historians who are not specialists in the history of medicine routinely exaggerate the professional power of the AMA. As late as the 1990s, most physicians still didn't take out memberships, though the organization, proportionally, enrolled greater numbers of American doctors than it did between the 1850s and the 1930s. Howard Markel: Communication with author.

[23] New York Academy of Medicine, *Preventive Medicine* (New York, 1942), 133. During these years many state public health departments had quarantine regulations against measles and pertussis. Regulations in Illinois were typical. If a child became ill with either disease, that fact was to be reported in writing or by telephone to the local health department. The sick child and any other children who had come into close contact were to be quarantined in their homes, upon whose doors large signs reading "Danger: Measles" or "Danger: Whooping Cough" were to be affixed. Only a public health officer could officially end the quarantine, at which time the patient would be required "to bathe and put on clean clothing which has been kept away from the sick room." However, as was the case with enforcement of smallpox vaccination, quarantines were not generally rigorously enforced, except in times of a measles or whooping cough epidemic. See Isaac Rawlings, Director, Illinois Department of Public Health, *Rules and Regulations for the Control of Measles and Whooping Cough, Revised and in Force Throughout Illinois* (Springfield, 1927), 5–9.

[24] Hearings, Intensive Immunization Programs, Before the Committee on Interstate and Foreign Commerce, House of Representatives, Eighty-Seventh Congress, Second Session (Washington, DC, 1962) (hereafter Hearing, Intensive Programs); Hearings, Communicable Disease and Immunization Programs, Before the Subcommittee on Public Health and Welfare of the Committee on Interstate and Foreign Commerce, House of Representatives, Ninety-First Congress, Second Session (Washington, DC, 1970) (hereafter Hearing, Communicable Disease).

The Polio Miracle

Epidemic poliomyelitis was very much a disease of the twentieth century, and a particular scourge of American children. Before 1907, no state health departments listed polio as a reportable disease. No epidemic outbreaks of the disease occurred until 1916. Polio, however, had likely always been present as an endemic intestinal virus, as was true almost everywhere else in the world. In unsanitary conditions, exposure was universal. Mothers gave passive immunity to their offspring in the womb; those babies who contracted the disease rarely showed symptoms. At most, polio caused infants mild distress.

However, when American children did not routinely come into contact with water or soil polluted by human feces, they no longer acquired automatic lifelong immunity to polio. Each year of delayed exposure increased the risk that an older child could contract the far more serious paralytic form of polio, in which the virus left its victim's gut and lodged instead in the central nervous system.

Although parents, physicians, and public health officials in the early twentieth century believed just the opposite, polio was a disease of cleanliness, not filth. The nation with the world's most sophisticated indoor plumbing was also the one with the greatest number of polio outbreaks. But polio was elusive and struck unpredictably. Symptoms varied dramatically. Sometimes only one person in a household became ill; other times all. One family member might suffer chills and a sore throat, another permanent paralysis. Even its most dreaded consequence took a range of forms. Some victims lost complete use of their muscles, only to recover within a matter of weeks or months. Others experienced paralysis of a particular group of muscles, ranging from those that controlled eyelids to those that enabled lungs to function.[25]

The appearance of a seemingly new disease that randomly struck children and young adults understandably attracted the attention of medical professionals. The fact that polio became a national obsession, however, cannot be explained by a recitation of its symptoms. America's rising standards for sanitation helped polio spike in the years between 1938 and 1952, but another

---

[25] For discussions of polio's symptoms and impact, see Naomi Rogers, *Dirt and Disease: Polio Before FDR* (New Brunswick, NJ, 1990); Kathryn Black, *In the Shadow of Polio, A Personal and Social History* (New York, 1996); Jane Smith, *Patenting the Sun: Polio and the Salk Vaccine* (New York, 1991); Nancy Bradshaw, "Polio in Kentucky – From Birthday Balls to the Breakthrough," *The Register of the Kentucky Historical Society* 87 (1989): 20–40; Saul Benison, "The Enigma of Poliomyelitis: 1910," in Harold Hyman and Leonard Levy, Eds., *Freedom and Reform, Essays in Honor of Henry Steele Commager* (New York, 1967), 228–53; Stuart Galishoff, "Newark and the Great Polio Epidemic of 1916," *New Jersey History* 54 (1976): 101–11.

particularly American phenomenon, public relations, made the disease the one parents most feared.[26]

Polio was America's first mass-media disease, its conquest marketed as a product to purchase. The same industry that sold the nation cereal, cigarettes, and cars, sold polio prevention. And the disease was a natural – a charismatic president as starring victim, adorable kids in fearsome iron lungs as supporting players.

The extent of Franklin Roosevelt's paralysis was minimized publicly. Political cartoons regularly featured him tugging a Democratic donkey or racing ahead of his rivals. Many citizens were unaware that he could not walk unaided. White House aides tore film from the cameras of photographers who defied an informal gentleman's agreement with the press not to describe Roosevelt's infirmities or photograph him in leg braces or a wheelchair.[27] Nonetheless, the president never hid the fact that he had suffered an attack of polio and from the moment he entered the national spotlight exerted his enormous charm to raise funds to fight the disease.

In 1933, he endorsed the suggestion of a New York public relations agency that President's Birthday Balls be held, with the proceeds going to polio research and treatment. On January 30, 1934, the first party occurred in Washington, DC, and during the ensuing decade the nation annually raised millions of dollars on Roosevelt's birthday through the sale of tickets granting admittance to hundreds of hugely successful, simultaneously staged, dances. In many communities, the balls became much more than "dances so others can walk." During grim times, they became excuses for cake auctions, parades, astrology readings, and performances by acrobats. One year the citizens of Louisville, Kentucky, included boxing matches between blind pugilists at their ball. Questionable taste, but a crowd pleaser, and all for a good cause.[28]

In 1937, the president gave his blessing to another effort and announced the establishment of the National Foundation for Infantile Paralysis, which quickly became one of the film industry's favorite charities. The March of Dimes emerged from a suggestion made at a Hollywood fundraiser, when the singer Eddie Cantor urged every American eager to fight polio to send FDR a dime. Within days, the White House mailroom was completely overwhelmed. Americans sent their dimes to Washington and their checks to the Foundation, which by the mid-1940s had raised more than $20 million.

---

[26] Even in one of the nation's most poverty-stricken states, Kentucky, domestic sanitation improved dramatically during the period. In 1940, 29 percent of the state's single family homes had a flush toilet. By 1950 40 percent did. Bradshaw, "Polio in Kentucky," 31.

[27] Rogers, *Dirt and Disease*, 168–9.

[28] Nancy Bradshaw, "Polio in Kentucky," 24–25; For Roosevelt's involvement, see Hugh Gregory Gallagher, *FDR's Splendid Deception* (New York, 1988).

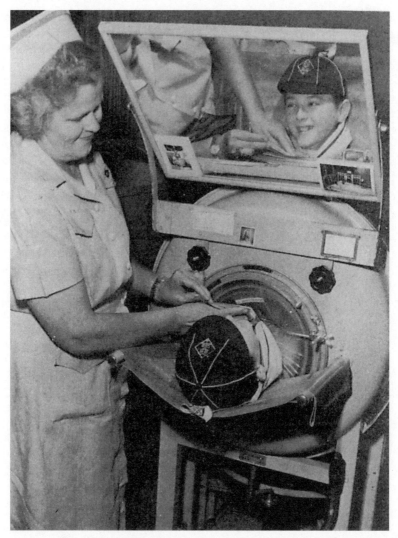

PHOTO 9.1 The caption reads, "James Headley wears his Cub Scout cap, getting ready for a troop meeting at Rancho los Amigos Respiratory Center, Hondo, California." Alton Blakeslee, *Polio and the Salk Vaccines: What You Should Know About It* (New York, 1956), no page numbers.

Citizens sobbed through films featuring tow-headed child actors pretending to struggle to walk again, stories that often merged seamlessly with the real-life efforts of similarly appealing March of Dimes poster children. They picked up their morning newspapers and, on the front pages, read the heart-breaking details of yet another stricken child's ordeal. Even the good gray *New York Times* prominently printed a daily tally of polio deaths and hospitalizations in the New York metropolitan area.[29]

Lost in all this publicity was the fact that, even at its peak in 1952, polio killed less than 5 percent of its 57,879 reported victims. Most among the approximately one third of cases with paralytic symptoms eventually regained use of their muscles. Typically, those who fell ill suffered nothing worse than headache, fever, and chills. But the average American thought that a diagnosis of polio was a virtual sentence to an iron lung, and children in iron lungs had become the nation's intellectual property. The search for their salvation altered public health policy.[30]

[29] Polio did seem to increase in ferocity after 1940, perhaps reflecting the rising living standards that increased the risk that older children and young adults would get the disease. Deaths and paralysis were, of course, terrible family tragedies, but in advertising polio as a national scourge, the Foundation blurred for most Americans the fact that their children's chances of suffering death or serious crippling were relatively remote. Even at its worst, in 1952, polio killed, on average, about sixty people in any given state. Scholars have placed relatively little emphasis on the battle against polio as a public relations triumph. Most are medical historians whose attention has been focused on the Salk-Sabin rivalry or on the conquest of polio as an episode in the history of virology. The activities of the Foundation generally have been discussed within the context of its sponsorship of medical research. Aaron Klein is representative of other scholars in his portrayal of the Foundation as forcing scientists to work too quickly, publicize their results too soon, and become, in effect, an adult group of poster-children. Aaron Klein, *Trial by Fury: The Polio Vaccine Controversy* (New York, 1972), 67–109. However, neither Klein nor anyone else has discussed the centrality of public relations to the choice of polio as a disease to conquer. Institutes like the Rockefeller Institute for Medical Research had more funding in the 1940s and 1950s, but they had a sole philanthropic patron and did not raise money through massive publicity campaigns. Naomi Rogers's excellent *Dirt and Disease* discusses the marketing of polio, but only in a brief epilogue to a book whose focus is American response to the polio epidemic of 1916. Many authors, perhaps unwittingly, echo the tone of Foundation literature, portraying polio as the horrific crippler of innocents, which, of course, it was, but authors downplay, as did the Foundation, the fact that polio only rarely left its victims permanently disabled. Unfortunately, there is no comprehensive history of the Foundation.

[30] In fact, the chance of suffering a form of permanent paralysis rose with age, and young adults between the ages of twenty and thirty-five were at greatest risk of suffering the worst terrors of polio. However, they never appeared on the Foundation for Infantile Paralysis's posters. Unquestionably, polio caused terrible suffering and was a significant American health threat in the years between 1900 and 1955. But so did many other diseases, including several which were greater killers of children. Between 1938 and 1955, the years of most fertile activity in polio research, other organizations existed to combat diseases, among them: the American Cancer Society, and the National Tuberculosis Association. But these groups did not raise funds in the same aggressive way as did the National Foundation for Infantile Paralysis, nor did the victims of the diseases they sought to fight, no matter how greatly they suffered, tug at the general public's heart and purse strings in the same way. Indeed, until the discovery in the mid-1940s that streptomycin could effectively treat the disease, tuberculosis sufferers were shunned or confined in remote sanatoriums. Some state legislatures tried, unsuccessfully, to ban the entry of tuberculosis patients. The measures failed, not because of sympathy for the disease's victims, but because of worries about the potential high cost of policing borders.

Between 1938 and 1955, funded from the deep pockets of the Foundation for Infantile Paralysis, several groups of researchers raced to find a vaccine. Virology itself was a new field, providing full time employment for a handful of research scientists. As late as the 1930s specialists still disagreed about the basic nature of viruses. Were they smaller versions of bacteria? Were they unique organisms? Were they inorganic poisons? Each view had adherents. On one subject, however, virologists agreed. Edward Jenner had gotten lucky. Smallpox, it turned out, was the exception to the rule. An injection of cowpox induced immunity to smallpox. Most vaccines worked only if made from the virus they sought to subdue, and that was much more difficult.

Scientists seeking a preventive for polio employed one of two experimental techniques. The first required that the virus be killed by heat, radiation, or formaldehye, then injected to stimulate the body to produce antibodies. The second "bred" weakened live viruses – by passing the disease from lab monkey to lab monkey to lab monkey. Such a live, but greatly weakened, virus could then be administered by mouth to stimulate immunity. With live vaccine, however, there was always the rare chance that the virus would naturally revert to a more potent form and cause the disease it was meant to prevent. Moreover, recipients might act as disease carriers, since they continued to excrete live virus in their stools for several weeks after receiving vaccine. In the tiny world of institute science, adherents of killed versus live virus techniques vehemently challenged each other's methods.

The killed virus group was the first to produce a successful vaccine. On April 12, 1955, the anniversary of Franklin Roosevelt's death, the ever-media-savvy Basil O'Connor, head of the Foundation for Infantile Paralysis, organized a news conference in Ann Arbor, Michigan, to announce that Dr. Jonas Salk's killed-virus injectable vaccine successfully immunized against polio. The story hit front pages everywhere; strangers hugged and wept in the streets.[31]

As a harbinger of a changed public health policy, the events of April through June 1954 were even more important. The parents of more than 440,000 American children eagerly volunteered their offspring as "Polio Pioneers" to receive a totally new, potentially deadly vaccine. After decades of hesitation, Americans dramatically changed their minds about childhood vaccination.

See Sheila Rothman, *Living in the Shadow of Death: Tuberculosis and the Social Experience of Illness in American History* (New York, 1994), 181–95.

[31] The story of the development of polio vaccines has been well told and is not the focus of this chapter. For good overviews, see Klein, *Trial by Fury*; Smith, *Patenting the Sun*; Allan Brandt, "Polio, Politics, Publicity, and Duplicity: Ethical Aspects in the Development of the Salk Vaccine," *International Journal of the Health Sciences* 8 (1978): 257–70.

"Lem Sikes has had his hogs immunized against cholera. His children are still unprotected against diphtheria and smallpox but of course his pigs are thorobreds."

© A.P.H.A

PHOTO 9.2   George Truman Palmer, Mahew Derryberry, and Philip Van Ingen, *Health Protection from the Preschool Child: A National Survey of the Use of Preventive Medical and Dental Service for Children Under Six*. Proceedings of the White House Conference on Child Health and Protection (New York, 1931), 95.

The Rush to Immunize

Since the early twentieth century, public health officials tried to promote immunization of children against smallpox and diphtheria. Their tactics ranged from persuading school districts to create honor rolls of immunized students, to offering magazine subscriptions to parents who brought their youngsters in to clinics, to organizing "vaccination round-ups" – parties complete with nurses, trays of needles, and ice cream. Dr. W. J. French, a physician who worked for the New York–based philanthropy, the Commonwealth Fund, spoke for many other public health doctors when he wearily ended a 1931 report on efforts to immunize with "As yet, no great results."[32]

Suddenly, in 1954, hundreds of thousands of parents frantically volunteered their children as test subjects in the Salk vaccine's first major field trial. Some tried to bribe health officials to make sure their youngsters had a chance – even though they knew that some children would receive placebos and had been told of the risk that the injection itself might cause polio.

With the welcome news on April 12, 1955, that this unprecedently large experimental program had been successful, the Division of Biologics Standards at the NIH quickly licensed six companies to produce polio vaccine. Indeed, the word "quickly" does not begin to describe the speed of the actual process. Federal approval of Salk vaccine took all of two hours. An open phone line connected a Washington, DC, auditorium packed with hundreds of reporters to the Ann Arbor hotel room where William Workmann of the Division sat with a review committee of well-known virologists. Workmann and his assistants carried in hundreds of pages of summary reports and stacked them on a table in the hotel room. In the madly ebullient atmosphere of the day, however, it was clear the committee was not really going to read anything. After all, reporters were interrupting radio and television programs to count down the minutes until victory over polio, and Surgeon-General Leonard Scheele stood in front of a bank of microphones, ready to celebrate. The good mood continued throughout the summer, even in the face of revelations that one company licensed to distribute vaccine, Cutter Laboratories, accidentally released a batch containing live virus. The arms of six California children into which the vaccine had been injected were permanently paralyzed.[33]

The "Cutter Incident" did not deter Congress from rapidly passing the Poliomyelitis Vaccination and Assistance Acts of 1955, a bill that established a new national health care policy – that no child should be denied the right to vaccination. It was a startling shift. Any municipal public health official who had enlisted during the early-twentieth-century vaccination wars could have justifiably wondered if he still lived in the same country. State after state enacted legislation making polio immunization mandatory before a child entered first grade. The pace quickened after 1960, when Jonas Salk's rival, Albert Sabin, received federal licensure for his live-virus oral polio vaccine. Sabin's vaccine could be distributed on sugar cubes by untrained volunteers, cutting the costs of a three-dose regime for polio vaccination in half. Received as a godsend by public health officials organizing mass

---

[32] Report by W. J. French, "Visit to Athens, Georgia," January 17–19, 1931, Records of the Commonwealth Fund, Series 12, Box 2, Folder 28, RAC.

[33] Klein, *Trial by Fury*, 110–19; Bert Spector, "The Great Salk Vaccine Mess," *The Antioch Review* 38 (1980): 291–304.

immunization programs, it rapidly displaced Salk's injected killed-virus vaccine. By 1965, all fifty states demanded polio vaccination of schoolchildren. Pictures of lines of children happily gobbling pink sugar cubes symbolized a public health triumph.

In 1949 an elderly Texas farmer was the last American to suffer a reported case of smallpox. Nonetheless, all states added smallpox vaccination to their compulsory vaccination laws. Polio vaccine not only finally made that ancient among vaccines respectable, it spurred exciting advances in the now hot field of virology. By 1970, more effective vaccines existed to immunize against diphtheria, pertussis, and tetanus, and new vaccines prevented measles, mumps, and rubella. By 1977, when mumps vaccine became widely available, most states had added these six childhood diseases to their lists of required immunizations.[34]

In the early twentieth century, state and national politicians avoided the issue of vaccination. Why suffer furious editorials in hometown newspapers? Why become the target of anti-immunization referendums? After 1956, politicians at all levels embraced childhood immunization as a holy cause.

In compliance with the terms of the Poliomyelitis Assistance Act, the federal government assumed a new role, as a major procurer of childhood vaccines. State health departments could apply for federal grants to aid them to supply vaccine to all children, and, in a notable departure from traditions firmly established by New Deal cost-sharing programs, federal assistance was outright.[35]

When called in 1962 to Washington to testify about his state's immunization campaign, a confused Dr. Russell Teague, Frankfort, Kentucky's, Health Commissioner, found himself engaged in bewildered conversation with Representative Walter Rogers, a man never previously on record as a champion of Big Government. Rogers asked Teague what the federal government might do to speed along mandatory compulsion, and noted, "Like now you say to a family, 'Now your child cannot go to school unless it is vaccinated.'" The puzzled Teague responded, "Yes, that can be done at the state level, but not at the federal level." To which Mr. Rogers of Texas replied,

---

[34] Measles vaccine was licensed in 1963 and became widely available in 1964. Mumps vaccine was selectively available in 1967, but not widely used in the United States until 1977. Vaccine against rubella was introduced in 1969. Sharon Snider, "Childhood Vaccines," 24 *FDA Consumer* (1990): 19–26.

[35] Beginning with a $30 million allocation in the 1956 budget, federal resources allocated to childhood immunization gradually, but steadily, climbed in the next several decades, spiking dramatically upwards beginning in the late 1980s. By 1991, even before the Clinton Vaccines for Children Initiative, the federal government spent at least $185 million on childhood vaccine procurement. Gary Freed, W. Clayton Bordley, and Gordon Defriese, "Childhood Immunization Programs: An Analysis of Policy Issues," *Milbank Quarterly* 71 (1993): 65–96.

"Yes, I understand, but the fact is that you can say to the state, 'Unless you (pass a) compulsory vaccination law then you will not be allowed to participate in these grant funds.'"[36]

Neither the Poliomyelitis Assistance Act of 1955 or the subsequent Vaccine Assistance Act of 1962 required states to institute compulsory programs in order to receive federal monies. Both charged the Public Health Service and the new Department of Health, Education, and Welfare (HEW) with the duty to assist state administration of vaccine programs. State legislatures, however, got the message. They might as well come out against motherhood – or School Lunch – as challenge the importance of mandatory vaccination.

In the early 1960s, the following predictions would have seemed entirely reasonable: federal-state cooperative programs to immunize the nation's young would be a politician's best friend, popular and effective; America's pharmaceutical companies would continue to dominate world vaccines' markets; public officials would only have to exercise oversight to ensure that manufacturers did not engage in price fixing.[37]

Nothing like this occurred. Instead, by 1976, the fourteen companies making the seven required childhood vaccines dwindled to four. Of these four, three announced plans to quit the U.S. vaccine market. The fourth, Lederle Laboratories, temporarily suspended its production of live-virus oral polio vaccine as it searched for an insurer. Spot shortages of measles, pertussis, and polio vaccines prevented an estimated thirty million American kids from receiving their vaccinations on schedule. Arkansas Senator Dale Bumpers assailed the nation's vaccine policy as "bordering on insanity."[38] What had happened? Simply put, vaccination became a litigated issue. To understand that development requires a review of changes in American tort and product liability law between 1967 and 1985. The fact that punitive damage awards became commonplace had major unexpected consequences.

---

[36] Exchange between Representative Walter Rogers, Texas, and Dr. Russell Teague, May 15, 1962, 14 Hearing, Intensive Programs.

[37] Indeed, in 1957 House Committee on Government Operations investigated charges that the five companies then in the business of making polio vaccine had engaged in a lucrative price-fixing conspiracy to double their product's price from 35 cents per cubic centimeter to 79 cents per cubic centimeter. The Department of Justice convened a federal grand jury, but the case went no further, since jurors found the evidence inconclusive. See "Activities of the Department of Health, Education, and Welfare Relating to Polio Vaccine," Fifteenth Report: August 15, 1957, House Committee on Government Operations (Washington, DC, 1957), 17–21.

[38] "Remarks of Senator Dale Bumpers," Polio Immunization Program, 1976, Hearing before the Subcommittee on Health of the Committee on Labor and Public Welfare, Senate, Ninety-Fourth Congress, Second Session (Washington, DC, 1976): 100 (hereafter Hearing, Polio, 1976).

Childhood Vaccines and the Revolution in Product Liability Law

Under American tort law, the manufacturer is responsible for injuries caused by a faulty product, even if it exercised all possible care in the item's preparation and sale. There are, however, exceptions to this strict standard. If, for instance, society finds a product valuable, but in some way inherently unsafe, its maker is protected and incurs liability only in two instances: if the plaintiff can establish that the item was improperly prepared or can prove that the product lacked an adequate warning about its risks. Vaccines all use a killed or live organism and contain potential dangers that the most scrupulous manufacturer can never eliminate.[39]

In the early twentieth century, a significant number of citizens sued states and localities, demanding the right to send their children to school unvaccinated. Uniformly, courts rejected their claims, found forcible vaccination to be an appropriate state police power, and narrowly defined a person's right to claim exemptions on religious or philosophical grounds. So, at least smallpox vaccine had already been on trial. However, these early vaccination disputes were very different from the suits that altered the nation's vaccine policy between 1968 and 1986. In the latter cases, a private manufacturer, not the state, was the defendant. Morever, the charges did not center on disagreements about privacy rights, as did most early-twentieth-century smallpox cases. Instead, they disputed arcane points in tort law concerning liability.

Before the mid-1970s, a handful of suits alleging vaccine-related injuries hinted of a soon-to-come full fledged legal assault on producers of childhood vaccines. Averaging two or three through the early 1970s, the number of cases mushroomed after 1977, linked to a dramatic change in court awards involving product liability claims. Before 1977, punitive damages were virtually unknown. By 1980, they were common.

American civil law had always said that an innocent party should be able to shift the costs of injury to those responsible. However, attorneys in the 1970s convinced juries that huge awards granted for pain and suffering could force industries to make safer products. Plaintiffs began to demand millions in actual damages and tens of millions in punitive awards. By 1985, lawsuits against vaccines producers escalated to an annual average of 150, and yearly totals for damages claimed exceeded four billion dollars. Realizing that punitive product liability damages were the least likely to be reduced on appeal, manufacturers often settled cases out of court. Corporate litigation defense costs not reimbursed by insurance soared.[40]

---

[39] Michael Sanzo, "Vaccines and the Law," *Pepperdine Law Review* 19 (1991): 29–48; Mary Elizabeth Mann, "Mass Immunization Cases: Drug Manufacturers' Liability for Failure to Warn," *Vanderbilt Law Review* 29 (1976): 235–66.

[40] *Ibid.* See also: Mary Beth Neraas, "The National Vaccine Injury Act of 1986: A Solution to the Vaccine Liability Crisis?" *Washington Law Review* 63 (1988) 150–68.

Most immunization cases involved either the three-dose sequence of oral polio vaccine or the four to five dose series of injections against diphtheria, tetanus, and pertussis (DTP) that every state required schoolchildren to take. All revolved around one question – had the producers of these vaccines sufficiently described their dangers? Different jurisdictions gave different answers, some of which ignored the traditional "learned intermediary" rule that held that a pharmaceutical company fulfilled its obligations to warn when it provided written notice to the prescribing physician.

In 1974, Epifanio Reyes, a resident of rural Hidalgo County, Texas, took Wyeth Laboratories to court, charging that a dose of vaccine his then-eight-month-old daughter Anita received at a public health clinic in 1970 gave the child polio. Wyeth distributed its vaccine with a package insert stating that paralytic disease following the ingestion of live polio virus had been reported in individuals receiving the vaccine or in persons in close contact with them, but that such incidents were overwhelmingly uncommon, fewer than one in three million. The nurse who gave baby Anita her sugar cube read the warning but did not explain it to Anita's parents before asking them to sign a release form, freeing the clinic from liability. The United States Court of Appeals for the Fifth Circuit ruled for the Reyes, arguing that Anita's parents could not have assumed a risk of which they were unaware.[41]

In 1977, the Fifth Circuit, in another precedent-setting ruling, further challenged the "learned intermediary" rule. Six years earlier a Florida housewife, Sherry Givens, drove her daughter Wendy to the family's private pediatrician for the baby's first dose of Sabin vaccine, obtained this time from the vaccine's other manufacturer, Lederle Laboratories. Lederle's package insert replicated the one used by Wyeth, and again, a medical professional read it and concluded that the risk incurred was so fantastically small that it was not worth mentioning to Mrs. Givens.

Sherry Givens, however, *did* contract polio. She was that oddity, someone who did not beat the live oral vaccine's one in three million chances against coming down with the disease. Changing Wendy's diapers exposed Mrs. Givens to the virus, and she lost all motor function in her legs. Again the Court found for the plaintiff.[42]

In essence, judges in some jurisdictions took on not just the vaccine manufacturers but also the medical and scientific communities. The presiding judge in the Reyes Appeal excluded testimony from the virologist who examined Anita Reyes's stool and concluded that the virus that paralyzed her was a "wild" variant, not one that could have possibly been excreted from vaccine. He also dismissed comments raised in briefs of *amici curiae* filed by

---

[41] *Epifanio Reyes and Anita Reyes v. Wyeth Laboratories*, 72-2251, United States Court of Appeals for the Fifth Circuit, 498 F. 2d 1264; 1974, U.S. App.

[42] *Sherry Givens and Wendy Givens v. Lederle Laboratories*, 75-3573, 75-3672, United States Court of Appeals for the Fifth Circuit, 556 f 2d 1341: 1977, U.S. App.

the American Academy of Pediatrics, which argued that if legal guardians of every child who received a vaccine had to be personally advised of its potential to cause harm, however remote, large scale immunization programs would stall. Even on a one-to-one basis such personally delivered warnings would, the AAP cautioned, "needlessly frighten and confuse" parents. The Court curtly responded? "The AAP's answer to this problem is to warn no one. That is no answer."[43] The *Reyes* and *Givens* decisions set the scene for a decade of strange legal skirmishes, in which judges without medical training offered opinions about wild versus cultured viruses and challenged the decisions of board-certified pediatricians.

In odd ways, suits featuring polio victims revived the bitterly personal feud between killed and live virus advocates. One commentator reviewing the brief for a case on appeal correctly concluded in 1986 that "The evidence introduced herein could well bear the caption, *Salk v. Sabin.*"[44] In several cases, Dr. Darrell Salk stood in for his late father and testified that Salk vaccine was a far better product, and that, given its risks, Sabin vaccine had no place in American public health programs.[45] American pediatricians who heard this must have found the statement Kafkaesque. Salk condemned them for not using a vaccine that had not been generally distributed in the United States since 1968.

Parents of children who claimed injuries caused by mandatory vaccinations against pertussis sought their day in court as well and argued, in the words of one child's attorney, that DTP's manufacturers caused "death and brain damage" by distributing a vaccine that "can and should be made better."[46] Again, judges without medical backgrounds excluded the testimony of prominent virologists who said that the immunity-producing antigens of the live virus pertussis organism continued to evade scientists, requiring the use of a potentially riskier, whole-virus, killed organism vaccine. Labels on DTP vials told physicians not to continue with the whole-cell pertussis component if a child convulsed, developed a fever, or began high-pitched, persistent crying, but hundreds of lawsuits claimed that this provided insufficient warning, even to physicians, much less parents.

In 1954 hundreds of thousands of American parents excitedly volunteered their children as test subjects in experimental polio field trials. They rushed to their pediatricians and public health clinics in 1955 when government and academic experts decided polio vaccine was safe. The relatively few

---

[43] *Reyes v. Wyeth Laboratories.*

[44] *Emil Johnson v. American Cyanamid Company and Lederle Laboratories* 57, 368, Supreme Court of Kansas, 239 Kan. 279; 718 P. 2d 1318; 1986.

[45] *Ibid.*

[46] "Testimony of Anthony Colantoni, Response to Questions Submitted by Senator Orrin Hatch," National Childhood Vaccine Injury Compensation Act, Hearing before the Committee on Labor and Human Resources, United States Senate, Ninety-Ninth Congress, First Session (Washington, DC, 1985): 65.

court cases involving charges of vaccine injury were straightforward. Cutter Laboratories, for instance, paid for the hospitalization and treatment of the California children injected with a batch of killed vaccine virus it readily acknowledged had been inadvertently tainted. Even if unwittingly, it had sold a defective product and was liable.[47]

Thirty years later, definitions of liability were no longer clear-cut. Courts assessed actual and punitive damages even when vaccine companies sold "pure" products carefully made to government standards and distributed with package inserts approved by the Division of Biologic Standards, now an agency within the Food and Drug Administration. Since vaccines were obviously not an over-the-counter item parents could pick up at a drugstore, would a representative from a vaccine maker have to sit in every physician's office or stand at the door of every health clinic to make sure that warnings about potential harm were given? Even if a company could trust all of the tens of thousands of health care workers who administered vaccines never to neglect this duty, it was not at all obvious exactly what sort of warning would meet a court's approval. Most American manufacturers of childhood vaccines assessed their chances in battle, surrendered, and abandoned field.

The two major companies left hinted that they too might cease making vaccines without the sort of indemnity against liability the federal government granted the makers of swine flu vaccine in 1976. Fearing an episode similar to the horrific Spanish Flu of 1918–1919, Congress quickly approved a program of publicly sponsored mass immunization and agreed to accept liability. All lawsuits would be brought against the federal government. The pandemic never came, but forty-five million Americans received a vaccine, which, it was soon charged, caused or promoted Guillian-Barre Syndrome, a neurological disorder. Thousands filed claims, and by 1986, the government had paid $65 million dollars to the victims or survivors of the condition. With that disastrous precedent fresh in mind, politicians were not eager to agree to manufacturers' requests again to be protected from liability.[48] In the face of this impasse, vaccine supplies dwindled and costs rose, between 1980 and 1986, on average, one thousand percent annually. A single shot of DTP vaccine that cost ten cents in 1980 cost $2.80 in 1984, and more than $5 by 1986.[49]

---

[47] *Gottsdanker v. Cutter Laboratories*, Cal. App. 1960, 182 Ca. App. 2d 602, 6 Cal. Rptr. 320.

[48] Barton Bernstein, "The Swine Flu Vaccination Campaign of 1976: Politics, Science, and the Public," *Congress and the Presidency* 10 (1983): 96–103; see also "Statements of Daniel Shaw: Vice President, Wyeth Laboratories," Vaccine Injury Compensation, Hearings before the Subcommittee on Health and the Environment of the Committee on Energy and Commerce, House of Representatives, Ninety-Eighth Congress, Second Session (Washington, DC): 295–311.

[49] "Testimony of Claude Earl Fox," *Ibid.*, 214–17; see also "Statutory Compensation Urged," *Nature* 316 (1985): 476–77; David Wood and Neal Halfon, "The Impact of the Vaccine for Children's Program on Child Immunization Delivery," 577–79. Notably as costs in the U.S.

The lawyers who represented disabled children accepted no blame for these price increases. They argued that every state required schoolkids to be immunized against communicable diseases. If this policy caused injury, why should families who had no choice suffer financially? Moreover, the willingness to accept the conclusions of scientific experts that ordinary citizens displayed in 1954 and 1955 had dimmed.

By the early 1990s chapters of two advocacy groups, Informed Parents Against Vaccine-Associated Polio and Dissatisfied Parents Together, existed all over the country. Members were usually parents who traced their child's disabilities to a vaccination.[50] Most disputed the unanimous verdict of government and medical agencies that mandatory vaccines were statistically safe, posing risk of injury on the order of one case in three million for polio vaccine and a slightly greater, but still miniscule, danger of one case per three hundred thousand for pertussis.[51] They agreed with attorney and spokesman for Dissatisfied Parents Together, Jeffrey Schwartz: "The Department of Health and Human Services has kept vaccine public policymaking in the hands of the few and out of sight of many. [It] has refused to get the facts, know the facts, or share the facts with the public."[52] Another Dissatisfied Parents member, Donna Gary, echoed Schwartz: "If it is true that adverse reactions to pertussis vaccine are so very rare, then how can one ordinary person like me know about . . . so many?"[53]

Some vaccination opponents believed that required childhood vaccines were inherently dangerous. They alleged that immunization was responsible for an estimated doubling of the number of American youngsters who suffered asthma. They argued that dramatically higher reported incidences of childhood autism in Britain, the United States, and other developed countries

---

escalated, they remained relatively stable in the rest of the world. By 1993, when a full series of shots averaged more than $500 at a private American pediatrician's office, UNICEF still continued to purchase the same series to distribute throughout the developing world for less than one dollar. No U.S. manufacturer has participated in the bidding or procurement process for UNICEF childhood vaccines since 1982. Violaine Mitchell, Nalini Philipose, and Jay Sanford, Eds., *The Children's Vaccine Initiative: Achieving the Vision* (Washington, DC, 1993), 6–7.

[50] Bridget Lyne, "The People v. VAPP," *Exceptional Parent* 28 (1998): 56–60; "The Vaccine Dilemma," *The Washington Post*, December 5, 1987.

[51] In 1985, the AMA's Ad Hoc Commission on Vaccine Compensation concluded that, out of 13.5 million doses administered, the P in DTP caused 43 children to suffer brain damage. Out of eighteen million polio doses, five people contracted the disease; all were parents who had changed babies' diapers. "American Medical Association, Report of Ad Hoc Commission on Vaccine Injury Compensation," *Connecticut Medicine* 49 (1985): 172–76.

[52] "Testimony of Jeffrey Schwartz," National Childhood Vaccine Injury Compensation Act, Hearing before the Committee on Labor and Human Resources, United States Senate, Ninety-Eighth Congress, Second Session (Washington, DC, 1984): 49 (hereafter Injury Compensation, 1984).

[53] "Testimony of Donna Gary," 68, *Ibid.*

coincided with a growth in the number of inoculations given young children. They connected learning disabilities to mandatory vaccination. They worried quite publicly that a significant number of genetically susceptible children just could not handle an ever-increasing number of mandated vaccines.[54] Whether in the minority that generally opposed all laws requiring immunization or the majority that focused on the dangers of one particular antiviral vaccine, all advocacy groups demanded compensation for injuries caused by vaccines.

In 1985, plaintiff groups and vaccine companies united to lobby for the passage of the measure both sides hoped would get the vaccines issue out of the courts. The National Childhood Vaccine Injury Act of 1986 established a no-fault system with compensation awarded for medical bills, rehabilitation expenses, and projected lost wages not covered by insurance.

Petitioners claiming injury caused by any of the seven commonly required childhood vaccines filed documented claims in U.S. district courts, whose judges determined settlements through uniform use of HHS's "Vaccine Injury Table," which listed all known injuries and adverse reactions. A vaccine company was not liable for "unavoidable" injury – if it could prove that it had properly prepared its product. Moreover, and more important, it no longer had to verify that the injured party or a legal guardian had received a direct warning of potential risk.[55]

By 1998, the new system had distributed cash settlements to more than twenty-six hundred people whose children had died or been seriously disabled after vaccination. The overwhelming majority of claims involved pertussis vaccine. On average the program cost $60 million annually, a substantial figure, but far below that predicted in 1984, when the Assistant Secretary for Health and Human Services, Edward Brandt, thought that the annual bill would exceed $225 million.[56]

---

[54] For a summary of these views, see Rosie Waterhouse, "Autism Linked to Vaccine," *The London Sunday Times*, May 27, 2001. Other experts linked these increases in certain childhood ailments to nutritional and environmental causes. In February 2002, the National Institutes of Medicine released the results of a long-term study – investigating charges that vaccines caused harm. It concluded that childhood shots did not worsen risks for autism or juvenile diabetes, nor did they prompt increases in serious infections, such as meningitis. However, the report, the product of a panel chaired by Harvard professor of public health, Dr. Marie McCormick, called for further study – saying that, with the evidence at hand, it could not dismiss potential links between immunizations and escalating rates of childhood asthma. Nor could it state categorically that immunizations were not related to immune system problems in some children. Clearly twentieth century battles continued. Report summarized in Sheryl Stolberg, "Panel Discounts Some Fears Over Vaccinations for Babies," *New York Times*, February 21, 2002.

[55] Neraas, "The National Childhood Vaccine Injury Act of 1986," 156–58. Petitioners could reject the court verdict and file civil actions.

[56] Allen, "Injection Rejection," 22–23; "Statement of Edward Brandt," Hearing, Injury Compensation, 1984, 13–16.

Vaccine manufacturers, along with most physicians and medical researchers, vigorously denied that anything like the number of people who received compensation under the terms of the Vaccine Injury Act had actually been harmed by a vaccination. Even in the late twentieth century, the causes of adverse reactions to pertussis vaccine were little understood. Many virologists thought that problems might be triggered by hereditary immune system defects that were rarely detectable in a baby only two months old, when doctors recommended infants begin routine immunization. Babies and toddlers, of course, continued to get sick, sometimes for reasons that mystified their physicians, and since several courses of vaccines were normally given before a child reached the age of two, it was inevitable that a few would suffer seizures, convulsions, or other serious health problems around the time of an inoculation. Especially after almost all health professionals adopted a less-risky acellular pertissus vaccine that became available in the 1980s, medical experts argued that if a baby suffered a seizure after a DTP vaccination, it was coincidence.

Debates about the actual harm caused any baby by pertussis vaccine continued, though they pitted a majority of pediatricians and research scientists against nonexperts. However, no authority had ever challenged the fact that on very rare occasion, oral polio vaccine could revert to virulence and paralyze.[57] Justifiably, families with members sickened by a vaccine the law required did not see themselves as statistically insignificant unfortunates. They thought themselves wronged victims of a bad public policy. In 1996, in very belated acknowledgment of the arguments advocates of killed virus vaccine had been making for forty years, CDC recommended a major change in U.S. polio vaccination practices. It urged physicians to change the three dose regime of oral vaccine that had become near-universal by the mid-1960s to a four-dose sequential schedule – two doses of injected Salk-type vaccine, to be followed by two doses of oral vaccine. The first two shots of killed vaccine protected against even the miniscule chance of infection from the

---

[57] Advocates of the live virus, however, argued that using live virus vaccine was the only possible way to eliminate wild virulent strains in nature, and the only way to make the gastrointestinal tract resistant to wild strains. Virologist Harold Cox, who worked with the Minnesota Department of Health to develop the Cox Live Polio Vaccine, explained: "The principle of the live virus vaccine in polio is analogous to protecting your house against the weather. You don't fill the rooms with concrete. All you do is paint the outside walls because they are the site of exposure. In the case of a natural polio infection, if you are one of the 999 lucky ones out of a thousand who does not get the disease, the virus grows in the cells of the gut, and viruses are shed anywhere from ten days to as long as six months without symptoms. During this process, antibodies appear in the blood. If you imitate the norms of nature as a model for improvement, you are on solid ground." Dr. Harold Cox, Panel: "The Present Status of Polio Vaccines," Presented Before the Section on Preventive Medicine and Public Health at the 120th Annual Meeting of the ISMS in Chicago, May 20, 1969, Transcript of Discussion Reprinted in Hearings, Intensive Programs: quotation on 105.

last two oral live vaccine doses, while retaining some of the cost benefits of the much cheaper second product.[58]

By then, three decades had passed since any American company sold killed virus polio vaccine but, because of its greater relative safety, several European firms continued to produce it. Connaught Laboratories, a Canadian subsidiary of the French pharmaceutical giant, Pasteur-Merieux, announced it would be pleased to extend its sales territory to the United States.

Immunization at the end of the century was a victim of its own success. Only Americans born before 1955 could vividly remember being terrified of polio and a host of other infectious childhood killers. By the 1990s, few that age were taking babies and toddlers in for vaccinations. Younger parents, moreover, were less willing to accept what their physicians told them: that bad luck, not a bad vaccine, left them with a disabled child. As Dr. Regina Rabinovich, chief of clinical studies in microbiology at the National Institute for Allergy and Infectious Disease, explained, "In science, we're not very good at proving the negative."[59] Since that was true, the Childhood Vaccine Injury Act, through compromise, ended a legal stalemate and helped ensure the nation's vaccine supply. However, its passage did not conclude the story of publicly mandated childhood vaccination in the twentieth century. The final chapter began during President Bill Clinton's first year in office.

The Vaccines for Children Initiative

The Childhood Vaccine Injury Act brokered a welcome truce, but it did not produce clear victory for advocates of cheap and universal childhood immunization. Indeed, even with the threat of most punitive damage suits removed, private market prices for vaccines continued to rise. In some parts of the country, immunization rates for some of the mandatory vaccines declined significantly between 1986 and 1992, and incidence of preventable disease increased. In 1983, public health agencies reported fewer than fifteen hundred measles cases nationwide. By 1989–1990, the country was in the midst of a "measles epidemic" that defied earlier epidemiological predictions that the disease would disappear in the United States by 1995. Instead, in 1990 almost twenty-eight thousand kids got the measles, a larger reported number than in any year since 1977.[60]

On February 12, 1993, President Bill Clinton chose a public health clinic in nearby Alexandria, Virginia, for a major policy announcement. It was,

[58] "Polio Vaccination Recommendations Changed in the U.S.," *Antiviral Agents Bulletin*: 9.
[59] Quoted in Allen, "Injection Rejection," 23.
[60] Gary Freed, W. Clayton Bordley, and Gordon Defriese, "Childhood Immunization Programs: An Analysis of Policy Issues," 66–67; The National Vaccine Advisory Committee, "The Measles Epidemic: The Problem, Barriers, and Recommendations," *Journal of the American Medical Association* 266 (1991): 1547–52.

he declared, completely "unacceptable that the United States is the only in-dustrial country that does not guarantee childhood vaccination for all chil-dren."[61] Every American child should receive recommended vaccinations at the appropriate age against every preventable disease. By the year 2000, no child in the country should celebrate a second birthday unimmunized. To achieve the goal, the Clinton Administration proposed that the federal gov-ernment buy up all childhood vaccine and distribute it. Congress rejected the idea but during the next eight years regularly approved annual spending increases for the Vaccines for Children (VFC) program, with money to be used to establish a national immunization tracking system, to buy vaccines for free distribution to children enrolled in Medicaid or without health insur-ance coverage, and to help local communities improve their immunization efforts.[62]

The Poliomyelitis and Vaccination Assistance Acts, which offered fed-eral financial assistance to states to extend vaccination programs, expired in 1968. The timing was propitious. The nation's attention was focused on poverty in the midst of plenty. Reports that poor children suffered not only hunger, but preventable diseases, helped spur the passage, in 1970, of the Communicable Disease Control Amendments to the Public Health Service Act. Successor to the Poliomyelitis Acts, this legislation provided additional funding to allow the federal government to purchase vaccines for free distri-bution to needy children.

Initially authorized at approximately the same levels of spending approved by Congress in the heady aftermath of the victory over polio, around $30 million, funding inched upward annually. By 1991, the federal government spent about $185 million annually to help states reach nonimmunized chil-dren. Appropriations for purchase of childhood vaccines even survived a Reagan era veto in 1982.[63] Then, the Clinton vaccination inititiative sweet-ened the pot. From under $500 million in 1994, spending increased to more than $1 billion yearly.

The federal financial contribution increased dramatically, but from 1970 to 2000, the questions were the same. Most agreed that, with laws in place in fifty states requiring their immunization, virtually all American schoolkids were immunized against a series of infectious childhood diseases. At issue was the number of preschool children between the ages of two and six who remained unprotected. Politicians and public health officials asked, who and how many were they?

[61] Quoted in Chester Robinson, "The President's Child Immunization Initiative – A Summary of the Problem and the Response," 108 *Public Health Reports* (1993): 419.

[62] *Ibid.*, 419–22.

[63] United States Department of Health and Human Services, *Fiscal Year Justifications of Ap-propriation Estimates for Committee on Appropriations* (Washington, DC, 1983), 170–75; Robert Pear, "Proposal Would Tie Welfare To Vaccinations of Children," *New York Times*, November 29, 1990.

Experts exchanged volleys of statistics that disputed preschool immunization levels. Some charged that between one third and one half of American two-year-olds had not received a complete schedule of immunizations. Others thought that figure grossly exaggerated, arguing that 90 percent of toddlers that age were fully protected.

The only consistency in this debate was perpetual confusion. A testy exchange in 1995 between Senator Bob Packwood of Oregon and Drs. Walter Orenstein and David Satcher, of the National Immunization Program of the CDC, accurately reflected its tone:

The Chairman (Packwood): "This is your chart. It says 1993 diphtheria, tetanus, pertussis, 90 percent in 1993. Are we higher than that now?
Dr. Satcher: "No, that is not our chart. That is not an official CDC report."
The Chairman: "It is not? It says, 'Source: CDC' at the bottom of it."
Dr. Orenstein: "I think there is at least one error on that chart that I am aware of, on polio vaccination."
The Chairman: "Is this your chart?"
Dr. Orenstein: "It is not our chart, no."
The Chairman: "Now hold on just a minute."
Dr. Satcher: "In fact, polio immunization is 76 percent."
The Chairman: "But this *is* from the CDC."[64]

Weird exchanges of this sort were common for several reasons. First, experts did not accept a standard definition of completed immunization. Especially in the 1990s, when several new vaccines became available, some included vaccination for Hib, two strains of Hepatitis, and chickenpox in their lists of immunizations a two-year-old needed. Others did not or added one, two, or three, but not all, of the more recent childhood vaccines. Finally, recommendations for an older vaccine sequence, DTP, varied. Whether children needed a fourth booster shot at around fifteen months before they could be registered as fully immunized remained in dispute.

Political agendas complicated these scientific disagreements. During the 1992 presidential campaign, Bill Clinton repeatedly charged that the measles epidemics of 1989 and 1990 were caused by the Bush Administration's failure to provide poor children with access to vaccines. After victory, he justified the huge increases for federal vaccine purchase as necessary catch-up, after twelve years of Republican inaction. In turn, Clinton critics counterattacked that Health and Human Services chief Donna Shalala intentionally used outdated data when she cited evidence that one half of the country's preschool kids had not completed their immunizations on time.[65] As the

---

[64] Testimony of David Satcher and Walter Orenstein, "Vaccines for Children Program," Hearing before the Committee on Finance, United States Senate, One Hundred-Fourth Congress, First Session (Washington, DC 1995): 7. Satcher soon left the CDC to become Clinton's second Surgeon-General (hereafter Hearing, VFC).

[65] Robert Goldberg, *The Vaccines for Children Program: A Critique* (Washington, DC, 1995), 4–8.

strife-torn Clinton presidency ended, analysts still battled over the impact of the Vaccines for Children program. One result, however, was clear: the federal government emerged as the dominant purchaser of pediatric vaccine.

Before Bill Clinton took office in 1993, there were two major buyers of childhood vaccines – the public sector, including governments at all levels; and the private sector – physicians, hospitals, pharmacies. The balance between the two was evenly divided. That had been true since the first mass immunizations against polio in the mid-1950s. By 1996, when all children under the age of eighteen were eligible for free vaccine, except those able to get immunizations covered by private insurance, the federal government was the elephant in the parlor – the purchaser of about 80 percent of childhood vaccine used in the United States.[66]

The money was wasted. The fastest growing federal entitlement of the 1990s, Vaccines for Children should have been called Vaccines for the Insurance Industry. Lost in the rhetoric about guarantees of free vaccines for every uninsured child was the late-twentieth-century reality that many noninsured children were not really needy. In fact, most conventional employer-based health insurance plans did not reimburse parents for childhood immunizations. Some states tried to attack the problem by passing laws demanding that insurance carriers cover such inoculations. Such efforts provided politicians with a chance to indulge in meaningless posturing.

ERISA, the Employment Retirement Income Security Act of 1974, exempted employers' self-insured health plans from state regulation. The pols knew that, even if the audiences their television ads targeted did not, and the corporations which strongly supported ERISA exemptions gave generously when party fundraisers called.[67] Vaccines for Children provided unnecessary federal subsidies to middle- and upper-class parents, who, had they not been relieved of the costs of vaccines, would have had greater reason to demand that their private insurance plans pay for childhood vaccines.[68]

---

[66] Henry Garbowski and John Vernon, *The Search for New Vaccines: The Effects of the Vaccines for Children Program* (Washington, DC, 1997), 2–5.

[67] ERISA was designed to protect employees who lost pension benefits due to employer bankruptcy or fraud, but many health insurance companies soon found that its language could be used to deter lawsuits and avoid state regulation. Generally, patients could sue physicians, but not, under most circumstances, their insurance companies. It was not a situation that put much pressure on insurance companies to expand coverage to childhood immunizations, especially in years when the industry focused on cutting costs. David Wood and Neal Halfon, "The Impact of the Vaccine for Children's Program on Child Immunization Delivery," 579–80.

[68] Many thousands of middle-class families were *not* relieved of the costs of vaccines. Insurance companies got a windfall, but many insured families did not, since few of the 79,000 private pediatricians the Clinton Administration claimed were eager to sign up for the VFC program ever materialized. Those who did described the paperwork processes required as a nightmare. Many dropped out. Only pediatricians approved by the VFC's Advisory Committee on Immunization Practices could distribute free vaccine to children whose shots were not

Moreover, immunization statistics for the group of preschool children most at risk of having incomplete vaccinations, those receiving Medicaid, did not improve. They may have worsened. The abolition of Title IV in 1996 pushed over three million people off the welfare rolls within a year. One in five became uninsured when she lost Medicaid benefits. At the cost of many billions of dollars, had the eight-year Vaccines for Children Initiative met its goal – complete vaccination of all American children before a second birthday? Nobody was claiming victory.[69]

Moreover, the program unwittingly provided a disincentive for American companies to invest in research and development of new or improved childhood vaccines. Compared to innovations in other classes of pharmaceuticals, vaccine development required heavier investments of time and money. Typically, a lag of two or more years separated successful culture of a new vaccine and its first use in a human. In addition, as biologics sensitive to heat, vaccines had to be shipped quickly and be kept cold at all times. They also could only be made in relatively small batches and could not easily be stockpiled, since many lost a portion of their effectiveness rapidly. These limitations characterized vaccine manufacture throughout the twentieth century, and researchers doubted that new technologies that might reduce companies' expenses were on the horizon. If, after risking hundreds of millions of dollars on a new vaccine, a company faced the reality that it could sell it only to one big customer, it might rethink its R&D plans. Indeed, by the mid-1990s, the few American companies still in the business shifted many of their research efforts from pediatric to adult vaccines.

These years were ones during which virologists regularly celebrated breakthroughs for "DNA vaccines." Genes injected directly into the body showed promise of stimulating particular kinds of immune defenses. In the year 2000, hundreds of fascinating initiatives were under way that explored possibilities for genetic immunization against tuberculosis, HIV-AIDS, cancer, malaria, as well as parasitic and fungal infections. Almost all of the research, however, involved adult diseases. The prospect existed that in the decades to come American children would be dependent on non-American companies for their immunizations.

---

insured. Therefore, a large number of middle-class families ended up paying out of pocket. Even had they been willing to tend to a restless child, while standing on line for hours at a public health clinic, they couldn't, since most middle-class parents made too much money to be eligible for any service provided by a public health clinic. See Prepared Statement of Lloyd Novick, First Deputy Commissioner, New York Department of Health, "Vaccines for Children Program," 41–43, Hearing, VFC.

[69] "Study Links Medicaid Drop to Welfare Changes," *New York Times*, May 14, 1999; "New Effort Aims to Enroll Children in Insurance Plans," *New York Times*, February 23, 1999; "Low-Cost Insurance," *New York Times*, July 4, 1999; "Kids' Care Plan Has Few Takers," *Detroit News*, June 7, 1999; "Child Health Program Gets Off to a Slow Start," *Washington Post*, April 13, 1999; "Texas Is Too Rich to Leave Its Poor Children Behind," *Houston Chronicle*, May 2, 1999.

Before the 1980s, producers of vaccines rarely competed outside national borders, but a decade later major mergers and joint development agreements "internationalized" the pharmaceuticals industry. Were vaccines used in the United States to be manufactured abroad, the FDA's insistence on close regulation of production facilities would certainly be challenged.[70] Triumph, then, was not the word to use to describe late-twentieth-century childhood vaccination policy. A better one would be that chosen by Dr. Daniel Shea, former president of the American Academy of Pediatrics: "crazy."[71]

Smallpox: Coda

Speaking of the need to protect against smallpox, the early-twentieth-century American state first walked on stage as an active decision maker about children's medical treatment – and for decades received hisses and boos. Only much later did it receive well-earned applause for its leading role in the disease's conquest. Nonetheless, and contrary to all predictions, the defeat of smallpox did not end the drama. Debates about vaccination against smallpox ended the century just as they began it.

In 1971, the United States Public Health Service recommended that routine childhood vaccinations against smallpox be discontinued in the United States. By 1974, all fifty states accepted the advice and repealed their laws demanding smallpox vaccination before school entrance.[72] In 1980, the World Health Organization (WHO) declared the world to be free of smallpox and recommended that all laboratory samples of the virus be destroyed or sent to one of two official smallpox repositories – one in the Soviet Union, one in the United States. The WHO had no inspection authority, however, and relied on a nation's word that it had complied.

---

[70] For changes in the vaccine industry in the 1990s, see Mitchell Mowery, "Improving the Reliability of the U.S. Vaccine Supply: An Evaluation of Alternatives," *Journal of Health Politics, Policy, and Law* 20 (1995): 973–1000; Mark Pauly, *Et Al.*, Eds., *Supplying Vaccines: An Economic Analysis of Critical Issues* (Amsterdam, 1996); Tracy Lieu, "Cost Effectiveness of a Routine Varicella Vaccination Program for U.S. Children," *Journal of the American Medical Association*, 271 (1994): 375–81; Marilyn Gosse, Joseph DiMasi, and Toben Nelson, "Recombinant Protein and Therapeutic Monoclonal Antibody Drug Development in the United States: 1980–94," *Clinical Pharmacology and Therapeutics* 60 (1996): 608–18; Joseph DiMasi, "A New Look at United States Drug Development and Approval Times," *American Journal of Therapeutics* 3 (1996): 1–11.

[71] Senator Dale Bumpers of Arkansas, a Clinton Administration ally on many other initiatives, accurately described VFC. It is, he said, "indescribably complicated. A fairly simple law, designed to benefit a relatively small group of uninsured children, was transformed into a bureaucratic nightmare that put the safety and availability of the nation's vaccine supply at risk." Statements of Daniel Shea and Senator Dale Bumpers, Appendix Materials, 80–83, Hearing, VFC.

[72] "Smallpox Vaccination Repeal," Hearing before the Subcommittee on Labor, Social Services, and the International Community of the Committee on the District of Columbia, House of Representatives, Ninety-Third Congress, Second Session (Washington, DC, 1974): 4–5.

The victory over smallpox was one of the great achievements of the twentieth century.[73] Both the United States and Russia agreed to destroy all remaining samples of virus by 1999. However, neither nation did so. In 1992, Ken Alibek, a high-ranking former Soviet official, defected to the U.S. and began telling bone-chilling tales of massive Soviet-era germ warfare programs that produced tons of genetically enhanced smallpox virus. In 1999, he went public with a book alleging that Russia, along with several of the world's rogue states, might have large, secret supplies of smallpox virus.[74]

Since the United States stopped routine immunization of schoolchildren against smallpox nearly a decade ahead of most other countries, its citizens might be particularly vulnerable to smallpox used as an agent of germ warfare or terrorist attack. None of the 114 million Americans born since 1972 have any protection against smallpox. Easy solutions are not apparent. Virologists know that the creation of an effective vaccine against smallpox virus that had been altered genetically in some unknown way would be tremendously difficult. The "wild" virus was no longer endemic anywhere in the world and was far too dangerous to unleash simply to facilitate clinical trials with human subjects. Some scientists believe that vaccination to safeguard against smallpox used as a weapon makes no sense. Enemies would learn of any mass immunization campaign and alter the virus. Better, they said, to devote resources to a search for antiviral drugs that could be administered after, not before, infection.[75]

---

[73] By the 1990s, most American medical schools no longer taught the disease, though, in fact, the only really effective treatment for smallpox had been immunization against contracting it. As Dr. Bruce Dull, of the CDC, admitted in 1974, "Generally speaking there is not a great deal one can do once the disease has been acquired." *Ibid.*, 14.

[74] Ken Alibek, with Stephen Handelman, *Biohazard: The Chilling True Story of the Largest Covert Biological Weapons Program in the World: Told From the Inside by the Man Who Ran It* (New York, 1999).

[75] In the wake of the terrorist attacks that destroyed New York City's World Trade Center on September 11, 2001, and after an ensuing spate of anthrax-contaminated letters sent through the U.S. mails, Congress authorized the federal Department of Health and Human Services to buy a stockpile of enough smallpox vaccine to innoculate all Americans. In the immediate aftermath of September 11, shocked officials began hesitantly to discuss the possibility of reintroducing mandatory smallpox vaccination. Soon, legislators were debating vaccine product liability, an issue most Americans had forgotten about in the aftermath of the passage of the Childhood Vaccine Injury Act of 1986. Senator Edward Kennedy of Massachusetts drafted a bill to create a federal fund to compensate victims of any vaccines distributed against bioterrorist attacks that later turned out to cause injuries. Representative Billy Tauzin of Louisiana responded tartly to Kennedy's proposal that he doubted "... whether in the middle of a bioterrorism crisis we can have a tort reform debate." Once again, problems unsolved by the failed Century of the Child loomed. Tauzin's remarks quoted in Keith Bradsher, "Three Smaller Companies Say Their Vaccines Are Cheaper," *New York Times*, November 8, 2001. In 2003, Democrats in Congress demanded that compensation systems be established for anyone injured by smallpox innoculations. Some suggested a new fund to parallel the one established by the Childhood Vaccine Injury Act. Others argued that

In 1900, relatively few Americans became ill with smallpox, but it remained a dreaded disease that prompted unprecedented government intervention in decisions about medical care of the nation's children. One hundred years later, no American got smallpox, but in its new guise as a potentially catastrophic terror weapon, it still inspired fear.[76] Obviously, the context had changed totally. Nonetheless, those most at risk were the country's young, especially those aged twenty-five and under.[77] Americans did not end the century with worry-free celebrations marking the conquest of epidemic disease. Rather, many asked, "Would smallpox return in the future in an even more horrific form? Would it claim American children among its first victims?"

this precedent would not work, since children rarely received compensation for lost wages. Obviously, the tort debates had *not* ended. See Denise Grady, "Medical Panel Has Doubts about Plans for Smallpox," *New York Times*, January 16, 2003.

[76] Indeed, due process considerations added further layers of complications to fears about reinstituted smallpox innoculation. Dr. Anthony Fauci, Director of the National Institute of Allergy and Infectious Diseases, noted that children under the age of eighteen were not able under American law to give informed consent. Therefore, making smallpox vaccination again mandatory for children raised "ethical and legal problems" that had not concerned policy makers in the early to mid-twentieth century. Many physicians thought smallpox innoculations potentially more dangerous to children than any of the vaccines required as a condition of entrance to school. Encephalitis from innoculation, a serious inflammation of brain tissues, occurred, they said, almost exclusively among children. Moreover, some argued that, during the decades of mandatory smallpox vaccination, few in the medical community carefully monitored the actual incidence of vaccinial encephalitis. Such a diagnosis could only be made after a brain biopsy, not standard procedure in any state with mandatory smallpox innoculation laws. See Michael Pollan, "Distant, Troubling Echo from '47 Smallpox War," *New York Times*, December 17, 2002.

[77] "Smallpox: the Once and Future Scourge?" *New York Times*, June 15, 1999.

Conclusion

Two Cheers for a "Failed" Century

As the historian Robert Darnton once reminded, historical "raw material" doesn't exist. It is, he said, "all cooked."[1] Every piece of paper, every photo, every song, every bit of information humans record can only be understood in context, and historians face the daunting task of creating it. They are judges, not just collectors, of knowledge, and, as such, must remind themselves regularly of Darnton's warning that every source embodies a rhetorical convention, argues a hidden agenda, and must be scanned between the lines.

Moreover, most historical evidence, even during the technology-driven twentieth century, has disappeared without a trace. However, the fragments left that enable analysis of the ways Americans governed their young between 1900 and 2000 fill so many shelves and so many archival boxes that anyone committed to reading them all will invariably fail. It would take a century. This book, like any work of history, has argued from documents. It has not assembled all possible information on its subject. Information, "by its very nature, is bottomless."[2]

Therefore, historical writing demands a wise detective's wary recognition that all the data unearthed can never exactly replicate what occurred. Yet, detectives must eventually end their investigations, hoping the bits of fiber, the trace of blood, the shard of glass led them to the right conclusions.

Smallpox, fittingly, ended the last topical chapter of this book. The conquest of one of the most awful diseases ever to strike humanity occurred because twentieth-century "welfare" states, importantly including the United States, bankrolled medical innovation, preached worldwide vaccination, and embraced an ambitious "progressive" vision that said the future, through

---

[1] Darnton's concern with his students' habit of using information on the Internet to write term papers, without any concern for the context in which the information existed, sparked the remark. Robert Darnton, "No Computer Can Hold the Past," *New York Times,* June 12, 1999.

[2] *Ibid.*

organized public action, could be better than the past. Through the 1970s, American children entered first grade bearing the distinctive welts of a small-pox innoculation. After 1950, none died of the disease. It was a triumph of state policy that youngsters born in the United States after 1975 might ask what the mark on their parents' arms indicated.

Few of the other programs examined in these pages provided the kind of permanent physical mark that a smallpox vaccination gave millions of Americans. However, they should be remembered. Collectively, they changed the experience of growing up – in ways still incompletely charted by those who study children and those who analyze government. Together, they left a record of public decision making that deserves the "two cheers" the novelist E. M. Forster famously awarded societies that praise ability over inheritance and defend protection of the weak, even if they incompletely institute such ideals.[3] Some of the public policies analyzed here improved the prospects of great numbers of children. The CCC redirected the lives of millions of drifting, despairing Depression-era boys. Required vaccination significantly reduced infectious illness in the young. Others had troubled histories. But programs such as Head Start or special education were ones earlier gener-ations would not likely have conceptualized. They reached out to children other centuries enslaved or ignored.

Twentieth-century America's inability to create an ideal institution to pun-ish criminal boys, or universally applaude public school curriculums, or a "cure" for child abuse, reflected the difficulties inherent in the tasks em-braced – and the thorny path down which public issues that confront pas-sionately held ideological beliefs travel. The "century of the child" failed in part because ideas central to attempts to improve childhood also enshrined contradictions in American culture. Americans wanted privacy – *and* bu-reaucracies that exposed the usually private activity of child abuse. They esteemed family stability, but married, divorced, remarried again. They said they loved the company of children, during decades marked by policies that separated people by age and sent youngsters out of the home to school, peer culture activities, and part-time jobs. Fewer and fewer adults spent more than a fraction of their lives with children underfoot. They said a good so-ciety was one that nurtured its young but more easily justified care for the politically influential, dependent old. They expected more of governments they tried to restrain through divided spheres of power.

The "century of the child," then, offers cautionary tales, worth noting by those interested in current public policy making or the future of state agency. For almost all of recorded history a preadolescent child was any society's most representative inhabitant. That this was no longer true in the late-twentieth-century United States was a change whose significance the country had not really absorbed. Yet, it was important that it do so. When the

[3] E. M. Forster, *Two Cheers for Democracy* (London, 1951), 1–15.

century began in 1900, the statistically average American was still a child – an eleven-year-old boy who lived on a farm in Pennsylvania. By 1999, the nation's demographically average citizen was a thirty-four-year-old divorced mother from California.[4]

A notably grayer early-twenty-first-century population needed to know that regulation of twentieth-century children's lives provided an important model for U.S. state interactions with the citizenry at large. In 1931, Judge Ben Lindsey predicted that "Society will be more willing to accept changes for children than for adults. It will, grudgingly perhaps, finally accept them (for everyone)."[5]

Time proved Lindsey right, though his faith that such a development would demonstrably improve American life was misplaced. Children were the first group whose futures depended on social policies that codified their intelligence. They were the first, in significant numbers, to carry government-issue identity cards – the work certificates that early-twentieth-century local labor investigators issued to school-leavers. By the end of the century, American adults who lacked birth certificates, driver's licenses, Social Security cards, or other forms of official identification were essentially non-persons, unable to carry on routine tasks. Social science's collaboration with public policy making had measured, labeled, and numbered the entire American population, starting first with the young. Consciously made public decisions caused this to happen. But even policy makers themselves often forgot the chain of particulars.

When Gulliver visited the Kingdom of the Laputans, he noted with amazement that servants trotted just behind all eminent thinkers – carrying little sticks topped with a blown fish bladder filled with dried peas, which, now and then, they used gently to strike the ears of their masters. It seems, Jonathan Swift sardonically observed, that Laputan intellectuals were "so taken up with intense speculations" that they could neither speak, nor listen to the ideas of others, without this physical reminder.[6]

The larger frame this study has employed attempts the same sort of flailing. Anecdotal memories convinced the politicians who supported Early Head Start that they had embarked on an "unprecedented" effort to teach mothers about the proper care of newborns and toddlers. The Sheppard-Towner Act clearly presaged the 1995 initiative by seventy years, but it had been forgotten.

At century's end, social scientists who thought a five- or ten-year span of time was "long term" surveyed the implications of "returning" welfare to the states. For those for whom "history" went back no further than 1988,

---

[4] Bill Dedman, "Portraying a Century of Changes in America," *New York Times*, December 13, 1999.

[5] Ben Lindsey and Rube Borough, *A Dangerous Life* (New York, 1931), 113.

[6] Jonathan Swift, *Gulliver's Travels* (London, England, 1962 Ed.), 174–75.

the federal government had always been a major presence in state programs of aid to dependent children and their families. But discussion of poverty policy demands a recognition that the final decades of the twentieth century were anomalous – indeed, so out of keeping with long traditions of locally controlled outdoor relief that they invited rebellion.

Educators and politicians who thought standardized testing would improve American children's math and English composition abilities talked constantly between 1980 and 2000 about "restoring" rigor to the public schools. If they recognized that they were imposing a different expectation on state-sponsored education, they might have fully grasped the difficulties inherent in expecting all graduates to meet academic minimums.

Fiercely waged debates about genetic research marked the start of the twenty-first century. Should embryonic tissue be used for medical experimentation? Should life be sacrificed to save life? What, indeed, *was* human life? No one acknowledged it, but the twentieth century began similarly, although the heated discussions took place in county departments of health, not in the well of the U.S. Senate. Then, too, politicians tried to set limits on medical research, and policies that affected the young centered controversy. During decades when scientists still wondered whether bacilli *were* living things, vaccination "wars" pitted those who argued that mandatory innoculation would provide great potential benefit to society against those who thought that children injected with as-yet-mysterious substances were in mortal danger.

These twentieth-century disputes offer lessons to those now seeking to navigate the always-dense thickets of domestic policy making, whether the issue is the best way to educate children, or free them from poverty, or improve their chances for a healthy life.

Moreover, while discussing numerous policy "failures," this assessment of the century of the child has attempted to outline a larger field of reference that challenges common notions about the supposedly incomplete development and slow growth of an American welfare state. It is, hopefully, a tap with a pea-filled fish bladder, a reminder of the ambition of American social policy making – even when the dreams described derailed. Compared to other technocracies, early-twentieth-century American states, especially below the national level, increased public spending with astonishing rapidity.

They did so, in part, because they believed more expansively in the powers of education than did their European or Japanese counterparts and embraced a vision of free public schooling centering a shared civic culture.[7]

---

[7] In 1995, the political scientist Robert Putnam fretted that large numbers of Americans had ceased to value the bonds of civic life and were instead content to "bowl alone." Robert Putnam, "Bowling Alone: America's Declining Social Capital," *Journal of Democracy* 6 (1995): 64–79. Neither Putnam nor most Progressives, however, paid sufficient attention to the perils of association. The historian James Kloppenberg notes that Timothy McVeigh, executed for

They wanted to do so despite the presence of a population that was far more ethnically diverse than was that of any other twentieth-century highly developed welfare state – in a society that celebrated the fact that citizenship could be a choice, not just a matter of birthright or blood.

Clearly, birthright and blood still mattered. For much of the twentieth century, nonwhite children suffered discrimination. Even as policies changed after the 1960s, Latino and African-American youth were, far and away, more likely to be arrested and imprisoned than were whites for identical crimes; minority kids were overrepresented among the poor; they were more likely to be sick.

However, they were also the face of the future. In 1900, 85 percent of all newcomers to the country were Europeans. By 1999, almost 70 percent were "people of color" – Asians and Latinos, as immigration restrictions based on ethnicity disappeared.[8] Moreover, there were signs that teenage members of "Generation Y" were more tolerant than their "Generation X" parents or Baby Boomer grandparents. A 1997 Gallup Poll found that 57 percent of its sample population had dated someone not a member of their own racial or ethnic group. Another 30 percent were quite willing to do so, but had not yet met the right person. Perhaps after a century of talk about America-as-melting-pot this generation might actually make it happen?[9] That the "failed" century of the child helped make this possible deserves two cheers.

Epilogue: The Twenty-First Century?

The twentieth "century of the child" failed, if judged by its own ambition. That is the central argument of this book, which began with questions and ends with speculative inquiry. The regulations explored in these pages changed American children's lives. Doubtless those children's children will live differently in the twenty-first century, but will they, too, face dilemmas the "century of the child" did not solve?

What will children's work lives be like? In the early twentieth century, middle-class investigators from the National Child Labor Committee regularly expressed surprise when working-class girls pridefully told them that they enjoyed being "little mothers" for the babies in the family. That was not what they wanted to hear, so they discounted the need for such family

---

the 1995 bombing of the Oklahoma City Federal Building, bowled regularly with his fellow suspects James and Terry Nichols. Concludes Kloppenberg: "American society would have been better off had each of them gone bowling alone." James Kloppenberg, *The Virtues of Liberalism* (New York, 2000), 79.

[8] United States Bureau of the Census, *Statistical Abstract of the United States, 1999* (Washington, DC, 2000); http://www.census.gov/us.html.

[9] Corey Takahashi, "Selling to Gen Y: A Far Cry From Betty Crocker," *New York Times*, April 8, 2001. For an interesting take on "Gen Y," see Neil Howe and William Strauss, *Millennials Rising: The Next Great Generation* (New York, 2000).

arrangements.[10] As the century ended, middle-class investigators still under-estimated the importance of the working-class "housechild."

By the 1970s, the non-income-earning American housewife had begun to disappear. By 2000, she comprised a tiny minority among adult women. Had "little mothers" returned in force without analysts quite noticing? At the end of the century, one in three American children lived with only one parent, and the great majority of American kids grew up in families where all adults worked outside the home. Increasingly, parents asked for help with household tasks. Cookbooks appeared with "easy" recipes children between the ages of eight and ten could use to get a family's dinner on the table by the time working parents returned home. They featured helpful tips for young cooks, such as: "Once the chicken is in the pan, *do not* leave to watch TV."[11] Even a child too young to read could be taught to operate a microwave oven. By the 1990s, smaller vacuums, mops, and other cleaning implements showed up in stores. American adults were not getting any shorter, and these items were not displayed as toys. Who was using them?

In 1981, the sociologist Viviana Zelizer's *Pricing the Priceless Child* argued that twentieth-century American children had a vastly different "social value." In strict economic terms, they were worthless to their parents. Indeed, they were incredibly expensive. They cost hundreds of thousands of dollars to raise to the age of eighteen, and, in return, parents expected "neither money, nor labor" – only: "love, smiles, and emotional satisfaction."[12] America's young were financially worthless, but emotionally "priceless."

Certainly no parent needed to be reminded of the costs of feeding, clothing, and educating a child, but late-twentieth-century social scientists, as had their predecessors, confidently exaggerated the economic "uselessness" of children. Shared wages and the cooperation of girls and boys were important to working class families' economic survival for at least the first fifty years of the twentieth century. Children never really disappeared into economic "worthlessness," and twentieth-century labor law never effectively regulated the agricultural work that occupied many child workers' time. Will twenty-first-century politicians dare to cross the threshold of a home?

[10] For examples of such stories, see Edward Clopper, *Rural Child Welfare: An Inquiry by the National Child Labor Committee* (New York, 1922), 4–35. Nor did reformers want to hear working class children tell them that they felt proud to contribute to household survival, but that is exactly what many interviewers who talked with child workers or former child workers learned. See Valerie Quinney, "Childhood in a Southern Mill Village," *International Journal of Oral History* 3 (1982): 167–92.

[11] This genre of "how-to" books teaching parents and kids how to cooperatively run a household began to appear in the 1970s and only grew during the rest of the century. For an example, see Eleanor Berman, *The Cooperating Family* (Englewood Cliffs, NJ, 1977), quotation: 85.

[12] Viviana Zelizer, *Pricing the Priceless Child: The Changing Social Value of Children* (New York, 1981), 3.

How will a new century's leaders cope with aging and different family structures? Throughout human history, most old people personally knew many more of their descendents than their ancestors. Likely that would no longer continue be true for elderly citizens of the twenty-first-century United States. Demographers predicted that growing numbers of adults would choose to be childless and that a majority of American couples who wanted offspring would have only one child. The number of persons who were another living person's child or grandchild would drop; the number of great-grandchildren and great-great-grandchildren would grow.[13]

By the end of the twentieth century, children were no longer the numerical majority in the societies of the developed world. If children's percentages within the total U.S. population continue to dwindle, what will happen? If people begin regularly to live into their eighties, or even their nineties, will "childhood" still legally end at sixteen, or eighteen, or twenty-one? Twentieth-century American governments never managed to agree on a consistent chronology that divided babies from children, and children from adults. Will a period forming an ever-shorter percentage of life be increasingly lengthened through state policy? That definitely happened in the twentieth century. In 1900, most Americans thought that those age fourteen were perfectly capable of full-time employment. Few retained that belief in 2000, when labor policy banned fourteen-year-olds from the "adult" world of forty-hour weeks. Parents whose twenty-something or thirty-something daughters and sons returned home in the 1990s to enjoy free rent between career changes might be forgiven for wondering if a greater statistical infantilization had not already occurred. Could expanded immigration quotas produce the families with several young children native-born Americans eschewed?

Few thought an open-door immigration policy alone would stem the aging of American society. How will a grayer United States react to a world filled with societies bursting with children, where most people die young? Jerome Groopman, a professor of medicine at Harvard, guessed that in the twenty-first century very long lives "won't be for the poor."[14]

Nor, he thought, would expensive health care be available to the disadvantaged. Already, at the end of the twentieth century, biotechnology and genetics research offered new ways for people to play God. Cells extracted from embryos, some said, offered exciting promises of cures for Alzheimer's

---

[13] Peterson, *Gray Dawn*, 57–63. The one-child family was already the modal family in China in the late twentieth century, imposed through state-mandated population planning, and in Germany, where the personal choices of millions of couples resulted in the same demographic.

[14] Jerome Groopman's book of essays, *Second Opinions* (New York, 2000), is highly recommended – not the least for its thoughts about how an aging, developed world might cope with a younger, poorer one.

and Parkinson's diseases, diabetes, and a host of other ailments. Others called the use of embryonic material the killing of a child.

By the 1990s, growing numbers of parents able to afford the costly procedure used *in vitro* fertilization to avoid genetically transmitted disease. They employed "pre-implantation genetic diagnosis" (PGD) to test embryos for the presence of hereditary scourges such as Franconia anemia or Tay-Sachs Syndrome. A new baby would, some hoped, save an older sibling, by "donating" stem cells from its umbilical cord to be used in a bone marrow transplant for a brother or sister.[15] Will the twenty-first century encourage a proliferation of such practices? Will greater numbers of parents harvest the cells from a second youngster to combat the diseases of a first? Will time prove Dr. Gregory Stock, Director of UCLA's Program on Medicine and Society, right? "In the not-too-distant future it [will] be looked upon as kind of foolhardy to have a child by normal conception."[16] Will parents routinely insert genes *in vitro* – to prevent cancer, or change eye color, or make an offspring musical?[17] How will the United States govern its young when children can be recreated genetically before being implanted into a womb, not necessarily their biological mother's?

In the twentieth century, women became "surrogate" mothers. They also became mothers at ever-advanced ages. Throughout time, a male ancient in his eighties or nineties occasionally fathered a child – eliciting wonder or scorn. In 1994, Severino Antinori, an Italian obstetrician, helped a sixty-two-year-old woman become pregnant.[18] Will the next century see seventy-, or eighty-, or ninety-year-old mothers, as well as fathers?[19]

In the absence of social consensus about how children should behave around elders, about how men should act around women, about how one group should interact with another, twentieth-century Americans legalized relationships. People once brought up children to resolve most disputes through "manners." Communities regulated behavior, through praise or through shunning, sometimes, in extreme situations, through duels. Often "manners" or "civility" let both sides pretend that an awkward situation just hadn't occurred.[20] Will a twenty-first-century nation of "legalized selves" make such solutions rarer?[21]

---

[15] For a review of this research, see Allen Goldberg, "Stem Cell Research and a Parent's Hopes," *New York Times*, July 21, 2001.

[16] Quoted in Sheryl Stolberg, "A Small Leap to Designer Babies," *New York Times*, January 1, 2000.

[17] *Ibid.*

[18] For a review of efforts by European physicians during the 1990s to help women into their sixties give birth, see "Cloning," *New York Times*, February 4, 2001.

[19] In 1999, the novelist Saul Bellow, at age eighty-four, fathered another baby. His other adult children were all old enough to be the infant's grandparents. Did his kind of family life presage the future?

[20] These are arguments made by the George Washington University law school professor Jeffrey Rosen in "In Lieu of Manners," *New York Times Magazine*, February 4, 2001, 46–48.

[21] The phrase is Rosen's: *Ibid.*, 46.

Or will Americans choose, instead, to curb their appetite for attorneys? There were hints that the decades between 1960 and 2000 might have marked a highpoint for the legal profession. Attorneys faced growing hostility and an explosion of what a worried American Bar Association (ABA) called "delawyering."[22] The ABA was concerned enough to initiate a major investigation of the thousands of websites, many run by nonattorneys, which gave legal advice over the Internet, although the attorney Richard Granat, chair of the study, admitted, "A large component [of the law] is just information."[23] One half of the 1.2 million couples divorcing in 1999 did so without consulting an attorney. Thousands visited "divorce-kit" sites on the Internet and downloaded copies of necessary documents for relatively small fees – usually around $200.[24] Lawyers had been in the forefront of the century's civil rights struggles. America was a fairer place because of many of their efforts, yet by the 1990s Americans routinely said attorneys were liars and cheats.[25] Early-twentieth-century Americans shunned lawyers. Will their great-grandchildren?

Will children's issues continue to act as harbinger of trends in social activism? Like the continued dominance of the legal profession, that was not guaranteed. In the 1960s, children's rights advocates confidently proclaimed that all distinctions between "legitimate" and "illegitimate" offspring would soon disappear, a quaint holdover from the Victorian age. They thought that most children would retain separate counsel if their parents divorced. Neither prediction materialized.[26] Indeed, the "personal responsibility" the Personal Responsibility and Work Opportunity Reconciliation Act of 1996 emphasized was the obligation of impoverished single mothers on welfare to find husbands. The century ended with old-fashioned marriage promoted as good public policy, even as marriage declined as the social bedrock all couples demanded before considering having a child.

Finally, early-twentieth-century "child savers" were among the first well-organized advocates of "special issues" politics. Would this model of non-partisan political lobbying continue to change American political life? In

---

[22] Michael Lewis, "Faking It," *New York Times*, July 15, 2001.

[23] *Ibid.*

[24] For example, for a fee of $249, www.completecase.com asked customers to answer an extensive onscreen questionnaire that included questions about everything from financial assets to plans for child care. Using this information, the web service then created documents for a couple to download and submit to a family court judge.

[25] Michael Lewis, "Faking It," *New York Times*, July 15, 2001.

[26] *Levy v. Louisiana*, 391 U.S. 68 (1986) held that the denial to illegitimate children of the right to recover for wrongful death of a mother was itself "wrongful discrimination." However, as the country's mood turned more conservative in the 1990s, efforts to erase legal distinctions between children born in and out of wedlock stalled, as did much of the rest of the "children's rights" agenda. For surveys of the "children's rights movement" and the late-twentieth-century state of the American family, see Joseph Hawes, *The Children's Rights Movement: A History of Advocacy and Protection* (Boston, 1991); Richard Gill, *Posterity Lost: Progress, Ideology, and the Decline of the American Family* (Lanham, MD, 1997).

the twentieth century, political parties' influence declined, and special interest groups' authority increased. That change affected public responses to childhood, as well as all other policy processes. It also altered the average citizen's connections to government decision making. Thousands of early-twentieth-century "anticruelty" crusaders personally hunted for mistreated youngsters. By the 1980s, those disturbed by child abuse were more likely to mail a check to the Children's Defense Fund. Ordinary citizens interacted with policy making in a detached way. They read a flyer picked from a pile of second-class mail, watched television, surfed the Web. Interest groups organized nationally and hired paid staff. Members of such organizations often numbered in the millions, but few knew each other personally. As state regulations governed ever more aspects of children's – and adults' – lives, citizens disconnected from politics.[27]

They said they hated politicians, but Americans had crossed a threshold. Most accepted the bigger governments that childhood policies had helped to form. In the year 2000, few really advocated returning to 1900 – when the federal government employed a few hundred thousand people, primarily to deliver the mail and send out pension checks to Union veterans – when most citizens were not graduates of public high schools – when a great number of people still viewed income taxation as completely unconstitutional.[28]

Late-twentieth-century American adults accepted more government but scorned the people who occupied the offices an enlarged public sphere created. They embraced public policy's changed rules for childhood but worried about many of their consequences. If their twenty-first-century children and grandchildren fulfilled a prediction first made in 1900 and made their era truly "the century of the child," they would have to think hard about ways to reconcile such contradictions.[29]

---

[27] This is a point made convincingly by R. Shep Melnick, "Governing More But Enjoying It Less," in Morton Keller and R. Shep Melnick, *Taking Stock*, 302–3. For an interesting discussion of the origins of these phenomena, see Elisabeth Clemens, *The People's Lobby: Organizational Innovation and the Rise of Interest Group Politics in the United States, 1890–1925* (Chicago, 1997).

[28] In 1900, the federal government included about 380,000 employees, about half of whom worked for the Post Office. Most of the rest worked for the Department of Agriculture and the Pension Office. James Q. Wilson, "The Growth of the Bureaucratic State," in Nathan Glazer and Irving Kristol, Eds., *The American Commonwealth* (New York, 1976), 86–89.

[29] This final argument draws heavily on one made by the political scientist R. Shep Melnick that "Reconciling our expansive expectations of government with our low estimation of politics will be the central task of the next century." "Governing More But Enjoying it Less," 306.

Index

Abbott, Edith, 20
Abbott, Grace, 31, 110, 112, 114, 232
Abt, Henry, 265–66
Adult retirement 97–98
Addams, Jane, 26, 189
Administration of Children, Youth, and
    Families, 79, 252
Adoption Assistance and Child Welfare
    Act (AACWA), 68–69, 84–85, 88
Age-grading, 2–3, 11–12, 24, 34, 220,
    275, 279, 356, 361
Agricultural Adjustment Act, 121
Aid to Dependent Children (ADC), 16,
    107, 112–16, 118–19, 130
Aid to Families of Dependent Children
    (AFDC), 92, 107, 117–25, 127
Alexander, Lamar, 212
Alger, Horatio, 35
Alibek, Ken, 353
American Academy of Pediatrics (AAP),
    342, 352
American Association for the Retarded,
    284
American Association of Retired Persons
    (AARP), 131
American Bar Association (ABA), 37,
    363
    see also legal profession
American Child Health Association, 107,
    232
American Civil Liberties Union (ACLU),
    39–41, 50, 119
American Council on Education, 301
American Dietetic Association, 305

American Humane Association, 57,
    62–64, 73
American Medical Association (AMA),
    62, 230–31, 233, 257, 330
American Psychological Association
    (APA), 79, 199
American Public Welfare Association,
    122
Amnesty International, 20
Anti-cruelty societies: see societies for the
    prevention of cruelty to animals;
    see societies for the prevention of
    cruelty to children
Anthropology and children's policy, 6,
    251–53
    see also social science theory
Asylums, 261–62, 275–76, 286
Attorneys: see legal profession

Baby Boom, 11–12, 33–34, 50, 97, 127,
    359
Baby Boomlet, 50
Baker, Newton, 113, 199
Bane, Mary Jo, 247
Basketball, 299–300, 307, 312, 314–16
Battered Child Syndrome, 62, 64, 72, 89
Behavior modification, 43
    see also juvenile justice
Behaviorism, 35, 224–25, 228–30, 233–34,
    236, 240, 298
Bell, Winifred, 117
Bennett, William, 211
Binet, Alfred, 198
Bloom, Benjamin, 240

Board of Education of Hedrick Hudson Central School District v. *Rowley*, 285–6
Botstein, Leon, 220–21
Bowen, Louise de Koven, 26
Brademas, John, 267
Brandt, Edward, 345
Breckinridge, Sophonisba, 20
Brown v. *Board of Education*, 270, 272
Buckey, Peggy, 81–82
Buckey, Ray, 81–82
Bumpers, Dale, 339
Bush, George H. W., 258, 349

California Conservation Corps, 181–82
Canady, Charles, 83
Cantor, Eddie, 332
Cardinal Principles, 193–94, 196–97, 200, 203, 208–10, 212
Carnegie Corporation, 113
Carstens, C.C., 22
Carter, Jimmy, 246, 279
Centers for Disease Control (CDC), 325, 346, 349
Charity organization societies, 22, 101
    see also societies for the prevention to the cruelty to children;
    see also Progressivism
Chickenpox, 324, 326
Child abuse, 53–91, 116–17, 138, 356
    and "Battered Child Syndrome," 62, 64, 72, 89;
    and definitions of, 68, 73, 78, 81;
    and early twentieth century responses to, 56–60, 70;
    and federal laws, 54–55, 68;
    and incidence of, 53–54, 70, 78, 89;
    and state child protective services, 11, 16, 56, 65–7, 70, 80–81, 83–85, 87, 168;
    and state reporting laws, 54, 64, 70, 79, 114;
    and the "child abuse industry," 54, 73, 78–79;
    consequences of public policy about, 78–91
Child Abuse Prevention and Treatment Act (CAPTA), 68, 71, 75
Child advocacy, 15, 71, 84, 87

Child Development Group of Mississippi (CDGM), 243, 253
Child Development Institute, Princeton University, 287
Child Health Association, 107
Childfree Network, 12
Child labor, 5, 13, 32, 137–83, 190, 205, 220, 247, 359–60
    and estimates of numbers of child workers, 138–44, 180, 359;
    federal laws restricting, 137–38, 148, 151–53, 175;
    and Progressive campaigns against, 143–44;
    and public work programs for adolescents, 5, 13, 138, 156–59, 161–75, 181–83, 196–97, 205, 207, 219–20, 238–39, 247, 249;
    and realities of, 143, 178, 181;
    and state legislation restricting, 5, 138–41, 144, 178;
    see also Civilian Conservation Corps;
    see also Job Corps;
    see also Child Labor Amendment
Child Labor Amendment, 3, 150–51, 153–55, 228, 231
Child Labor Tax Act, 149, 226
Childhood, 1–16, 24, 39
    as a cultural abstraction, 6,8;
    a brief history of, 7–9, 356–7;
    chief characteristics of American state regulation of, 1–4, 356–9
Childhood poverty, 60, 70, 73, 79, 91–134, 237, 240, 348, 357–58
    and definitions of, 97–98, 102, 116, 127–28;
    and government programs to combat, 99–133;
    and realities of, 94–98, 128–33;
    see also mothers' pensions;
    see also ADC;
    see also AFDC;
    see also Head Start;
    see also social science theory;
    see also welfare
Child protective services, 11, 16, 56–60, 65–67, 70, 80–81, 83–85, 87
    see also child abuse
Child psychology: see developmental psychology

Child-saving, 4, 9–10, 15, 70, 75, 107, 111, 137, 142, 150, 153, 225, 228, 244, 298, 363
Child-study clubs, 233
Child welfare: see welfare
Child Welfare League of America, 22
Child Welfare Research Center, 87, 237
Children's Bureau: see United States Children's Bureau
Children's courts: see juvenile justice
Children's culture, 6
Children's Defense Fund, 3, 71, 83–84, 363
Children's Health Insurance Program, 128
Children's rights movement, 36–39, 363
Civilian Conservation Corps (CCC), 138, 156–59, 161–69, 172–73, 175, 181–83, 196–97, 205, 207, 302, 356
Claxton, Philander, 187
Clinton, Bill, 79, 168, 212, 320, 347–50
Clopper, Edward, 142
Cloward, Richard, 168
Cohen, Wilbur, 118
Commission on the Reorganization of Secondary Education, 195
Commonwealth Fund, 336
Communicable Disease Control Amendments to the Public Health Service Act, 348
Community action: see Head Start
Compulsory Education, 2, 11, 187–221, 228, 255, 259–60, 266, 278, 285, 290, 298, 356, 358
  and attendance policies, 219–21;
  and curriculums, 188, 193–98, 204–14, 356;
  and nineteenth century precedents, 188–90;
  and Progressive support for expansion of, 187, 189, 195–97, 200, 217;
  and students' reactions to, 217–23;
  and reorganized school systems, 199–201, 277–78;
  and responses of teachers, 209–10, 213–15;
  see also educational standards movement;
  see also Intelligence Quota (I.Q. exams);
  see also physical education;
  see also vocational education

Connaught Laboratories, 347
Consent decrees, 87–88, 272
Cooke, Robert, 239, 241–42
Coops, Helen, 315
Coordinating Council for Handicapped Children, 274
Costin, Lela, 67
Crime and children: see Juvenile justice
Cultural deprivation theory, 116–118, 122, 239–40
Cutter Laboratories, 337, 342–43

Darwinism, 55, 60
Davis v. *Monroe County Board of Education*, 317
Davis, Nancy (Mrs. Ronald Reagan), 273
Day nurseries, 224, 234–35, 255
Deinstitutionalization, 275–77
De Wine, Mike, 70, 82
Dean, James, 31, 35
Deutsch, Albert, 30
Devine, Edward, 101
Developmental psychology and children's policy, 5, 14, 22–23, 34–35, 54, 73, 105, 197–99, 201–4, 207–9, 219, 222–25, 236, 239–40, 256–58, 265, 288–89, 297–99
  see also intelligence quota (IQ) exams;
  see also social science theory
Dewey, John, 194, 196
Digre, Peter, 85
Diphtheria, 16, 230, 323, 326–27, 336, 338, 341
Disabled children, 259–90
  and eugenics, 260, 263–64, 272;
  and federal law, 260, 266–67, 281, 283–84, 287–88;
  and medical breakthroughs, 269–70, 287;
  and nineteenth century reform, 259–60;
  and public education, 5, 259, 264, 273, 279, 281, 284–90;
  and spurs to change in attitudes towards, 262, 273–75, 288;
  and state laws, 265, 274, 285–86;
  and Supreme Court rulings about, 263–64, 272–73, 282–83, 285–86;
  see also Education of All Handicapped Children Act (EHCA);

Disabled children (*cont.*)
  see also learning disabilities;
  see also special education
Dissatisfied Parents Together, 344
Diversion, 43, 48–9
  see also juvenile justice
Dodd, Christopher, 78, 142, 254
Dolman, Glen, 257
Douglas, William, 119
Due process rights, 20, 39, 42–43, 119–20,
    123, 267, 271, 278–79, 281–82, 363
  and challenges to AFDC, 120, 123;
  and education of disabled children,
    267, 271, 279, 281–82;
  and child abuse statutes, 73, 78;
  and juvenile justice, 20, 39, 42–43

Early childhood education, 222–258
  and federal encouragement of, 226–30,
    234–41;
  and growth of, 255–58
  and nineteenth century precedents,
    222–24;
  and social science theory, 237–44, 256;
  and United States Children's Bureau,
    225–26, 228, 231;
  see also Head Start;
  see also Infant schools;
  see also Sheppard-Towner Maternity
    and Child Protection Act;
  see also WPA Emergency Nursery
    Schools
Early Head Start, 253–54, 357
Eastman, George, 75
Economic Opportunity Act, 167
Edelman, Marion Wright, 3–4
Education of All Handicapped Children
    Act (EHCA), 15, 260, 267–68,
    279–80, 284–89
Education Amendments Act, 316
Educational standards movement, 211–14,
    322, 358
Educational Testing Service (ETS), 202–3
Eisenhower, Dwight, 319
Elementary and Secondary Education Act
    of 1965, 278
Employment certificates, 146, 177, 218,
    357
Employment Retirement Income Security
    Act of 1974 (ERISA), 350

Erickson, Erik, 240, 255
Espionage and Sedition Acts, 1917–1918,
    39
Eugenics, 116, 260, 262–63, 265,
    272

Fair Labor Standards Act (FLSA), 137,
    154–56, 175, 177, 180, 274
Family Preservation and Support Initiative
    of the Omnibus Budget
    Reconciliation Act of 1993, 69
Family reunification, 85–86
Family Support Act, 123, 125
Fechner, Robert, 158, 161, 196
Federal Emergency Relief Administration
    (FERA), 111, 234–35
Federal Security Administration, 63
Female suffrage: see woman suffrage
Finch, Robert, 63
Finn, Chester, 211
Folks, Homer, 106, 142
Fontana, Vincent, 69
Food and Drug Administration (FDA),
    324, 343, 352
Food stamps, 127, 134
Ford, Gerald, 246, 266, 287
Fortas, Abe, 41–42
Fosdick, Raymond, 299
Foster care, 11, 68–69, 86, 88
Fowler, Frank, 81
Frank, Barney, 83
Fuller, Raymond, 153

Gang Violence and Juvenile Crime
    Prevention Act, 50–51
General Federation of Women's Clubs,
    103
Generation X, 359
Generation Y, 359
German measles: see rubella
Gesell, Arnold, 240, 255
Gil, David, 72
Givens v. *Lederle Laboratories*, 341–42
Glueck, Eleanor, 29, 35
Glueck, Sheldon, 29, 35
Grassley, Charles, 83
Great Depression, 32, 95, 102, 110, 143,
    158, 166, 182, 197, 235, 296, 302,
    318, 356
Green, Edith, 169
Guillian-Barre Syndrome, 343

Gulick, Luther, 298, 307, 315, 322
Gun-Free Schools Act, 283

Hall, G. Stanley, 24, 224, 240, 298
Hammer v. *Dagenhart*, 148, 156
Handicapped children: see disabled
    children
Hart-Celler Act, 178
Hatch, Orrin, 143
Head Start, 223, 237–39, 241–53, 255–56,
    303, 350
    and connections to expanded
        preschool education, 237–38, 242,
        255, 283–87;
    and reality of, 243–44, 250–55;
    and studies of, 239, 245–46, 248;
    as a part of Great Society initiatives,
        238–41;
    see also childhood poverty;
    see also Intelligence Quota (IQ) exams;
    see also social science theory
Healthy Start, 24, 253–54
Heiser, Annette, 90
Hill, Charles, 245–46
Hine, Lewis, 144
Hobson v. *Hansen*, 271
Honing v. *Doe*, 282
Home Rule movement, 300
Hoover, Herbert, 34, 107, 231–32
Hoover, J. Edgar, 33
Hopkins, Harry, 111–12, 234
Hull House, 26, 189
Humphrey, Hubert, 166, 274
Hunt, J. McViker, 240, 255

Illegitimacy, 130, 363
Illinois Juvenile Court Act, 1899, 21, 27
Immigration to the United States, 28, 51,
    59–60, 160, 177, 190–92, 195–97,
    199, 271, 298, 356, 359, 361
    and changing demographics of, 298,
        359, 361;
    and impact on mandatory education
        statutes, 190–92, 195, 223;
    as a spur to the emergence of child
        abuse as a public issue, 60, 70
Immunization of children, 15, 323–354,
    358
In re Gault, 41, 43, 45
In re Winship, 42–43
Individuals with Disabilities Act, 289

Individuals with Disabilities Education
    Act, 289
Infancy defense, 21, 35
Infant mortality, 7, 10–11, 226, 231, 253,
    294, 296
Infant schools, 223–24, 256
Infantile diarrhea, 294, 324
Infantile paralysis: see poliomyelitis
Informed Parents Against
    Vaccine-Associated Polio, 344
Intelligence Quota (I.Q.) exams, 2,
    198–201, 203–4, 240–42, 244–45,
    256–57, 263, 266, 271
    and American public school
        curriculums, 201, 204, 257, 263;
    and influence on early childhood
        development theory, 240–41, 257;
    and the growth of early childhood
        education, 200, 240–41, 257, 266;
    as a spur to Head Start 240, 242, 248
Intensive Family Services (IFS), 88
Instinct theory, 224, 298
In vitro fertilization, 362
Iowa Child Welfare Research Station, 237

James, William, 157
Jeffords, Jim, 172, 247, 251
Jenner, Edward, 325, 335
Jessup, Albert, 30–31, 48
Jim Crow laws, 2, 40, 48
Job Corps, 166–75, 205, 219, 238–39,
    247–49
Johnson, Lady Bird, 241, 244
Johnson, Lyndon, 41, 63, 166, 183,
    262–3, 265, 271167, 237–41, 245
Juvenile delinquency, 2, 16, 22, 24–31,
    33–35, 45, 50, 80, 117, 168, 359
    see also juvenile justice
Juvenile gang violence, 36–39, 59
    see also juvenile justice
Juvenile justice, 16, 19–53, 57, 66–67, 70,
    101, 114, 118, 132, 225, 293, 326
    and emergence of separate juvenile
        courts, 20–34;
    and goals of, 20–25, 31, 35, 45, 47;
    and problems of, 25–31, 45–52;
    and reality of adolescent crime, 19–26,
        29–34, 48–52, 172;
    and reorganization of, post 1960,
        43–48;

Juvenile justice (*cont.*)
  see also due process rights;
  see also social science theory;
  see also United States Supreme Court;

Kassebaum, Nancy, 173
Kean, Thomas, 309
Keating, Edward, 147
Keating-Owen Bill, 148–50, 155–56, 226
Kefauver, Estes, 33
Kellogg Corporation, 217
Kempe, C. Henry, 61, 72
Kennedy, Anthony, 317
Kennedy, Edward, 260
Kennedy, John, 117, 240, 278, 319–20
Kent v. *United States*, 40–41, 43
Kindergartens, 224, 255–57, 321–22
  see also early childhood education
King v. *Smith*, 118
Kingsley, Clarence, 195
Kirk, Samuel, 270
Kraus, Hans, 319
Knutson, Harold, 112

Lamm, Margaret, 115
Largent, Steve, 83
Laura Spellman Rockefeller Memorial,
  28, 225
Lawrence, Francis, 203
Learning disabilities, 270, 282, 288
  see also special education
Lederle Laboratories, 339, 341
Legal profession, 14, 19, 39, 41, 67,
  78–79, 279–81, 281, 285, 306–12,
  317, 324–27, 340–47, 362–63
  and impact on children's policies, 67,
  279–81, 310–12, 317, 324, 340–47
Lee, Joseph, 298
Lenroot, Katharine, 111
Levin, Tom, 243
Life adjustment education, 208–11
Lindsey, Ben, 22, 37, 51, 137, 143, 357
Livingston, Dodie, 79
Long, Huey, 111
Lovejoy, Owen, 151, 153

Mack, Julian, 26, 106, 137
Malnutrition of children, 295–96, 302–6
Manpower Training Corporation, 167
Malcolm X, 119
March of Dimes, 332–33

Maternal Mortality Thermometers,
  226–27
McCollum, Bill, 20
McGovern, George, 16
McEntee, J.J., 161, 164, 196, 207
McMartin Preschool trials, 81–82
McMartin, Virginia, 81–82
McNamara, Robert, 245
Measles, 24, 323, 338, 347, 349
Medicaid, 120, 127–28, 348, 351
Medicare, 96
Miller, George, 280
Miller, Zell, 257
Mistreatment and neglect of children: see
  child abuse
Modernization theory, 8, 10–11
Molloy, Paul, 115
Mondale, Walter, 67, 71, 76, 90
Morgenthau, Henry, 111
Mothers' pensions, 101–5, 110, 119–20,
  228
Moynihan, Daniel Patrick, 123, 132
Mumps, 212, 338
Municipal recreation: see planned play
Murphy, Patrick, 92, 132
Musial, Stan, 319

Naismith, James, 307
National Affordable Housing Act, 182
National Amateur Athletic Federation
  (AAF), Women's Division,
  314–15
National Bureau of Economic Research,
  95
National Center on Child Abuse and
  Neglect, 75, 79
National Center on Institutions and
  Alternatives, 77
National Child Labor Committee, 142,
  144, 148, 151, 153, 234, 359
National Childhood Vaccine Injury Act of
  1986, 345–46
National Commission on Excellence in
  Education, 211
National Commission on Life Adjustment
  Education, 209
National Committee for the Prevention of
  Child Abuse (NCPCA), 71
National Education Association (NEA),
  83, 194–95

National Education Standards and
    Improvements Council, 212
National Foundation for Infantile
    Paralysis, 332, 335
National health insurance, 111
National Institute for Allergy and
    Infectious Disease, 347
National Institutes of Health (NIH), 328,
    337
National Origins Act of 1924, 60
National Organization of Non-Parents, 12
National School Lunch Act of 1946, 303
National Society for the Promotion of
    Industrial Education, 204
Nelson, Gaylord, 171
New York Society for the Prevention of
    Cruelty to Children, 56, 90, 106
Nineteenth Amendment: see woman
    suffrage
Nixon, Richard, 63, 168, 245–46, 316
Nursery schools, 234–37, 256–57
    see also Works Progress Administration
    (WPA) Emergency Nursery Schools
Nutrition education, 217, 293, 303–5, 321

Obesity in children, 305–6
O'Connor, Basil, 335
O'Grady, John, 231
Office of Economic Opportunity (OEO),
    63, 167–68, 238–39, 241–42,
    245–46, 250
Ohlin, Lloyd, 168
Omnibus Budget Reconciliation Act
    (OBRA), 68–69, 123–24, 126
Opportunity theory, 168, 172, 239
Orenstein, Walter, 349
Orphanages, 10, 99, 101–2, 110,
    115
Orphan trains, 59
Owen, Robert, 147

Packwood, Bob, 180–81, 349
Parent education, 224–34, 242, 244, 247,
    250, 252–54
    see also Head Start;
    see also Sheppard-Towner Maternity
    and Child Protection Act
Parental Rights and Responsibilities Act,
    83
Pasteurization, 295–96
Peebles, J.M., 328–29

Pennsylvania Association of Retarded
    Citizens (PARC) v. Commonwealth of
    Pennsylvania, 372
Perkins, Frances, 63, 111, 118
Perry Preschool Project, 248
Personal Responsibility and Work
    Opportunity Act (PRA), 125, 127,
    133, 363
Pertussis, 24, 323, 338, 341–42, 344
Philanthropy, 22, 56–57, 59–60, 95, 99,
    101, 104–5, 224, 298–99, 321, 336
    and aid to poor children, 95, 99, 101,
    104–5;
    and child abuse, 56–57, 59–60;
    and child labor, 137, 142–43;
    see also March of Dimes;
    see also mothers' pensions;
    see also societies for prevention of
    cruelty to children;
    see also planned play;
    see also PRAA;
    see also Russell Sage Foundation;
    see also Rockefeller Institute
Physical education (P.E.), 306–12, 316,
    318, 320–21
    and reality of, 306–7, 310;
    and sex-segregation, 312, 314–17;
    and state minimum requirements, 307,
    309–10;
    as subject of litigation, 310–12, 317
Pierce v. Hill Military Academy, 192, 214
Pisani, Joseph, 84
Planned play, 296, 298–301, 308, 315,
    318, 321
Playground and Recreation Association of
    America (PRAA), 298
Polio: see Poliomyelitis
Poliomyelitis, 5, 15, 323, 325, 268, 271,
    331–32, 334–35, 337–38, 341–42,
    348
Poliomyelitis Vaccination and Assistance
    Acts of 1955, 337–39, 348
Preschools: see early childhood education
Probation, 25–26, 28, 41, 46, 66, 177
Progressivism, 3–4, 21, 23, 34, 53, 56, 62,
    64, 103, 111, 116, 137, 141,
    143–46, 187, 189, 194–95, 197,
    217, 260, 265, 355
    and chief characteristics of, 54–55, 137,
    144–46;

Progressivism (*cont.*)
  and child labor, 143–44, 146–47, 187;
  and early twentieth century
    reorganization of municipal
    government, 137;
  and juvenile justice, 21–23;
  and legacies of, 57–60, 153, 187–198,
    210, 355;
  and organized recreation, 296;
  and poor children, 103, 110, 116;
  and support for compulsory education,
    187, 189, 194, 196–97, 200, 265
Prosser, Charles, 204–5, 208–9
Psychology: see developmental psychology
Public Health Service Act, 348
Pure milk campaigns, 294–96

Randolph, Jennings, 285
Ravitch, Diane, 211
Reagan, Ronald, 79, 122, 123
Reformatories, 21, 29–30, 41
Reno, Janet, 255
Res ipsa loquitor, 65
Retirement: see adult retirement
Revenue Act of 1918: See Child Labor
    Tax Act
Reyes v. *Wyeth Laboratories*,
    341–42
Ribicoff, Abraham, 118
Richmond, Mary, 104
Robertson, Alice, 228
Rockefeller, John D. Jr., 299
Rockefeller, John D. Sr., 60
Rockefeller Institute, 273
Rogers, Walter, 338
Romanticism, 55, 223
Roosevelt, Franklin, 63, 107, 110, 138,
    156–58, 234, 332, 335
Roosevelt, Theodore, Jr., 106
Roosevelt, Theodore Sr., 106
Rousseau, Jean-Jacques, 10
Rubella, 323, 338
Russell Sage Foundation, 104,
    298–99

Sabin, Albert, 337, 341
Sage, Olivia, 298
Salk, Darrell, 342
Salk, Jonas, 330, 335, 337–38
Satcher, David, 349
Scheele, Leonard, 337

Scholastic Achievement Test (SAT),
    202–3
School Board v. *Malone*, 283
School leavers: see truancy
School Lunch Act: see National School
    Lunch Act of 1946
School lunch programs, 303–6, 339
Schroeder, Patricia, 68
Schwarzenegger, Arnold, 320
Shalala, Donna, 349
Shaw, E. Clay, 125
Shea, Daniel, 352
Sheppard, Morris, 226, 231
Sheppard-Towner Maternity and Child
    Protection Act, 223, 226, 228–34,
    254, 294, 302, 327, 357
Sherman, Lawrence, 199
Shriver, Sergeant, 167, 240–41, 243
Simon, Paul, 170
Sinatra, Barbara, 78
Smallpox, 230, 325–29, 335–36, 338, 340,
    352–56
Smith, Al, 231
Smith, Hoke, 204
Smith-Hughes Act, 205
Smith-Lever Act, 204, 307
Snedden, David, 195
Social science theory, 2, 14, 19, 23, 26,
    34–35, 48, 66, 70–79, 81, 84, 89,
    101, 105, 116, 167–68, 172, 197,
    207–8, 215, 237–44, 256, 280,
    283–86, 294, 298–99, 357–60
  and analyses of poverty, 84, 101, 105,
    116–119;
  and child abuse, 66, 70–79, 81;
  and concepts of child development,
    34–35, 237–56, 298;
  and influence on policy making, 14,
    23–24, 48, 70–79, 168, 197, 207–8,
    237–44, 280, 283, 289–90, 297–99,
    357–60
Social Security Act, 92, 107, 111–12,
    130–31
Society of the Directors of Physical
    Education, 300
Societies for the prevention of cruelty to
    animals, 55–57, 75
Societies for the prevention of cruelty to
    children, 55–59, 62, 192, 224–25,
    293, 364

Sociology and children's policy, 10–11, 14, 67, 89, 101, 168, 180, 213, 242–43, 265–66, 268, 360
see also social science theory
Spanish Flu, 343
Special education, 203, 264, 266, 278–90, 310, 356
see also disabled children;
see also Education of All Handicapped Children Act (EHCA)
Specter, Arlan, 48
Spencer, Herbert, 55
Standards education: see educational standards movement
Stanton, Jessie, 236
Stanford-Binet tests, 198–99, 201
Status crime, 22–23, 28–29, 44, 47, 50
see also juvenile justice
Stoddard, George, 237
Studebaker, John, 208
Sugarman, Jule, 242, 244, 266, 270
Supplemental Social Security, 95, 131
Supreme Court: See United States Supreme Court
Survey, 102, 226
Sweatshops, 178–79, 181
Swine flu vaccine, 343

Tay-Sachs Syndrome, 362
Teague, Russell, 338
Terman, Lewis, 199, 203, 206–7, 257, 266
Temporary Assistance for Needy Families (TANF), 125
Tetanus, 323, 338, 341, 349
Texas Youth Works, 181, 183
Thomas, Charles, 144
Thompson, Tommy, 126
Thorndike, Edward, 224
Title III Social Security Act, 266
Title IV Social Security Act, 107, 112–14, 118–19, 122, 125, 351
Title IX of the Education Amendments Act of 1972, 310, 312, 316–17
Towner, Horace, 226
Townsend, Francis, 111
Truancy, 80, 192, 218, 220, 264
Trujillo, Jackie, 176–77
Tuberculosis, 263, 265, 269, 294–96, 326
Tuition vouchers, 214
Typhoid fever, 24, 294

Ungraded classrooms: 266, 268–69, 283
United States Advisory Board on Child Abuse and Neglect, 71
United States Bureau of Education: see United States Office of Education
United States Children's Bureau, 26–27, 29, 31, 62–4, 105–6, 110, 148, 194, 225, 228, 230, 232–3, 294, 302, 306, 315
United States Congress, 3, 83, 92, 114, 118–19, 122–23, 128, 133, 137, 148–51, 153–54, 156, 158, 174, 179, 193, 199, 226, 228, 230, 246, 248–49, 253, 255, 266, 272, 281, 283–84, 286–87, 302, 305, 309, 327, 337, 343, 348, 358
and House Committee on Education and Labor, 169, 249;
and House Select Subcommittee on Education, 267;
and House Ways and Means Committee, 112, 118–19;
and Senate Committee on Labor and Human Relations, 249;
and Senate Committee on Labor and Public Welfare, 285;
and Senate Hearings on Juvenile Delinquency, 33;
and Senate Subcommittee on Employment, Manpower, and Poverty, 171;
and Senate Subcommittee on Juvenile Justice, 48;
and Senate Subcommittee on Social Security and Family Policy of the Committee on Finance, 123;
and Senate Subcommittee on Children and Youth, 72, 90;
and Senate Subcommittee on Children, Family, Drugs, and Alcoholism, 78
United States Council of Mayors, 128
United States Department of Agriculture, 111, 158, 162–63, 236, 302, 306
see also School lunch programs
United States Department of Education, 193, 246, 267, 281
United States Department of Health, Education, and Welfare, 63–64, 238, 246, 319, 339

United States Department of Health and
Human Services, 79, 247, 252, 306,
320–21, 344–45, 349, 349
United States Department of Interior, 56,
158, 163, 167
United States Department of Justice, 30
United States Department of Labor, 63,
111, 158, 172, 174–75, 177,
238
United States Office of Education, 188,
193, 195, 208–9, 234–36, 314
United States Public Health Service, 232,
352
United States Supreme Court, 39–43, 49,
117–20, 146, 148–49, 156, 192,
263–64, 270, 282, 285–86, 317
and aid to poor children, 117–18;
and childhood disability, 263–64, 270,
282, 285–86;
and compulsory education, 192,
270;
and due process, 39, 42;
and juvenile justice, 39–43;
and rulings on child labor law, 146,
148–49, 156;
and sexual harassment, 317

Vaccine Act of 1813, 327, 339
Vaccination: see immunization of children
Vaccines for Children Initiative (VFC),
348–52
Van Vorst, Emily, 176
Van Waters, Miriam, 24, 31, 217
Victims of Child Abuse Laws (VOCAL),
79–80
Virology, 335, 338, 341–42, 351, 353
Virus Anti-Toxin Act of 1902, 327
Vocational education, 169–71, 204–9,
214

Walker, Sydnor, 28
Wallace, Henry, 111
War Risk Insurance, 113
Warren, Earl, 42
Watson, John, 35, 224–25, 233, 240

Welfare, 4, 16, 21, 28, 45, 48, 65, 67, 79,
92–3, 97, 107, 114–5, 118–9,
121–30, 132, 177, 189, 355, 358
see also Aid to Dependent Children
(ADC);
see also Aid to Families of Dependent
Children (AFDC)
White House Conference on Care
Dependent Children, 106
White House Conference on Child Health
and Protection, 102–3, 107
Whooping cough: see pertussis
Weiss, Ted, 79
Wilkinson, Bud, 319
Willowbrook State School, 276–77
Wise, Henry, 121
Wilbur, Ray Lyman, 232
Wilson, Mary Ellen, 75, 90, 144
Wilson, Pete, 51
Wilson, Woodrow, 148, 226
Woman suffrage, 151, 226–28, 231
Workfare, 124
Working papers: see employment
certificates
Workmann, William, 337
Works Progress Administration (WPA)
Emergency Nursery Schools, 165,
223–37, 302
Workers' compensation, 104
World Health Organization (WHO), 352
World War I, 38, 150–51, 158–161, 217,
225, 296, 299, 302, 306–8, 314
World War II, 35, 95, 98, 116, 143, 163,
175, 207, 235, 240, 267, 270, 272,
273, 305, 307–8, 318, 328
Wright, Henry, 268
Wyeth Laboratories, 341

Yerkes, Robert, 199
Youth-Build Boston, 181–83
Youth peer cultures, 3, 19, 31–34, 165, 356
Youthful violent crimes, 32–34, 40–41,
49–52

Zigler, Edward, 239, 241–42, 244, 258